The Race is Run

TOMLINSON

"For that ye strove in neighbour love, it shall be written fair,
But now ye wait at Heaven's Gate and not in Berkeley Square,
Though we called your friend from his bed this night, he could not speak for you,
For the race is run by one and one and never by two and two."

RUDYARD KIPLING

The Race is Run

an Indictment of Creedal Christianity

VYNETTE HOLLIDAY

Publishing
Vynette Holliday
theraceisrun@gmail.com

Copyright © Vynette Holliday, July 2020

All rights reserved. No part of this book may be reproduced in any form by electronic or mechanical means, including information storage and retrieval systems, without permission in writing from the publisher, except by a reviewer who may quote brief passages in a review.

First Paperback Edition: 11 February 2020
Revised Paperback Edition: 15 July 2020

ISBN 978-0-646-81377-6

 A catalogue record for this book is available from the National Library of Australia

Permissions

Scripture quotations marked (NIV) are taken from the Holy Bible, New International Version®, NIV®. Copyright © 1973, 1978, 1984, 2011 by Biblica, Inc.™ All rights reserved worldwide. Used by permission.

Scripture quotations marked (NASB) are taken from the New American Standard Bible® Copyright © 1960, 1962, 1963, 1968, 1971, 1972, 1973, 1975, 1977, 1995 by The Lockman Foundation. Used by permission.

Scripture quotations marked (ESV) are taken from The Holy Bible, English Standard Version®, Copyright © 2001 by Crossway Bibles, a publishing ministry of Good News Publishers. All rights reserved. Used by permission.

Scripture quotations marked (ISV) are taken from The Holy Bible: International Standard Version® Release 2.1 Copyright © 1996-2012 The ISV Foundation. All rights reserved internationally. Used by permission.

Scripture quotations marked (ASV) are taken from the American Standard Version 1901. Public Domain.

Scriptures quotations marked (KJV) are taken from the King James Version. Public Domain.

Publishing
Vynette Holliday
Email: theraceisrun@gmail.com

Cover Design: Naomi McKenzie

for the six million

and for

Deborah
1963-2003
"full of grace and truth"

and

Edward Patrick (Ted) Wixted
1927-2001
friend, mentor, inspiration

Acknowledgements

In heartfelt gratitude to those members of my family who supported and encouraged this work and to the members of T.M. Wixted & Co. without whose pioneering research and patient attention to detail this work could never have been written.

Table of Contents

PART I	**The Context** 1	
Chapter 1.	Setting the scene 3	
Chapter 2.	Centres of Israelite life in the 1st Century AD 5	
PART II	**The Documents** 11	
Chapter 1.	The Canon of the Hebrew Scriptures 13	
Chapter 2.	The Canon of the New Testament 15	
Chapter 3.	Christian Fables 18	
Chapter 4.	New Testament Target Groups 19	
Chapter 5.	Dating the New Testament Documents 28	
Chapter 6.	Language in 1st Century Judea 34	
Chapter 7.	The Language of the Gospels 36	
Chapter 8.	Hebraisms in the Gospels 39	
Chapter 9.	Understanding literary styles 44	
Chapter 10.	The Interpretation Methodology 47	
PART III	**Creeds & Christologies** 51	
Chapter 1.	The Creeds 53	
Chapter 2.	Christologies 55	
PART IV	**Virgin Birth and Incarnation** 59	
Chapter 1.	Introduction 61	
Chapter 2.	The Book of Isaiah the Prophet 63	
Chapter 3.	The Gospel of Matthew 66	
Chapter 4.	The Gospel of Luke Part I 73	
Chapter 5.	The Gospel of Luke Part II 78	
Chapter 6.	The Gospel of Luke Part III 83	
Chapter 7.	Supplementary Materials 87	
PART V	**The Divine Court** 89	
Chapter 1.	Introduction 91	
Chapter 2.	Appeals to precedent 92	
Chapter 3.	Appeals to concepts 102	
Chapter 4.	Appeals to Descriptions and Titles 136	
PART VI	**Trinity on Trial** 161	
Chapter 1.	The Triune God 163	
Chapter 2.	Common Core 169	

Chapter 3.	Proof-texts	173
PART VII	**Paul**	**191**
Chapter 1.	Introduction	193
Chapter 2.	Paul and his world	194
Chapter 3.	Paul the Jew	198
Chapter 4.	Paul and his Theology	202
PART VIII	**Sin and Salvation**	**233**
Chapter 1.	Original Sin	235
Chapter 2.	Sin and its Atonement	241
Chapter 3.	Salvation	246
PART IX	**The Papacy**	**249**
Chapter 1.	Introductory Notes	251
Chapter 2.	Common Beliefs	252
Chapter 3.	Unequivocal Assertions	255
Chapter 4.	Irreconcilable Inconsistencies	257
Chapter 5.	Paul's Mission	259
Chapter 6.	Peter's Mission	265
Chapter 7.	Clement & the Corinthians	273
Chapter 8.	Centres of Israelite Life in the 1st Century AD	277
Chapter 9.	Luke's Pentecost	282
Chapter 10.	The General Epistles	286
Chapter 11.	'Rock-Stone' Imagery	294
Appendix	The 'Bones' of Peter	302
PART X	**Aftermath**	**307**
Chapter 1.	Introduction	309
Chapter 2.	Immortal Souls	311
Chapter 3.	Heaven	315
Chapter 4.	Hell	323
Chapter 5.	Judgement Day	331
PART XI	**In the beginning**	**333**
Chapter 1.	Introduction	335
Chapter 2.	In the beginning	336
Chapter 3.	Anti-Myth in Genesis	340
Chapter 4.	The Days	342

| Chapter 5. | The Trees | 343 |
| Chapter 6. | The end of the beginning | 346 |

PART XII	**The Israelite God**	**349**
Chapter 1.	The God of Israel	351
Chapter 2.	Man and his purpose	355
Chapter 3.	Manifestations	356
Chapter 4.	The Holy Spirit	358

PART XIII	**The Israelite Messiah**	**363**
Chapter 1.	Great Expectations	365
Chapter 2.	The Unexpected Messiah	367
Chapter 3.	The Prophet like Moses	374
Chapter 4.	Jesus Anointed	377
Chapter 5.	The Ideal Israelite	379
Chapter 6.	A Right Hand Man	382
Chapter 7.	Minister Plenipotentiary	384
Chapter 8.	The Author of Life	386
Chapter 9.	A Man of Authority	387
Chapter 10.	A Priest Forever	390
Chapter 11.	The Saviour	394
Chapter 12.	The end of the charge	402
Chapter 13.	Ignorance or deception?	404

PART XIV	**Trial and Death**	**407**
Chapter 1.	Introductory Notes	409
Chapter 2.	Dating	411
Chapter 3.	Personalities of the Period	413
Chapter 4.	The Conflict	421
Chapter 5.	The Last Supper	423
Chapter 6.	Betrayal	428
Chapter 7.	Arrest and Interrogation	431
Chapter 8.	Crucifixion	453
Chapter 9.	Burial	469

PART XV	**Resurrection**	**479**
Chapter 1.	Introduction	481
Chapter 2.	Roadblocks	484
Chapter 3.	Altered states	491

Chapter 4.	The eye-witnesses	496
Chapter 5.	The Empty Tomb	499
Chapter 6.	The Parallels	510
Chapter 7.	Three Days	517
Chapter 8.	Community Promises	524
Chapter 9.	Individual promises	527
Chapter 10	The Kingdom of God	531
Chapter 11.	Now, but not yet	534
Chapter 12.	Elijah	541
Chapter 13.	Signs of the times	545
Chapter 14.	Resurrection Revelations	555
Chapter 15.	Double Jeopardy	558
Chapter 16.	Hiding in plain sight	560
Chapter 17.	Timelines	564
Chapter 18.	Choices	566
PART XVI	**The Israelite People**	**569**
Chapter 1.	Introduction	571
Chapter 2.	The Judeans	575
Chapter 3.	Jesus the Jew	577
Chapter 4.	Supersessionism	579
Chapter 5.	Poison Pens	581
Chapter 6.	'Superior' Hellenist-Western thought	586
Chapter 7.	Millennial Rivals	588
Chapter 8.	The Holy See and the Holy Places	590
Chapter 9.	European Fascism	598
Chapter 10.	The Holy See and European Fascism	602
Chapter 11.	Pope Pius XII	610
Chapter 12.	The State of Israel	623

Select Bibliography 647

Preface

Arrangement

This work is arranged in the form of a collection of critical essays and research papers written over a considerable length of time. Each of these critical essays and research papers sets forth arguments and draws specific conclusions from the relevant data.

The task of separating the entwined maze of mainstream Christian doctrine and associated teachings into discrete and coherent strands has proved immensely difficult. This work has therefore been arranged according to topical divisions which, it is hoped, will make it easier for the reader to navigate. However, essays applicable to one or more of these divisions have, of necessity, been repeated in whole or in part if deemed essential to a thorough explication of the subject under examination. The readers' indulgence is therefore sought from the outset.

Definition

The term "Creedal Christianity" should be taken to encompass the doctrines, teachings, confessions and statements of faith all ultimately deriving in full or in part from the Christian Creeds formulated and formalised by the Ecumenical Councils convened between the years 325 AD and 451 AD.

Scope of Work

- To provide a detailed analysis of the core teachings deemed necessary to conform to the mainstream beliefs shared by the major denominations of Christianity, as well as further detailed analysis of various non-core beliefs;

- To compare this *mélange* of core and non-core beliefs of mainstream Christianity with the teachings of the Hebrew Scriptures and the New Testament;

- To demonstrate how the Christian teaching of Supersessionism was one of the major contributing factors behind the centuries of Jewish persecution which ultimately led to the Holocaust.

Notes

Hebrew and Greek words take many different forms all deriving from the same basic root. To avoid unnecessary complexity, only the basic root forms and their meanings will be reproduced in this work.

If necessary to draw attention to specific words or phrases, the author has added bold or italic text for emphasis.

The Biblical citations which appear in this work were not chosen because of a preference for either Byzantine or Alexandrian text-type families but solely on the basis of translations which attempt to capture and convey the meaning of terms, concepts and idiomatic references particular to an ancient Israelite cultural and religious context.

Introduction

The Israelite People

From the Law, the Prophets, and the Writings of the Hebrew Scriptures through to the books of the New Testament, what is laid out for us is the evolution of the human mind. A gradual development from darkness into light. It is our greatest anthropological storehouse and would be valuable for that reason alone. It marks the progress of human ethical and intellectual development and an evolution in human thinking about the nature of God.

From a tribal God of the Israelites only, a god among many gods, who first lived on a mountain, then was carried about in a box, who was vengeful and terrible, and who could be approached only with fear and appropriate ceremony, all the way through to the perception that there is only one God, a God who was not vengeful but full of endless mercy, a God who did not have to be appeased, a God of love and truth who did not have to be approached through ceremony, but could be approached privately through prayer. From the birth of the first Adam, made in the potential image of God, through to the death of Jesus, the last Adam, and thereafter the resurrection of a new creature, a man realising the full potential of humanity, a man finally made in the *imago dei*, the image of God.

If not for the writings of the Israelite people, the core principles of the Ten Commandments, specifically the prohibitions against murder, theft and perjury, would never have become the basis for so many of the world's legal codes. We would never have known that concepts such as justice, peace, equality and, above all, the sanctity of human life, were first articulated in the Hebrew Scriptures. We would never have known that Jesus existed at all and we would never have heard about the golden rule and other New Testament maxims that have elevated and energised millions.

The debt we all owe to these ancient peoples is vast. And yet some of their descendants, the tribe of Judah, have been demonised and delegitimised throughout these long centuries by those whose motives primarily stem from the concept of "replacement theology", otherwise known as "Supersessionism", and the consequent need to demonstrate Jewish unworthiness to remain the "people of God".

The teaching of Supersessionism asserts that because the majority of Jews in the First Century AD did not accept Jesus as their Messiah, God poured out his wrath upon them and destroyed both nation and Temple in 70 AD. God also terminated his Covenants with the Israelite people and transferred them to the followers of Christianity who are the new "people of God". Christianity is the "true" Israel and the sole heir to God's Covenant blessings.

"Fathers" of the church indulged themselves in tirades of demonisation and condemnation, which only increased in fervour and ferocity when Christianity was declared the official religion of the Roman Empire in 380 AD. This now state-sanctioned vitriol was to rain down relentlessly upon the heads of the Jews throughout these long centuries, all the while smoothing a path to the gas chambers.

The religious leaders in Jerusalem are rightly held accountable for the crucifixion of one Jew. The Christian teaching of Supersessionism must rightly be held accountable for the lives of six million. Those who continue to preach this doctrine unwittingly stand in the ashes of the dead. Essays on Supersessionism have been included in relevant sections of this work as this concept is the source of centuries of festering hostility towards the Jews, boiling over into the occasional pogrom, but finding its inevitable and ultimate realisation in the Holocaust.

Jesus of Nazareth

The Christian Churches ostensibly preach Jesus of Nazareth while, at the same time, through their doctrines, they misrepresent him and actually further the viewpoint of those who crucified him. The personality cult built up around "Jesus Christ", and his elevation to divine status, destroys the central figure with far greater definition than the crucifixion itself accomplished. The real man has been effectively buried for nearly two thousand years so it's time, more than time, that he was resurrected from the stranglehold imposed by Christian theology. No matter what terminology has been devised in its justification, a teaching that seeks to characterise the relationship between God and Jesus of Nazareth as anything other than "ethical" and "spiritual" is demeaning to both.

PART I

The Context

CHAPTER ONE

Setting the Scene

The Biblical Narrative

The House of Jacob/Israel

The House of Jacob/Israel consisted of twelve tribes, descendants of the twelve sons of Jacob, who was renamed Israel (Genesis 35:10).

These tribes were allotted various homelands in Canaan after the Exodus from Egypt and the conquest of the Canaanites. (The males of the tribe of Levi were set apart for priestly and administrative duties so they and their families were distributed amongst the other tribes.)

After the allocation of tribal lands, the Israelites lived in a type of confederate system and, at times of crisis, were governed by military/judicial leaders known as "Judges", some of the most notable of whom were Deborah, Samson and Samuel. Following a period of extreme threats from non-Israelite neighbours, Samuel, the last Judge of Israel, was forced to "anoint" Saul of the tribe of Benjamin as the first King of Israel.

It is unnecessary for our purposes to recount the long and complicated story of how and why Saul was overthrown by David of the tribe of Judah, or the events of David's reign, so we will content ourselves by noting that the twelve tribes were united under David's kingship and that they lived in peace and prosperity during the reign of his son Solomon who built the First Temple in the capital Jerusalem.

After the death of Solomon, the Kingdom fractured into two sections. The ten northern tribes became known as the northern House of Israel while the two southern tribes, Judah and Benjamin (with its requisite number of Levites), became known as the southern House of Judah. The territory of Judah included the city of Jerusalem which had been previously captured by David from the Jebusites, a Canaanite tribe.

Just to add to the complexity, the ten northern tribes were known specifically as the "House of Israel", but when general reference is made to the collective of the twelve tribes, they are also known as the "House of Israel". For example, when Jesus referred to the "House of Israel", he intended to embrace the twelve tribes because he appointed twelve disciples as a representative number.

Centuries before Jesus was born, however, the Kingdoms of Israel and Judah had both been defeated in war and some of their populations deported to the East: Israel by the Assyrians circa 720 BC:

> In the ninth year of the reign of Hoshea, the king of Assyria captured Samaria and carried away the Israelites to Assyria, where he settled them in Halah, in Gozan by the Habor River, and in the cities of the Medes (2 Kings 17:6 NIV).

and Judah by the Babylonians circa 586 BC:

> But because our fathers had angered the God of heaven, he gave them into the hand of Nebuchadnezzar king of Babylon, the Chaldean, who destroyed this house (the Temple of Solomon) and carried away the people to Babylonia (Ezra 5:12 ESV).

The Kingdoms of Israel and Judah came to an end with these conquests and deportations but that did not serve to quell the people's yearning for a restored monarchy ruled by a king of Davidic descent.

Whilst it can be difficult to grasp Israelite tribal particularities, the effort will be well rewarded in the long run as we will encounter references to these different groups in the New Testament. If we keep in mind the following benchmark provided by Paul, it may help to dispel the confusion. Even though he was born in a Diaspora community outside the land of Judea, Paul described his ancestry in three different ways. Let us proceed, then, from the general to the particular:

1. As a member of the "people of Israel". That is, in a general sense, he belonged to the twelve-tribed House of Jacob/Israel.

2. As a "Jew". That is, in a more specific sense, he not only belonged to the two-tribed southern House of Judah but also followed the customs and practices of the Judeans who worshipped in the Temple at Jerusalem.

3. As a "Benjamite". That is, in the particular sense, he belonged to one of the two tribes which originally comprised the House of Judah.

Note that all Jews are Israelites, but not all Israelites are Jews.

CHAPTER TWO

Centres of Israelite life in the 1st Century AD

Although readers may find it tedious, we must take a necessarily brief and incomplete journey through the geography and demography of the ancient Near East if a full understanding of some vital aspects of both the Hebrew Scriptures and the New Testament is desired.

In addition to the people of the tribes of Judah and Benjamin then living in the land of Israel, there were also many Jewish communities scattered around the shores of the Mediterranean. By far the largest groups, however, lived beyond the sway of Rome in various locations controlled by client kings of the Parthian Empire, the successor of the previous Achaemenid (Persian) and Seleucid dynasties.

According to Pliny the Elder,[1] the Parthian empire consisted of 18 kingdoms (or satrapies), 11 of which were called the upper kingdoms, while 7 were called the lower kingdoms, meaning that they were located on the plains of Mesopotamia. The centre of the lower kingdoms was ancient Babylonia.

We will concern ourselves with the three Parthian satrapies of Media, Elam and Babylonia in which were situated the three great cities of the former Persian period, known to contemporary Greeks and Jews as Ecbatana, Shushan, and Babylon.[2]

Ecbatana in Media

The modern city of Hamadan is located in North-West Iran and is identified with ancient Ecbatana (Biblical Achmetha), capital of Media Magna. According to the Book of Ezra, an edict by the Persian King Cyrus to rebuild the Temple in Jerusalem was discovered in the fortress of Ecbatana during the reign of Darius who decreed that the edict be honoured. This Cyrus Edict (see Ezra 6:1-12) was found in Ecbatana in 1879.[3]

Ecbatana had been the summer residence of Persian royalty and, according to Josephus, also the burial place of the kings of "Media, of Persia, and of Parthia".[4] Also

---

1 Pliny the Elder. *Natural History, VI. 112.*
2 Olmstead A.T. *History of the Persian Empire.* University of Chicago Press: Chicago, 1970, p.162.
3 Known as the Cyrus Cylinder, the Akkadian script confirms that Cyrus had a policy of restoring cult sanctuaries and repatriating deported peoples.
4 Josephus, *Antiquities,* X.263.

in Ecbatana is a little mausoleum, supposedly containing the remains of the biblical figures Esther and Mordecai.

The detailed accounts of two celebrated twelfth-century Jewish tourists—Benjamin of Tudela[5] and Petahiah of Regensburg—are among the most crucial sources of geographic and demographic information about ancient Jewish communities of the Persian and Parthian periods.

Benjamin of Tudela reported that by the middle of the 12th Century AD, the descendants of the Jewish populations of various towns in ancient Media, such as Hamadan, Fars and Isfahan, numbered into the many tens of thousands. In addition to these Jewish communities of Media were also thousands of Israelites who had been deported to "Halah, in Gozan by the Habor River, and in the cities of the Medes" (2 Kings 17:6) circa 720 BC by the Assyrian Sargon II after his capture of Samaria, the capital of the Northern Kingdom of Israel.[6] Prior to the discovery of the Khorsabad Annals of Sargon in 1847, most historians had regarded the following biblical story of this Israelite deportation as mythical:

> In the ninth year of the reign of Hoshea, the king of Assyria captured Samaria and carried away the Israelites to Assyria, where he settled them in Halah, in Gozan by the Habor River, and in the cities of the Medes (2 Kings 17:6 NIV).

Josephus, a contemporary of both Peter and Paul, confirmed that these ten tribes were still an identifiable group in his own time, dwelling beyond the Euphrates and not subject to the Romans:

> Wherefore there are but two tribes (the Jews) in Europe and Asia subject to the Romans, while the ten tribes (Israelites) are beyond the Euphrates till now, and are an immense multitude, and not to be estimated by numbers.[7]

Shushan in Elam

The ancient city of Shushan (Susa) was the capital of Elam. It lay in the northern portion of the modern province of Khuzistan in the South-West corner of Iran. The city proper lay to the North-East of the head of the Persian Gulf. We find reference to Shushan in the biblical books of Daniel, Esther and Nehemiah:

---

5 www.jewishencyclopedia.com/articles/2988-benjamin-of-tudela

6 *Annals: 2nd year of Sargon II*, J. B. Pritchard (ed.), *Ancient Near Eastern Texts Relating to the Old Testament*, 3rd edition; Princeton University Press: Princeton. 1969.

7 Josephus, *Antiquities*, XI.5.2

> In my vision I saw myself in the palace of Shushan in the province of Elam; in the vision I was beside the Ulai Canal (Daniel 8:2 NIV).

> Now it came to pass in the days of Ahasuerus, (this is Ahasuerus which reigned, from India even unto Ethiopia, over an hundred and seven and twenty provinces:) That in those days, when the king Ahasuerus sat on the throne of his kingdom, which was in Shushan the palace, In the third year of his reign, he made a feast unto all his princes and his servants; the power of Persia and Media, the nobles and princes of the provinces, being before him (Esther 1:1-4 KJV).

> The words of Nehemiah the son of Hachaliah. And it came to pass in the month Chisleu, in the twentieth year, as I was in Shushan the palace… (Nehemiah 1:1 KJV).

Our 12th Century Spanish globetrotter, Benjamin of Tudela, gave an account of his visit to Shushan and the reputed place of the tomb of Daniel the prophet:

> The River Tigris divides the city, and the bridge connects the two parts. On one side, where the Jews (7,000) dwell, is the sepulchre of Daniel. [8]

Babylon in Babylonia

Although we can discern a measure of status enjoyed at certain times by the Jewish communities scattered throughout the Persian and later Parthian Empire, such as those in Media and Elam, those communities never attained the status, wealth, power and influence possessed by the 1st Century descendants of the Jewish elite class of royals and nobles who had been deported to Babylon after the capture of Jerusalem and the destruction of the Temple of Solomon by the Babylonian King Nebuchadnezzar in 586 BC.

The wealth and influence of Babylonian Jewry

The head of the Jewish community of Babylon—who was officially recognized by the Persian authorities—was called *Resh Galusa* in Aramaic, which means *Rosh Galut* in Hebrew, and *Head of the Diaspora* in English. The Jewish community in Babylon was the "mother" of the world Diaspora.

---

8   *The Itinerary of Benjamin of Tudela*. Trans. Marcus Nathan Adler. Selzer Books, 2018.

Both Philo[1] and Josephus[2] inform us that, in the apostolic age, Babylonian Jews were very numerous and very wealthy and every year sent large amounts of silver and gold to the Temple in Jerusalem, whereas Jews were comparatively few in Rome, about eight thousand according to Josephus.[3]

Hillel the Elder

Hillel the Elder, one of the Jewish elite of Babylonia, re-located to Jerusalem during the reign of Herod the Great, became prominent circa 30 BC, and died circa 10 BC. Hillel was the renowned sage and scholar who founded the school named after him, was head of the Great Sanhedrin and, according to Rabbinic tradition, the ancestor of the patriarchs who headed Palestinian Judaism till about the 5th Century AD.

High Priest Hananel

Herod the Great was sole ruler of the Roman province of Judea from 37 BC to 4 BC. His first appointment to the position of High Priest in Jerusalem was Hananel, a Jew from Babylonia. (Only two years later, Hananel was deposed as High Priest by Herod at the behest of the Roman Triumvir, Marc Antony.)

Herod the Great

So influential were those Babylonians who could claim royal descent from King David that Herod himself, although an Idumean by birth, tried to insinuate himself into this royal Babylonian stock in order to increase his honour status. It was conventional at this time for any claimant to legitimate power in Israel to allege Davidic lineage, as is evident by the entire New Testament's insistence on Jesus being a descendant of David "according to the flesh".

Connections

A constant flow of correspondence passed back and forth between the Jerusalem establishment and the heads of Babylonian Jewry right up until the destruction of the Jerusalem Temple in 70 AD:

> For example, Gamaliel I, a 'teacher of the law,' a Pharisee, and member of the council of the Temple (Acts 5:34) sent letters to Jews in other parts of the world, including specifically Babylonia, concerning tithing regulations and intercalations of the calendar, as did R. Johanan ben Zakai and R. Simeon ben Gamaliel afterwards. They addressed themselves to 'our brethren in the

---

1 Philo, *Legatio ad Cajum*, 36.

2 Josephus, *Antiquities*, XV.2.2; XXIII.12

3 ibid XVII.2

Exile of Babylonia' as well as to those in Media and elsewhere...Thus through pilgrimages, through correspondence on matters of law and doctrine, and through exerting authority over the designation of the sacred days (intercalation of the calendar), as well as through collections of Temple funds, frequent and normal relations were maintained between Jerusalem and the diaspora, including Babylonia, and the influence of Palestine was exerted throughout the golah (diaspora).[4]

It is important for our purposes to note here that the centre of the lower Parthian satrapies was Babylonia, which was located on the plains of Mesopotamia. Thus the Babylonian Jews were included among the Mesopotamian Jews whom Peter addressed specifically at Pentecost (Acts 2:9).

From all the foregoing we can determine that, in addition to the many Jewish communities scattered around the shores of the Mediterranean and under the control of the Roman Empire, there were also many Jews and Israelites living beyond the sway of Rome in the various locations previously mentioned. These particulars become important when the missions of the Apostles Peter and Paul are addressed in Part IX: *The Papacy*.

---

4   Nuesner, Jacob. *A History of the Jews of Babylonia : Vol I. The Parthian Period.* E.J.Brill: Netherlands, 1969, pp. 37-45.

PART II

The Documents

CHAPTER ONE

The Canon of the Hebrew Scriptures

The Hebrew canon is a collection of narrative traditions, legal materials, historical chronicles, oracles, and poetry and songs and their interpretations over time, produced and transmitted by priests, scribes, prophets and other community leaders. The common thread underlying the selection of a considerable portion of the material is the hope of the eventual redemption of the people of Israel by the God of Israel.

The canon comprises twenty-four books, the five of the Pentateuch (Torah), eight books of the Prophets (Joshua, Judges, Samuel, Kings, Isaiah, Jeremiah, Ezekiel, the Minor Prophets), and eleven Hagiographa (Psalms, Proverbs, Job, Song of Solomon, Ruth, Lamentations, Ecclesiastes, Esther, Daniel, Ezra, and Chronicles). Samuel and Kings form but a single book each, as is seen in Aquila's Greek translation.

The most radical criticism agrees that the Torah is the first and oldest part of the canon. The narrative of Nehemiah Chapters 8-10, which describes an actual canonisation, is of prime importance for the history of the collection. It is generally agreed that by the middle of the fifth century BC, the first part of the canon was extant.[1] By the time of Jesus, however, an expanded canon identical to one used today was available to the New Testament authors.

The TaNaKH, an acronym comprised of initial letters, is a term used to describe the three chief divisions of the Hebrew Scriptures. These three divisions are:

- The five books of Moses, also called the Law or the Teaching (Torah);
- The Prophets (Nevi'im);
- The Writings (Ketuvim)

These three chief divisions of the Hebrew Scriptures are designated in Luke 24:44 as the "Law", the "Prophets", and the "Psalms". Usually, however, only the Law and the Prophets are mentioned (Matthew 5:17; Luke 26:16).

The following statement by Jesus demonstrates that the canonical order of books appearing in Christian Bibles is not the same as that used by the New Testament

---

[1] Jewish Encyclopaedia Article : *Bible Canon*. Accessed 9 September 2018 : www.jewishencyclopedia.com/articles/3259-bible-canon

authors, who obviously made use of the Hebrew order where Chronicles is listed as the final book of the canon:

> From the blood of Abel unto the blood of Zacharias, which perished between the altar and the temple: verily I say unto you, It shall be required of this generation (Luke 11:51 KJV, cf. 2 Chronicles 24:20).

The canonical order of books becomes an important interpretive issue when analysing Matthew's "Great Commission", as will be seen in the forthcoming Chapter: *New Testament Target Groups*.

The Canon of the New Testament

In the apostolic preaching age, there was not yet a need to collect the body of writings we know as the New Testament. The Hebrew Scriptures were sufficient for Jesus, as they were for Paul and the other Jesus followers. The Hebrew Scriptures were:

> ...breathed out by God and profitable for teaching, for reproof, for correction, and for training in righteousness, that the man of God may be complete, equipped for every good work (2 Timothy 3:16-17 ESV).

In the immediate post-apostolic age, however, the earliest Christian communities in Jerusalem, Samaria, Lydda, Caesarea, Antioch, and etcetera, began to collect the various materials which form our present New Testament. The formation of the canon was due to a growing grass-roots consensus that these materials were the "expression of revealed faith". It was certainly not a decision handed down from above by ecclesiastical authorities. The canon was not imposed by Eastern or Western church leaders or by councils. Those bodies stand at the end of the process rather than at the beginning.

When the first official canonical list identical to the New Testament we have today appeared in 367 AD, it was prepared by Athanasius, the Bishop of Alexandria.

> ...Again (after a list of the Old Testament books) it is not tedious to speak of the (books) of the New Testament. These are, the four Gospels, according to Matthew, Mark, Luke, and John. After these, the Acts of the Apostles and Epistles called catholic (general), of the seven apostles: of James, one; of Peter, two; of John, three; after these, one of Jude.
>
> In addition, there are fourteen Epistles of Paul the apostle, written in this order: the first, to the Romans; then, two to the Corinthians; after these, to the Galatians; next, to the Ephesians; then, to the Philippians; then, to the Colossians; after these, two of the Thessalonians; and that to the Hebrews; and again, two to Timothy; one to Titus; and lastly, that to Philemon. And besides, the Revelation of John (Athanasius' Thirty-Ninth Festal Epistle. AD 367).

This Athanasian canon did not impose anything new upon Christian communities—it merely codified what had been the general practice of those communities for nearly three centuries. No action of a council or a synod was early enough to have had a decisive influence on the course of events. The council decrees have the form:

> This council declares that these are the books which have always been held to be canonical.

Until the close of the fourth century, the list of New Testament works recognised as "apostolic" by Rome and the Western Churches excluded Hebrews, James, 1 Peter and 2 Peter. It was not until then, as the Roman Catholic Encyclopaedia states, that:

> The West began to realize that the ancient Apostolic Churches of Jerusalem and Antioch, indeed the whole Orient, for more than two centuries had acknowledged Hebrews and James as inspired writings of Apostles, while the Alexandrian Church, supported by the prestige of Athanasius, and the powerful Patriarchate of Constantinople, with the scholarship of Eusebius behind its judgment, had canonised all the disputed Epistles.[2]

Moreover, the Pontifical Biblical Commission published in 1993 a document entitled *The Interpretation of the Bible in the Church*, in which the following statement was made:

> Sacred Scripture has come into existence on the basis of a consensus in the believing communities recognizing in the texts the expression of revealed faith.[3]

The preface to this document was written by none other than Cardinal Joseph Ratzinger, later Pope Benedict XVI, now Pope Emeritus.

In his work *Who Chose the Gospels? Probing the Great Gospel Conspiracy*, C.E. Hill makes the compelling case that the early and universal acceptance of Matthew, Mark, Luke and John, as well as their ascendancy over all fictitious and heretical writings, depended simply on apostolic authority. Christians never regarded themselves as having a choice about which Gospels to accept. Rather, it was partly the acceptance of the Gospels which made one a Christian in the first place. On the final page, he states:

> In one sense, of course, the answer to the question: "Who chose the Gospels?" is, everybody who has known something of that indemonstrable power and majesty and, like Aristides, Justin, Irenaeus, Clement, and countless others, has chosen to live by their telling of the story of Jesus. But second-century Christian leaders would have said that neither individuals nor churches had the authority

---

[2] Catholic Encyclopaedia Article : *Canon of the New Testament*. Accessed 9 September 2018 : http://www.newadvent.org/cathen/03274a.htm

[3] Pontifical Biblical Commission : *The Interpretation of the Bible in the Church*. Accessed 9 September 2018 : http://catholic-resources.org/ChurchDocs/PBC_Interp-FullText.htm

to 'choose' which of the many Gospels they liked, but to receive the ones given by God and handed down by Christ through his apostles.[4]

The early church viewed the books which now make up the New Testament as having apostolic authority and thus worthy to stand with the Hebrew Scriptures used by Jesus and the apostles.

---

[4] Hill, C.E. *Who Chose the Gospels? Probing the Great Gospel Conspiracy*. Oxford University Press: Reprint edition, April 7, 2012, p. 246.

CHAPTER THREE

Christian Fables

A thirst to know more about Jesus than the New Testament revealed gave rise to the concoction of various stories tailored specifically to resonate with certain audiences and to meet perceived needs. In addition to most of these works being produced under a strong Gnostic influence, they are also riddled with historical errors, theological incongruities, fantastical Christologies and, unlike the four theologically consistent canonical Gospels, betray a fundamental incoherence.

There is a very good reason why early writings such as the *Shepherd of Hermas*, the *Epistle of Barnabas*, and the *Didache* for example were not included in the canon of the New Testament—they lacked authority in the eyes of early Christians.

Note that it is becoming more and more the practice that modern theologians and academics are framing their arguments using some of these non-canonical, non-authoritative works, including a selection of the mainly Gnostic texts found at Nag Hammadi in Egypt in 1945. Such practices must always be viewed with more than a hint of skepticism. If theologians or academics are incapable of presenting a theology based on the canon, then they have no business being in the business.

The Qur'an's adoption of Christian Fables

Islam claims that the Qur'an is the final revelation from God to humanity and also that it is an exact word-for-word copy of tablets which have always existed in heaven. Centuries after Jesus was born, redactors of Islam's Qur'an believed the Hellenist-Latin fathers of Christianity when they claimed that the doctrine of the Virgin Conception/Birth was a teaching of the New Testament so, along with a few embellishments, included the Virgin Mary story in the Qur'an (Sura 19).

The question is: when the Virgin Conception/Birth story is revealed as fraudulent, what then happens to the holy Qur'an? Strangely, also included in Islam's holy book are snippets from other Christian fables such as the *Gospel of the Infancy of Jesus Christ* and the *Gospel of Thomas the Israelite*.

CHAPTER FOUR

New Testament Target Groups

Note

Before one first picks up the book containing the writings of the New Testament, it should be understood that these documents were never intended for "outsiders", that is, for people who did not belong to Jesus-groups. In the wider context, every document is firmly embedded within what may be described as a "pan-Israelite" framework.

Section 1

The Synoptic Gospels

The Synoptic Gospels were written to specific communities of Jesus-followers who had been expecting the establishment of the Kingdom of God on Earth to be ruled over by the King-Messiah Jesus whom God had raised from the dead. They were not written for all peoples, at all times, and in all circumstances, as is commonly believed. In the following pages, we will comment briefly on the Kingdom of God, which is addressed more comprehensively elsewhere in this work, before turning our attention to the Gospel of Matthew which, because of its structural method, is the most informative about intended target groups, specifically those encompassed by the "Great Commission".

The Kingdom of God

Out of the welter of messianic expectations and longings arising from successive waves of tribulation, disaster and disappointment, there emerged a picture of an ideal King-Messiah who would inaugurate the eschatalogical Messianic Age, God's Kingdom on Earth, a holy and righteous Kingdom of brotherhood, peace and justice modelled on a restored, perfected, Kingdom of David.

All Israel's intellectual, spiritual and moral resources were to be dedicated to building this holy and righteous society, the radical political and national components of which were not envisioned as separate from the ethical and universal but formed part of a unified whole. The Kingdom of Israel was to serve as a model for the nations.

John the Baptist had proclaimed the "good news" that the God of Israel was about to overturn the existing establishment and set up this Kingdom of God in the land of Israel. The first disciples became Jesus' followers in the belief that he was the promised King-Messiah who would inaugurate the Kingdom.

John the Baptist, the disciples, and some of the people to whom Jesus preached, all assumed that the Kingdom was imminent. Jesus corrected their assumption with the parable concerning a certain nobleman who went into a "far country" to receive a Kingdom, and then returned (Luke 19:11-12). It is clear that Jesus did not expect the establishment of the Kingdom until after he returned from that "far country". The disciples continued to hope for the establishment of the Kingdom of God in their own lifetimes so, after the Resurrection, Jesus was forced to correct them once again:

> So when they had come together, they asked him, "Lord, will you at this time restore the kingdom to Israel?" He said to them, "It is not for you to know times or seasons that the Father has fixed by his own authority" (Acts 1:6-7 ESV).

However, Jesus assured his disciples that the Kingdom would indeed be established upon his return from the "far country":

> And I appoint unto you a kingdom, as my Father hath appointed unto me; That ye may eat and drink at my table in my kingdom, and sit on thrones judging the twelve tribes of Israel (Luke 22:29-30 KJV).

> And Jesus said unto them, Verily I say unto you, That ye which have followed me, in the regeneration when the Son of man shall sit in the throne of his glory, ye also shall sit upon twelve thrones, judging the twelve tribes of Israel (Matthew 19:28 KJV).

The Gospel of Matthew

If we consider the organisation of the Hebrew Scriptures used by Israelites we find that, unlike Christian Bibles, the final book is Second Chronicles. The book of Second Chronicles ends with a decree:

> Thus saith Cyrus king of Persia, "All the kingdoms of the earth hath the LORD God of heaven given me; and he hath charged me to build him an house in Jerusalem, which is in Judah. Who is there among you of all his people? The LORD his God be with him, and let him go up" (2 Chronicles 36:23 KJV).

Cyrus, having received "all the kingdoms of the earth" from YHWH, God of Heaven, commissions Israel to "go up" to Jerusalem to rebuild the temple. In both Matthew 28:18-20 and 2 Chronicles 36:23, we find the following sequence:

- Universal authority is claimed;
- The source of authority is identified;
- Finally there is a commission to "go".

Jesus, being greater than Cyrus, has received authority in Heaven as well as on Earth and, on the strength of that authority, he commissions the disciples to "go" (and build the Kingdom of God).

The very first words of Matthew's Gospel:

> The book of the generation(s) of Jesus Christ…

recall for the reader the words of Genesis 5:1:

> This is the book of the generations of Adam…

Matthew's Gospel begins like Genesis and ends like Chronicles thereby encompassing the entirety of the Hebrew Scriptures. Owing to the Christian re-organisation of the Hebrew Scriptures, this authorial intent is lost.

The Great Commission

Before the Resurrection, the disciples had been directed *not* to go among the Gentiles (*ethnē*):

> These twelve Jesus sent forth, and commanded them, saying, "Go nowhere among the Gentiles (*ethnē*), and into any city of the Samaritans enter ye not: But go rather to the lost sheep of the house of Israel (Matthew 10:5-6 KJV).

Throughout the Gospels we see Jesus described as the great exemplar of all the moral and ethical principles necessary to build the Kingdom. If this Kingdom were to become a model for the nations, however, the concept must first take root among those who could hear his voice. There can be no doubt that Jesus believed his days were numbered and that it was only a matter of time before the authorities silenced him forever. It is no surprise therefore that Jesus directed all his remaining time and effort towards teaching and healing those Israelites who lived in the region of his personal ministry.

However, after the Resurrection, the disciples are directed to extend their mission, which clarifies his statement made earlier in Matthew:

> And I say unto you, That many shall come from the east and west, and shall sit down with Abraham, and Isaac, and Jacob, in the kingdom of heaven (Matthew 8:11 KJV).

In this verse, Jesus speaks of the many Israelites who would eventually be gathered from East and West to celebrate the establishment of the Kingdom of Heaven (God) in the land of Israel.

The Text

> But the eleven disciples proceeded to Galilee, to the mountain which Jesus had designated. When they saw Him, they worshiped him; but some were doubtful. And Jesus came up and spoke to them, saying, "All authority has been given to Me in heaven and on earth. Go therefore and make disciples of all the nations (*ethnē*), baptizing them in the name of the Father and the Son and the Holy Spirit" (Matthew 28:16-19 NASB).

Firstly, it should be obvious that one cannot "disciple" or "baptise" a nation. Secondly, given Jesus' reluctance to teach and heal non-Israelites, his original command could only have been to make disciples of Israelites living *among* all the nations, i.e. in those regions where countless Israelites lived among majority non-Israelite populations. (See Part I.2: *Contex*t*-Centres of Israelite life in the 1st Century AD.*)

Notes

The authenticity of Matthew 28:19 has long been called into question on historical as well as textual grounds. The Trinitarian formula of "Father, Son, and Holy Spirit" did not make its appearance until relatively late in creedal terms. It is not this author's intention to delve into this long history of controversy except to point out that there is not a single instance of the disciples obeying this disputed direction by Jesus. Instead they baptised *in* or *into* the name of Jesus.

The inconsistent and confused translation of various Greek words appearing in English as "Gentile" has obscured the correct identification of target groups (see The Pauline Epistles below).

As outlined in the forthcoming Chapter: *Dating the New Testament Documents*, Matthew's Gospel would have had little or no relevance for non-Israelites.

Section 2

The Gospel of John

Although the Gospel of John was also written to Jesus-group members embedded within the pan-Israelite framework, it differs from the Synoptics in the following fundamental ways:

- Its main setting is Jerusalem, which was the centre of religious/political life because Israelites believed that God ruled from a place beyond the vault of the firmament of the sky directly above the Jerusalem Temple's Holy of Holies;

- It portrays Jesus as the representative of God's values, and portrays the Judean priestly establishment as the representative of the opposite values, hence truth versus lies; the spirit of the law rather than the letter; humility versus arrogance; personal integrity versus institutional formalism; selflessness; and commitment to principle to the extent of laying down one's own life.

Because John framed his Gospel in this manner—as a collision of values that are timeless and universal—it can be described as applicable to all peoples, at all times, and in all circumstances. Therefore the Kingdom of God can also be regarded as ruling over the hearts and minds of all those who live by the timeless and universal principles embodied by Jesus. Tragically, also timelessly and universally, John's Gospel has been used to foment anti-Semitic sentiment for nearly two thousand years.

Because the Gospel is set in Jerusalem and portrays the Judean establishment as the main force of opposition to both God and Jesus, the Greek word *Ioudaios* appears seventy-one times compared to five times in Matthew and Luke and seven times in Mark. Besides being a preposterous assertion just on the face of it, there has been a universal failure to recognise that, in John's Gospel, this word *Ioudaios*, always translated into English in an ethnic sense as "Jew", should most often be translated into English in a geographic sense as "Judean". (See *Paul's Mission* in following pages for the various categories of persons designated as *Ioudaios* in the New Testament.)

When John uses the word *Ioudaios* in a condemnatory sense, he is always referring to the elite class ruling from Jerusalem. He is certainly not referring to those descendants of the tribe of Judah then living in Galilee, such as Jesus and the disciples, or to the many then living in the Diaspora. (See Part I.2: *Context-Centres of Israelite life in the 1st Century AD* for a description of Israelite tribal distributions.)

Note

Some scholars assert that the word *Ioudaios* always means "Judean" but they fail to take into account the other categories of *Ioudaios* mentioned in the New Testament.

Section 3

The Pauline Epistles

The inability to recognise the "in-group" Israelite context for Paul's letters is the major factor which led to his writings becoming the most abused, misused, misinterpreted and misunderstood body of work in all of human history.

For many theologians past and present, the Pauline "good news" is one that declares a universalism, subsuming lesser entities such as the law and cultural differences. Nothing could be more deceptive. Just like all of his 1st Century AD contemporaries, Paul himself was not a universalist but an ethnocentrist.

Paul's Mission

The correct identification of Paul's target groups has been obscured by ambiguous, incorrect and inconsistent translations. For example:

Jews (Greek Ἰουδαὶός: Transliteration Ioudaios)

Ambiguous translation: The Greek New Testament has been translated into many different languages over time. If translators of all these versions had correctly identified the various categories of persons all designated as *Ioudaios* in the New Testament, that word would not have become the most consequential single word in all of human history. Since this work is in English, we will confine our remarks on this topic to the English version but its content applies equally to all translations of the Greek New Testament regardless of era, language or version.

Whilst an understanding of the particularities of the Israelite tribal system is both complex and challenging, such understanding should not have been beyond the capacity of professionally-qualified translators. No attempt has been made to determine both context and authorial intent and differentiate accordingly: all *Ioudaios* are carelessly lumped together and rendered into English as "Jew/s".

Persons designated as "Jews" could fall into one or more of the following categories:

1. Descendants of the Israelite tribe of Judah who lived in the Roman Province of Judea and worshipped at the Temple in Jerusalem;
2. Descendants of the Israelite tribe of Judah regardless of where they lived. For example, Jesus was a Jew because he belonged to the tribe of Judah even though he came from Galilee;

3. Persons who followed the customs and practices of the Judeans who worshipped at the Temple in Jerusalem regardless of where they lived. For example, Paul self-identified as a "Jew" because he followed the customs and practices of the Judeans who worshipped at the Temple in Jerusalem even though he came from Tarsus and belonged to the Israelite tribe of Benjamin.

Note that Jesus falls into categories 2 and 3 above: not only did he belong to the Israelite tribe of Judah but he also followed the customs and practices of the Judeans who worshipped at the Temple in Jerusalem.

Correctly identifying the category of person the author has in view at any one time is daunting but not impossible if context is studied and fully appreciated. Given the fact that the word *Ioudaios* was to become the most important single word in all of human history, the consequences of not differentiating between the various categories of *Ioudaios* mentioned in the New Testament can hardly be overestimated.

Greeks (Greek Ἕλλην : Transliteration Hellēn)

No consistency of translation: e.g. sometimes rendered Gentile. In the 1st Century AD, there was no nation state of Greece. "Greeks" are civilised people who speak the Greek language and follow the customs and practices of Hellenists. Among those designated as "Greeks" were both Israelites living in diaspora communities and non-Israelites. Israelite "Greeks" do not follow the "barbaric" customs and practices of the Judeans but rather the customs and practices of Hellenists.

Gentiles (Greek ἀλλοφύλῳ :Transliteration allophylō) (Greek ἐθνῶν :Transliteration ethnē)

No consistency of translation: e.g. variously Greek, heathen, pagan, nation, race. There are various Greek words that have been translated into English as "Gentile". As with the word "Greek", there is no consistency of translation.

The complexity of the above terminology is daunting so, as always, we must determine meaning by context. Even though it is almost universally believed that Paul is the Apostle to the Gentiles, i.e. non-Israelites, it is obvious from his statement to Agrippa when he appeared before him in Caesarea that his mission was to the twelve tribes of Israel. (The correct translation of "Jews" appears in brackets):

> King Agrippa, I consider myself fortunate to stand before you today as I make my defense against all the accusations of the Jews (Judeans) and especially so because you are well acquainted with all the Jewish (Judean) customs and controversies. Therefore, I beg you to listen to me patiently. The Jewish (Judean) people all know the way I have lived ever since I was a child, from the beginning of my life in my own country, and also in Jerusalem. They have known me for

a long time and can testify, if they are willing, that I conformed to the strictest sect of our religion, living as a Pharisee. And now it is because of my hope in what God has promised our ancestors that I am on trial today. **This is the promise our twelve tribes are hoping to see fulfilled as they earnestly serve God day and night.** King Agrippa, it is because of this hope that these Jews (Judeans) are accusing me (Acts 26:2-7 NIV).

Paul was an Israelite who had persecuted Jesus groups in Judea. After his "road to Damascus" experience, he believed he had been called to be an Israelite prophet standing in the same tradition as the prophets of old and to proclaim the "Gospel of God" to Israelites. Paul's appeal to other Israelites is based on their common genealogy through Abraham and it is this commonality that forms the framework for all his theology.

Paul did not focus on the story of Jesus' life. Rather, his focus was on what the God of Israel had done in raising up Jesus. He announced that the Crucifixion and Resurrection was a signal to Israelites living in the Diaspora that they would one day be "resurrected" from their dispersion, regarded as a type of death, and ingathered to Israel to form the Kingdom of God to be ruled over by God's Messiah.

Many modern scholars claim that there are only seven genuine Epistles written by Paul himself, viz. 1 Thessalonians, Galatians, Philemon, Philippians, 1 & 2 Corinthians, and Romans. Their view that the other six pseudepigraphic epistles were written by later followers of Paul is borne out by the fact that these epistles are not Israelite-specific, as are the seven that can be directly attributed to Paul himself, and they do not require a knowledge of the Hebrew scriptures in order to be understood.

Since Paul's arguments would have made sense only to an Israelite audience, his mission then was to proclaim the Gospel of God to Israelites living among majority non-Israelite populations scattered throughout the Roman Empire. The one exception to this pattern is the Epistle to the Romans which was addressed to Jesus groups that Paul did not found. These Roman Jesus groups contained a few non-Israelite members and Paul issued them with some specific warnings about their status in Chapter 11:13-24. Still later generations of non-Israelites adopted Christianity after the Church Fathers, using their own philosophies and theologies, imposed upon the New Testament texts a synthesis of paganism and Hellenism more appealing to the peoples of the Roman Empire.

Paul's letters have been subjected to multiple doctrinal overlays and the distractions of theological hair-splitting over issues such as Faith, Works, Righteousness, Justification, Grace, Election, and so on. If we had not been subjected to these distractions, we would perhaps have recognised long ago that the letters directly attributable to Paul were addressed to those who could understand them, viz. fellow Israelites.

As it is, Pauline theology is largely based on non-Israelite concepts and would therefore collapse under the weight of its utter irrelevance and total absurdity. As Malina and Pilch state:

> It is quite significant to note that Paul's proclamation (of the gospel of God) was Israelite-specific in all of its dimensions: in its means of transmission (Paul received it through a revelation ascribed to the God of Israel who calls prophets), in its origin (the God of Israel), in its medium (a revelation of Israel's Messiah, the crucified and resurrected Jesus), in its content (an Israelite theocracy), and in its rationale (spelled out according to Israel's scriptures). Hence it is fairly obvious that the proclamation was meant specifically for Israelites.[5]

As well as the original Pauline epistles and the Gospels, the remainder of the New Testament documents were also Israelite-specific. See for example James 1:1 and Revelation 21:10-14.

---

[5] Malina, B.J, Pilch, J.J. *Social Science Commentary on the Letters of Paul*. Augsburg Fortress: Minneapolis, 2006, p 12

CHAPTER FIVE

Dating the New Testament Documents

Despite there being very little basis for many of the dates so confidently assigned to the New Testament documents, the mainstream scholarly view is that, with the exception of Paul's letters, the remaining material was composed after the destruction of the Jerusalem Temple by the Romans in 70 AD.

Mainstream scholars hold this view despite the fact that the most datable and climactic event of the era—the destruction of Jerusalem and the attendant collapse of the Temple sacrificial system—is not once mentioned as a past event. The destruction of the Holy City would have been more significant for Israelites than was the 1945 destruction of Berlin for the Germans, or the destruction of Hiroshima and Nagasaki for the Japanese in that same year. Despite the fact that there are many New Testament references to Jerusalem, the Temple, and to Temple worship, there is not a single mention or allusion to their destruction. This absence in the Gospels, Acts, Epistles, and Apocalypse is remarkable.

In regard to the Synoptics, Bo Reicke puts it succinctly:

> An amazing example of uncritical dogmatism in New Testament studies is the belief that the Synoptic Gospels should be dated after the Jewish War of 66-70 because they contain prophecies ex events of the destruction of Jerusalem by the Roman in the year 70.[6]

The "late date" theories were first advanced by the German historical-critical school of the early nineteenth century and, since that time, mainstream scholars have become habituated into this way of thinking. There is a certain tyranny in this uncritical dogmatism. Once orthodoxy is fixed, it becomes almost impossible to swim against the tide without inviting ridicule from one's peers. Nevertheless, some scholars have questioned the late date theories and claimed that the Gospels were written within the lifetime of the contemporaries of Jesus. Most notable of these were *Claude Tresmontant*, Hebrew scholar, Hellenist, philosopher, member of the faculty of the Sorbonne, and author of numerous studies in the history of Hebrew and Christian thought; *Bishop J.A.T. Robinson*, Dean of Trinity College, Cambridge; and *Abbé Jean Carmignac*, philologist, Dead Sea Scrolls translator and annotater, and editor of the

---

6 Reicke, B. *Synoptic Prophecies on the Destruction of Jerusalem*' in D.W.Aune (ed.), Studies in New Testament and Early Christian Literature: Essays in Honour of Allen P.Wikgren (Nov. Test. Suppl.33). Leiden, 1972, pp. 121-34.

Revue de Qumran (RQ). The writings of these scholars have been dismissed or ignored by the majority of their peers for two major reasons:

- it is considered rather simple-minded to believe in prophecy, to believe that Jesus actually predicted the destruction of the Temple, and yet these same scholars will credulously and confidently assert the "Deity" of Jesus of Nazareth;
- many eminent past and present reputations are at stake.

The majority of their peers ascribe to a linear, data-driven view of history and not to the Israelite cyclical view which searches for repeating patterns of history. It is not so remarkable that Jesus, a man with great insight and a profound sense of Israel's history, would be able to correctly identify all the gathering forces of destruction and to predict the downfall of the Temple.

It appears that many academics and theologians have little or no knowledge of Hebrew literary devices used throughout both the Hebrew Scriptures and the New Testament. (For more on this subject see the forthcoming Chapter: *Understanding Literary Techniques*.)

Consider the following passage from the Kingdom of Heaven parable:

> The king was enraged. He sent his army and destroyed those murderers and burned their city (Matthew 22:7 NIV).

It is often asserted that this passage concerns the destruction of Jerusalem and that it was written after the event. However, many nearly-identical passages are found in the Hebrew Scriptures and Jesus is here drawing on that type of language to talk about who, and who is not, worthy to enter the Kingdom of Heaven.

It is beyond the scope of this work to describe in detail the complexity of New Testament dating issues raised by scholars. However, a brief look at the Epistle of James and the Gospel of John should serve as case studies for pre-destruction dating.

The Epistle of James

In the earliest and best manuscripts of the New Testament, the seven general epistles of James, 1 & 2 Peter, 1, 2 & 3 John, and Jude are placed before the fourteen epistles of Paul in accord with the recognition of their superior authority. Professor Ernest F. Scott of Columbia University says:

> In our English New Testament, the General Epistles are placed near the end of the volume, just before the Book of Revelation. The Greek manuscripts put them as a rule, immediately after the Gospels and Acts, and before the writings

of Paul. This was no doubt in recognition of the fact that they bore the names of the Apostles who were directly associated with Jesus, and whose authority, therefore, might be considered superior to that of Paul. In keeping with this principle, the first place of all was accorded to the Epistle of James. Its author was assumed to be no other than James, the Lord's own brother.[7]

This ordering of the General Epistles follows Paul's exact ranking order:

> James, Cephas (Peter) and John, those esteemed as pillars… (Galatians 2:9 NIV).

The epistle of James lacks any specific line of demarcation between the messianic followers of Jesus and Temple religion. It attacks the exploiting classes in the manner of the Israelite prophets, and of Jesus himself:

> The local Christian gathering referred to as a 'synagogue' within Judaism (2:2; cf Acts 6:9). The basis of everything he says is the fundamental Jewish doctrine of the unity of God (2:19), who is invoked as 'the Lord of Sabbath' (5:4)…The appeal is to the Jewish law and its giver (2:9-11; 4:11f), and there is no hint that the Christian message represents anything but its (the law) fulfilment…[8]

No clear-cut break had yet occurred at the time of the Epistle's writing. The Jesus movement was still a sect embedded within the Judean pattern of worship.

Gospel of John

Contrary to the assertion that the Gospel of John is of a very late date because of its supposed Hellenist influence, there is internal evidence which dates this work well before the destruction of the Temple in 70 AD.

The Gospel presents Jesus as the ultimate truth and fullness of Israel. Its literary methods would have been practically unintelligible outside an Israelite context. Apart from the Ebionite sect, there is no possible milieu where this presentation could have been significant after 70 AD. It was hoped by the author that his arguments concentrating on the typical categories of the manna and the vine would enable his readers to accept that Jesus was the fulfillment of Israelite hopes.

Consider the following passages:

---

[7] Scott, Ernest F. *The Literature of the New Testament*. Columbia University Press: New York, 1936, pp. 209-210.

[8] Robinson, Bishop J.A.T. *Redating the New Testament*. Wipf & Stock: Oregon, 1976, p.121.

> Jesus answered them, "Destroy this temple, and I will raise it again in three days." They replied, "It has taken forty-six years to build this temple, and you are going to raise it in three days?" (John 2:29-20 NIV).

In the passage above, some interlocutors of Jesus observed that Herod's temple had been in the process of building for forty-six years. This passage dovetails with the time Jesus is presumed to be speaking as Herod the Great had begun building the Temple and its outbuildings and courts around 20 BC.[9] (According to Josephus, the temple was not completed until circa 63 AD.[10])

> Now there is in Jerusalem by the Sheep Gate a pool, in Aramaic called Bethesda, which has five roofed colonnades (John 5:2 ESV).

In the passage above, the author implies that he is familiar with all the geographical features of the pool of Bethesda and that it is still intact at the time of writing. Note that the "five roofed colonnades", long buried in rubble, have only recently been unearthed by archaeologists.

> If a man on the sabbath day receive circumcision, that the law of Moses should not be broken; are ye angry at me, because I have made a man every whit whole on the sabbath day? (John 7:23 KJV).

The passage above reflects contemporary rabbinic disputes.

> They will put you out of the synagogues. Indeed, the hour is coming when whoever kills you will think he is offering service to God (John 16:2 ESV).

In the passage above, Jesus warns the disciples that they had much to suffer at the hands of the Jerusalem establishment, not at the hands of the Romans. The God to whom Jesus refers is the God of Israel. Certainly, the Romans would never have thought in terms of doing the God of Israel a service. (See also Luke 21:12.)

As demonstrated in the above examples, the author's inclusion of many temporal and specific details provides the most compelling evidence that his account was committed to writing well before the destruction of the Temple in 70 AD.

---

9 Jewish Encyclopaedia Article : *Temple of Herod*. Accessed 26 February 2018. www.jewishencyclopedia.com/articles/14304-temple-of-herod

10 Josephus, *Antiquities*, XX:219

Worship patterns of early Jesus followers

The first Jesus followers were still embedded within the Judean pattern of worship prior to 70 AD. Thus the Synoptic Gospels are not arranged chronologically but according to episodes in the life of Jesus which were considered to belong to the complementary and appropriate passages from the Hebrew Scriptures used in the liturgical year. The Gospel of Matthew is the most striking in this regard. Matthew's five discourses by Jesus relate to the five great festivals of the Israelite liturgical year: Pentecost (*Shavuot*), New Year (*Rosh Hashanah*), Tabernacles (*Sukkot*), Dedication (*Hanukkah*), and Passover (*Pesach*).

In addition, Matthew represents Jesus as recapitulating in his individual existence a selection of deliverance-themed passages in the Hebrew Scriptures, especially those associated with Moses. For Matthew, Jesus is the representative Israelite, the one standing for the many, the "corporate personality", the one who fulfills in his individual existence God's salvation plan for the whole people of Israel.

As such, Matthew's Gospel would have had little or no relevance for non-Israelites. What would non-Israelite communities have thought about the following injunctions by Jesus?:

> These twelve Jesus sent forth, and commanded them, saying, Go not into the way of the Gentiles, and into any city of the Samaritans enter ye not: But go rather to the lost sheep of the house of Israel. And as ye go, preach, saying, The kingdom of heaven is at hand (Matthew 10:5-7 KJV).
>
> He answered, "I was sent only to the lost sheep of Israel" (Matthew 15:24 ESV).

Matthew's Gospel was written for the Israelite followers of Jesus before the end of the apostolic age. In the post-apostolic age, the original message became obscured by an overlaid synthesis of religious thought common to the peoples of the Roman Empire.

Summary

In 1964, when writing about the Apocalypse in relation to the Gospels of Matthew, Luke and John, Austin Farrer summed it all up very engagingly:

> The datings of all these books are like a line of tipsy revellers walking home arm-in-arm; each is kept in position by the others and none is firmly grounded.

The whole series can lurch five years this way or that, and still not collide with a solid obstacle.¹¹

In due course, these "tipsy revellers" will prove to be far more than just "five years" out either way but they will hold each other upright until their theories finally take a last unlamented breath.

Valuable works on early dating

Redating the New Testament, Bishop J.A.T. Robinson, Wipf & Stock: Oregon, 2000.

The Birth of the Synoptics, Abbé Jean Carmignac, Franciscan Herald Press: Chicago, 1987.

The Hebrew Christ, Professor Claude Tresmontant, Franciscan Herald Press: Chicago, 1989.

---

11   Farrer, A.M. *The Revelation of St. John the Divine.* Wipf & Stock: Oregon 1964, p. 37.

CHAPTER SIX

Language in 1st Century Judea

Discovering the scrolls

The conviction that 1st Century Israelites in the land of Israel predominantly spoke Aramaic was widespread from the end of the nineteenth century until the discovery of the Dead Sea Scrolls. Despite this discovery, the old conviction continues to circulate in academic and popular literature.

The Dead Sea Scrolls from Qumran (circa 250 BC - 68 AD) and those from other locations concerning the Bar-Kochba revolt (132-135 AD), conclusively settled the question of whether Mishnaic Hebrew had been an artificial or a living language. Hymns, prayers and biblical works written in Hebrew were discovered, as well as documents composed in the Mishnaic Hebrew dialect. Among them were letters containing Hebrew slang and abbreviated Hebrew forms characteristic of everyday speech.[12]

These discoveries prompted the biblical scholar J. T. Milik to conclude:

> The thesis of such scholars as Segal, Ben-Yehuda and Klausner that Mishnaic Hebrew was a language spoken by the population of Judea in the Persian and Græco-Roman periods can no longer be considered an assumption, but rather an established fact.[13]

According to Michael Wise, Martin Abegg Jr. and Edward Cook:

> Prior to the discovery of the Dead Sea Scrolls, the dominant view of the Semitic languages of Palestine in this period was essentially as follows: Hebrew had died; it was no longer learned at mother's knee. It was known only by the educated classes through study, just as educated medieval Europeans knew Latin…The spoken language of the Jews had in fact become Aramaic…The discovery of the scrolls swept these linguistic notions into the trash bin…Apart from copies of biblical books, about one out of six of the Dead Sea Scrolls is inscribed in Aramaic. Clearly the writing of an Aramaic Gospel was eminently

---

12   Safrai, Shmuel. *Spoken Languages in the time of Jesus*. Accessed 15 October 2016. www.jerusalemperspective.com/2551

13   Milik, Abbé J.T. *Discoveries in the Judaean Desert*. Clarendon Press: Oxford. 1961, Vol.2:70

possible. Yet the vast majority of the scrolls were Hebrew texts. Hebrew was manifestly the principal literary language for speech as well as writing…A small minority of the scrolls were written in Greek. Their discovery has vouchsafed us a further glimpse into the linguistic complexity of first-century Jewish society. Hebrew, Aramaic, Greek: each was being used in particular situations of speech and writing.[14]

Taking into account all of the above, we can safely conclude that, during the 1st Century AD, Hebrew could be spoken and written by Israelites. Additionally, Hebrew was the "sacred" language insisted upon by the Judean priestly and scribal classes at least until the destruction of the Jerusalem Temple by the Romans in 70 AD.

At the time of Jesus, Hebrew still remained the only language linking Israelites to their cultural, historical and religious origins.

---

14 Wise, M. Abegg, M Jr. Cook, E. *The Dead Sea Scrolls: A New Translation.* HarperCollins Publishers: New York. 1996, pp 8-10.

CHAPTER SEVEN

The Language of the Gospels

Very soon after the apostolic age, Christianity began to embrace anti-Israelite ideas and doctrines. It should come as no surprise, therefore, to discover that Christians have always had little or no awareness of the real roots of their faith. However, a new and searching light began to penetrate into the dark recesses of this millennial ignorance soon after the Second World War when two remarkable events occurred in swift succession—the adoption of Modern Hebrew as the official language of the State of Israel and the discovery of the Dead Sea Scrolls.

Since the establishment of the State, and the adoption of modern Hebrew as the official State language, New Testament scholars based at the Hebrew University in Jerusalem have acquired a conversational knowledge of the language, thereby enabling enhanced recognition of the Hebrew subtext behind the Greek copies of the Gospels, while the simultaneous study of the Dead Sea Scrolls and coinage of the period is making it increasingly clear that Hebrew was a living language spoken and written at the time of Jesus.

Nowhere in the ancient world was the written word more revered than amongst the Israelites. For an example of this reverence, we need look no further than the Book of Jeremiah where we learn that as soon as the prophet received the word of God, his scribe, Baruch, committed it to writing.

Israelite religious thought centred on the written Hebrew Scriptures which Israelites were, and still are, admonished to know and teach their children. The following points should be kept in mind when considering the relative importance attached to the written word:

- 1st Century Israelite boys were taught Torah and how to read Hebrew from an early age. According to the Babylonian Talmud (Sukkah 42a), boys were taught the *Shema*, the foundational creed of the Israelite religion, as soon as they could speak;

- It is clear from the Gospels that Jesus could read, quote, interpret and debate the Hebrew Scriptures with priests, professional scribes, theologians and scholars;

- Luke described both Jesus and Paul as speaking in Hebrew (Acts 21:40; 22:2; 26:14). In all three places, however, some English translations render the Greek word Ἑβραΐς (*Hebra'is*) as "Aramaic";

- The *titulus* inscription was in Latin, Greek and Hebrew and was placed in a position where it could be read by "many".

Despite the educated environment of Jerusalem, with its abundance of written literature, its reverence for the written word, and the presence of the aforementioned priests, scribes, theologians, and religious scholars, the majority Christian theological and academic view is that the Gospels were orally transmitted, gradually embellished, and not committed to writing (Greek) until decades after the crucifixion, first by Mark.

They would have us believe that no one recorded so much as a syllable issuing from the mouth of the man whom some believed to be no less than the awaited Davidic Messiah.

The evidence — ancient and modern

There is an abundance of ancient evidence from Papias, Hegesippus, Irenaeus, Origen, Eusebius and Jerome that Matthew's Gospel was originally composed in Hebrew.

However, we do not have to rely on ancient witnesses who knew of the existence of at least one Gospel which had been originally composed in Hebrew because as Claude Tresmontant, Abbé Jean Carmignac, and other eminent scholars have convincingly and irrefutably demonstrated, the Greek Gospels we now have are full of Hebrew idioms, literalisms, thought patterns, literary devices and syntactical structures. Indeed, sections contain such slavishly transparent transliterations that they can only be based on Hebrew originals. These sections are mainly those which record the words of Jesus and those of his opponents. Luke's Gospel is the most remarkable in this regard. Since the intricacies and peculiarities of the Hebrew language could not possibly have survived years of oral transmission, particularly in a foreign Hellenist environment far removed from their source, before being committed to writing, it has now become clear that the sayings of Jesus and those of his opponents were taken down at the time of their utterance, in the language in which they were uttered.

The authors of the original Greek Gospels arranged their accounts according to their own particular purposes, including the degree to which their target readers were familiar with *Midrashic* analogies (see Chapter Nine: *Understanding Literary Styles*). They utilised documents, notes, witness statements and so on, reproducing in whole or in part the various sayings, incidents, parables and the like in no consistent temporal or logical relationship to one another. This compilation process naturally resulted in the loss of the original chronology of events; in textual variants; and in the inclusion or otherwise of certain passages according to authorial discretion. What is truly remarkable, however, is the coherent, homogenous, and self-consistent point of view that was preserved throughout.

The good news for followers of Jesus

The good news for followers of Jesus is that because these translations of the Hebrew words of Jesus have been rendered into Greek with such scrupulous attention and care, we can have a high degree of confidence in the fidelity of the Gospel authors. We can therefore have a high degree of confidence that the words of Jesus have been faithfully transmitted to us.

The bad news for Creedal Christianity

The bad news for the theological establishment is that we can no longer have confidence in their views. By continuing to assert that the Gospels were only committed to writing after a long period of oral transmission in a language and culture far removed from their original Israelite context, they stand opposed to the rising tide of knowledge and understanding. Such opposition is in certain cases based on a residue of deep dislike for "Jewish" thought, widely regarded as narrow-minded, exclusive and legalistic, as opposed to "Hellenist" thought, widely regarded as spiritual, cosmic, and universal.

At a very early stage, Christianity cut itself off from the tree onto which it was grafted, and it remains cut off to this day. However, because knowledge is no longer the exclusive preserve of the theological establishment, and because of the rapid pace of its dissemination, we now see all too clearly that the Christian age, characterised more by war, hatred and division than by love, peace and unity, is soon to die.

Unless Christianity returns to its Israelite roots, and re-grafts itself onto the tree from which it sprang, its sickness is terminal.

When the major doctrines of mainstream Christianity centred upon Jesus are examined, and we compare them with the New Testament texts on which they are supposedly based, we will find that these doctrines have absolutely nothing to do with Jesus or with the original Jesus followers. Worse than that, we will find that they distort and misrepresent the central redemptive theme of the Bible from start to finish. In fact, if it had been deliberately determined by someone or something, right from the beginning, to destroy everything that Jesus was born, lived and died for, then the outcome could not have been more desirable for that someone or something.

CHAPTER EIGHT

Hebraisms in the Gospels

It would be too lengthy a task to list the numerous occurrences of Hebraisms found in the Gospels. However, a few examples should suffice for the purposes of demonstration.

Word Order and Phrase Structure

It is evident that the thought and language of the Hebrew Scriptures came naturally to the authors of the original documents on which our Greek Gospels are based. In some places, the Hebrew word order and phrase structure has been carefully retained by those who first translated the Hebrew originals into Greek. When we find phrases that have the form, structure and composition of Hebrew, we can be sure that the translator attempted to respect what had been handed down to him.

Hebrew phrase structure of initial verb followed by either subject or complements/prepositional phrases expressing circumstances, place, etc. are easily identifiable. Out of the tens of thousands of such phrase structures in the Hebrew Scriptures, just one example from Genesis 18:1a demonstrating the difference between English and Hebrew word order should suffice:

> The Lord appeared to Abraham near the great trees of Mamre… (English word order)
>
> And appeared to him, by the oaks of Mamre, the Lord… (Hebrew word order)

In certain places in the New Testament, this original Hebrew word order has been faithfully retained. For example, after quoting from Isaiah 7:14, the author of Matthew's Greek Gospel preserves the Hebrew original word order when explaining the meaning of the name Emmanuel which is, "with (*im*) us (*nu*) God (*el*)". Below is a literal English translation of the Greek:

> Behold, the virgin (*parthenos*)[15] in womb will hold, and will bear a son and they will call the name of him Emmanuel which is being translated, with us God (Matthew 1:23).

Consider the following passage, also from Matthew:

---

15 For an analysis of the 1st Century AD meaning of *parthenos* see Part IV : *Virgin Birth and Incarnation*.

> Then came to him the disciples of John, saying, Why do we and the Pharisees fast oft, but thy disciples fast not? And Jesus said unto them, Can the children of the bridechamber mourn, as long as the bridegroom is with them? but the days will come, when the bridegroom shall be taken from them, and then shall they fast (Matthew 9:14-15 KJV).

In Greek, the original Hebrew word order has been preserved and can be rendered into English as:

> Advanced towards him, the disciples of John, saying, "Why do we and the Pharisees fast, but your disciples do not fast?" Said to them, Jesus, "They cannot fast, the sons of the bridechamber (*benei hahuphah*), while the bridegroom (*hatan*) is still with them. The days will come when he will be taken away, the bridegroom, and then they will fast."

Note that the terms "the sons of the bridechamber" and "the bridegroom" would have been simply unintelligible to Greek speakers unacquainted with the Hebrew Scriptures and the symbolism of the Song of Songs. (See also Mark 2:19 and Luke 5:34.)

Idioms

Son of Man

The idiomatic differences between Hebrew and English are vital to facilitate understanding of certain terms and phrases when we find them in the New Testament. As an example of a popular Hebrew idiom found in the New Testament, we will focus on the term "son of man".

To identify an individual man, the Israelites used the phrase "son of man". A son of man was simply an individual belonging to the class of humans. Similarly, for example, an individual belonging to the class of prophets was often referred to as "son of a prophet". This of course did not imply that the individual had a biological father who was a prophet: it simply meant that he belonged to a class of those who prophesied. On some occasions, the term was used as "a cumbersome but solemn and formal substitute for the personal pronoun". [16]

"Son of man" is a common term found in the Psalms. When used in passages such as those in Psalms 8:4 and 144:3, it implies "mortality", "impotence", and "transientness", as opposed to the omnipotence and eternality of God:

---

[16] Hirsch, Emil G. *Son of Man*. Jewish Encyclopaedia 1906. Accessed 3 March 2019. http://jewishencyclopedia.com/articles/13913-son-of-man

O LORD, what is man, that You take knowledge of him? Or the son of man, that You think of him? (Psalm 144:3 NASB).

In the Book of Ezekiel, God addresses the prophet about ninety times as "son of man". As in the Psalms, the vast difference between God and man is accentuated.

The term is the favorite self-designation of Jesus in the Gospels. It occurs over thirty times in Matthew, twenty-five times in Luke, fifteen times in Mark, and twelve times in John. Other than the Gospels, it occurs once in Acts (7:56), and twice in the Book of Revelation (1:13; 14:14). Jesus used the term in the following senses:

As a basic idiom indicating a specific type of human:

> And if a son of peace is there, your peace will rest upon him. But if not, it will return to you (Luke 10:6 ESV).

As a basic idiom indicating the general species of human:

> Verily I say unto you, All sins shall be forgiven unto the sons of men, and blasphemies wherewith soever they shall blaspheme (Mark 3:28 KJV).

And as a formal substitute for the personal pronoun:

> And Jesus said to him, "Foxes have holes, and birds of the air have nests, but the Son of Man has nowhere to lay his head" (Matthew 8:20 ESV).

Unfortunately, these Hebrew idioms are lost in some modern English versions of Scripture where, for example, a "son of peace" is translated as "someone who promotes peace" and "sons of men" is translated as "people".

Setting the Face

Those acquainted with the Hebrew Scriptures would be familiar with the expression in these passages:

> For I have set my face against this city for evil, and not for good, saith the LORD: it shall be given into the hand of the king of Babylon, and he shall burn it with fire (Jeremiah 21:10 KJV).

> Son of man, set your face against the mountains of Israel; prophesy against them (Ezekiel 6:2 NIV).

> Likewise, thou son of man, set thy face against the daughters of thy people, which prophesy out of their own heart; and prophesy thou against them (Ezekiel 13:17 KJV).

It should come as no surprise therefore to find the author of Luke using this Hebraic expression in three different ways in one passage:

> And it came to pass, when the time was come that he should be received up, he stedfastly set his face to go to Jerusalem, And sent messengers before his face: and they went, and entered into a village of the Samaritans, to make ready for him. And they did not receive him, because his face was as though he would go to Jerusalem (Luke 9:51-53 KJV).

In addition to these Hebraic expressions, Luke's Gospel contains sections with such transparent transliterations, mainly those that record the words of Jesus and those of his opponents, that they can only be based on Hebrew originals. Also included in Luke are the Canticles of Mary and Zechariah, both derived almost exclusively from Hebrew models found countless times in the Hebrew Scriptures. It is truly remarkable that all this compelling evidence pointing to a Hebrew substratum in the Gospels can be ignored or overlooked by theologians, academics and translators alike.

Patterns

Amen

"Amen" is a Hebrew word that was simply transliterated from Hebrew into the Greek ἀμήν. The Greek was then translated into English as "truly" or "verily". The word is used an impressive number of times in the Gospel of John where it is even doubled in the typical Hebraic fashion. For example:

> Jesus answered and said unto him, Verily, verily, I say unto thee, Except a man be born again, he cannot see the kingdom of God (John 3:3 KJV).

> Jesus said to them, "Truly, truly, I say to you, before Abraham was, I am" (John 8:58 ESV).

Parent and Child

For Israelites, children were not only the result of the biological process but were also generated in the intellectual and spiritual order. For instance, a pupil who learned from a rabbi became a type of son and could therefore call his teacher "father".

Paul taught that one could join the Abrahamic covenant and become a child of Abraham if one adopted Abraham as a spiritual father:

> Understand, then, that those who have faith are children of Abraham (Galatians 3:7 NIV).

And if you belong to the Messiah, then you are Abraham's descendants indeed, and heirs according to the promise (Galatians 3:29 ISV).

When this concept of intellectual or spiritual generation is used in the New Testament, it is a reflection of Israelite thought patterns.

CHAPTER NINE

Understanding Literary Styles

The writings of the Hebrew Scriptures and the New Testament comprise many literary forms including parallelism, allegory, typology, pesher and parables. New Testament readers would be most familiar with the parable—the favoured teaching method of Jesus.

Since copious material is already available on the most well-known of these forms, it would serve no important purpose to reproduce it here. However, for an enhanced understanding of the New Testament, it is most important to become familiar with two forms used throughout the Hebrew Scriptures. Being ancient Israelite in origin, they are mainly overlooked by literary analysts embedded in the Western tradition.

Midrash

If one is familiar with the Israelite literary style of *Midrash*, and knows a little about the major themes of the Hebrew Scriptures, it is quite a simple matter to identify passages where the Gospel authors, perceiving that the events of Jesus' life and death were invested with a much deeper meaning than the bare circumstances would suggest, enlivened those events by analogous association with prior events already holding great significance for a contemporary reader.

Hence we see an abundance of *Midrashic* analogy between individual events in the life of Jesus and previous events in the national life of Israel, the purpose of which was to demonstrate Jesus' central role in the redemptive plan of God. We see the literary style of *Midrash* most strikingly employed in Matthew's Gospel.

Unfamiliarity with the *Midrashic* style leads many to relegate the Gospel accounts to myth by pointing out their minor inconsistencies, additions, or omissions. In reality, these features are mostly the result of individual writers doing *Midrash*.

When the author of Luke wrote the book of Acts, he put into Paul's mouth sermons full of quotations and references to the Hebrew scriptures demonstrating that, in his day, sermons for Jesus followers were composed according to *Midrashic* analogies.

Parallelism

One of the main characteristics of the Hebrew language is known as parallelism, a feature which is abundant in the Hebrew Scriptures:

> It is now generally conceded that parallelism is the fundamental law, not only of the poetical, but even of the rhetorical and therefore of higher style in general in

the Old Testament. By parallelism in this connection is understood the regularly recurring juxtaposition of symmetrically constructed sentences. The symmetry is carried out in the substance as well as in the form, and lies chiefly in the relation of the expression to the thought.[17]

The most basic and frequent form is the simple distich, in which two lines balance each other in thought and expression. For example:

> But let judgment run down as waters, and righteousness as a mighty stream (Amos 5:24 KJV).

The parallelism may extend to several lines with the same variety of relationships as in the distich. For example, the tripstich form:

> Blessed is the man that walketh not in the counsel of the ungodly, nor standeth in the way of sinners, nor sitteth in the seat of the scornful (Psalm 1:1 KJV).

Another form of this feature is the tetratstich—two distich balanced against each other:

> When you pass through the waters, I will be with you; and through the rivers, they shall not overwhelm you; when you walk through fire you shall not be burned, and the flame shall not consume you (Isaiah 43:2 ESV).

New Testament parallelisms

As noted in a previous Chapter: *The Language of the Gospels*, there is compelling evidence that the sections of the Gospels which record the words of Jesus and those of his opponents were originally composed in Hebrew before the destruction of the Jerusalem Temple in 70 AD.

This view is further strengthened by the fact that Hebrew parallelisms are scattered throughout the Gospels. For example, Mary used a typical distich parallelism in her poetic praise of God:

> My soul glorifies the Lord and my spirit rejoices in God my Savior (Luke 1:46-47 NIV).

Jesus also expressed his thoughts in Hebrew parallelisms of different types on many occasions. For example:

---

[17] The Jewish Encyclopaedia Article : *Parallelism in Hebrew Poetry*. Accessed 26 February 2018. www.jewishencyclopedia.com/articles/11902-parallelism-in-hebrew-poetry

> The disciple is not above his master, nor the servant above his lord (Matthew 10:24 KJV).

Gabriel's words to Mary were similarly expressed by Luke:

> And the angel answered her, "The Holy Spirit will come upon you, and the power of the Most High will overshadow you; therefore the child to be born will be called holy—the Son of God (Luke 1:35 ESV).

Parallelisms can be very instructive in unexpected ways as, for example, we can plainly see a negation of the Trinity doctrine in the above verse where the "Holy Spirit" is synonymous with the "power of the Most High" thus demonstrating that the Holy Spirit is not to be considered as separate in any way from God himself. The Holy Spirit is not the third part of the Trinity but rather God acting on humans through his Spirit, a concept repeatedly expressed throughout the Hebrew Scriptures and the New Testament.

CHAPTER TEN

The Interpretation Methodology

Biblical texts can be meaningless unless interpreted from within a linguistic, authorial, theological and cultural context vastly different to our own, and separated in time by thousands of years. Further complications arise when the significance and meaning of various passages is obscured by imposing on the texts doctrinal imperatives, personal value systems, modern Western cultural assumptions, and even emotional needs.

Linguistic Context

The distinctive language, terminology, and broad range of figurative speech characteristic of the peoples we encounter in the pages of the Bible is crucial to comprehension.

Authorial Context

Every word of the New Testament was written after the Resurrection by members of the Jesus community. With the perspective afforded by hindsight, they could reflect and interpret events, beginning with Creation and ending with Jesus, which may have held little significance for some of the participants at the actual time. Thus when talking about Jesus, their descriptive terms such as Messiah, son of God, only-begotten son, etcetera, all reflect post-resurrection awareness.

Theological Context

The theological intent of both the Hebrew Scriptures and the New Testament, beginning in Genesis, is to convey an understanding about our relationship with God, how that understanding has been revealed over time, and how that relationship impacts upon human life in all ages. To read the Bible in a linear, historical, data-driven type of way is to impose on the texts the relatively modern science of history recording. This approach fails to recognise that many passages are not concerned with merely recording "facts", as we understand them, but with interpreting the significance and meaning of God's encounters with Israel's history and using that interpretation to explain present theological truths to the community (see previous Chapter: *Understanding Literary Styles*). Fact, as opposed to fiction, is a modern construct. Truth, as opposed to lies, is a more appropriate Biblical construct.

Cultural Context

Ethnocentrism

1st Century AD Mediterranean peoples were ethnocentric. When reading the New Testament we should always be aware of the social boundaries existing between Israelites (in-groups) and everyone else (out-groups). Israelite in-group attitudes were derived from the perception of shared values existing within the sub-groups of family, village community, and country-dweller.

Religion and State

Ancient Israel did not separate various aspects of its society into modern categories. Hence, there was no distinction between religion and politics. All aspects were embedded in the social structure of the day. Take, for example, the Jerusalem Temple compound which served as an economic centre, as a military fortress, and as a place of religious observance. The view that Christians should be concerned only with religious issues is based on the assumption that the priests and scribes with whom Jesus interacted were solely focused on religious questions and were not part of the state apparatus. This view betrays a lack of knowledge of the conditions in Judea in the 1st Century AD. The government of the day was a coalition of king, aristocratic families, high government officials, Roman military representatives and the ruling elites of the priesthood. The High Priests, Annas and Caiaphas, both appointed by the Roman authorities, were two such members of the elite priestly establishment (John 18:13).

Family

Great emphasis was placed on family tradition and continuity. At least from the period of the Babylonian Exile, (see Ezra and Nehemiah), genealogies, the purity of blood, and the symbolic importance of the twelve tribes were basic. Significant social roles such as the priesthood, requirements for admission to the temple, and appropriate marriage depended on genealogical purity.

Betrothal and Marriage

To begin the process, the prospective bridegroom would negotiate an agreement with the head of the prospective bride's family. If successful, the bridegroom would go to his own father's house where he would prepare either an existing room or build a separate room for himself and his new bride. To complete the betrothal and marriage process, the bridegroom would take his bride to the room in his father's house that he had prepared beforehand where they would begin their life together. Note how this custom illuminates Jesus' statement in John 14:2, "In my Father's house are many rooms: if it were not so, I would have told you. I go to prepare a place for you".

Note that Simon Peter's mother-in-law resided in Simon's house along with Andrew (Mark 129-30), presumably also with Simon and Andrew's wives and children.

Limited Goods

Unlike the modern Western world with its abundance of goods, 1st Century Israel was a society of limited goods. To exist within a society of limited goods meant that one could not be described as a "rich" person owning many goods without the existence of its corollary—a "poor" person deprived of goods. This reality can be most instructive when reading New Testament passages about the interactions between Jesus and the "rich young ruler" for example.

Honour-Shame

Concern for one's honour permeated every aspect of life in Mediterranean antiquity. Honour served as the prime indicator of social position and prescribed how persons should interact with superiors, inferiors and equals in appropriate ways. Public insults were an attempt to shame another and must be challenged to defend one's honour. All of the trial exchanges between Pilate and the Jerusalem elites, and between Pilate and Jesus, are set within the framework of this honour-shame society.

PART III

Creeds & Christologies

CHAPTER ONE

The Creeds

Notes

The Council of Nicea was convened by the Emperor Constantine in 325 AD. Except for a few Latin attendees from the West, the remainder of the traditional number of 318 were Greek-speaking bishops from the Eastern churches where most Christians then lived.

This work will not address the content of the Apostles Creed or the Athanasian Creed but only those which today remain the most influential in terms of authority and recognition.

Niceno-Constantinopolitan Creed : 381 AD

The Nicene Creed was first adopted at the Council of Nicea in an attempt to unify the Christian Churches with one statement of belief. The original Creed was later revised and accepted by both Eastern and Western branches of Christendom at the First Council of Constantinople in 381 AD.

The final version reads:

> I believe in one God, the Father almighty, maker of heaven and earth, of all things visible and invisible. I believe in one Lord Jesus Christ, the Only Begotten Son of God, born of the Father before all ages. God from God, Light from Light, true God from true God, begotten, not made, consubstantial with the Father; through him all things were made. For us men and for our salvation he came down from heaven, and by the Holy Spirit was incarnate of the Virgin Mary, and became man. For our sake he was crucified under Pontius Pilate, he suffered death and was buried, and rose again on the third day in accordance with the Scriptures. He ascended into heaven and is seated at the right hand of the Father. He will come again in glory to judge the living and the dead and his kingdom will have no end. I believe in the Holy Spirit, the Lord,the giver of life, who proceeds from the Father and the Son, who with the Father and the Son is adored and glorified, who has spoken through the prophets. I believe in one, holy, catholic* and apostolic Church. I confess one baptism for the forgiveness of sins and I look forward to the resurrection of the dead and the life of the world to come. Amen.

Note that the word "catholic" here means "universal" and does not, as some have claimed, refer to the Roman Catholic Church.

Chalcedonian Creed: 451 AD

The Chalcedonian Creed was adopted at the Fourth Ecumenical Council held at Chalcedon as a response to certain "heretical" views concerning the nature of Christ. It established the orthodox view that Christ has two natures (human and divine) that are unified in one person:

> We, then, following the holy Fathers, all with one consent, teach men to confess one and the same Son, our Lord Jesus Christ, the same perfect in Godhead and also perfect in manhood; truly God and truly man, of a reasonable [rational] soul and body; consubstantial (co-essential) with the Father according to the Godhead, and consubstantial with us according to the Manhood; in all things like unto us, without sin; begotten before all ages of the Father according to the Godhead, and in these latter days, for us and for our salvation, born of the Virgin Mary, the Mother of God, according to the Manhood; one and the same Christ, Son, Lord, only begotten, to be acknowledged in two natures, inconfusedly, unchangeably, indivisibly, inseparably; the distinction of natures being by no means taken away by the union, but rather the property of each nature being preserved, and concurring in one Person and one Subsistence, not parted or divided into two persons, but one and the same Son, and only begotten, God Logos, the Lord Jesus Christ; as the prophets from the beginning (have declared) concerning Him, and the Lord Jesus Christ Himself has taught us, and the Creed of the holy Fathers has handed down to us.

Despite the efforts of these Councils, both Eastern and Western branches of Christendom disagreed over elements of the Trinity so, eventually, attempts at unity were abandoned and Western Christendom adopted the Athanasian Creed in which the equality of the three persons of the Trinity is made explicit.

There are practically no statements in these Creeds that bear any similarity to the Israelite Jesus revealed to us in the New Testament. Essays appearing elsewhere in this work will address the claims made in these Creeds in their appropriate contexts.

Christologies

Christology (from Greek Χριστός *Khristós* and λογία *logia*), the "study of Christ", is that part of theology that is concerned with the nature and work of Jesus, including such matters as the Miraculous Incarnation and the relationship between his human and divine natures. All Christologies, past and present, are based on the incorrect assertion that the New Testament teaches the twin doctrines of the Virgin Conception/Birth and the Miraculous Incarnation, an assertion which eventually culminated in the formulation of the Trinity.

It would be at least one of the labours of Hercules to deal extensively with Christological thought spanning almost two thousand years. Rather, we will look briefly at its beginnings and endings to determine whether anything at all has changed since the days of the Church Fathers who retrojected onto the New Testament texts a fabricated synthesis of their own Hellenist-Latin theologies and philosophies.

The Christology of Modernism

The Enlightenment marked a move away from the theocentric world view of the Church Fathers to one where human beings replaced God. Henceforth, humans would be the masters of their own fate and all external authority would be replaced by human reason as the final arbiter of truth. Christianity's pessimistic view of a hopelessly corrupted and sinful human nature abated in favour of the optimistic view that, through self-development, humans could eventually triumph over ignorance and social evil by the application of reason and science.

Enlightenment theologians began searching for a new Christological paradigm more befitting to the modern era. It is impossible in this work to even attempt to describe the bewildering array of new perspectives and new model Christologies emerging from Enlightenment philosophy, theology and science. A complex succession of these new perspectives and new model Christologies began to proliferate on bookshelves, all appealing to "age of reason" modernity and all using their particular brand of esoteric and impenetrable terminology.

The Christology of Post-Modernism

The definition of post-modernism is fluid and difficult to define. Generally speaking, unlike modernism, post-modernism denies the existence of any ultimate principles and lacks the optimism of the modern mind, which was characterised by a conviction that there was a scientific, philosophical, or religious truth which would explain everything for everybody. For post-moderns, there is no such thing as a universal truth: all is relative to the individual's personal experience, social and cultural context, and historical perspective.

Marching along to the same drumbeat is post-modern Christology, which also finds universality and non-contextual truth abhorrent. Consequently, another complex succession of new perspectives and new model Christologies are again proliferating on our bookshelves, although now appealing to post-modern relativism but still using similar esoteric and impenetrable terminology. The current crop of theological tomes may appear more profound, may display greater subtlety of thought, more visionary insight, and more exalted spirituality, but they are just as profoundly incorrect as all the works of their theological ancestors.

It is claimed that these new Christologies are diverse yet complementary ways of explaining the central tenet that Jesus of Nazareth was the "Son of God, begotten from all ages, sent from heaven to become flesh in, or as the son of, Mary". [1]

In other words, ***nothing has changed since the days of Nicea and Chalcedon.***

Theologians and academicians claim that Christology is a long and never-ending task which will continue to yield many interpretations in different ages and different cultures. Thus they ensure for themselves and their theological descendants a cornucopia of ever-more sublime and complex theories which, in turn, spawn yet more, and yet more *ad infinitum.* In terms of providing some inspirational value to the vast multitude of Christians who just want to live according to the golden rule, past and present Christologies have been, and still are, exceptionally useless.

If one were to seek an example of Orwellian double-think—holding two opposing positions at the same time—one could hardly do better than to fasten on the Doctrine of the Incarnation. If one were to seek an example of group-think, one could hardly do better than settle on today's crop of theologians, speaking only the language of the academy and seeking only the approval of the academy.

And most of this modern and post-modern effort has been directed towards *explaining away* the Doctrine of the Miraculous Incarnation.

Note

The renowned scholar, Jaroslav Pelikan, spoke of the consequences of the early identification of Jesus with the title "Logos":

---

[1] Dunn, James D. *Christology in the Making: A New Testament Inquiry Into the Origins of the Doctrine of the Incarnation.* Wm. B. Eerdmans Publishing Company: 2 Edition, 1996, p. 251.

By the fourth century, it had become evident that all the various "titles of majesty for Christ" adapted and adopted during the first generations after Jesus, none was to have more momentous consequences than the title 'Logos', consequences as momentous for the history of thought as were those of the title King in the history of politics.[2]

We will critically examine the consequences of adopting the Hellenist concept of "Logos" as a "title of majesty for Christ" in an essay appearing elsewhere in this work.

---

[2] Pelikan, Jaroslav. *Jesus Through the Centuries: His Place in the History of Culture.* Yale University Press: 1999, p.58.

PART IV

Virgin Birth & Incarnation

CHAPTER ONE

Introduction

The Doctrine of the Virgin Conception/Birth teaches that Jesus had no human father and that his mother Mary conceived him through supernatural means while still a virgin. The Doctrine of the Incarnation teaches that God became flesh in Jesus through the supernatural event of the Virgin Conception/Birth. Thus the doctrines of Virgin Concpetion/Birth and Incarnation are wholly dependent upon each other.

After promulgating the teaching of the Virgin Conception/Birth, the early Hellenist-Latin Fathers of the Church subsequently found scriptural problems which could only be addressed and answered by promulgating yet more teachings, culminating in the doctrine of the Trinity. In the case of the Roman Catholic Church, these adaptations continued until the 19th Century with the adoption of the doctrine of the "Immaculate Conception" which teaches that Mary was conceived without spot or stain of Original Sin.

If, however, there was no supernatural birth, there was no supernatural Incarnation. If the child, Jesus of Nazareth, were a human conceived in the same way as the rest of humanity, then the entire doctrinal apparatus of Christianity collapses. Notwithstanding its current status in the different denominations of Christendom, the doctrine of the Virgin Conception/Birth is the foundation stone upon which the entire structure rests.

Doctrines such as the Virgin Conception/Birth were developed by the Fathers in almost total ignorance of the Israelite God or the Israelite Jesus or the Israelite Apostles. They knew almost nothing about Israelite messianic expectations, Hebrew language terminology, or Israelite modes of thinking and expression.

The propagation of the doctrine served two purposes:

1. It allowed for the seamless integration of the Jewish Jesus into the synthesis of Hellenist and Latin theological and philosophical thought characteristic of the general populace of the Roman Empire;

2. It allowed for the concealment of the "embarrassing" fact that Jesus of Nazareth was the son of a man other than the man to whom his mother was betrothed.

For nigh on two thousand years, ecclesiastics, scholars, popes and theologians have continued to assert, as did their forbears, that the doctrine of the Virgin Conception/Birth of Jesus is based on the Bible. As their evidence they quote:

- The Book of the prophet Isaiah in the Hebrew Scriptures;
- The New Testament Gospel of Matthew;
- The New Testament Gospel of Luke.

We shall examine their evidence in the following Chapters.

CHAPTER TWO

The Book of Isaiah the Prophet

Isaiah 7:14

The context of Isaiah Chapter 7 is the threatened destruction of the House of David by the armies of Rezin, King of Syria, and Pekah, King of Israel. Isaiah the prophet gave King Ahaz a sign of deliverance from these enemies.

Chapter 7 verses 14-16 read:

> Therefore the Lord himself shall give you a sign; Behold, a virgin shall conceive, and bear a son, and shall call his name Immanuel. Butter and honey shall he eat, that he may know to refuse the evil, and choose the good. For before the child shall know to refuse the evil, and choose the good, the land that thou abhorrest shall be forsaken of both her kings (Isaiah 7:14-16 KJV).

The Hebrew words of verse 14 reproduced below are taken from the *Leningrad Codex B19A (L)*, dated 1008-1009 AD, as reproduced in *Biblica Hebraica Stuttgartensia*.[1]

The word signifying "the young woman" appears highlighted below.

הִנֵּה הָעַלְמָה הָרָה וְיֹלֶדֶת בֵּן וְקָרָאת שְׁמוֹ עִמָּנוּ אֵל׃

The literal translation of verse 14 is:

> Behold · the young woman (*almah*) · is pregnant/will be pregnant · and is bearing/and will bear (*harah*)· son · and she will call · his name · with us · God. (*im nu el*)

This sign had absolutely nothing to do with the manner of the child's conception or birth. It was a sign of deliverance. The child soon to be born would function as a living clock, a growing reminder to the King that by the time the child reached the age of reason, the House of David (Judah) would be delivered from its enemies. Even the child's name, *Immanuel* (with us God), would serve as another reminder of their deliverance.

According to Brown-Driver-Briggs (BDB), the authoritative Hebrew-English Lexicon, the word *almah* means "young woman (ripe sexually, maid or newly

---

[1] *Biblica Hebraica Stuttgartensia*. Deutsche Bibelgesellschaft: Stuttgart, 1983.

married)". If Isaiah had wished to specify virginity, he would have used the Hebrew word *bethulah* (virgin), as he did five times elsewhere (23:4, 23:12, 37:22, 47:1, 62:5).

The crucial section of verse 14 is a verbless clause introduced by *hinneh* (behold). Such clauses refer to the present or to the immediate future. Therefore the translation must be either:

> Behold, the young woman is pregnant and is bearing a son...
> *or* Behold, the young woman will be pregnant and bear a son...

The former interpretation is preferable as the child referred to here is obviously the same child born to Isaiah in Chapter 8. Note that the child is named *Immanuel* (with us God) by the mother in Chapter 7 to symbolise that God would be with the House of David in its struggle against the kings *Rezin* and *Pekah*, and then named *Maher-shalal-hashbaz* (the spoil speeds, the prey hastes) by the father and God in Chapter 8 to symbolise the impending destruction of these two kings by the king of Assyria. Isaiah goes on to tell us that:

> Behold, I and the children whom the LORD hath given me are for signs and for wonders in Israel from the LORD of hosts, which dwelleth in mount Zion (Isaiah 8:18 KJV).

Note that mention is made in 7:3 of another son of Isaiah, *Shear-jashub*.

The name *Immanuel* has no special or extraordinary significance (see Judges 6:12-13). It is no different to many other Hebrew names possessed of similar meanings: *Boel* (in him is God); *Abijah* (my father is YHWH); *Zebadiah* (gift of YHWH); *Ahijah* (brother of YHWH); *Elihu* (my God is He).

It is important to take note that:

- the child *Immanuel* of Isaiah 7:14 was a child born in Isaiah's own time;

- Jesus was not named *Immanuel*.

The Hebrew Scriptures were eventually translated into Greek at some point between the 3rd and 1st Centuries BC. This Greek version is commonly referred to as the Septuagint (LXX standing for the seventy scholars supposedly engaged upon the translation). Without going into laborious detail, scholarly opinions vary widely as to the Septuagint's origin, its transmission, its textual integrity (especially the Book of Isaiah), whether it first included only the Torah, the dating of the first translation, and so on. Many excellent works on the subject are readily available.

The Greek Septuagint rendered the Hebrew word *almah* (young woman) of Isaiah 7:14 into the Greek word *parthenos* (virgin). The translation of this one single word has been a source of controversy ever since. However, all these long centuries of dispute have been pointless because *parthenos* had varied usage in ancient Greek and never carried the narrowly defined meaning of strictly biological virginity. The Septuagint itself in Genesis 34:2-4 twice describes *Dinah* after her rape by *Shechem* as a *parthenos* and the word was also used in classical Greek literature to refer to women who had not retained their virginity biologically.

The Liddell-Scott-Jones Greek-English Lexicon (LSJ) is the most comprehensive and up-to-date Greek dictionary in the world. It is an essential library item in universities and used by every student of ancient Greek. The main dictionary covers every surviving ancient Greek author and text discovered up to 1940, from the Pre-Classical Greek of the 11th-8th Century BC (for example *Homer* and *Hesiod*), through Classical Greek (7th-5th Century BC) to the Hellenistic Period, including the Greek Old and New Testaments.)

There are four citations under *parthenos*. Two use *parthenos* to refer to a woman who had already borne a child (*Homer, Iliad* 2.514; *Aristophanes, Clouds* 530). The other two references are to young women who had slept with men (*Pindar, Pythian* 3.34; *Sophocles, Trachiniae* 129). According to the Bauer–Danker–Arndt–Gingrich Greek-English Lexicon of the New Testament (BDAG), the primary meaning of *parthenos* is "generally a young woman of marriageable age…" hence BDAG gives essentially the same meaning as the LSJ and BDB.

But over and above all the foregoing semantic disputes is the central issue that the book of Isaiah is an Israelite book reflecting Israelite thought. The concept of a virgin conception/birth is utterly alien to Israelite thought. It was alien to Isaiah, it was alien to the Israelites of the New Testament, it is alien to Israelites now and always will be.

CHAPTER THREE

The Gospel of Matthew

Allusions to the theme of a Davidic Messiah were expressed repeatedly in the Hebrew Scriptures but the Second Book of Samuel, Chapter 7 verses 12-17, is undoubtedly the primary text upon which Israelite expectations of a Messiah of Davidic ancestry is based:

> "When your days are fulfilled and you lie down with your fathers, I will raise up your offspring after you, who shall come from your body, and I will establish his kingdom. He shall build a house for my name, and I will establish the throne of his kingdom forever. I will be to him a father, and he shall be to me a son. When he commits iniquity, I will discipline him with the rod of men, with the stripes of the sons of men, but my steadfast love will not depart from him, as I took it from Saul, whom I put away from before you. And your house and your kingdom shall be made sure forever before me. Your throne shall be established forever." In accordance with all these words, and in accordance with all this vision, Nathan spoke to David (2 Samuel 7:12-17 ESV).

The three major elements of this text are:

- The Davidic descent of the Messiah;
- The father-son relationship between God and the Messiah;
- The perpetual nature of the Davidic throne.

Matthew's Genealogy

An accurate rendering of Matthew 1:1 into English is vital if we are to understand the premise on which the author bases his entire set of arguments. Whether wholly or in part, current translations fail to provide this essential accuracy so the author must supply the deficiency. An accurate translation is:

> The book of the generation(s) of Jesus Anointed, the son of David, the son of Abraham.

Within this single verse are contained several points of great significance to Israelite peoples:

- Matthew's very first words, "The book of the generation(s)" recall for the reader the words of Genesis 5:1, "This is the book of the generation(s) of man…" With this phrase, Matthew introduces the theme of the new beginning, the new creation, a theme which underscores the entire New Testament;

- Matthew's selection of Abraham and David was not merely because Abraham was the "father" of the Israelite people and David was Israel's greatest King but, more importantly, because both men were the recipients of great and enduring promises from God;

- Matthew states his belief that Jesus is the Anointed one of God (Messiah), but more precisely that he is the Messiah of the royal House of David. Thus Matthew's Jesus is not only the fulfilment of the primary Israelite expectation—that the Messiah will be a descendant of David, according to God's promise—but also that, in Jesus, all the hopes and promises, indeed all the Scriptures given to his ancestors have now been fulfilled and embodied.

The unique religious and political character of ancient Israelite society mandated the keeping of genealogies. Genealogies were a testament to God's providential rule of history and defined a person's identity within the family and the tribe. By the time of Jesus, the two major genealogical registers considered most vital were those of the descendants of the kingly House of David and those of the priestly House of Levi. *Josephus*, in his autobiographical *Life* (6[1]), refers to the "public registers" from which he extracts his own genealogical information. (See also Josephus *Contra Apion* I, 28-56 [6-10]) and *Genesis Rabbah* 98:8 which records that Rabbi Hillel was proved to be a descendant of David because a genealogical scroll was found in Jerusalem.)

Matthew's genealogy is similar to that of Ruth 4:18-22 in that it is concerned with recording only the highlights of God's saving plan for Israel through the Davidic line. When we read through the genealogy, we see in verses 2-17 that it serves three major purposes:

To demonstrate God's salvation plan for Israel

By removing what he considers unimportant generational steps, Matthew is able to construct a genealogy around the three great rise and fall periods of Israelite history. Captivity-Freedom; Freedom-Captivity; Captivity-Freedom.

1. From Abraham's Babylonian Captivity (Ur of the Chaldees) rising to freedom with the Davidic Kingship;

2. From the freedom of the Davidic Kingship sinking to the depths of the Babylonian Captivity;
3. From the depths of the Babylonian Captivity rising again to the glorious freedom of the new Kingdom of God under a new Davidic King.

To demonstrate that the plan was achieved in the past through unusual circumstances

If one refers to the stories of the four women mentioned in Matthew's genealogy—*Tamar*, *Rahab*, *Ruth*, and *Bathsheba*—one will find that all of them took decisive steps vital to the fulfillment of God's purposes for Israel, regardless of whether their actions had contravened normal social relationships or whether they were "insiders" or "outsiders" (non-Israelites). For Israelites, the names of these women would have evoked memories of the inscrutable yet saving purposes of God, which have never been constrained by biology, social norms, or ethnicity (see Ruth 4:17).

To demonstrate that the plan is being achieved in the present through similarly unusual circumstances

Unlike other genealogies in the Hebrew Scriptures, Matthew mentions Jesus first, then switches back to Abraham and then down through the generations to Joseph. Jewish readers would have been immediately alerted to something not altogether regular. Matthew has thus carefully prepared the ground for the two revelations of verse 18:

> Now the birth of Jesus the Messiah (anointed) happened in this way. When his mother Mary was engaged to Joseph, before they lived together she was discovered to be pregnant by the Holy Spirit (Matthew 1:18 ISV).

Firstly, God is working out his present salvation plan through another woman, Mary, just as he did those four times previously through *Tamar, Rahab, Ruth* and *Bathsheba*.

Secondly, Joseph is not the father of Jesus. Matthew knows that his readers will wonder why he has gone to considerable trouble to carefully construct and provide a genealogy, only to then inform them that Jesus is not the son of Joseph. He also knows that his readers, his Jewish readers, will search back through the genealogy to find the answer, and they will find it and understand.

The contemporaries of Jesus, if they ever gave it more than a passing thought, believed that Jesus was the son of the parents who raised him—Joseph and Mary—but Matthew found it necessary to deny this common perception for a compelling reason that had absolutely nothing to do with a virgin conception/birth.

Write this man childless

So what was Matthew's compelling reason for denying Joseph's biological connection to Jesus? The answer is provided in verse 11:

> And Josias begat Jechonias[2] and his brethren, about the time they were carried away to Babylon (Matthew 1:11 KJV).

The following passages from the Book of Jeremiah reveal to us why Matthew went to such pains to stress that Jesus was not the son of Joseph:

> As I live, saith the LORD, though Coniah the son of Jehoiakim king of Judah were the signet upon my right hand, yet would I pluck thee thence… (Jeremiah 22:24 KJV).
>
> O earth, earth, earth, hear the word of the LORD. Thus saith the LORD, Write ye this man childless, a man that shall not prosper in his days: for no man of his seed shall prosper, sitting upon the throne of David, and ruling any more in Judah (Jeremiah 22:29-30 KJV).

Matthew's Gospel was written for the purpose of convincing Israelites that their expected Messiah had come. However, before presenting his credentials, the author had to demonstrate the prerequisite that Jesus was not descended from David through this disinherited Jeconias, as was Joseph. (Some scholars have asserted that by Joseph exercising a father's right to name the child, he took legal responsibility for Jesus, but Matthew cannot be arguing for legal rather than biological paternity because Joseph's own disinherited status would apply also to Jesus.)

Matthew knows that Jesus is not the son of Joseph when he begins to construct his genealogy, yet he still prefaces his account by calling Jesus the "son of David". How is he able to have the *Magi* ask the question "where is he who was born King of the Jews…" with such superb assurance? Only a patrilineal descendant of King David would qualify to be called the "King of the Jews".

Matthew is certainly sure of the Davidic ancestry of Jesus, but how detailed was his information? As we will discover when we come to examine Luke's infancy narrative, more comprehensive information about the biological ancestry of Jesus was available to an earnest seeker like Luke, but the question of whether or not Matthew had access to this information remains an open question. It is obvious that Matthew's infancy account is told from Joseph's point of view so Matthew's source originated, in whatever chain of transmission, from someone close to Joseph. Therefore, we would

---

2 *Jeconias* is the Greek form of *Jeconiah* (1 Chronicles 3:16-17; Jeremiah 24:1), and *Coniah* (Jeremiah 22:24,28; 37:1).

not expect Matthew's source to have access to the type of intimate information that could have originated only with Mary herself.

The Holy Spirit

Two verses from Matthew Chapter 1 are commonly adduced to support the Virgin Conception/Birth doctrine:

> ...she was found to be with child from the Holy Spirit (Matthew 1:18 ESV).
>
> ...that which is conceived in her is from the Holy Spirit (Matthew 1:20 ESV).

It is obvious in 1:20 that the "Holy Spirit" does not refer to the manner of conception but to "that which is conceived in her".

A consistent theme of the Hebrew Scriptures is that the Holy Spirit of God (the *ruach ha-kodesh*) is the agent of *every* human birth:

> Now Adam knew Eve his wife, and she conceived and bore Cain, saying, "I have gotten a man with the help of the LORD" (Genesis 4:1 ESV).
>
> And the LORD visited Sarah as he had said, and the LORD did unto Sarah as he had spoken. For Sarah conceived, and bare Abraham a son in his old age, at the set time of which God had spoken to him (Genesis 21:1-2 KJV).
>
> The Spirit of God hath made me, and the breath of the Almighty hath given me life (Job 33:4 KJV).
>
> So Boaz took Ruth, and she became his wife. And he went in to her, and the LORD gave her conception, and she bore a son (Ruth 4:13 ESV).
>
> And the LORD visited Hannah, so that she conceived, and bare three sons and two daughters... (1 Samuel 2:21 KJV).

To use this theme in a particular or exclusive way *only* where it refers to Jesus is to wrest the words of Gospel authors for purposes they could never have conceived.

One need only to consult Luke to appreciate how insupportable it is to use these verses from Matthew to justify a Virgin Conception/Birth. References to the workings of the Holy Spirit abound in Luke Chapters 1 and 2, e.g. John the Baptist was "filled with the Holy Spirit even from his mother's womb" (1:15), and a few months before John was born, his mother Elizabeth was "filled with the Holy Spirit" (1:41).

What's in a name?

In Matthew 1:21, we read:

"She will give birth to a son, and you are to name him Jesus (*Yeshua*), because he is the one who will save his people from their sins" (Matthew 1:21 ISV).

It should be immediately apparent that the logical and causal relationship indicated by "because" is missing. This causal relationship is also missing in the Greek. (I have argued elsewhere that there is compelling evidence for the existence of a Hebrew subtext underlying our present Greek Gospels.)

The Hebrew name *Yeshua* is a shortened form of *Yehoshua* (Joshua). It is derived from YH, a shortened form of the Tetragrammaton YHWH, and the Hebrew verb root *yasha* meaning to save or to deliver. Only on the basis of a Hebrew original is this logical and causal relationship between the name and the function explicit, i.e. 'you will call his name *Yeshua* (YH is our salvation) because he will save…"

Note that the child was not named *Immanuel*. Again pointing to a Hebrew original is the fact that while the explanatory note providing the meaning of the name *Immanuel* (verse 23) has been translated into English according to English word order, the Greek preserves the original Hebrew word order—*Im* (with) *nu* (us) *El* (God).

Corporate Personality

The Israelite religion, both past and present, is communal. In the words of the Jewish scholar Nicholas de Lange:

> To be a Jew means first and foremost to belong to a group, the Jewish people, and the religious beliefs are secondary, in a sense, to this corporate allegiance.[3]

Most prayers were, and still are, communal, as we see in the Lord's Prayer. An old Hasidic saying goes like this, "A prayer which is not spoken in the name of all Israel is no prayer at all". [4]

Central to the idea of Israelite community is the concept of "corporate personality". From ancient times, the entire community of past, present and future Israelites was seen as one personality, as "a living whole, a single animated mass of blood, flesh and bones". [5] Even today, at Passover, modern Jews are required to think of themselves as personally taking part in the Exodus and receiving the Torah at Sinai. Matthew draws on this Israelite concept of the "corporate personality" in his presentation of Jesus.

---

3   De Lange, Nicholas. *Judaism*. Oxford University Press: New York, 1986, p. 4.

4   Buber, Martin, ed. *Ten rungs: Hasidic Sayings*. Schocken Books: New York, 1947, p. 31.

5   Robinson, H.Wheeler. *Corporate Personality in Ancient Israel*, rev.ed. Fortress Press: Philadelphia, 1980, p. 28. Quotation from W. Robertson Smith. *Lectures on the Religion of the Semites*, 2nd ed. A.& C. Black: London, 1894, pp. 273-74.

Signs of Deliverance

Drawing on the meaning of Jesus' name, to "save" or "deliver", Matthew paints Jesus as recapitulating in his individual existence a selection of deliverance-themed passages in the Hebrew Scriptures, especially those associated with Moses. For Matthew, Jesus is the representative Israelite, the one standing for the many, the "corporate personality", the one who fulfils in his individual existence God's salvation plan for the whole people of Israel. Jesus is Israel: Israel is Jesus.

Discover Matthew's method by checking the Gospel passage and then the source of his quote in its original context:

- Chapter 1:23 quoting Isaiah 7:14;
- Chapter 2:6 quoting Micah 5:2-5;
- Chapter 2:15 quoting Hosea 11:1;
- Chapter 2:18 quoting Jeremiah 31:15;
- Chapter 3:3 quoting Isaiah 40:3;
- Chapter 4:14 quoting Isaiah 9:1-2

Verse 1:23

One of the deliverance-themed Scripture passages Matthew presents as being fulfilled in Jesus was the sign given to King Ahaz by the prophet Isaiah (Isaiah 7:14). The one and only significance of Verse 1:23 is that it forms part of Matthew's overall presentation of Jesus as the representative Israelite. As such, Jesus can very obviously be no different in any essential respect from his fellow Israelites. To assert otherwise is to utterly destroy Matthew's Jesus.

Notes on parallels

The original Joseph son of Jacob is associated with three sets of dreams: he had his own dreams of supremacy over his brothers (Genesis 37:5-11); he interpreted dreams while in Egypt for the baker and cup-bearer (40:1-23); and for Pharaoh (41:1-36). Matthew's Joseph, (also son of a man named Jacob) has three dreams (1:20; 2:13, 19).

Similarly, the original Joseph brings his family to Egypt, where they find food and safety, as does the later Joseph. (See Part II.8: *The Documents-Understanding Literary Styles.*)

CHAPTER FOUR

The Gospel of Luke : Part I

As we discovered in Chapter Two: *The Book of Isaiah the Prophet*, and in Chapter Three: *The Gospel of Matthew*, there is no justification for asserting that the doctrine of the Virgin Conception/Birth is based on either Isaiah 7:14 or on the Gospel of Matthew. Now we will see if there is any justification for asserting that the doctrine is based on the Gospel of Luke.

The Preparation

Regardless of the identity of Theophilus—and there are many scholarly suggestions—his identity does not detract from the fact that the work we have come to know as the Gospel of Luke is actually a private letter. As such, we may expect it to contain information not publicly available. And so it proves to be. There is such an intimate knowledge of Mary, her family, and the time of Jesus' conception, that Luke's source can only have been derived, by whatever means of transmission, from someone directly connected to Mary herself.

Luke introduces his Gospel by assuring Theophilus that he has done his research and "investigated everything carefully from the beginning". As we shall presently see, one of the most important of his discoveries is that he has verified the circumstances surrounding the birth of Jesus. This is, for him, a cause of great celebration because he can now demonstrate that Jesus has a claim by right of birth to sit on the earthly throne of David.

The author first sets out to demonstrate to Theophilus that he has done his research by describing the circumstances surrounding the birth of John the Baptist. He establishes his credentials by going into great detail about the Levite priest Zacharias, even going so far as to identify Zacharias as belonging to the priestly "course of Abia". One of Luke's major purposes here is to identify Zacharias' wife Elizabeth as one of the "daughters of Aaron". Thus, husband and wife both belong to the tribe of Levi (Luke 1:5).

He is laying the groundwork, painting an intimate and detailed picture of a priestly family, so that when he goes on to describe the events in Nazareth, Mary will appear no stranger to Theophilus: as a *suggenes* (tribal kin) of Elizabeth, she will fit neatly into the framework he has already set out (see Luke 1:36).

The crucially important fact that Mary was of the tribe of Levi has been ignored by theologians and biblical scholars intent on promulgating the doctrine of Virgin Conception/Birth. These theologians, knowing that the New Testament states several times that Jesus is the Israelite Messiah of the "seed of David", and knowing that Joseph is not the father of Jesus, erroneously assert that it is through Mary that Jesus can claim Davidic descent.

Luke's infancy narrative lays particular emphasis on Jesus as the fulfillment of Messianic promises, as we can see in the Canticles of Mary, Zachariah and Simeon, and in the response of Anna the "prophetess". (Note that the emphasis on David and Israel and the frequent mention of "our fathers" rule out the assertion that these hymns of praise in Luke were originally products of a non-Israelite Christian community.)

It is risible to assert that Luke would attempt to portray Jesus as a descendant of David through the matrilineal line as Israelite tribal affiliation and family genealogy was at that time traced only through the patrilineal line.

The Annunciation

Elizabeth, the wife of Zacharias, had been regarded as barren but had conceived a child and was six months pregnant when the angel [6] appeared to Mary.

Luke 1:26-27

> In the sixth month the angel Gabriel was sent from God to a city of Galilee named Nazareth, to a virgin (*parthenos*) betrothed to a man whose name was Joseph, of the house of David. And the virgin's (*parthenos*) name was Mary (Luke 1:26-27 ESV).

Luke testifies that, at this time, Mary was a *parthenos*. (In ancient Greek, the word *parthenos* had varied usage and did not necessarily imply physical virginity. See Chapter Two for Lexical references.) However, even if the word did specify physical virginity, as proponents of the Virgin Conception/Birth claim, it would be irrelevant because Jesus was not conceived until some indeterminate time after the angel's departure:

> And when eight days were accomplished for the circumcising of the child, his name was called Jesus, which was so named of the angel before he was conceived in the womb (Luke 2:21 KJV).

---

6 The English word "angel" is a transliteration of the Greek ἄγγελος *angelos* which is derived from the Hebrew מַלְאָךְ *malakh* meaning "messenger".

Luke, writing these words to Theophilus, having no personal knowledge but having traced the course of all things accurately from the first, was nevertheless able to specify that the conception took place *after* the Annunciation. Need it be pointed out that every young woman is a virgin before she first has a sexual relationship and that only a woman could specify the timing of conception in terms of *before* and *after*? (As noted previously, Luke's source must have derived, in whatever chain of transmission, from Mary herself.)

Luke 1:28

> The angel went to her and said, "Greetings, you who are highly favored! The Lord is with you" (Luke 1:28 NIV).

Note that it was the same Gabriel who told the prophet Daniel that he was also "highly favoured". (Daniel 9:23;10:11;12,19). "The Lord be with you" was a standard form of Jewish greeting.

Luke 1:29-31

> But she was greatly troubled at the saying, and tried to discern what sort of greeting this might be. And the angel said to her, "Do not be afraid, Mary, for you have found favor with God. And behold, you will conceive in your womb and bear a son, and you shall call his name Jesus" (Luke 1:29-31 ESV).

At first, we are told that Mary could not understand the angel's greeting for, unlike Zacharias, she had made no supplication to God.

Luke 1:32a

> "He will be great and will be called the Son of the Most High…" (Luke 1:32a ESV).

Sonship and Fatherhood

"Sonship" of God was a concept applied to the anointed kings of ancient Israel and to the whole House of Israel long before the time of Jesus:

> He (Solomon) shall build an house for my name; and he shall be my son, and I will be his father; and I will establish the throne of his kingdom over Israel for ever (1 Chronicles 22:9-10 KJV).
>
> I will be his father, and he will be my son (2 Sam. 7:12-17 NIV).
>
> He shall cry to me, "You are my Father, my God, and the Rock of my salvation" (Psalm 89:26 ESV).

> When Israel was a child, then I loved him, and called my son out of Egypt (Hosea 11:1 KJV cf. Exodus 4:22).

This concept was also expressed by Jesus:

> Blessed are the peacemakers, for they shall be called sons of God (Matthew 5:9 ESV).
>
> But love your enemies, and do good, and lend, expecting nothing in return, and your reward will be great, and you will be sons of the Most High, for he is kind to the ungrateful and the evil (Luke 6:35 ESV).

Adam is called the "son of God" because he was created in God's image (Luke 3:38; Acts 17:26-29). All who are led by the Spirit of God are "sons of God" (Romans 8:14), and Jesus is the "firstborn of many brothers" (Romans 8:29). The author of Hebrews speaks explicitly of the many "sons of God" who are to come (Hebrews 2:10) and, for John, those who are united with Jesus become "children of God" (John 1:12-13). The essential difference between Jesus and all other "sons of God" was that he was also the promised deliverer (Messiah).

We read in Luke 2:46-50 about Mary and Joseph's search for Jesus:

> After three days they found him in the temple courts, sitting among the teachers, listening to them and asking them questions. Everyone who heard him was amazed at his understanding and his answers. When his parents saw him, they were astonished. His mother said to him, "Son, why have you treated us like this? Your father and I have been anxiously searching for you." "Why were you searching for me?" he asked. "Didn't you know I had to be in my Father's house?" But they did not understand what he was saying to them (Luke 2:46-50 NIV).

Thus, Mary, who had supposedly conceived a child fathered by the Holy Spirit of God while still a virgin, did not know what Jesus was talking about when he called God his Father. Her amazement would be that a child born in such lowly circumstances would use language reserved for the nation as a whole, or for Kings.

The above evidence demonstrates that to regard God as a Father, and to thereby be called a "son of God" carries with it no implication whatsoever of Deity. Any assertion to the contrary is to read texts according to the demands of Christian theology.

Son of God synonymous with Messiah

When the term "son of God" is used in reference to Jesus, it is synonymous with the term "Messiah", as we can see in Mark, John and Acts where the two concepts are merged into the one person of Jesus, thus demonstrating that they are interchangeable terms in the New Testament:

> But Jesus remained silent and gave no answer. Again the high priest asked him, "Are you the Messiah, the Son of the Blessed One?" (Mark 14:61 NIV).
>
> "Yes, Lord," she told him. "I believe that you are the Messiah, the Son of God, the one who was to come into the world" (John 11:27 ESV).
>
> But these are written that you may believe that Jesus is the Messiah, the Son of God, and that by believing you may have life in his name (NIV John 20:31 ESV).
>
> And we declare unto you glad tidings, how that the promise which was made unto the fathers (of a Messiah), God hath fulfilled the same unto us their children, in that he hath raised up Jesus again; as it is also written in the second psalm, Thou art my Son, this day have I begotten thee (Acts 13:32-33 KJV).

Note that one of the creedal pillars of Christianity is the assertion that Jesus is the "eternally-begotten son" of the Father. The above statement by Paul (Acts 13:33), that Jesus became the only-begotten son of the Father on the day of his resurrection, should be more than enough to consign the creedal formulations of "eternally begotten not made" to oblivion because there was a time before Jesus was "begotten".

To say that he was begotten from all eternity is a self-contradiction and absurd in the extreme. Eternity has no "beginning" whereas sonship implies time—a time before the generation of the son.

The Gospel of Luke : Part II

The Promise to King David

> "When your days are fulfilled and you lie down with your fathers, I will raise up your offspring after you, who shall come from your body, and I will establish his kingdom. He shall build a house for my name, and I will establish the throne of his kingdom forever. I will be to him a father, and he shall be to me a son. When he commits iniquity, I will discipline him with the rod of men, with the stripes of the sons of men, but my steadfast love will not depart from him, as I took it from Saul, whom I put away from before you. And your house and your kingdom shall be made sure forever before me. Your throne shall be established forever." In accordance with all these words, and in accordance with all this vision, Nathan spoke to David (2 Samuel 7:12-17 ESV).

Imminent Fulfillment

Luke 1:32b -1:33

Gabriel announces the imminent fulfillment of this Davidic promise:

> ...and the Lord God shall give unto him the throne of his father David: And he shall reign over the house of Jacob for ever; and of his kingdom there shall be no end (Luke 1:32b-33 KJV).

At this time, Mary was betrothed to Joseph, a descendant of David. As we have already discovered in the Gospel of Matthew, Joseph's line had been debarred forever from sitting on the throne of David.

It is important to note here that Luke has already identified Mary as a Levite and that her relative Zacharias served in the temple. The Levitical priesthood kept the genealogical records, paying particular attention to those of the Levites and the descendants of King David. As such, Mary would have been well acquainted with Joseph's genealogy. (*Josephus*, in his autobiographical *Life* (6[1]), refers to the "public registers" from which he sought information about his own genealogy.)

Knowing that her betrothed could not father a child entitled to sit on the throne of David, Mary asked the angel the most logical of questions.

Luke 1:34

Since no Greek text of Luke 1:34 contains the word *parthenos* (virgin), the following rendering of this verse by many well-known English translations such as the NIV, ESV, and NASB is blatantly dishonest and doctrinally driven:

> "How will this be," Mary asked the angel, "since I am a virgin (*parthenos*)?" (Luke 1:34 NIV).

One of the few versions which do provide an honest and correct translation is the KJV:

> Then said Mary unto the angel, "How shall this be, seeing I know (*ginóskó*) not a man?" (Luke 1:34 KJV).

Not content with the almost complete doctrinal subjugation of translators, proponents of the Virgin Conception/Birth doctrine attack the only remaining honest translations and assert that the word "know" (*ginóskó*) in versions such as the KJV refers to knowing sexually whereas most New Testament occurrences of the word *ginóskó* refer to a state of knowledge. The only interpretation that fits with Luke's narrative is that Mary did not know—did not have knowledge of—a man who could father a child entitled to sit upon the throne of David.

As we have seen, the angel has made some startling promises concerning the child to be born, promises that cannot be fulfilled if Joseph is to be the father. So what was Gabriel's response to Mary's question in the previous verse?

Luke 1:35a

> The angel answered, "The Holy Spirit will come on you, and the power of the Most High will overshadow you..." (Luke 1:35a NIV).

Hebrew parallelism is evident here (expressing the same thought twice using equivalent words). The "Holy Spirit" is synonymous with the "power of the Most High". It is this divine power, the "Holy Spirit", which will "overshadow" or protect Mary. The image of the Spirit overshadowing Mary is drawn from the image of Boaz covering Ruth with the "wings" of his garment (Ruth 3:7-9) and from the Hebrew theme of overshadowing protection which is found in the Psalms, "He shall cover thee with his feathers, and under his wings shalt thou trust: his truth shall be thy shield and buckler" (Psalm 91:4).

Luke 1:35b

> "…So the holy one to be born…" (Luke 1:35b NIV).

There is nothing singular or exclusive about the word "holy" in reference to Jesus. In memory of the deaths of the first-born of the Egyptians, every first-born Israelite male who opened the womb was a sanctified "holy" child and had to be redeemed by his parents. A comparison of texts will place the matter in its correct perspective:

> And the LORD spake unto Moses, saying, Sanctify unto me all the firstborn, whatsoever openeth the womb among the children of Israel, both of man and of beast: it is mine (Exodus 13:1-2 KJV).

> When Pharaoh stubbornly refused to let us go, the Lord killed the firstborn of both people and animals in Egypt. This is why I sacrifice to the Lord the first male offspring of every womb and redeem each of my firstborn sons (Exodus 13:15 NIV).

> And she brought forth her firstborn son, and wrapped him in swaddling clothes, and laid him in a manger… (Luke 2:7 KJV).

> And when the days of her purification according to the law of Moses were accomplished, they brought him to Jerusalem, to present him to the Lord; (As it is written in the law of the Lord, Every male that openeth the womb shall be called holy to the Lord) (Luke 2:22-23 KJV).

Luke 1:35c

> "…shall be called the Son of God" (Luke 1:35c NASB).

As demonstrated exhaustively in the Gospel of Luke: Part I, the term "son of God" is not exclusive to Jesus.

Luke 1:36-38

> And, behold, thy cousin Elisabeth, she hath also conceived a son in her old age: and this is the sixth month with her, who was called barren. For with God nothing shall be impossible (Luke 1:36-38 KJV).

Just as God had ensured the conception of the aged and barren Sarah (Genesis 18:14), so has God now ensured the conception of the aged and barren Elizabeth. These conceptions were of a far more miraculous nature than the relatively simple task of finding an eligible man to father a child with a young and fertile woman.

Luke 1:38

> And Mary said, Behold the handmaid of the Lord; be it unto me according to thy word. And the angel departed from her (Luke 1:38 KJV).

A suitable descendant of King David was found because the New Testament authors go on to record the fulfillment of the promise first made to King David and then to Mary:

> Paul, a servant of Christ Jesus, called to be an apostle, set apart for the gospel of God, which he promised beforehand through his prophets in the holy Scriptures, concerning his Son, who was descended from David according to the flesh and was declared to be the Son of God in power according to the Spirit of holiness by his resurrection from the dead (Romans 1:1-3 ESV).

> "I have found in David the son of Jesse a man after my heart, who will do all my will." Of this man's offspring God has brought to Israel a Saviour, Jesus, as he promised (Acts 13:22-23 ESV).

> Hath not the scripture said, That Christ cometh of the seed of David, and out of the town of Bethlehem, where David was? (John 7:42 KJV).

> Remember that Jesus Christ of the seed of David was raised from the dead according to my gospel (2 Timothy 2:8 KJV).

Aside from contradicting every one of these texts, as well as many others, the doctrine of the Virgin Conception/Birth was formulated in almost total ignorance of Israelite thought as expressed in the Hebrew Scriptures. Only through artificial contrivance and theological sophistry have theologians been able to justify ignoring the clear intent of these passages. But we shall press on with the Gospel of Luke and see what remains to be discovered.

Notes

Before proceeding, important points to keep in mind:

- The Kingdom of David originally included the entire twelve-tribed Israel originating from the twelve sons of Jacob. After the death of his son Solomon, the Kingdom fractured into two sections: the northern Kingdom of Israel consisting of 10 tribes, and the southern Kingdom of Judah consisting of two tribes. Around 721 BC, the Assyrians invaded the northern Kingdom. The Assyrians had a policy of removal and replacement of native populations so they deported substantial numbers of Israelites and replaced them with another group of captive people. These replacement people later became known as the Samaritans;

- Around 604 BC, the Babylonian King, Nebuchadnezzar, invaded the southern Kingdom of Judah, inhabited by the people we know by the term "Jews", destroyed the Temple of Solomon, and carried off the leading citizens to Babylon. Some returned from Babylon, and rebuilt the Temple in Jerusalem. The descendants of these returnees and those who had always remained in the land are the people we meet in the New Testament;

- Gabriel's promise is that the child to be born will reign over the "house of Jacob" (1:33). The term "house of Jacob" signifies the whole twelve tribes of Israel, whereas the "house of David" signifies just two tribes—those of Judah (David's own tribe) and Benjamin, as well as a sprinkling of Levites;

- Out of the entire New Testament, only Luke makes mention of a descendant of one of the ten northern tribes—Anna of the tribe of Asher (Luke 2:36. His purpose in mentioning "the house of Jacob" and Anna of the tribe of Asher is to reinforce the memory that Messianic promises were made to all twelve tribes of Israel.

CHAPTER 6

The Gospel of Luke : Part III

As pointed out previously, in ancient Greek usage a *parthenos* was "generally a young woman of marriageable age…", whether she be a physical virgin or not. If proponents of the Virgin Conception/Birth doctrine insist that *parthenos* means physical virginity then they are still confronted with an insurmountable problem because at the time of the angel's visit there had, as yet, been no conception. That Jesus was not conceived until some time after the angel's departure is confirmed later by Luke:

> And when eight days were accomplished for the circumcising of the child, his name was called Jesus, which was so named of the angel before he was conceived in the womb (Luke 2:21 KJV).

Luke 1:38

> And Mary said, "Behold, the bondslave of the Lord; may it be done (*genoito*: let it happen) to me according to your word." And the angel departed from her (Luke 1:38 NASB).

Luke used the Greek word γένοιτό (*genoito*) in the aorist tense "let it happen". If Luke had wished to signify that conception happened at the word of the angel then he would not have used *genoito*. As one of the most renowned and respected exegetes of Luke's New Testament Greek, Frederick Godet, points out:

> The evangelist shows his tact in the choice of the aorist γένοιτό (*genoito*). The present (tense) would have signified, 'Let it happen to me this very instant?' The aorist (tense) leaves the choice of the time to God."[7]

Godet's statement is correct since no other New Testament occurrence of γένοιτό (*genoito*) refers to something to happen/not happen instantly but at some indeterminate time in the future.

Luke tells us that after the angel's departure, Mary left "with haste" to travel to Elizabeth's house, a journey of four or five days (1:39). By the time Mary reached Elizabeth's house, she knew that she was pregnant, knew that the angel's promise of a son entitled to sit on the throne of David was already in the process of being fulfilled, enabling her to exclaim "he that is mighty has done to me great things" (1:49).

---

7   Godet, Frédéric Louis. *Commentary on the Gospel of Luke*. T & T Clark: Edinburgh, 1889, p. 95.

If it were a miraculous conception, the only way Mary could possibly know any of the above would be by the continued absence of menstruation. We know that only a few days had passed between the angel's visit and her arrival at Elizabeth's house, not enough time for pregnancy to be confirmed by these means. Mary's state of knowledge could only be the result of an encounter which took place on the journey to Elizabeth's house, and which led to Mary's conviction that she had already become pregnant.

Briefly and bluntly put, Luke tells us that conception took place by normal means, after the angel's visit but before Mary arrived at Elizabeth's house, through an encounter with a descendant of David who could father a son entitled to sit upon David's throne, and who Luke names in Chapter 3:23.

All of the angel's promises to Mary and to Israel have been fulfilled: that is the whole point of the story. Luke's Gospel is a private letter and, as such, contains private and confidential information which some may find uncomfortable to confront. However, Luke's overriding concern was to confirm to Theophilus that God keeps his salvation promises regardless of the contravention of social norms.

In essence, Matthew delivers the same message. Even though he does not name the biological father of Jesus, he also found it necessary to stress that God's salvation plan for Israel had often been achieved through strange and unusual circumstances. All four women mentioned in Matthew's genealogy—*Tamar, Rahab, Ruth, and Bathsheba*—took decisive steps vital to the fulfillment of God's purposes for Israel, regardless of whether their actions had contravened normal social relationships or whether or not they were "outsiders", i.e. non-Israelites. For Israelites, the names of these women would have evoked memories of the inscrutable yet saving purposes of God, which have never been constrained by biology, social norms, or ethnicity (see Ruth 4:17).

The Translation Games

Translators have played yet more games with Luke 3:23, which begins the genealogy of Jesus. A selection of English Translations:

> And Jesus himself began to be about thirty years of age, being (as was supposed) the son of Joseph, which was the son of Heli…(KJV).
>
> Jesus, when he began his ministry, was about thirty years of age, being the son (as was supposed) of Joseph, the son of Heli…" (ESV).
>
> Now Jesus himself was about thirty years old when he began his ministry. He was the son, so it was thought, of Joseph, the son of Heli…" (NIV).

In these English versions, translators have disguised the meaning of the verse by either inserting parenthesis in the incorrect place or by inserting the following words which do not appear in the Greek texts—"which was the son" or "the son" immediately preceding "of Heli...". It was surprising to discover that scholars of the Roman Catholic Church have actually known and recorded the correct translation of Luke 3:23.

The Roman Catholic Encyclopaedia article entitled *Genealogy* has the following to say:

> St. Matthew's genealogy is that of St. Joseph; St. Luke's, that of the Blessed Virgin. This contention implies that St. Luke's genealogy only seemingly includes the name of Joseph. It is based on the received Greek text, *on (os enomizeto ouios Ioseph) tou Heli*, "being the son (as it was supposed, of Joseph, but really) of Heli. This parenthesis really eliminates the name of Joseph from St. Luke's genealogy, and makes Christ, by means of the Blessed Virgin, directly a son of Heli. [8]

So, the Catholic Encyclopaedia's translation of 3:23 is:

> And Jesus himself began to be about thirty years old, being the son (as it was supposed of Joseph, but really) of Heli.

In his Commentary on the Gospel of Luke,[9] the above mentioned exegete and scholar of Biblical Greek, Frédéric Louis Godet, inserts dashes in the text and says: "The text, therefore, to express the author's meaning clearly, should be written thus:

> And Jesus himself began to be about thirty years old, being a son—as was thought, of Joseph—of Heli, of Matthat...

Although Frédéric Godet and the Roman Catholic Church assert that Luke's genealogy is that of Mary, i.e. "Jesus, (Mary), Heli, Matthat".... to maintain the doctrine of the Virgin Conception/Birth, Godet's arguments as to the original genealogical information provided by Luke and the correct translation of the passage remain overwhelmingly convincing. The one issue upon which these scholars are united is that the name of Joseph does not belong in the original genealogy.

---

8   Roman Catholic Encyclopaedia Article: *Genealogy*. Accessed 15 October 2015. www.newadvent.org/cathen/06410a.htm

9   Godet, Frédéric Louis. *Commentary on the Gospel of Luke.* T & T Clark: Edinburgh, 1889, pp. 195-204. Godet's commentary is frequently referenced to this day as a reliable source for the study of Luke's Gospel. It is one of the most significant studies of Luke from the 19th century and is respected for its exegetical style and ability to address the authenticity and origins of Luke's Gospel with precision.

Luke was confiding to Theophilus that Jesus was the biological son of a man named Heli. He then gives Heli's genealogy in a direct line back to King David. Jesus is, therefore, entitled by birth to be Israel's Messiah-King and God's promises to David have been fulfilled. This is the reason why Luke emphasises that he has investigated everything from the beginning and why he is happy to impart the good news to Theophilus that Israel's Messiah has been identified.

Despite the fact that Luke has clearly identified Mary as a Levite, some theologians and biblical scholars continue to claim that Luke is tracing Mary's descent from David. This assertion is ludicrous and ignores ancient Israelite culture where tribal affiliation and family genealogy could only be traced through the patrilineal line. It is a clumsy attempt to conceal the stark reality of the very point that Luke is making and conflicts with every other New Testament statement about the birth of Jesus. As Longnecker quite rightly observes:

> It need not be supposed that the church's ascription of messiahship to Jesus made him a descendant of David in their eyes when in fact he was not. Neither the acclaim of Jesus as "son of David" on the part of the people nor the Evangelists' recording of that fact are plausible had it been believed that he did not satisfy the genealogical conditions implied by the name. And, as Dalman has further pointed out: As the scribes held to the opinion that the Messiah must be a descendant of David, it is certain that the opponents of Jesus would make the most of any knowledge they could procure, showing that Jesus certainly did not, or probably did not, fulfil this condition. And there can be no doubt that Paul, as a persecutor of the Christians, would be well instructed in regard to this point. As he, after mingling freely with members of the Holy Family in Jerusalem, shows that he entertained no sort of doubt on this point, it must be assumed that no objection to it was known to him. Nowhere in the New Testament do we find a single trace of conscious refutation of Jewish attacks, based on the idea that the derivation of Jesus from David was defective.[10]

As is evident, the endlessly-debated "conflict" between the two genealogies of Matthew and Luke is simply an illusion necessitated by adherence to the doctrine of the Virgin Conception/Birth.

---

10 Longnecker, Richard N. *The Christology of Early Jewish Christianity.* Regent College Publishing: Bellingham, USA, 1994, pp. 110-111.

CHAPTER SEVEN

Supplementary Materials

Marriage and Betrothal Customs in First Century Israel

Valuable insights are to be gained by referring to the marriage and betrothal customs of the 1st Century AD.

The prospective bridegroom, in this case Joseph, would have negotiated a contract with the head of Mary's family and then returned to his own father's house to build a separate room for himself and his bride. At the end of this process, he would come to take Mary away to the room in his father's house that he had prepared beforehand.

In Lightfoot's *Hebrew and Talmudical Exercitations,* we discover that:

> A woman is espoused three ways; by money, or by a writing, or by being lain with. And being thus espoused, though she were not yet married, nor conducted into the man's house, yet she is his wife... [11]

The author of Matthew has already ruled out that Mary was espoused to Joseph by "being lain with" (Matthew 1:18). Now note the interesting detail in Luke 1:56:

> And Mary abode with her (Elizabeth) about three months, and returned to her own house (Luke 1:56 KJV).

Luke specified that Mary stayed with Elizabeth for "about three months" because ninety days separation between couples was necessary to establish paternity. As Lightfoot points out, Mary was already Joseph's wife, so if she had returned to her own house at any time before the three months period had expired, Joseph could have exercised his right to take her into his own house and to "lay" with her. Thus the paternity of Jesus would always have been in doubt.

Mary had faith in Gabriel's word that she would be protected from the consequences of what was then a social taboo punishable by death. And she was protected: from the law; from social shunning; and by having the good fortune to be betrothed to a "just" man. Notwithstanding, even without an assurance of protection, where love and/or sex is concerned, men and women have always broken laws, conventions and taboos, even at great danger to themselves. And they always will.

---

[11] Lightfoot, Rev. John. *Hebrew and Talmudical Exercitations* in Vol. XI, *The Whole Works of the late Rev. John Lightfoot*, G. Cowie & Co: London, 1825, p. 20.

The Queen of Heaven

The idolatry and pagan practices associated with the worship of the Queen of Heaven, under her various names of *Ishtar*, *Isis*, *Ashtaroth*, and etcetera, was roundly condemned by the Israelite prophets, e.g. Jeremiah:

> We will not listen to the message you have spoken to us in the name of the Lord! We will certainly do everything we said we would: We will burn incense to the Queen of Heaven and will pour out drink offerings to her just as we and our ancestors, our kings and our officials did in the towns of Judah and in the streets of Jerusalem (Jeremiah 44:16-17 NIV).

One of the Virgin Mary's titles is "Queen of Heaven". The concept of virgin mothers belongs to the pagan world: it is not only absent from the Bible but is the very antithesis of Israelite thought.

As if the many titles bestowed upon Mary by the Christian Churches were not enough, the proponents of "New Age" spiritualism have now fused Mary with the "Great Mother" concept beloved of occultism, feminism, paganism and etcetera. This "Great Mother" concept is nothing more than a new attempt to resurrect the old pagan mythologies.

We would find it extremely difficult to imagine the profound shock and abhorrence the Jewish Jesus and his Jewish mother would have experienced if they could only have known what fate would befall them at the hands of those who claim to be their representatives.

PART V

The Divine Court

CHAPTER ONE

Introduction

When the writings of the New Testament fell into the hands of the Hellenist and Latin Church Fathers, they retrojected onto those documents their own prevailing philosophies and theologies and framed the core doctrines of Creedal Christianity.

The Hypostatic Union

The Council of Chalcedon, held in 451 AD, produced the official definition of faith known as the Hypostatic Union. Briefly stated, this doctrine asserts that the incarnation of the Son of God united inseparably and forever the human nature with the divine nature in the one person of Jesus Christ. Yet the two natures remain distinct, whole, and unchanged, without mixture or confusion so that the one person, Jesus Christ, is *truly God and truly man*. This doctrine of the Hypostatic Union, together with the vast theological edifice of Creedal Christianity, rests entirely on the correct interpretation of key New Testament texts which, it is asserted, prove that Jesus of Nazareth is *truly God and truly man*.

Deity

Throughout these many centuries, from immediate post-apostolic times to this present moment, ecclesiastics, scholars, sages, theologians and popes have proclaimed with one voice the Deity of Jesus of Nazareth. This Deity proclamation is based on a false foundation first laid down in ignorance of Israelite concepts, terminology and culture, and further exacerbated by contextual blindness and the practice of "proof-texting".

This work will prosecute the case against the Deity teaching. Readers are encouraged to weigh all the evidence that will be presented and then determine whether that which is so confidently asserted is based on the contents of the documents or on the theological and philosophical predilections of the Hellenist-Latin Fathers.

CHAPTER TWO

Appeals to Precedent

Section 1

A last resort

The central claim of the New Testament is that Jesus of Nazareth was the long-awaited Israelite Messiah according to Scripture. To provide justifications for this claim, the New Testament authors liberally quoted from, and alluded to, passages from the Hebrew Scriptures which were generally regarded as written in "expectation" of the Messiah. They then demonstrated how these "expectations" were fulfilled in Jesus of Nazareth.

Unfortunately for the Hellenist-Latin Fathers, all of these Israelite expectations depicted a man born in the normal fashion, one chosen from among his fellows, one like his brethren in every respect. (See Deuteronomy 18:18 for "expectation" and Acts 3:22 for "fulfillment".)

Undaunted nevertheless, Anti-Nicene Fathers such as Justin Martyr and Irenaeus searched the Hebrew Scriptures in an effort to find justification for the interdependent Virgin Conception/Birth and Incarnation teachings. From these very lean pickings they plucked out two passages from the Book of Isaiah and claimed that these were Messianic expectations fulfilled in Jesus of Nazareth. We will now proceed with an analysis of both passages and discover to what extent, if any, these claims are justifiable.

Section 2

Isaiah 7:14

Immanuel

The context of Isaiah Chapter 7 is the threatened destruction of the House of David by the armies of *Rezin*, King of Syria, and *Pekah*, King of Israel. Isaiah the prophet gave King Ahaz a sign of deliverance from these enemies. Chapter 7 verses 14-16 read:

> Therefore the Lord himself shall give you a sign; Behold, the young woman shall conceive, and bear a son, and shall call his name Immanuel. Curd and honey shall he eat, that he may know to refuse the evil and choose the good. But before the child shall know to refuse the evil and choose the good, the land whose two kings you have a horror of shall be forsaken (Isaiah 7:14-16 KJV).

The Hebrew words of verse 14 reproduced below are taken from the *Leningrad Codex B19A (L)*, dated 1008-1009 AD, as reproduced in *Biblica Hebraica Stuttgartensia*.[1] The word signifying "the young woman" appears highlighted below.

הִנֵּה הָעַלְמָה הָרָה וְיֹלֶדֶת בֵּן וְקָרֵאת שְׁמוֹ עִמָּנוּ אֵל:

The literal translation of verse 14 is:

> Behold · the young woman (*ha almah*) · is pregnant/will be pregnant · and is bearing/and will bear · son · and she will call · his name · with us · God. (*im nu el*)

This sign had absolutely nothing to do with the manner of the child's conception or birth. It was a sign of deliverance. The child soon to be born would function as a living clock, a growing reminder to the King that by the time the child reached the age of reason, the House of David (Judah) would be delivered from its enemies. Even the child's name, *Immanuel* (with us God), would serve as another reminder of their deliverance.

According to Brown-Driver-Briggs (BDB), the authoritative Hebrew-English Lexicon, the word *almah* means "young woman (ripe sexually, maid or newly married)". If Isaiah had wished to specify virginity, he would have used the Hebrew word *bethulah* (virgin), as he did five times elsewhere (23:4, 23:12, 37:22, 47:1, 62:5).

The crucial section of verse 14 is a verbless clause introduced by *hinneh*. Such clauses refer to the present or to the immediate future. Therefore the translation must be either:

> Behold, the young woman is pregnant and is bearing a son…
> *or* Behold, the young woman will be pregnant and bear a son…

The latter interpretation is to be preferred as the child spoken of here is obviously the same child born to Isaiah in Chapter 8. Note that the child is named *Immanuel* (with

---

[1] *Biblica Hebraica Stuttgartensia*. Deutsche Bibelgesellschaft: Stuttgart, 1983.

us God) by the mother in Chapter 7 to symbolise that God would be with the House of David in its struggle against the Kings *Rezin* and *Pekah*, and then named *Maher-shalal-hashbaz* (the spoil speeds, the prey hastes) by the father and God in Chapter 8 to symbolise the impending destruction of these two kings by the king of Assyria. Isaiah goes on to say in 8:18 that:

> Behold, I and the children whom the LORD hath given me are for signs and for wonders in Israel from the LORD of hosts, which dwelleth in mount Zion (Isaiah 8:18 KJV).

(Mention is made in 7:3 of another son of Isaiah, *Shear-jashub*.)

The name *Immanuel* has no special or extraordinary significance (see Judges 6:12-13). It is no different to many other Hebrew names possessed of similar meanings: *Boel* (in him is God); *Abijah* (my father is YHWH); *Zebadiah* (gift of YHWH); *Ahijah* (brother of YHWH); *Elihu* (My God is He).

It is important to take note that:

- the child *Immanuel* of Isaiah 7:14 was a child born in Isaiah's own time;
- Jesus was not named *Immanuel*.

The Hebrew Scriptures were eventually translated into Greek at some point between the 3rd and 1st Centuries BC. This Greek version is commonly referred to as the Septuagint (LXX standing for the seventy scholars supposedly engaged upon the translation). Without going into laborious detail, scholarly opinions vary widely as to the Septuagint's origin, its transmission, its textual integrity (especially the Book of Isaiah), whether it first included only the Torah, the dating of the first translation, and so on. Many excellent works on the subject are readily available.

The Greek Septuagint rendered the Hebrew word *almah* (young woman) of Isaiah 7:14 into the Greek word *parthenos* (virgin). The translation of this one single word has been a source of controversy ever since.

However, all these long centuries of dispute have been pointless because *parthenos* had varied usage in ancient Greek and never carried the narrowly defined meaning of strictly biological virginity. The Septuagint itself in Genesis 34:2-4 twice describes *Dinah* after her rape by *Shechem* as a *parthenos* and the word was also used in classical Greek literature to refer to women who had not retained their virginity biologically.

The Liddell-Scott-Jones Greek-English Lexicon (LSJ) is the most comprehensive and up-to-date Greek dictionary in the world. It is an essential library item in universities and used by every student of ancient Greek. The main dictionary covers every surviving ancient Greek author and text discovered up to 1940, from the

Pre-Classical Greek of the 11th-8th Century BC (for example *Homer* and *Hesiod*), through Classical Greek (7th-5th Century BC) to the Hellenistic Period, including the Greek Old and New Testaments.)

There are four citations under *parthenos*. Two use *parthenos* to refer to a woman who had already borne a child (*Homer, Iliad* 2.514; *Aristophanes, Clouds* 530). The other two references are to young women who had slept with men (*Pindar, Pythian* 3.34; *Sophocles, Trachiniae* 129). According to the Bauer–Danker–Arndt–Gingrich Greek-English Lexicon of the New Testament (BDAG), the primary meaning of *parthenos* is "generally a young woman of marriageable age…" hence BDAG gives essentially the same meaning as the LSJ and BDB.

But over and above all the foregoing semantic disputes is the central issue that the book of Isaiah is an Israelite book reflecting Israelite thought. The concept of a virgin conception/birth is utterly alien to Israelite thought. It was alien to Isaiah, it was alien to the Israelites of the New Testament, it is alien to Israelites now and always will be.

Isaiah 7:14 in the Gospel of Matthew

Signs of Deliverance

Drawing on the meaning of Jesus' name, to "save" or "deliver", Matthew paints Jesus as recapitulating in his individual existence a selection of deliverance-themed passages from the Hebrew Scriptures, especially those associated with Moses. For Matthew, Jesus is the representative Israelite, the one standing for the many, the "corporate personality", the one who fulfils in his individual existence God's salvation plan for the whole people of Israel. Jesus is Israel: Israel is Jesus.

Discover Matthew's method for by checking the Gospel passage and then the source of the quote in its original context:

- Chapter 1:23 quoting Isaiah 7:14;
- Chapter 2:6 quoting Micah 5:2-5;
- Chapter 2:15 quoting Hosea 11:1;
- Chapter 2:18 quoting Jeremiah 31:15;
- Chapter 3:3 quoting Isaiah 40:3;
- Chapter 4:14 quoting Isaiah 9:1-2

Verse 1:23

One of the deliverance-themed Scripture passages Matthew presents as being fulfilled in Jesus was the sign given to King Ahaz by the prophet Isaiah (Isaiah 7:14).

The one and only significance of Verse 1:23 is that it forms part of Matthew's overall presentation of Jesus as the representative Israelite. If a representative, then he can be no different in any essential respect from his fellow Israelites. To assert otherwise is to utterly destroy Matthew's Jesus.

For more on Matthew's presentation of Jesus, including the concept of "corporate personality", see Part IV.3: *Virgin Birth and Incarnation-The Gospel of Matthew*.

Section 3

Isaiah 9:6-7

Note

In both the Hebrew Scriptures and the New Testament, the divisions into chapter and verse were introduced long after the original accounts were written in order to facilitate reference. Some numbering differences exist, as is the case here where the verses we are examining are numbered in Hebrew texts as 5 and 6 whereas in our English translations they are numbered 6 and 7.

Mighty God, Everlasting Father...

The Hebrew words of verses 5-6 (see note) are taken from the *Leningrad Codex B19A (L)*, dated 1008-1009 AD, as reproduced in *Biblica Hebraica Stuttgartensia*.[2]

כִּי־יֶ֣לֶד יֻלַּד־לָ֗נוּ בֵּ֚ן נִתַּן־לָ֔נוּ וַתְּהִ֥י הַמִּשְׂרָ֖ה עַל־שִׁכְמ֑וֹ וַיִּקְרָ֨א שְׁמ֜וֹ פֶּ֠לֶא יוֹעֵץ֙ אֵ֣ל גִּבּ֔וֹר אֲבִיעַ֖ד שַׂר־שָׁלֽוֹם׃

לְמַרְבֵּ֨ה הַמִּשְׂרָ֜ה וּלְשָׁל֣וֹם אֵֽין־קֵ֗ץ עַל־כִּסֵּ֤א דָוִד֙ וְעַל־מַמְלַכְתּ֔וֹ לְהָכִ֤ין אֹתָהּ֙ וּֽלְסַעֲדָ֔הּ בְּמִשְׁפָּ֖ט וּבִצְדָקָ֑ה מֵעַתָּה֙ וְעַד־עוֹלָ֔ם קִנְאַ֛ת יְהוָ֥ה צְבָא֖וֹת תַּעֲשֶׂה־זֹּֽאת׃

The King James Version numbers these verses 6 and 7 (see note) and translates into English thus:

> For unto us a child is born, unto us a son is given: and the government shall be upon his shoulder: and his name shall be called Wonderful, Counseller, The mighty God (el), The everlasting Father, The Prince of Peace. Of the increase of his government and peace there shall be no end, upon the throne of David, and upon his kingdom, to order it, and to establish it with judgment and with justice from henceforth even for ever. The zeal of the LORD of hosts will perform this (Isaiah 9:6-7 KJV).

---

2 *Biblica Hebraica Stuttgartensia*. Deutsche Bibelgesellschaft: Stuttgart, 1983.

Verse 5

The Soncino edition of the Book of Isaiah translates Isaiah 9:5 into English thus:

> For a child is born unto us, A son is given to us;
> And the government is upon his shoulder;
> And his name is called Pele-joez-el-gibbor-Abi-ad-sar-shalom. (Many would perhaps recognise the Hebrew word "shalom" meaning peace.) [3]

Soncino Commentary

- *For a child is born unto us, a son is given to us;*
  This verse is actually in the Hebrew perfect tense which means the action has been completed and the child has already been born;

- *…the government is upon his shoulder;* This verse referred to Hezekiah, the son of King Ahaz who served as Crown Prince during his father's lifetime;

- *…and his name is called Pele-joez-el-gibbor-Abi-ad-sar-shalom.* The meaning of the Hebrew words is "Wonderful in counsel is god the mighty, the everlasting father, the ruler of peace". The child will bear these significant names in order to recall to the people the message which they embodied.

Verse 6

The Soncino edition of the Book of Isaiah translates Isaiah 9:6 into English thus:

> That the government may be increased,
> And of peace there be no end,
> Upon the throne of David, and upon his kingdom,
> To establish it, and to uphold it
> Through justice and righteousness
> From henceforth even for ever,
> The zeal of the Lord of hosts (YHWI I) doth perform this. [4]

Soncino Commentary:

- *That the government may be increased…*
  The kingdom of Ephraim, destroyed by the Assyrians in the reign of Ahaz,

---

[3] Slotki, Rev. Dr. Israel W. *Isaiah: Soncino Books of the Bible.* Ed. Rev.Dr. A.Cohen. The Soncino Press: London, 1970, pp 44-45.

[4] Slotki, Rev. Dr. Israel W. *Isaiah: Soncino Books of the Bible.* Ed. Rev.Dr. A.Cohen. The Soncino Press: London, 1970, pp 44-45.

passed over to Hezekiah when Assyria was showing signs of weakness. He (Hezekiah) was this the first ruler…to combine the entire nation, both in the north and the south as in the days of David and Solomon;

- *…From henceforth even for ever…*
  During the lifetime of Hezekiah. The Hebrew word olam (ever) also signifies "a considerable time";

- *…the zeal of the Lord…*
  Either God's zeal on behalf of His people, or Hezekiah's zeal to perform the Divine will by promoting the welfare of his subjects and his passion for justice;

- *…doth perform this.*
  Assures the fulfillment of the promise by YHWH.

Notes

It is the Israelite God YHWH who will fulfill the promise whereas the "mighty god" component of the name *Pele-joez-el-gibbor-Abi-ad-sar-shalom* is simply an *el*, a generic word for "god" that is incorporated into scores of Hebrew names.

It is the child's name which embodies all the attributes of God, not the child himself. Further, it cannot be the child himself that embodies these attributes because, if it were so, the child Hezekiah to whom the verse applied originally is also "god the mighty, the everlasting father, the ruler of peace".

Messianic Expectations in Ancient Israel

As noted in Section 1: *A last resort*, it is asserted that Isaiah 9:6-7 is an Israelite Messianic expectation of the Deity of Jesus of Nazareth. Before considering whether or not this claim is justified, we must first examine Messianic expectations as they existed at the time of Jesus.

The Messiah concept had its genesis in the longings of the Israelite people for deliverance from its sufferings, its humiliations, its oppressions, and its martyrdoms. Over the course of ancient Israelite history, prophets, priests and kings had been hailed as Messiahs (anointed ones) but these had served only temporary or specific purposes, e.g. Cyrus, King of Persia (see Isaiah 41:1).

Out of the welter of messianic expectations and longings arising from successive waves of tribulation, disaster and disappointment, there emerged a picture of an ideal King-Messiah who would inaugurate the eschatalogical Messianic Age, God's Kingdom on Earth, a holy and righteous Kingdom of brotherhood, peace and justice modelled on a restored, perfected, twelve-tribed Kingdom of David. All Israel's intellectual, spiritual and moral resources were to be dedicated to building this holy and righteous society which would serve as a model for the nations.

The King-Messiah would sit on the throne of this Kingdom and, because of God's dynastic promises to David, it was imagined that he therefore must be a biological "son of David". In the course of fulfilling his mission, it was envisioned that the Messiah would prove himself to be the greatest of all the prophets of righteousness in the line which began with Moses in Egypt. Because both the Messiah, individually, and the people of God, collectively, are spoken of by the prophets in terms of grief, humiliation, and suffering, it was therefore presumed that the glorious reign of God would emerge only after their passage through the refining furnace of affliction which would burn off the dross of the reign of man. This advent period, also likened to the travail of a woman in childbirth, was termed by later Rabbis as the "birth pangs of the Messiah".

All these elements, together with the suggestive force of other passages in the Hebrew Scriptures, came to constitute the following selection of criteria which the anointed one was expected to satisfy on his appearance:

- he would be an Israelite of the tribe of Judah;
- he would be descended from King David and entitled by birth to sit on David's earthly throne;
- he would usher in the Kingdom of God on earth;
- he would be a deliverer like the prophet Moses who would save the Israelites from their enemies;
- he would restore and gather into one the scattered tribes of Israel;
- he would cleanse the world by fire.

Then, as now, in the more rarified air of academia, there existed messianic speculations of greater purity, of more exquisite transcendence, of more exalted spirituality, of loftier learning and insight but, by the time of Jesus, a great majority of the "simple" people awaited the promised Messiah of the house of David who would deliver them from the tribulations of the Roman yoke and establish God's Kingdom of peace, justice and righteousness in its place.[5]

---

5   Fredriksen, Paula. *From Jesus to Christ: The Origins of the New Testament Images of Christ, Second Edition.* Yale University Press: 2000, pp. 141-42.

> The messiah everyone expected was the Davidic messiah. Paul himself attests to the strength of the royal tradition: if Jesus is the Christ, then he must be "descended from David according to the flesh," and so, without troubling to argue the case, Paul states he was (Romans 1:3; cf. 15:12 quoting Isaiah 11:10). [6]

It is not necessary, however, to rely on the analyses of expert academics regarding the messianic expectations of 1st Century Israelites. The New Testament itself contains more than enough evidence to reach an independent conclusion. For instance, when Zechariah, the father of John the Baptist, was moved to speak of his unborn son, he provided us with a magnificent encapsulation of these hopes.

> Blessed be the Lord God of Israel, for he has visited and redeemed his people and has raised up a horn of salvation for us in the house of his servant David, as he spoke by the mouth of his holy prophets from of old, that we should be saved from our enemies and from the hand of all who hate us; to show the mercy promised to our fathers and to remember his holy covenant, the oath that he swore to our father Abraham, to grant us that we, being delivered from the hand of our enemies, might serve him without fear, in holiness and righteousness before him all our days. And you, child, will be called the prophet of the Most High; for you will go before the Lord to prepare his ways, to give knowledge of salvation to his people in the forgiveness of their sins, because of the tender mercy of our God, whereby the sunrise shall visit us from on high to give light to those who sit in darkness and in the shadow of death, to guide our feet into the way of peace (Luke 1:68-69 ESV).

---

6 Vermes, Geza. *Jesus the Jew*. Fortress Press: Philadelphia, 1981, pp, 130-140.

Section 4

Justification? No...and...yes

Isaiah 7:14

As previously demonstrated, there is absolutely no justification for claiming that Isaiah 7:14 is a Messianic expectation of a Virgin Conception/Birth that was fulfilled in Jesus.

Isaiah 9:6-7

There is also no justification for claiming that Isaiah 9:6-7 is an Israelite Messianic expectation of the Deity of Jesus of Nazareth. As noted, it is the child's name which embodies all the attributes of God, not the child himself. Further, it cannot be the child himself that embodies these attributes because, if it were so, the child Hezekiah to whom the verse applied originally is also "god the mighty, the everlasting father, the ruler of peace".

Having said that, however, it is justifiable to claim that Isaiah 9:6-7 prefigures Jesus in terms of some of the Israelite Messianic expectations outlined above. Unfortunately for mainstream theology, these expectations depict a man born in the normal fashion: one chosen from among his fellows; one like his brethren in every respect. Consider Deuteronomy 18:18 for the "expectation" and Acts 3:22 for the "fulfillment":

> I will raise them up a Prophet from among their brethren, like unto thee (Moses), and will put my words in his mouth; and he shall speak unto them all that I shall command him (Deuteronomy 18:18 KJV).

> For Moses truly said unto the fathers, A prophet shall the Lord your God raise up unto you of your brethren, like unto me; him shall ye hear in all things whatsoever he shall say unto you (Acts 3:22 KJV).

The crude belief that God would assume human form belongs to the world of ancient paganism, not to the world of the Israelites portrayed in the Hebrew Scriptures and the New Testament. Just like the arsenal of other "proof" texts of mainstream Christian teachings, Isaiah 7:14 and Isaiah 9:6-7 have been shamelessly removed from their contexts and used for purposes unimaginable to their original authors. There is not now, nor has there ever been, any precedent in the Hebrew Scriptures justifying the Virgin Coneeption/Birth or Deity teachings.

CHAPTER THREE

Appeals to Concepts

Section 1

Pre-Existence

The Pre-existence teaching asserts the ontological or personal existence of Jesus before his conception. Support for this assertion is drawn from several key "proof-texts" in the New Testament. However, after a close examination of all these proof-texts, it will become apparent that they have been plucked out of their Israelite milieu and the contexts in which they occur to support a pre-existing theological position.

It will also become apparent that the New Testament teaching is the *foreknowledge* of God, not the *pre-existence* of Jesus. For example, the author of 1 Peter could not make the position any clearer:

> Forasmuch as ye know that ye were not redeemed with corruptible things, as silver and gold, from your vain conversation received by tradition from your fathers; But with the precious blood of Christ, as of a lamb without blemish and without spot: Who verily was foreordained before the foundation of the world, but was manifest in these last times for you (1 Peter 1:18-20 KJV).

In the following sections, the proof-texts most often cited to support the concept of a pre-existent Jesus will be examined.

Section 1a

Note

In Greek philosophy and theology, *Logos* is a term signifying the divine mind or reason which brought order and harmony to the cosmos. Christian philosophers identified Jesus as this *Logos*:

> The identification of Jesus as Logos also made intellectual, philosophical and scientific history. For by applying this title to Jesus, the Christian philosophers of the fourth and fifth centuries who were trying to give account of who he was

and what he had done were enabled to interpret him as the divine clue to the structure of reality (metaphysics) and, within metaphysics, to the riddle of being (ontology) - in a word, as the "Cosmic Christ." [7]

The Word made flesh

The theology of the Incarnate Word, based largely on the first few verses of the Gospel of John, was developed by Hellenist philosophers and metaphysicians because the style of John's writing, while actually focussed on Israelite norms, appealed to the speculative Greek mind.

Dabar

The Hebrew Scriptures state that God's creation came into existence through the *Word*:

> By the word (Hebrew: *dabar*) of the LORD the heavens were made, and by the breath of his mouth all their host (Psalm 33:6 ESV).

When John's Gospel passed into the hands of Hellenists, the introduction of the Greek philosophical concepts attached to *Logos* obscured John's understanding of the functions of God's *Word* (*dabar*) and masked what otherwise would have been obvious to all but the most doctrinaire of theologians: his total commitment to the fundamental tenet of Judaism—unitary monotheism. For John, there is the one true and only God (John 5:44; 17:3) and everything else is idols (1 John 5:21).

John gives the spiritual presentation of Jesus that the other Gospels lack and, unfortunately, it is from a banal interpretation of these spiritual words that the Incarnation and Pre-existence doctrines draw their support. One major reason for the universal misunderstanding of John's Gospel is a fixation on non-existent Hellenist concepts to the detriment of passages which stands in the starkest contrast to the orthodox theological position. For example:

- The author speaks of others besides Jesus as being "sent" by God and being "begotten" of God (1:6,12);

- The yardstick for determining if a man is really sent from God is whether he does, or does not, speak the words of God (3:34);

- In the case of those "begotten" of God, it is obvious that the author is speaking figuratively as they were procreated by normal means (see 1 John

---

[7] Pelikan, Jaroslav. *Jesus Through the Centuries: His Place in the History of Culture.* Yale University Press: 1999, p.58.

4:7 where it is clear that the "begotten of God" are those who love the brethren);

- Being written after the resurrection, there is no anomaly in John's reference to Jesus as the "only-begotten" son of God as it was not until the day of the resurrection that Jesus became that "only-begotten" son (Acts 13:33);

- The author, along with four disciples, believed that Jesus was the son of Joseph, thus of human parentage, "Philip findeth Nathanael, and saith unto him, 'We have found him, of whom Moses in the law, and the prophets, wrote, Jesus of Nazareth, the son of Joseph'." (1:45);

- The author did not find this thought incompatible with the Baptist's previous identification of Jesus as "the son of God" (1:34), nor with the subsequent similar identification by Nathaniel, "Nathaniel answered him, 'Rabbi, thou art the Son of God; thou art King of Israel'." (1:49);

- When the Baptist spoke of Jesus as being "before" him, he was not referring to time but to status;

- John could not be testifying to the Deity of Jesus because he states that, "No man has seen God at any time; the only-begotten son, he has declared him." (1:18).

Keeping these points in mind, the opening words of John's Gospel will be examined.

The author draws upon the language of Genesis 1 to emphasise the Israelite concept that God's "word" initiated Creation, e.g. "and God said 'let there be light'." According to the KJV, this is how the passage should be translated:

> In the beginning was the Word, and the Word was with God, and the Word was God. The same was in the beginning with God. All things were made by him; and without him was not any thing made that was made. In him was life; and the life was the light of men. And the light shineth in darkness; and the darkness comprehended it not (John 1:1-5 KJV).

These verses transition from Creation to Jesus. However, John did not provide the connecting link between the Word and Jesus until a few verses later:

> And the Word became flesh, and dwelt among us, and we saw His glory, glory as of the only begotten from the Father, full of grace and truth (John 1:14 NASB).

This last verse puts all into perspective and we see that:

- The *Word* existed from the "beginning";
- the *Word* cannot be "with" God, and also "be" God at one and the same time. The second God in verse 1 is not identical to the first God but is the anarthrous use of the predicate. Therefore the second God is a quality of the first, as many Greek scholars have attested.[8]
- The *Word* cannot be identical to God because God is "eternal, immortal, invisible" (2 Timothy 1:17) and has no beginning and no ending (Psalm 90:2);
- The *Word* was made flesh and dwelt among us;
- Jesus' life—the *Word* made flesh—was the light of men.

Before one can understand what John is trying to convey here, it is necessary to determine just what the *Word* was before it became flesh. Fortunately, John provides the answer himself in his First Epistle:[9]

> That which was from the beginning, which we have heard, which we have seen with our eyes, which we have looked upon, and our hands have handled, of the Word of life; (For the life was manifested, and we have seen it, and bear witness, and shew unto you that eternal life, which was with the Father, and was manifested unto us) (I John 1:1-2 KJV).

It is the impersonal concept of the "Word of Eternal Life" which was "with the Father" before the birth of Jesus, not Jesus himself pre-existing. John intended us to understand that when the *Word* became flesh, the transition was not that of a divine person becoming a human person, but of an impersonal concept—the Word of Eternal Life—becoming embodied in a human being.

There is further confirmation in John's Gospel that the *Word* is the "Word of Eternal Life":

> And I (Jesus) know that his commandment is eternal life. What I say, therefore, I say as the Father has told me (John 12:50 ESV).
>
> Simon Peter answered him, "Lord, to whom shall we go? You have the words of eternal life" (John 6:68 ESV).

---

8   See for example Phillip B. Harper's article "Qualitative Anarthrous Predicate Nouns" published in the Journal of Biblical Literature, Vol. 92, Philadelphia, 1973, p. 85.

9   "The three Epistles and the Gospel of John are so closely allied in diction, style, and general outlook that the burden of proof lies with the person who would deny their common authorship." (Streeter, B. H. *The Four Gospels*, rev. ed. Macmillan: London, 1930 p. 460.

The Epistle of Paul to Titus also confirms that it is the "Word of Eternal Life" that existed from the beginning:

> Paul, a servant of God, and an apostle of Jesus Christ, according to the faith of God's elect, and the acknowledging of the truth which is after godliness; In hope of eternal life, which God, that cannot lie, promised before the world began (Titus 1:1-2 KJV).

Jesus was presented by John as the embodiment of God's "Word of Eternal Life" which *dwelt* in Jesus, in precisely the same manner as Paul argued in 1 Corinthians 1:30 that Jesus was the embodiment of God's Wisdom.

The word "dwelt" in John 1:14 is derived from the Greek *skenoo* which, in the Greek Septuagint, is based on the Hebrew *shakan* which means to "inhabit", to "tabernacle" or to "settle". We can observe the intended meaning of this Hebrew word in passages such as Exodus 24:16, Judges 5:17, and 1 Kings 8:12. The passage in Exodus 25:8, however, most accurately expresses the meaning of John 1:14:

> And let them make me a sanctuary; that I may dwell (*shakan*) among them (Exodus 25:8 KJV).

There is no difference between the concept of God dwelling in the sanctuary and God dwelling in Jesus. No difference whatsoever. It is the "Word of Eternal Life" promised by God "before the world began" (Titus 1:2) that was "with" God and was "godlike", not Jesus.

The Wisdom of God made flesh : a parallel principle

Wisdom and *Word* are aspects of God's activity. These are Israelite concepts which carry with them no thought or suggestion of Deity or Pre-existence.

After the death of his father King David, Solomon requested God for the wisdom to govern well. God gave Solomon more than he had asked for: he would receive unparalleled wisdom and, with it, wealth and fame (1 Kings 3:6-13).

Just as God's *Word* was made flesh in Jesus, so also was God's *Wisdom* made flesh in Solomon. The 8th Proverb demonstrates this principle.

> I, wisdom, dwell with prudence; I possess knowledge and discretion. ...From everlasting I was established, From the beginning, from the earliest times of the earth...When He established the heavens, I was there, When He inscribed a circle on the face of the deep...When He marked out the foundations of the earth; Then I was beside Him, as a master workman... (Proverbs 8:12-30 ESV).

At first glance, this Proverb seems to speak of Solomon, but a few moments reflection will convince that it speaks of the Wisdom given him by God, of which he was the physical embodiment. Just as the Wisdom of Solomon was pre-existent, so too was the Word of Eternal Life. Solomon the man was not, neither was the man Jesus.

The New Testament understanding of pre-existent entities such as the impersonal *Wisdom* and *Word* is naturally the same as the Jewish understanding both past and present. I will therefore leave the last word to Sigmund Mowinckel:

> Rabbinic theology speaks of the Law, of God's throne of glory, of Israel and of other important objects of faith as things which had been created by God, and were already present with Him before the creation of the world. The same is also true of the Messiah. It is said that his name was present with God in heaven beforehand, that it was created before the world, and that it is eternal. But the reference here is not to genuine pre-existence in the strict and literal sense. This is clear from the fact that Israel is included among these pre-existent entities. This does not mean that either the nation Israel or its ancestor existed long ago in heaven, but that the community Israel, the people of God, had been from all eternity in the mind of God, as a factor of His purpose…This is true of references to the pre-existence of the Messiah. It is his 'name,' not the Messiah himself, that is said to have been present with God before creation. In Preikta Rabbati 152b it is said that 'from the beginning of the creation of the world the King Messiah was born, for he came up in the thought of God before the world was created.' This means that from all eternity it was the will of God that the Messiah should come into existence, and should do his work in the world to fulfil God's eternal saving purpose. [10]

Section 1b

The Carmen Christi

It is asserted that Philippians 2:5-11, also known as the "Carmen Christi", was utilised by the early Christian church to teach and magnify the Pre-existence, the Incarnation, and the full Deity of Jesus. Rather than accept this verdict, we will allow Paul himself to have the final say:

---

10 Mowinckel, Sigmund. *He That Cometh: The Messiah Concept in the Old Testament and Later Judaism.* Transl. G.W. Anderson. Abingdon: Nashville, 1954, p.334.

Have this mind among yourselves, which is yours in Christ Jesus who, though he was in the form (*morphē*) of God, did not count equality with God a thing to be grasped, but emptied himself, by taking the form of a servant, being born in the likeness of men. And being found in human form, he humbled himself by becoming obedient to the point of death, even death on a cross. Therefore God has highly exalted him and bestowed on him the name that is above every name, so that at the name of Jesus every knee should bow, in heaven and on earth and under the earth, and every tongue confess that Jesus Christ is Lord (*kurios*), to the glory of God the Father (Philippians 2:5-11 ESV).

Analysis

Verses 5-11 are all about an attitude of mind which Paul hopes that the Philippians will adopt. He sets forth his arguments by drawing an analogy between Jesus and the righteous servant of Isaiah 52:13 - 53:12 and then exhorts them to imitate this example by embracing humility and rejecting self-righteousness.

The passage is in keeping with the remainder of Paul's theology in which Jesus reverses the sin of Adam, which is why he refers to Jesus as the "last Adam" and the "first-born" of the New Creation (Colossians 1:15).

Just like Adam, Jesus was created in the "image" (form) of God with free will. Although Jesus imaged God in his character and demeanour, and possessed free will, he did not choose to grasp at equality with God, as did Adam (Genesis 3:5), but deliberately abased himself to the status of the Isaiah servant. Unlike the disobedience of Adam, Jesus became "obedient to the point of death, even death on a cross". Therefore God "highly-exalted" him (cf. Isaiah 52:13) and bestowed on him the "name that is above every name".

Jesus was not given the "name above every name" until after his exaltation. A change of name in the Bible indicates the commencement of a new relationship. Henceforth, all the authority and sovereignty of YHWH would be invested in his human delegate Jesus. Jesus is, therefore, to be accorded an honour and a glory—"every knee should bow"—similar to that accorded to YHWH.

The Greek word *kurios* is simply the equivalent of the Hebrew *adonai* (Lord). The fact that Jesus is referred to as "Lord" in no way implies that he is to be equated with God. There are many human Lords mentioned in the Hebrew Scriptures: it is simply a word denoting authority.

Rather than this Pauline exhortation proclaiming the Pre-existence, the Incarnation, and the full Deity of Jesus, it proclaims precisely the opposite: if Jesus, born as a normal man, can attain such exalted status in the eyes of God, then so too can the Philippians, and everyone else.

A comparison of texts

In his exhortation to the Philippians, Paul employed quite complicated imagery and language. In Romans Chapter 1, however, Paul uses more forthright language to impart what is essentially the same sequence of events:

> Concerning his Son Jesus Christ our Lord, which was made of the seed of David according to the flesh; And declared to be the Son of God with power, according to the spirit of holiness, by the resurrection from the dead (Romans 1:3-4 KJV).

Section 1c

The Canticle of Colossians

Much of the argumentation for Pre-existence and Incarnational Christology derives from passages such as the so-called Canticle of Colossians. It has been demonstrated in the previous Section that, in regard to Philippians 2:5-11, orthodox Pauline Christology is totally incorrect in its interpretation of Paul's teachings. In this section, we will focus out attention on Colossians 1:15-17 as these verses are much-quoted and would appear at first glance to provide orthodox theology with a veritable cornucopia of support for the doctrines of Pre-existence, Incarnation, and Deity. However, the context in which these verses were written will provide a correct perspective.

The New Creation of Life

The writers of the New Testament recorded that a New Creation had come into being—that a revolution in thinking had taken place. Whereas before, the earth had been filled with death and corruption, the disciples saw it spring to life once again in the teachings of Jesus of Nazareth. They witnessed a New Creation coming into existence, brought into being by and through Jesus.

In the beginning, as recorded in the Hebrew Scriptures, the Israelite God "made the earth by his power; he founded the world by his wisdom and stretched out the heavens by his understanding" (Jeremiah 10:12).

But in the new "beginning", as described in the Gospel of John, when the Word of Eternal Life was made flesh in Jesus, the old things passed away, they became new (2 Corinthians 5:17).

What came into existence by means of Jesus was Life (John 1:4; Acts 3:15). At his resurrection, he became the firstborn creature in this New Creation of Life, the firstborn of many brethren to follow (Romans 8:29) who, together, constitute the Kingdom of God. It is to Jesus as the architect of this New Creation of Life, not as co-creator of the old world of dead matter, that the following texts apply:

> …yet for us there is but one God, the Father, from whom all things came and for whom we live; and there is but one Lord, Jesus Christ, through whom all things came and through whom we live (1 Corinthians 8:6 NIV).

> Long ago, at many times and in many ways, God spoke to our fathers by the prophets, but in these last days he has spoken to us by his Son, whom he appointed the heir of all things, through whom also he created the world (Hebrews 1:1-2 ESV).

And of course, the subject of our present enquiries, the much-quoted verses from Colossians reproduced below:

> Who is the image of the invisible God, the firstborn of every creature: For by him were all things created, that are in heaven, and that are in earth, visible and invisible, whether they be thrones, or dominions, or principalities, or powers: all things were created by him, and for him: And he is before all things, and by him all things consist (Colossians 1:15-17 KJV).

When these verses are quoted, they usually terminate immediately before verse 18 in which Paul puts all into perspective:

> And he is the head of the body, the church: who is the beginning, the firstborn from the dead; that in all things he might have the preeminence (Colossians 1:18 KJV cf. Revelation 1:5, 3:14).

(See also related texts such as Galatians 6:15 and 2 Corinthians 5:17.)

None of the above texts apply to the old Creation of matter. Jesus is the first-born of the New Creation of Life brought into existence on the day of his resurrection.

If the difference between theological teachings and New Testament teachings could be reduced to one simple concept it is this: the theological teaching is that God became manly whereas the New Testament teaching is that man became godly.

Section 1d

The rejoicing of Abraham

The Gospel of John 8:56-58 is yet another "proof-text" drummed into service to support the teaching of Pre-existence:

> Your father Abraham rejoiced to see my day: and he saw it, and was glad. Then said the Jews (Judeans) unto him, Thou art not yet fifty years old, and hast thou seen Abraham? Jesus said unto them, Verily, verily, I say unto you, Before Abraham was, I am (John 8:56-58 KJV).

The priestly establishment opposed to Jesus claimed that their descent from Abraham and then Moses conferred upon them the authority to pronounce judgement on him because they had been divinely appointed according to Scripture. They picked up stones to stone him because he was claiming a greater authority than Abraham and Moses. The only person who would be presumed to have a greater authority than either men would be the Messiah at his advent so this response by Jesus is a proclamation that he is indeed the Messiah and that he has indeed arrived. Since it was commonly believed that the promise of a Messiah existed from the "beginning", from before the time of Abraham, Jesus quite rightly claims that Abraham was able to look forward and see his "day", the day of his advent.

We will first examine verse 56:

> Your father Abraham rejoiced to see my day: and he saw it, and was glad.

Then consider these similar statements by and about Jesus:

> For had ye believed Moses, ye would have believed me: for he wrote of me (John 5:46 KJV).
>
> These things said Esaias, when he saw his glory, and spake of him (John 12:41 KJV).

The Foreknown Brethren

Only the most determined and doctrinaire apologist for the teaching of Pre-existence could find any essential difference whatsoever between the statements reproduced above and these below.

> According as he hath chosen us in him before the foundation of the world, that we should be holy and without blame before him in love (Ephesians 1:4 KJV).

And we know that all things work together for good to them that love God, to them who are the called according to his purpose. For whom he did foreknow, he also did predestinate to be conformed to the image of his Son, that he might be the firstborn among many brethren (Romans 8:28-29 KJV).

But we are bound to give thanks always to God for you, brethren beloved of the Lord, because God hath from the beginning chosen you to salvation through sanctification of the Spirit and belief of the truth (2 Thessalonians 2:13 KJV).

And that he might make known the riches of his glory on the vessels of mercy, which he had afore prepared unto glory, Even us, whom he hath called... (Romans 9:23-24 KJV).

Who hath saved us, and called us with an holy calling, not according to our works, but according to his own purpose and grace, which was given us in Christ Jesus before the world began (2 Timothy 1:9 KJV).

The Foreknown Witnesses

Him God raised up the third day, and shewed him openly; Not to all the people, but unto witnesses chosen before of God, even to us, who did eat and drink with him after he rose from the dead (Acts 10:40-41 KJV).

The Foreknown Messiah

Concerning this salvation, the prophets, who spoke of the grace that was to come to you, searched intently and with the greatest care, trying to find out the time and circumstances to which the Spirit of Christ in them was pointing when he predicted the sufferings of the Messiah and the glories that would follow (1 Peter 1:11 NIV).

Who verily was foreordained before the foundation of the world, but was manifest in these last times for you (1 Peter 1:20 KJV).

The Foreknown Works

Now we who have believed enter that rest. As for the others, it is just as God has said: "So I swore on oath in My anger, 'They shall never enter My rest'." And yet His works have been finished since the foundation of the world (Hebrews 4:3 ESV).

The Foreknown Kingdom

> ...Come, ye blessed of my Father, inherit the kingdom prepared for you from the foundation of the world (Matthew 25:34 KJV).

The correct interpretation of John 8:56 is that, just as all the persons and entities noted above, Jesus was *foreknown* and *foreordained*, not *pre-existent*.

Even though verse 58 could rightly belong elsewhere in this work, we will continue with it in the next sub-section so as to maintain context and flow.

Section 1e

Note

It has been conclusively demonstrated by Claude Tresmontant and others that the Greek Gospels were originally composed from Hebrew originals or from Hebrew notes. It makes no difference whether Jesus spoke in Aramaic or Hebrew—his words were originally recorded in Hebrew, the "sacred" language. (See Part II.7: *The Documents-The Language of the Gospels*.)

The "I am"

In the previous section, we have demonstrated that John 8:56 does not indicate the *pre-existence* of Jesus but rather the *foreknowledge* of God. It is now time to address the final words of verse 8:58 which are incorrectly translated into English as "I am". The verse reproduced once again:

> Verily, verily, I say unto you, Before Abraham was, I am (*ego eimi*) (John 8:58 KJV).

Firstly, Jesus could not have spoken the words translated into English as "I am" because the simple copulative forms of the Hebrew present tense "to be" are merely implied, e.g. I (am) sick; she (is) pretty; we (are) happy. The appropriate form, in this case "am", has been simply added, first to the Greek and then to the English, to conform with the linguistic demands of these languages.

The "I am" of John 8:58 is an incomplete translation of the Greek *ego eimi* which, in turn, is based on the Hebrew *ani hou* (I, he). Jesus simply responded to his interrogators questions by answering, "I (am) he". We are entitled to ask why verse 58 was singled out for an incomplete translation when Jesus's use of the same Greek phrase was correctly translated into English in other passages. For example:

> Many will come in my name, claiming, "I am he, (*ego eimi*) and will deceive many (Mark 13:6 ESV).

> And he said, "See that you are not led astray. For many will come in my name, saying, 'I am he!' (*ego eimi*) and, 'The time is at hand!' Do not go after them" (Luke 21:8 ESV).

The answer to the question is that theological considerations drove the translators to render John 8:58 incompletely as "I am" in the hope of identifying Jesus with the "burning bush" episode in the Book of Exodus.

Exodus 3:13-14

It is now time to take a closer look at this crucial passage, reproduced below:

> And Moses said unto God, Behold, when I come unto the children of Israel, and shall say unto them, The God of your fathers hath sent me unto you; and they shall say to me, What is his name? (*mah semo*) what shall I say unto them? (Exodus 3:13 KJV).

> And God said unto Moses, I AM THAT I AM (*Ehyeh Asher Ehyeh*): and he said, Thus shalt thou say unto the children of Israel, I AM hath sent me unto you (Exodus 3:14 KJV).

Verse 13

The English interpretation of the Hebrew *mah semo* is "what is his name?" In Biblical Hebrew, where the interrogative particle *mah* (what) is associated with *semo* (his name), the force of the question asked is "what is concealed or lies beneath that name?"

Verse 14

The answer given in verse 14 corresponds with the question asked in verse 13. It is the significance of the name that is given—not the name itself. It is therefore a statement about God's essence, suggesting that the God of Israel is not able to be manipulated by humans in a manner reminiscent of the gods of Egypt with whom the Israelites were well acquainted.

The phrase *Ehyeh Asher Ehyeh* has been wrongly translated into English as "I am that I am". Without going into laborious detail about Hebrew tenses and linguistic forms, the Hebrew words actually spoken at the burning bush were *Ehyeh* (1st person singular imperfect form of the verb "to be"), *Asher* (relative pronoun), *Ehyeh* (1st person singular imperfect form of the verb "to be"). The verbs here are in the "imperfect" tense meaning that the action may have begun in the past but will be completed in the future, or will continue in the future. *Ehyeh,* being in the imperfect tense, is more correctly translated as "I will be" as it is in Judges 6:16 and Hosea 1:9. Hence we are left with the more correct but still inadequate "I will be what I will be".

Given this range of the imperfect Hebrew tense, and the difficulties of translating its significance from Hebrew into English, the precise meaning of this mysterious phrase *Ehyeh Asher Ehyeh* has been debated by Hebrew scholars and Rabbis for many centuries. We, however, have most fortunately been provided with two Greek New Testament passages which, although not stated to be such, convey a similar but more comprehensive expression of God's essence—*which is, which was, and which is to come*:

> John to the seven churches which are in Asia: Grace be unto you, and peace, from him which is, and which was, and which is to come; and from the seven Spirits which are before his throne; And from Jesus Christ, who is the faithful witness, and the first begotten of the dead, and the prince of the kings of the earth… (Revelation 1:4-5 KJV cf. Revelation 1:8).

The farce

Regardless of whether or not one accepts the evidence given above, the hope of identifying Jesus with the "burning bush" episode is revealed as farcical by Stephen's address to the Sanhedrin:

> And when forty years were expired, there appeared to him in the wilderness of mount Sinai an angel of the Lord in a flame of fire in a bush. When Moses saw it, he wondered at the sight: and as he drew near to behold it, the voice of the Lord came unto him, Saying, I am the God of thy fathers, the God of Abraham, and the God of Isaac, and the God of Jacob. Then Moses trembled, and durst not behold. Then said the Lord to him, Put off thy shoes from thy feet: for the place where thou standest is holy ground. I have seen, I have seen the affliction of my people which is in Egypt, and I have heard their groaning, and am come down to deliver them. And now come, I will send thee into Egypt. This Moses whom they refused, saying, Who made thee a ruler and a judge? the same did God send to be a ruler and a deliverer by the hand of the angel which appeared to him in the bush (Acts 7:30-35 KJV).

So, it was not God but an "angel of the Lord" who appeared to Moses in flames of fire from within a bush (Exodus 3:2). Stephen added that the angel spoke to Moses with the "voice of the Lord" (Acts 7:30-35).

The Abode of God

Yet more justification for the Pre-existence teaching is drawn from other passages in the Gospel of John.

Bread of Heaven

John Chapter 6 is mainly about food, and the difference between merely *physical* food and a vastly more nourishing *spiritual* food. John sets the scene by beginning with the miracle of the physical loaves and fishes and then continues on to describe quite clearly the difference between the *physical manna* of the wilderness and the *spiritual manna* which Jesus would give them:

> I am that bread of life. Your fathers did eat manna in the wilderness, and are dead. This is the bread which cometh down from heaven, that a man may eat thereof, and not die. I am the living bread which came down from heaven: if any man eat of this bread, he shall live for ever: and the bread that I will give is my flesh, which I will give for the life of the world (John 6:48-51 KJV).

Those who ate from the spiritual bread that Jesus offered would not die spiritually, unlike those who ate from the physical bread in the wilderness but eventually died. He went on to tell the people that:

> Whoso eateth my flesh, and drinketh my blood, hath eternal life; and I will raise him up at the last day (John 6:54 KJV).

Jesus was not recommending cannabalism. Such pagan practices as eating human flesh and drinking human blood would have been abhorrent in the extreme to the Israelite Jesus. Eating the flesh and drinking the blood of Jesus is symbolic of living the way Jesus lived by following in his footsteps and obeying his commandments. The words he spoke were "spirit and life" (6:63). To eat Jesus spiritually is to partake of eternal life, sent as a gift from Heaven.

In this chapter of John is found yet another verse used to justify the teaching of the Pre-existence of Jesus:

> What and if ye shall see the Son of man ascend up (*anabainonta*) where he was before? (John 6:62 KJV).

Because the Greek word *anabainonta* has been translated into English as "ascend", it is asserted that this verse refers to the Ascension of Jesus, as recorded in Acts 1:9.

However, Acts 1:9 uses a different Greek word *epairó* meaning to "lift up" whereas *anabainó* means to "get up".

The Greek word *anabainó* is used in its various verbal forms to refer to Jesus "coming up" from under the water at his baptism (Matthew 3:16; Mark 1:10), to refer to plants that "grow up" out of the ground (Matthew 13:7; Mark 4:7, 8, 32), and even to refer to the act of climbing a tree.

Verse 6:62 does not refer to Jesus returning to Heaven, i.e. "where he was before" as the Pre-existence teaching would have us believe. Rather, this verse refers to the Resurrection and Jesus "coming up" out of the grave to the earth, i.e. "where he was before" his death. It is a contextless absurdity to claim otherwise.

Up and Down the Ladder

When the High Priest entered the Jerusalem Temple's Holy of Holies on the Day of Atonement, into the presence of God, he symbolically ascended to God's abode in Heaven above and, as near-contemporary texts show, on his return to the people from the inner sanctuary, he symbolically descended from Heaven back to Earth. (Note that God was believed to rule through an opening in the sky directly above the Jerusalem Temple, the *axis mundi*, the place of connection between God in Heaven and his covenant people on Earth.)

Similarly, those who are described in the New Testament as being "sent" from God to work his will on Earth, symbolically descend from Heaven to Earth. With that concept in mind, consider the following passages:

> But I have greater witness than that of John: for the works which the Father hath given me to finish, the same works that I do, bear witness of me, that the Father hath sent me (John 5:36 KJV).

> For I came down from heaven, not to do mine own will, but the will of him that sent me (John 6:38 KJV).

As well as applying this concept to Jesus, the author of John's Gospel also applied it to John the Baptist:

> There was a man sent from God, whose name was John (John 1:6 NIV).

In Luke Chapter 20, when Jesus' authority to teach was challenged, he responded with a question expressing the same concept:

> The baptism of John, was it from heaven, or of men? And they reasoned with themselves, saying, If we shall say, From heaven; he will say, Why then believed

ye him not? But and if we say, Of men; all the people will stone us: for they be persuaded that John was a prophet (Luke 20:4-6 KJV).

When Jesus used phrases such as "came down from heaven" or "the Father hath sent me", he was speaking symbolically and actually indicated so on most occasions.

Notes

The Greek words *aion* denoting an "age" or "ages", and *aionios* meaning "age-lasting", are usually translated into English with words like "eternal". The concept of "eternity" or "endlessness" was not conveyed by these Greek words until theologians assigned such meanings to them centuries after the New Testament was written. God alone possesses "eternity". The phrase "eternal life" actually means "age-long life in the age to come".

Section 1g

The Rock

The various "rock" descriptions of Jesus are arguments used to advance both the Pre-existence and Deity teachings. Since, a major analysis of these arguments appears in Chapter 4: *Appeals to Descriptions and Titles*, it is only necessary here to provide a brief commentary on the Pre-existence component of these teachings.

One of the apologetic texts is taken from Paul's First Epistle to the Corinthians, which must be reproduced in full in order to grasp its context:

> For I do not want you to be ignorant of the fact, brothers and sisters, that our ancestors were all under the cloud and that they all passed through the sea. They were all baptized into Moses in the cloud and in the sea. They all ate the same spiritual food and drank the same spiritual drink; for they drank from the spiritual rock that accompanied them, and that rock was Christ (1 Corinthians 10:1-4 NIV).

In the Hebrew Scriptures, two occasions are mentioned when Moses struck a rock and the Israelites miraculously received water (Exodus 17:1–7; Numbers 20:1–14). Since the rocks were apparently in different places, an Israelite folk tradition arose about a "physical" rock that accompanied them on their journey through the wilderness. In the above passage, Paul refutes this folk tradition and explains that it was not a "physical" but a "spiritual" rock that accompanied them in expectation of the Messiah. The smiting of the rock from which "physical" waters flowed prefigured the smiting of the Messiah from whom "spiritual" waters now flow.

The Alpha and Omega

Theological support for both the Pre-existence and Trinity teachings is drawn in part from the "Alpha and Omega" phrase found in the Book of Revelation and also from certain texts found in the Book of Isaiah.

It is asserted that the Israelite God and Jesus are both described as "the Alpha and Omega", "the first and the last", and "the beginning and the end", thereby demonstrating that Jesus should be equated with God. This assertion will be examined from a Pre-existence standpoint. (An analysis of the Trinity teaching appears in Part VI: *Trinity on Trial*.)

The New Creation of Life

Although it has already been pointed out in Section 1c: *The Canticle of Colossians*, that certain passages have been commandeered by mainstream theology to serve the Pre-existence teaching, it is unavoidably necessary to draw attention to a selection of these texts yet again as they provide the all-important backdrop to phrases such as the ones we are at present addressing.

The New Testament position is that Jesus brought into being a New Creation of Life (John 1:4; Acts 3:15).

The following texts apply to this New Creation of Life, the new Heavens and the New Earth brought into existence by and through Jesus. These texts speak of a new world of spiritual life, not of an old world of dead matter:

> ...yet for us there is but one God, the Father, from whom all things came and for whom we live; and there is but one Lord, Jesus Christ, through whom all things came and through whom we live (1 Corinthians 8:6 NIV).

> Long ago, at many times and in many ways, God spoke to our fathers by the prophets, but in these last days he has spoken to us by his Son, whom he appointed the heir of all things, through whom also he created the world (Hebrews 1:1-2 ESV).

The following text tells us *when* this New Creation came into existence:

> Who is the image of the invisible God, the firstborn of every creature: For by him were all things created, that are in heaven, and that are in earth, visible and invisible, whether they be thrones, or dominions, or principalities, or powers: all things were created by him, and for him: And he is before all things, and

by him all things consist. And he is the head of the body, the church: who is the beginning, the firstborn from the dead; that in all things he might have the preeminence (Colossians 1:15-18 KJV cf. Revelation 1:5, 3:14).

The New Creation of Life came into existence at the Resurrection, at which time Jesus became the "firstborn of every creature", the firstborn of many brethren to follow in the New Creation of Life. Note also that verse 15 states unambiguously that Jesus is a created being. (See also related texts such as Galatians 6:15; 1 Corinthians 8:6; 2 Corinthians 5:17; Romans 8:29.)

Now that the New Testament position has been established, we can proceed.

The Book of Isaiah

Hebrew Scriptural support for the "first and last" component of the Pre-existence teaching is drawn mainly from the Book of Isaiah:

> Who hath wrought and done it, calling the generations from the beginning? I the LORD, the first, and with the last; I am he (Isaiah 41:4 KJV).
>
> Thus says the LORD, the King of Israel and his Redeemer, the LORD of hosts: "I am the first and I am the last; besides me there is no god" (Isaiah 44:6 ESV).
>
> "Listen to me, Jacob, Israel, whom I have called: I am he; I am the first and I am the last" (Isaiah 48:12 NIV).

The "first" and "last" of these verses describes God's rank. It reflects the common Israelite theme that there is no God before him, and there is no God after him. He is the eternal, immortal and invisible God who has no beginning and no ending. He is "from everlasting to everlasting" (Psalm 90:2).

The Book of Revelation

It has been asserted that analysis of the Book of Revelation is notoriously difficult for scholars given that it is a genre combining three literary styles described as apocalyptic, epistolary, and prophetic. While this assertion is warranted to a certain extent, it is undeniable that certain difficulties stem from an unwillingness or inability to grasp the Book's interpretive themes of the *New Creation* and the *Absolute Sovereignty of God*.

The New Creation

The author of Revelation continues with the overall New Testament theme of a New Creation brought into existence by Jesus. In the following texts, all referring to the New Creation, Jesus is variously described as the "firstborn from the dead"; as the "beginning of God's creation"; and as the "first and last" who "was dead and is alive":

> ...and from Jesus Christ, who is the faithful witness, the firstborn from the dead, and the ruler of the kings of the earth (Revelation 1:5 NIV).
>
> When I saw him, I fell at his feet as though dead. But he laid his right hand on me, saying, "Fear not, I am the first and the last, and the living one" (Revelation 1:17 ESV).
>
> And unto the angel of the church in Smyrna write; These things saith the first and the last, which was dead, and is alive (Revelation 2:8 KJV).
>
> And to the angel of the church in Laodicea write: "The words of the Amen, the faithful and true witness, the beginning of God's creation" (Revelation 3:14 ESV).

A moment's reflection will demonstrate that by referring to Jesus as the "first and the last", the author of John was not equating Jesus with the God described as the "first and last" in the previously quoted texts from Isaiah because he also informs us that Jesus was a created being subject to death and therefore with a beginning and an ending.

Just as Hebrews 12:2 describes Jesus as the "author and finisher of our faith", so does the author of Revelation express the same conviction by describing Jesus as the "first and the last" of God's great salvation plan for Israel.

The Absolute Sovereignty of God

Throughout the Book, the author emphasises the absolute sovereignty and "otherness" of God. He draws many distinctions between God and Jesus: distinctions that preclude any possibility that the author intends to equate Jesus with God. Consider the following verses from Chapter 1:

> The Revelation of Jesus Christ, which God gave unto him, to shew unto his servants things which must shortly come to pass; and he sent and signified it by his angel unto his servant John (Revelation 1:1 KJV).
>
> John, To the seven churches in the province of Asia: Grace and peace to you from him who is, and who was, and who is to come, and from the seven spirits before his throne, and from Jesus Christ, who is the faithful witness, the firstborn from the dead, and the ruler of the kings of the earth. To him who loves us and has freed us from our sins by his blood, and has made us to be a kingdom and priests to serve his God and Father—to him be glory and power for ever and ever! Amen (Revelation 1:4-6 NIV).

In verse 1 and in verses 4-6, John states that:

- the revelation was given to Jesus by God and delivered to John by an angel;
- there are three distinct entities: God; the seven spirits; and Jesus;
- Jesus is a faithful and true witness to God;
- Jesus died and was resurrected;
- Jesus serves his God and his Father.

These first verses of the Book of Revelation draw categorical distinctions between the eternal, immortal and invisible God who has no beginning and no ending and the man Jesus who is not only described as God's servant and witness but was also subject to death and therefore had a beginning and an ending. A few verses later, John again draws our attention to the fact that Jesus died:

> When I saw him, I fell at his feet as though dead. But he laid his right hand on me, saying, "Fear not, I am the first and the last, and the living one. I died, and behold I am alive forevermore, and I have the keys of Death and Hades" (Revelation 1:17-18 ESV).

In addition to the foregoing, an examination of the references to Jesus as a "son of man" and as a "slain lamb", will provide additional insight into John's conviction of the absolute sovereignty and "otherness" of God.

The son of man

In Chapter 1, verses 12-14, John identifies one that spoke to him and goes on to describe his appearance:

> And I turned to see the voice that spake with me. And being turned, I saw seven golden candlesticks; And in the midst of the seven candlesticks one like unto the Son of man, clothed with a garment down to the foot, and girt about the paps with a golden girdle. His head and his hairs were white like wool, as white as snow; and his eyes were as a flame of fire; And his feet like unto fine brass, as if they burned in a furnace; and his voice as the sound of many waters (Revelation 1:12-15 KJV).

In passages from Chapter 7 of the Book of Daniel, the "Ancient of Days" (God) is described in terms similar to the "son of man" in the passage above. It is asserted, therefore, that Jesus must be equated with God. In the Book of Daniel, however, the "Ancient of Days" and the one like a "son of man" are separate entities. They cannot be separate in Daniel, yet the same in Revelation.

If any doubt should still remain, it is only necessary to consider John's other reference to a "son of man" to settle the matter once and for all. In Chapter 14, verses 14-16, we see thrown into sharp relief the risible nature of the assertion that the "son of man" term is a divine title:

> I looked, and there before me was a white cloud, and seated on the cloud was one like a son of man with a crown of gold on his head and a sharp sickle in his hand (Revelation 14:14 NIV).
>
> Then another angel came out of the temple and called in a loud voice to him who was sitting on the cloud, "Take your sickle and reap, because the time to reap has come, for the harvest of the earth is ripe" (Revelation 14:15 NIV).
>
> So he who was seated on the cloud swung his sickle over the earth, and the earth was harvested (Revelation 14:16 NIV).

Although some scholars demur, appreciating the difficulties that this verse presents for the Deity teachings, the majority view is that the "son of man" of verse 14 is Jesus. If so, and if the Deity teachings are correct, then the angel of verse 15 has the authority to issue orders to God, and to have those orders obeyed.

A more comprehensive treatment of the term "son of man" appears in Chapter 4: *Appeals to Descriptions and Titles*.

The slain lamb

The depiction of Jesus as a slain lamb is introduced in Revelation Chapter 5. Throughout this Chapter, the "one who sits on the throne", is entirely separate and distinct from the lamb. It is the throne figure who hands the sealed scroll to the lamb who has been found worthy to open it. The reason given for the lamb's worthiness again emphasises the distinction between God and Jesus:

> And they sang a new song, saying: "You are worthy to take the scroll and to open its seals, because you were slain, and with your blood you purchased for God persons from every tribe and language and people and nation" (Revelation 5:9 NIV).

In subsequent chapters, John draws more distinctions between God and Jesus. For example:

> After this I beheld, and, lo, a great multitude, which no man could number, of all nations, and kindreds, and people, and tongues, stood before the throne, and before the Lamb, clothed with white robes, and palms in their hands; And cried

with a loud voice, saying, Salvation to our God which sitteth upon the throne, and unto the Lamb (Rvelation 7:9-10 KJV).

Then I looked, and behold, on Mount Zion stood the Lamb, and with him 144,000 who had his name and his Father's name written on their foreheads. (Revelation 14:1 ESV).

…They held harps given them by God and sang the song of God's servant Moses and of the Lamb: "Great and marvelous are your deeds, Lord God Almighty (*Pantokratōr*). Just and true are your ways, King of the nations. Who will not fear you, Lord, and bring glory to your name? For you alone are holy. All nations will come and worship before you, for your righteous acts have been revealed (Revelation 15:2-4 NIV).

Note that this song of praise to Almighty God (*Pantokratōr*) is attributed to Moses and Jesus. Note also the statement that "you (God) alone are holy". (See also Hebrews 2:12 where Jesus praises God.)

Alpha and Omega

Now that we have established a framework, we can finally turn our attention to the three proof-texts used to support the assertion that Jesus should be equated with God because both are described as "the Alpha and Omega".

Revelation 1:8

In Revelation 1:8, the speaker is Almighty God (*Pantokratōr*):

> I am Alpha and Omega, the beginning and the ending, saith the Lord, which is, and which was, and which is to come, the Almighty (*Pantokratōr*) (Revelation 1:8 KJV).

Revelation 21:6

Verse 21:6, the oft-cited proof-text, has been completely divorced from its context. Reading Verses 5 through 7 will demonstrate that the speaker is Almighty God (*Pantokratōr*):

> And he that sat upon the throne (God) said, Behold, I make all things new. And he said unto me, Write: for these words are true and faithful. And he said unto me, It is done. I am Alpha and Omega, the beginning and the end. I will give unto him that is athirst of the fountain of the water of life freely. He that overcometh shall inherit all things; and I will be his God, and he shall be my son (Revelation 21:5-7 KJV).

Revelation 22:13

The last few verses of the Book present us with voices from a variety of speakers, as if all the players are brought back on stage to utter parting words. It therefore appears difficult to determine exactly who is speaking. However, an honest application of the author's consistent themes from beginning to end demand the conclusion that, just as in 1:8 and 21:6, the speaker in 22:13 is Almighty God (*Pantokratōr*):

> "I am the Alpha and the Omega, the First and the Last, the Beginning and the End" (Revelation 22:13 NIV).

It is beyond any reasonable doubt that on all three occasions under discussion, the term "Alpha and Omega" refers to Almighty God, the *Pantokratōr*. Note that the author of Revelation uses this supreme title of *Pantokratōr* seven times to refer to the God of Israel. Not once does he use it to refer to Jesus.

Conclusion

The author of Revelation's insistence on the absolute sovereignty of God, and his many statements confirming the vast gulf separating Jesus from that divine sovereign, cannot be defied or overcome by the theological establishment no matter how many proof-texts be drummed up to serve the doctrines which have been the hallmark of the establishment since time immemorial.

Section 2

Oneness

It is often asserted that Jesus was claiming equality with God when he made the following statement:

> "…I and the Father are one" (John 10:30 NIV).

Consider the context:

> At that time the Feast of Dedication took place at Jerusalem. It was winter, and Jesus was walking in the temple, in the colonnade of Solomon. So the Jews (Judeans) gathered around him and said to him, "How long will you keep us in suspense? If you are the Christ, tell us plainly." Jesus answered them, "I told you, and you do not believe. The works that I do in my Father's name bear witness about me, but you do not believe because you are not among my sheep. My sheep hear my voice, and I know them, and they follow me. I give them eternal

life, and they will never perish, and no one will snatch them out of my hand. My Father, who has given them to me, is greater than all, and no one is able to snatch them out of the Father's hand. I and the Father are one." The Jews (Judeans) picked up stones again to stone him. Jesus answered them, "I have shown you many good works from the Father; for which of them are you going to stone me?" The Jews (Judeans) answered him, "It is not for a good work that we are going to stone you but for blasphemy, because you, being a man, make yourself God" (John 10:22-33 ESV).

Apologists point to verse 33 and claim that the Judean opponents of Jesus must have understood that Jesus was claiming equality with God because they picked up stones to stone him. However, if one could characterise with a single word the interactions between Jesus and the Jerusalem religious establishment, that word would be "entrapment". They feigned indignation and conveniently misunderstood Jesus' responses to their loaded questions on many occasions, a ploy designed to lay the groundwork for a charge of blasphemy. The Gospel of John Chapter 10 is certainly a prime example of this style of entrapment.

For the sake of intellectual honesty, if for nothing else, doctrinal apologists should test their resolve by using the following comparative method of interpretation:

> Holy Father, keep them in thy name which thou hast given me, that they may be one even as we are…
>
> Neither for these only do I pray, but for them also that believeth on me through their word, that they may all be one…
>
> …even as thou, Father, art in me and I in thee that they also may be in us…
>
> And the glory which thou hast given me, I have given unto them, that they may be one as we are one…
>
> I in them and thou in me, that they may be perfected into one… (John 17:11, 20-23 KJV).

This concept of "Oneness" refers to an affinity of spirit between those that love truth, those that love God, and those who pray for the coming of God's reign on Earth. This affinity of spirit binds Jesus, his disciples, the believers and God into "one" body. We see exactly the same concept expressed by Paul:

> For we being many are one bread, and one body: for we are all partakers of that one bread (1 Corinthians 10:17 KJV).

Because of the human propensity to draw the wrong conclusions, Jesus was on many occasions particularly careful to draw a clear distinction between himself and God, e.g. "of myself, I can do nothing" (John 5:30).

Just as he castigated the religious leaders of his day for not understanding, or for deliberately misunderstanding his words, the present theological establishment perpetuates that same misunderstanding, e.g. thinking Jesus was claiming to be God, misunderstanding the designation "son of God", and etcetera.

Section 3

Forgiveness

Minister Plenipotentiary

An interpretive principle of the New Testament is that Jesus is depicted as God's minister plenipotentiary on Earth, a man anointed (invested) with full power and authority to speak and act in the name of the God of the Israelites (see Isaiah 61:1; Luke 4:17).

The concept of delegated authority exercised by a plenipotentiary appears to be quite incomprehensible to those who promulgate the doctrines of mainstream Christianity. One assertion is that if Jesus had no claim to equality with God, then he had no right to forgive sins. The most quoted passage is taken from Mark 2:5-12 when Jesus is in Capernaum. It must be quoted in full to grasp a sense of the exchange between Jesus and the scribes:

> When Jesus saw their faith, he said unto the sick of the palsy, Son, thy sins be forgiven thee. But there were certain of the scribes sitting there, and reasoning in their hearts, Why doth this man thus speak blasphemies? who can forgive sins but God only? And immediately when Jesus perceived in his spirit that they so reasoned within themselves, he said unto them, Why reason ye these things in your hearts? Whether is it easier to say to the sick of the palsy, Thy sins be forgiven thee; or to say, Arise, and take up thy bed, and walk? But that ye may know that the Son of man hath power on earth to forgive sins, (he saith to the sick of the palsy,) I say unto thee, Arise, and take up thy bed, and go thy way into thine house. And immediately he arose, took up the bed, and went forth before them all; insomuch that they were all amazed, and glorified God, saying, We never saw it on this fashion (Mark 2:5-12 KJV).

Before proceeding, it is important to recognise the following conventions and practices followed by Israelites in the 1st Century AD:

- The forgiveness of sin is a prerogative of God;
- In Hebrew language usage, passive voice statements such as "thy sins be forgiven thee" are pious conventions used to avoid accidentally invoking the name of God; [11]
- These passive voice statements about God's prerogatives always imply that God is the doer of the action;
- It is Jesus presuming to act on God's behalf that the scribes object to.

In Matthew's parallel account of the incident recorded in Mark, we find that the multitude "marvelled" that God had "given such power unto men". According to Matthew, Jesus is one of these "men", therefore a created being—the ultimate theological spoiler:

> And, behold, they brought to him a man sick of the palsy, lying on a bed: and Jesus seeing their faith said unto the sick of the palsy; Son, be of good cheer; thy sins be forgiven thee. And, behold, certain of the scribes said within themselves, This man blasphemeth. And Jesus knowing their thoughts said, Wherefore think ye evil in your hearts? For whether is easier, to say, Thy sins be forgiven thee; or to say, Arise, and walk? But that ye may know that the Son of man hath power on earth to forgive sins, (then saith he to the sick of the palsy,) Arise, take up thy bed, and go unto thine house. And he arose, and departed to his house. But when the multitudes saw it, they marvelled, and glorified God, which had given such power unto men (Matthew 9:2-8 KJV).

Just as Jesus, the minister plenipotentiary, had been delegated his authority to forgive sins by God, so also were the disciples delegated the same authority by Jesus:

> Jesus said to them again, "Peace be with you. As the Father has sent me, even so I am sending you." And when he had said this, he breathed on them and said to them, "Receive the Holy Spirit. If you forgive the sins of any, they are forgiven them; if you withhold forgiveness from any, it is withheld" (John 20:21-23 ESV).

In all cases, however, God is perceived to be the one from whom forgiveness flows.

---

[11] The term "Heaven," as in Matthew's "Kingdom of Heaven," is another pious substitute for "God."

Note

The Apostle Peter, it is asserted, was the first Pope of the Roman Catholic Church. Through a chain of transmission starting with God, passing through Jesus and then through Peter, the priests of that church claim the delegated authority to forgive sins. (See Part IX: *The Papacy*.)

Section 4

God and gods

The specific Hebrew word for the God of Israel is the Tetragrammaton YHWH. The generic Hebrew word for "god" is *elohim*. The designation *elohim* (god) can refer to the God of Israel but also to men who had been divinely appointed to serve a specific function for the God of Israel. These "gods" included Moses:

> And the Lord (YHWH) said unto Moses, See, I have made thee a god (*elohim*) to Pharaoh: and Aaron thy brother shall be thy prophet (Exodus 7:1 KJV).

These human "gods" were not to be confused with YHWH and had no claim at all to divinity. According to Israelites, there is only one divine being and that being is YHWH. Because the New Testament contains numerous quotes from, or allusions to, passages from the Hebrew Scriptures, it is vital to research original word meanings and the original contexts in which they came to be written. Failure to adopt this basic research procedure has produced the following results:

- the numerous false doctrines of orthodox Christianity;
- the loss of faith in these false doctrines and the concomitant and unstoppable decline in numbers of the "faithful";
- the betrayal of the man Jesus of Nazareth and all he represents.

The Gospel of John

While none of the writings of the New Testament imply or teach the Deity of Jesus of Nazareth, the Gospel of John in particular provides us with the most transparent and unambiguous evidence of the falsity of this teaching. Jesus himself assured his listeners that those to whom the word of God came were themselves "gods". In John Chapter 10 we find Jesus quoting a passage from the Hebrew Scriptures:

Jesus answered them, Is it not written in your law, I said, Ye are gods? If he called them gods, unto whom the word of God came, and the scripture cannot be broken; Say ye of him, whom the Father hath sanctified, and sent into the world, Thou blasphemest; because I said, I am the Son of God? (John 10:34-36 KJV).

The passage to which Jesus referred is taken from Psalm 82:

"I said, 'You are "gods" (*elohim*); you are all sons of the Most High' (Psalm 82:6 NIV).

Jesus reminds his accusers that those to whom the word of God came were themselves described as "gods" in the Hebrew Scriptures so he asks how they can charge him with blasphemy for calling himself the "son of God"? In this passage, Jesus categorically denies his Deity, accuses the religious authorities of not understanding their own Scriptures, and castigates them for misunderstanding or distorting his words in order to fabricate a charge of blasphemy.

Therefore, in addition to Moses, the prophets of old to whom the word of God came, such as Jeremiah, Ezekiel, and Elijah, were regarded by Jesus himself as "gods". For Christians, there can be no greater authority than Jesus so continuing to proclaim his Deity in the face of his own denials places one in the same category of condemnation as that of his opponents.

Section 5

Note

As it has no effect on their essential meanings, only the simple root forms of the Greek or Hebrew verbs will appear below.

Worship

Both the Hebrew Scriptures and the New Testament affirm that God, as a divine being, is to be worshipped and served. It is asserted by proponents of the Deity teaching that because Jesus allowed himself to be worshipped, he is therefore also a divine being. Before we can determine the truth or otherwise of this assertion, it is first necessary to discover the meaning of the Greek word προσκυνέω.

προσκυνέω is transliterated *proskuneó* and is formed from *prós* (towards) and *kyneo* (to kiss). The word *kyneo* reflects the Eastern custom of prostrating oneself before a person of superior rank and prestige and kissing the feet. This Greek word *proskuneó* is frequently translated into English as "worship".

The Septuagint, commonly referred to as the LXX, is the Greek version of the Hebrew Scriptures. The use of the Greek word *proskuneó* in the LXX shows that this word was frequently used to translate the Hebrew word שָׁחָה (*shachah*). שָׁחָה (*shachah*), meaning "to bow down", or "to pay homage to", or "to prostrate oneself", was an act of obeisance performed to kings and various other dignitaries as well as to the God of Israel. Numerous examples can be found in the Hebrew Scriptures:

> And Abraham stood up, and bowed himself (*shachah*) to the people of the land, even to the children of Heth (Genesis 23:7 KJV).
>
> When Abigail saw David, she hurried and got down from the donkey and fell before David on her face and bowed (*shachah*) to the ground (1 Samuel 25:23 ESV).

See also Exodus 23:24; Deuteronomy 8:19; 1 Samuel 24:8; and 2 Kings 2:15. Now that the meaning and semantic range of the Greek *proskuneó* and its derivation from the Hebrew *shachah* is clear, we can proceed.

Before the resurrection

Jesus is portrayed throughout the New Testament as a minister plenipotentiary, as one invested with supreme authority to speak and act in the name of God. Given the semantic range of *shachah*, it is extremely misleading and dishonest to claim that New Testament references to Jesus being "worshipped" *(proskuneó)* constitute proof that he was a divine being. The type of worship accepted by Jesus during his lifetime is nothing more than a reflection of the typical and pervasive Eastern custom of paying homage to a person one regards as having superior authority and status to oneself. The context in which Jesus accepts worship closely corresponds with the homage paid to kings and various other dignitaries. For example, in Matthew 2:2, it is in his role as King, not as a divine being, which makes Jesus worthy of worship:

> …Where is he that is born King of the Jews? for we have seen his star in the east, and are come to worship (*proskuneó*) him (Matthew 2:2 KJV).

After the resurrection

One favoured verse in the New Testament often advanced as proof of the Deity teaching is Hebrews 1:6. Its introductory verses provide necessary context.

Hebrews 1:3-6

Verses 1:3 and 1:4 tell us that because Jesus is the "express image" of God, and therefore superior to the angels, he is worthy to receive worship:

> Who being the brightness of his glory, and the express image of his person, and upholding all things by the word of his power, when he had by himself purged our sins, sat down on the right hand of the Majesty on high (Hebrews 1:3 KJV).

> Being made so much better than the angels, as he hath by inheritance obtained a more excellent name than they (Hebrews 1:4 KJV).

Verses 5 and 6 tell us that the angels were instructed to worship Jesus at a particular point in time:

> For unto which of the angels said he at any time, Thou art my Son, this day have I begotten thee? And again, I will be to him a Father, and he shall be to me a Son? (Hebrews 1:5 KJV).

> And again, when he bringeth in the firstbegotten into the world, he saith, And let all the angels of God worship (*proskuneó*) him (Hebrews 1:6 KJV).

Jesus became the "firstbegotten" son of God on the day of his Resurrection (Acts 13:33), at which time the angels were instructed to "worship him" as the exalted son of God, not as a divine being himself. The New Testament position is simple: as God's anointed, as the divinely-appointed representative of God on earth, Jesus is worthy of receiving all the honour, glory and worship appropriate to the exalted status bestowed on him at the Resurrection:

> They sang with a loud voice, "Worthy is the lamb who was slaughtered to receive power, wealth, wisdom, strength, honor, glory, and praise!" (Revelation 5:12 ISV).

Consider also the episode in Matthew commonly known as the "temptation in the wilderness". Firstly, God cannot be tempted (James 1:13). Secondly, the opponent treats Jesus as a human being with very human aspirations of kingship and glory. Jesus himself must have the last word—God alone should receive the type of worship due a divine sovereign:

> Again, the devil taketh him up into an exceeding high mountain, and sheweth him all the kingdoms of the world, and the glory of them; And saith unto him, All these things will I give thee, if thou wilt fall down and worship (*proskuneó*) me. Then saith Jesus unto him, Get thee hence, Satan: for it is written, Thou

shalt worship (*proskuneó*) the Lord thy God, and him only shalt thou serve (Matthew 4:8-10 KJV).

See also Luke 4:8 and Deuteronomy 6:13.

Section 6

Wonders and Signs

Jesus

Throughout the New Testament we find "wonders and signs" attributed to Jesus of Nazareth. Many claim that proof of his Deity lies in his performance of these wonders and signs, and in his raising of the dead:

> Men of Israel, hear these words: Jesus of Nazareth, a man attested to you by God with mighty works and wonders and signs that God did through him in your midst, as you yourselves know (Acts 2:22 ESV).

Note particularly that Jesus acts as the agent of God in the above verse, "God did *through* him". Consider also the following passages where others act as agents of God in the performance of wonders and signs:

> And fear came upon every soul: and many wonders and signs were done by the apostles (Acts 2:43 KJV).
>
> Now Stephen, a man full of God's grace and power, performed great wonders and signs among the people (Acts 6:8 NIV).

The performance of wonders and signs is not intrinsic to the humans involved but is an extrinsic power bestowed on those humans by God. Perhaps the most striking example of how this Godly power manifests itself is found in Mark 5:30 where a woman who had suffered from bleeding for twelve years is cured by touching Jesus' cloak:

> At once Jesus realized that power had gone out from him. He turned around in the crowd and asked, "Who touched my clothes?" (Mark 5:30 NIV).

The English word "power" in this verse is a translation of the Greek word *dunamis* meaning *might, power, marvellous works*. What is important to recognise here is that if Jesus was able to discern the power of God leaving him, he must also have been able to discern its arrival. It is therefore evident that this power from God was only with Jesus at certain times. We need only to reflect upon Jesus' cry from the cross, "My God, my God, why have you forsaken me?" to perceive that Jesus possessed no intrinsic power of his own.

An analysis of relevant passages in the Hebrew Scriptures and the New Testament will reveal that, in all cases, it is the power of God working in individual humans that enables the performing of wonders and signs and the raising of the dead.

Moses

> And there arose not a prophet since in Israel like unto Moses, whom the LORD knew face to face, In all the signs and the wonders, which the LORD sent him to do in the land of Egypt to Pharaoh, and to all his servants, and to all his land, And in all that mighty hand, and in all the great terror which Moses shewed in the sight of all Israel (Deuteronomy 34:10-12 KJV).

In his speech to the Sanhedrin, Stephen claimed that Jesus was the promised prophet like Moses. Among the parallels which Stephen drew to bolster his argument was the following:

> He brought them out, after that he had shewed wonders and signs in the land of Egypt, and in the Red sea, and in the wilderness forty years. This is that Moses, which said unto the children of Israel, A prophet shall the Lord your God raise up unto you of your brethren, like unto me; him shall ye hear (Acts 7:36-37 KJV cf. Deuteronomy 18:15).

The working of wonders and signs did not confer Deity upon men such as Moses, Stephen or the Apostles so there is no justification for claiming that the working of wonders and signs confers Deity on Jesus.

The raisers of the dead

The Hebrew Scriptures and the New Testament provide us with three accounts of persons "raising the dead".

Elijah

> And he stretched himself upon the child three times, and cried unto the LORD, and said, O LORD my God, I pray thee, let this child's soul come into him again. And the LORD heard the voice of Elijah; and the soul of the child came into him again, and he revived (1 Kings 17:21-22 NIV).

Elisha

> And when Elisha was come into the house, behold, the child was dead, and laid upon his bed. He went in therefore, and shut the door upon them twain, and prayed unto the LORD. And he went up, and lay upon the child, and put his mouth upon his mouth, and his eyes upon his eyes, and his hands upon his hands: and he stretched himself upon the child; and the flesh of the child waxed warm. Then he returned, and walked in the house to and fro; and went up, and stretched himself upon him: and the child sneezed seven times, and the child opened his eyes (2 Kings 4:32-35 KJV).

Jesus

In the story of the raising of Lazarus we find the following passage:

> Then said Martha unto Jesus, Lord, if thou hadst been here, my brother had not died. But I know, that even now, whatsoever thou wilt ask of God, God will give it thee… Then they took away the stone from the place where the dead was laid. And Jesus lifted up his eyes, and said, Father, I thank thee that thou hast heard me (John 11:21-22, 41 KJV).

All three of these "raisings" were performed by God working through the agency of the prophets and the Messiah. Just as no Deity attaches to Elijah or Elisha because of these "raisings", so also does no Deity attach to Jesus.

In conclusion, a popular misconception is that Jesus raised himself from the dead. It is important to realise that the apostles were preaching that God raised Jesus, not that Jesus raised himself. Despite any misinterpretation of the account as given in the Gospels, it is made abundantly clear that God raised Jesus in Acts 2:24, 32; 3:15, 26; 4:10; 5:30, Romans 4:24; 10:9; Colossians 2:12; and Hebrews 13:20.

CHAPTER FOUR

Appeals to Descriptions and Titles

Section 1

The Christ

The words "Jesus Christ" appear in the very first sentence of the English New Testament. The word "Christ" is an English transliteration of the Greek Χριστός (*Khristós*), which is the equivalent of the Hebrew מָשִׁיחַ (*Mashiach*) meaning "anointed one". The *Mashiach* refers to a person chosen by the God of Israel to be his vice-regent on behalf of the people of Israel. Over the course of ancient Israelite history, prophets, priests and kings had taken office by having oil poured over their heads, thus becoming "anointed ones". For example, the prophet Samuel anointed Saul as ruler:

> Then Samuel took the flask of oil, poured it on his head, kissed him and said, "Has not the LORD anointed (*Mashiach*) you a ruler over His inheritance? (1 Samuel 10:1 NASB).

Even non-Israelites could be anointed to perform a specific function:

> Thus saith the LORD to his anointed (*Mashiach*), to Cyrus, whose right hand I have holden, to subdue nations before him; and I will loose the loins of kings, to open before him the two leaved gates; and the gates shall not be shut (Isaiah 45:1 KJV).

However, Messiahs such as those mentioned in the passages above had served only for temporary or specific purposes whereas the New Testament affirms that Jesus of Nazareth was the long-awaited King-Messiah whose role was perceived as being much greater than those of his predecessors.

The term *Mashiach* appears 39 times in the Hebrew Scriptures. Except for a few occasions where it is rendered into English as "Messiah", it is mostly translated as "anointed one". In the New Testament, however, its Greek equivalent *Khristós* is rarely translated into English: it is merely transliterated. By not translating the word *Khristós* into "anointed one", translators have achieved several outcomes:

- concealed the fact that there were other Israelite Messiahs before the time of Jesus;
- masked the premise upon which every book of the New Testament is based;
- muted the questions that should have arisen about the person, nature and role of the Israelite Messiah;
- caused millions of Christians to wrongly assume that "Christ" is a name rather than a title.

As a name, the words "Jesus Christ" invite no question, but as a combination of name and title, the words "Jesus anointed", immediately pose a question for the reader—anointed by whom and for what purpose? Phrases such as "the total Christ" and "the cosmic Christ", frequently employed in a bewildering array of model Christologies, would disappear from the academy as they would invite the same undesirable question.

It is asserted that Paul used the word "Christ" as a name. If we translate it into English, however, we see that Paul was calling Jesus the "anointed one", which is merely a shorthand way of referring to the man he at other times described more fully as the "Lord Jesus anointed". This type of assertion deflects attention away from the fact that, just like all the other writers of the New Testament, Paul was stating his belief that Jesus was the Israelite Messiah, the anointed one of God.

Note

As far as non-canonical sources are concerned, it is asserted that in works such as 1 Enoch there were expectations of a divine, pre-existent Messiah but these assertions are merely the result of reading Jewish texts through the lens of Christian theology.[12]

---

12 VanderKam, James C. *From Revelation to Canon: Studies in the Hebrew Bible and Second Temple Literature*, Brill, 2002.

Section 2

The son of God

That the term "son of God" would in future come to imply the Deity of Jesus would have been profoundly shocking to Jesus himself and to all his contemporaries. Can we imagine that Judas knew he was betraying his God? Did the disciples believe that God was washing their feet at the last supper? Did they believe that their "eternal, immortal and invisible" God of Israel had actually died? "Ridiculous" doesn't even begin to describe the scenario postulated by Christian theology. Fundamental to the problem is a misunderstanding of the term "son of God" when applied to Jesus.

Sonship and Fatherhood

Theological ignorance of the concepts of Israelite Sonship and Fatherhood was a major factor in the development of mainstream doctrines. These concepts were applied to the anointed kings of ancient Israel and to the whole House of Israel long before the time of Jesus:

> His name will be Solomon…He is the one who will build a house for my Name. He will be my son, and I will be his father (1 Chronicles 22:9-10 NIV).
>
> I will be to him a father, and he shall be to me a son (2 Samuel 7:14 ESV).
>
> He shall cry unto me, Thou art my father, my God, and the rock of my salvation (Psalm 89:26 KJV).
>
> When Israel was a child, then I loved him, and called my son out of Egypt (Hosea 11:1 KJV cf. Exodus 4:22).

These concepts were also expressed in the New Testament on many occasions, most notably by Jesus himself:

> Blessed are the peacemakers, for they shall be called sons of God (Matthew 5:9 ESV).
>
> But love your enemies, do good to them, and lend to them without expecting to get anything back. Then your reward will be great, and you will be children of the Most High, because he is kind to the ungrateful and wicked (Luke 6:35 ISV).

Adam is called the "son of God" because he was created in God's image (Luke 3:38; Acts 17:26-29). All who are led by the Spirit of God are "sons of God" (Romans 8:14) and Jesus is the "firstborn of many brothers" (Romans 8:29). The author of

Hebrews speaks explicitly of the many "sons of God" who are to come (Hebrews 2:10) and, for the author of John's Gospel, those who are united with Jesus become "children of God" (John 1:12-13).

We read in Luke 2:46-50 about Mary and Joseph's visit to Jerusalem for Passover and their subsequent search for the missing Jesus:

> Three days later, they found him in the Temple sitting among the teachers, listening to them, and posing questions to them. All who heard him were amazed at his intelligence and his answers. When Jesus' parents saw him, they were shocked. His mother asked him, "Son, why have you treated us like this? Your father and I have been worried sick looking for you!" He asked them, "Why were you looking for me? Didn't you know that I had to be in my Father's house?" But they did not understand what he told them (Luke 2:46-50 ISV).

Thus, Mary, who had supposedly conceived a child fathered by the Holy Spirit of God while still a virgin, did not know what Jesus was talking about when he called God his Father. Her amazement would be that a child born in such lowly circumstances would use language reserved for the nation as a whole, or for Kings.

It is recorded in the Gospel of John 1:40-50 that when first joined by his disciples, Jesus was described by them as:

- the Christ (the anointed one);
- he of whom Moses in the law and the prophets wrote;
- Jesus of Nazareth, the son of Joseph;
- the son of God;
- the King of Israel.

As is abundantly clear from the above, the disciples believed that Jesus was the son of God while still acknowledging his human parentage, which demonstrate that to regard God as a Father, and to thereby be called a "son of God" carries with it no implication whatsoever of Deity.

Note

When the term "son of God" is used in reference to Jesus, it is synonymous with the term "Messiah", as we can see in Mark 14:61, John 11:27 and John 20:31 where the two terms are merged into the one person of Jesus.

Section 3

The only-begotten son of God

One of the pillars on which the Deity of Jesus of Nazareth rests is the assiduous cultivation of the idea that Jesus was the "only-begotten son of God born of the Father before all ages".

Niceno-Constantinopolitan Creed : 381AD

The Nicene Creed was first adopted in 325 AD at the Council of Nicea in an attempt to unify the Christian church with one statement of belief. The original creed was later revised and accepted by both eastern and western branches of Christendom at the First Council of Constantinople. The section of the revised creed with which we are presently concerned reads:

> I believe in one Lord Jesus Christ,
> *the Only Begotten Son of God,*
> *born of the Father before all ages.*
> God from God, Light from Light,
> true God from true God,
> *begotten, not made*, consubstantial with the Father;
> through him all things were made.

There are slightly different English renderings of the Creed in use today. The most popular versions use the words "eternally-begotten of the Father" instead of "born of the Father before all ages". However, the substance remains the same. Theologians and ecclesiastics routinely use the phrase "eternally-begotten son" to describe Jesus of Nazareth. Let us now turn to the New Testament passage upon which they base their doctrinal claim:

John 1:18

> …No man hath seen God at any time; the only begotten son, which is in the bosom of the Father, he hath declared him (John 1:18 KJV).

If we turn to the teachings of Paul we will find an explanation of the term used in John. The central tenet of Paul's teaching is that Jesus of Nazareth is the Israelite Messiah (Christ), the man appointed by God to be his delegate on earth. It is no surprise therefore that he draws constantly upon the Hebrew Scriptures to support his arguments and he does so by using passages he regards as messianic expectations.

Hebrew Scriptures

> I will declare the decree: the LORD hath said unto me, Thou art my Son; this day have I begotten thee (Psalm 2:7 KJV).

Paul

> And we declare unto you glad tidings, how that the promise which was made unto the fathers, God hath fulfilled the same unto us their children, in that he hath raised up Jesus again; as it is also written in the second psalm, Thou art my Son, this day have I begotten thee (Acts 13:33 KJV).

This single statement by Paul, that Jesus became the only-begotten son of the Father on the day of his Resurrection, should be more than enough to consign the creedal formulations of "eternally-begotten of the Father" and "begotten not made" to the ash heap of theology because there was a time before Jesus was "begotten". Eternity has no beginning whereas sonship implies time, a time before the generation of the son.

(Paul is similarly instructive about other related terms he uses to describe Jesus such as the "first-born", and the "first-fruits". These terms are discussed in different contexts elsewhere in this work.)

Translators of such English versions as the NIV, the ESV and the NASB have chosen to follow a different textual family than that of the KJV and have rendered John 1:18 as follows:

> No one has ever seen God, but the one and only Son, who is himself God and is in closest relationship with the Father, has made him known (John 1:18 NIV).

This translation represents theologians who believe that the original text read "ho monogenes theos" (the unique, or only begotten God), while the KJV is representative of theologians who believe that the original text was "ho monogenes huios" (the only begotten Son). Although it is true that the earliest Greek manuscripts contain the reading "theos" (God), every one of those texts is of the Alexandrian text type whereas the other textual traditions, including the Western, Byzantine, Caesarean and secondary Alexandrian texts, read "huios" (Son). The famous textual scholars, Westcott and Hort, known for their defense of the Alexandrian text type, consider John 1:18 to be one of the few places in the New Testament where it is not correct.

It should also be taken into consideration that leading Church Fathers such as Irenaeus, Clement and Tertullian quoted the verse with "Son," and not "God". Since Tertullian argued aggressively for the Incarnation and is credited with being the one who developed the concept of "one God in three persons", this is especially significant. (For a much more detailed account of why the word "Son" should be favoured over the word "God," see *The Orthodox Corruption of Scripture*, by Bart Ehrman. Oxford University Press: New York, 1993, pp. 78-82.)

However, the best argument for the KJV text type renderings is based on simple common sense. Consider the ludicrous consequences of adopting the reading according to the NIV quoted above:

- Jesus has the closest relationship with the Father, but Jesus is God so therefore he has the closest relationship with himself;

- No one has ever seen God, but Jesus is God so therefore can only be seen by himself; *or this author's personal favourite -*

- No one has ever seen God, but Jesus is God and was seen by humans so therefore he can be both "seen" and "unseen" at the same time.

Section 4

That Holy Thing

In the Gospel of Luke, we find the words "the holy thing (one)" used to describe Jesus. Among the portfolio of arguments used to justify the Deity teaching, this description of Jesus has been drummed into service by legions of theologians and ecclesiastics past and present.

Regardless of the identity of Theophilus, to whom Luke's Gospel is addressed—and there are many scholarly suggestions—his identity does not detract from the fact that the work we have come to know as the Gospel of Luke is actually a private letter. As such, we may expect it to contain information not publicly available. And so it proves to be. There is such an intimate knowledge of Mary, her family, and the time of Jesus' conception, that Luke's source can only have been derived, by whatever means of transmission, from someone directly connected to Mary herself.

Luke introduces his Gospel by assuring Theophilus that he has done his research—that he has a investigated everything carefully from the beginning. One of the most important of his discoveries is that he has verified the circumstances surrounding the birth of Jesus. This is, for him, a cause of great celebration. He can demonstrate that Jesus has a claim by right of birth to sit on the earthly throne of David. (For a detailed analysis of Luke's birth narrative see Part IV.4,5,6: *Virgin Birth and Incarnation-The Gospel of Luke I,II,III.*)

At this point, however, we will focus only on the words contained in Luke 1:35b:

>...So the holy one to be born...(Luke 1:35b NIV).

There is nothing singular or exclusive about the word "holy" in reference to Jesus. In memory of the deaths of the first-born of the Egyptians, every first-born Israelite male was sanctified to God and had to be redeemed by the child's parents. Such male children were designated "holy". A comparison of texts from the Hebrew Scriptures and the New Testament will place the matter in its correct perspective:

Hebrew Scriptures

> And the LORD spake unto Moses, saying, Sanctify unto me all the firstborn, whatsoever openeth the womb among the children of Israel, both of man and of beast: it is mine (Exodus 13:1-2 KJV).

> When Pharaoh stubbornly refused to let us go, the Lord killed the firstborn of both people and animals in Egypt. This is why I sacrifice to the Lord the first male offspring of every womb and redeem each of my firstborn sons (Exodus 13:15 NIV).

New Testament

> And she brought forth her firstborn son, and wrapped him in swaddling clothes, and laid him in a manger... (Luke 2:7 KJV).

> And when the days of her purification according to the law of Moses were accomplished, they brought him to Jerusalem, to present him to the Lord; (As it is written in the law of the Lord, Every male that openeth the womb shall be called holy to the Lord;) And to offer a sacrifice according to that which is said in the law of the Lord, A pair of turtledoves, or two young pigeons (Luke 2:22-24 KJV).

Just as all other parents of a "holy" child, Joseph and Mary had to redeem the first-born male child Jesus, the price in this case being a "pair of turtledoves or two young pigeons".

Section 5

The Son of Man

The Hebrew term בֶּן־אָדָם (*ben-adam*) translates into English as "son of man".

Hebrew Idiom

The idiomatic differences between Hebrew and English are vital to facilitate understanding of the term "son of man" when we find it in the Hebrew Scriptures and in the New Testament.

To identify an individual man, the Israelites used the phrase "son of man". A "son of man" was simply an individual belonging to the class of humans. Similarly, for example, an individual belonging to the class of prophets was often referred to as "son of a prophet". On some occasions, the term was used as "a cumbersome but solemn and formal substitute for the personal pronoun". [13]

Scripture usage

"Son of man" is a common term found in the Psalms. When used in passages such as those in Psalms 8:4 and 144:3, it implies mortality, impotence, and transientness, as opposed to the omnipotence and eternality of God. In the Book of Ezekiel, God addresses the prophet about ninety times as "son of man". As in the Psalms, the vast difference between God and man is accentuated.

The term "son of man" is the favorite self-designation of Jesus in the Gospels. It occurs over thirty times in Matthew, twenty-five times in Luke, fifteen times in Mark, and twelve times in John. Other than the Gospels, it occurs once in Acts (7:56), and twice in the Book of Revelation (1:13; 14:14). Jesus used the term in the following senses:

As a basic idiom indicating a specific type of human:

> And if the son of peace be there, your peace shall rest upon it: if not, it shall turn to you again (Luke 10:6 KJV).

As a basic idiom indicating the general species of human:

> Truly I say to you, all sins shall be forgiven the sons of men, and whatever blasphemies they utter (Mark 3:28 NASB).

---

13 Hirsch, Emil G. *Son of Man*. Jewish Encyclopaedia 1906. Accessed 3 March 2019. http://jewishencyclopedia.com/articles/13913-son-of-man

And as a formal substitute for the personal pronoun:

> And Jesus said to him, "Foxes have holes, and birds of the air have nests, but *the* Son of Man has nowhere to lay his head" (Matthew 8:20 ESV).

As demonstrated, the idiom is used in various ways but the subject is always human. However, when Jesus uses it in a self-referential way, it is transformed by Christian theology into a quasi-mystical, divine title. Let us now examine a selection of texts which will put the matter in its correct perspective and shed light on the purpose behind the imagery.

The High Priest

The author of the Book of Hebrews asserts that Jesus is the new High Priest of Israel:

> And being made perfect, he became the author of eternal salvation unto all them that obey him; Called of God an high priest after the order of Melchisedec (Hebrews 5:9-10 KJV).

Coming with the Clouds of Heaven

Consider the following verse from Daniel Chapter 7:

> In my vision at night I looked, and there before me was one like a son of man, coming with the clouds of heaven. He approached the Ancient of Days and was led into his presence (Daniel 7:13 NIV).

Jesus draws directly on this verse from Daniel when he makes the following statement:

> "…they will see the Son of Man coming on the clouds of heaven with power and great glory" (Matthew 24:30 ESV cf. Matthew 26:63-64).

The son of man coming to God with the clouds of Heaven evokes the Day of Atonement when the High Priest entered the Jerusalem Temple's Holy of Holies, into God's presence, surrounded by clouds of incense. He symbolically ascended from Earth to God's abode in Heaven, and as near-contemporary texts show, on his return to the people from the inner sanctuary, the High Priest is a plenipotentiary of God's own power and glory, symbolically descending from Heaven down to Earth. (Note that God was believed to rule through an opening in the sky directly above the Jerusalem Temple, the *axis mundi*, the place of connection between God in Heaven and his covenant people on Earth.)

Plenipotentiary of God's own Power and Glory

> For whoever is ashamed of me and of my words in this adulterous and sinful generation, of him will the Son of Man also be ashamed when he comes in the glory of his Father with the holy angels (Mark 8:38 ESV cf. Mark 3:26; Matthew 16:27).

The son of man comes clothed in the "glory of his Father", just as the High Priest, when clothed in his sacred garments, embodied the glory of God (Exodus 28:2, 40). This perception of Jesus is of course a reflection of the Jewish understanding of agency, viz. the agent was regarded as the person himself. According to *The Encyclopedia of the Jewish Religion*:

> Agent (Heb. *Shaliah*): The main point of the Jewish law of agency is expressed in the dictum, "a person's agent is regarded as the person himself" (Ned. 72b; Kidd. 41b). Therefore any act committed by a duly appointed agent is regarded as having been committed by the principal, who therefore bears full responsibility for it with consequent complete absence of liability on the part of the agent.[14]

In his ceremonial role, the High Priest was God's representative—his "image". (See for example Josephus, *Antiquities* XIII.294.) This Jewish understanding of agency casts further light on other New Testament passages such as:

> In whom the god of this world hath blinded the minds of them which believe not, lest the light of the glorious gospel of Christ, who is the image of God, should shine unto them (2 Corinthians 4:4 KJV).

Although the High-Priestly analogy is made most explicit in the Book of Hebrews, it can be seen clearly in the above passage that other New Testament authors such as Paul also portrayed Jesus using language and descriptive terminology most suited to the contemporary perception of the High Priest as the image of God who reflects the glory of God.

In addition to all of the above, the author of Revelation depicts the son of man dressed in the distinctive foot-length robe and golden girdle that the High Priest wore on the Day of Atonement:

---

14 Werblowsky, R. J. Zwi. *The Encyclopedia of the Jewish Religion*. ed. Geoffrey Wigoder. Adama Books: New York, 1986, p.15.

> ...and among the lampstands was someone like a son of man, dressed in a robe reaching down to his feet and with a golden sash around his chest (Revelation 1:13 NIV).

When Jesus was taken before the Sanhedrin, the High Priest asked him the following question:

> ...Again the high priest asked him, "Are you the Messiah, the Son of the Blessed One?" "I am," said Jesus. "And you will see the Son of Man sitting at the right hand of the Mighty One and coming on the clouds of heaven" (Mark 14:61-62 NIV).

From the perspective of the Sanhedrin, this response by Jesus represented a blasphemous challenge to the current, God-ordained High Priest.

Finally, consider the following passage from the Book of Revelation which provides much needed perspective:

> And I looked, and behold a white cloud, and upon the cloud one sat like unto the Son of man, having on his head a golden crown, and in his hand a sharp sickle (Revelation 14:14 KJV).
>
> And another angel came out of the temple, crying with a loud voice to him that sat on the cloud, Thrust in thy sickle, and reap: for the time is come for thee to reap; for the harvest of the earth is ripe (Revelation 14:15 KJV).
>
> And he that sat on the cloud thrust in his sickle on the earth; and the earth was reaped (Revelation 14:16 KJV).

Although some scholars demur, appreciating the difficulties that this passage presents, the majority view is that the "Son of man" of verse 14 is Jesus. If so, and if the Deity teachings are correct, then the angel of verse 15 has the authority to issue orders to God...and to have those orders obeyed.

Note

Unlike most of the Hebrew Scriptures, the Book of Daniel was written partly in Hebrew and partly in the closely-related Aramaic language. Daniel 7:13 is in Aramaic so instead of the Hebrew בֶּן־אָדָם *(ben-adam)*, we find its Aramaic equivalent בַּר־אֱנָשׁ *(bar-enash)*.

My Lord and my God

> And Thomas answered and said unto him, My Lord and my God (John 20:28 KJV).

John 20:28 has been chosen as the focal point of this section because, firstly, it is much-quoted by those intent on promulgating the Deity of Jesus and, secondly, it combines the two titles most used to justify this teaching and is, therefore, most in need of clarification. Before proceeding with an analysis of this verse, however, we must first determine derivations and meanings.

The Greek Septuagint

The Hebrew Scriptures were translated into Greek at some point between the 3rd and 1st Centuries BC. This Greek version is commonly referred to as the Septuagint (LXX), standing for the seventy scholars supposedly engaged upon the translation.

The divine name of God is known as the four-letter Tetragrammaton. Although the Tetragrammaton, YHWH, was not easily translatable into Greek, there is ample evidence from Qumran and elsewhere that in the earliest pre-Christian Septuagint manuscripts, attempts had been made to preserve the Tetragrammaton by writing it in either Hebrew, or Paleo Hebrew, or Greek characters.

The New Testament contains innumerable quotes from, and allusions to, the Hebrew Scriptures. There can be little doubt that the earliest copies of the Greek New Testament continued the Septuagint practice of preserving the divine name, thus preserving the same unambiguous distinction between God and man as found in the Hebrew Scriptures. However, preservation attempts were to prove fruitless because, aside from fragments, the only complete copies of the New Testament still in existence are those produced centuries after the originals were written, during which time scribal awareness of the sacred nature of the divine name had gradually diminished, or was not understood, and it was eventually replaced with either *Kurios* (Lord) or *Theos* (God).

The only certain path to understanding the meaning of crucial passages in the New Testament is to consult the Hebrew documents on which both the Septuagint and the New Testament are based and seek the original meanings of words and phrases, and the contexts in which those words and phrases came to be written.

Kurios

The Greek word Κύριος *(Kurios)* is most often translated into English as "lord", as is its Hebrew equivalent אֲדֹנָי *(Adonai)*. In all three languages the word denotes a person exercising superior or absolute authority and can be variously translated as "lord", "master" or "owner". The word *can* refer to the Israelite God YHWH, but also to other gods, angelic beings, and even humans.

Because of our reliance on the only copies of the Greek New Testament still available to us, the distinction between YHWH and *Kurios*, between the divine name of Almighty God and a word which could refer to any authority, earthly or otherwise, has been lost. A demonstration of this point is provided in the Gospel of Matthew:

> The Lord (*Kurios*) said to my Lord (*Kurios*): "Sit at my right hand until I put your enemies under your feet" (Matthew 22:44 ESV).

In Greek, there is no distinction between the two "Lords" of this passage: they are both *Kurios* and seemingly both of equal stature. Yet if we check Psalm 110:1 from which this quote was taken, we find the clarifying distinction:

> The LORD (YHWH) says to my Lord (*Adonai*): "Sit at my right hand, until I make your enemies your footstool." (Psalm 110:1 ESV).

Both the above quotations are from the ESV version. Note that in the quote from the Psalms, an attempt has been made to distinguish YHWH from *Adonai*, the Hebrew equivalent of *Kurios*, by capitalising "LORD". In the quote from Matthew, however, no attempt has been made to distinguish one *Kurios* from the other.

Theos

The Greek word θεός *(Theos)* is the common word for God in the Greek New Testament. The word normally refers to YWVH the God of Israel but is sometimes used to refer to false gods (1 Corinthians 8:5) and even humans (John 10:34-36), as is its Hebrew counterpart אֱלֹהִים *(Elohim)*.

Consider Hebrews 1:8, a verse which is often used to justify the Deity and Trinity teachings as it appears to say that God calls Jesus "God":

> But unto the Son he saith, Thy throne, O God (*Theos*), is for ever and ever: a sceptre of righteousness is the sceptre of thy kingdom (Hebrews 1:8 KJV).

However, when we refer to Psalm 45:6 from which this quote is taken, we find that it is not the Tetragrammaton YHWH that has been translated into Greek as *Theos* but the Hebrew word *Elohim:*

> Your throne, O God (*Elohim*), is forever and ever. The scepter of your kingdom is a scepter of uprightness (Psalm 45:6 ESV).

As demonstrated elsewhere in this work, *Elohim* is a word that *can* be used to refer to the Israelite God, YHWH, but is also used to refer to other gods, angelic beings and even humans such as Moses:

> And the LORD (YHWH) said unto Moses, See, I have made thee a god (*Elohim*) to Pharaoh: and Aaron thy brother shall be thy prophet (Exodus 7:1 KJV).

The following quote from the Hebrew Scriptures is most instructive because the Tetragrammaton, the Hebrew word for God, and the Hebrew word for Lord are all present in a single verse. Note that Abraham is twice referred to as an *Adonai*, the Hebrew equivalent of the Greek *Kurios* (Lord):

> And he said, "O LORD (YHWH), God (*Elohim*) of my master (*Adonai*) Abraham, please grant me success today and show steadfast love to my master (*Adonai*) Abraham" (Genesis 24:12 ESV).

Context

With an enhanced understanding of terminology, we may now return to an examination of John 20:28 which is much-quoted by apologists as if they had never heard of the word "context", such is their disregard for it. We will now supply the deficit.

When speaking to Mary in verse 20:17, Jesus had drawn a definite distinction between himself and God, "I ascend unto my Father, and your Father; and to my God, and your God". The subsequent exchanges between Jesus, Thomas and the other disciples centred on Thomas' refusal to believe that God had raised Jesus from the dead. After touching the wounds of Jesus, Thomas not only acknowledges Jesus' resurrection but also his now exalted status by addressing him as "My Lord":

> And Thomas answered and said unto him, My Lord (*Kurios*) and my God (*Theos*) (John 20:28 KJV).

In this verse, Thomas addresses two separate entities: Jesus as his Lord (*Kurios*) and the God (*Theos*) who raised his Lord Jesus from the dead.

In verse 31, the author announces his purpose for writing the gospel:

> But these are written, that ye might believe that Jesus is the Christ, the Son of God; and that believing ye might have life through his name (John 20:31 KJV).

The context of John Chapter 20 rules out any claim that Thomas is addressing Jesus as both his Lord and his God. In verse 17, Jesus calls God "my Father" and in verse 31 John affirms that Jesus is indeed God's son. Regardless of esoteric theological justification, Jesus cannot be God and the son of God at one and the same time yet this is the type of Orwellian double-think imposed upon us by Christian doctrines.

Section 7

The Rock

Amongst the portfolio of arguments used to advance both the Pre-existence and Deity teachings is the New Testament application of the "rock-stone" image to Jesus. The argument is based largely on the fact that because God and Jesus are described using similar imagery, they must therefore be the same divine being. As with other simplistic arguments which appeal to the similarity of descriptions and titles, this also can be readily demolished as the "rock-stone" image recurs throughout the Hebrew Scriptures and was used to refer to the Israelite God, to the gods of other peoples, to humans, and also to the Kingdom.

Rock-stone imagery in the Hebrew Scriptures

The "rock-stone" image of course is one of strength and, in the case of YHWH, also the associated ideas of reliability, faith and trust in God.

Of YHWH the God of Israel

> He is the Rock, his work is perfect: for all his ways are judgment: a God of truth and without iniquity, just and right is he (Deuteronomy 32:4 KJV).
>
> The LORD is my rock, my fortress and my deliverer; my God is my rock, in whom I take refuge, my shield and the horn of my salvation, my stronghold (Psalm 18:2 NIV).

Of the gods of other peoples

> And he shall say, Where are their gods, their rock in whom they trusted (Deuteronomy 32:37 KJV).

Of humans

> Listen to me, you who pursue righteousness and who seek the Lord: Look to the rock from which you were cut and to the quarry from which you were hewn;

look to Abraham, your father, and to Sarah, who gave you birth (Isaiah 51:1-2 NIV).

Therefore thus says the Lord GOD, "Behold, I am the one who has laid as a foundation in Zion, a stone, a tested stone, a precious cornerstone, of a sure foundation…" (Isaiah 28:16 ESV).

The stone which the builders rejected Has become the chief corner stone. This is the LORD'S doing; It is marvelous in our eyes (Psalm 118:22-23 NASB).

Of the Kingdom

In the Book of Daniel, Chapter 2, we read that the prophet is brought before King Nebuchadnezzar, not only to recount a dream troubling the king, but also to provide an interpretation. Daniel tells Nebuchadnezzar that, in the dream, the king saw a great statue with a head of gold, chest and arms of silver, belly and thighs of bronze, legs of iron, and feet a combination of iron and clay. This symbol of earthly empires is then struck on its feet of iron and clay by a stone cut out of a mountain without human hands. The stone utterly destroys the statue and in turn becomes a great mountain that fills the whole earth (Daniel 2:1-23).

Daniel's Interpretation

After the fall of the Babylonian empire, other empires of gradually diminishing worth will arise until the last, the empire of iron and clay, will be destroyed by the stone cut out of the mountain without human hands. The stone, the *eben* (אֶבֶן), is the kingdom which the God of Heaven is about to set up, and which shall never be destroyed (Daniel 2:24-48.)

Rock-stone imagery in Israelite thought

> As recorded in the Mishnah, while building the second temple, the masons cleared the floor of the original Holy of Holies (Solomon's Temple). In the center of that floor they found a single stone three fingerbreadths higher than the rest of the flagstones. They left it and the community named it eben shetiyah, "the foundation stone" (Mishnah. Moed, Yoma, 5:2. Danby Translation, p.167)[15] …it is highly probably that this especially honoured stone was called eben shetiyah because the building of the Second Temple was seen as a fulfilment of the prophecy of Isaiah 28. They were building in Zion. Here was a precious stone, a sure foundation on which the entire temple complex, with its

---

15 Published at the end of the second century AD, the Mishnah is an edited record of the complex body of material known as Oral Torah that was transmitted in the aftermath of the destruction of the Jerusalem Temple in 70 AD.

rich and meaningful liturgies, was based…The importance of the "foundation stone" was not lost by Jesus and the NT writers…[16]

Rock-stone imagery in the New Testament

In the First Epistle of Peter, a work entirely dependent on the Hebrew Scriptures, the author draws on several "rock-stone" passages to give weight and authority to his presentation of Jesus as the ultimate expression of Israelite thought, as the chief corner-stone of a new spiritual Temple built without human hands, the same *eben* (אֶבֶן) of Daniel, that destroyed the kingdoms of the earth and is now the foundation of the kingdom which the God of Heaven is about to set up.

In 1 Peter 2:4-8, the author includes three quotes from the Hebrew Scriptures which he affirms are messianic expectations fulfilled in Jesus:

> As you come to him, a living stone rejected by men but in the sight of God chosen and precious, you yourselves like living stones are being built up as a spiritual house, to be a holy priesthood, to offer spiritual sacrifices acceptable to God through Jesus Christ. For it stands in Scripture: "Behold, I am laying in Zion a stone, a cornerstone chosen and precious, and whoever believes in him will not be put to shame" (Isaiah 28:16). So the honor is for you who believe, but for those who do not believe, "The stone that the builders rejected, has become the cornerstone"(Psalm 118:22) and "A stone of stumbling, and a rock of offense" (Isaiah 8:14). (1 Peter 2:4-8 ESV).

The author regards himself and his readers as living rocks-stones, a holy priesthood, building up this new spiritual Temple upon the foundation laid by Jesus Messiah. Compare this passage with the following from Romans 9:33 and Ephesians 2:20 where Paul makes use of a combination of the same Hebrew texts to portray Jesus as both a "stone of stumbling" laid in Zion and as the "cornerstone".

> As it is written, "Behold, I am laying in Zion a stone of stumbling, and a rock of offense and whoever believes in him will not be put to shame" (Romans 9:33 ESV).

> Now therefore ye are no more strangers and foreigners, but fellow citizens with the saints, and of the household of God; And are built upon the foundation

---

16 Bailey, K.E. Inverted Parallelisms and Encased Parables in Isaiah and their significance for Old and New Testament Translation and Interpretation in *Literary Structure and Rhetorical Strategies in the Hebrew Bible*. (eds.) L. J. de Regt, Jan de Waard, J. P. Fokkelman. K. Van Gorcum & Co: Netherlands, 1996, p.18.

of the apostles and prophets, Jesus Christ himself being the chief corner stone (Ephesians 2:19-20 ESV).

Jesus makes a veiled self-reference to the cornerstone in three parallel passages (Mark 12:10, Matthew 21:42, Luke 20:17), and Peter again states that Jesus is the cornerstone in Acts 4:11.

The authors of the New Testament viewed Jesus as the living embodiment of the "rock-stone" imagery found in the Hebrew Scriptures and also that this "rock-stone" was messianic in nature, as Paul states:

> For I do not want you to be ignorant of the fact, brothers and sisters, that our ancestors were all under the cloud and that they all passed through the sea. They were all baptized into Moses in the cloud and in the sea. They all ate the same spiritual food and drank the same spiritual drink; for they drank from the spiritual rock that accompanied them, and that rock was Christ (1 Corinthians 10:1-4 NIV).

In the Hebrew Scriptures, two occasions are mentioned in which Moses struck a rock and the Israelites miraculously received water (Exodus 17:1–7; Numbers 20:1–14). Since the rocks were apparently in different places, an Israelite folk tradition arose about a "physical" rock that accompanied them on their journey through the wilderness. In the above passage, Paul refutes this folk tradition and explains that it was not a "physical" but a "spiritual" rock that accompanied them in expectation of the Messiah. The smiting of the rock from which "physical" waters flowed prefigured the smiting of the Messiah from whom "spiritual" waters now flow.

Note

The claim by the Papacy that Jesus regarded Simon son of Jonah as this "rock" is insupportable. An exhaustive analysis of this claim appears in Part IX: *The Papacy*.

Section 8

Note

Hebrew and Greek words take many different forms all deriving from the same basic root. To avoid unnecessary complexity, only the basic root forms and their meanings will be reproduced here.

Agency

Equating God with Jesus simply because similar descriptions and titles are ascribed to them both overlooks or ignores the biblical principle of agency. When the scripture authors state that God *did* something, it is always understood that the *doing* was actually *done* by humans chosen by God to implement his purposes on Earth. It was simply a way of giving praise to God who is credited with putting into the hearts and minds of humans the will and the spirit to do his work.

Throughout the New Testament, Jesus is presented as God's minister plenipotentiary, an agent invested with an authority superior to all the others who had preceded him. This perception of Jesus is of course a reflection of the Jewish understanding of agency viz. the agent was regarded as the person himself. According to The Encyclopedia of the Jewish Religion:

> Agent (Heb. *Shaliah*): The main point of the Jewish law of agency is expressed in the dictum, "a person's agent is regarded as the person himself" (Ned. 72b; Kidd. 41b). Therefore any act committed by a duly appointed agent is regarded as having been committed by the principal, who therefore bears full responsibility for it with consequent complete absence of liability on the part of the agent.[17]

Depending on the function perceived to have been performed on behalf of Israelites, the God of Israel was described at various times by titles such as Judge, Saviour and Shepherd of his people. Because the New Testament authors attributed these same titles to Jesus, many have no doubt been misled into believing that Jesus could be Almighty God. This belief founders on the rocks of agency and terminology.

Judge

Broadly speaking, eschatology is the study of last things, variously the end of individual life, the end of the world, the end of the age, and so on. It is asserted

---

17 Werblowsky, R. J. Zwi. *The Encyclopedia of the Jewish Religion*. ed. Geoffrey Wigoder. Adama Books: New York, 1986, p.15.

that Deity must be ascribed to Jesus because of his role as eschatological judge. This assertion overlooks the fact that Jesus' authority to execute judgement has been delegated to him by God. For example:

> ...because he (God) has fixed a day on which he will judge the world in righteousness by a man whom he has appointed; and of this he has given assurance to all by raising him from the dead (Acts 17:13 ESV).

Also overlooked is the fact that other eschatological judges besides Jesus have been delegated similar authority and all of them are most definitely mortal. For example:

> ...do you not know that the Lord's people will judge the world?...Do you not know that we will judge angels?...(1 Corinthians 6:2-3 NIV).

Saviour

The Hebrew Scriptures teach that Almighty God is the Saviour of Israel:

> For I am the LORD thy God, the Holy One of Israel, thy Saviour (Isaiah 43:3 KJV).

Apologists claim that because the New Testament also describes Jesus as a "Saviour", this means that he is to be equated with God. Yet another Deity assertion: yet another overlooked fact that, according to the Hebrew Scriptures, God delegates authority to perform all his works on Earth to humans of his choice.

The English word "saviour" derives from the Greek σῴζω *(sózó)* and the Hebrew root יָשַׁע *(yasha)*, both of which mean to "save" or "deliver". The Hebrew name *Yeshua* is a shortened form of *Yehoshua*, the name of *Joshua* the successor of Moses. It is derived from YH, a shortened form of YHWH and the Hebrew verb root *yasha*. Because of the meaning of the name "Jesus", a transliteration of *Yeshua*, Joseph was instructed to name him accordingly:

> She will bear a son, and you shall call his name Jesus (Yeshua), for he will save his people from their sins (Matthew 1:21 ESV).

However, works of "salvation" had been delegated to others long before the time of Jesus. Just two examples should suffice:

> But when the people of Israel cried out to the LORD (YHWH), the LORD (YHWH) raised up a deliverer *(yasha)* for the people of Israel, who saved *(yasha)* them, Othniel the son of Kenaz, Caleb's younger brother (Judges 3:9 ESV).

And the people said unto Saul, Shall Jonathan die, who hath wrought this great salvation (*yasha*) in Israel?... (1 Samuel 14:45 KJV).

Just as the other humans mentioned above, Jesus was delegated authority by God to perform a "saving" role:

> The Spirit of the Lord God is upon me...I will greatly rejoice in the LORD, my soul shall be joyful in my God; for he hath clothed me with the garments of salvation, he hath covered me with the robe of righteousness (Isaiah 61:1,10 KJV quoted partly in Luke 4:18-19. See also Psalm 98:1).

In addition to Jesus and other individual Saviours, the whole people of Israel were delegated this role by Jesus:

> Ye worship ye know not what: we know what we worship: for salvation is of the Jews (John 4:22 KJV).

Shepherd

We know from that much-quoted and most-beloved biblical hymn that Almighty God is the Shepherd of the whole flock of Israel:

> The LORD is my shepherd; I shall not want. He maketh me to lie down in green pastures: he leadeth me beside the still waters. He restoreth my soul: he leadeth me in the paths of righteousness for his name's sake. Yea, though I walk through the valley of the shadow of death, I will fear no evil: for thou art with me; thy rod and thy staff they comfort me. Thou preparest a table before me in the presence of mine enemies: thou anointest my head with oil; my cup runneth over. Surely goodness and mercy shall follow me all the days of my life: and I will dwell in the house of the LORD for ever (Psalm 23: 1-6 KJV).

However, just as in all the roles thus far mentioned, God delegates authority to humans to "shepherd" the flock for particular purposes.

To feed them with knowledge and understanding:

> And I will give you shepherds after my own heart, who will feed you with knowledge and understanding (Jeremiah 3:15 ESV).

To lead the people as their King:

> All Israel came together to David at Hebron and said, "We are your own flesh and blood. In the past, even while Saul was king, you were the one who led

Israel on their military campaigns. And the Lord your God said to you, You will shepherd my people Israel, and you will become their ruler" (2 Chronicles 11:1-2 NIV).

To rebuild the Temple at Jerusalem:

> That saith of Cyrus, He is my shepherd, and shall perform all my pleasure: even saying to Jerusalem, Thou shalt be built; and to the temple, Thy foundation shall be laid (Isaiah 44:28 KJV).

The Chief Shepherd

The prophet Ezekiel foretold that God would one day appoint a descendant of David to represent him as chief Shepherd of Israel:

> And I will set up one shepherd over them, and he shall feed them, even my servant David; he shall feed them, and he shall be their shepherd (Ezekiel 34:23 KJV).

The prophet Zechariah foretold that this chief Shepherd would be "smitten":

> Awake, O sword, against my shepherd, and against the man that is my fellow, saith the LORD of hosts: smite the shepherd, and the sheep shall be scattered… (Zechariah 13:7 KJV)

Jesus recognised his delegated role of chief Shepherd by quoting this exact verse:

> Then saith Jesus unto them, All ye shall be made to stumble because of me this night: for it is written, I will smite the shepherd, and the sheep of the flock shall be scattered abroad (Matthew 26:31 KJV).

Other authors of the New Testament also spoke of Jesus' role as chief shepherd:

> And when the chief Shepherd shall appear, ye shall receive a crown of glory that fadeth not away (1 Peter 5:1 KJV).

> Now the God of peace, that brought again from the dead our Lord Jesus, that great shepherd of the sheep, through the blood of the everlasting covenant, Make you perfect in every good work to do his will… (Hebrews 13:20-21 KJV).

It would be wearisome in the extreme for readers to be subjected to yet more evidence that, on occasion, certain types of authority represented by a title or a description are delegated by the God of Israel to humans of his choice so we will conclude this section with a short commentary on the difference between Jesus and other human agents.

The Investiture

The New Testament position is that, after the Resurrection, Jesus was invested with an authority superior to all those other agents who had preceded him:

> Therefore God has highly exalted him and bestowed on him the name that is above every name, so that at the name of Jesus every knee should bow, in heaven and on earth and under the earth, and every tongue confess that Jesus Christ is Lord, to the glory of God the Father (Philippians 2:9-11 ESV).

Jesus is, therefore, to be accorded an honour and a glory—"every knee should bow" — similar to that accorded to the God of Israel. Note the unambiguous distinction between Jesus and God in these verses: all this was to be done "to the glory of God the Father".

The principle of agency pervades the whole of Scripture. It is the supreme irony that while theologians and academicians can devise the most tortuous and complex of theories, the simplicity of the agency principle appears to elude them completely. An inconvenient truth for theologians and academicians to digest—every single work ascribed to God is in fact carried out by human agents.

PART VI

Trinity on Trial

CHAPTER ONE

The Triune God

The doctrine of the Trinity is a teaching which says, in effect, that there is one God, but that this God may take on any one of three divine persons—the Father, the Son, and the Holy Spirit. This teaching is generally stated to be a "great truth" or a "mystery". In fact it is an attempt to marry two opposing concepts: monotheism versus the plurality of pagan theology.

Section 1

The Creeds

Niceno-Constantinopolitan Creed : 381 AD

The Nicene Creed was first adopted at the Council of Nicea in an attempt to unify the Christian Churches with one statement of belief. The original Creed was later revised and accepted by both Eastern and Western branches of Christendom at the First Council of Constantinople in 381 AD.

Chalcedon: 451 AD

The Chalcedonian Creed was adopted at the Fourth Ecumenical Council held at Chalcedon as a response to certain "heretical" views concerning the nature of Jesus of Nazareth. This Creed established the orthodox view that Jesus has two natures (human and divine) and that those natures are unified in one person. Despite the efforts of these Councils, both Eastern and Western branches of Christendom disagreed over elements of the Trinity so, eventually, attempts at unity were abandoned and Western Christendom adopted the Athanasian Creed in which the equality of the three persons of the Trinity is made explicit.

Section 2

Philosophical Roots

Opponents of the Trinity doctrine often claim it is derived from paganism and cite as their evidence the Hindu triad of *Brahma, Vishnu* and *Siva,* or the Persian triad of *Oromasdes, Mithras,* and *Arimanes.* However, a much closer version of the Christian Trinity can be found in the writings of the Neoplatonist Plotinus:

> Another influence may have been the Neoplatonist Plotinus' (204–70 CE) triad of the One, Intellect, and Soul, in which the latter two mysteriously emanate from the One, and "are the One and not the One; they are the one because they are from it; they are not the One, because it endowed them with what they have while remaining by itself" (Plotinus Enneads, 85). Plotinus even describes them as three hypostases, and describes their sameness using homoousios (Freeman 2003, 189). Augustine tells us that he and other Christian intellectuals of his day believed that the Neoplatonists had some awareness of the persons of the Trinity (Confessions VIII.3; City X.23). Many thinkers influential in the development of trinitarian doctrines were steeped in the thought not only of Middle Platonism and Neoplatonism, but also the Stoics, Aristotle, and other currents in Greek philosophy (Hanson 1988, 856–869).[1]

None of these trinitarian currents can be found in the Hebrew Scriptures or in the New Testament. The Hellenist-Latin Fathers responsible for the Trinity doctrine viewed the New Testament writings through the prism of their already developed philosophical and religious thought. This is particularly evident in the Gospel of John.

Despite the fact that the New Testament utterly repudiates such Hellenist-Latin thought, patristic writers such as Justin Martyr and Irenaeus had already searched the Hebrew Scriptures and collected "proof-texts" to find justification for the Virgin Conception/Birth and Incarnation teachings. (See Part V.2: *The Divine Court-Appeals to Precedent*). With the adoption of the Athanasian Creed, however, the search went into overdrive and the entire biblical corpus was scoured anew to find doctrinal justification. Regardless of culture, narrative, context and theme, verses were simply plucked out of the thinnest biblical air and used as a basis for promulgating the Trinity doctrine. Over these long centuries, until this very day, apologists repeat these proof-texts *ad infinitum*. (These texts are addressed in forthcoming sections and in other relevant categories elsewhere in this work.)

---

[1] *History of Trinitarian doctrines: Introduction.* Stanford Encyclopedia of Philosophy. Accessed 16 February 2017. https://plato.stanford.edu/entries/trinity/trinity-history.html

Section 3

A thoroughly modern god

The doctrine of the Trinity had always been the cornerstone of Christian theology but seen as rather irrelevant in its practical application to daily life. Over the last few decades, however, many theological movements have been reflecting upon the doctrine's meaning for modern life.

Forests of paper and excessive amounts of bandwidth have now been swallowed up in the rush to affirm the doctrine's critical importance to each and every relationship: from that of the marriage bed all the way through to that between member states of the United Nations.

Trinitarian theologians have now defined for themselves a god more in harmony with the modern world-view. The Father, the Son, and the Holy Spirit represent mutual love, co-operation and understanding, they say. This three-in one structure provides a basis for accepting a multiplicity of viewpoints, and is the model for the ideal society, they say. It is more conducive to peace and less likely to provoke conflict, they say.

The exclusive and particular claims of the Scriptures, they say, are stumbling blocks to people today, especially in a democratic, egalitarian culture. And so we find that many academics and theologians who live on the fruits of the Bible actually find Israelite monotheism offensive.

An eminent theologian, Jurgen Moltmann, had this to say:

> The social doctrine of the Trinity is in a position to overcome both monotheism in the concept of God and individualism in the doctrine of man, and to develop a social personalism and personalist socialism…that is important for the divided world in which we live and think. [2]

The words of Catholic intellectual, G. K. Chesterton, capture with artful and awful clarity the irreconcilable intellectual differences between modern Western society and the ancient Middle-Eastern peoples who gave us the Scriptures. Over a century ago, Chesterton reflected on the difference between Allah of the Muslims (and by implication YHWH of the Israelites) and the Triune god of the Christians. His words are well worth repeating at length:

---

[2] Moltmann, Jurgen. "The Reconciling Power of the Trinity in the Life of the Church and the World" in *Triune God: Love, Justice, Peace.* ed K.M. Tharakan. Mavelikkara: Youth Movement of Indian Orthodox Church, 1989, p 32.

> The complex God of the Athanasian Creed may be an enigma for the intellect; but He is far less likely to gather the mystery and cruelty of a Sultan than the lonely god of Omar or Mahomet. The god who is a mere awful unity is not only a king but an Eastern king…
>
> The heart of humanity, especially of European humanity, is certainly much more satisfied by the strange hints and symbols that gather round the Trinitarian idea, the image of a council at which mercy pleads as well as justice, the conception of a sort of liberty and variety existing even in the inmost chamber of the world. For Western religion has always felt keenly the idea 'it is not well for man to be alone'…
>
> For to us Trinitarians (if I may say it with reverence) to us God Himself is a society. It is indeed a fathomless mystery of theology…Suffice it to say here that this triple enigma is as comforting as wine and open as an English fireside; that this thing that bewilders the intellect utterly quiets the heart: but out of the desert, from the dry places and, the dreadful suns, come the cruel children of the lonely God; the real Unitarians who with scimitar in hand have laid waste the world. For it is not well for God to be alone…[3]

The Triune god of Christianity is nothing more than a philosophical concept first existing in the minds of the Hellenist-Latin Fathers, a God who was much more suited to their tastes and their values. This Triune god of the Fathers has now been newly fashioned to suit the tastes and values of a democratic, egalitarian society. Rather than reflecting the "image of God", Christian theologians and academics have created a god in their own image. God is no longer an infinite and unchanging rock in a sea of troubles, but is now infinitely malleable and subject to change according to the whims of the moment.

The bizarre position in which Trinitarians find themselves hopelessly enmeshed is that, having created mankind in his own image, God has now found it necessary to become the image of himself in the person of Jesus.

---

3 Chesterton, G.K. "The Romance of Orthodoxy" in *Orthodoxy*. John Lane: The Bodley Head, London, 1909.

Section 4

A personality cult

Where in the Gospels will you find a description of Jesus' personality? The example set by the life of Jesus lay in his character in action, his principles, his teachings, and the words that he spoke which were "never to pass away". In total opposition to the benchmarks set by Jesus, the doctrine of the Trinity focuses completely upon the personality of Jesus and the effect which it is assumed he produced upon his contemporaries. To accept this view is to accept that the issues for which he lived and died were issues applicable only to that time, and only to those circumstances.

The priestly establishment in the Jerusalem of 30 AD had their own concept of the divine will and saw themselves as its expression. The followers of Jesus took a contrary view and saw him as embodying and projecting the divine will. The Jerusalem of Pilate and Herod Antipas became a stage where two opposing points of view based on two opposing sets of values were played out. In its self-righteous arrogance, the priestly establishment of Jerusalem asserted that Jesus could not be the representative Israelite, the anointed one of God, because he did not appear to meet their criteria for Messiahship.

The churches of Christendom, in turn, assert that the anointed one of God must meet their criteria, as proclaimed through their doctrines. The disinformation projected by church doctrine imposes a barrier between Jesus and the rest of humanity; it misrepresents the values he stood for; it falsifies the issues that brought him into collision with the religious establishment; and it conceals the motives of those who caused him to be crucified.

So far have these teachings strayed from the original New Testament message that what we mainly see manifested today is no more than devotion to a personality cult called "Jesus Christ". Life in the age to come is to be found in spirit, not doctrines. Jesus' true message, unfettered by doctrines, brings hope and a sense of human dignity to the despised and rejected of the Earth. The New Testament authors enumerate principles to follow in order that his followers living many centuries later may become *one* with Jesus.

The Trinity can deliver no such message. If Jesus of Nazareth walked the earth and preached the same message today, he would be unidentifiable in terms of the Trinity. Perhaps he would again be branded a heretic, a blasphemer, a companion of undesirables, a malcontent, and so on. Of one thing we could be absolutely certain: a large body of so-called Christians would be in the forefront of those shouting "away with him".

Our predicament, when faced with the man himself, would mirror that of the disciples who had to choose between the teachings, authority and weight of tradition represented by the religious establishment, or the weight of moral authority represented by Jesus. They chose Jesus and what he represented over the religious establishment and what it represented. They recognised that the man described as being destined to rule the world in righteousness would be a man possessing certain qualities of character; a man who would be chosen by God and not by any earthly authority.

CHAPTER TWO

Common Core

Note

The Trinity and Deity teachings of mainstream Christianity are inextricably entwined. A necessity to separate teachings applicable to both into a more easily navigable order has necessitated the inclusion of many components of the Trinity teaching into Part V: *The Divine Court*. The following brief commentaries will therefore focus on a selection of arguments which were not included in Part V.

Section 1

Foundations

The writings of both the Hebrew Scriptures and the New Testament are based on a fundamental set of beliefs, values, principles and attitudes common to the ancient Israelite people. In what follows, we will test various elements of the Trinity teaching against this common core.

The eternal, immortal and invisible God

The Hebrew Scriptures attest to the following qualities of God which are found linked together in the New Testament:

> Now unto the King eternal, immortal, invisible, the only wise God, be honour and glory for ever and ever. Amen (1 Timothy 1:17 KJV).

> ...God, the blessed and only Ruler, the King of kings and Lord of lords, who alone is immortal and who lives in unapproachable light, whom no one has seen or can see. To him be honor and might forever. Amen (1 Timothy 6:15-16 NIV).

The unchanging God

Between God and man is a vast gulf fixed, a simple concept which was obvious to those who wrote the Hebrew Scriptures millennia ago:

God is not man, that he should lie, or a son of man, that he should change his mind. Has he said, and will he not do it? Or has he spoken, and will he not fulfill it? (Numbers 23:19 ESV cf. 1 Samuel 15:29; Malachi 3:6).

And also obvious to those who wrote the New Testament:

> Every good gift and every perfect gift is from above, and cometh down from the Father of lights, with whom is no change, neither shadow of turning (James 1:17 KJV).

The God of our Fathers

From the Hebrew Scriptures:

> And when we cried unto the LORD God of our fathers, the LORD heard our voice, and looked on our affliction, and our labour, and our oppression (Deuteronomy 26:7 KJV).

From the New Testament:

> The God of Abraham, Isaac and Jacob, the God of our fathers, has glorified his servant Jesus… (Acts 3:13 NIV).

> And he said, "The God of our fathers appointed you to know his will, to see the Righteous One and to hear a voice from his mouth" (Acts 22:14 ESV).

> "But this I admit to you, that according to the Way which they call a sect I do serve the God of our fathers, believing everything that is in accordance with the Law and that is written in the Prophets" (Acts 24:14 NASB).

Zechariah's song of praise is a magnificent encapsulation of faith and hope in the God of Israel—the God of his fathers. Its crucial importance is ignored and its substance never addressed by those whose responsibility it is. As such, it is reproduced in full here:

> Blessed be the Lord God of Israel; for he hath visited and redeemed his people, And hath raised up an horn of salvation for us in the house of his servant David; As he spake by the mouth of his holy prophets, which have been since the world began: That we should be saved from our enemies, and from the hand of all that hate us; To perform the mercy promised to our fathers, and to remember his holy covenant; The oath which he sware to our father Abraham, That he would grant unto us, that we being delivered out of the hand of our enemies might serve him without fear, In holiness and righteousness before him, all the days of our life. And thou, child, shalt be called the prophet of

the Highest: for thou shalt go before the face of the Lord to prepare his ways; To give knowledge of salvation unto his people by the remission of their sins, Through the tender mercy of our God; whereby the dayspring from on high hath visited us, To give light to them that sit in darkness and in the shadow of death, to guide our feet into the way of peace (Luke 1:68-79 KJV).

This single passage sounds the death knell for the masquerade that passes for Christianity today. It contradicts almost every aspect of mainstream theology as well as challenging accepted theories about Gospel dating and transmission, about the messianic role, about the identity of the people of God, and so on. (These theories are discussed in full elsewhere in this work.)

Section 2

The Agents

The biblical principle of agency appears quite beyond the grasp of those who continue to equate God with Jesus.

Throughout the New Testament, Jesus is presented as God's minister plenipotentiary, an agent invested with an authority superior to all the others who had preceded him. This perception of Jesus is of course a reflection of the Jewish understanding of agency, viz. the agent was regarded as the person himself. According to The Encyclopedia of the Jewish Religion:

> *Agent* (Heb. *Shaliah*): The main point of the Jewish law of agency is expressed in the dictum, "a person's agent is regarded as the person himself" (Ned. 72b; Kidd. 41b). Therefore any act committed by a duly appointed agent is regarded as having been committed by the principal, who therefore bears full responsibility for it with consequent complete absence of liability on the part of the agent.[4]

The delegation of God's authority to agents is termed "anointing". The passage below from the Gospel of Luke does not lend itself to any sort of misinterpretation or manipulation: it demonstrates very clearly that Jesus is not to be equated with God in any way, shape or form; that he is a human being embedded in a human community; but with the essential difference being that he has been "anointed" to act on behalf of God:

---

[4] Werblowsky, R. J. Zwi. *The Encyclopedia of the Jewish Religion*. ed. Geoffrey Wigoder. Adama Books: New York, 1986, p.15.

And he came to Nazareth, where he had been brought up. And as was his custom, he went to the synagogue on the Sabbath day, and he stood up to read. And the scroll of the prophet Isaiah was given to him. He unrolled the scroll and found the place where it was written (Isaiah 61:1), "The Spirit of the Lord is upon me, because he has anointed me to proclaim good news to the poor. He has sent me to proclaim liberty to the captives and recovering of sight to the blind, to set at liberty those who are oppressed, to proclaim the year of the Lord's favor." And he rolled up the scroll and gave it back to the attendant and sat down. And the eyes of all in the synagogue were fixed on him. And he began to say to them, "Today this Scripture has been fulfilled in your hearing" (Luke 4:16-21 ESV).

As is evidenced from this passage, the concept of "anointing" agents to carry out God's will was not simply a relic from the past but was a living and active concept in the New Testament. (This concept has a very long history and has been carried through to our own modern times. Just like many of her ancestors, Queen Elizabeth II was "anointed" on the occasion of her crowning, and the heirs to the British throne will be similarly "anointed".)

Long before the time of Jesus, other Israelites had been anointed for specific purposes. Just as they had been normal men born of normal parents into a normal human community, so also was Jesus. The merest suggestion that, centuries later, this anointed Israelite would be refashioned into a type of pagan god would have been greeted with incomprehension and incredulity.

CHAPTER THREE

Proof-texts

Many of the proof-texts cited by Trinitarian apologists resemble nothing more than a bunch of straws grasped in desperation so they are just not worth either space or time to reproduce. However, in the following sections, those remaining bulwark texts most beloved and much quoted will be addressed, some only briefly. The reader is encouraged to study the contexts from which these orphaned texts were "cherry-picked" to serve the interests of mainstream theology.

Section 1

Matthew 28:19

The Great Commission

Advocates claim that Jesus specifically teaches the doctrine of the Trinity in the following verse from Matthew Chapter 28, commonly known as "The Great Commission":

> Go ye therefore, and make disciples of all the nations, baptizing them into the name of the Father and of the Son and of the Holy Spirit (Matthew 28:19 ASV).

The authenticity of the baptismal formula given in verse 19 has long been called into question on historical as well as textual grounds and mainly centres on the fact that every extant manuscript of the New Testament post-dates the adoption of the Trinity teaching. Critics claim, therefore, that the formula is a scribal substitution for the original. The only sure method of ascertaining the original formula is to compare verse 19 with the actual baptismal formula found in other passages from the New Testament.

Baptism, when connected with mention of a formula, is twice "in the name of Jesus Christ" (Acts 2:38; 10:48), twice "in the name of the Lord Jesus" (Acts 8:16; 19:5), once "to Christ" (Galatians 3:27), and once "into Christ Jesus" (Romans 6:3).

Given the fact that the Trinitarian formula in Matthew 28:19 is never used in baptism, or even alluded to elsewhere in the New Testament, the conclusion must be that it was never part of the original commission. To assert otherwise is to also assert that the disciples disobeyed Jesus' final instructions to them.

A further observation

It should be obvious that one cannot *disciple* a nation, or *baptise* a nation. Given Jesus' reluctance to teach and heal non-Israelites, his original command could only have been to make disciples of Israelites living *among all the nations,* that is in those regions where countless Israelites lived among majority non-Israelite populations. (See Part II.3: *The Documents-New Testament Target Group*s.)

Section 2

Genesis 1:1

It is often claimed by Trinitarian advocates that the first three verses of Genesis portray their Triune God creating the Heavens and the Earth, viz. verse 1 refers to the Father; verse 2 to the Spirit; and verse 3 to the Son as the eternal Word speaking light into existence.

This Trinitarian claim is based on the Hebrew word אֱלֹהִים (*Elohim*) found in the first verse. This word is in plural form and therefore, they say, the truth of the three-fold Trinity was embedded in the Hebrew Scriptures right from the beginning, as if waiting for the doctrine to be later revealed. This claim would be risible if it were not so serious and had not led to such deadly serious consequences so we must address it.

The Sacred Name

The sacred name reserved for God alone is known as the four-letter Tetragrammaton and is usually referred to by substituting the Latin characters YHVH or YHWH for the Hebrew form, which is never pronounced such is the reverence and awe in which it is held. This sacred name represents the Israelite conception of the divine nature, character and attributes as revealed through the Deity's activity on behalf of those who worship and serve him.

The Generic Name

The Hebrew word *Elohim*, or its short form *El*, is a generic word for God occurring more than 2500 times in the Hebrew Scriptures. *Elohim can* be used to refer to the God of Israel, but is also used to refer to false gods, supernatural beings, and human leaders.

In the Hebrew language, the ending *im*, as in *Elohim*, mainly indicates a masculine plural noun so the presence of the word *Elohim* in Genesis 1 would appear to be simple, straightforward evidence for Trinitarians. However, a little more knowledge about the Hebrew language will demonstrate otherwise.

Hebrew Grammar

The scope of this work precludes any comprehensive analysis of the varied usage of the word *Elohim*. Given this limiting factor, it would appear that any attempt to determine whether the word is meant to indicate a singular or plural entity presents an insurmountable difficulty. However, such a comprehensive analysis is not necessary and the difficulty is only apparent because there is a straightforward rule of Hebrew grammar that will cut through all the complexity and leave us with a simple answer.

That rule is this: *a verb or adjective must agree with its subject in number and gender.* With this rule in place, we can proceed to examine the text of Genesis 1:1, commonly translated into English as:

In the beginning, God created the heavens and the earth.

Hebrew word order is different to that of English so a simple translation into English without changing the Hebrew word order is:

In the beginning, create God the heavens and the earth.

The Hebrew words of verse 1 reproduced below are taken from the *Leningrad Codex B19A (L)*, dated 1008-1009 AD, as reproduced in *Biblica Hebraica Stuttgartensia*.[5] The crucial words are highlighted:

בְּרֵאשִׁית **בָּרָא אֱלֹהִים** אֵת הַשָּׁמַיִם וְאֵת הָאָרֶץ׃

The subject of this verse is the masculine noun *Elohim* אֱלֹהִים
The action verb in this verse is the masculine singular *bara* בָּרָא

As stated, the rules of Hebrew grammar stipulate that verbs must agree with their subject in number and gender. The masculine singular verb *bara*, when used as the verb of action by the masculine subject *Elohim* precludes any possibility that this particular *Elohim* in Genesis 1:1 is anything but a masculine singular entity.

In addition, more than half the Scriptural verses containing the word *Elohim* couple it with the divine name YHWH, as in Genesis 2:4 where the creator is referred to as *YHWH Elohim*. *Elohim*, the word for God in Genesis 1:1, therefore carries with it all the attributes of YHWH in whose honour is recited the *Shema*, that great statement

---

5   *Biblica Hebraica Stuttgartensia*. Deutsche Bibelgesellschaft: Stuttgart, 1983.

of faith in the one true God of Israel (See Deuteronomy 6:4). To carve out this particular *Elohim* from its entire biblical context and apply to it a special Trinitarian interpretation is pure sophistry.

In any case, whether described as *Elohim* or *YHWH Elohim*, when the God of Israel is in action, is *doing* something, the verb of action is always masculine singular. The renowned scholar of Biblical Hebrew, Wilhelm Gesenius, had this to say:

> That the language has entirely rejected the idea of numerical plurality in אֱלֹהִים (whenever it denotes one God), is proved especially by its being almost invariably joined with a singular attribute (cf. § 132 h), e.g. אֱלֹהִים צַדִּיק ψ 7¹⁰, &c. Hence אֱלֹהִים may have been used originally not only as a numerical but also as an abstract plural (corresponding to the Latin numen, and our Godhead), and, like other abstracts of the same kind, have been transferred to a concrete single god (even of the heathen). [6]

The plural of majesty

There can be no doubt about the above facts, but some will still quibble and no doubt point to passages in which God makes self-referential statements using plural pronouns. These instances number only four: Genesis 1:26, 3:22, 11:7, and Isaiah 6:8. Particular attention is given to this use of the plural pronoun in Genesis:

> And God said, Let us make man in our image, after our likeness (Genesis 1:26 KJV).

> And the LORD God said, Behold, the man is become as one of us, to know good and evil…(Genesis 3:22 KJV).

> "Come, let Us go down and there confuse their language, so that they will not understand one another's speech" (Genesis 11:7 NASB).

Trinitarian advocates will ask—what entities could be included in the "us" if God is not a plurality of persons?

Firstly, we answer, God is depicted as presiding over a divine council. The plural pronouns in these verses refer to God and to those entities portrayed as gathering around the throne of God, all of whom existed prior to the creation account in Genesis. No creative action is attributed to these entities: they are merely onlookers who worship and serve God. (For references to this divine council see Job 1:6-12, 15:8, 38:4-7; Isaiah 6:1-8; Jeremiah 23:18; and I Kings 22:19-23.)

---

6 Gesenius, Wilhelm. *Gesenius' Hebrew Grammar.* eds Kautzsch, E; Cowley, A. E. Oxford: Clarendon Press, 1910, p.399.

Secondly, we answer, the "us" in these verses is spoken by the God of Israel. The authors used this literary device, called by linguists the "majestic plural", to emphasise the fullness of honour, majesty, and totality of deity attaching to him. The God of Israel is a "God of gods", an "*Elohim* of *Elohim*":

> For the LORD your God is God of gods, and Lord of lords, a great God, a mighty, and a terrible, which regardeth not persons, nor taketh reward (Deuteronomy 10:17 KJV).

Note that although the Scripture authors used the generic *Elohim* to describe the gods of pagan peoples, such as *Ashteroth, Ba'al, Chemosh, Dagon*, and etcetera, they did not believe that these entities were actually divine beings. One has only to read Isaiah 44:9-20 to appreciate just how scorned and derided were the representations of these pagan gods. Finally, if we must accept the assertion that the word *Elohim* indicates a multi-person God, then we must also accept the idea of a multi-person Moses:

> And the LORD (YHWH) said unto Moses, See, I have made thee a god (*Elohim*) to Pharaoh: and Aaron thy brother shall be thy prophet (Exodus 7:1 KJV).

If doubt should remain, other sources of clarifying information are available to us.

The Septuagint

In the ancient Greek translation of the Hebrew Scriptures known as the Septuagint (LXX), where the word *Elohim* refers to the God of Israel, the translators substituted *Theos*, the singular Greek word for God. Compare the Hebrew and Greek versions of the word for God in Genesis 1:1:

> In the beginning, *Elohim* created the heavens and the earth (Hebrew Scriptures).
>
> In the beginning, *Theos* made the heavens and the earth (Greek Septuagint).

The New Testament

The New Testament provides even further clarification. When quoting passages from the Hebrew Scriptures containing the word *Elohim* or variants, the New Testament uses the singular Greek form *Theos* or variant singular forms. For example, in the following verse from Matthew 4:10, Jesus quotes from Deuteronomy 6:13. The word for God in Deuteronomy is *Elohim*. The Greek substitute in Matthew is the singular *Theos*:

Then saith Jesus unto him, Get thee hence, Satan: for it is written, Thou shalt worship the Lord thy God (*Theos*), and him only shalt thou serve (KJV Matthew 4:10).

The Qur'an

Allah, the God of Islam, speaks of himself in the collective "we" (Qur'an 6:112; 10:87; 15:23,26; 20:77; 25:50; 32:21,24; 47:31; 56:57; 78:40), yet Muslims proclaim Allah to be one (Qur'an 112:1-4) and regard the Christian doctrine of the Trinity to be a monstrous idolatry.

Section 3

2 Corinthians 5:18-19

God in Christ

A passage in 2 Corinthians 5:18-19 is often used to support the doctrine of the Trinity. The passage reads:

> And all things are of God, who hath reconciled us to himself by Jesus Christ, and hath given to us the ministry of reconciliation; To wit, that God was in Christ, reconciling the world unto himself, not imputing their trespasses unto them; and hath committed unto us the word of reconciliation (2 Corinthians 5:18-19 KJV).

The concept of God dwelling in humans is a common theme throughout the Bible therefore it can only be for doctrinal reasons that the following similar passages are ignored:

> The one who keeps God's commands lives in him, and he in them. And this is how we know that he lives in us: We know it by the Spirit he gave us (1 John 3:24 NIV).

> No man hath seen God at any time. If we love one another, God dwelleth in us, and his love is perfected in us (1 John 4:12 KJV).

> And what agreement hath the temple of God with idols? for ye are the temple of the living God; as God hath said, I will dwell in them, and walk in them; and I will be their God, and they shall be my people (2 Corinthians 6:16 KJV).

Particular attention should be paid to Isaiah 45:14 which is addressed to Cyrus, the Medo-Persian King who had been "anointed" by the God of Israel to carry out his will on Earth. We read how various people will say to Cyrus:

> ...Surely God is in thee; and there is none else, there is no God (Isaiah 45:14 KJV).

When God's will is carried out by humans, including Jesus, God is perceived to be *dwelling in them*.

Section 4

John 14:9

Apologists for the Trinitarian doctrine often quote texts such as John 14:9:

> Jesus saith unto him, "Have I been so long time with you, and yet hast thou not known me, Philip? he that hath seen me hath seen the Father; and how sayest thou then, Shew us the Father?" (John 14:9 KJV).

Seeing God

When the Biblical authors speak in terms of *seeing, hearing*, and *speaking* with God, it is meant to be understood figuratively. As the following texts emphasise, God has never been seen by the human eye:

> And he said, Thou canst not see my face: for there shall no man see me, and live. (Exodus 33:20 KJV).
>
> No man hath seen God at any time... (John 1:18 KJV cf. 1 John 4:12).
>
> ...God, the blessed and only Ruler, the King of kings and Lord of lords, who alone is immortal and who lives in unapproachable light, whom no one has seen or can see... (1 Tim 6:15-16 NIV).

The New Testament authors teach that Jesus is the "image" of the invisible God, that he perfectly reflected God's character attributes of truth, justice, mercy, righteousness and etcetera. Thus, as in John 14:9, it is possible to "see" that reflection in Jesus. It is also possible for others to "see" God by doing good or by being pure in heart:

> Beloved, do not imitate what is evil, but what is good. The one who does good is of God; the one who does evil has not seen God (3 John 1:11 NASB).

> Blessed are the pure in heart: for they shall see God (Matthew 5:8 KJV).

The same figurative concept applies to the Spirit of Truth:

> …The world cannot accept him, because it neither sees him nor knows him. But you know him, for he lives with you and will be in you (John 14:17 NIV).

Hearing God

The following text explains in what sense humans "hear" God:

> But he (Jesus) answered them, "My mother and my brothers are those who hear the word of God and do it" (Luke 8:21 ESV).

Speaking with God

God "speaks" to humans through agents, in the following case the prophets:

> In the past God spoke to our ancestors through the prophets at many times and in various ways… (Hebrews 1:1 NIV).

The concepts of *seeing*, *hearing*, and *speaking* with God are interpreted literally if they slot neatly into a particular doctrinal apparatus. However, if literal interpretation of a particular text or concept stands in opposition to doctrine, then it is quickly assigned a figurative sense. The bizarre situation has developed where some texts which are intended to be taken figuratively are taken literally, and vice versa.

Section 5

Romans 9:5

Although many scholars do not accept the Trinitarian assertion that Romans 9:5 identifies Jesus as God, some advocates still persist so we must therefore persist in discrediting the claim. First, the context:

> I am speaking the truth in Christ—I am not lying; my conscience bears me witness in the Holy Spirit— that I have great sorrow and unceasing anguish in my heart. For I could wish that I myself were accursed and cut off from Christ for the sake of my brothers,a my kinsmen according to the flesh. They are Israelites, and to them belong the adoption, the glory, the covenants, the giving of the law, the worship, and the promises (Romans 9:1-4 ESV).

In verses 1-4 above, Paul lists the great spiritual honors given to Israel: the sonship, the glory, the covenants, the law, the temple worship and the promises. The greatest of these promises were those made to Abraham and David concerning the eventual birth of a Messiah:

> And in thy seed shall all the nations of the earth be blessed; because thou hast obeyed my voice (Genesis 22:18 KJV).
>
> And when thy days be fulfilled, and thou shalt sleep with thy fathers, I will set up thy seed after thee, which shall proceed out of thy bowels, and I will establish his kingdom. He shall build an house for my name, and I will stablish the throne of his kingdom for ever (2 Samuel 7:12-13 KJV).

Note that Paul states explicitly in Galatians 3:16 that the "seed" promised to Abraham was the Messiah.

Now the proof-text in which we see that Paul was indeed referring to the promise of a Messiah:

> To them belong the patriarchs, and from their race, according to the flesh, is the Christ, who is God over all, blessed forever. Amen (Romans 9:5 ESV).

In verse 5 above, Paul explains that God's promises to the patriarchs Abraham and David have now been fulfilled and that the Messiah Jesus is descended from them "according to the flesh".

Paul concludes verse 5 with the typical 'Blessed" or 'Blessed be" ascription of thanks and praise used exclusively for God in the Hebrew Scriptures and in the New Testament. The assertion that Paul is here identifying Jesus with God rests on practically no foundation whatsoever. Translated word for word into English, the Greek reads:

> ...and of whom the Christ according to flesh being over all God be blessed (*eulogetes*) to the ages amen.

Note that there is no punctuation in the original Greek. Reading aids such as commas and full stops have been provided for us in our English translations. Without the guidance provided by authorial punctuation, translators must rely on Greek grammar to render the verse correctly into English. Unlike the English language, word order in Greek is far less important. Intended meaning is derived from word inflection rather than order. It is agreed by all reputable scholars of Ancient Greek that the grammar of verse 5 admits of three viable translations:

1. ...Christ according to the flesh who is God over all be blessed to the ages. Amen.
2. ...Christ according to the flesh who is over all. God be blessed to the ages. Amen.
3. ...Christ according to the flesh. God who is over all be blessed to the ages. Amen.

Given this array from which to pick and choose according to one's commitment to doctrinal orthodoxy, there is only one correct method of ascertaining Paul's intended meaning and that is to compare this verse with other unambiguous New Testament statements by Paul and others. For example:

> Blessed be the Lord God of Israel... (Luke 1:68 ESV).

> Who changed the truth of God into a lie, and worshipped and served the creature more than the Creator, who is blessed for ever. Amen (Romans 1:25 KJV).

> Blessed be the God and Father of our Lord Jesus Christ... (2 Corinthians 1:3 ESV).

Every New Testament occurrence of the word *eulogetes* (blessed be) refers exclusively to God the Father. Thus the correct translation of Romans 9:5 given below should never have been in doubt for those committed to intellectual honesty rather than doctrinal orthodoxy:

> To them belong the patriarchs of whom (is) the Christ according to the flesh. God who is over all be blessed to the ages. Amen.

Section 6

Colossians 2:9

The fullness of God

Colossians 2:9 would seem to provide a veritable cornucopia for Trinitarian advocates:

> For in him dwelleth all the fullness of the **Godhead** (θεότης) bodily (Colossians 2:9 KJV.)

In virtually every English translation of this passage, such as the KJV above, the Greek word θεότης (*theotētos*) is translated as "Godhead" or as "Deity". It is asserted by advocates that the word expresses Godhead in the absolute sense. It does not merely signify a divine attribute, they say, but indicates that Jesus possesses the very essence of Deity.

This must be tiresome for readers but, yet again, we must point out their absolute contempt for the basics of scholarship. Firstly, this Greek word occurs only once in the Bible therefore there is no comparative biblical evidence on which to base its translation into English as "Godhead", or to make bold assertions about the meaning of the word.

Secondly, in Liddell and Scott, the classic Greek-English lexicon of the ancient Greek language used by scholars the world over, *theotētos* is translated into English as "divinity, divine nature". The lexicon cites works by various ancient Greek authors on which to base its translation.

There is a vast gulf separating the God of Israel from a mere mortal, albeit one perceived as possessing god-like attributes such as a "divine nature". This is a basic interpretive principle of the New Testament and perhaps the most misunderstood. Consider if you will the gigantic edifice built upon an inability or an unwillingness to grasp this principle.

Contrary to the basics of good scholarship, those committed to a theological viewpoint begin with the false premise that Paul preaches the Trinity, and then begin to construct their assertions and arguments from that false foundation. If one really wishes to clarify the meaning of Colossians 2:9, then it is a simple matter to refer back to Colossians 1:19:

> For it pleased the Father that in him (Jesus) should all fullness dwell (Colossians 1:19 KJV).

Note that in the above verse, indeed in the entire Pauline corpus, Paul draws clear and definite distinctions between the Father and Jesus. In his letter to the Ephesians, he sounds the death knell for this particular Trinitarian assertion by telling us that, just as Jesus was filled with the fullness of God, so would his followers also be filled:

> ...and to know this love that surpasses knowledge-that you may be filled to the measure of all the fullness of God (Ephesians 3:19 NIV).

Naturally enough, determining meaning through context and comparative analysis is much feared by those who cling desperately to a fatally-flawed belief system.

Section 7

1 Timothy 1:16

Revealing the mystery

The following passage in 1 Timothy 3:16 had always been considered essential to the Trinity doctrine as it appeared to contain the requisite Deity and Pre-existence teachings:

> And without controversy great is the mystery (*mustérion*) of godliness: God (*Theos*) was manifest in the flesh, justified in the Spirit, seen of angels, preached unto the Gentiles, believed on in the world, received up into glory (1 Timothy 3:16 KJV).

However, Trinitarian scholars have now been forced to admit that the word "*Theos*" in English translations such as the KJV above was interpolated into the Greek text by some overzealous scribe of the 8th-9th Century AD. Many modern English versions such as the NIV no longer dare to perpetuate such an obvious fraud and translate according to the earliest and best manuscripts that do not contain the word "*Theos*" but rather "*hos*" (he who) or just "*ho*" (he).

Concerning 1 Timothy 3:16, Bruce Metzger, the late professor emeritus at Princeton Theological Seminary, had the following to say:

> ["He who"] is supported by the earliest and best uncials...no uncial (in the first hand) earlier than the eighth or ninth century supports theos; all ancient versions presuppose hos or ho ["he who" or "he"]; and no patristic writer prior to the last third of the fourth century testifies to the reading theos. The reading theos arose either (a) accidentally, or (b) deliberately, either to supply a substantive for the following six verbs [the six verbs that follow in the verse], or, with less probability, to provide greater dogmatic precision [i.e., to produce a verse that more clearly supports the Trinitarian position]. [7]

The interpolation of the word "*Theos*" in 1 Tim 3:16 also places this passage in direct conflict with other Pauline passages where he unequivocally states that, far from God being revealed in the flesh, it was by God's commandment that Jesus and the prophets

---

[7] Metzger, Bruce. *A Textual Commentary on the Greek New Testament*. United Bible Society: New York, 1975, p. 641

before him had revealed the "mystery" that had been "hidden for long ages past" and "from ages and from generations":

> Now to him who is able to establish you in accordance with my gospel, the message I proclaim about Jesus Christ, in keeping with the revelation of the mystery (*mustérion*) hidden for long ages past, but now revealed and made known through the prophetic writings by the command of the eternal God, so that all the Gentiles might come to the obedience that comes from faith…(Romans 16:25-27 NIV).

> Whereof I am made a minister, according to the dispensation of God which is given to me for you, to fulfil the word of God; Even the mystery (*mustérion*) which hath been hid from ages and from generations, but now is made manifest to his saints (Colossians 1:25-26 KJV).

Mystery or Secret

From the Greek word *mustérion* in the passages above is derived the English word "mystery". However, unlike in English where the word implies something that is unknowable, the Greek word *mustérion* more properly implies something that is "secret", something that is knowable and can be revealed. Therefore, phrases in the New Testament such as "the mystery of the Kingdom" should rather read "the secret of the Kingdom".

Section 8

Titus 2:13

Honour and Glory

Scholars often engage in debate about the correct translation of Titus 2:13, a debate that is reflected in the various English translations. The crux of the matter is this: do we wait for the "appearing of the glory of our great God and Savior, Jesus Christ?" Or do we wait for the "glorious appearing of the great God and our Saviour Jesus Christ?" Consider these two translations of verse 13 in context:

> For the grace of God has appeared that offers salvation to all people. It teaches us to say "No" to ungodliness and worldly passions, and to live self-controlled, upright and godly lives in this present age, while we wait for the blessed hope— the appearing of the glory of our great God and Savior, Jesus Christ… (Titus 2:11-13 NIV).

> For the grace of God that bringeth salvation hath appeared to all men, Teaching us that, denying ungodliness and worldly lusts, we should live soberly, righteously, and godly, in this present world; Looking for that blessed hope, and the glorious appearing of the great God and our Saviour Jesus Christ… (Titus 2:11-13 KJV).

Throughout the New Testament, Jesus is depicted as God's human representative on earth. As such, he stands in the place of God and receives the type of worship, honour and glory befitting his position. For example, see the song of praise to the resurrected Jesus in Revelation 5:12-13. However, the glory that is bestowed on the resurrected Jesus is not of the same order as the incomprehensible glory of the God of Israel. We see the distinction drawn between the two types of "glory" in the following passage:

> For whoever is ashamed of me and of my words, of him will the Son of Man be ashamed when he comes in his glory and the glory of the Father and of the holy angels (Luke 9:26 ESV).

See also Matthew 16:27, Mark 8:38; 2 Peter 1:17.

Reflected glory

Whilst the resurrected Jesus is entitled to his own honour and glory, he also reflects God's own glory:

> He is the reflection of God's glory and the exact likeness of his being, and he holds everything together by his powerful word… (Hebrews 1:3 ISV).

The potential to reflect God's own glory is not restricted to Jesus. For example:

> But we all, with open face beholding as in a glass the glory of the Lord, are changed into the same image from glory to glory, even as by the Spirit of the Lord (2 Corinthians 3:18 KJV).

> For it was fitting for Him, for whom are all things, and through whom are all things, in bringing many sons to glory, to perfect the author of their salvation through sufferings (Hebrews 2:10 NASB).

> If you are insulted because of the name of Christ, you are blessed, for the Spirit of glory and of God rests on you (1 Peter 4:14 NIV).

Comparative textual analysis makes it abundantly clear that Jesus comes "in the glory of his Father", and that the "spirit of glory" rests upon many others besides Jesus. Therefore, it is the appearing of the "glory" of God in the person of Jesus upon which we wait, not upon the appearing of God himself in the person of Jesus.

Section 9

Hebrews 1:1-13

The premise of the Book of Hebrews is that Jesus communicates the ultimate revelation of God to man, superior to all the methods of divine communication that had come before him. The book is deeply reliant on the Hebrew Scriptures, from which it quotes directly 29 times and to which it makes a further 53 allusions.

It is not feasible in this work to provide a complete book-length commentary addressing all these quotes and allusions so we will confine our remarks to a few verses from Chapter One, which will be more than enough to dispel the dominant theological narrative arising from selective quoting in combination with a disregard for major New Testament themes and cultural contexts.

1:1-2

> Long ago, at many times and in many ways, God spoke to our fathers by the prophets, but in these last days he has spoken to us by his Son, whom he appointed the heir of all things, through whom also he created the world (Hebrews 1:1-2 ESV).

The first question to be asked is this: what "world" did God create through Jesus? We do not have to read very far into the book to discover that it is the "world to come", the New Creation, to which the author refers:

> It is not to angels that he has subjected the world to come, about which we are speaking (Hebrews 2:5 NIV).

1:3

> He is the reflection of God's glory and the exact likeness of his being, and he holds everything together by his powerful word. After he had provided a cleansing from sins, he sat down at the right hand of the Highest Majesty (Hebrews 1:3 ISV).

The New Testament authors taught that Jesus imaged the invisible God in his character: that he was a perfect human representation of all the divine attributes. The reason for the teaching is twofold—to encourage others to follow in the footsteps of Jesus, and to warn that because it was possible for one man to perfectly reflect God's attributes, it was therefore possible, indeed expected, of all humankind. No excuses, no rebates.

1:4

> So he became as much superior to the angels as the name he has inherited is superior to theirs (Hebrews 1:4 NIV).

Another question that springs to mind is this: why did the author find it necessary to compare Jesus with created beings such as angels and prophets if Jesus is equal to God? Of course the author believed no such absurdity, which is why the introduction to his book is all about giving would-be followers of Jesus reasons to have faith in him as the ultimate revelation from God.

1:5

> For unto which of the angels said he at any time, Thou art my Son, this day have I begotten thee? And again, I will be to him a Father, and he shall be to me a Son? (Hebrews 1:5 KJV).

Note that Jesus became the only-begotten son of the Father on the day of his Resurrection (Acts 13:33). For an in-depth analysis of the terms *son of God* and *only-begotten son* see Part V.4: *The Divine Court-Appeals to Descriptions and Titles*.

1:8-9

> But unto the Son he saith, Thy throne, O God (*Theos*), is for ever and ever: a sceptre of righteousness is the sceptre of thy kingdom (Hebrews 1:8 KJV).
>
> Thou hast loved righteousness, and hated iniquity; therefore God, even thy God, hath anointed thee with the oil of gladness above thy fellows (Hebrews 1:9 KJV).

Verses 8 and 9 are direct quotations from a single passage in the Psalms:

> Thy throne, O God (*Elohim*), is for ever and ever: the sceptre of thy kingdom is a right sceptre. Thou lovest righteousness, and hatest wickedness: therefore God, thy God, hath anointed thee with the oil of gladness above thy fellows (Psalm 45:6-7 KJV).

Verse 8 is very often used to justify the Trinity doctrine as it appears to say that God calls Jesus "God". However, we now discover from Psalm 45:6 that the god (*Theos*) of Hebrews 1:8 is based on the Hebrew word *Elohim* and not on YHWH, the sacred name of the God of Israel. As demonstrated in Section 2 and elsewhere in this work, the word *Elohim can* be used to refer to the Israelite God YHWH but is also used to refer to false gods, supernatural beings, and human leaders. Considering that Hebrews 1:9 and Psalm 45:7 both continue on to speak of a man chosen by God for his qualities of character and set *above his fellows* to fulfill God's purposes, it is clear that the *Elohim* of 45:7 cannot possibly refer to YHWH and therefore any attempt to justify the Trinity based on Hebrews 1:8 is doomed to failure.

1:10-12

> And "You, Lord, laid the foundation of the earth in the beginning, and the heavens are the work of your hands; they will perish, but you remain; they will all wear out like a garment, like a robe you will roll them up, like a garment they will be changed. But you are the same, and your years will have no end" (Hebrews 1:10-12 ESV).

In verses 10-12 above, the author quotes directly from Psalm 102:

> In the beginning you laid the foundations of the earth, and the heavens are the work of your hands. They will perish, but you remain; they will all wear out like a garment. Like clothing you will change them and they will be discarded. But you remain the same, and your years will never end (Psalm 102:25-27 NIV).

It has been asserted that Hebrews 1:10-12 is a demonstration of God attributing to the Son the same role in creation and the same eternality as that ascribed to himself in Psalm 102. Consider the folly of maintaining this assertion despite the fact that, in the immediately preceding verse 9, the author has drawn on Psalm 45:6 and characterised Jesus as a man *anointed by God and set above his fellows*. Those who make these assertions would have us believe that the New Testament authors were subject to the same type of confused, muddled, and inconsistent thinking which they themselves demonstrate.

1:13

> But to which of the angels did he ever say, "Sit at my right hand until I make your enemies a footstool for your feet"? (Hebrews 1:13 ISV).

The author is once again quoting directly from the Psalms:

> ...The LORD says to my lord: "Sit at my right hand until I make your enemies a footstool for your feet"(Psalm 110:1 NIV).

For an in-depth analysis of this and similar verses, see Part XIII.6: *The Israelite Messiah-A Right Hand Man*.

In case any doubt should remain about the status of Jesus, the author states definitively in a subsequent Chapter that Jesus was a man descended from the tribe of Judah:

For it is evident that our Lord was descended from Judah... (Hebrews 7:14 ESV).

Only through theological sophistry or wilful blindness can the clear intent of these and many similar New Testament passages be ignored.

PART VII

Paul

CHAPTER ONE

Introduction

Many Christian theological teachings regarding Faith, Works, Righteousness, Justification, Grace, and etcetera, are un-scriptural and demonstrably so. These un-scriptural teachings are mainly drawn from the writings of Paul and arose for the following reasons:

- a failure to recognise the Israelite Covenant framework within which Paul sets all his teachings;
- a failure to identify the peoples to whom Paul addressed these teachings;
- a failure to understand the cultural milieu from which Paul's teachings emerged.

These monumental failures have resulted in his writings becoming the most abused, misused, misinterpreted and misunderstood corpus of works in all of human history.

Separating out the interconnected web of Pauline teachings into individual strands is profoundly difficult but we will nevertheless make the attempt although a certain amount of repetition is unavoidable.

Whilst it is to Paul we must turn for much of the material in the following Chapters, we will also address some of the subjects in question from an overall scriptural perspective.

CHAPTER TWO

Note

For a thorough understanding of Paul's letters it is necessary here to reproduce in part an Essay appearing in Part II.4: *The Documents-New Testament Target Groups.*

Paul and his world

For many theologians past and present, the Pauline "good news" is one that declares a universalism, subsuming lesser entities such as the law and cultural differences. Nothing could be more deceptive. Just like all of his 1st Century AD contemporaries, Paul himself was not a universalist but an ethnocentrist.

Much has been made of a supposed conflict between Paul's theology and the rest of the New Testament but the reality is that the conflict exists only because of confused and inconsistent theological teachings.

Section 1

Paul's Mission

Paul's "Gospel of God" is ultimately about a forthcoming Israelite theocracy—the Kingdom of God. Therefore it is only natural that his target groups are Israelites. However, the correct identification of these groups has been obscured by ambiguous, incorrect and inconsistent translations. For example:

Jews (Greek Ἰουδαῖός: Transliteration Ioudaios)

Ambiguous translation: The Greek New Testament has been translated into many different languages over time. If translators of all these versions had correctly identified the various categories of persons all designated as *Ioudaios* in the New Testament, that word would not have become the most consequential single word in all of human history. Since this work is in English, we will confine our remarks on this topic to the English version but its content applies equally to all translations of the Greek New Testament regardless of era, language or version.

Persons designated in the English New Testament as "Jew/s" could fall into one or more of the following categories:

1. Descendants of the Israelite tribe of Judah who lived in the Roman Province of Judea, worshipped at the Temple in Jerusalem, and followed the Law of Moses;
2. Descendants of the Israelite tribe of Judah regardless of where they lived. For instance, Jesus was a Jew because he belonged to the tribe of Judah even though he came from Galilee;
3. Persons who followed the customs and practices of the Judeans regardless of where they lived. For instance, Paul self-identified as a Jew because he followed the customs and practices of the Judeans who worshipped at the Temple in Jerusalem even though he came from Tarsus and belonged to the Israelite tribe of Benjamin.

Note that Jesus falls into categories 2 and 3 above: not only did he belong to the Israelite tribe of Judah but he also followed the customs and practices of the Judeans who worshipped at the Temple in Jerusalem.

Correctly identifying the category of person the author has in view at any one time is daunting but not impossible if context is studied and fully appreciated. Given the fact that the word rendered into English as "Jew" was to become the most important single word in all of human history, the consequences of not differentiating between the various categories of *Ioudaios* mentioned in the New Testament can hardly be overestimated.

Note

Some scholars assert that the word *Ioudaios* always means "Judean" but they fail to take into account the other categories of *Ioudaios* mentioned in the New Testament.

Greeks (Greek Ἕλλην : Transliteration Hellēn)

No consistency of translation: e.g. sometimes rendered Gentile. In the 1st Century AD, there was no nation state of Greece. "Greeks" were civilised people who spoke the Greek language and followed the customs and practices of Hellenists. Among those designated as "Greeks" were both Israelites living in diaspora communities and non-Israelites. Israelite "Greeks" did not follow the "barbaric" customs and practices of the Judeans but rather the customs and practices of Hellenists.

Gentiles (Greek ἀλλοφύλῳ :Transliteration allophylō) (Greek ἐθνῶν :Transliteration ethnē)

No consistency of translation: e.g. variously Greek, heathen, pagan, nation, race. There are various Greek words that have been translated into English as "Gentile". As with the word "Greek", there is no consistency of translation.

The complexity of the above terminology is daunting so, as always, we must determine meaning by context.

Even though it is almost universally believed that Paul is the Apostle to the Gentiles, i.e. non-Israelites, it is obvious from Paul's statement to Herod Agrippa when he appeared before him in Caesarea that his mission was to the twelve tribes of Israel. (The correct translation of "Jews" appears in brackets):

> King Agrippa, I consider myself fortunate to stand before you today as I make my defense against all the accusations of the Jews (Judeans), and especially so because you are well acquainted with all the Jewish (Judean) customs and controversies. Therefore, I beg you to listen to me patiently. The Judean people all know the way I have lived ever since I was a child, from the beginning of my life in my own country, and also in Jerusalem. They have known me for a long time and can testify, if they are willing, that I conformed to the strictest sect of our religion, living as a Pharisee. And now it is because of my hope in what God has promised our ancestors that I am on trial today. This is the promise our twelve tribes are hoping to see fulfilled as they earnestly serve God day and night" (Acts 26:2-7 NIV).

Paul was an Israelite who had persecuted Jesus groups in Judea. After his "road to Damascus" experience, he believed he had been called to be an Israelite prophet standing in the same tradition as the prophets of old and to proclaim the Gospel of God to Israelites. Paul's appeal to other Israelites is based on their common genealogy through Abraham and it is this commonality that forms the framework for all his theology.

Paul did not focus on the story of Jesus' life. Rather, his focus was on what the God of Israel had done in raising up Jesus. He announced that the Crucifixion and Resurrection was a signal to Israelites living in the Diaspora that they would one day be "resurrected" from this dispersion, regarded as a type of death, and ingathered to Israel to form the Kingdom of God to be ruled over by God's Messiah.

Many modern scholars claim that there are only seven genuine Epistles written by Paul himself, viz. 1 Thessalonians, Galatians, Philemon, Philippians, 1 & 2 Corinthians, and Romans. Their view that the other six pseudepigraphic epistles were written by later followers of Paul is borne out by the fact that these epistles are not Israelite-specific, as are the seven that can be directly attributed to Paul himself, and they do not require a knowledge of the Hebrew scriptures in order to be understood. Paul directed his letters to Israelite Jesus groups that he founded and there is no evidence that he showed any interest whatever in non-Israelites.

Seeing that Paul's arguments would have made sense only to an Israelite audience, his mission then was to proclaim the Gospel of God to Israelites living among majority non-Israelite populations scattered throughout the Roman Empire. The one exception to this pattern is the Epistle to the Romans which was addressed to Jesus groups that Paul did not found. These Roman Jesus groups contained a few non-Israelite members and he issues them with some specific warnings about their status in Chapter 11:13-24. For example:

> But if some of the branches were broken off, and you, being a wild olive, were grafted in among them and became partaker with them of the rich root of the olive tree, do not be arrogant toward the branches; but if you are arrogant, remember that it is not you who supports the root, but the root supports you (Romans 11:17-18 NASB).

Later generations of non-Israelites adopted Christianity after the Hellenist-Latin fathers, using their own philosophies and theologies, imposed upon the New Testament texts a synthesis of Paganism and Hellenism more appealing to the peoples of the Roman Empire.

Paul's letters have been subjected to multiple doctrinal overlays and the distractions of theological hair-splitting over issues such as Faith, Works, Righteousness, Justification, Grace, Election and so on. If we had not been subjected to these distractions, we would perhaps have recognised long ago that the letters directly attributable to Paul were addressed to those who could understand them, viz. fellow Israelites living among majority non-Israelite societies beyond the confines of the land of Israel.

As it is, Pauline theology is largely based on non-Israelite concepts and would therefore collapse under the weight of its utter irrelevance and total absurdity. As Malina and Pilch state:

> It is quite significant to note that Paul's proclamation (of the gospel of God) was Israelite-specific in all of its dimensions: in its means of transmission (Paul received it through a revelation ascribed to the God of Israel who calls prophets), in its origin (the God of Israel), in its medium (a revelation of Israel's Messiah, the crucified and resurrected Jesus), in its content (an Israelite theocracy), and in its rationale (spelled out according to Israel's scriptures). Hence it is fairly obvious that the proclamation was meant specifically for Israelites.[1]

---

1   Malina, B.J, Pilch, J.J. *Social Science Commentary on the Letters of Paul.* Augsburg Fortress Press: Minneapolis, 2006, p 12.

CHAPTER THREE

Note

Paul self-identified as a "Jew" because he followed the customs and practices of the Judeans who worshipped at the Temple in Jerusalem and followed the Law of Moses even though he came from Tarsus and belonged to the Israelite tribe of Benjamin. (See previous Chapter on categories of persons designated as "Jews".)

Paul the Jew

Before his "road to Damascus" experience, Paul identified himself with the Israelite people and the Israelite God. If possible, his allegiance to both was further strengthened when, as if in a flash of light, he realised that God had kept his promises to Israel and raised up among them a Messiah, born of the "seed of David according to the flesh" (Romans 1:3).

Although Christian theology would have us believe otherwise, Paul's new convictions did not change his pattern of behaviour in any way: he continued to observe the Law of Moses; he urged others to keep God's commandments; he declared to all who would listen his faith in the Israelite God; and he taught in Israelite synagogues on many occasions.

Paul's commitment to his ancestral beliefs and customs never wavered despite all his trials and tribulations. Many examples could be cited but the following quote from the Book of Acts is probably the most important. With the permission of the Roman authorities, Paul recounts his "road to Damascus" experience to a crowd gathered in the Jerusalem Temple precincts:

> I am a Jew, born in Tarsus of Cilicia, but brought up in this city. I studied under Gamaliel and was thoroughly trained in the law of our ancestors. I was just as zealous for God as any of you are today…
>
> As I was on my way and drew near to Damascus, about noon a great light from heaven suddenly shone around me. And I fell to the ground and heard a voice saying to me, "Saul, Saul, why are you persecuting me?" And I answered, "Who are you, Lord?" And he said to me, "I am Jesus of Nazareth, whom you are persecuting…"
>
> And I said, "What shall I do, Lord?" And the Lord said to me, "Rise, and go into Damascus, and there you will be told all that is appointed for you to do."

> And since I could not see because of the brightness of that light, I was led by the hand by those who were with me, and came into Damascus…
>
> And one Ananias, a devout man according to the law, well spoken of by all the Jews who lived there, came to me, and standing by me said to me, "Brother Saul, receive your sight." And at that very hour I received my sight and saw him. And he said, "The God of our fathers appointed you to know his will, to see the Righteous One and to hear a voice from his mouth" (Acts 22:3-14 ESV).

The importance of Ananais' statement cannot be overestimated. From it, we discover that Paul receives his commission from the *"God of our fathers"* who has appointed Paul to know his will, to see a vision of Jesus, and to hear the voice of Jesus. (Despite popular belief, Jesus did not appear by his own volition to Paul or any of the resurrection witnesses, as we will discover in Part XV: *Resurrection*.)

From this day forward, all Paul's teachings must be based on what Paul perceives to be the "will" of the God of Israel. Would Paul have somehow forgotten this direct instruction along the way? Would he have begun preaching a new and different religion which, in essence, equates to a new and different God? (Note that Paul receives his commission through the hand of Ananias, "a devout man according to the law".)

The Defender of the Law and the Prophets

The Ten Commandments given at Sinai (also known as the "Ten Words") served as a counterpoint to the slavery, oppression, idolatry, immorality and injustice characterising the Israelite experience in Egypt. For Paul, those Ten Words always remained "holy, just and good" (Romans 7:5-13). The original stone tablets contained the Ten Words *only* (see Exodus 34:28) and were given directly by God to Israel in the wilderness when, "The Lord spoke to you face to face at the mountain, out of the fire" (Deuteronomy 5:4). Thus, they were given to Moses by God before the Golden Calf incident.

When Paul refers to the Law given by Moses, he is not referring to the Ten Words given at by God at Sinai but rather to the broad range of other commandments, ethical teachings, regulations and prescribed rituals covering all the aspects of Israel's political, social, and religious life given at various times throughout Israel's subsequent sojourn in the wilderness. Unlike the Ten Words given directly by God to Israel, this additional material was given to Israel by God through angelic intermediaries (Acts 7:53; Galatians 3:19-20).

From Paul's perspective, all this additional material, especially the prescribed rituals such as circumcision, dietary restrictions, calendrical observations and etcetera, was added to the Ten Words because of the Golden Calf incident (see Mosaic Covenant below). These prescribed rituals had become vital to the life of the Jews (Judeans) but had become optional for other Israelites.

Paul, being a self-described Jew, followed the customs and practices of the Judeans who worshipped at the Jerusalem Temple and followed the Law of Moses. Regardless of his publicly stated view that the observance of these customs and practices of the Law, i.e. the "works", was no longer necessary for followers of Jesus, they still remained a vital part of Paul's inner life and he continued to perform rituals such as purification, sacrifice and worship. Despite these recorded occasions, he was still accused of breaking the Law of Moses, accusations he always strenuously denied.

For instance, when he was arrested in Jerusalem on trumped-up charges, Paul was sent under guard to Ceasarea to appear before Governor Felix. A group of his Judean accusers, including the High Priest Ananais, had also travelled to Ceasarea to witness against him and Paul mounted a spirited defence before them all:

> You (Felix) can verify that it is not more than twelve days since I went up to worship in Jerusalem, and they did not find me disputing with anyone or stirring up a crowd, either in the temple or in the synagogues or in the city. Neither can they prove to you what they now bring up against me. But this I confess to you, that according to the Way, which they call a sect, I worship the God of our fathers, believing everything laid down by the Law and written in the Prophets, having a hope in God, which these men themselves accept, that there will be a resurrection of both the just and the unjust (Acts 24:11-15 ESV).

Although his accusers were never able to demonstrate that he broke the Law of Moses in any way, Paul was detained in Caesarea before having once again to defend himself, now before Governor Festus and Herod Agrippa:

> Having therefore obtained the help that is from God, I stand unto this day testifying both to small and great, saying nothing but what the prophets and Moses did say should come; how that the Christ must suffer, and how that he first by the resurrection of the dead should proclaim light both to the people and to the Gentiles (Acts 26:22-23 ASV).

This single statement by Paul— "saying *nothing* but what the prophets and Moses did say should come"—should be enough to consign the entire edifice of Creedal Christianity to its richly deserved place in the theological rubbish bin of history. However, it is simply ignored, or worse, not even noticed.

According to Acts, Paul was a Roman citizen by birth and this gave him the right to appeal directly to Caesar in any dispute over which he felt aggrieved. It was because

Paul wished to avoid being handed over to his Judean opponents that he appealed to Caesar during his witness before Festus and Herod Agrippa. Festus and Agrippa both agreed that Paul was innocent of any crime and could have been set free if he had not appealed to Caesar. But appeal to Caesar he had, so to Caesar he must go. By the time Paul was handed over to the custody of the Centurion Julius and had boarded ship for Rome, he had spent about 18 months in detention in Caesarea Maritima.

After a harrowing sea voyage, Paul eventually arrived in Rome where he, along with a guard, settled in a house for which Paul paid. Then:

> Three days later he called together the local Jewish leaders. When they had assembled, Paul said to them: "My brothers, although I have done nothing against our people or against the customs of our ancestors, I was arrested in Jerusalem and handed over to the Romans. They examined me and wanted to release me, because I was not guilty of any crime deserving death. The Jews (Judeans) objected, so I was compelled to make an appeal to Caesar. I certainly did not intend to bring any charge against my own people. For this reason I have asked to see you and talk with you. It is because of the hope of Israel that I am bound with this chain." They replied, "We have not received any letters from Judea concerning you, and none of our people who have come from there has reported or said anything bad about you. But we want to hear what your views are, for we know that people everywhere are talking against this sect." They arranged to meet Paul on a certain day, and came in even larger numbers to the place where he was staying. He witnessed to them from morning till evening, explaining about the kingdom of God, and from the Law of Moses and from the Prophets he tried to persuade them about Jesus (Acts 28:17-23 NIV).

Paul speaks with these Jewish leaders for an entire day concerning the forthcoming Israelite religious/political theocracy to be established by Israel's Messiah Jesus whom the God of Israel had raised from the dead according to the Law and the Prophets.

As we can see from the above passages, Paul was commissioned by the God of Israel; he worshipped the God of Israel in the Jerusalem Temple; he preached nothing against his people or their customs; he preached nothing but what Moses and the prophets said should come concerning Jesus; and he believed everything that was according to the Law and everything written in the prophets. There is nothing about this Paul that is even remotely similar to the Paul of Christian theology who, it is claimed, sought to establish a new religion.

CHAPTER FOUR

Paul and his Theology

Floods of ink, forests of paper, and the sometimes life-long efforts of thousands of theologians and academics, have been expended on the so-called "problems" of Pauline theology. Profoundly complex doctrinal systems and entire branches of Christendom seem to stand or fall on their interpretations of the Pauline corpus. Battles continue to be waged in citadels of learning over the concepts of Faith, Works, Righteousness, Justification, Grace, Election, and etcetera. In the following sections, we will see if these problems exist in reality, or are only manufactured.

Section 1

Note

Despite the profusion of learned tomes dedicated to the concepts of Faith, Works, Righteousness, Justification, and Grace, these terms cannot be properly understood unless clearly defined according to the anti-introspective, collectivist culture of Israelite society in the First Century AD. Once defined, however, implications deriving from their usage become readily apparent.

Interpretive Principles

Paul's target groups are Israelites living in Greco-Roman societies beyond the confines of the land of Israel.

When Paul uses the designation "Jew", he is referring mainly to those who follow the customs and practices of the Judeans who worship in the Jerusalem Temple and follow the Law of Moses. (See Chapter 2 for categories of persons designated "Jews".) When he uses the designation "Greek", he is referring mainly to Greek-speaking Jews and other Israelites who live in these Greco-Roman societies beyond the confines of the land of Israel. Except for the Epistle to the Romans, Paul directed his Epistles to Israelite Jesus groups that he founded and there is no evidence that he showed any interest whatever in non-Israelites.

Because some Israelites followed the Law of Moses and some did not, Paul found it necessary to develop a set of arguments based on their shared ancestry through Abraham: to focus on what united them rather than the observance of the Law of

Moses that had hitherto divided them. Thus, Paul set his entire body of work within the framework of the Abrahamic Covenant.

The consequences of mainstream theology's inability, or unwillingness, to recognise or accept these interpretive principles have been catastrophic. Tragically, it is far too late for the many whose lives have been sacrificed on the altars of dogmatism and Supersessionism by that particular brand of authoritarian mentality characterising the majority of "Christian" denominations.

Section 2

The Covenants

The Abrahamic Covenant

The Abrahamic Covenant was established when Abraham was called to the service of God (Genesis 12:1-3). The Covenant's promises were to be realised only through Abraham and Sarah's yet unborn son Isaac:

> And God said, Sarah thy wife shall bear thee a son indeed; and thou shalt call his name Isaac: and I will establish my covenant with him for an everlasting covenant, and with his seed after him (Genesis 17:19 KJV).

The sacrifice

The story of the attempted sacrifice of Isaac has no doubt puzzled many. We read that Abraham hears a voice telling him to sacrifice his son despite the fact that the prior promises of posterity, land and blessings were to be established only through Isaac:

> Then God said, "Take your son, your only son, whom you love—Isaac—and go to the region of Moriah. Sacrifice him there as a burnt offering on a mountain I will show you" (Genesis 22:2 NIV).

The answer to this puzzle is found in the Book of Joshua where we read that Abraham's ancestors had "served other gods":

> And Joshua said to all the people, "Thus says the LORD, the God of Israel, 'Long ago, your fathers lived beyond the Euphrates, Terah, the father of Abraham and of Nahor; and they served other gods (Joshua 24:2 ESV).

The journey towards the place of sacrifice, which Abraham reaches on the "third day," is a journey from death to life foreshadowing the Crucifixion and Resurrection of Jesus. The journey also symbolises progressive revelation of the one, true God. The God who had called Abraham to Canaan to serve him is not the "gods" of his ancestors. This God would not renege on his promises; both he and Isaac would return; God would provide the lamb; and even if Isaac's death were required, God could raise him from the dead. When Isaac was spared, Abraham received him back figuratively from the dead (Hebrews 11:17-19).

Abraham's faith in the power of God is established and his absolute obedience extolled and rewarded. The concept of human sacrifice is explicitly repudiated, both then by the "angel of the Lord", and later by such prophets as Micah (6:7) and Jeremiah (7:31).

The Covenant was once more confirmed in his son Isaac—in him and his seed would all the nations of the earth be blessed (Genesis 22:15-18). Thus the promises made to Abraham passed to his son Isaac, then to his grandson Jacob-Israel, and then in turn to Jacob's descendants—twelve-tribed Israel. The Israelite people are defined in all ages by God's binding covenant with Abraham, Isaac and Jacob.

The purpose of the story of Abraham is threefold: to establish Abraham as a model for obedience and faith; to demonstrate that God keeps his promises to Israel; and to dramatise the difference between the "old" religion of Abraham's ancestors and the henceforth "new" religion of Abraham's descendants.

The Mosaic Covenant

According to the Hebrew Scriptures, the Ten Commandments (also known as the Ten Words) were given at Sinai after the Exodus from Egypt. At this time, the Israelites entered into another Covenant with God and were constituted a "kingdom of priests and a holy nation" (Exodus 19:6).

The key to interpreting Paul's teachings about "works" is to recognise that the original tablets contained the Ten Words *only* (see Exodus 34:28). These Ten Words were given directly by God to Israel in the wilderness before the Golden Calf incident when, "The Lord spoke to you face to face at the mountain, out of the fire" (Deuteronomy 5:4). For Paul, these Ten Words always remained holy, just, and good. (See Romans 7:5-13.)

The Golden Calf

To ancient Israelites, the making of an image of God was seen as an attempt to control God. The destruction of the wilderness generation of Israelites was due to their dishonouring of the God who had brought them out of Egypt by making an image of God, a molten Calf of Gold (Exodus 32).

The Golden Calf was to serve as a place for the apparition of God. Those who controlled the image could presume to speak in the name of God and say, "This is your god, O Israel, who brought you up out of the land of Egypt" (Exodus 32:4) and use the image to lead the people wherever they wished them to go. With the controllable Golden Calf, Israelites could be steered back to Egypt, thus reversing the act of the God who had freed them.

According to the Exodus story, the incident of the Golden Calf occurred while Moses was still on the mountain receiving the Ten Words engraved by the "finger" of God on stone steles (Exodus 31:18; 32:15-16). It was these stone steles that Moses threw down and broke upon seeing the Israelites' attempt to control God.

After the Golden Calf "transgression", God ceased direct communication with the people. Moses returned up the mountain to receive the Ten Words again but now, and at various times throughout Israel's subsequent sojourn in the wilderness, with the gradual addition of other commandments, ethical teachings, regulations and prescribed rituals covering all aspects of Israel's political, social, and religious life.

Paul refers to all this additional material as the Law given by Moses which was added to the Ten Words because of the Golden Calf transgression. Observing all these "works" of the Law given by Moses is therefore no longer obligatory for Paul's groups because Jesus has made a corporate atonement for their ancestors' former transgressions (Romans 3:25-26). Those Israelites who accept that God has acted on their behalf by raising up Jesus in preparation for the forthcoming establishment of the Kingdom of God have behaved in a way that honours God, thereby reversing the wilderness sin of dishonouring God. The slate has been wiped clean.

Blessings and curses

Although the Mosaic Covenant carried with it the promise of great blessings, it was conditional in that it was predicated on the faithfulness of Israelites:

> Now therefore, if ye will obey my voice indeed, and keep my covenant, then ye shall be a peculiar treasure unto me above all people: for all the earth is mine: And ye shall be unto me a kingdom of priests, and an holy nation. These are the words which thou shalt speak unto the children of Israel (Exodus 19:5-6 KJV).

In Deuteronomy Chapter 28, Moses sets out a detailed account of the blessings for fidelity, and the corresponding punishments for infidelity. In Deuteronomy Chapter 30, he offers the people a choice:

> This day I call the heavens and the earth as witnesses against you that I have set before you life and death, blessings and curses. Now choose life, so that you and your children may live (Deuteronomy 30:19 NIV).

Subsequent warnings by the prophets that the Israelites were not keeping Covenant faith with God went unheeded. After the destruction of Jerusalem and the First Temple by the Babylonians circa 597 BC, the prophet Daniel wrote that the "curses" spoken of by Moses had now been poured out upon the Israelites. (See Daniel 9:4-11).

By the time of Jesus, it had become a distinct possibility that Jerusalem and the Second Temple may suffer the same fate under the Romans as they had under the Babylonian King Nebuchadnezzar. Jesus saw it as inevitable rather than possible and so predicted its destruction.

The New Covenant

From the outset, Paul set himself the extremely difficult task of convincing his fellow Israelites that God had entered into yet another Covenant with them. This New Covenant was based on the Resurrection of Jesus, which Paul claimed was a signal to Israelites living in the Diaspora that they would one day be "resurrected" from their dispersion, regarded as a type of symbolic death, and ingathered to Israel to form the Kingdom of God to be ruled over by the Messiah.

The following points represent a few covenant-specific arguments extracted from the wealth of complex and occasionally tortuous material found in Paul's letters:

- The Abrahamic covenant was everlasting and unconditional and had been confirmed by God hundreds of years before the Mosaic Covenant came into existence. Therefore it could never be broken;

- The Mosaic differed from the Abrahamic in that it was conditional and national and its blessings were dependent on the faithfulness of the Israelites as a group. When the conditions were broken, the people suffered "nationally". Having been broken nationally, it was no longer a vehicle for conferring blessings on individuals;

- The Law of Moses was added to the original Ten Words because of the Golden Calf incident in the wilderness (Galatians 3:19 cf. Romans 3:20; 7:7);

- In bringing the knowledge of these transgressions, the Law of Moses was a disciplinarian bringing the people to the Messiah (Galatians 3:24);

Now that the Messiah had come, the people were no longer under a disciplinarian (Galatians 3:25);

- Abraham, the ancestor of all Israelites, was acceptable to God before the Law of Moses came into existence. Therefore, those Israelites living among non-Israelite populations who did not follow the Law of Moses could also be acceptable to God;

- What makes them acceptable is what made Abraham acceptable. Just as Abraham had faith in the power of God to raise Isaac from the dead, so also do the Israelite recipients of Paul's Gospel of God have faith in the power of God to raise Jesus from the dead;

- Just as Abraham's faith in the Israelite God was counted to him for righteousness (Genesis 15:6), so also are all Israelites accounted righteous and acceptable to God if they have the faith of their ancestor Abraham (Galatians 3:5-14) and believe in God's activity on their behalf, specifically in raising Jesus from the dead. These Israelites are the authentic descendants of Abraham;

- The Covenant of Abraham was of faith and faith was not limited to those of physical descent. Those of physical descent, who also had faith, had a natural advantage, but this did not preclude the grafting in of faithful who were of non-Israelite stock. But, as a warning, those who were grafted in should take heed that if the casting away of the Israelite was their reconciliation, then what would the receiving of them be but life from the dead? (Romans 11:15);

- Jesus is the singular heir to the Abrahamic promise of posterity and land (Galatians 3:16). Thus those who have faith in Jesus as the Israelite Messiah are Abraham's descendants and also heirs according to the promise (Galatians 3:26; 29).

Perhaps more than any other passage drawn from the Hebrew Scriptures, Paul modelled his teachings on this promise:

> "The days are coming," declares the Lord, "when I will make a new covenant with the people of Israel and with the people of Judah. It will not be like the covenant I made with their ancestors when I took them by the hand to lead them out of Egypt, because they broke my covenant, though I was a husband to them," declares the Lord. "This is the covenant I will make with the people of Israel after that time," declares the Lord. "I will put my law in their minds and write it on their hearts. I will be their God, and they will be my people. No

longer will they teach their neighbor, or say to one another, 'Know the Lord,' because they will all know me, from the least of them to the greatest" (Jeremiah 31:31-34 NIV).

Section 3

Faith

In traditional Israelite terms, to have "faith" (Hebrew: *emunah*) meant to have steadfast faithfulness towards the God of Israel and to trust that God would act on behalf of Israelites. This trust and faithfulness was expressed by appropriate behaviour towards God and other Israelites.

In the New Testament, the authors supplied the Greek word *pístis* to reflect the meaning of its Hebrew counterpart *emunah*.

In the majority of cases, the Greek *pístis* has been translated into English as "faith", derived from the Latin *fides*, or as "belief", derived from the Latin *cred*. Unfortunately, the English words "faith" and "belief" have come to imply little more than an unquestioning acceptance of the doctrines and creeds of religion. If we define these terms in their original Hebrew and Greek contexts, we will see that "blind belief" was a foreign concept to ancient Israelites.

emunah (Hebrew: אֱמוּנָה)

The first definition of *emunah* in Brown, Driver and Briggs Hebrew-English Lexicon is "firmness, steadfastness, fidelity". Also implied in the word are the concepts of trustworthiness, faithfulness, reliability, and the like. For example, in Romans 1:17 and Galatians 3:11, Paul quotes the final words of Habbakuk 2:4. The majority of English translations render these words as, "…the righteous shall live by faith", wheras the correct translation should be, "…the righteous shall live by his faithfulness (*emunah*)".

The Israelite concept of *emunah* is therefore not an intellectual assent to a creed or list of doctrinal propositions but implies trust in someone or something and steadfast faithfulness to someone or something.

pístis (Greek Πίστις)

The word *pístis* is found in the writings of the ancient Greeks including those of Aristotle, Plato, Herodotus, and etcetera. The Liddell and Scott Greek-English Lexicon is used by every student of ancient Greek in the English-speaking world and is an essential library item in universities. The first definition of *pístis* in Liddell and Scott is "trust in others".

New Testament "faith" and "belief" in Jesus is therefore not blind belief in a set of religious doctrines but unwavering trust that God has once again acted on behalf of Israelites by sending them Messiah Jesus, a man who is to establish the Kingdom of God on Earth, and whom God has raised from the dead. In John's Gospel in particular, we find that "belief" in Jesus means trust that he represents the values and principles of God and not those of God's opposition. One became a follower of Jesus by demonstrating commitment to those same values and principles.

Unquestioning acceptance of doctrine—blind belief—produced a credulity throughout Christendom which became indifferent to the laws of nature and which deprecated reason, research and learning. A craving for the miraculous and supernatural created ever new superstitions or sanctioned, under the form of relic-worship, old pagan forms of belief. One has only to consider the centuries of religious warfare and the multitude of victims slain on the altar of dogmatism to appreciate just how devastating, how diabolical, and how "un-Christian" blind belief can be. Surely a warning for our times with the rise of yet another deadly band of blind believers.

Section 4

Works

There has been a widespread failure to understand that when Paul contrasts "faith" with "works", he is referring to the "works" of the Law of Moses.

As noted previously, Paul's target groups are Israelites living in Greco-Roman societies beyond the confines of the land of Israel. Some of these Israelites practiced the customs of the Judeans who followed the Law of Moses while others did not. The ancestors of some of these Israelites groups had lived in far-flung diaspora communities, perhaps for centuries. Paul argued that if those ancestors had not in the past followed the "works" of the Law such as circumcision, it was unnecessary for their descendants to now revert to a way of life unfamiliar to them. However, whether they did, or did not, was of little account to Paul:

> Circumcision is nothing and uncircumcision is nothing. Keeping God's commands is what counts (1 Corinthians 7:19 NIV).

What did matter to Paul was convincing fellow Israelites that one could not be made acceptable to God simply by observing the "works" of the Law and that their mere performance did not constitute "keeping God's commands". (It should, however, be kept in mind that Jesus and all his disciples observed the Law of Moses.)

Spirit

From time immemorial, humans have attempted to reduce to writing those principles regarded by society as just, worthy and good. However, the written words, the "letter" of the Law, can actually be used to defeat justice unless its underlying "spirit" informs every judgement. Paul recognised this fact nearly two thousand years ago. For him, the deficiency of the Law lay in its "letter":

> But now we have been released from the Law (of Moses), having died to that by which we were bound, so that we serve in newness of the Spirit and not in oldness of the letter (Romans 7:6 NASB).

The New Covenant, says Paul in his letter to the Corinthians, cannot be written in ink. It can only be written by the spirit of God working in people:

> He has made us competent as ministers of a new covenant—not of the letter but of the Spirit; for the letter kills, but the Spirit gives life (2 Corinthians 3:6 NIV).

Section 5

Righteousness

All of Paul's arguments about Faith, Righteousness, Justification, Grace, Election and etcetera are set within a context that has simply been ignored by mainstream Christian theology.

Paul's purpose throughout his letters was to convince Israelites that one could not be made righteous, i.e. made acceptable to God, simply by observing the works of the Law of Moses and that their mere performance did not constitute keeping God's commands. To answer objections from those who believed that in order to keep faith with the God of Israel, all that was required was to observe of the Law of Moses, Paul had to develop a set of arguments based on an entirely new way of thinking about the God of Israel and his actions on behalf of Israelites down through the ages.

Abraham

Thus we find Paul's reliance on the example of Abraham. He taught that just as Abraham's faith in the Israelite God was counted to him for righteousness (Genesis 15:6), so also are all Israelites accounted righteous and acceptable to God if they have the faith of their ancestor Abraham (Galatians 3:5-14) and believe in God's activity on their behalf, specifically in raising Jesus from the dead. Those Israelites could share in the resurrection life of Jesus by emulating his righteousness. Those who do so are "justified", i.e. they are made righteous and acceptable in God's sight.

Orphaned Ignorance

Mainstream Christian theology has removed Paul's teachings from their context and developed a set of arguments based mainly on ignorance of 1st Century AD Israelite cultural norms and modes of expression coupled with an abundance of orphaned "proof" texts.

The common teaching that human righteousness is beyond reach because "fallen" man is incapable of overcoming sin apart from divine enablement derives from the Augustinian doctrine of Total Depravity. These teachers of "total depravity" not only ignore the existence of the many righteous persons mentioned throughout the Bible but also have no compunction about lifting verses out of context to support their doctrinal position. The passage below is an all-time favourite, quoted countless times:

> But we are all as an unclean thing, and all our righteousnesses are as filthy rags; and we all do fade as a leaf; and our iniquities, like the wind, have taken us away (Isaiah 64:6 KJV).

The preceding verses of this passage are simply ignored. Verse 4 actually confirms the existence of righteous persons and their premature "taking away" is given as the cause of the present state of the nation. According to the Soncino Commentary, verses 4-6 are:

> A humble confession of sins and weaknesses, preceded by the plea that the death of the righteous men, whom God had prematurely taken away because of the people's iniquities, was the cause of the nation's degeneration and moral and religious helplessness. [2]

Isaiah 64:4-6 is a community confessional statement applying to the ritually "unclean" such as the leper or the menstruant, hence the "filthy rag/s" (Hebrew: garment of the menstrual period). The term "unclean" has two applications. Firstly, it refers to ritual

---

2   *Isaiah*, Soncino Books of the Bible. Ed. Rev. Dr. A. Cohen. The Soncino Press: London, 1970, p 311.

contamination which rendered a person or thing unfit to participate in religious worship. Secondly, the term could figuratively describe sin and its resulting guilt as contaminating a person, thus rendering that person unacceptable to God.

"Unclean" is the opposite of "holy" (Leviticus 10:10-11). The unclean are not fit to approach God while the holy are set apart for service to God. The Israelites were to be a "holy people" (Leviticus 19:2) so to describe them as "unclean" was a severe reproach.

The righteous ones

Finally, let us consider the doctrine of Total Depravity:

- original sin is both universally debilitating and insuperable without the aid of unmerited grace;
- the human will is free only to sin;
- the human race is comprised of a *massa damnata* (a condemned crowd, a mass of perdition), out of which God, in a manner inscrutable to us, has predestined a small number to be saved.

Now let us allow the New Testament itself to deliver the *coup de grâce* to this teaching by considering the following *massa damnata*, the following condemned crowd of unsaved persons.

Elizabeth and Zechariah

> There was in the days of Herod, the king of Judaea, a certain priest named Zacharias, of the course of Abia: and his wife was of the daughters of Aaron, and her name was Elisabeth. And they were both righteous before God, walking in all the commandments and ordinances of the Lord blameless (Luke 1:5-6 KJV).

Simeon

> Now there was a man in Jerusalem, whose name was Simeon, and this man was righteous and devout, waiting for the consolation of Israel, and the Holy Spirit was upon him (Luke 2:25 ESV).

Abraham, Isaac and Jacob

> I say to you that many will come from the east and the west, and will take their places at the feast with Abraham, Isaac and Jacob in the kingdom of heaven (Matthew 8:11 NIV).

The little ones

> Take heed that ye despise not one of these little ones; for I say unto you, That in heaven their angels do always behold the face of my Father which is in heaven (Matthew 18:10 KJV).

Paul's position is that all who choose to emulate the righteousness of Jesus and to spiritually share in his death and resurrection by crucifying the old "earthy" man and resurrecting the new "spiritual" man have also become righteous and holy, born of God, and fashioned after God's own image:

> You were taught, with regard to your former way of life, to put off your old self, which is being corrupted by its deceitful desires; to be made new in the attitude of your minds; and to put on the new self, created to be like God in true righteousness and holiness (Ephesians 4:22-24 NIV).

Section 6

Justification

To be "justified" is to be declared righteous. Righteousness means being acceptable to God.

Abraham had unswerving loyalty to God and faith in the power of God to raise Isaac from the dead. Because Abraham had that faith in God's power, and he demonstrated that faith by his actions in journeying to Moriah and building there an altar (James 2:20-23), he was therefore "justified", i.e. was declared to be righteous. He was made acceptable to God.

Paul argued that one could not be justified (made righteous) by the outward signs of the "letter" of the Law of Moses—circumcision, dietary laws, calendrical observances etcetera—but one could be justified after the manner of Abraham by having faith in the power of God to raise Jesus from the dead. Just as Abraham demonstrated his faith by actions, so also do those who believe in the resurrection demonstrate their faith by actively emulating the righteousness of Jesus.

Contrast the simplicity of Paul's message with the following commentary on complex Justification theologies.

The Theologies of Justification

The various theologies of Justification supposedly based on the writings of Paul, is the fault line which divided the Catholic and Eastern Orthodox Churches from the Lutheran and Reformed branches of Protestantism during the Reformation.

Significant differences exist between these major denominations as to the means by which a person becomes "justified". The resulting variety of arguments used to either confirm or deny these many conflicting views are of such theological complexity that they stand in defiance of any attempt to provide a concise analysis.

However, because the concept of Justification is claimed to be fundamental to Protestantism, indeed its *raison d'être*, we will therefore make some general remarks focusing on the Protestant view. Before proceeding, however, it must be pointed out that although all the Creeds of Christianity fatally undermine the teachings of the New Testament, Protestant Justification in its most extreme form, such as that taught by Calvinism, is by far the most pernicious in that it distorts the good news of the Gospel into a message of deep and hopeless despair over the human condition, a viewpoint which ultimately derives from the Augustinian doctrine of Total Depravity which holds that all mankind is fallen, sinful, under a curse, and incapable of saving itself.

Justification by faith alone

The doctrine of Justification holds that salvation is the free gift of God received by "grace alone" (*sola gratia*) through "faith alone" (*sola fide*), excluding all works. When a person accepts the free gift of salvation, that person is said to be "justified". The process of justification is God's act of removing the guilt and penalty of sin while at the same time declaring a sinner righteous through Christ's atoning sacrifice. Justification through "faith alone" is also commonly known as "Justification by grace alone through faith alone in Christ's righteousness alone".

For the purposes of demonstration, the author has reproduced below a sample set of arguments used by proponents to explain the doctrine of Justification. Contrast Paul's simple message with the following impenetrable and esoteric jargon so beloved by the theological class:

- The sole ground of our justification is the righteousness of God, expressed in the alien, imputed, active obedience of Christ, climaxing in his sin-bearing, substitutionary death;

- Faith alone is the sole means of justification. In other words, it is faith only, and not our deeds in any way (whether the external manifestation or the internal God-glorifying motive behind them), that connect us savingly to Jesus Christ;

- Faith is distinct from its fruit, the obedience of faith, yet faith is of such a nature that it must and will produce love for people and a life of genuine, though imperfect, holiness in this world. Therefore, as the Westminster Confession of Faith (11.2) says, the faith that alone justifies (as the instrument which unites us to Christ, not as the ground or content of our justifying righteousness) is never alone;

- Therefore, this reality of forensic righteousness, which is imputed to us on the first act of saving faith (as the seed of subsequent persevering faith), is different from transformative sanctification, which is imparted by the work of the Holy Spirit through faith in future grace.

A favourite New Testament quote drummed up in service of the Justification doctrine is:

> For by grace are ye saved through faith; and that not of yourselves: it is the gift of God: Not of works, lest any man should boast (Ephesians 2:8-9 KJV).

However, in the following verses from Romans Chapter 3, it is quite clear that Paul does not contrast faith with good works, but faith with the works of the Law of Moses:

> Therefore no one will be declared righteous in God's sight by the works of the law; rather, through the law we become conscious of our sin...For we maintain that a person is justified by faith apart from the works of the law... (Romans 3:20, 28 NIV).

Compare also the following two statements by Paul where he quotes the same passage from Habakkuk 2:4:

> For in it the righteousness of God is revealed from faith for faith, as it is written, "The righteous shall live by faith" (Romans 1:17 ESV).

> Now it is evident that no one is justified before God by the law, for "The righteous shall live by faith" (Galatians 3:11 ESV).

Note that in the above passages, Paul clarifies in Galatians 3:11 the intent of his statement in Romans 1:17, yet again confirming that when he contrasts "faith" with "works", he is referring specifically to the "works" of the Law of Moses. The passage from Habakkuk 2:4 is claimed to be one of the greatest declarations of faith in the entire Bible:

See, the enemy is puffed up; his desires are not upright—but the righteous person will live by his faithfulness (*emunah*) (Habakkuk 2:4 NIV).

Note

It is interesting to note that the NIV above has at least attempted a more correct translation of the Hebrew *emunah* which, as pointed out previously, implies trust, unwavering conviction, steadfast loyalty and faithfulness *to* "someone", in this context to God.

Section 7

Grace

Origins

The New Testament concept of Grace, regarded by many as the most important concept in Christianity, is drawn exclusively from the Hebrew Scriptures. The New Testament Greek word for this concept is χάρις *(charis)*, which occurs around 160 times (the reading is uncertain in places), and is variously translated into English as "grace", "favour", "gift", "thankfulness", and similar.

To understand the concept that Paul and others meant to convey when they used this Greek word χάρις *(charis)*, we must first determine which of the concepts attached to the following two Hebrew terms were in the forefront of the author's mind at the time of writing a particular passage.

חֶסֶד *(chesed)*

The concept of *chesed* is a central theme of the Hebrew Scriptures, occurring 248 times. Although it can be used of human relationships, when used of the God of Israel in covenant with Israelites, it encapsulates all the positive attributes of such a relationship: steadfast love, covenant faithfulness, mercy, grace, loving kindness, everlasting loyalty and the like. Unfortunately, all the attributes associated with the concept of חֶסֶד *(chesed)* cannot be captured in a single word, either in Greek or in English.

חֵן *(chen)*

The Hebrew term *chen* occurs 69 times in the Hebrew Scriptures. Its two basic meanings are "grace" and "favour". The term refers primarily to the positive disposition one person has towards another and is used in familiar expressions such as "find favour in the eyes/sight of…".

Comparisons

The term *chen* is not as profound as the concept of *chesed*. The words rarely occur together and are found in altogether different environments despite that fact both can be translated with similar words. *Chesed* is a covenant term, most often expressing "covenant love". It presupposes mutual rights and obligations whereas *chen* is not mutual but bestowed by one party on the other. A relationship built on *chesed* is meant for the long-term whereas a *chen* type of relationship may be for a specific time or circumstance and is sustained only so long as the giver desires. Unlike *chesed*, *chen* can be withdrawn freely at any time without consequence.

That *chesed* is both mutual and timeless is expressed eloquently in the following passage:

> Know therefore that the LORD your God is God; he is the faithful God, keeping his covenant of love (*chesed*) to a thousand generations of those who love him and keep his commandments (Deuteronomy 7:9 NIV).

Now consider the purely temporary nature of the *chen* enjoyed by, for example, Joseph in the house of Potiphar the Egyptian:

> And Joseph found grace (*chen*) in his sight, and he served him: and he made him overseer over his house, and all that he had he put into his hand (Genesis 39:4 KJV).

Whether drawing on the attributes attaching to *chen*, or those attaching to the profound concept of *chesed*, the New Testament authors had recourse only to the Greek word *charis* to convey meaning. It is therefore only by context that authorial intent can be established. Before turning to Paul, we may take the following as an example of how to determine authorial intent:

> And the Word was made flesh, and dwelt among us, (and we beheld his glory, the glory as of the only begotten of the Father,) full of grace (*charis*) and truth (*alētheia*) (John 1:14 KJV).

This statement in John 1:14 that Jesus was "full of grace and truth" is drawn directly from the pairing of the Hebrew words *chesed* and *emeth* in Exodus 34:6:

The LORD passed in front of him and proclaimed, "The LORD, the LORD God, compassionate and gracious, slow to anger, and filled with gracious love (*chesed*) and truth (*emeth*)" (Exodus 34:6 ISV).

It is clear from the comparison with Exodus 34:6 that when the author of John used *charis* in 1:14, he was not referring to the short-term attributes of *chen* but rather to the timeless attributes associated with the concept of *chesed*.

Pauline Grace

As noted previously, Paul's target groups are Israelites living in Greco-Roman societies beyond the confines of the land of Israel. Some of these Israelites practiced the "barbaric" customs of the Jews (Judeans) who followed the Law of Moses, while other Israelites practiced the customs of "civilised" Hellenists.

Paul's grace teachings were designed to counter the arguments of his Jewish (Judean) opponents, i.e. those who taught that it was obligatory for all Israelites to practice the works of the Law of Moses. Paul argued that it was not necessary for any Israelite to continue to perform these works, as the Judeans did, because if they had faith in what the God of Israel had done on their behalf in raising up Jesus, then they had already been declared righteous and justified apart from the Law of Moses. As Israelites who had faith in what God had done on their behalf, they were joint heirs to the Abrahamic Covenant promises and therefore already recipients of Covenant grace.

The following passage from Romans is oft-quoted and much-beloved by proponents of certain theological understandings of Pauline grace so it will be focal point of our analysis of Paul's teachings:

> And if by grace (*charis*), then it cannot be based on works; if it were, grace (*charis*) would no longer be grace (*charis*) (Romans 11:6 NIV).

This brief statement cannot be viewed in isolation, as is the preferred habit of many theologians and academics, but must be viewed in both its immediate and overall context, a context which is rich in meaning, and more so in consequence for mainstream Christianity.

Context

The letter is addressed to Jesus group members in Rome. This group consists of:

- Jews, i.e. those who follow the customs and practices of the Judeans who worship at the Temple in Jerusalem and observe the works of the Law of Moses including the practice of circumcision;

- A sprinkling of non-Israelites.

In Romans 10:21, Paul has already expressed his sorrow over the reality that many of his brethren have rejected Jesus although they are still considered to be "Israel", and this is a fact witnessed in the Hebrew Scriptures (cf. Isaiah 65:2).

Now for the all-important verses preceding verse 6:

> I say then, Did God cast off his people? God forbid. For I also am an Israelite, of the seed of Abraham, of the tribe of Benjamin. God did not cast off his people which he foreknew. Or know ye not what the scripture saith of Elijah? how he pleadeth with God against Israel: "Lord, they have killed thy prophets, they have digged down thine altars; and I am left alone, and they seek my life"(1 Kings 19:10, 14). But what saith the answer of God unto him? "I have left for myself seven thousand men, who have not bowed the knee to Baal" (1 Kings 19:18). Even so then at this present time also there is a remnant according to the election of grace (*charis*) (Romans 11:1-5 ASV).
>
> But if it is by grace (*charis*), it is no more of works: otherwise grace (*charis*) is no more grace (*charis*)" (Romans 11:6 ASV).

Consider all that is encapsulated in this one passage:

- God has not rejected his Covenant people;

- Just as there had been a remnant faithful to the Covenant in the time of Elijah, so also is there still a faithful remnant;

- The remnant are the recipients of Covenant grace despite the fact that they do not observe the works of the Law of Moses practiced by the Jews of Rome who follow the customs and practices of the Judeans who worship at the Temple in Jerusalem.

When considering that this passage is all about the Israelite Covenant, there can be no doubt that when Paul used the word *charis* here, he is referring directly to *chesed*, the grace of God which is bestowed on "those who love him and keep his commandments" (Deuteronomy 7:9).

Many would disagree with the connection between *chesed* and New Testament grace for the simple reason that if grace is the equivalent of *chesed*, then it originally applied to the Israelite Covenant people and more broadly to those non-Israelites who subsequently joined the Covenant on the terms laid down by Paul in Romans Chapter 11.

Perhaps because of a negative view of the Israelite Covenant, combined with the teaching of Supersessionism, c*hesed* is never translated as "grace" in English versions of the Hebrew Scriptures but more often with inadequate words such as "mercy" or "love".

However, as already noted, all the attributes associated with the concept of חֶסֶד (*chesed*) cannot be captured in a single word, either in Greek or in English. Although a compromise, for once this author agrees with Martin Luther who realised that the nearest New Testament single word equivalent to the Hebrew *chesed* was the Greek word χάρις *(charis)*.

Given that all Paul's teachings are set within an Israelite Covenant framework, his use of *charis* therefore refers to the Hebrew concept of *chesed*, except where it obviously refers to something more transitory such as that expressed by the Hebrew term *chen*.

Once again, the bewildering variety of grace teachings reflects ignorance on the part of mainstream Christian theology: ignorance about the Israelite Covenant framework within which all Paul's teachings are set; ignorance about the composition of Paul's target groups; and ignorance about Paul specifically referring to the works of the Law of Moses when contrasting "faith" with "works" and "faith" with "grace".

Theological Grace

Notes

Mainstream theological grace teachings are inextricably entwined with their teachings on Justification, Righteousness, Election and Pre-Destination.

The many and varied disputes about the means by which grace is conferred upon recipients divides Catholicism from Protestantism, Calvinism from Arminianism, and modern theological liberalism from theological conservatism. While this author does not intend to indulge the proponents of all this theological nit-picking by delving into the maze, the central role that the concept of grace has assumed in Christian theology makes it nevertheless necessary to address the doctrine that represents the most extreme distortion of Pauline teachings—Sovereign Grace.

Sovereign Grace

Although not limited to Calvinism or Reformed Theology, it is Calvinism's doctrine of Sovereign Grace which appears to excite the most heated debates in the closed corridors of academia. As with the doctrine of Protestant Justification in its most extreme form, the doctrine of Sovereign Grace distorts the good news of the Gospel into a message of deep and hopeless despair over the human condition, a viewpoint which ultimately derives from the Augustinian doctrine of Total Depravity which holds that all mankind is fallen, sinful, under a curse, and incapable of saving itself.

TULIP

The five points of Calvinism's doctrine of Sovereign Grace, more commonly known by the acronym TULIP, are Total Depravity; Unconditional Election; Limited Atonement; Irresistible Grace; and the Perseverance of the Saints. Whilst there are slightly different explanations of these terms, their core meanings remain essentially the same. The teachings of Total Depravity and Atonement (limited or otherwise) are addressed in Part VIII: S*in and Salvation,* so we will deal here with the remaining three of these five points.

- *Unconditional Election*
  Before Creation, God chose a group of people, the elect, not based on anything they would do in the future, either good or bad, but based solely on the merit of Jesus. God's purpose was to save these elect people before they even sinned.

- *Irresistible Grace*
  God, using the same power it took to raise Jesus from the dead, works in the heart of the elect to give them eternal life by imputing to them the righteousness of Jesus and regenerating them by the Holy Spirit, giving them both faith and repentance to trust in God and reject their own righteousness.

- *Perseverance of the Saints*
  God preserves the elect based solely upon the work Jesus did for them, which put them in the unchanging, legal state of Justification. This means they are not only forgiven but also placed in the state where sin cannot be imputed or charged to them. They are forgiven for all past, present and future sins and are judged perfectly righteous based on the imputation of the righteousness of Jesus. God dwells in the justified through the Spirit and works in them to produce good works by faith throughout life.

These three points are only sets of inferences drawn from teachings on Righteousness, Justification, Election and Pre-Destination. To examine these points in detail is to reverse the logical order of argument. One must first examine whether the particular view of the teachings on which they are based is valid. If invalid, then all drawn inferences are also invalid. Since we have examined the teachings of Righteousness and Justification and found them to be invalid, then so also are their drawn inferences. All that remains now is to address the twin teachings of Election and Pre-Destination. Firstly, however, a brief reflection on the subject of "free will".

Section 8

Free Will

The extent to which man is able to exercise free will is a question that has plagued philosophers and theologians for millennia. It is not a question that has ever been answered with any degree of satisfaction or certainty. Whilst the aim of this work is to compare the scriptural record with the theologies that have been taught in its name, the twin subjects of Election and Pre-Destination demand a little philosophical reflection on the subject of free will from a Biblical perspective.

Before proceeding, however, it is advisable to keep in mind the following factors:

- The Bible would never have been written if its authors had not believed that the God of Israel intervened in human history;

- The Bible is for the most part a record of those interventions;

- Every word of the Bible emerged from a uniquely Israelite cultural milieu, and from an authorial perspective afforded by hindsight;

- At every stage, scripture authors could reflect upon the past and interpret the present impact of events, beginning with Adam and ending with Jesus, which may have held little significance for some of the participants at the actual time;

- Thus when scripture authors describe a person as being "elected" by God, it is only because they can reflect on the impact that person has had on subsequent events;

- Whether applied to an entire people, or to sub-groups, or to individuals, the Biblical concept of election is always for the specific purpose of furthering what was perceived to be God's will on earth.

The question for us to answer is the same as that sought by said philosophers and theologians: if humans possess free will, how can it be claimed that anyone is "elected" to perform God's will?

Perhaps this question should be framed differently. Did God choose Abraham? Or did Abraham freely choose the one God rather than the many gods of his pagan ancestors? Did God choose the Israelite people to be his standard bearers on earth? Or did the Israelites freely choose to follow the God of their ancestors Abraham, Isaac and Jacob? Did God choose the members of Paul's Jesus groups? Or did those members freely choose to follow Jesus? The same question could be asked of all those the Bible describes as being "elected" by God, including Moses, the prophets, the disciples, and Jesus of Nazareth.

The God of the Israelites is consistently depicted as a God of truth who has everlasting love for his people. The drawing power of love being greater by many orders of magnitude than the coercive power of fear, is it not a possibility that successive generations of Israelites were drawn by a reciprocal love of God and love of truth to serve him and strive to accomplish what they perceived to be his will?

Or is it a combination of both? Paul certainly believed after his Road to Damascus experience that God had directly called him to be a prophet in the tradition of the Israelite prophets of old, as did Jesus at his baptism. It is impossible for any of us to be certain of the inner thoughts and motivations of others, especially of those so removed in terms of time, cultural norms and common beliefs. Through our own experience, however, we can be certain of the ageless drawing power of that self-sacrificing love witnessed by so many down through the ages.

Finally, humans cannot exist in a state of untrammeled free will. Whether imposed externally by nature and by the requirements of community living, or internally by the dictates of conscience, we are at all times subject to certain boundaries. This human condition has never changed and is reflective of the allegory of the Garden of Eden in which we are told that man was created with free will but subject to certain boundaries. Adam and Eve possessed the freedom to choose good over evil, and the freedom to choose life rather than death. They chose instead to step outside the boundaries of behaviour set by God in the pursuit of self-interest and self-glorification. They fell from favour through the exercise of their own untrammeled free will.

Having presented these personal reflections and perceptions, we must return to the stated aim of this work, which is to compare the scriptural record with the theologies taught in its name. To do justice to these comparisons, it is necessary to take the scriptural record and the perceptions of its authors at face value and proceed on the basis that God does the "electing".

Section 9

Election

The concept of "election" derives from the Hebrew Scriptures and the New Testament where the Israelites are presented as a "chosen people", i.e. chosen to be in Covenant with the God of Israel for the purpose of spreading the knowledge of God to all the peoples of the earth:

> They shall not hurt nor destroy in all my holy mountain: for the earth shall be full of the knowledge of the LORD, as the waters cover the sea (Isaiah 11:9 KJV).

The Hebrew Scriptures clearly state that being "elected" does not imply superiority or privilege but rather entails a host of obligations and duties both to God and to fellow humans, such obligations and duties being commensurate with the awesome responsibility of being chosen by the God of Israel.

Consider first the conditional nature of election:

> "... 'Now therefore, if you will indeed obey my voice and keep my covenant, you shall be my treasured possession among all peoples, for all the earth is mine; and you shall be to me a kingdom of priests and a holy nation.' These are the words that you shall speak to the people of Israel" (Exodus 19:5-6 ESV).

Now consider that the corollary of being singled out and then failing to keep the Covenant obligations means to be singled out for punishment:

> You only have I chosen of all the families of the earth; therefore I will punish you for all your sins (Amos 3:2 NIV).

Yet Israelites were exhorted to remember that even if they descended into sin and darkness, God's *chesed*, his Covenant loyalty and love for them would endure forever. (See Psalm 136 where praise of God's *chesed* is repeated 26 times.)

Choice

It is self-righteous and arrogant in the extreme to make judgements on the ultimate fate of others or to decide for oneself if an individual or group has, or has not, been chosen to perform God's will on Earth. With those reservations in mind, it is possible, however, to discern values which contributed to the choice or election of Jesus and his followers:

For example, in Romans 8:28, Paul declares that the "called" ones, the "chosen" ones are those who already love God, i.e. those who already obey the first and greatest commandment:

> And we know that all things work together for good to them that love God, to them who are the called according to his purpose (Romans 8:28 KJV).

The author of the Book of Hebrews, in applying Psalm 45:7 to Jesus, states that Jesus was chosen because of his love of "righteousness" and his hatred of "iniquity":

> Thou hast loved righteousness, and hated iniquity; therefore God, even thy God, hath anointed thee with the oil of gladness above thy fellows (Hebrews 1:9 KJV).

In Matthew 5:6, Jesus blesses those who hunger and thirst for that same "righteousness":

> Blessed are they which do hunger and thirst after righteousness: for they shall be filled (Matthew 5:6 KJV).

Similarly, in John 18:37, Jesus states that his voice will be heard by those in whom "truth" is already present:

> "…Everyone who is of the truth hears My voice" (John 18:37 NASB).

In the context of the New Testament, these fundamental values already present in the disciples—love of God, love of neighbour, love of truth and righteousness—led them to identify with Jesus, just as the absence of these values led others to oppose him.

All that being said, however, and whether applied to an entire people, or to sub-groups, or to individuals, election is always for the specific purpose of furthering God's will on Earth.

The refiners fire

Millennia ago, the prophet Isaiah recognised that the sterling qualities of character able to withstand the forces of opposition to God could only be forged through suffering in the "refiner's fire".

His "suffering servant" theme (Isaiah 52:13-53:12) not only applies to the nation in a corporate sense but also finds its fullest expression in the ideal Israelite, Jesus of Nazareth, the *imago dei*, a man who perfectly reflected the holiness and righteousness of God and demonstrated by example how we may live lives of similar holiness and righteousness, i.e. he brought the knowledge of salvation. As we know, the author of this salvation was made perfect through suffering (Hebrews 2:10).

One has only to consider the fate of the elect—the Israelite people as a whole, the prophets, the disciples, Jesus of Nazareth—to recognise that they are not chosen for any sort of reward, not chosen to live while others die. Rather, they are chosen for a purpose, for greater responsibility, to be God's instruments for fulfilling the Abrahamic promise to spiritually bless all nations with the true knowledge of God, thereby bringing many to salvation.

However, this spiritual blessing has been purchased through wholesale physical suffering and death. Indeed the badge of election is suffering. One should rather pray *not* to be chosen. How then can it be claimed that, for some inscrutable reason, the elect are chosen to live and the non-elect to die? Jesus of Nazareth died so that the non-elect may live.

The drawing power of love is greater by many orders of magnitude than the coercive power of fear. Thus Jesus' exhortation to love your enemies, and his demonstration of a love that will lay down its life for others, has motivated and energised untold numbers of persons over these long centuries to follow in his footsteps and live lives of service and self-sacrifice leading to salvation (1 Corinthians 11:1; 1 Peter 2:21).

However, the really "good news" of the Gospel is that salvation can be earned by all who emulate the righteousness of Jesus, whether they consciously follow in his footsteps or not. The values which he embodied—truth versus lies; the spirit of the law rather than the letter; humility versus arrogance; personal integrity versus institutional formalism; selflessness; and commitment to principle even to the extent of laying down his own life—are universal and timeless. They cut across every human division. Therefore, one does not need to be a Christian, or have ever heard of Jesus, to enter the Kingdom (be "saved"). All that matters in the final analysis is the living of a "christ-like" life, whether one realises it or not.

Contrary to the claims of the Calvinists and their co-religionists that only the elect are saved through the merits of Jesus and all the rest are damned, the elect are only a fraction of these saved, only a part of the "great multitude, which no man could number, out of every nation and of all tribes and peoples and tongues…" (Revelation 7:9).

The God of Israel is consistently portrayed as exemplifying the qualities of love, mercy, righteousness and justice. For the characters peopling the pages of the New Testament, the God of the Calvinists and their co-religionists would have been perceived as a ruthless and cruel despot, merciless, unjust, and utterly foreign.

Few beliefs have been the primary reason for so much death and destruction as this concept of election. Mainstream Christian thought is that God first entered into a covenant with the Israelite people but because Jesus was rejected by Israelites, the God of Israel felt snubbed, played a type of tit-for-tat, rejected Israelites, and entered into a new covenant with a new religion called Christianity whose adherents became the new "people of God". (See *Supersessionism* in forthcoming Chapter.)

Section 10

Pre-Destination

For ancient Israelites, the God of Israel was the Creator of Heaven and Earth and everything contained therein. God was omnipotent and omniscient and must be accorded appropriate homage, worship and respect. It was a common belief that if something happened, no matter how small or how great, God had decreed it and therefore had foreknowledge of the event.

Given the type of reasoning behind this common Israelite belief, it is no surprise to discover that a major premise of the Bible is that the God of Israel knew the end from the beginning and made provision for mans' redemption before Creation. Jesus of course plays *the* major redemptive role:

> He was foreknown before the foundation of the world but was made manifest in the last times for the sake of you who through him are believers in God, who raised him from the dead and gave him glory, so that your faith and hope are in God (1 Peter 1:20-21 ESV).

Whilst it is also used in support of the Sovereign Grace teachings on Election and Justification, the following passage from Romans is primarily called upon by proponents to support their Pre-Destination teaching:

> For those God foreknew he also predestined to be conformed to the image of his Son, that he might be the firstborn among many brothers and sisters. And those he predestined, he also called; those he called, he also justified; those he justified, he also glorified (Romans 8:29-30 NIV).

This passage from Romans has nothing to do with genuine pre-destination: it is simply a reflection of Paul's belief that God had in past times decreed the present and must be accorded retrospective credit.

As pointed out previously, Adam and Eve possessed the freedom to choose good over evil and the freedom to choose life rather than death. Their choices were theirs alone, and their destiny solely in their hands. There is no room in this or any other Biblical story for the teaching of Pre-Destination, as is clearly illustrated in this passage from Deuteronomy where the Israelites are exhorted to "choose life":

> This day I call the heavens and the earth as witnesses against you that I have set before you life and death, blessings and curses. Now choose life, so that you and your children may live (Deuteronomy 30:19 NIV).

No person's destiny is pre-determined—it is possible to fall out of favour with God, as did King Solomon (1 Chronicles 28:5-7).

Although Solomon had been elected by God to sit on the throne of Israel, it was conditional on his carrying out the commands and laws of God. Solomon subsequently fell from favour for leading Israel into idolatry, the consequences of which were catastrophic both for the nation and for Solomon's descendants.

Section 11

The Greatest Commandment

In the anti-introspective, collectivist society of the First Century AD, "love" always possessed the underlying meaning of attachment to God or group of persons. In this society, there was no term for an internal state that did entail a corresponding external action. "Love" always meant appropriate public actions which supported the well-being of the persons to whom one was attached.

The type of "love" most commonly referenced in today's popular culture is characterised mainly by self-interest, a weak sentimentality and an excess of emotion. The type of "love" embodied in Jesus of Nazareth, however, is of an entirely different order—strength of character, determined will, sacrifice of self-interest, and a clear head unclouded by an excess of feeling. And, yes, one that will lay down its life for others if necessary (John 15:13).

For Jesus, love of God and love of neighbour were the greatest commandments of the Law (Matthew 12:29-31). For Paul also, love was the greatest commandment of the Law (Galatians 5:14). Both Jesus and Paul upheld the Hebrew Scriptures and everything contained therein. Both claimed that their teachings fulfilled the Law and were all reducible to this one commandment of love.

Section 12

Supersessionism

Interpretive Principles of Paul's theology:

- Except for the Epistle to the Romans, Paul directed his Epistles to Israelite Jesus groups that he founded and there is no evidence that he showed any interest whatever in non-Israelites;

- When Paul uses the designation "Jew", he is referring mainly to those who follow the customs and practices of the Judeans who worship in the Jerusalem Temple and follow the Law of Moses (see Chapter 2 for categories of persons designated "Jews"). When he uses the designation "Greek", he is referring mainly to Greek-speaking Jews and other Israelites who live in diaspora communities scattered throughout the Roman Empire;

- Paul is fully immersed in the history of his own people and all his teachings are set within an Abrahamic covenantal framework.

Failure to recognise and accept these interpretive principles has led to the teaching of "Supersessionism", more recently known as "Replacement Theology", which essentially voids all of Paul's teachings. Consider his warning to the non-Israelites among the Roman Jesus Group:

> If some of the branches have been broken off, and you, though a wild olive shoot, have been grafted in among the others and now share in the nourishing sap from the olive root, do not consider yourself to be superior to those other branches. If you do, consider this: You do not support the root, but the root supports you. You will say then, 'Branches were broken off so that I could be grafted in.' Granted. But they were broken off because of unbelief, and you stand by faith. Do not be arrogant, but tremble. For if God did not spare the natural branches, he will not spare you either (Romans 11:17-21 NIV).

Paul's warning to non-Israelites has either been rejected or simply ignored for nearly two millennia, during which time the theological teaching of Supersessionism, first developed by such men as Justin Martyr (circa 100 to 165 AD), Irenaeus of Lyon (circa 130 to 202 AD) and Origen of Alexandria (185-254), became the dominant interpretation of Christian history.

This teaching asserts that because the majority of Jews (Judeans) in the First Century AD did not accept Jesus as their Messiah, God poured out his wrath upon them and destroyed both nation and Temple in 70 AD. God also terminated his Covenants with the Israelite people and transferred them to the followers of Christianity who are the new people of God. Christianity is the true Israel and the sole heir to God's Covenant blessings.

Fathers of the church indulged themselves in tirades of demonisation and condemnation, which only increased in fervour and ferocity when Christianity was declared the official religion of the Roman Empire in 380 AD. This now state-sanctioned vitriol was to rain relentlessly down upon the heads of the Jews throughout these long centuries, all the while smoothing an inevitable path to the gas chambers.

Responsibility for this descent into the abyss must be attributed in large measure to a multi-generational failure by those many teachers who either did not know, or did not care to know, to whom the designation "Jew" referred, or to whom Paul addressed his letters. (See Chapter 2: *Paul and his world*.)

In the wake of the Holocaust, many mainstream Christian churches began the work of hand-washing, back-tracking, modifying, excusing, and even attempting to undo the teaching of Supersessionism. But there will be no redemption for the major institutions of Christianity.

Section 13

Wrapping-Up Paul

It is difficult to find words in the English language to adequately describe Paul's horror had he known to what use his writings would be put in the service of Hellenist-based Christian doctrines and teachings.

Those who accept these doctrines and teachings without question would assert that "faith" is the ability to accept as reality what one cannot fully understand. However, as demonstrated previously, the English word "faith" has come to imply nothing more than an unquestioning belief in the doctrines of religion whereas such "blind belief" was a concept utterly foreign to those who wrote the Bible. Thus Paul's injunction to his brethren that they should present their bodies as a living sacrifice which is holy and pleasing to God and that their service should conform to human reason, a "logiken latreian", has fallen on deaf ears (Romans 12:1).

However, the inexorable forward march of knowledge will ensure that, one day, the doctrines, the traditions, the forms, the rituals, the theological empire-building, and the mind-numbing complexities introduced by the Christian churches over the last two millennia will be tossed into the theological rubbish bins of history.

And what will be left of Paul's teachings then? Just one simple dictum—follow the old man, Adam, or the new man, Jesus. Our choice.

Finally, lest it be thought that the teachings of Protestantism in general, and of Calvinism in particular, receive an undue share of critical attention, it must be pointed out that all the Creeds, doctrines and teachings of mainstream Christianity fatally undermine the teachings of the New Testament and, therefore, all major denominations of Christendom stand under the same indictment.

Note

Some topics raised only in passing are addressed in detail elsewhere in this work.

PART VIII

Sin and Salvation

CHAPTER ONE

Original Sin

The Augustinian View

Although Augustine of Hippo (354-430 AD) is largely credited with devising the theory of Original Sin, its genesis as early as the 2nd Century can be found in the writings of Church Fathers such as Irenaeus.

Before Augustine's conversion to Christianity in 386 AD, he had embraced the teaching of Hellenist dualism which views the world as a battle between light and dark, between spirit and flesh.

After Augustine's conversion, he began to sift through the Bible searching for scriptural justification for the theory of Original Sin. Unfortunately for the many generations of Christians to follow, he interpreted his findings through the lens of Hellenist philosophy, especially Neoplatonism, and concluded that sin was passed biologically from Adam to all his descendants through the sexual act.

The abridged article below is taken from the Stanford Encyclopedia of Philosophy:

> By the time Augustine completed De Civitate Dei in 427 C.E., he came even more emphatically to insist upon the conclusion to which his discussion in Ad Simplicianum had led him, i.e., that original sin is both universally debilitating and insuperable without the aid of unmerited grace [De Civitate Dei XIV.1]. Furthermore, there is a predestination at work that is as rigorous as the foreknowledge by which God knows its results [De Civitate Dei XIV.11]. Here too Augustine insists that we are morally culpable for the sinful choices that the will makes [De Civitate Dei XIV.3], but under the pressures of the Pelagian controversy—a controversy in which he will find his earlier words being cited against him [see Retractationes I.9.3–6]—he presents these views in a manner that is austere and uncompromising. So damaging are the effects of the original sin that the human will is free only to sin [De Correptione et Gratia 1.2; 11.31; Rist 1972, pg. 223]. Thus, the human race is comprised of a massa damnata [De Dono Perseverantiae 35; see also De Civitate Dei XXI.12], out of which God, in a manner inscrutable to us [De Civitate Dei XII.28], has predestined a small

number to be saved [De Civitate Dei XXI.12], and to whom he has extended a grace without which it is impossible for the will not to sin. [1]

For Augustine then:

- original sin is both universally debilitating and insuperable without the aid of unmerited grace;
- the human will is free only to sin;
- the human race is comprised of a *massa damnata* (a condemned crowd, a mass of perdition), out of which God, in a manner inscrutable to us, has predestined a small number to be saved.

Augustinian adoption...more and less

Most Christian denominations teach that humans are born in Original Sin but in varying degrees ranging from a "slight tendency" towards sin without collective guilt, all the way through to "total depravity" with automatic collective guilt.

The vast array of Original Sin teachings are so complex, so confused, and even contradictory, that it is not possible to document the resulting theological stew here. Suffice to say that some of these teachings, especially those of Calvinism and like-minded denominations, are utterly alien to Israelite thought and misrepresent everything that the Bible teaches about God's relationship with humans.

The Biblical View

The Hebrew Scriptures

Genesis Chapter 3 describes humans who know what God's boundaries are, who know the consequences of stepping outside those boundaries, and who deliberately choose to do so anyway. When the humans disobey, they destroy their relationship with God, with each other, and even with the world in which they live. Through their premature aspiration to be like God (Genesis 3:5), they instead bring disorder, disharmony, and the threat of death into the world.

In Biblical terms, "sin" is shaming or dishonouring the God of Israel. This is clearly the nature of the "sin" committed by Adam and Eve whose behaviour shamed and dishonoured their Creator.

---

[1] Stanford Encyclopedia of Philosophy: *Saint Augustine*. First published Fri Mar 24, 2000; substantive revision Fri Nov 12, 2010. Accessed 5 May 2017. https://plato.stanford.edu/entries/augustine/

Their "sin" is not the type of sin that we in the English-speaking world commonly associate with the word, e.g. murder, theft, bearing false witness and etcetera. Rather it is the type of sin referred to in the New Testament as *hamartia*.

The New Testament

The Greek word *hamartia* is by far the most common Greek word for "sin" in the New Testament, where it is used in its various forms over 220 times. It is derived from the root word *hamartanō* which, historically, was an archer's term that meant to "miss the mark", to "fall short of the objective". Thus, according to context, it may mean heading in the wrong direction, or reaching the wrong destination, or making an error of judgement due to ignorance, or taking any action which, for whatever reason, ends in failure rather than success.

Paul

The Pauline idea of "sin" is widely misunderstood. For Paul "…everything that does not come from faith is sin (Romans 14:23).

The Israelite view had been that all non-Israelites were "sinners," regardless of whether or not they had actually sinned, e.g. murder, theft, bearing false witness etcetera. Paul contrasts this view with his New Covenant of faith proposition that "sinners" are the unredeemed, and that persons commit "sin" whether they are Israelite insiders or non-Israelite outsiders.

We can see this clearly in Romans 4 where Abraham's pre-covenantal status is synonymous with the state of the "sinner." For Paul, those truly inside the New Covenant of faith are "non-sinners" whether Israelite or non-Israelite.

This idea is also expressed so clearly in 1 John 3:7-9 that it bears repeating:

> Little children, let no one deceive you. Whoever practices righteousness is righteous, as he is righteous. Whoever makes a practice of sinning is of the devil, for the devil has been sinning from the beginning. The reason the Son of God appeared was to destroy the works of the devil. No one born of God makes a practice of sinning, for God's seed abides in him; and he cannot keep on sinning, because he has been born of God (1 John 3:7-9 ESV).

We can see from the above passage that, in New Testament terms, "righteousness" is the equivalent of "sinlessness". When persons such as Zechariah and Elizabeth are described as "righteous", it means they are non-sinners.

Baptism

Biblical View

The author of Mark opens his account of the life of Jesus by telling his readers that he has good news to tell them. Mark then identifies John the Baptist with the messenger from Malachi 3:1 and the voice crying in wilderness from Isaiah 40:3. With the appearing of John, the one who prepares the way, his readers know that he is about to announce the arrival of the long-awaited Israelite Messiah:

> The beginning of the gospel of Jesus Christ, the Son of God; As it is written in the prophets, Behold, I send my messenger before thy face, which shall prepare thy way before thee. The voice of one crying in the wilderness, Prepare ye the way of the Lord, make his paths straight. John did baptize in the wilderness (*erémos*), and preach the baptism of repentance (*metanoias*) for the remission of sins (*hamartiōn*) (Mark 1:1-4 KJV).

Whether considered necessary to wash away original sin or not, whether considered necessary for salvation or not, whether considered necessary for infants or not, Baptism is the central rite of identity governing the great majority of Christian denominations. It is, therefore, vitally important to acquire a correct understanding of the Greek words *erémos*, *metanoia* and *harmatia*.

erémos - wilderness

In Israelite thought, the wilderness was a place of renewal and hope where God revealed himself through Moses; where God provided the water and the manna; and where God prepared the way into the promised land.

metanoia - repentance

The Greek word *metanoia* translated into English as "repentance", means to change one's mind, to take a new direction, to think differently. In the New Testament, it is a call for total change, a reorientation of one's entire being away from the world in which one now lives and towards the coming Kingdom of God.

harmatia - sin

As already pointed out, the Greek word *hamartia*, translated into English as "sin", conveys the idea of heading in the wrong direction; or reaching the wrong destination; or making errors of judgement due to ignorance; and, finally, of failure.

Thus, these three Greek words complement each other perfectly. John is preaching in the wilderness, a place of renewal, and proclaiming that both collective Israel and individual Israelites have been heading in the wrong direction. They need to start heading in the right direction and show their willingness to do so by immersing themselves in the waters of the Jordan in preparation for the coming of the Messiah.

Extra-Biblical View

The Jewish Encyclopaedia describes Baptism in the following terms:

> Baptism is a Jewish religious ablution signifying purification or consecration… Baptism is not merely for the purpose of expiating a special transgression, as is the case chiefly in the violation of the so-called Levitical laws of purity; but it is to form a part of holy living and to prepare for the attainment of a closer communion with God. [2]

According to the Encyclopaedia, Baptism is not merely for the purpose of expiating a purity transgression but to prepare one for a closer communion with God. However, since the historian Josephus wrote about John the Baptist and therefore provides us with a contemporary view, his record is of paramount importance:

> But to some of the Jews the destruction of Herod's defeat is attributed to his murder of John the Baptist. Herod's army seemed to be divine vengeance, and certainly a just vengeance, for his treatment of John, surnamed the Baptist. For Herod had put him to death, though he was a good man and had exhorted the Jews to lead righteous lives, to practise justice towards their fellows and piety towards God, and so doing to join in baptism. In his view this was a necessary preliminary if baptism was to be acceptable to God. They must not employ it to gain pardon for whatever sins they committed, but as a consecration of the body implying that the soul was already thoroughly cleansed by right behaviour.[3]

According to Josephus, John's view was that Baptism could not be acceptable to God unless one had already been cleansed by righteous behaviour towards God and towards fellow Israelites. Neither should it be employed as a mechanism to gain pardon for sin because Baptism stands at the end of the process rather than the beginning.

After weighing the evidence noted above, it becomes clear that the Christian understanding of Baptism is based on a flawed understanding that the ritual was intended to "wash" away sin when, in reality, it was mainly a symbolic consecration

---

[2] Jewish Encyclopaedia, Article: *Baptism*, Kaufmann Kohler, Samuel Krauss. Accessed 10 May 2017 http://www.jewishencyclopedia.com/articles/2456-baptism

[3] Josephus: *Jewish Antiquities*. xviii. 116-119 in Books 18-19, Loeb Classical Library, No. 433, trans. Louis H. Feldman, Harvard University Press: 1965.

of one who had been already cleansed by righteous behaviour and wished to demonstrate commitment to a new way of life.

John the Baptist came preaching a message of renewal, hope and joy. Rather than reflecting this message, certain Christian denominations such as Calvinism teach the hopeless, joyless, doctrine of Total Depravity. Rather than allow ourselves to sink into this morass with the Calvinists, we will instead allow the New Testament to deliver the *coup de grâce* to this teaching by considering the following *massa damnata*, the following condemned crowd of unsaved and unbaptised persons.

Elizabeth and Zechariah

> There was in the days of Herod, the king of Judaea, a certain priest named Zacharias, of the course of Abia: and his wife was of the daughters of Aaron, and her name was Elisabeth. And they were both righteous before God, walking in all the commandments and ordinances of the Lord blameless (Luke 1:5-6 KJV).

Simeon

> Now there was a man in Jerusalem, whose name was Simeon, and this man was righteous and devout, waiting for the consolation of Israel, and the Holy Spirit was upon him (Luke 2:25 ESV).

Abraham, Isaac and Jacob

> I say to you that many will come from the east and the west, and will take their places at the feast with Abraham, Isaac and Jacob in the kingdom of heaven (Matthew 8:11 NIV).

The little ones

> Take heed that ye despise not one of these little ones; for I say unto you, That in heaven their angels do always behold the face of my Father which is in heaven (Matthew 18:10 KJV).

The belief in Original Sin and the necessity to wash it away only developed centuries after the New Testament was written. Thus the concept of inheriting Original Sin and a "fallen" nature from Adam would have been viewed as preposterous by Jesus, by John the Baptist, and by all their contemporaries.

CHAPTER TWO

Sin and its Atonement

The violations of God's boundaries, with the resulting defilement of the community and the world, were taken very seriously by ancient Israelites. Sin, even if accidental, brought a disruption of God's order and harmony that needed correction. Their worship rituals, especially those associated with blood sacrifice, symbolised their acknowledgement of the magnitude of the sin they had brought into the world. If retributive justice were exacted, then it is they who should die rather than the animals. Yet God in his grace and mercy allowed them to atone for their sins with a lesser sacrifice, thus effecting reconciliation with a people who were deserving of death. The entire sacrificial system of the ancient Israelites was designed to testify to the grace and mercy of Israel's God.

Sin and Atonement in the Hebrew Scriptures

Both the Hebrew Scriptures and the New Testament draw clear distinctions between intentional and unintentional sin, and between individual and corporate atonement. A failure to recognise these distinctions is certainly the basis for all the disputations on this subject between the various denominations of Christendom and has given rise to all the fatally flawed teachings about sin and its atonement.

The shedding of blood

Israelites were forbidden to eat blood. Blood was sacred and it was considered that the most fitting use for something sacred was upon the altar:

> For the life of the flesh is in the blood, and I have given it for you on the altar to make atonement for your souls, for it is the blood that makes atonement by the life. Therefore I have said to the people of Israel, No person among you shall eat blood, neither shall any stranger who sojourns among you eat blood (Leviticus 17:11-12 ESV).

The Holy of Holies

The Holy of Holies was that part of the Tabernacle of the Temple which was regarded as possessing the utmost degree of holiness. So sacred was this space that the High Priest was permitted to enter only once a year on the Day of Atonement.

On that Day of Atonement, the High Priest offered up the innocent blood of unblemished animals to make a corporate, vicarious atonement for the whole people of Israel for sins they had committed *in ignorance*:

> Now if you as a community unintentionally fail to keep any of these commands the Lord gave Moses…and if this is done unintentionally without the community being aware of it, then the whole community is to offer a young bull for a burnt offering as an aroma pleasing to the Lord, along with its prescribed grain offering and drink offering, and a male goat for a sin offering. The priest is to make atonement for the whole Israelite community, and they will be forgiven, for it was not intentional and they have presented to the Lord for their wrong a food offering and a sin offering. The whole Israelite community and the foreigners residing among them will be forgiven, because all the people were involved in the unintentional wrong (Numbers 15:22-26 NIV).

The shedding of blood under the Mosaic Law did not vicariously atone for an individual's intentional sin: it was merely a corporate and symbolic atonement for sins committed *in ignorance*. The Israelites were warned throughout the Hebrew Scriptures that there was no vicarious atonement for individual intentional sin, as we can see just a few verses further on:

> But the person who does anything with a high hand, whether he is native or a sojourner, reviles the LORD, and that person shall be cut off from among his people. Because he has despised the word of the LORD and has broken his commandment, that person shall be utterly cut off; his iniquity shall be on him (Numbers 15:30-31 ESV).

And again:

> The next day Moses told the people, "You committed a great sin, and now I'll go up to the LORD, and perhaps I can make atonement for your sin." Moses returned to the LORD and said, "Please, LORD, this people committed a great sin by making a god of gold for themselves. Now, if you will, forgive their sin—but if not, blot me out of your book which you have written." The LORD told Moses, "Whoever sins against me, I'll blot him out of my book (Exodus 32:30-33 ISV).

Moses' plea was denied on the basis that he could not suffer vicariously for *corporate intentional sin*. See also Jeremiah 31:30; Psalm 49:7; Deuteronomy 24:16; and 2 Kings 14:6 where it is made clear that neither can there be vicarious atonement for *individual intentional sin*.

Sin and Atonement in the New Testament

Corporate Atonement

The Israelite concept of vicarious corporate atonement is reinforced in the New Testament, especially in the Book of Hebrews. Whereas under the Mosaic Law, the High Priest once a year atoned for the unintentional sins of corporate Israel by making a sacrificial offering of the blood of "unblemished" animals in the Holy of Holies, the author of Hebrews teaches that the New Covenant's High Priest, as the representative of corporate Israel, made a sacrificial offering of his own "unblemished" blood to atone for the *sins of the people committed in ignorance*:

> …but into the second (the Holy of Holies), only the high priest enters once a year, not without taking blood, which he offers for himself and for the sins of the people committed in ignorance (Hebrews 9:7 NIV).

The atoning blood of Jesus was to be offered once only:

> Nor did he go into heaven to sacrifice himself again and again, the way the high priest goes into the Holy Place every year with blood that is not his own. Then he would have had to suffer repeatedly since the creation of the world. But now, at the end of the ages, he has appeared once for all to remove sin by his sacrifice (Hebrews 9:25-26 ISV).

The Mosaic sacrificial system had begun with blood and had now ended with blood. The slate had been wiped clean.

The Pauline Perspective

The story of the Garden of Eden presents us with the failings of mankind portrayed in an allegory. "Adam" simply means "man" and is derived from the Hebrew *ha adamah* which means "the ground" or "the earth". "Eve" simply means "living one" or "source of life".

Paul identifies the sins of Adam, symbolic of mankind, as:

- exchanging the truth of God for a lie (Romans 1:25);
- worshipping and serving the creature rather than the Creator (Romans 1:25);
- disobedience to the commands of the Creator (Romans 5:19).

Paul taught that by subordinating the will of his own flesh, by choosing the truth of God instead of lies, and by choosing obedience to God instead of disobedience, Jesus restored man to his position as it existed in the beginning. Hence, Paul describes Jesus as the "last Adam":

> So it is written: "The first man Adam became a living being," the last Adam, a life-giving spirit (1 Corinthians 15:45 NIV).

(As noted in a previous Chapter, the sins of Adam are not the types of sin that we in the English-speaking world commonly associate with the word, e.g. murder, theft, bearing false witness and etcetera. Rather, they are the types of sins for which there could be a corporate atonement.)

Life not death

Paul argued that death rather than sin had been the common inheritance of mankind ever since Adam and Eve disobeyed God (Romans 6:23). But now, new life was available for those who, in a spiritual sense, crucified the old man after the fashion of Adam and resurrected the new man after the fashion of Jesus (1 Corinthians 15:21-22).

Because blood symbolised life, and there is new life in Jesus, Paul depicts Jesus as corporately atoning once only for the sins of Adam and purging them with redeeming blood (see Leviticus 17:11). Paul's description of Jesus as the "last Adam" completely discredits the doctrine of Original Sin. Even if mankind had inherited sin from Adam, then that inheritance would have ceased automatically with the "last Adam".

The claim that only a divinity can atone for corporate sin leaves the concept of atonement utterly devoid of meaning. Only a normal man fashioned after the first Adam, subject to all the weaknesses and temptations of the first Adam, can make such corporate atonement.

Individual Atonement

While Living

Individual sins deliberately committed with a so-called "high hand" were considered to be a total rejection of God and his Covenant and placed a person outside of any relationship with God.

The Israelites had been consistently warned that there was no vicarious atonement for individual intentional sin—no atonement through the ritual blood sacrifices that had become a "cover" for such sin in the minds of some. By the time of Jesus, ritual observance of the letter of the Law while ignoring the obligations of its spirit was commonplace among those members of the Jerusalem establishment charged with upholding the Mosaic Law. Their exaggerated show of ritual observance was no more than a pretense, a convenient cover for the sin of failing to fulfill their most important duties, and was roundly condemned by Jesus:

> Woe to you, scribes and Pharisees, hypocrites! For you tithe mint and dill and cummin, and have neglected the weightier provisions of the law: justice and mercy and faithfulness; but these are the things you should have done without neglecting the others (Matthew 23:23 NASB).

Jesus warned that there would henceforth be no more excuses, no more cover for sin that the Law had been seen to provide, but that every individual was fully responsible for his or her own sin:

> If I had not come and spoken to them, they would not be guilty of sin; but now they have no excuse for their sin (John 15:22 NIV).

(Note also that this statement by Jesus is another rebuttal of the doctrine of Original Sin which, in effect, replaces the cover for sin that the Mosaic Law had been seen to provide in the minds of some.)

Biblically speaking, the only way it has ever been possible for an individual to atone for his or her own intentional sin and to receive God's forgiveness is through prayer and repentance followed by good works and righteous behaviour. (See for example Psalm 51:16-17; Psalm 32:5; Daniel 4:27; Micah 6:6-8.)

When Dead

For 1st Century Israelites, death was a process, not a moment in time. Mourning would continue for a year as the body underwent decomposition, considered a type of penal atonement for whatever sins the dead person may have committed in life. Such sins were thought to be embedded in the flesh and to dissolve along with the body.

After a year of decay and purification, the bones were often collected and placed in a stone box called an ossuary, which was just long enough to accommodate the thigh bones. It was believed that the bones retained the personality and that God would use these bones to support new flesh for the Resurrection (see Ezekiel 37 and his vision of the Valley of Dry Bones).

The day of placing the bones in the ossuary, a type of second burial, would mark the end of the family's mourning period and the beginning of hope in eventual reunion and Resurrection. These cultural practices and beliefs are the context in which the Resurrection accounts were written. (See Part XIV.9: *Trial and Death-Burial*.)

CHAPTER THREE

Salvation

The Hebrew Scriptures teach that Almighty God is the Saviour of Israel:

> For I am the LORD your God, the Holy One of Israel, your Savior… (Isaiah 43:3 NIV).

Because the New Testament also describes Jesus as a "Saviour", it is asserted that he is to be equated with God. This claim overlooks or ignores the fact that, according to the Hebrew Scriptures, God delegates authority to perform all his works on Earth to humans of his choice and that works of "salvation" had been delegated to others long before the time of Jesus. Just two examples should suffice:

> But when the people of Israel cried out to the LORD (YHWH), the LORD (YHWH) raised up a deliverer (*yasha*) for the people of Israel, who saved (*yasha*) them, Othniel the son of Kenaz, Caleb's younger brother (Judges 3:9 ESV).
>
> Then the people said to Saul, "Shall Jonathan die, who has worked this great salvation (*yasha*) in Israel?…" (1 Samuel 14:45 ESV).

The English word "saviour" derives from the Greek σώζω *(sózó)* and the Hebrew root ישע *(yasha)*, both of which mean to "save" or "deliver". The Hebrew name *Yeshua* is a shortened form of *Yehoshua*, the name of *Joshua* the successor of Moses. It is derived from YH, a shortened form of YWVH and the Hebrew verb root *yasha*. Because of the meaning of the name "Jesus", a transliteration of *Yeshua*, Joseph was instructed to name him accordingly:

> She will bear a son, and you shall call his name Jesus (Yeshua), for he will save his people from their sins (Matthew 1:21 ESV).

Just as the other humans mentioned above, Jesus was delegated authority by God to perform a "saving" role:

> The Spirit of the Lord God is upon me…I will greatly rejoice in the LORD, my soul shall be joyful in my God; for he hath clothed me with the garments of salvation, he hath covered me with the robe of righteousness (Isaiah 61:1,10 KJV quoted partly in Luke 4:18-19 cf. Psalm 98:1).

In addition to Jesus and other individual Saviours, the whole people of Israel were delegated a "saving" role by Jesus himself:

> Ye worship ye know not what: we know what we worship: for salvation is of the Jews (John 4:22 KJV).

A belief held by countless Christians is that they will be magically "saved" from their sins simply by reciting some incantation, e.g. *I accept the Lord Jesus Christ as my Saviour*. Jesus did not then, and does not now, possess the authority to "save" anyone. God alone is Saviour, as many biblical texts affirm. (See for instance Luke 1:47 where Mary describes God as her Saviour.)

The passport to life

In his own words, Jesus tells us that Salvation is entry into life in the Kingdom of God. In the Gospel of Luke, in answer to the question, "Are many saved?", Jesus replied:

> Strive (*agónizomai*) to enter through the narrow door. For many, I tell you, will seek to enter (the Kingdom of God) and will not be able (Luke 13:24 ESV).

The Greek word *agónizomai* translated above as "strive", means *to fight, to labour fervently, to contend as with an adversary,* and suchlike. In all cases, the word conveys hard work and struggle. In the Gospel of Matthew, Jesus tells that the narrow gate/door represents entrance to life in the Kingdom of God:

> Enter by the narrow gate. For the gate is wide and the way is easy that leads to destruction, and those who enter by it are many. For the gate is narrow and the way is hard that leads to life (in the Kingdom), and those who find it are few (Matthew 7:13-14 ESV).

The importance of the above warnings by Jesus cannot by overstated. Those who repose blind trust in teachers who assert that salvation rests on mental assent to some proposition or belief would do well to heed the gravity of Paul's injunction to his friends:

> Therefore, my dear friends…continue to work out your salvation with fear and trembling (Philippians 2:12 NIV).

Note

Essays on the Kingdom of God appear elsewhere in this work.

The Way, the Truth, and the Life

The farewell discourse in John 14: 1-14 was specifically modelled on the farewell discourse in Deuteronomy 30:16 in order to identify Jesus with Moses. The central message of Moses' discourse to the Israelite community was that the only way to God was by loving God, walking in God's ways, and observing God's commandments. If they did, they would live. In verse 6, Jesus tells his followers that the only way to God was by emulating him, a man who loved God, walked in God's ways, and kept God's commandments. If they did, they too would live. Note that the New Testament claims that Jesus was the promised "prophet like Moses" (See Part XIII.3: *The Israelite Messiah - The Prophet like Moses*.)

PART IX

The Papacy

CHAPTER ONE

Introductory Notes

- The aim of Part Nine of this work is to present an exhaustive investigation into the Papacy's claim to Primacy and Apostolic Succession through Simon bar Jonah;

- In the time of Jesus, there were no individuals with the personal name of "Peter". It is merely a form of the New Testament Greek word Πέτρος (*Petros*), drawn from the Aramaic *kêfâ* (*cephas*), having the essential meaning of "rock" in both Greek and Aramaic. *Cephas* was Jesus' nickname for the man known to his contemporaries as Simon bar Jonah. In common parlance, it would be like us giving the name "rocky" to one who appeared to be either physically or mentally tough. Only later did the word "Peter" become a personal name. Following customary usage, however, the name "Peter" will be used in forthcoming Chapters rather than Simon bar Jonah;

- The term "Catholic Church", properly known as the "Holy Roman Catholic and Apostolic Church", refers to the Latin Church of the Catholic communion headquartered in Rome, in contradistinction to the 21 other particular Churches of the Catholic communion, including the Byzantine, Alexandrian, Armenian, Antiochian and Chaldean Catholic Churches;

- The term "Pope" refers to the Bishop of Rome who is also known as the Supreme Pontiff (*Pontifex Maxiumus*). The Pope exercises world-wide dominion over the congregations of the Catholic Church;

- The terms "Papacy", "Holy See", "Apostolic See", and "Vatican", are often used interchangeably but all refer the central administration comprising the Pope and his Curial Government which is headquartered in the independent Vatican City State enclave in Rome;

- As an aid to understanding, it is necessary to reproduce a description of the various categories of persons mentioned in the New Testament found in Part VII.1: *Paul-Paul and his world*. For the purposes of scene-setting, it is also necessary to reproduce certain material from Part I: *Context*.

CHAPTER TWO

Common Beliefs

The most common beliefs held by Catholics in communion with Rome are:

- that Peter was the first to preach the gospel in Rome;
- that Peter founded the Church in Rome;
- that as a result of his residence in Rome, Peter passed on his primacy to his successors the Popes, as Bishops of Rome.

These beliefs are neatly summed up by the Very Rev. Joseph Faà Di Bruno:

> St. Peter was the first to preach the gospel in Rome, and owing to his sanctity, zeal, prudence and power of working miracles, it was not long before he made many converts. The number of Christians increasing steadily each year, he chose the most distinguished among them and sent them as bishops or priests to different parts of the world as recorded in the Roman Martyrology...St. Peter having fixed his See in Rome to the end of his life and having died there a martyr, it follows as a matter of course, that his heirs and successors in that See should enjoy the prerogatives of that episcopate, that is, the supremacy which St. Peter received...[1]

It is only natural that Catholics should believe without question what the Church has claimed for so many centuries. Unfortunately, when these common beliefs are examined, they prove to be no more than a mixture of errors, confusions, and downright deceptions.

What Catholics are required to believe

Any doctrine of faith or morals which is necessary for all Catholics to believe at all times is classified as a *de fide dogma*. All *de fide dogmas* are listed in *Fundamentals of Catholic Dogma* by Dr. Ludwig Ott. Although it may come as a surprise to many Catholics, there is no *de fide dogma* requiring them to believe that Peter either went to Rome, or that he established a church there. Nevertheless, Dr. Ott makes the unequivocal assertions that:

---

1 Faà Di Bruno, Joseph. *Catholic Belief: Or A Short And Simple Exposition Of Catholic Doctrine*. Burns and Oates: London, 2nd ed. 1878, pp. 353, 358

> According to Christ's ordinance, Peter is to have successors in his primacy over the whole church and for all time.
>
> The successors of St. Peter in the primacy are the Bishops of Rome. [2]

According to sacred Canon Law which binds all believing Catholics, they are required to believe these unequivocal assertions about Papal Primacy and Apostolic Succession despite the fact that they are not required to believe that Peter was present in Rome at any time:

> The bishop of the Roman Church, in whom continues the office given by the Lord uniquely to Peter, the first of the Apostles, and to be transmitted to his successors, is the head of the college of bishops, the Vicar of Christ, and the pastor of the universal Church on earth. By virtue of his office he possesses supreme, full, immediate, and universal ordinary power in the Church, which he is always able to exercise freely. [3]

These unequivocal assertions are also enshrined in the Catechism of Catholic Church:

> The Lord made St. Peter the visible foundation of his Church. He entrusted the keys of the Church to him. The bishop of the Church of Rome, successor to St. Peter, is head of the college of bishops, the Vicar of Christ and Pastor of the universal Church on earth. [4]
>
> The college or body of bishops has no authority unless united with the Roman Pontiff, Peter's successor, as its head. As such, this college has supreme and full authority over the universal Church; but this power cannot be exercised without the agreement of the Roman Pontiff. [5]

In the Catholic Encyclopaedia article *The Pope,* Papal Primacy is defined under pain of anathema for doubters and disbelievers:

> The primacy of St. Peter and the perpetuity of that primacy in the Roman See are dogmatically defined in the canons attached to the first two chapters of the Constitution *Pastor Aeturnus:*

---

2 Ott, Dr. Ludwig. *Fundamentals of Catholic Dogma*, Mercier Press Ltd: Cork, Ireland, 1955, pp. 282, 283.

3 Code of Canon Law: 331. Accessed 30 July 2019 http://www.vatican.va/archive/cod-iuris-canonici/eng/documents/cic_lib2-cann330-367_en.html

4 Catechism of the Catholic Church: 936. Accessed 12 November 2017 http://www.vatican.va/archive/ENG0015/__P2A.HTM

5 *Catechism of the Catholic Church*: 883. Accessed 12 November 2017 http://www.vatican.va/archive/ENG0015/__P2A.HTM

> If any one shall say that Blessed Peter the Apostle was not constituted by Christ our Lord as chief of all the Apostles and the visible head of the whole Church militant: or that he did not receive directly and immediately from the same Lord Jesus Christ a primacy of true and proper jurisdiction, but one of honour only: let him be anathema.
>
> If any one shall say it is not by the institution of the Christ our Lord Himself or by divinely established right that Blessed Peter has perpetual successors in his primacy over the universal Church: or that the Roman Pontiff is not the successor of Blessed Peter in the same primacy: - let him be anathema. (Denzinger-Bannwart, "Enchiridion", nn. 1823, 1825) [6]

So we have established that although many Catholics believe that Peter travelled to Rome and established the church there, they are under no obligation to do so. Dr. Ludwig Ott, Sacred Canon Law, the Catechism, and the Constitution *Pastor Aeturnus* all claim that the Roman Pontiff holds the primacy from Peter by a divine ordinance. How this primacy was transferred from Peter to the Bishop of Rome is left totally unexplained. Dr. Ott merely states that he records "the more usual theological viewpoint". From this it follows that Catholics are simply required to believe, under pain of anathema, that Peter passed on primacy to the popes, yet the authorities are under no obligation to produce evidence by way of explanation or substantiation.

Asserting Peter's ministry in Rome would surely imply that the required historical evidence is available. We will now examine what evidence the authorities can produce.

Note

Pastor Aeternus (First Dogmatic Constitution on the Church of Christ) was issued by the First Vatican Council on July 18, 1870. The document defines four doctrines of the Catholic faith: the Apostolic Primacy conferred on Peter, the perpetuity of the Petrine Primacy in the Roman pontiffs, the meaning and power of the Papal Primacy, and Papal Infallibility.

---

6   Catholic Encyclopaedia article: *The Pope*. Accessed 10 November 2017 http://www.newadvent.org/cathen/12260a.htm

CHAPTER THREE

Unequivocal Assertions

The Congregation of the Doctrine of the Faith

> In Peter's person, mission and ministry, in his presence and death in Rome attested by the most ancient literary and archaeological tradition—the Church sees a deeper reality essentially related to her own mystery of communion and salvation: 'Ubi Petrus, ibi ergo Ecclesia'. From the beginning and with increasing clarity, the Church has understood that, just as there is a succession of the Apostles in the ministry of Bishops, so too the ministry of unity entrusted to Peter belongs to the permanent structure of Christ's Church and that this succession is established in the See of his martyrdom.[7]

The Catholic Encyclopaedia

> It is an indisputably established historical fact that St. Peter laboured in Rome during the last portion of his life, and there ended his earthly course in martyrdom. As to the duration of his Apostolic activity in the Roman Capital, the continuity or otherwise of his residence there, the details and success of his labours, and the chronology of his arrival and death, all these questions are uncertain, and can be solved only on hypotheses more or less well-founded. The essential fact is that Peter died at Rome: this constitutes the historical foundation of the claim of the Bishops of Rome to the Apostolic Primacy of Peter. St. Peter's residence and death in Rome are established beyond contention as historical facts by a series of distinct testimonies.[8]

It would seem from all the foregoing that the Papacy's unequivocal assertions about Peter, about its authority deriving from Peter, and about Peter's ministry and death in Rome, were historical certainties, able to be demonstrated and verified. These assertions, however, quickly unravel when tested, not the least from the fact that traditions about Peter's presence in Rome only surfaced in the latter half

---

7 *The Primacy of the Successor of Peter in the Mystery of the Church:* Reflections of the Congregation for the Doctrine of the Faith by Cardinal Joseph Ratzinger, Prefect, and Tarcisio Bertone, Archbishop emeritus of Vercelli, Secretary. Reported in *Il Primato del Successore di Pietro, Atti del Simposio teologico*, Rome, 2-4 December 1996, *Libreria Editrice Vatican*a, Vatican City, 1998.

8 Catholic Encyclopaedia Article: *St. Peter, Prince of the Apostles : Activity and death in Rome—Burial Place.* Accessed 29 November 2017 http://www.newadvent.org/cathen/11744a.htm

of the Second Century AD, at around the same time as the various apocryphal/ pseudigraphical works and the Clementine literature, with their elaborate and fanciful tales about Simon Peter and Simon Magus, began to proliferate. Elements from these fables crept into subsequent writings until the fully fledged legend of Peter's twenty-five year episcopacy and martyrdom in Rome reached its final form with Jerome. It is a task of epic proportions to attempt an analysis of all the afore-mentioned works from antiquity that resulted in these assertions by Jerome so we will instead focus on the fact that without Peter's alleged death in Rome, there is no basis at all for the Bishop of Rome to claim Apostolic Succession from Peter.

CHAPTER FOUR

Irreconcilable Inconsistencies

For Peter to have died in Rome, it is obviously necessary that he should have first arrived there. Yet the authorities cannot come up with any evidence, not even a consistent story, regarding his arrival, his ministry, his sojourn, or his death in Rome.

The Dating Game

- Did Peter's Pontificate begin in Rome in 32 AD as claimed in the Catholic Encyclopaedia Pope List? [9]
- Or did it begin in 42 AD, the second year of Claudius, as claimed by Jerome? [10]
- Or would it have been impossible for Peter to arrive in Rome before 62 AD as stated by the acclaimed Catholic Church historian Msgr. Philip Hughes?

Msgr. Hughes has the following to say on the subject of Peter's residence in Rome:

> …The precise date at which the Roman Church was founded we do not know, nor the date at which St. Peter first went to Rome. But it is universally the tradition of this primitive Christianity that St. Peter ruled the Roman Church and that at Rome he gave his life for Christ in the persecution of Nero.

Hughes goes on:

> …About the origins of Christianity in Rome we know nothing. It is already a flourishing church in 56 AD when St. Paul refers to it. Three years later he arrived in Rome himself, a prisoner, for the hearing of his appeal to Caesar.
>
> …St. Peter first appeared there apparently some three years later, about the time St. Paul, acquitted, had left the city. [11]

According to Hughes then:

---

9 Catholic Encyclopaedia Article: *The List of Popes*. Accessed 29 November 2017 http://www.newadvent.org/cathen/12272h.htm

10 Jerome, *Lives of Illustrious Men*, trans. by Ernest C. Richardson, Vol. III, *The Nicene and Post-Nicene Fathers*, ed. Philip Schaff and Henry Wace, Wm. B. Eerdmans Publishing Company: Grand Rapids, 1953 p. 361.

11 Hughes, Msgr Philip. *A Popular History of the Catholic Church*. Macmillan & Co: New York, 1951, pp 14, 17, 18.

- There was a "flourishing" Christian community in Rome when Paul first arrived there, as we already knew from the New Testament;
- The earliest time he can place Peter in Rome is between Paul's two captive visits;
- Peter, therefore, could not have arrived in Rome before 62 AD.

Even though Peter's alleged death in Rome constitutes the historical foundation for the claims of the Bishops of Rome, the authorities cannot produce one scintilla of evidence to support claims so monumental in their historical implications.

As Richard P. McBrien, Crowley-O'Brien Professor of Theology at the University of Notre Dame, states:

> Few, if any, traditions associated with the Papacy have anything at all to do with the Apostle Peter, or with the Lord himself for that matter.[12]

If Peter was never in Rome, then where would he have been most likely to go to further the mission entrusted to him by Jesus? In the following Chapters we will examine the evidence available to us.

---

12 McBrien, Richard P. *Lives of the Popes: The Pontiffs from St. Peter to John Paul II*. Harper: San Francisco, 1997, p.392.

CHAPTER FIVE

Paul's Mission

Notes

As noted in the previous Chapter, the fully fledged tradition of Peter's twenty-five year episcopacy and martyrdom in Rome reached its final form with Jerome. This tradition is not only bereft of any evidence but is also demonstrably false as it contradicts statements from the New Testament as well as events of secular history.

Also in the previous Chapter, the question was posed, "If Peter was never in Rome, then where would he have been most likely to go to further the mission entrusted to him by Jesus?" The interplay between two sources of information—the New Testament and the record of secular history—may provide us with the answer.

Section 1

Target Groups

Paul's "Gospel of God" is ultimately about a forthcoming Israelite theocracy—the Kingdom of God. Therefore it is only natural that his target groups are Israelites. However, the correct identification of these groups has been obscured by ambiguous, incorrect and inconsistent translations. For example:

Jews (Greek Ἰουδαῖός: Transliteration Ioudaios)

Ambiguous translation: The Greek New Testament has been translated into many different languages over time. If translators of all these versions had correctly identified the various categories of persons all designated as *Ioudaios* in the New Testament, that word would not have become the most consequential single word in all of human history. Since this work is in English, we will confine our remarks on this topic to the English version but its content applies equally to all translations of the Greek New Testament regardless of era, language or version.

Persons designated in the English New Testament as "Jew/s" could fall into one or more of the following categories:

1. Descendants of the Israelite tribe of Judah who lived in the Roman Province of Judea, worshipped at the Temple in Jerusalem, and followed the Law of Moses;
2. Descendants of the Israelite tribe of Judah regardless of where they lived. For instance, Jesus was a Jew because he belonged to the tribe of Judah even though he came from Galilee;
3. Persons who followed the customs and practices of the Judeans regardless of where they lived. For instance, Paul self-identified as a "Jew" because he followed the customs and practices of the Judeans who worshipped at the Temple in Jerusalem even though he came from Tarsus and belonged to the Israelite tribe of Benjamin.

Note that Jesus falls into categories 2 and 3 above: Not only did he belong to the Israelite tribe of Judah but he also followed the customs and practices of the Judeans who worshipped at the Temple in Jerusalem.

Correctly identifying the category of person the author has in view at any one time is daunting but not impossible if context is studied and fully appreciated. Throughout this work, the correct rendering of *Ioudaios* has been supplied where appropriate. Given the fact that the word rendered into English as "Jew" was to become the most important single word in all of human history, the consequences of not differentiating between the various categories of *Ioudaios* mentioned in the New Testament can hardly be overestimated.

Greeks (Greek Ἕλλην : Transliteration Hellēn)

No consistency of translation: e.g. sometimes rendered Gentile. In the 1st Century AD, there was no nation state of Greece. "Greeks" were civilised people who spoke the Greek language and followed the customs and practices of Hellenists. Among those designated as "Greeks" were both Israelites living in diaspora communities and non-Israelites. Israelite "Greeks" did not follow the "barbaric" customs and practices of the Judeans but rather the customs and practices of Hellenists.

Gentiles (Greek ἀλλοφύλῳ :Transliteration allophylō) (Greek ἐθνῶν :Transliteration ethnē)

No consistency of translation: e.g. variously Greek, heathen, pagan, nation, race. There are various Greek words that have been translated into English as "Gentile". As with the word "Greek", there is no consistency of translation.

The complexity of the above terminology is daunting so, as always, we must determine meaning by context. Even though it is almost universally believed that Paul is the Apostle to the "Gentiles", i.e. non-Israelites, it is obvious from Paul's statement to

Agrippa when he appeared before him in Caesarea that his mission was to the twelve tribes of Israel. (The correct translation of "Jews" appears in brackets):

> King Agrippa, I consider myself fortunate to stand before you today as I make my defense against all the accusations of the Jews (Judeans), and especially so because you are well acquainted with all the Jewish (Judean) customs and controversies. Therefore, I beg you to listen to me patiently. The Judean people all know the way I have lived ever since I was a child, from the beginning of my life in my own country, and also in Jerusalem. They have known me for a long time and can testify, if they are willing, that I conformed to the strictest sect of our religion, living as a Pharisee. And now it is because of my hope in what God has promised our ancestors that I am on trial today. This is the promise our twelve tribes are hoping to see fulfilled as they earnestly serve God day and night" (Acts 26:2-7 NIV).

Paul was an Israelite who had persecuted Jesus groups in Judea. After his "road to Damascus" experience, he believed he had been called to be an Israelite prophet standing in the same tradition as the prophets of old and to proclaim the "Gospel of God" to Israelites. Paul's appeal to other Israelites is based on their common genealogy through Abraham and it is this commonality that forms the framework for all his theology.

Paul did not focus on the story of Jesus' life. Rather, his focus was on what the God of Israel had done in raising up Jesus. He announced that the Crucifixion and Resurrection was a signal to Israelites living in the Diaspora that they would one day be "resurrected" from this dispersion, regarded as a type of death, and ingathered to Israel to form the Kingdom of God to be ruled over by God's Messiah.

Many modern scholars claim that there are only seven genuine Epistles written by Paul himself viz. 1 Thessalonians, Galatians, Philemon, Philippians, 1 & 2 Corinthians, and Romans. Their view that the other six pseudepigraphic epistles were written by later followers of Paul, is borne out by the fact that these epistles are not Israelite-specific, as are the seven that can be directly attributed to Paul himself, and they do not require a knowledge of the themes and motifs of the Hebrew scriptures in order to be understood.

Paul directed his letters to Israelites living in Greco-Roman societies beyond the confines of the land of Israel. Some of these Israelites practiced the customs of the Judeans (Jews) who followed the Law of Moses, including the practice of circumcision, while others practiced the customs of Hellenists. Paul argued that it was not necessary for these "Hellenist" Israelites to now revert to a way of life unfamiliar to them in order to belong to one of his Jesus groups. However, whether they did, or did not, was of little account to Paul:

> Circumcision is nothing, and uncircumcision is nothing, but the keeping of the commandments of God (1 Corinthians 7:19 KJV).

Seeing that Paul's arguments would have made sense only to an Israelite audience, his mission to the *ethnē* then was to proclaim the "Gospel of God" to Israelites living among majority non-Israelite populations scattered throughout the Roman Empire. The one exception to this pattern is the Epistle to the Romans which was addressed to Jesus groups that Paul did not found. These Roman Jesus groups contained a few non-Israelite members and he issues them with some specific warnings about their status in Chapter 11:13-24. For example:

> But if some of the branches were broken off, and you, being a wild olive, were grafted in among them and became partaker with them of the rich root of the olive tree, do not be arrogant toward the branches; but if you are arrogant, remember that it is not you who supports the root, but the root supports you (Romans 11:17-18 NASB).

Later generations of non-Israelites adopted Christianity after the Hellenist-Latin fathers, using their own philosophies and theologies, imposed upon the New Testament texts a false synthesis of Paganism and Hellenism more appealing to the peoples of the Roman Empire.

Paul's letters have been subjected to multiple doctrinal overlays and the distractions of theological hair-splitting over issues such as Faith, Works, Righteousness, Justification, Grace, Election and so on. If we had not been subjected to these distractions, we would perhaps have recognised long ago that the letters directly attributable to Paul were addressed to those who could understand them, viz. fellow Israelites living among majority non-Israelite societies beyond the confines of the land of Israel.

As it is, Pauline theology is largely based on non-Israelite concepts and would therefore collapse under the weight of its utter irrelevance and total absurdity. As Malina and Pilch state:

> It is quite significant to note that Paul's proclamation (of the gospel of God) was Israelite-specific in all of its dimensions: in its means of transmission (Paul received it through a revelation ascribed to the God of Israel who calls prophets), in its origin (the God of Israel), in its medium (a revelation of Israel's Messiah, the crucified and resurrected Jesus), in its content (an Israelite

theocracy), and in its rationale (spelled out according to Israel's scriptures). Hence it is fairly obvious that the proclamation was meant specifically for Israelites.[13]

Section 2

Rome

In Romans Chapter 15, Paul states that he had already "fully proclaimed the good news of Christ" in the Eastern Mediterranean, having preached from "Jerusalem as far around as Illyricum" (north of Macedonia on the Adriatic), and that his intention was to travel westwards to Rome and thence to Spain. He must first, however, deliver to the "saints" in Jerusalem some poor-relief resources collected from Jesus communities in Macedonia and Achaia.

Paul arrived in Jerusalem circa 58 AD and met with James and "all the elders" (Acts 21:17-18). For our purposes, there is little to be gained by recounting Paul's subsequent tribulations, except to say that circumstances allowed him to witness to the Gospel of the God of Israel before the Sanhedrin, before the Roman Governors Felix and Festus, and before Herod Agrippa.

According to Acts, Paul was a Roman citizen by birth and this gave him the right to appeal directly to Caesar in any dispute over which he felt aggrieved. It was because Paul wished to avoid being handed over to his Judean opponents that he appealed to Caesar during his witness before Festus and Herod Agrippa in Caesarea Maritima. Festus and Agrippa both agreed that Paul was innocent of any crime and could have been set free if he had not appealed to Caesar. But appeal to Caesar he had, so to Caesar he must go. By the time Paul was handed over to the custody of the Centurion Julius and had boarded ship for Rome, he had spent about 18 months in detention in Caesarea Maritima.

After a harrowing sea voyage, Paul eventually arrived at Puteoli on the Gulf of Naples circa 60 AD. Paul stayed in Puteoli for a week, enough time for word of his arrival to spread to Rome, about 200 km distant. Upon receipt of this news, some Jesus group members set out from the city along the Appian Way to meet Paul. Some travelled as far as the Appian Forum, about 65 km from Rome, while others travelled a lesser distance to the Three Taverns, about 50 km from Rome.

---

13   Malina, B.J, Pilch, J.J. *Social Science Commentary on the Letters of Paul*. Augsburg Fortress: Minneapolis, 2006, p 12

Paul was greatly heartened by his enthusiastic welcome and the entire entourage gathered together and proceeded towards the city. Upon his arrival, Paul along with a guard settled in a house for which Paul paid. Then:

> Three days later he called together the local Jewish leaders. When they had assembled, Paul said to them: "My brothers, although I have done nothing against our people or against the customs of our ancestors, I was arrested in Jerusalem and handed over to the Romans. They examined me and wanted to release me, because I was not guilty of any crime deserving death. The Jews (Judeans) objected, so I was compelled to make an appeal to Caesar. I certainly did not intend to bring any charge against my own people. For this reason I have asked to see you and talk with you. It is because of the hope of Israel that I am bound with this chain." They replied, "We have not received any letters from Judea concerning you, and none of our people who have come from there has reported or said anything bad about you. But we want to hear what your views are, for we know that people everywhere are talking against this sect." They arranged to meet Paul on a certain day, and came in even larger numbers to the place where he was staying. He witnessed to them from morning till evening, explaining about the kingdom of God, and from the Law of Moses and from the Prophets he tried to persuade them about Jesus (Acts 28:17-23 NIV).

We can see from the above that the leaders of the Roman Jews had not heard any negative reports about Paul himself but had heard people "everywhere" speaking against Paul's "sect". Nevertheless, they expressed a wish to know more so Paul later witnessed to these Jewish leaders for an entire day concerning the forthcoming Israelite religious/political theocracy (the Kingdom of God) to be established by Israel's Messiah Jesus whom the God of Israel had raised from the dead according to the Law and the Prophets.

It is clear from the above exchanges that, prior to 60 AD, the Jews to whom Paul spoke had no knowledge of any of the teachings of the Jesus group, the "sect" which had been widely spoken against, the "sect" to which Peter also belonged.

Chapter 28, the conclusion of the Book of Acts, takes us forward to circa 62 AD, at which time Paul had been kept under house arrest for about two years. During that period, he had continued to proclaim the forthcoming Kingdom of God and teach about Jesus Messiah unhindered. The Book of Acts ends on a positive note, claims Paul's preaching as a fulfillment of Scripture, makes no mention of Peter, and lacks any hint of a coming persecution at the hands of Roman authorities.

CHAPTER SIX

Peter's Mission

Note

In Galatians 2:9 we read of a clear division of ministries: Paul and Barnabas were to preach to the Gentiles (*ethnē*), i.e. those who followed the customs and practices of Hellenists while Peter and the other disciples were to preach to the circumcised, i.e. those who followed the customs and practices of the Judeans who worshipped at the temple in Jerusalem:

> And when James and Cephas and John, who seemed to be pillars, perceived the grace that was given to me, they gave the right hand of fellowship to Barnabas and me, that we should go to the Gentiles (*ethnē*) and they to the circumcised (Galatians 2:9 ESV).

Section 1

Directions

Before the death of Jesus...

Before his death, Jesus instructed Peter and the other disciples not to go into the "way of the Gentiles" or to enter "any city of the Samaritans". Thus their preaching was restricted to the area of Jesus' own ministry—Judea, Samaria and Galilee:

> These twelve Jesus sent forth, and commanded them, saying, Go not into the way of the Gentiles, and into any city of the Samaritans enter ye not: But go rather to the lost sheep of the house of Israel (Matthew 10:5-6 KJV).

The care of these same "lost sheep of the house of Israel" is committed to the care of Peter and the other disciples:

> Be shepherds of God's flock that is among you, watching over it, not because you must but because you want to, and not greedily but eagerly, as God desires. Do not lord it over the people entrusted to you, but be examples to the flock.

Then, when the Chief Shepherd appears, you will receive the victor's crown of glory that will never fade away (1 Peter 5:2-4 ISV).

After the death of Jesus...

The role of the Messiah is Israelite-specific, a role undertaken on behalf of Israel. After the Resurrection, the disciples are told not to confine their preaching to Israelites living in Judea, Samaria and Galilee, as in the former command of Matthew 10:5-6, but to also go to those regions where countless "lost sheep of the House of Israel" lived among majority non-Israelite populations. As Malina and Rohrbaugh correctly point out:

> The move away from the region of Jesus' ministry to the wider reaches of the Roman Empire where countless Israelite émigrés lived, served to clarify and justify how Matthew's followers of an Israelite Jesus got to be his disciples although they did not live in the land of Israel. In the Gospel story, sayings such as 'I tell you, many will come from east and west and eat with Abraham, Isaac and Jacob in the kingdom of heaven' (Matthew 8:11) refer to the many Israelites who would be gathered from east and west to feast in the forthcoming theocracy, to be located in Israel's promised land. [14]

Section 2

Mission Locations

In a previous Chapter, the question was posed, "If Peter was never in Rome, then where would he have been most likely to go to further the mission entrusted to him by Jesus?" Now we will try to pinpoint Peter's locations in places other than Rome at various times. This task requires us to glean every possible grain of information available to us from the New Testament and from the record of secular history.

Peter is recorded in Acts as being present in Jerusalem from the death of Jesus until the execution of Stephen. Thereafter, he is recorded as being either in Jerusalem or travelling on various missionary journeys throughout Judea, Samaria, and Galilee. This period extends from 30 AD to 50 AD. A pinpoint in time from which we can establish more specific details, however, is given to us in Acts 18:12:

---

[14] Malina, Bruce J. Rohrbaugh, Richard. L. *Social-Science Commentary on the Synoptic Gospels*. Second Ed. Fortress Press: Minneapolis, 2003, pp 141-142

> But when Gallio was proconsul of Achaia, the Jews made a united attack on Paul and brought him before the tribunal (Acts 18:12 ESV).

Gallio was the son of the rhetorician Seneca the Elder and the elder brother of Seneca the Younger. He was adopted by Lucius Junius Gallio from whom he took the name of Junius Gallio. It is now possible to establish the exact year of Gallio's proconsulship through the discovery of the Delphi Inscription of the Emperor Claudius in which Gallio is referred to as the Proconsul of Achaia. By combining the date of the Claudius Inscription with other historical factors, Gallio's proconsulship in Achaia can be precisely dated between late spring and late October 52 AD.

Using this pinpoint in time, in combination with other information provided in Acts and in Paul's letters, we can now work backwards from this precise date of 52 AD to establish an early chronology of Paul's travels. We will focus only on those aspects of this chronology which enable us to also fix Peter's presence with reasonable accuracy at various times and in various places.

Peter in Jerusalem : 30-33 AD

Peter confronts Jerusalem elites from Pentecost until the execution of Stephen, which took place before Paul's epiphany on the road to Damascus (see Acts 1-7 and Galatians 1).

Peter in Jerusalem : 36-37 AD

Paul meets Peter and James in Jerusalem three years after the road to Damascus experience:

> Then after three years, I went up to Jerusalem to get acquainted with Cephas and stayed with him fifteen days. I saw none of the other apostles—only James, the Lord's brother (Galatians 1:18-19 NIV. Read in conjunction with Acts 9:26).

Peter in Jerusalem : March-April 43 or 44 AD

Peter is jailed by Herod Agrippa I, "about that time" (of the famine reported in Acts 11):

> About that time Herod the king laid violent hands on some who belonged to the church. He killed James the brother of John with the sword, and when he saw that it pleased the Jews, he proceeded to arrest Peter also. This was during the days of Unleavened Bread. And when he had seized him, he put him in

prison, delivering him over to four squads of soldiers to guard him, intending after the Passover to bring him out to the people (Acts 12:1-4 ESV).

Peter escapes before his trial is due to begin and departs to "another place" (Acts 12:6-17). Note that the parallels between the recounting of the death of Herod Agrippa in Acts 12:19-23 and Josephus' account of the same event are quite striking. [15]

Peter in Jerusalem : 48-49 AD

Jerusalem Council

The question of whether or not followers of Jesus should be circumcised had caused conflict in Antioch. Paul and Barnabas, along with "some other believers", were appointed to go and discuss the issue with the elders and apostles in Jerusalem. A decision was reached by the elders and apostles in the name of the whole Jerusalem church that followers should not be required to be circumcised although they should still observe some Levitical laws regarding diet and morality. The elders and apostles sent a letter to that effect to the believers in Antioch, Syria and Cilicia (see Acts 15:1-35). The scholarly consensus is that the Jerusalem Council described in Acts 15 is the same meeting that Paul describes in Galatians 2.

In Galatians 2:9 we read of a clear division of ministries: Paul and Barnabas were to preach to the Gentiles *(ethnē)*, i.e. those who followed the customs and practices of Hellenists while Peter and the other disciples were to preach to the circumcised, i.e. those who followed the customs and practices of the Judeans who worshipped at the temple in Jerusalem.

By analysing all the above information, it is reasonable to conclude that between 30 AD and 49-50 AD, between Pentecost and the Jerusalem Council, Peter had been pursuing his mission to the circumcised in Judea, Samaria and Galilee and, according to Paul, his intention in 50 AD was to continue the way he had begun.

Peter in Antioch

> But when Cephas came to Antioch, I opposed him to his face, because he stood condemned. For prior to the coming of certain men from James, he used to eat with the Gentiles; but when they came, he began to withdraw and hold himself aloof, fearing the party of the circumcision (Galatians 2:11-12 NASB).

Scholars are divided on the date of this conflict between Paul and Peter. It can be narrowed down, however, to just before the Jerusalem Council or just after so it makes

---

15 Josephus, *Antiquities*, XIX.8.3

little difference for our purposes, which are to demonstrate that there is sufficient data in Acts and Paul's letter to the Galatians to situate Peter either in Jerusalem, or engaged on various missionary journeys in the regions of Judea, Samaria, Galilee and Antioch between 30 AD and 49-50 AD. As we have arrived in Antioch, it is perhaps noteworthy to point out that the Papacy is not the only claimant to Apostolic Succession through Peter.

The Syrian Orthodox Church claims an unbroken Apostolic Succession beginning with Peter founding the Church at Antioch and continuing to this day. They give the dates 37-67 AD for Peter's Patriarchate. Even though there is as little credence in their supposed line of succession as there is in that of the Papacy, there was at least a great deal of apostolic activity in Antioch and Peter was recorded in the New Testament as actually being in that city whereas the only New Testament reference that supporters for Peter's presence in Rome can muster up is:

> The church that is at Babylon, elected together with you, saluteth you; and so doth Marcus my son (1 Peter 5:13 KJV).

It is necessary to deal with this assertion at length so, once we have exhausted all other sources, we will deal with the Petrine Epistles.

Note

It is extremely important to keep in mind when reading the following material that the designations "Jew/s" and "Jewish", which will be used from this point, refer to those particular Israelites who practised the customs of the Judeans who worshipped at the Temple in Jerusalem and followed the Law of Moses including the requirement for circumcision.

Peter's whereabouts 50-54 AD

Before we attempt to discover Peter's possible whereabouts after 50 AD, we must first turn our attention to source material that militates against Peter being in Rome in the period immediately following the Jerusalem Council.

As noted previously, Gallio was proconsul of Achaia in late 52 AD. According to Acts 18:11, Paul resided for 18 months in Corinth before he was brought before Gallio. Therefore, we can date his arrival in that city to early in 51 AD.

It is recorded in Acts that Paul meets Priscilla and Aquila in Corinth:

> There he met a Jew named Aquila, a native of Pontus, who had recently come from Italy with his wife Priscilla, because Claudius had ordered all Jews to leave Rome…(Acts 18:2 NIV).

The Jewish believers Priscilla and Aquila were already present in Corinth when Paul arrived there having "recently come from Italy". According to the Roman historian Suetonius, "Since the Jews constantly made disturbances at the instigation of Chrestus, he (Emperor Claudius) expelled them from Rome".[16] This expulsion of the Jews from Rome can be dated to 49 AD.

Most scholars agree that this statement does not refer directly to "Christ" or to an individual named "Chrestus" but most likely refers to preachers who caused a disturbance among Jewish residents of Rome by proclaiming that "Jesus is the Christ". The edict probably did not apply to non-Jewish converts but, whatever the case, the expulsion order certainly applied to Jewish believers such as Priscilla and Aquila, whom Paul met in Corinth in early 51 AD. Just like Priscilla and Aquila, if Peter had been in Rome at that time, then he would certainly have been expelled along with them. The expulsion edict would have gone out of effect at the death of Claudius in 54 AD and, since the following emperor (Nero) did not renew the edict, those expelled could have returned to Rome after 54 AD.

It is therefore reasonable to conclude that Peter did not go to Rome after the Jerusalem Council of 50 AD because of the Claudian edict. It is also reasonable to conclude that the earliest possible time that he could journey to Rome was after 54 AD when the edict lapsed.

Peter's whereabouts 54-62 AD

Material that militates against Peter journeying to Rome after 54 AD can be found in Paul's letters and in Acts.

In Acts 2:9-10, we find that visitors from Rome, both Jews and proselytes, were present in Jerusalem at Pentecost and heard Peter preach that Jesus was their long-awaited Israelite Messiah. It is more than likely therefore that the Gospel message was carried to Rome at a very early stage. However, on the question of when the Jesus community in Rome was established, and by whom, the New Testament is silent.

When Paul writes to these Roman believers circa 56-57 AD, after the Claudian edict had lapsed, they had re-established themselves and were flourishing. As Paul said: "…your faith is proclaimed throughout the whole world", i.e. where the Gospel had been proclaimed in the provinces of the Roman Empire (Romans 1:8).

In Romans Chapter 16, we find a named list of believers resident in Rome, including those of Priscilla and Aquila who must have returned to Rome after the Claudian edict had lapsed. Note that Paul does not directly greet these friends and co-workers,

---

16 Suetonius, *Life of Claudius*, 25:4

but rather has them pass on his greetings to one another. Conspicuously absent from this list of names is the one person we would most expect to find included if he were present in Rome, the only man who had known Jesus face to face—Peter the Apostle.

Section 3

Life Expectancy in the 1st Century AD

Richard Ascough has this to say on the subject of life-expectancy in the First Century AD:

> Mortality rates from antiquity are not easy to determine, particularly since the records we have are rather sketchy and are localised. The attempts that have been made paint a picture of life expectancies that are rather bleak. Although much of the evidence comes from the late Roman period and/or from Egypt, it is probably safe to assume that the overall conditions across the empire in the first century were not particularly better. We find that there was a very high infant mortality rate, especially up to age one, assuming that the child even made it past the threats of miscarriage and still-birth. One third of those who survived infancy were dead by age six and half of the children died by age ten. Nearly 60% of these survivors died by age sixteen and by age twenty-six 75% were dead. By age forty-six 90% had passed away, and less than 3% if the population made it to age sixty. [17]

Ascough goes on to say that a disproportionate number of deaths fell upon the lower rank residents of the villages and cities. We can see from this data that if Peter were still alive in 62 AD, as was Paul, he would have already beaten the odds against him by a considerable margin.

What age would Peter have been in 62 AD? At the time he met Jesus around 28 AD, he was already married, was in a business partnership with Andrew, James and John, and was the owner of his own fishing boat. Even by the most generous estimates, Peter would have been at least in his late fifties and possibly much older in 62 AD so, given the terrible hardships of travel through the Mediterranean for anyone, let alone a person of advanced age by 1st Century standards, I don't propose to go beyond this date in our quest for a Roman Peter.

---

17 Ascough, Richard S. Malina, Bruce J. (ed). *Lydia: Paul's Cosmopolitan Hostess (Paul's Social Network: Brothers and Sisters in Faith)*. Liturgical Press: Minnesota, 2009, pp 43-44.

We have outlined above some objections to Peter's presence in Rome between 50 and 62 AD. So, if it were not westwards to Rome, where amongst the many communities of Diaspora Israelites would Peter have been most likely to go in furtherance of his personal commission by Jesus to preach the gospel to the "lost sheep of the House of Israel?"

Before we attempt to provide a reasonable answer to that question, we will first deal with another piece of alleged "evidence" that the authorities rely on to substantiate their claims to Universal Primacy through the Apostle Peter.

CHAPTER SEVEN

Clement and the Corinthians

Although it may be quite tedious for readers, it is nevertheless crucial to deal with the 1st Epistle of Clement to the Corinthians, written circa 96-100 AD. This Epistle is arguably the most important piece of alleged "evidence" upon which advocates of Papal Primacy rely, claiming that it demonstrates an early exercise of authority flowing from Peter's presence in Rome. The former Pope Benedict XVI, now Pope Emeritus, had this to say in 2007:

> "Already in the first century, popes exercised their primacy over the other Churches," Benedict XVI says. The Holy Father explained this on Wednesday at the general audience, which he dedicated to Pope St. Clement of Rome, the third successor of Peter. Speaking to some 16,000 people gathered both in Paul VI Hall and St. Peter's Basilica, the Pontiff began a new series of catecheses on the Apostolic Fathers. Benedict XVI mentioned that Clement's Letter to the Corinthians was given "[a]n almost canonical characteristic." The letter noted that the Church of Corinth was experiencing severe divisions. "The priests of the community, in fact, had been deposed by some young upstarts," the Holy Father said. And quoting St. Irenaeus, he explained the context of Clement's letter: "[t]he Church of Rome sent the Corinthians a very important letter to reconcile them in peace to renew their faith and to announce the tradition, a tradition they had so newly received from the apostles." Benedict XVI continued: "Therefore we could say that [Clement's letter] is a first exercise of a Primate of Rome after the death of St. Peter." He added that the letter "opened to the Bishop of Rome the possibility for vast intervention on the identity of the Church and its mission." [18]

Pope Benedict made two major claims in this address:

1. "Pope St. Clement of Rome" was the third successor of Peter;
2. The 1st Epistle of Clement to the Corinthians proves that in the First Century AD, popes already exercised their primacy over other churches.

---

18 *Benedict XVI Highlights 1st Century Papal Primacy*, Vatican City: March 8, 2007. Reproduced by Byzantine Catholic Church in America. Accessed 4 January 2018 http://byzcath.com/index.php/news-mainmenu-49/225-benedict-xvi-highlights-1st-century-papal-primacy

A closer look at the 1st Epistle of Clement to the Corinthians

Towards the end of the First Century AD, an upsurge of factionalism in the congregation at Corinth caused a divisiveness and resentment that resulted in widespread embarrassment to other Christian congregations. The Roman congregation wrote a letter to the Corinthian congregation pleading that they settle their differences and reminding them that the essence of the teachings of Jesus was love and humility.

Keep the following points in mind:

- The Epistle is anonymous. Therefore we know nothing about its author. Later tradition asserts it was written by a man named "Clement";

- The author is not named as head of the church in Rome;

- Nowhere does the author assert the primacy of Rome over other churches. On the contrary, the author makes his appeal to the Corinthians on the values of self-abasement, humility and love, as did Jesus in his sermons, "For Christ is with them that are lowly of mind, not with them that exalt themselves over the flock" (1 Clement 16:1);

- The author does not appeal to his own authority, or to that of his congregation, but to the authority of scripture, from which he quotes copiously to reinforce his arguments;

- For the writer of I Clement, the presbyterial college form of church government is normative and proper. The most important purpose in writing is the restoration of the Corinthian presbyters so that the faithful transmission of apostolic teaching is secured.

There is a broad consensus among scholars that 1 Clement does not establish the Primacy of the Church in Rome, or the succession of bishops from the Apostle Peter. I have chosen from amongst these scholars the following crucial observations by Peter Lampe:

> Before the middle of the second century in Rome, at no time did one single prominent person pass on the tradition: this was done by a plurality of presbyters…at the time that Rome experiences the development of a monarchical episcopacy, a twelve-member list of names going back to the apostles is constructed…the presence of a monarchical bearer of tradition is projected back into the past…the list of Irenaus (Haer.3.3.3) is with highest probability a historical construction from the 180's when the monarchical episcopacy developed in Rome. Above all, the framework of "apostolic" twelve

members (from Linus to Eleutherus) points in the direction of a fictive construction. The names that were woven into the construction were certainly not freely invented but were borrowed from the tradition of the city of Rome (for example "Clement" or "Pius" the brother of Hermas). They had belonged to presbyters of Roman church history. These persons, however, would never have understood themselves as monarchical leaders—especially Pius at the time of Hermas.[19]

Peter Lampe demonstrates that the purpose of this Pope list was to anchor the then current doctrine with a successive chain of authorities back to the apostles and not to prove a succession of monarchical bishops. Peter Lampe's account makes fascinating reading.

Chapter Five

It is important to keep in mind that the historical claims of the Papacy rest entirely on Peter's alleged death in Rome. The mention of both Peter and Paul in Chapter 5 of the Epistle has at times been put forward in support of these claims.

J.B. Lightfoot's translation of Chapter 5:

> But, to pass from the examples of ancient days, let us come to those champions who lived nearest to our time. Let us set before us the noble examples which belong to our generation. By reason of jealousy and envy the greatest and most righteous pillars of the Church were persecuted, and contended even unto death. Let us set before our eyes the good Apostles. There was Peter who by reason of unrighteous jealousy endured not one but many labors, and thus having borne his testimony went to his appointed place of glory. By reason of jealousy and strife Paul by his example pointed out the prize of patient endurance. After that he had been seven times in bonds, had been driven into exile, had been stoned, had preached in the East and in the West, he won the noble renown which was the reward of his faith, having taught righteousness unto the whole world and having reached the farthest bounds of the West; and when he had borne his testimony before the rulers, so he departed from the world and went unto the holy place, having been found a notable pattern of patient endurance.[20]

---

19 Lampe, Peter. *Christians at Rome in the First Two Centuries: From Paul to Valentinus*. Continuum International Publishing Group: London, 2006, pp. 405-406.

20 Early Christian Writings, *Clement of Rome, First Epistle*. Accessed 4 January 2018. http://www.earlychristianwritings.com/text/1clement-lightfoot.html

In the words "There was Peter who by reason of unrighteous jealousy endured not one but many labors, and thus having borne his testimony went to his appointed place of glory", is found evidence that Peter was martyred in Rome.

Although the apostles are bracketed together, the Epistle makes it as a distinguishing circumstance of Paul that he preached both *in the East and West*, implying that Peter never was in the West.

Only a determinedly preconceived motive could possibly extract from this Epistle one shred of evidence that Peter died in Rome, or that the "Primate of Rome" exercised authority over other churches in the 1st Century. Even Pope Benedict's use of the term "Primate of Rome" is anachronistic as the monarchical episcopate was not in existence at the time of the Epistle's writing, either in Rome or in Corinth.

Despite no evidence whatever, the Papacy continues to repeat the age-old mantra of Universal Primacy and Apostolic Succession through the Apostle Peter because Peter was allegedly martyred in Rome:

> In Peter's person, mission and ministry, in his presence and death in Rome attested by the most ancient literary and archaeological tradition—the Church sees a deeper reality essentially related to her own mystery of communion and salvation: 'Ubi Petrus, ibi ergo Ecclesia'. From the beginning and with increasing clarity, the Church has understood that, just as there is a succession of the Apostles in the ministry of Bishops, so too the ministry of unity entrusted to Peter belongs to the permanent structure of Christ's Church and that this succession is established in the See of his martyrdom.[21]

The 1st Epistle of Clement to the Corinthians is a two-edged sword for the Church. On the one hand, as a genuine piece of early correspondence from one Christian community to another, the Church must hang its monumental claims to Papal Primacy upon this single slender thread. On the other hand, however, the Epistle reflects none of the Church's superimposed doctrines such as the Virgin Birth. The author refers to "Jesus Christ the High Priest by whom our gifts are offered", and nowhere is Jesus presented as anything other than man of God.

---

21   *The Primacy of the Successor of Peter in the Mystery of the Church:* Reflections of the Congregation for the Doctrine of the Faith by Cardinal Joseph Ratzinger, Prefect, and Tarcisio Bertone, Archbishop emeritus of Vercelli, Secretary. Reported in *Il Primato del Successore di Pietro, Atti del Simposio teologico*, Rome, 2-4 December 1996, *Libreria Editrice Vaticana*, Vatican City, 1998.

CHAPTER EIGHT

Centres of Israelite life in the 1st Century AD

Although readers may find it tedious, we must take a necessarily brief and incomplete journey through the geography and demography of the ancient Near East if a full understanding of some vital aspects of the New Testament is desired.

In addition to the people of the tribes of Judah and Benjamin then living in the land of Israel, there were also many Jewish communities scattered around the shores of the Mediterranean. By far the largest groups, however, lived beyond the sway of Rome in various locations controlled by client kings of the Parthian Empire, the successor of the previous Achaemenid (Persian) and Seleucid dynasties.

According to Pliny the Elder,[22] the Parthian empire consisted of 18 kingdoms (or satrapies), 11 of which were called the upper kingdoms, while 7 were called the lower kingdoms, meaning that they were located on the plains of Mesopotamia. The centre of the lower kingdoms was ancient Babylonia.

We will concern ourselves with the three Parthian satrapies of Media, Elam and Babylonia in which were situated the three great cities of the former Persian period, known to contemporary Greeks and Jews as Ecbatana, Shushan, and Babylon.[23]

Ecbatana in Media

The modern city of Hamadan is located in North-West Iran and is identified with ancient Ecbatana (Biblical Achmetha), capital of Media Magna. According to the Book of Ezra, an edict by the Persian King Cyrus to rebuild the Temple in Jerusalem was discovered in the fortress of Ecbatana during the reign of Darius who decreed that the edict be honoured. This Cyrus Edict was found in Ecbatana in 1879 (see Ezra 6:1-12).[24]

Ecbatana had been the summer residence of Persian royalty and, according to Josephus, also the burial place of the kings of "Media, of Persia, and of Parthia".[25] Also

---

22 Pliny the Elder. *Natural History, VI. 112*.

23 Olmstead A.T. *History of the Persian Empire*. University of Chicago Press: Chicago, 1970, p. 162.

24 Known as the Cyrus Cylinder, the Akkadian script confirms that Cyrus had a policy of restoring cult sanctuaries and repatriating deported peoples.

25 Josephus, *Antiquities*, X.263

in Ecbatana is a little mausoleum, supposedly containing the remains of the biblical figures Esther and Mordecai.

The detailed accounts of two celebrated twelfth-century Jewish tourists—Benjamin of Tudela[26] and Petahiah of Regensburg—are among the most crucial sources of geographic and demographic information about ancient Jewish communities of the Persian and Parthian periods.

Benjamin of Tudela reported that by the middle of the 12th Century AD, the descendants of the Jewish populations of various towns in ancient Media, such as Hamadan, Fars and Isfahan, numbered into the many tens of thousands. In addition to these Jewish communities of Media were also thousands of Israelites who had been deported to "Halah, in Gozan by the Habor River, and in the cities of the Medes" (2 Kings 17:6) circa 720 BC by the Assyrian Sargon II after his capture of Samaria, the capital of the Northern Kingdom of Israel.[27] Prior to the discovery of the Khorsabad Annals of Sargon in 1847, most historians had regarded the following biblical story of this Israelite deportation as mythical:

> In the ninth year of the reign of Hoshea, the king of Assyria captured Samaria and carried away the Israelites to Assyria, where he settled them in Halah, in Gozan by the Habor River, and in the cities of the Medes (2 Kings 17:6 NIV).

Josephus, a contemporary of both Peter and Paul, confirmed that these ten tribes were still an identifiable group in his own time, dwelling beyond the Euphrates and not subject to the Romans:

> Wherefore there are but two tribes (the Jews) in Europe and Asia subject to the Romans, while the ten tribes (Israelites) are beyond the Euphrates till now, and are an immense multitude, and not to be estimated by numbers. [28]

Shushan in Elam

The ancient city of Shushan (Susa) was the capital of Elam. It lay in the northern portion of the modern province of Khuzistan in the South-West corner of Iran. The city proper lay to the North-East of the head of the Persian Gulf. We find reference to Shushan in the biblical books of Daniel, Esther and Nehemiah:

---

26 www.jewishencyclopedia.com/articles/2988-benjamin-of-tudela

27 *Annals: 2nd year of Sargon II*, J. B. Pritchard (ed.), *Ancient Near Eastern Texts Relating to the Old Testament*, 3rd edition; Princeton University Press: Princeton. 1969.

28 Josephus, *Antiquities*, XI.5.2

> In my vision I saw myself in the palace of Shushan in the province of Elam; in the vision I was beside the Ulai Canal (Daniel 8:2 NIV).

> Now it came to pass in the days of Ahasuerus, (this is Ahasuerus which reigned, from India even unto Ethiopia, over an hundred and seven and twenty provinces:) That in those days, when the king Ahasuerus sat on the throne of his kingdom, which was in Shushan the palace, In the third year of his reign, he made a feast unto all his princes and his servants; the power of Persia and Media, the nobles and princes of the provinces, being before him (Esther 1:1-4 KJV).

> The words of Nehemiah the son of Hachaliah. And it came to pass in the month Chisleu, in the twentieth year, as I was in Shushan the palace… (Nehemiah 1:1 KJV).

Our 12th Century Spanish globetrotter, Benjamin of Tudela, gave an account of his visit to Shushan and the reputed place of the tomb of Daniel the prophet:

> The River Tigris divides the city, and the bridge connects the two parts. On one side, where the Jews (7,000) dwell, is the sepulchre of Daniel.[29]

Babylon in Babylonia

Although we can discern a measure of status enjoyed at certain times by the Jewish communities scattered throughout the Persian and later Parthian Empire, such as those in Media and Elam, those communities never attained the status, wealth, power and influence possessed by the 1st Century descendants of the Jewish elite class of royals and nobles who had been deported to Babylon after the capture of Jerusalem and the destruction of the Temple of Solomon by the Babylonian King Nebuchadnezzar in 586 BC.

The wealth and influence of Babylonian Jewry

The head of the Jewish community of Babylon—who was officially recognized by the Persian authorities—was called *Resh Galusa* in Aramaic, which means *Rosh Galut* in Hebrew, and *Head of the Diaspora* in English. The Jewish community in Babylon was the "mother" of the world Diaspora.

---

29 *The Itinerary of Benjamin of Tudela*. Trans. Marcus Nathan Adler. Selzer Books, 2018.

Both Philo[30] and Josephus[31] inform us that, in the apostolic age, Babylonian Jews were very numerous and very wealthy and every year sent large amounts of silver and gold to the Temple in Jerusalem, whereas Jews were comparatively few in Rome, about eight thousand according to Josephus.[32]

Hillel the Elder

Hillel the Elder, one of the Jewish elite of Babylonia, re-located to Jerusalem during the reign of Herod the Great, became prominent circa 30 BC, and died circa 10 BC. Hillel was the renowned sage and scholar who founded the school named after him, was head of the Great Sanhedrin and, according to Rabbinic tradition, the ancestor of the patriarchs who headed Palestinian Judaism till about the 5th Century AD.

High Priest Hananel

Herod the Great was sole ruler of the Roman province of Judea from 37 BC to 4 BC. His first appointment to the position of High Priest in Jerusalem was Hananel, a Jew from Babylonia. (Only two years later, Hananel was deposed as High Priest by Herod at the behest of the Roman Triumvir, Marc Antony.)

Herod the Great

So influential were those Babylonians who could claim royal descent from King David that Herod himself, although an Idumean by birth, tried to insinuate himself into this royal Babylonian stock in order to increase his honour status. It was conventional at this time for any claimant to legitimate power in Israel to allege Davidic lineage, as is evident by the entire New Testament's insistence on Jesus being a descendant of David "according to the flesh".

Connections

A constant flow of correspondence passed back and forth between the Jerusalem establishment and the heads of Babylonian Jewry until the destruction of the Jerusalem Temple in 70 AD:

> For example, Gamaliel I, a 'teacher of the law,' a Pharisee, and member of the council of the Temple (Acts 5:34) sent letters to Jews in other parts of the world, including specifically Babylonia, concerning tithing regulations and intercalations of the calendar, as did R. Johanan ben Zakai and R. Simeon ben Gamaliel afterwards. They addressed themselves to 'our brethren in the

---

30 Philo, *Legatio ad Cajum*, 36.

31 Josephus, *Antiquities*, XV.2.2; XXIII.12

32 ibid XVII.2

Exile of Babylonia' as well as to those in Media and elsewhere…Thus through pilgrimages, through correspondence on matters of law and doctrine, and through exerting authority over the designation of the sacred days (intercalation of the calendar), as well as through collections of Temple funds, frequent and normal relations were maintained between Jerusalem and the diaspora, including Babylonia, and the influence of Palestine was exerted throughout the golah (diaspora).[33]

It is important for our purposes to note here that the centre of the lower Parthian satrapies was Babylonia located on the plains of Mesopotamia. Thus the Babylonian Jews were included among the Mesopotamian Jews whom Peter addressed specifically at Pentecost (Acts 2:9).

From all the foregoing we can determine that, in addition to the many Jewish communities scattered around the shores of the Mediterranean and under the control of the Roman Empire, there were also many Jews and Israelites living beyond the sway of Rome in the various locations previously mentioned.

---

33 Nuesner, Jacob. *A History of the Jews of Babylonia : Vol I. The Parthian Period.* E.J.Brill: Netherlands, 1969, pp. 37-45.

CHAPTER NINE

Luke's Pentecost

Pentecost (Hebrew *Shavuot*) was the name given by Greek-speaking Jews to the festival which occurred fifty days after the offering of the barley sheaf during the Passover feast.

> In Palestine the grain harvest lasted seven weeks and was a season of gladness (Jer. v. 24; Deut. xvi. 9; Isa. ix. 2). It began with the harvesting of the barley (Men. 65-66) during the Passover and ended with the harvesting of the wheat at Pentecost, the wheat being the last cereal to ripen. Pentecost was thus the concluding festival of the grain harvest, just as the eighth day of Tabernacles was the concluding festival of the fruit harvest (comp. Pesik. xxx. 193). According to Ex. xxxiv. 18-26 (comp. ib. xxiii. 10-17), the Feast of Weeks is the second of the three festivals to be celebrated by the altar dance of all males at the sanctuary…[34]

The festival of *Shavuot* (Pentecost) is the traditional anniversary of the day on which God spoke at Sinai, which is believed to have occurred fifty days after the first Passover lamb was eaten on the eve of the Exodus from Egypt.

Acts 2:1-4

The author of Luke's Gospel draws on a wealth of parallels from the Hebrew Scriptures to makes it abundantly clear that the first *Shavuot* in the New Creation represents a new Sinai:

> When the day of Pentecost had come, they were all together in one place. And suddenly there came from heaven a noise like a violent rushing wind, and it filled the whole house where they were sitting. And there appeared to them tongues as of fire distributing themselves, and they rested on each one of them. And they were all filled with the Holy Spirit and began to speak with other tongues, as the Spirit was giving them utterance (Acts 2:1-4 NASB).

Just as God's presence on Sinai was represented by earthquake, thundering sounds and fire, so also is God's presence at this Pentecost represented by thundering sounds and tongues of fire. Luke's account also evokes an early rabbinic teaching that the voice of God on Sinai divided into seventy tongues and all the nations received God's Law in their own language. (Note also that the concept of "tongues of fire" appears

---

[34] Jewish Encyclopaedia Article: *Pentecost*. Accessed 4 January 2018. http://www.jewishencyclopedia.com/articles/12012-pentecost#ixzz1U0gc64Du

in at least two Dead Sea Scrolls fragments.) Consider also the "about 3000" people destroyed in Exodus 32:28 with the "about 3000" people baptised in Acts 2:41.

The concern of Luke-Acts is focused on Israel and, needless to say, all these parallels would have passed completely over the heads of non-Israelites. For our purposes it is not necessary to go on and further analyse the traditional Israelite basis for the Pentecost experience but only to be aware of the identity of the parties who saw and heard what happened on that day.

Acts 2:5

> Now there were staying in Jerusalem God-fearing Jews from every nation under heaven (Acts 2:5 NIV).

This verse refers to those ethnic in-groups who follow the customs of the Jews of Judea who worship at the Temple in Jerusalem and follow the Law of Moses including the practice of circumcision.

Acts 2:9-11

These verses go on to describe the "God-fearing Jews" according to where they lived among non-Israelites, i.e. Jewish Parthians, Jewish Medes, Jewish Elamites, Jewish Mesopotamians, Jewish Judeans and so on. (Jesus and most of his disciples were Jewish Galileans.)

Acts 2:14-41

Peter begins his witness to this group by addressing them as "Men of Judea and all who dwell in Jerusalem…" and finishes with "Therefore let the *entire house of Israel* know with certainty that God has made him both Lord and Messiah, this Jesus whom you crucified".

From Luke's account of Pentecost, we can determine the following:

- That Peter desired the *entire house of Israel* to know that the long-awaited Messiah of Israel had already been made manifest;
- That, for Luke, this day of Pentecost represented a new Sinai for the *entire house of Israel*;
- That Luke went to considerable pains to demonstrate that this day of Pentecost was a uniquely Israelite experience drawn from uniquely Israelite traditions.

In summary, the Pentecost experience recorded in Acts was written to Israel, for Israel, about Israel. It would have had absolutely no meaning or relevance for non-Israelites.

We discovered from the historical sources already provided that many of the dispersed of Israel were located in the very territories mentioned in Acts 2:9-11. We further discovered that the most influential, the most wealthy, and the most powerful of all the diaspora groups in the First Century AD was located on the Mesopotamian plain, in Babylon and its surrounds.

This question was posed in a previous Chapter:

> We have outlined above some objections to Peter's presence in Rome between 50 and 62 AD. So, if it were not westwards to Rome, where amongst the many communities of Diaspora Israelites would Peter have been most likely to go in furtherance of his personal commission by Jesus to preach the gospel to the "lost sheep of the House of Israel?"

The most reasonable answer to this question is that Peter would likely have travelled eastwards to the regions of Babylon on the Mesopotamian plain where the great majority of these "lost sheep of the House of Israel" then lived.

The Twelve Witnesses

In Acts 1:15, we find Peter addressing a group of 120 "brothers". The very first item on the agenda of this group is to appoint a replacement for Judas. Peter points out that because Judas had been "one of our number and shared in our ministry", it was necessary to replace him with one similarly qualified:

> Therefore it is necessary to choose one of the men who have been with us the whole time the Lord Jesus was living among us, beginning from John's baptism to the time when Jesus was taken up from us. For one of these must become a witness with us of his resurrection (Acts 1:21-22 NIV).

This first order of business underscores the importance Luke placed on the symbolism of there being twelve witnesses, one for each of the twelve tribes of Israel. These twelve witnesses were chosen because they had the necessary qualifications to offer first-hand authentication of Jesus' life from his baptism to his resurrection. The task and role of the twelve is to serve as eye-witnesses, to attest to the truth of what the God of Israel has done to Jesus on Israel's behalf (Acts 2:32; 3:15; 5:32; 10:39, 41; 13:31). It is surely stating the obvious that first-hand witnesses can have no successors.

Peter therefore can have no successor.

Note

While some translations of Acts 1:15 favour gender-inclusive language, the substitution of "brothers" with words like "believers" and "friends" conceals the reason why Luke specifies that there were 120 "names" (persons) present, such reason being that each of the twelve is affiliated with ten males, ten males being the number required to constitute an Israelite quorum.

CHAPTER TEN

The General Epistles

Section 1

Introduction

The First Epistle of Peter belongs to that section of the New Testament variously referred to as the "general" or "catholic" epistles. This section includes James, the Petrine Epistles, the Johannine Epistles and Jude. The terminology reflects the "general" or "catholic" (universal) nature of their contents in that they contain broad-based concepts rather than the specific issues we find Paul grappling with in his correspondence to specific communities. This group of epistles is also sometimes referred to as the "Jewish" epistles in recognition of their Jewish content and character and also because of the belief by some that the epistles bearing their names were penned by James, Peter and John, the "pillars" of the Jerusalem church.

A comparison between the numbers of scholarly works devoted to the Pauline corpus and those focusing on the general epistles will demonstrate that Paul has received far more than his fair share of attention while the general epistles have been largely ignored until relatively recently.

It could be argued that this neglect is not merely an oversight. The Pauline epistles have always been fertile ground for the teaching and preaching ministries of those who would tailor their contents to suit particular doctrinal purposes while the general epistles are far less subject to such manipulation. Even today, commentary on the general epistles is often focused on establishing authorship rather than on content and meaning. This misdirection is often compounded when such commentary is based on the premise that if Peter the Apostle wrote 1 Peter, then it must have been written in Rome.

Section 2

Relative Authority

Arguably, the most influential extant Greek Biblical manuscript is the 4th Century AD *Codex Vaticanus*, one of the four uncial codices. As its name suggests, it now resides in the Vatican Library. The order of the New Testament books included in *Codex Vaticanus* are:

- The Four Gospels;
- Acts;
- The general epistles (James, the Petrine Epistles, the Johannine Epistles, and Jude;
- Paul's epistles (including Hebrews).

Note that the epistles of Paul's three "pillars" (Galatians 2:9) are placed immediately after Acts, in precisely Paul's order—James, Peter and John—reflecting the recognition of superior teaching authority deriving from first-hand witnesses. Unfortunately, rather than reflecting superior teaching authority, the ordering of books in the New Testament now reflects the ordering found in Jerome's Latin Vulgate.

Section 3

The First Epistle of Peter

Although an exhaustive analysis of the entire text of 1 Peter would be of great value, and prove more than a little illuminating, space precludes all but a brief commentary on some key issues.

Section 3a

The recipients

> Peter, an apostle of Jesus Christ, to the elect (*eklektois*) who are sojourners (*parepidémos*) of the Dispersion (*diasporas*) in Pontus, Galatia, Cappadocia, Asia, and Bithynia (I Peter 1:1 ASV).

These five regions are all located in the Northern half of Asia Minor, now modern Turkey. Note that Paul did not preach in these areas of Asia Minor but spent his time in the Southern, or Greek half. The names of these areas need not imply that they were officially recognised Roman provinces: they could just as correctly have referred to geographical areas known informally by those names in antiquity.

Among those commentators who do focus on content and meaning rather than on authorship, some proceed on the basis that Peter writes mainly for Gentile (non-Israelite) converts, and some on the basis that 1 Peter was written specifically for Jewish communities. (Whatever the case, later Christian doctrinal concepts entirely foreign to Jews are often retrojected into their commentaries.)

Let us attempt to settle the question. Consider the following points:

1. We learn from Acts 2:5-11 that waiting at Jerusalem for the feast of *Shavuot* were God-fearing Jews from every nation (peoples, Gentiles) under heaven: Parthians, Medes and Elamites; residents of Mesopotamia, Judea, Cappadocia, Pontus, Asia, Phrygia, Pamphylia, Egypt and the parts of Libya near Cyrene; visitors from Rome (both Jews and converts); Cretans and Arabs. Note that three of these "nations"—Cappadocia, Pontus and Asia—are listed in 1 Peter 1:1;

2. Peter uses terminology and conceptual frameworks that imply the readers' sophisticated and intimate familiarity with the Hebrew Scriptures, a familiarity almost impossible to attain unless imbibed along with mother's milk;

3. The persons to whom Peter writes he calls a chosen generation, a royal priesthood, a holy nation, a peculiar people (1 Peter 2:9), a direct reference to the blessings pronounced by God upon the whole House of Israel at Sinai (Exodus 19:6). Further, the House of Israel had been declared by God to be *not his people* (Hosea 1:9) but then had been brought back to God to once again *be his people* (Hosea 1:10; 2:23). In 1 Peter 2:10, the author specifically applies these passages from Hosea to his letter's intended recipients and in 2:12 he tells these recipients that God expects them to behave righteously among the Gentiles (non-Israelites);

4. Peter had been directly commissioned by Jesus to preach only to the lost sheep of the House of Israel and, by agreement among the Apostles, had the ministry of the circumcision particularly committed to him (Galatians 2:8);

5. Therefore, it should come as no surprise that in 1:1 we find Peter describing his readers as *eklektois parepidémos diasporas* (chosen sojourners of the dispersion). Legally, these persons could fall into the Roman category of

"resident aliens" but if we check Chapter 2:11-12 we will find that Peter is not referring to their legal status in the eyes of the Romans but to their status in the eyes of God as his covenant people:

> Dear friends, I urge you as aliens (*paroikos*) and exiles (*parepidémos*) to keep on abstaining from the desires of the flesh that wage war against the soul. Continue to live such upright lives among the gentiles that, when they slander you as practicers of evil, they may see your good actions and glorify God when he visits them (1 Peter 2:11-12 ISV).

The theme of God's covenant people wandering the face of the earth as aliens and exiles is the interpretive principle for study of the Hebrew Scriptures and forms the backdrop to the stories of Abraham, Moses, and the whole House of Israel. However, all looked towards the promise of an ingathering of exiles to the land of Israel from which they would never again be removed. This theme underlies not only the First Epistle of Peter but also every New Testament reference to the Kingdom of God on earth to be ruled over by the Messiah.

Summing up the recipients

The First Epistle of Peter was addressed to Jewish Messianists, i.e. to Jews who believed that the promises to their fathers had been fulfilled in that God had sent the long-awaited Messiah in the person of Jesus of Nazareth. Consequently, they could hope for a further promise fulfillment that they would one day be "resurrected" from their dispersion, regarded as a type of death, and ingathered to the land of Israel to form the Kingdom of God. These Jews formed part of God's covenantal sojourners who were afflicted in the Diaspora because of their ethnicity and customs.

Section 3b

Authorship

There is much scholarly dispute about authorship of the First Epistle of Peter. It would serve no useful purpose to delve into this minutiae as it would only add to the general confusion. We can, however, offer the observation that one of the most ridiculous arguments advanced against its authorship by Peter is the view that Jesus Messiah groups could not have spread within Peter's lifetime as far as the Roman provinces of Pontus, Galatia, Cappadocia, Asia, and Bithynia, all of which Peter names in the opening verse.

Proponents of this view are seemingly oblivious to the fact that Jews from three of the five places specifically mentioned in these verses—Cappadocia, Pontus, and Asia—had travelled to Jerusalem for *Shavuot* (Pentecost) and thus were present to hear Peter's speech (Acts 2:5-11).

Some of these groups of Jews were undoubtedly among the "three thousand" baptised (Acts 2:41).

Section 3c

Babylon

It is generally assumed that the city of Babylon began to decline after its conquest by the Persian king Cyrus the Great, fell rapidly into decay after its later conquest by Alexander the Great, until it was finally deserted in the First Century AD. This assumption is mainly based on Greek and Roman authors of the period such as Pausanias, Strabo, Diodorus, and Pliny the Elder.

However, as we discovered in a previous Chapter, a constant flow of correspondence passed back and forth between the Jerusalem establishment and the heads of Babylonian Jewry until the destruction of the Jerusalem Temple in 70 AD.[35] We also discovered that the contemporary Jewish authors Philo[36] and Josephus[37] were in a much better position to know the facts than any Greek or Roman author and they tell us that, in the apostolic age, Babylonian Jews were very numerous and very wealthy and every year sent large amounts of silver and gold to the Temple in Jerusalem, whereas Jews were comparatively few in Rome, about eight thousand according to Josephus.[38] It is also important to note here that because Babylonia was located on the plains of Mesopotamia, some of these very same Babylonian Jews must have been included among the Mesopotamian Jews whom Peter addressed specifically at Pentecost (Acts 2:9).

The assumed desertion of the city of Babylon was, and still is, advanced as a reason why the Apostle Peter could not have written 1 Peter from Babylon. However, it must be emphasised that the word "Babylon" does not necessarily refer to the city proper:

---

35 Nuesner, Jacob. *A History of the Jews of Babylonia : Vol I. The Parthian Period*. E.J.Brill: Netherlands, 1969, pp. 37-45.

36 Philo, *Legatio ad Cajum*, 36

37 Josephus, *Antiquities*, XV.2.2; XXIII.12

38 ibid XVII.2

it was also used to refer to the regions around the city and, as stated previously, to the centre of the Parthian province located on the Mesopotamian plain.

Coding Babylon

As noted in a previous Chapter, traditions about Peter's presence in Rome only surfaced in the latter half of the Second Century AD upon the circulation of the Clementine literature and the apocryphal Gospels and Acts, with their grotesque and fanciful tales about Simon Peter and Simon Magus.

Before the seat of the Roman Empire moved from Rome to Byzantium (renamed Constantinople) in 330 AD, some of these early concoctions were only concerned with tying the new religion to Rome by placing Peter, the alleged Chief of the Apostles, in the same city as the great Emperor.

These concoctions certainly influenced writers such as Tertullian of Carthage (c. 155 – c. 240 AD), the so-called "father of Latin Christianity":

> How happy is its church, on which apostles poured forth all their doctrine along with their blood! where Peter endures a passion like his Lord's! where Paul wins his crown in a death like John's where the Apostle John was first plunged, unhurt, into boiling oil, and thence remitted to his island-exile! [39]

And, according to Theodor Zahn,[40] even the historian Eusebius confused Simon Magus with Simon Peter.

So something with more *cachet* was needed, something that would ground all the legends in reality, something from the New Testament itself. That something was duly found because marching along a parallel path with the authors of the romances and apocrypha had been other writers claiming that the "Babylon the Great" term used in the Book of Revelation was a coded reference to Rome. Fortunately for the supporters of Peter's presence in Rome, a single verse in 1 Peter also refers to "Babylon":

> She (the church) who is in Babylon, chosen together with you, sends you her greetings, and so does my son Mark (1 Peter 5:13 ISV).

So this verse was drummed into service even though there is no absolutely no evidence that in New Testament times the city of Rome was known by its authors as Babylon. On the contrary, wherever Rome is mentioned in the New Testament, it receives its proper name—Rome.

---

39 Tertullian. *De praescriptione haereticorum* (On the prescription of heretics), 36

40 Zahn, Theodor. *Introduction to the New Testament: Vol. II.* Kregel Publications: Grand Rapids, 1953, p. 169.

The "Babylon is a code word for Rome" chestnut is very hoary indeed. It is used in such works as the *Sibylline Oracles* (5:159f), the *Apocalypse of Baruch* (2:1), and *4 Esdras* (3:1). None of these works, however, could be considered remotely reliable because all of them are pastiches of various works of uncertain origins, uncertain authorship, and uncertain times.

Fantastic fables became irreversibly entwined with the biblical material that Christianity is supposedly based upon and later writers began to speak with absolute certainty on matters that were simply unknown or unrecorded by earlier writers. For instance, Eusebius, writing in the early 4th Century, states that:

> It is said that Peter's first epistle, in which he makes mention of Mark, was composed at Rome itself; and that he himself indicates this, referring to the city figuratively as Babylon.[41]

There is no evidence that "Babylon" was used by the Jews as a code-word for Rome prior to the destruction of the Jerusalem Temple in 70 AD, by which time the Jewish Apostle Peter would have been long since dead. Indeed, in the first centuries of our era, Jews were more accustomed to equate Rome with Edom/Esau, not Babylon:

> The first rabbi who is cited as apparently identifying Rome with Esau and Edom is Rabbi Akiva (c. 50-135)...[42]

and later:

> The Holy One, blessed be He, knows that Israel is unable to endure the cruel decrees of Edom (Rome) and exiled them to Babylonia.[43]

Section 3d

Babylon the Great and the Great Irony

Apparently heedless of the simple fact that the other geographical designations in the First Epistle of Peter undoubtedly carry a literal meaning, and that the plain language of letters cannot possibly be compared to the type of language used in the Book of

---

41 Eusebius. *Historia Ecclesiastica*. 2, 15, 4

42 Feldman, Louis H. *Remember Amalek!: Vengeance, Zealotry, and Group Destruction in the Bible According to Philo, Pseudo-Philo, and Josephus*. Hebrew Union College Press: Pittsburgh, April 2004.

43 *Babylonian Talmud, Pesahim 87b*, cited by Jacob Neusner in *A History of the Jews in Babylonia: Vol 1. The Parthian Period*. E.J.Brill: Netherlands, 1969, p. 74.

Revelation, the belief that the Apostle Peter used the word "Babylon" as a code-word for Rome and wrote 1 Peter from Rome is more widespread today ever and is pursued by its proponents with vehemence.

Of course, there is a divine irony here. The alacrity with which Roman Catholic authorities assert that "Babylon is a code word for Rome" in 1 Peter 5:13 suddenly evaporates when it comes to the Book of Revelation where commentaries and footnotes bend over backwards to assure all and sundry that the term "Babylon the Great" refers either to pagan Imperial Rome, or to evil cities generally, and not to the Catholic Church. That would be unthinkable, they say. Of course, many non-Catholic denominations of Christendom dare to think the unthinkable.

CHAPTER ELEVEN

Rock-stone imagery

Section 1

In the Hebrew Scriptures

The "rock-stone" image recurs all throughout the Hebrew Scriptures and was used to refer to the Israelite God, to the gods of other peoples, to ordinary humans, and also to concepts. The rock-stone image of course is one of strength and, in the case of YHWH, also the associated ideas of reliability, faith and trust in God.

Of YHWH the God of Israel

> He is the Rock, his work is perfect: for all his ways are judgment: a God of truth and without iniquity, just and right is he (Deuteronomy 32:4 KJV).

> The LORD is my rock, my fortress and my deliverer; my God is my rock, in whom I take refuge, my shield and the horn of my salvation, my stronghold (Psalm 18:2 NIV).

Of the gods of other peoples

> And he shall say, Where are their gods, their rock in whom they trusted (Deuteronomy 32:37 KJV).

Of humans

> Listen to me, you who pursue righteousness and who seek the Lord: Look to the rock from which you were cut and to the quarry from which you were hewn; look to Abraham, your father, and to Sarah, who gave you birth (Isaiah 51:1-2 NIV).

> Therefore thus says the Lord GOD, "Behold, I am the one who has laid as a foundation in Zion, a stone, a tested stone, a precious cornerstone, of a sure foundation..." (Isaiah 28:16 ESV).

> The stone which the builders rejected Has become the chief corner stone. This is the LORD'S doing; It is marvelous in our eyes (Psalm 118:22-23 NASB).

Of the Kingdom

In the Book of Daniel, Chapter 2, we read that the prophet is brought before King Nebuchadnezzar, not only to recount a dream troubling the king, but also to provide an interpretation. Daniel tells Nebuchadnezzar that, in the dream, the king saw a great statue with a head of gold, chest and arms of silver, belly and thighs of bronze, legs of iron, and feet a combination of iron and clay. This symbol of earthly empires is then struck on its feet of iron and clay by a stone cut out of a mountain without human hands. The stone utterly destroys the statue and in turn becomes a great mountain that fills the whole earth (Daniel 2:1-23).

Daniel's Interpretation

After the fall of the Babylonian empire, other empires of gradually diminishing worth will arise until the last, the empire of iron and clay, will be destroyed by the stone cut out of the mountain without human hands. The stone, the *eben* (אֶבֶן), is the kingdom which the God of Heaven is about to set up, and which shall never be destroyed (Daniel 2:24-48).

Section 2

In Israelite thought

> As recorded in the Mishnah, while building the second temple, the masons cleared the floor of the original Holy of Holies (Solomon's Temple). In the center of that floor they found a single stone three fingerbreadths higher than the rest of the flagstones. They left it and the community named it eben shetiyah, "the foundation stone" (Mishnah. Moed, Yoma, 5:2. Danby Translation, p.167)[44] ...it is highly probably that this especially honoured stone was called eben shetiyah because the building of the Second Temple was seen as a fulfilment of the prophecy of Isaiah 28. They were building in Zion. Here was a precious stone, a sure foundation on which the entire temple complex, with its rich and meaningful liturgies, was based...The importance of the "foundation stone" was not lost by Jesus and the NT writers...[45]

---

[44] Published at the end of the second century AD, the Mishnah is an edited record of the complex body of material known as Oral Torah that was transmitted in the aftermath of 70 AD.

[45] Bailey, K.E. Inverted Parallelisms and Encased Parables in Isaiah and their significance for Old and New Testament Translation and Interpretation in *Literary Structure and Rhetorical Strategies in the Hebrew Bible*. (eds.) L. J. de Regt, Jan de Waard, J. P. Fokkelman. K. Van Gorcum & Co: Netherlands, 1996, p.18.

Section 3

In the New Testament

In the First Epistle of Peter, a work entirely dependent on the Hebrew Scriptures, the author draws on several "rock-stone" passages to give weight and authority to his presentation of Jesus as the ultimate expression of Israelite thought, as the chief corner-stone of a new spiritual Temple built without human hands, the same *eben* (אֶבֶן) of Daniel, that destroyed the kingdoms of the earth and is now the foundation of the kingdom which the God of Heaven is about to set up.

In 1 Peter 2:4-8, the author includes three quotes from the Hebrew Scriptures which he affirms are messianic expectations fulfilled in Jesus:

> As you come to him, a living stone rejected by men but in the sight of God chosen and precious, you yourselves like living stones are being built up as a spiritual house, to be a holy priesthood, to offer spiritual sacrifices acceptable to God through Jesus Christ. For it stands in Scripture: "Behold, I am laying in Zion a stone, a cornerstone chosen and precious, and whoever believes in him will not be put to shame" (Isaiah 28:16). So the honor is for you who believe, but for those who do not believe, "The stone that the builders rejected, has become the cornerstone"(Psalm 118:22) and "A stone of stumbling, and a rock of offense" (Isaiah 8:14) (1 Peter 2:4-8 ESV).

The author regards himself and his readers as living rocks-stones, a holy priesthood, building up this new spiritual Temple upon the foundation laid by Jesus Messiah. Compare this passage with the following from Romans 9:33 and Ephesians 2:20 where Paul makes use of a combination of the same Hebrew texts to portray Jesus as both a "stone of stumbling" laid in Zion and as the "cornerstone".

> As it is written, "Behold, I am laying in Zion a stone of stumbling, and a rock of offense and whoever believes in him will not be put to shame" (Romans 9:33 ESV).

> Now therefore ye are no more strangers and foreigners, but fellow citizens with the saints, and of the household of God; And are built upon the foundation of the apostles and prophets, Jesus Christ himself being the chief corner stone (Ephesians 2:19-20 ESV).

Jesus makes a veiled self-reference to the cornerstone in three parallel passages (Mark 12:10, Matthew 21:42, Luke 20:17), and Peter again states that Jesus is the cornerstone in Acts 4:11.

The authors of the New Testament viewed Jesus as the living embodiment of the "rock-stone" imagery found in the Hebrew Scriptures and also that this "rock-stone" was messianic in nature, as Paul states:

> For I do not want you to be ignorant of the fact, brothers and sisters, that our ancestors were all under the cloud and that they all passed through the sea. They were all baptized into Moses in the cloud and in the sea. They all ate the same spiritual food and drank the same spiritual drink; for they drank from the spiritual rock that accompanied them, and that rock was Christ (1 Corinthians 10:1-4 NIV).

In the Hebrew Scriptures, two occasions are mentioned in which Moses struck a rock and the Israelites miraculously received water (Exodus 17:1–7; Numbers 20:1–14). Since the rocks were apparently in different places, an Israelite folk tradition arose about a "physical" rock that accompanied them on their journey through the wilderness. In the above passage, Paul refutes this folk tradition and explains that it was not a "physical" but a "spiritual" rock that accompanied them in expectation of the Messiah. The smiting of the rock from which "physical" waters flowed prefigured the smiting of the Messiah from whom "spiritual" waters now flow.

Section 4

The Rock of stumbling

Note

In the time of Jesus, there were no individuals with the personal name of "Peter". It is merely a form of the New Testament Greek word Πέτρος (*Petros*), drawn from the Aramaic *kêfâ* (*cephas*), having the essential meaning of "rock" in both Greek and Aramaic. *Cephas* was the nickname that Jesus bestowed on the man known to his contemporaries as Simon bar Jonah. In common parlance, it would be like giving the name "rocky" to one who appeared to be either physically or mentally tough.

Matthew 16:13-20

The following verses are reproduced according to the New International Version (NIV).

> When Jesus came to the region of Caesarea Philippi, he asked his disciples, "Who do people say the Son of Man is?" (verse 13)

They replied, "Some say John the Baptist; others say Elijah; and still others, Jeremiah or one of the prophets." (verse 14)

"But what about you?" he asked. "Who do you say I am?" (verse 15)

Simon Peter answered, "You are the Messiah, the Son of the living God." (verse 16)

Jesus replied, "Blessed are you, Simon son of Jonah, for this was not revealed to you by flesh and blood, but by my Father in heaven. (verse 17)

And I tell you that you are Peter (*Petros*), and on this rock (*petra*) I will build my church, and the gates of Hades will not overcome it. (verse 18)

I will give you the keys of the kingdom of heaven; whatever you bind on earth will be bound in heaven, and whatever you loose on earth will be loosed in heaven." (verse 19)

Then he ordered his disciples not to tell anyone that he was the Messiah. (verse 20)

Analysis

In verse 15, Jesus asks a question of all those present:

> "But what about you?" he asked. "Who do you say I am?"

In verse 16, Simon Peter answers the question:

> "You are the Messiah, the son of the living God." (The terms "Messiah" and "son of God" are synonymous. See for example Mark 14:61.)

In verse 17, Jesus responds to Peter with a "truth" statement:

> Jesus replied, "Blessed are you, Simon son of Jonah, for this was not revealed to you by flesh and blood, but by my Father in heaven."

In verse 18, Jesus then follows up by using the pun, that most favoured Jewish literary device. In this case the pun takes the form of a triplet based on the meaning of Simon's nickname:

> "And I tell you that you are Peter (*Petros*), and on this rock (*petra*) I will build my church (assembly)…"

The Triple Pun

1. It was Jesus who first bestowed the nickname "rocky" on Simon bar Jonah;

2. How prescient that nickname has proved to be because "rocky" now has faith in Jesus as the "rock" of Israel (see 1 Peter 2:4-8);
3. "Rocky's" faith in Jesus as the "rock" of Israel is the certain and sure "rock" of faith on which the assembly will be built.

The keys of the kingdom

In verse 19, Jesus states:

> "I will give you the keys of the kingdom of heaven; whatever you bind on earth will be bound in heaven, and whatever you loose on earth will be loosed in heaven."

The Papacy's claim that Simon alone is given the "keys of the kingdom" cannot be sustained when considering that the concomitant power of "binding and loosing" is also given to the other disciples in Matthew 18:18. Any analysis of how Matthew portrays Peter will demonstrate that the author alternates between praising and despising him and, in the end, makes no effort to rehabilitate him. Given the supposed significance of the "keys", Matthew's attitude is striking and militates against the Papacy's claim the Peter was ever regarded as the "Chief Apostle".

Richard P. McBrien, the noted Roman Catholic priest and scholar, rightly points out that Peter is not regarded by the other apostles as having sole or superior authority:

> The conferral of the power of the keys of the kingdom surely suggests an imposing measure of authority, given the symbolism of the keys, but there is no explicit indication that the authority conferred was meant to be exercised over others, much less that it be absolutely monarchical in kind...In Acts, in fact, Peter is shown consulting with other apostles and even being sent by them (8:14). He and John are portrayed as acting as a team (3:1-11; 4:1-22; 8:14). And Paul confronts Peter for his inconsistency and hypocrisy...Paul "opposed him to his face because he was clearly wrong" (Galatians 2:11; see also 12-14) [46]

Even the early Catholic writers did not teach that Peter was given sole authority, as the devout Catholic historian von Dollinger noted:

> Of all the Fathers who interpret these passages (Matthew 16:18; John 21:17), not a single one applies them to the Roman bishops as Peter's successors. How many Fathers have busied themselves with these three texts, yet not one of them who commentaries we possess—Origen, Chrysostom, Hilary, Augustine,

---
46 McBrien, Richard P. *Lives of the Popes: The Pontiffs from St. Peter to Benedict XVI*. Harper: San Francisco, 2005 updated ed., pp. 30-31.

Cyril, Theodoret, and those whose interpretations are collected in catenas—has dropped the faintest hint that the primacy of Rome is the consequence of the commission and promise to Peter! Not one of them has explained the rock or foundation on which Christ would build His Church as the office given to Peter to be transmitted to his successors, but they understood by it either Christ Himself, or Peter's confession of faith in Christ; often both together. [47]

It was not until the late Second or early Third Century that the Papacy appealed to the text of Matthew 16:18 as the basis for Roman Primacy:

> …Stephen I seems to have been the first pope to have appealed to the classic "you are Peter" text in Matthew's Gospel (16:18) as the basis for Roman primacy…Peter was not regarded as the first Bishop of Rome until the late second or early third century. [48]

The scene closes in verse 20 with Jesus warning all those present not to tell anyone that he was the Messiah.

Scene Notes

The scene opens at verse 13 and ends at verse 20. The entire conversation contained within this discrete unit is about the true identity of Jesus. Note that in the very next scene beginning at verse 21, Jesus calls Peter "Satan" and berates him for being a stumbling block (*skandalon*), i.e. an impediment placed in the way and causing one to stumble or fall.

Despite scholarly awareness of "word-play" or "punning" as a literary phenomenon in ancient Near Eastern literature, the claim by advocates of Papal Primacy that Jesus regarded Peter as the "rock" is allowed to stand virtually unchallenged, or else challenged for the wrong reasons. Those who make the claim lift this statement out of its context from within Israelite "rock-stone" imagery and ignore the comprehensive New Testament application of this imagery to Jesus.

Advocates who rely on this passage from Matthew to buttress claims for Papal Primacy are the butt of what must surely be a great cosmic joke—Jesus' love of "word-play" or "punning."

Jesus himself is the chief corner-stone, the foundation of a new spiritual Temple built without human hands, the same stone *eben* (אֶבֶן) of Daniel, that destroyed the kingdoms of the earth and is now the foundation of the kingdom which the God of

---

[47] von Dollinger, J.J.Ignaz. *The Pope and the Council*. Roberts: Boston, 1869. p 74.

[48] McBrien, Richard P. *Lives of the Popes: The Pontiffs from St. Peter to Benedict XVI*. Harper: San Francisco, 2005 updated ed., pp. 27-28.

Heaven is about to set up. All believers in Jesus as the Israelite Messiah, including Simon nicknamed Peter, are "rocks-stones" being built up to form this new spiritual Temple.

Summing up Part IX

What we can reasonably conclude from all the foregoing Chapters is that the Papacy has no claim whatsoever to Universal Primacy and Apostolic Succession through the Apostle Peter. As demonstrated, she has had to rely solely on myth, fable and legend to bolster her claims. In reality, beyond what is recorded in the New Testament, the Papacy knows absolutely nothing about the fate of Simon bar Jonah, also known as Peter.

APPENDIX

The "bones" of Peter

Lest it be assumed that all the foregoing belongs to the ancient past and has little or no relevance for modern times, two relatively recent articles from the *Guardian* newspaper reproduced below will dispel such notions.

Saint Peter's bones: Vatican exhumes old argument with plan to show 'relics'

Guardian: 19 Nov 2013: Lizzy Davies: Vatican City

For the first time in nearly 2,000 years, fragments of bone held to be those of the apostle will go on public display.

On 26 June 1968, as much of Europe was busy rebelling against authority and fighting for free love, Pope Paul VI made a dramatic announcement that put the Roman Catholic church back in the headlines for reasons other than its stance on women, abortion or contraception.

Bones discovered in a Roman cemetery in the Vatican, he declared, had been identified "in a way we believe to be convincing" as those of Saint Peter, the Christian martyr who is traditionally held to have been the first pope and died 1,950 years ago.

On Sunday, fragments of the bones are to be displayed in public as part of celebrations to mark the end of the Year of Faith, an initiative launched by Pope Benedict XVI, who resigned this year.

The fragments, contained in an urn usually kept in a private papal chapel, will be presented for public veneration in St. Peter's Square at a mass celebrated by Pope Francis. The decision to exhibit is controversial. No pontiff has ever said the bones are without doubt those of Saint Peter, and some within archaeological circles are fairly sure they are not.

The battle over the bones, which pits a rigorous Jesuit archaeologist against a pioneering female epigraphist, is one of the strangest stories to have come out of the Vatican during the 20th century and may also be one of the least dignified.

But, speaking on Monday, Monsignor Rino Fisichella said he had no qualms about thrusting the relics back into the spotlight. "We did not want to, and have no intention, of opening up any argument," said Fisichella who, in a carefully worded article for the semi-official Vatican newspaper *L'Osservatore Romano* last week, described the relics as those "recognised by tradition" as Saint Peter's.

"We believe… faith, the people of God, has always believed these to be the relics of the apostle Peter, and we continue to venerate them in this way and give them the honour they deserve," he said.

Fisichella, president of the pontifical council for the promotion of the new evangelisation, also said "the symbolic value" of the bones—their "underlying theological value"—was hugely important. Regardless of what scientific testing might reveal, he said, Christians would venerate the remains and pray at the tomb of Saint Peter.

The story of how the bones came to be proclaimed Peter's dates back to 1939, when Pope Pius XII ordered an excavation of an area below St Peter's basilica thought to contain his tomb. The digging, overseen by a German monsignor, Ludwig Kaas, lasted 11 years and led, in 1950, to a stunning papal radio broadcast announcing "the tomb of the prince of the apostles" had been found.

But the pope was forced to admit his team had been unable to prove with certainty the bones were Peter's.

Years later, Margherita Guarducci, an archaeologist and the first woman to lead Vatican excavations, began to question the original findings. She noted graffiti near the tomb reading *Petr eni*, which she believed was an abbreviation of *Petros enesti*, the Greek for "Peter is here".

She was told Kaas had been collecting bones out of concern that they were not being properly looked after, and putting them in boxes in a Vatican storeroom. Having located some bones she thought were the most interesting, she convinced Pope Paul VI to commission tests on them.

These revealed, among other things, that they belonged to a robust man who died approximately in his 60s. To the outrage of Antonio Ferrua, the Jesuit father who had been the chief archaeologist on the initial excavation, Guarducci told the pope he should say the bones were believed to be Saint Peter's. And, to the disquiet of Ferrua and some other Vatican experts, he did just that. Kaas, Ferrua and Guarducci have all since died.

In his book, *The Vatican Diaries*, longtime observer John Thavis calls the affair "an embarrassment for the church. The supposed bones of Saint Peter had been surreptitiously dug up by a meddling monsignor when the archaeologists weren't looking; then they were thrown into a box and forgotten for more than a decade; then they were rediscovered by accident and became the focus of a feud between church experts," he writes.

"The whole affair did not inspire confidence in the Vatican's ability to exhume its own history, and it is little wonder that none of it is mentioned in the Vatican guidebooks."

The Vatican, however, hopes the bones' moment has finally come. During its Year of Faith, which began in October 2012, 8.5 million pilgrims had prayed at St. Peter's tomb, Fisichella said, and it seemed only fitting that the year should be rounded off with "a unique moment".

"For the first time, the relics of the apostle will be displayed for the veneration of believers," he said. "Peter was called by the Lord to confirm his brothers in faith. Around the successor of Peter, but almost in the physical presence of the first of the apostles—to whom, with Paul, we owe the foundation of this church— we will be called to profess our faith once more with conviction and strength."

Guardian note: This article was amended on 10 January 2014 to make clear that the relics had never been "hidden" as stated in the original article; the novelty of the event was that the relics were being displayed publicly for the first time for veneration in a public ceremony. While the particular relics exhibited had previously been kept in an urn in a private chapel, pilgrims visiting St Peter's tomb beneath the basilica have been able to see others since the area was opened after excavations.

Vatican displays Saint Peter's bones for the first time

Guardian: 24 Nov 2013: Associated Press: Vatican City

The Vatican has publicly unveiled bone fragments purportedly belonging to Saint Peter, reviving the scientific debate and tantalising mystery over whether the relics found in a shoe box truly belong to the first pope.

The nine pieces of bone sat nestled like rings in a jewel box inside a bronze display case on the side of the altar during a mass commemorating the end of the Vatican's year-long celebration of the Christian faith. It was the first time they had ever been exhibited in public.

Pope Francis prayed before the fragments at the start of Sunday's service and clutched the case in his arms for several minutes after his homily.

No pope has ever definitively declared the fragments to belong to the apostle Peter, but Pope Paul VI in 1968 said fragments found in the necropolis under St Peter's Basilica were "identified in a way that we can consider convincing".

Some archaeologists dispute the finding.

The relics were discovered during excavations begun under St. Peter's Basilica in the years following the death in 1939 of Pope Pius XI, who had asked to be buried in the grottoes where dozens of popes are buried, according to the 2012 book by veteran Vatican correspondent Bruno Bartoloni, *The Ears of the Vatican*.

During the excavations, archaeologists discovered a funerary monument with a casket built in honour of Peter and an engraving in Greek that read:

"*Petros eni*", or "*Peter is here*".

The scholar of Greek antiquities Margherita Guarducci, who had deciphered the engraving, continued to investigate and learned that one of the basilica workers had been given the remains found inside the casket and stored them in a shoe box kept in a cupboard. She reported her findings to Paul VI, who later proclaimed there was a convincing argument that the bones belonged to Peter. Leading Vatican Jesuits and other archaeologists strongly denied the claim, but had little recourse.

"No pope had ever permitted an exhaustive study, partly because a 1,000-year-old curse attested by secret and apocalyptic documents, threatened anyone who disturbed the peace of Peter's tomb with the worst possible misfortune," Bartoloni wrote.

The Vatican newspaper, *L'Osservatore Romano*, published excerpts of the book last year, giving his account a degree of official sanction.

In 1971, Paul VI was given an urn containing the relics, which were kept inside the private papal chapel inside the apostolic palace and exhibited for the pope's private veneration every 29 June, for the feast of saints Peter and Paul. Sunday marked the first time they were shown in public.

Summing up the Bones

The supposed discovery of Peter's tomb under St. Peter's Basilica is a triumph of excessive piety masquerading as archaeology. It was an inside job, and the insiders found exactly what they wanted to find. The box supposedly containing the bones of Peter actually contained the unidentifiable remains of a man aged between 60-70. No mention was made of the fact that the box also contained sheep, ox and pig bones, plus the complete skeleton of a mouse.

PART X

Aftermath

CHAPTER ONE

Introduction

The inevitability of death and the uncertainty of death's aftermath has haunted mankind since the very first stirrings of self-awareness. Every person who has ever lived has pondered mortality and wondered if death meant total oblivion…or something else. Most religions have attempted to address this universal predicament and to provide the "something else" for their followers but no religion, no philosophy, no humanist, atheist, or any other belief system can ever successfully answer questions about purpose, tragedy, bereavement, or apparent futility; can ever convince of life's intrinsic value; can ever deliver the certainty of man's post-mortem existence; or ever fully quell man's fear of total oblivion.

Throughout the ages, writers, poets, sages, philosophers and such have attempted to give expression to this greatest of human predicaments, none more successfully so than William Shakespeare.

"To be or not to be", the opening words of Act III, Scene I of his play "Hamlet, Prince of Denmark", are possibly the most famous six words in English literature for the very good reason that they draw us into an exploration of death and its aftermath that is universal, timeless, and compelling. Hamlet's soliloquy posits the question of whether it is more noble to suffer through the known "slings and arrows of outrageous fortune", or to fight against this "sea of troubles", take the escape route of death, and suffer the unknown consequences in that "undiscovered country, from whose bourn no traveller returns". In the end, Hamlet fears that "undiscovered country" more than the "slings and arrows of outrageous fortune" and so decides on life rather than death.

This profound contemplation resonated with just as much significance for his audience yesterday, as it does for us today, and as it will for others tomorrow.

Upon conclusion of this brief general reflection, it is now time to turn our attention to the scriptural record and compare its teachings on death and its aftermath with those of the theologies taught in its name.

Note

The concepts of Immortal Souls, Eternal Life, Heaven, Hell, Resurrection, New Creation, and the Kingdom of God, are all inextricably entwined and therefore difficult to separate into individual strands. Although the structural form of this work demands at this stage the inclusion of the mainstream Christian beliefs about post-mortem existence, commentaries integrating some or all these strands appear elsewhere in this work so, for now, we will just make a few observations about Immortal Souls, Heaven and Hell, and Heaven's relationship to the Kingdom of God.

CHAPTER TWO

Immortal Souls

The Christian traditional teachings of human immortality and post-mortem existence in some disembodied *soul Heaven* or *soul Hell* are concepts ultimately derived from the Hellenist philosophy of immortal souls.

According to the Bible, God alone possesses "immortality":

> ...God, the blessed and only Ruler, the King of kings and Lord of lords, who alone is immortal (*athanasia*) and who lives in unapproachable light, whom no one has seen or can see. To him be honor and might forever. Amen (1 Timothy 6:15-16 NIV).

Because the minds of the Hellenist-Latin Fathers were set in the key of a different structure to that of the Israelite people, they retrojected onto documents containing uniquely Israelite concepts their own prevailing religious and philosophical outlook. Nowhere is this made more explicit than in the framing of doctrines through the lens of Plato's philosophy of the soul. Briefly stated, this philosophy holds that man is a duality composed of a pre-existing immortal soul imprisoned within a mortal body. Only upon death can the immortal soul of man be released from this body and return to its metaphysical home. This philosophy pervades almost all Christian doctrine and practice and gave rise to the traditional teachings of other-worldly soul destinations called Heaven and Hell and a soul fate called Eternal Life. (As noted elsewhere in this work, the Biblical promise of "eternal life" for humans (*zóé aiónios*) actually means "age-long life in the age to come".)

In stark contrast to these teachings based on Hellenist dualism, ancient Israelite thought held that man is one indivisible entity created by God to serve the Creator's purposes on Earth. There is no escape to some other world: the earth is man's home and ever will be. Man is expected to glorify God daily with all his actions, including with his bodily functions. He is expected to pursue justice, righteousness, mercy, and the knowledge of God with every fibre of his being in the physical world.

Consider this well-known verse:

> Then the LORD God formed man of dust from the ground, and breathed into his nostrils the breath of life; and man became a living being (*chai nephesh*) (Genesis 2:7 NASB).

For ancient Israelites, the dust of the ground (the body), together with the breath of life (the spirit), form the living being (*chai nephesh*). If there was a body, it had to be animated by the spirit to become a *chai nephesh*. Upon death, the now non-living being returns to the dust of the earth and the breath of life (spirit) returns to God who gave it:

> Then shall the dust return to the earth as it was: and the spirit shall return unto God who gave it (Ecclesiastes 12:7 KJV).
>
> Then Jesus, calling out with a loud voice, said, "Father, into your hands I commit my spirit!" And having said this he breathed his last (Luke 23:46 ESV cf. Matthew 27:50; John 19:30).

The Hebrew Scriptures state clearly that there is only oblivion in the grave:

> His spirit departs, he returns to the earth; In that very day his thoughts perish (Psalm 146:4 NASB).
>
> For the living know that they shall die: but the dead know not any thing, neither have they any more a reward; for the memory of them is forgotten… Whatsoever thy hand findeth to do, do it with thy might; for there is no work, nor device, nor knowledge, nor wisdom, in the grave, whither thou goest (Ecclesiastes 9:5,10 KJV).

The only post-mortem existence that humans have is what may be termed a "life" in the mind of God.

It is more than unfortunate that the indivisible living being (*chai nephesh*) was commonly rendered into Greek as *psuchi* and then into English as "soul". This rendering introduced Hellenist ideas about the separation of soul and body, whereas the ancient Israelite concept of "life" was the life of the whole person.

Note

Unlike other creatures, who are also living beings (*chai nephesh*) comprised of body and spirit, humans have the capacity to image God's own "spirit", hence man's intended status as the *imago dei*. It is this *imago dei* potential that differentiates man from the animals.

Sleeping and Waking

The Bible does not speak of disembodied souls existing in other-worldly realms called Heaven and Hell. Rather, the Bible speaks about man sleeping in the dust of the earth until awakening in the Resurrection. (Commentaries on the Resurrection and related subjects appear elsewhere in this work.)

Jesus himself described the dead Lazarus as "sleeping", then "waking":

> ..."Our friend Lazarus has fallen asleep, but I'm leaving to wake him up" (John 11:11 ISV).

Martha, the sister of Lazarus, provides us with a clear and unambiguous statement of what the followers of Jesus believed about death and its immediate aftermath:

> "Lord," Martha said to Jesus, "if you had been here, my brother would not have died. But I know that even now God will give you whatever you ask." Jesus said to her, "Your brother will rise again." Martha answered, "I know he will rise again in the resurrection at the last day." Jesus said to her, "I am the resurrection and the life. The one who believes in me will live, even though they die; and whoever lives by believing in me will never die..." (John 11:21-26 NIV).

Martha believes there is only the grave until that "last day" resurrection comes. Jesus assures her that all who believe in him, even though they will eventually sleep in the grave, have already undergone a spiritual resurrection and passed from death to life with God, thus enabling their resurrection "at the last day".

These statements by Jesus and Martha totally overturn traditional Christian teachings that, immediately upon death, immortal souls are rewarded in Heaven or punished in Hell. According to those teachings, the four days dead Lazarus should have already been judged and received into Heaven or banished to Hell.

Until the day of awakening comes, every person who has ever lived is now sleeping in the dust of the earth. The mechanism by which the Bible envisions man awakening from this sleep of death is addressed elsewhere in this work.

The Pharisees

By the time of Jesus, Hellenism had been the dominant culture of the peoples of the Hellenist-Roman world for centuries and Israelite intellectuals and others of similar social classes had not been immune to its influence. For instance, in the writings of Philo of Alexandria, we can see Hellenist philosophy tailored to suit Israelite sensibilities.

The Hellenist-inspired teachings of the Pharisees, however, are of particular interest to us and we are indebted to the contemporary historian Flavius Josephus for the following description:

> ...they (the Pharisees) also believe that souls have an immortal vigour in them, and that under the earth there will be rewards or punishments, according as they have lived virtuously or viciously in this life; and the latter are to be detained in

an everlasting prison, but that the former shall have the power to revive and live again; on accounts of which doctrines they are able to greatly persuade the body of the people...[1]

The remarkable application of this description to traditional Christian teachings should be apparent to all. Jesus told the people to beware of the teachings and traditions of the Pharisees because:

> You (the Pharisees) are destroying the word of God through your tradition that you have handed down. And you do many other things like that (Mark 7:13 ISV).

The only "word of God" in existence at that time were the Hebrew Scriptures, to which Jesus gives the ultimate authority. Thus any Christian teaching which similarly destroys the "word of God" stands under the same indictment as that pronounced by Jesus on the Pharisees.

---

[1] Flavius Josephus. "Antiquities of the Jews" in *The Works of Flavius Josephus*, xviii, Chapter 1. Transl. William Whiston. Milner and Sowerby: Halifax, 1864, p.390.

CHAPTER THREE

Heaven

Section 1

Introduction

Within the Christian churches and their many denominations, further divided into conservative and liberal wings, there is a significant amount of confusion regarding what happens after death. Some hold that after death, everyone "sleeps" until the final judgment, after which everyone will be sent to Heaven or Hell. Others believe that at the moment of death, people are instantly judged and sent to their eternal destinations. Still others claim that when people die, their souls/spirits are sent to a "temporary" Heaven or Hell to await a final resurrection, a final judgment, and then consigned to their eternal destination.

For all of us, especially those who have lost loved ones before their time, it is distressing to accept that the Bible speaks of no other existence for man but the one we have always shared together—this Earth. The comfort we seek often leads us to read into the Bible our own hopes and dreams but the sobering reality is that, whether living or dead, the Bible states unequivocally that this Earth is the only habitation we will ever know:

> The heaven, even the heavens, are the LORD'S: but the earth hath he given to the children of men (Psalm 115:16 KJV).

All that being said, however, there is the possibility of new earthly life posited for us in the Bible but so focused has mainstream Christianity been on teachings derived from Hellenist theology and philosophy that it appears to have gone unnoticed. Essays exploring this topic in depth appear elsewhere in this work and, it is envisaged, will replace old false hopes with new and vastly more meaningful ones.

Section 2

Note

The Kingdom of God (Heaven) is also known as the "Messianic Age" or the "Age to Come". All terms imply the same conditions and the same promises. On that premise, and for the sake of simplicity, the term Kingdom of God is used in this Chapter.

The Kingdom of God

As previously stated, the Bible speaks of no other existence for mankind but the one we have always shared together—this Earth. When it does speak of "Heaven" as a destination for man it always implies life in an ideal earthly Kingdom, envisioned as a re-establishment of the symbolic Garden of Eden from which humans were expelled. To complete the cycle of life on Earth, we must in a sense return to Eden and to our previous state of being ruled by God and not by man.

The Tree of Life

Consider the description of the symbolic Garden in the Hebrew Scriptures:

> And the LORD God planted a garden (Hebrew: *gan*) eastward in Eden; and there he put the man whom he had formed. And out of the ground made the LORD God to grow every tree that is pleasant to the sight, and good for food; the tree of life also in the midst of the garden (Hebrew: *gan*), and the tree of knowledge of good and evil (Genesis 2:8-9 KJV).

Also consider that the expulsion from the Garden was to deny human access to the "tree of life":

> And the LORD God said, Behold, the man is become as one of us, to know good and evil: and now, lest he put forth his hand, and take also of the tree of life, and eat, and live for ever: Therefore the LORD God sent him forth from the garden (*gan*) of Eden, to till the ground from whence he was taken. So he drove out the man; and he placed at the east of the garden of Eden Cherubims, and a flaming sword which turned every way, to keep the way of the tree of life (Genesis 3:22-24 KJV).

Now consider the New Testament promise about the "tree of life":

> …To the one who is victorious, I will give the right to eat from the tree of life, which is in the paradise (*paradeisos*) of God (Revelation 2:7 NIV).

The Greek Septuagint translation of Genesis 2:8-9 from the Hebrew Scriptures substitutes the equivalent Greek word *paradeisos* for the Hebrew *gan* (Garden) of Eden. The author of the Greek text of Revelation 2:7 similarly substitutes the equivalent Greek word *paradeisos* for the Hebrew *gan*.

Given that the author of Revelation locates the "tree of life" within the *paradeisos*, and given that *paradeisos* is synonymous with *gan*, it is clear that the author of Revelation is envisioning humanity's symbolic return to the Garden of Eden. "Heaven" for humans is, therefore, the right to eat from the "tree of life" in the new Garden of Eden, an earthly Kingdom that will pattern God's own kingship of the Heavens. The term used to express this hoped-for state of existence for humans is the "Kingdom of God".

The King

This hope for the establishment of God's kingship on Earth developed in parallel with the hope of an ideal earthly King, a man anointed by God for the purpose of ruling this earthly Kingdom as his viceroy. Such men, anointed by God for a purpose, were known by the title "Messiah". According to the Hebrew Scriptures, the Messiah was to be a descendant of King David and would sit on David's earthly throne:

> "Behold, days are coming," declares the LORD, "when I will fulfill the good word which I have spoken concerning the house of Israel and the house of Judah. In those days and at that time I will cause a righteous Branch of David to spring forth; and He shall execute justice and righteousness on the earth. In those days Judah will be saved and Jerusalem will dwell in safety; and this is the name by which she will be called: the LORD is our righteousness." For thus says the LORD, "David shall never lack a man to sit on the throne of the house of Israel" (Jeremiah 33:14-17 NASB).

> Of the greatness of his government and peace there will be no end. He will reign on David's throne and over his kingdom, establishing and upholding it with justice and righteousness from that time on and forever. The zeal of the LORD Almighty will accomplish this (Isaiah 9:7 NIV).

The New Testament records that these promises were fulfilled in Jesus of Nazareth:

> He shall be great, and shall be called the Son of the Highest: and the Lord God shall give unto him the throne of his father David: And he shall reign over the house of Jacob for ever; and of his kingdom there shall be no end (Luke 1:32-33 KJV).

> Of this man's seed hath God according to his promise raised unto Israel a Saviour, Jesus (Acts 13: 22-23 KJV).

These passages could not be clearer: the Kingdom envisioned here is an earthly Kingdom to be ruled by a descendant of David seated on his ancestor David's throne. The New Testament accurately reflects the ancient and enduring synagogue prayer which expresses the hope that God "will establish His kingdom in your lifetime and during your days, and within the life of the entire House of Israel, speedily and soon".

Kings enthroned

Contributing to the dire and almost irredeemable situation in which Christian theology finds itself is the inability or unwillingness to recognise the following major factors:

- the Bible speaks of two thrones: one on Earth as well as one in Heaven. (Israelite thought perceived God as a King reigning on his heavenly throne.)

- the infancy narratives of Matthew and Luke were not written to record a Virgin Birth but to present Jesus' credentials for Messiahship, i.e. his right *by birth* to sit upon David's earthly throne;

- the throne of David did not magically change into a "spiritual" throne in the New Testament;

- the New Testament authors state clearly that Jesus was a biological descendant of David (e.g. Romans 1:3; John 7:42; Acts 2: 29-36).

Before the Ascension, Jesus was asked a specific question concerning the timing of the establishment of his earthly throne:

> When they therefore were come together, they asked of him, saying, Lord, wilt thou at this time restore again the kingdom to Israel? And he said unto them, It is not for you to know the times or the seasons, which the Father hath put in his own power (Acts 1:6-7 KJV).

Jesus made it clear that he did not know when the Kingdom would be established on Earth. He knew only that it would be in a future period he called the "regeneration" that he would sit on his earthly throne as the viceroy of YHWH, the King of Heaven who sits on his heavenly throne.

> And Jesus said to them, "Truly I say to you, that you who have followed Me, in the regeneration when the Son of Man will sit on His glorious throne, you

also shall sit upon twelve thrones, judging the twelve tribes of Israel" (Matthew 19:28 NASB).

The man who uttered the following words had no difficulty distinguishing between himself and the God who sits on the heavenly throne:

> But I say unto you, Swear not at all; neither by heaven; for it is God's throne: Nor by the earth; for it is his footstool…(Matthew 5:34-35 KJV).

Because of the confusion engendered by mainstream Christian teachings, it is extremely difficult for many to recognise that the Bible speaks of an earthly King seated on an earthly throne who is destined to rule in the name of the King who sits on the heavenly throne. However, being Israelites and accustomed to the Biblical principle of delegated authority, the people who welcomed Jesus on his ride into Jerusalem were under no such illusions:

> Blessed is the king who comes in the name of the Lord! Peace in heaven and glory in the highest! (Luke 19:38 NIV).

Section 3

An Ethical Kingdom

Except for the author of the Gospel of John, all other New Testament authors envisioned the Kingdom of God as a theocracy to be set up in the land of Israel and ruled by the Israelite Messiah enthroned as King.

Unlike his fellow authors, however, the author of John did not speak of this type of Kingdom but rather one based on the shared ethics and morality of his Jesus group and manifested in their righteous words and deeds which testified to their loyalty to Jesus, to the group, and to the God of Israel.

John's World

A variety of claims have been made about Jesus' statement to Pilate in John 18:36. Despite the fact that Jesus taught his followers to pray for the coming of God's Kingdom on Earth, some continue to assert that this Kingdom was other-worldly, a spiritual Heaven that has nothing to do with the physical world. All such claims defy the overwhelming scriptural evidence to the contrary, perhaps none more so than a ludicrous claim that in 18:36 Jesus was denying his Israelite identity:

> Jesus answered, "My kingdom is not of this world (*kosmos*): if my kingdom were of this world, then would my servants fight, that I should not be delivered to the Jews (Judeans): but now is my kingdom not from hence" (John 18:36 KJV).

John's entire Gospel is presented as a conflict of opposites: the values represented by the "world" of Jesus and his followers, as opposed to the values represented by the "world" of the Judeans, i.e. the Jerusalem establishment and their followers. That conflict of values, however, always occurs between humans confined to living on this Earth, as we can see clearly by referencing John's use of "world" *(kosmos)* in 15:18-19:

> If the world (*kosmos*) hates you, keep in mind that it hated me first. If you belonged to the world (*kosmos*), it would love you as its own. As it is, you do not belong to the world (*kosmos*), but I have chosen you out of the world (*kosmos*). That is why the world (*kosmos*) hates you (John 15:18-19 NIV).

See also John 8:23 and John 12:31.

Section 4

Note

Matthew and Mark describe the men crucified with Jesus as *lēstai* (robbers, brigands) while Luke describes them as *kakourgoi* (criminals, malefactors).

Paradise

As with Jesus' statement to Pilate in John 18:36, Jesus' promise to the malefactor on the cross in Luke 23:42-43 has been subjected to the same assertions by advocates of an other-worldly Heaven.

First consider verse 42:

> And he said unto Jesus, Lord, remember me when thou comest into thy kingdom (Luke 23:42 KJV).

When the man asked Jesus to remember him when he came into his Kingdom, he was referring to the Kingdom of God on Earth. As noted previously, this Kingdom was envisioned as a symbolic re-establishment of the Garden of Eden. As also noted previously, "paradise" is the "paradise of God" (Revelation 2:7) which is synonymous with the Garden of Eden because the "tree of life" is located within it.

Now verse 43:

> Jesus answered him, "Truly I tell you, today you will be with me in paradise (*paradeisos*)" (Luke 23:43 NIV).

The punctuation of verse 43 is critical. The placement of the comma after "you" and before "today" is a doctrinally-driven assertion by the translators that Jesus and the malefactor both went to "paradise" on the day they died. Aside from the merely temporal use of various forms of "day", the particularly Hebrew emphatic expression, "today" or "this day" is used in the Bible to indicate something that is ordained in the present, but its fulfilment lies in the future. For example:

> Behold, I set before you this day a blessing and a curse (Deuteronomy 11:26 KJV).

Since the man was promised a place with Jesus, let us just recall that Jesus did not go to "paradise" on the day he died:

> For just as Jonah was three days and three nights in the belly of the great fish, so will the Son of Man be three days and three nights in the heart of the earth (Matthew 12:40 ESV cf. Matthew 16:21).

Neither did he go to "paradise" after "three days and three nights in the heart of the earth":

> After his suffering, he presented himself to them and gave many convincing proofs that he was alive. He appeared to them over a period of forty days and spoke about the kingdom of God (Acts 1:3 NIV).

Jesus did not go to "paradise" on the day he died. Neither did the malefactor. Both men went into the grave that same day. Therefore, the author has supplied below the common sense punctuation of Luke 23:43:

> Jesus answered him, "Truly I tell you today (or this day), you will be with me in Paradise" (i.e. when Jesus comes into his Kingdom).

Section 5

Matthew's Heaven

During the Second Temple period, the commandment against taking the name of YHWH in vain was so strictly interpreted that pious substitutions were used to avoid unintentionally vocalising the name of God. Given that Matthew's Gospel is totally focused on Israelite norms, it is not surprising therefore to find the author substituting the term "Kingdom of Heaven" for the term "Kingdom of God".

Despite the fact that these terms are fully interchangeable, a degree of confusion persists with some equating the "Kingdom of Heaven" with the soul Heaven taught by Christian theology.

This confusion can be dispelled by teachers informing their followers that Matthew's substitution of "Heaven" for "God" is simply a reflection of Israelite piety norms. That is, of course, if they are not so wedded to teachings about a soul Heaven that they would prefer not to draw attention to this uncomfortable truth.

Final Note

Whether it be of physical or ethical dimensions, the Kingdom of God (Heaven, Paradise) envisioned by all Biblical authors has always been here on this Earth. Scripture cannot be tailored to suit the psychological and emotional needs of humans. There is no other place for us, there is no escape to somewhere else. This is our home and always will be.

CHAPTER FOUR

Hell

Notes

In English versions of both the Hebrew Scriptures and the New Testament, words meaning the "grave" have been translated indiscriminately. In the Hebrew Scriptures, the Hebrew word *Sheol* has been variously translated as "Hell", "Pit", or "Grave". In the New Testament, the Greek word *Hades* has either been left untranslated as "Hades" or translated as "Hell", the Greek word *Tartarus* translated as "Hell" or the "Deepest Abyss", and the Greek word *Géenna* transliterated as "Gehenna" or translated as "Hell".

To most Christians, the word "Gehenna" conjures up a visionary place of eternal torment, often equated to the "Lake of Fire" mentioned in Revelation. As the most common New Testament Greek word translated into English as "Hell", the following analysis will focus on this word *Géenna* and its attached symbolism.

Section 1

Gehenna

The Greek word γέεννα (*Géenna*) is drawn from the Hebrew term *Gey Ben Hinom* which means "Valley of the Son of Hinom". *Géenna* or its variations is used twelve times in the New Testament, eleven of those times by Jesus, and is either translitered as *Gehenna* or translated as "Hell" in English versions.

Unless one is acquainted with the geographical features of Jerusalem, one would not be aware that *Gehenna* (Valley of the Son of Hinom) is a physical location south-west of the Old City Walls or that there is a modern street, *Gey Ben Hinom Street*, which takes its name from the Valley through which is now winds.

In the time of Jesus, *Gehenna* was a very deep ravine situated south-west of the Herodian Temple Mount and well below the staircases, ramps and gates leading up to the Temple. It was the local rubbish dump, a place of vile things, animal carcasses and the bodies of executed criminals. Permanent fires burned there (according to some stories, with the addition of brimstone) to prevent outbreaks of disease. In former times, hideous practices had been carried out there in the name of *Moloch* (otherwise known as the Canaanite Sun-God, *Baal*). The worship of *Moloch* involved sacrificing children by making them "pass through the fire".

The Valley of the Son of Hinom (*Gehenna*) eventually came to symbolise fire, human sacrifice, and idolatry. Any reference to it would immediately have conjured up the prophet Jeremiah's warning that the practices carried out there in the name of *Moloch* would lead to the destruction of Jerusalem and the Temple of Solomon:

> Then came the word of the LORD unto Jeremiah…Behold, I will give this city into the hand of the Chaldeans, and into the hand of Nebuchadrezzar king of Babylon, and he shall take it: And the Chaldeans, that fight against this city, shall come and set fire on this city, and burn it with the houses, upon whose roofs they have offered incense unto Baal, and poured out drink offerings unto other gods, to provoke me to anger…Because of all the evil of the children of Israel and of the children of Judah, which they have done to provoke me to anger, they, their kings, their princes, their priests, and their prophets, and the men of Judah, and the inhabitants of Jerusalem. And they have turned unto me the back, and not the face: though I taught them, rising up early and teaching them, yet they have not hearkened to receive instruction. But they set their abominations in the house, which is called by my name, to defile it. And they built the high places of Baal, which are in the valley of the son of Hinnom, to cause their sons and their daughters to pass through the fire unto Molech; which I commanded them not, neither came it into my mind, that they should do this abomination, to cause Judah to sin (Jeremiah 32:26-35 KJV).

By the time of Jesus, the magnitude of the disaster eventually visited upon Israelites because of these practices had long been imprinted on the minds of their descendants.

For ancient Israelites, Jerusalem was the centre of religious/political life because they believed that God ruled from his heavenly abode which lay beyond the vault of the firmament of the sky directly above that part of the Tabernacle of the Temple known as the Holy of Holies. So sacred was the Holy of Holies that the High Priest was permitted to enter only once a year on *Yom Kippur* (the Day of Atonement).

Jesus used the word *Gehenna* to illustrate the difference between life with God (symbolised by the Temple and the Holy of Holies) and life without God (symbolised by *Gehenna*). Life with God meant entering into the coming Kingdom on earth: life without God meant exile from the Kingdom through self-imposed isolation and ignorance of the one God of Israel, which would inexorably lead to a personal destruction symbolic of the destruction visited upon Jerusalem and the Temple of Solomon in the time of Jeremiah.

This author has visited the Temple Mount and the Valley of the Son of Hinom (*Gehenna*) on several occasions. Although vastly different in scale now, the symbolism attached to these two opposing sites is still readily apparent, and how much more so to the persons peopling the New Testament? The impact of looking down from a midway point into the fiery pit, and then up towards the Temple and the abode of God above it, must have been dramatic and enduring for all, including for Jesus himself.

Israelite contemporaries of Jesus would have understood that the type of language he used when speaking in parables was never intended to be taken literally. Consider for example the parables of the Weeds and the Talents:

> Just as the weeds are gathered and burned with fire, so will it be at the end of the age. The Son of Man will send his angels, and they will gather out of his kingdom all causes of sin and all law-breakers, and throw them into the fiery furnace. In that place there will be weeping and gnashing of teeth (Matthew 13:40-42 ESV).

> And cast the worthless servant into the outer darkness. In that place there will be weeping and gnashing of teeth (Matthew 25:30 ESV cf. Matthew 8:12).

The "fiery furnace" and the "outer darkness" are mutually exclusive concepts, therefore figurative expressions.

The Bosom of Abraham

Consider also the parable of the Rich Man and Lazarus, the context of which is Jesus' rebuke of the Pharisees for their callous disregard, not only of the poor but also of Moses and the Prophets. This parable is of great interest, not only for its heightened moral and spiritual lessons, but also because it references the unique Israelite belief that the righteous dead are sleeping in the "Bosom of Abraham" until the Resurrection:

> Now there was a rich man, and he habitually dressed in purple and fine linen, joyously living in splendor every day. And a poor man named Lazarus was laid at his gate, covered with sores, and longing to be fed with the crumbs which were falling from the rich man's table; besides, even the dogs were coming and licking his sores. Now the poor man died and was carried away by the angels to Abraham's bosom; and the rich man also died and was buried. In Hades he lifted up his eyes, being in torment, and saw Abraham far away and Lazarus in his bosom. And he cried out and said, "Father Abraham, have mercy on me, and send Lazarus so that he may dip the tip of his finger in water and cool off my

tongue, for I am in agony in this flame." But Abraham said, "Child, remember that during your life you received your good things, and likewise Lazarus bad things; but now he is being comforted here, and you are in agony. And besides all this, between us and you there is a great chasm fixed, so that those who wish to come over from here to you will not be able, and that none may cross over from there to us." And he said, "Then I beg you, father, that you send him to my father's house—for I have five brothers—in order that he may warn them, so that they will not also come to this place of torment." But Abraham said, "They have Moses and the Prophets; let them hear them." But he said, "No, father Abraham, but if someone goes to them from the dead, they will repent!" But he said to him, "If they do not listen to Moses and the Prophets, they will not be persuaded even if someone rises from the dead" (Luke 16:19-31 NASB).

Firstly, *Hades* is the Greek equivalent of the Hebrew *Sheol*. As pointed out previously, *Sheol* simply means the grave, the place of darkness to which all the dead go, both the righteous and the unrighteous, regardless of the moral choices made in life.

However, in ancient Israelite thought, when righteous Israelites died and were consigned to *Sheol*, they were perceived to sleep in the bosom of their remote ancestor Abraham. Just as a fatigued or troubled child may be taken to sleep in the comfort and security of a parent's arms, so also was Abraham supposed to act towards his children after the fatigues and troubles of the present life, hence the figurative expression "Bosom of Abraham" which meant to sleep in comfort and security with him. In contrast, the unrighteous dead were imagined as being in a state of torment because they too will rise in the "resurrection" but only to face judgement (John 5:28-29).

All the contemporaries of Jesus would have understood that this is the type of parable known as an exemplary story which uses one specific case to illustrate a general moral principle, in this case an exhortation to be a righteous person in life as in death you can do nothing to change your status. The righteous cannot become unrighteous and vice versa, hence the great gulf is fixed.

Secondly, it is claimed that Jesus was here confirming the teaching of a "soul" Heaven and a "soul" Hell even though the parable describes characters who have physical bodies with eyes that can see, tongues that can speak, ears that can hear, and who can interact with each other even though they are supposedly in different places.

It is remarkable that we who use a wide range of literary devices and techniques to communicate with others deny the same latitude of expression to the authors who composed the books of the Bible.

Section 2

Note

It has been asserted that analysis of the Book of Revelation is notoriously difficult for scholars given that it is a genre combining three literary styles described as apocalyptic, epistolary, and prophetic. However, such excuses cover the reality that most difficulties stem from an unwillingness to correctly define context and terminology for fear that it will subject core teachings to unwanted scrutiny.

The Lake of Fire

Several passages in the Book of Revelation make reference to a "Lake of Fire". Each passage lists symbols, concepts, beings, and persons to be consigned therein. These are the *Shatan* (Satan), the beast, the false prophet, the grave, death, Hades, and various human beings whose names are not written in the "Book of Life".

These passages in Revelation expose the teachings of a literal fiery Hell and a literal Lake of Fire to be nothing more than nonsense. How can the *Shatan*, the beast, the false prophet, the grave, death, and Hades be cast into a literal Lake of Fire to be "tormented" forever? How can symbols, concepts, and beings not made of flesh and blood be literally burned with fire?

Nevertheless, because human beings are also said to be cast into the same Lake of Fire, we will determine the meaning of three of the terms contained in the passage below before turning our attention to the nature of Biblical "fire":

> And the devil that deceived them was cast into the lake of fire and brimstone (*theiou*), where the beast and the false prophet are, and shall be tormented (*basanisthēsontai*) day and night for ever and ever (*eis tous aionas ton aionon*) (Revelation 20:10 KJV.)

Brimstone

The word *theiou*, translated into English as "brimstone" or "sulfur", is a form of the Greek root *theion*. The verb derived from *theion* is *theioo* which means to hallow, to make divine, or to dedicate to a god. Among the ancient Greeks, brimstone (sulfur) was used to purify and cleanse in preparation for consecration to a deity.

To an ancient Greek, a "lake of fire and brimstone" would imply a lake of divine purification.

Torment

The word *basanisthēsontai*, translated into English as "shall be tormented", is a form of the Greek root *basanizo* derived from the cognate Oriental loan word *basanois*. A *basanois* was a Lydian touchstone used for the testing of precious metals.

These words belong to a family of New Testament Greek words, *basanos, basanismos, basanizo, basanistes*, all having the same primary meaning as the English word "touchstone", which is described as "a black siliceous stone related to flint and formerly used to test the purity of gold and silver by the streak left on the stone when rubbed by the metal" (Merriam-Webster Dictionary). In Greek, as well as in English, the word "touchstone" acquired the secondary idiomatic meaning of "a test or criterion for determining the quality or genuineness of a thing" (Merriam-Webster Dictionary).

Refining, purifying and testing by fire is a recurring theme throughout the Bible. Consider these statements:

> But who can endure the day of his (the messenger's) coming? Who can stand when he appears? For he will be like a refiner's fire or a launderer's soap (Malachi 3:2 NIV).

> Every man's work shall be made manifest: for the day shall declare it, because it shall be revealed by fire; and the fire shall try every man's work of what sort it is (1 Corinthians 3:13 KJV).

The "torment" of Revelation's Lake of Fire cannot refer to literal suffering since symbols, concepts and beings not made of flesh and blood are obviously not subject to physical torture. Rather, the torment conveys the idea of testing: a testing of one's sincerity, loyalty and worth.

Note

The Lazarus and the rich man parable from Luke 16:19-31 has obvious parallels with Revelation's Lake of Fire and therefore the "torment" mentioned twice in the parable must be considered from within that context.

For ever and ever

In Revelation 20:10, the phrase *eis tous aionas ton aionon* has been translated into English as "for ever and ever". This Greek phrase *eis tous aionas ton aionon* occurs about twenty times in the Greek New Testament in this combination.

The Greek nouns *aionas* and *aionon* are plural forms of the Greek *aion*, which simply means an "eon" or "age". The word *aion* always means a period of time. Otherwise it would be impossible to account for its plural forms, or for such qualifying expressions as "this age", or the "age to come" (see for example Matthew 12:32; 1 Corinthians 2:6; Ephesians 1:21). It is only necessary to reference one verse to recognise the inherent contradictions in English translations of all forms of the Greek word *aion:*

> In the hope of eternal life (*zoe aionios*), which God, who does not lie, promised before the beginning of time (*pro cronon aionion*) (Titus 1:2 NIV).

If *aionios* is translated as "eternal" in the first part of the verse then, to be consistent, the final *pro cronon aionion* must be translated as "before eternal times", which makes no sense whatever as eternity has no beginning and no ending. Common sense, however, seems to be on permanent, doctrinal by-pass for some translators.

The concept of "eternity" or "endlessness" was not conveyed by the Greek word *aion* or any of its various forms until theologians assigned such meanings to them centuries after the New Testament was written. Once it is recognised that *aion* denotes an "age" or "ages", and that *aionios* means "age-lasting", it can be seen clearly that the concepts of eternal bliss in some disembodied soul Heaven, eternal torments in Hell, and eternal life for humans, are without foundation and ultimately derived from the Hellenist philosophy of immortal souls. The Biblical promise of "eternal life" (*zóé aiónios*) for humans actually means "age-long life in the age to come":

> And this is what he promised us—eternal life (*zóé aiónios*) (1 John 2:25 NIV).

This "age to come" of which John speaks is the longed-for Messianic age, the age of the kingship of God on earth, described in the New Testament as the Kingdom of God.

Section 3

Biblical Fire

For centuries, the fear of hellfire and damnation has kept millions safely herded within walls constructed by Christian theologians and teachers. If those same theologians and teachers had devoted similar amounts of time and energy on discovering what the Bible really has to say on these subjects, then many would have been spared needless anguish over the possibility that they and their loved ones may be tortured by flames for all eternity.

It has been necessary to proceed step by step and unravel the theological assumptions about Gehenna and the Lake of Fire, before allowing the Bible itself to deliver the *coup-de-grace*. In Matthew 3:11-12, John the Baptist said:

> "I baptize you with water for repentance, but he who is coming after me is mightier than I, whose sandals I am not worthy to carry. He will baptize you with the Holy Spirit and fire. His winnowing fork is in his hand, and he will clear his threshing floor and gather his wheat into the barn, but the chaff he will burn with unquenchable fire" (Matthew 3:11-12 ESV).

When John said that Jesus would baptise them with "fire", and that he would burn up the chaff "with unquenchable fire", he was simply reinforcing the common Israelite belief that the "Word of God" was analogous to "fire":

> Therefore thus says the LORD, the God of hosts: "Because you have spoken this word, behold, I am making my words in your mouth a fire, and this people wood, and the fire shall consume them" (Jeremaiah 5:14 ESV).

> But if I say, "I will not mention his word or speak anymore in his name," his word is in my heart like a fire, a fire shut up in my bones. I am weary of holding it in; indeed, I cannot (Jeremiah 20:9 NIV).

> "Is not My word like fire?" declares the LORD, "and like a hammer which shatters a rock?" (Jeremiah 23: 29 NASB).

Consider also the following examples of figurative language describing the power of words:

> But with righteousness shall he judge the poor, and reprove with equity for the meek of the earth: and he shall smite the earth with the rod of his mouth, and with the breath of his lips shall he slay the wicked (Isaiah 11:4 KJV).

> And then the lawless one will be revealed, whom the Lord Jesus will overthrow with the breath of his mouth and destroy by the splendor of his coming (2 Thessalonians 2:8 NIV).

Biblical "fire" has nothing whatever to do with physical flames. It is symbolic of the pure, cleansing Word of God that burns up the dross and stubble of mankind's false values leaving nothing but ashes behind.

CHAPTER FIVE

Judgement Day

In Revelation 20:11, what is commonly called the "great white throne judgement" period is introduced. (This period corresponds with "the end" spoken of by Paul in 1 Corinthians 15:23-26 when the works of the Kingdom age are completed.)

> And I saw a great white throne, and him that sat on it, from whose face the earth and the heaven fled away; and there was found no place for them. And I saw the dead, small and great, stand before God; and the books were opened: and another book was opened, which is the book of life: and the dead were judged out of those things which were written in the books, according to their works. And the sea gave up the dead which were in it; and death and hell delivered up the dead which were in them: and they were judged every man according to their works. And death and hell were cast into the lake of fire. This is the second death. And whosoever was not found written in the book of life was cast into the lake of fire (Revelation 20:11-15 KJV).

We will begin with the simple observation that there would be no need for the dead to be raised to face this final judgement if judgement had already been pronounced on them immediately after their deaths.

Whilst the majority of Protestant Christian denominations have diverse and apparently ever-changing views and, in some cases, appear to have adopted a *laissez faire* approach, the Roman Catholic Church, being meticulous in terms of doctrine and practice, has correctly perceived the serious nature of the problem and devised the theory of two judgements— "particular" and "general". According to this theory, the immortal soul is separated from the body upon death and immediately faces a particular judgement which will decide the soul's eternal destiny. Depending on the outcome, the soul is either granted entrance to Heaven or sentenced to Hell. Then, at the "end of times", the soul is summoned from either Heaven or Hell and re-united with its body in a general resurrection. The same irreversible decree is pronounced at a general judgement, after which time the soul is sent back either to Heaven or to Hell for all eternity, this time in company with its body.

Aside from the fact that this theory is grossly offensive to the God of justice, mercy and love, it is remarkable that so many should accept a concoction so glaringly based on the necessity to bolster and preserve related teachings.

Finally, let us lay to rest all teachings that insist on judgement immediately upon death by considering once again the case of Lazarus, the brother of Mary and Martha. According to these teachings, the following sequence of events had to have transpired:

- Lazarus has died and his immortal soul has separated from his body;
- his dead body now lays in the grave;
- his soul has been judged and has either entered an eternal Heaven or been consigned to an eternal Hell;
- Jesus summons him from the grave after four days;
- the corollary of which is that his soul must be summoned from either Heaven or Hell to be re-united with his four days dead body;
- after which Lazarus lives again through the trials of this life;
- before being once more consigned to his eternal abode;
- keeping in mind that his eternal destiny was already decreed at the time of his first death.

All that one can really say about this pathetic example of what passes for serious theology is this:

> He that sitteth in the heavens shall laugh: the Lord shall have them in derision (Psalm 2:4 KJV).

Notes

For a commentary on the raising of Lazarus, see Part XV.7: *Resurrection-Three Days*.

It is beyond the scope of this work to consider the differences between ancient Israelite thought and those of the various branches of modern Judaism regarding the concept of an afterlife, except to remark that most Jewish ideas on this topic developed in post-biblical times.

PART XI

In the Beginning

CHAPTER ONE

Introduction

The Hebrew Bible is a collection of narrative traditions, legal materials, historical chronicles, and a selection of oracles, poetry and songs and their interpretations over time produced and transmitted by priests, scribes, prophets and other community leaders. The common thread underlying the selection of a considerable portion of the material is the hope of the eventual redemption of the people of Israel by the God of Israel.

It is a book written by Israelites, for Israelites, about Israelites. The allegorical story of the pair of humans in Eden is intended to represent the unknown progenitors of Israelites and other Ancient Near Eastern peoples at a time before the call of Abraham, after which point the story narrows its focus to the descendants of Abraham and their interactions with non-Israelites. The accounts in Genesis are therefore geographically, linguistically, and culturally limited in scope.

The intent of this commentary is not to deal exhaustively with all the issues in the early chapters of Genesis but rather to raise just a few important points for consideration.

CHAPTER TWO

Note

Without going into laborious detail, Hebrew words are formed from stem roots with the addition of prefixes and suffixes which determine particular meanings. A single word in Hebrew often represents several words in English.

In the beginning

Creation *ex-nihilo* is a term which refers to God creating everything from nothing. A majority of Jews, Christians and Muslims now believe in this concept although it has been the subject of classic disputes among theologians and philosophers from all religious traditions since the earliest of times, disputes which continue to this day.

Creation *ex-nihilo* is one of the foundational assumptions of Christian theology. It is based on the opening verses of the Bible which are usually translated into English as a sequence of independent statements:

1. In the beginning, God created the heavens and the earth.
2. And the earth was formless and void and darkness was upon the face of the deep. And the spirit of God was hovering over the face of the water.
3. And God said, "Let there be light," and there was light.

It is not generally recognised that this understanding of Genesis 1:1-3 has been challenged on a linguistic and exegetical basis since at least mediaeval times by great Jewish scholars and sages such as Rashi and Ibn Ezra, and by later scholars who adopted their views. According to these critics, the three verses are not a sequence of independent statements but depend absolutely on the correct understanding of the very first Hebrew word (*bereshith*) which then governs the meaning of the verses that follow.

Rashi

Because Rashi's reputation is unassailable, and because so much depends upon a correct understanding of this word, we will focus on his view.

Rashi's rendering of Genesis 1:1-3 is as follows:

1. In the beginning *of* (*bereshith*) God's creation *(bara)* of the heavens and the earth.

2. Now the earth was astonishingly empty, and darkness was on the face of the deep, and the spirit of God was hovering over the face of the water.

3. And God said, "Let there be light", and there was light.

The Hebrew word *bereshith* (בְּרֵאשִׁית) is formed from the root noun *reshith* meaning "beginning". Prefixed to this root is an inseparable prepositional form indicating "in the". The form of the noun *reshith* is in the "construct" state meaning that it is dependent on the word *bara* (בָּרָא) which follows it and indicates possession, hence "In the beginning *of*..."

Rashi also pointed out that there are five occurrences of the word *bereshith* in the Bible: one in Genesis and four in the Book of Jeremiah. In every case, except for perhaps the most important one in Genesis, the word has been rendered into English as "in the beginning of" e.g:

> The word of the LORD that came to Jeremiah the prophet against Elam in the beginning of (*bereshith*) the reign of Zedekiah king of Judah, saying...(Jeremiah 49:34 KJV).

According to Rashi, Verse 1 is a temporal clause stating when the action takes place, Verse 2 is a circumstantial clause describing the conditions in which the action takes place, and Verse 3 is the main clause stating what the action is: "Let there be light..."

There is a modern English version of the Hebrew Bible that reflects the general views of critics such as Rashi so let's take a look at the primary translation of Genesis 1:1-3 according to this version:

> When God began to create heaven and earth—the earth being unformed and void, with darkness over the surface of the deep and a wind from God sweeping over the water—God said, "Let there be light"; and there was light.[1]

If the above translations of Genesis 1:1-3 are correct, and one were to take a purely naturalistic approach to the story, then one could assume that the only difference between the Creation story and the view of modern science is one of agency. Modern science would claim that natural processes can explain the development of life on earth from primordial waters whereas the authors of Genesis would claim that the initiation of such development can only be explained by divine creative activity.

However, such a naturalistic approach does little justice to an account which is multi-levelled and rich in meaning. We will explore a different approach in a future Chapter.

---

[1] *Tanakh: The Holy Scriptures*. Philadelphia: Jewish Publication Society. 1985

Reflections

Further indications that Genesis is not describing Creation *ex-nihilo* are the several Biblical references to the "divine council" created previously. This council, consisting of God and the ministering messengers and servants, is called to witness God's creative activity in Genesis. For references to this divine council see Job 1:6-12, 15:8, 38:4-7; Isaiah 6:1-8; Jeremiah 23:18; and I Kings 22:19-23.

It has been asserted by certain critics that if the account in Genesis does not claim Creation *ex-nihilo*, then it is merely a reflection of ancient pagan and Hellenist cosmologies. For instance, Aristotle's view of the universe is not something created from nothing (*ex nihilo*) or created anew (*de novo*). The universe—as it is now—was eternally this way. Plato's view is similar to Aristotle in that uncreated matter always existed but, unlike Aristotle, God fashioned that matter from its chaotic state into refined substances and forms. Although the rendering of Genesis 1:1-3 according to the critics noted above appears to support these views, essentially that God imposed order upon eternal uncreated matter, the similarity is only superficial because the authors of Genesis would assert that since only God is eternal and uncreated, all matter in the universe must have been created *ex-nihilo* in the actual "beginning".

In their book *The Atheist Crusade: A Jewish rebuttal to Richard Dawkins' The God Delusion*, Sara Yoheved Rigler with Rabbi Moshe Zeldman wrote:

> The problem of "First Cause" is the knock-out argument against which Dawkins has no defense. Even if Dawkins, the evolutionary biologist, could prove that human beings evolved out of some primordial soup, evolution still begs the bigger questions: Where did the elements of the primordial soup come from? What caused the first particles to come into being? What caused the Big Bang? How can you believe in a beginning without also believing in a beginner?

Rigler and Zeldman also point out that:

> Einstein understood that the beginning of the universe implies a transcendent force that brought it into being. That's why for so long he clung to his belief in a static universe (one that had always existed, and therefore had no beginning) and resisted the mounting evidence for an expanding universe...Faced with evidence of an expanding universe discovered by astronomer Vesto Slipher and deduced by mathematicians Willem de Sitter and Alexander Friedman, Einstein refused to accept the inevitable conclusion. "I have not yet fallen into the hands of the priests," was Einstein's famous response to the possibility of

an expanding universe. Clearly he understood that an expanding universe must have a non-physical First Cause.[2]

A Rabbinical View

There are authentic, respected voices in the Jewish community that take a literalist position with regard to these issues; at the same time, Judaism has a history of diverse approaches to the understanding of the biblical account of creation. As Rabbi Joseph Hertz wrote, "While the fact of creation has to this day remained the first of the articles of the Jewish creed, there is no uniform and binding belief as to the manner of creation, i.e. as to the process whereby the universe came into existence. The manner of the Divine creative activity is presented in varying forms and under differing metaphors by Prophet, Psalmist and Sage; by the Rabbis in Talmudic times, as well as by our medieval Jewish thinkers." Some refer to the Midrash (Koheleth Rabbah 3:13) which speaks of God "developing and destroying many worlds" before our current epoch. Others explain that the word "yom" in Biblical Hebrew, usually translated as "day," can also refer to an undefined period of time, as in Isaiah 11:10-11. Maimonides stated that "what the Torah writes about the Account of Creation is not all to be taken literally, as believed by the masses" (Guide to the Perplexed II:29), and recent Rabbinic leaders who have discussed the topic of creation, such as Rabbi Samson Raphael Hirsch and Rabbi Abraham Isaac Kook, saw no difficulty in explaining Genesis as a theological text rather than a scientific account.[3]

---

2 Sara Yoheved Rigler with Rabbi Moshe Zeldman. T*he Atheist Crusade: A Jewish rebuttal to Richard Dawkins' The God Delusion*. Accessed 4 September 2017
http://www.aish.com/sp/ph/The-Atheist-Crusade.html

3 Rabbinical Council of America. *Creation, Evolution, and Intelligent Design*, accessed 1 September 2017
http://www.rabbis.org/news/article.cfm?id=100635

CHAPTER THREE

Anti-Myth in Genesis

Although the creation account in Genesis 1 is often described as a "myth", it is in reality an heroic attempt by ancient authors to de-mythologise the creation epics of other peoples. With the very first words, the authors of Genesis signal an intention to mount an anti-mythological refutation of those other ancient Near-Eastern cosmogonies by demonstrating the difference between the God of the Israelites and the gods of other peoples.

Most Ancient Near-Eastern creation accounts are theogonies, that is, they are accounts of the origin and genealogy of the gods. These gods produce their offspring, mainly through sexual acts, and engage in cosmic battles for supremacy. The Egyptian god *Ptah*, for example, masturbates and from his seed creates his divine family and the world.

Even though the Bible's view of the Israelite God is often criticised for being too "anthropomorphic", the reality is that the creation account in Genesis is notable for the absence of such crude anthropomorphisms. The Israelite God just *is*. He alone is sovereign. There is no trace of emanation or pantheism. No beginning, no end, no origins, no parents, no wife, no consort. By divine *fiat*, by his magisterial Word, the waters of chaos and darkness are defeated and the structured world we inhabit comes into existence.

In other creation epics, the visible heavens,[4] the "sky", not only *were* the gods but all the gods were contained *within them*. Contrast this view with that put forward in Genesis where the Israelite God is pictured as outside and in control of the visible heavens as is a potter his clay.

The story in Genesis was designed to confront the nature deities, the nature religions and the fertility myths of the Canaanites and the Babylonians. Genesis postulates that the Israelite God is not a nature deity but a God who intervenes in human history.

The Israelite God did not create humans to be lackeys and to perform menial tasks for the gods, as did the gods in the Babylonian epic *Enuma Elish*. Rather than humans being just an afterthought of the gods, as in other creation epics, they were created to reflect God's own image, the *imago dei*, and were expected to reflect God's righteous behaviour, thereby demonstrating God's presence in the world.

---

[4] The fifth word of verse 1 is שָׁמַיִם (*shamayim*) which means the "visible heaven" or "sky."

Genesis ridicules the perceived powers of the Sun, the Moon and other heavenly bodies to control human existence. These bodies, the "greater" and "lesser" lights and the stars, are relegated to the simple functionary roles of giving light on the earth, enabling humans to tell time, to order crop planting, to navigate, and so on. Humans cannot guarantee the return of the seasons by sacrificing to the "gods". Neither can sacrifice guarantee reproduction of plants and animals because every living thing reproduces "after its kind".

Genesis posits that the Israelite God has so arranged nature that nature takes care of itself. This view of nature may seem a given to the modern mind but, for its time, it is a model of sophisticated and enlightened thinking.

Note

Although pagan concepts and practices lingered on in certain sectors of the population, they were explicitly condemned by the prophets and historians of Israel throughout all generations.

CHAPTER FOUR

The Days

Despite its manifest absurdity, and despite overwhelming evidence to the contrary, many continue to insist on six literal twenty-four hour Creation days, no doubt for fear that to pull on just one thread may result in a wholesale unravelling of cherished beliefs.

The Hebrew word *yom* (day), as in English, is used both for a literal twenty-four-hour day and also for an indefinite period of time, such as in the expression "for the day of the Lord is at hand" (Joel 1:15) or the "Day of the Dinosaur". Because Genesis was compiled after the Exodus event, the authors chose to frame the story within six figurative days of Creation followed by a seventh figurative day of rest as a means of reinforcing the commandment of God given at Sinai:

> For six days, work is to be done, but the seventh day shall be your holy day, a day of sabbath rest to the LORD…(Exodus 35:2 NIV).

The Bible is replete with patterns and groups of seven. The words for "sabbath" and "seven" are derived from the same Hebrew root. In the world of the Genesis authors, seven was the perfect number, and seven days the perfect length of a process:

> Akkadian and Ugaritic literature…prove that a series of seven consecutive days was considered a perfect period in which to develop an important work, the action lasting six days and reaching its conclusion and outcome on the seventh day.[5]

The six periods of Creation given the term "day" (*yom*) can only be figurative because the same term (*yom*) is also used for the seventh-day period during which God rests from his creative labours (see Genesis 2:4). The elements of the day, the "evening" and "morning" periods into which the day is divided, must also be figurative for they are features of the three days before the creation of the lights in the firmament which were to divide day from night. Most important of all, however, is Jesus' understanding of the creation days, "…My Father is always at his work to this very day, and I too am working" (John 5:17).

For Jesus, the six days of Creation are not yet finished. God has not yet entered into the Sabbath rest.

---

[5] Cassuto, U. *A Commentary on the Book of Genesis.* The Hebrew University: Jerusalem, 1961, p. 13.

CHAPTER FIVE

The Trees

As stated in Part X: *Aftermath*, the Bible speaks of no other existence for mankind but the one we have always shared together—this Earth. When it does speak of "Heaven" as a destination for man it always implies life in an ideal earthly Kingdom, envisioned as a re-establishment of the Garden of Eden from which we were expelled. To complete the cycle of life on Earth, we must symbolically return to Eden and to our previous state of being ruled by God and not by man.

Of Life

Consider the description of the symbolic Garden in the Hebrew Scriptures:

> And the LORD God planted a garden (Hebrew: *gan*) eastward in Eden; and there he put the man whom he had formed. And out of the ground made the LORD God to grow every tree that is pleasant to the sight, and good for food; the tree of life also in the midst of the garden (Hebrew: *gan*), and the tree of knowledge of good and evil (Genesis 2:8-9 KJV).

Also consider that the expulsion from the Garden was to deny human access to the "tree of life":

> And the LORD God said, Behold, the man is become as one of us, to know good and evil: and now, lest he put forth his hand, and take also of the tree of life, and eat, and live for ever: Therefore the LORD God sent him forth from the garden (*gan*) of Eden, to till the ground from whence he was taken. So he drove out the man; and he placed at the east of the garden of Eden Cherubims, and a flaming sword which turned every way, to keep the way of the tree of life. (Genesis 3:22-24 KJV).

Now consider the New Testament promise about the "tree of life":

> ...To the one who is victorious, I will give the right to eat from the tree of life, which is in the paradise (*paradeisos*) of God (Revelation 2:7 NIV).

The Greek Septuagint translation of Genesis 2:8-9 substitutes the equivalent Greek word *paradeisos* for the Hebrew *gan* (garden) of Eden. The author of the Greek text of Revelation 2:7 similarly substitutes the equivalent Greek word *paradeisos* for the Hebrew *gan*.

Given that the author of Revelation locates the "tree of life" within the *paradeisos*, and given that *paradeisos* is synonymous with *gan*, it is clear that the author of Revelation is envisioning humanity's symbolic return to the Garden of Eden. "Heaven" for humans is, therefore, the right to eat from the "tree of life" in the new Garden of Eden, an earthly Kingdom that will pattern God's own kingship of the Heavens.

Of Wisdom

> And the LORD God commanded the man, saying, "Of every tree of the garden thou mayest freely eat: But of the tree of the knowledge of good and evil, thou shalt not eat of it: for in the day that thou eatest thereof thou shalt surely die" (Genesis 2:16-17 KJV).

The attributes of the "tree of knowledge of good and evil" come from the mouth of the serpent:

> But the serpent said to the woman, "You will not surely die. For God knows that when you eat of it your eyes will be opened, and you will be like God, knowing good and evil." So when the woman saw that the tree was good for food, and that it was a delight to the eyes, and that the tree was to be desired **to make one wise**, she took of its fruit and ate, and she also gave some to her husband who was with her, and he ate. Then the eyes of both were opened, and they knew that they were naked. And they sewed fig leaves together and made themselves loincloths (Genesis 3:4-7 ESV).

In both the Hebrew and English languages, to *see* with the eyes also carries the implication of *understanding* with the mind. Thus, for Eve, the prospect of having their eyes opened by eating from the tree was the prospect of gaining "wisdom". In some Biblical passages, the phrase "knowing good and evil" refers to the wise discernment of mature adults but in others it is an attribute of the wise ruler as, for example, King Solomon who prays for the ability to discern between good and evil:

> Give your servant therefore an understanding mind to govern your people, that I may discern between good and evil, for who is able to govern this your great people? (1 Kings 3:9 ESV cf. 2 Samuel 14:17; Hebrews 5:14).

According to the account in Genesis, humans were created to reflect God's image and to rule the created world as viceroys. By choosing to believe the lies of the serpent and grasp at a wisdom which could not be pre-empted, their eyes were indeed opened. Rather than reflecting the image of God and acquiring the knowledge and discernment of wise rulers, they instead acquired a knowledge of their own guilt at violating God's command. Their guilt and shame are represented by the nakedness of which they were now aware. They search to cover their guilt and shame before God but can find nothing but leaves. The humans have undergone a transformation—from innocence to guilt, from light to darkness, from blessing to curse, and from life to death. God in his mercy does not exact the full penalty for their disobedience but banishes them clothed in animal skins, clothing greater than leaves but less than the regal robes with which they would have been invested had they not disobeyed.

Note

There could be no better metaphor for cunning lies and slippery deceptions than a fork-tongued snake.

CHAPTER SIX

The end of the beginning

As noted in a previous Chapter, if the alternative translation of Genesis 1:1-3 is correct, and if one were to take a purely naturalistic approach to the story, then one could assume that the only difference between the Creation story and the view of modern science is one of agency. Modern science would claim that natural processes can explain the development of life on earth from primordial waters whereas the authors of Genesis would claim that the initiation of such development can only be explained by divine creative activity.

As also noted in a previous Chapter, such a naturalistic approach does not do justice to a story which is multi-levelled and rich in meaning.

As Jon D. Levenson, Albert A. List Professor of Jewish Studies at Harvard Divinity School, observes:

> Two and a half millennia of Western theology have made it easy to forget that throughout the ancient Near Eastern world, including Israel, the point of creation is not the production of matter out of nothing, but rather the emergence of a stable community in a benevolent and life-sustaining order. The defeat by YHWH of the forces that have interrupted that order is intrinsically an act of creation.[1]

Within the account of God's mastery over the forces of chaos and formless darkness is embedded a more meaningful story about the intention of God to bring "light", to bring wisdom, understanding and order to the chaotic darkness of the human mind.

According to this approach, Adam and Eve are the representative humans who portray their darkness of mind in an allegory using conflicting values: lies as opposed to truth; evil as opposed to good; guilt as opposed to innocence; curse as opposed to blessing; and death as opposed to life. They cannot master their darkness of mind and so fail to reach their *imago dei* potential. It is a message which is deep in consequence, a message quite lost on creationists and evolutionists alike.

Consider the ramifications if the authors of Genesis were not asserting Creation *ex-nihilo* of the material world but making theological statements about the human condition. Not only would those who espouse a fundamentalist, literalist doctrine

---

1   Levenson, Jon.D. *Creation and the Persistence of Evil: The Jewish Drama of Divine Omnipotence.* Princeton University Press: Princeton, New Jersey, 1988, p. 12.

of Creation have their positions finally and fully discredited, but also those who use this literalist view as a weapon of ridicule to promote wholesale rejection of the Bible would find themselves disarmed.

Imaging God

According to the account in Genesis, the representative humans are portrayed as knowing what God's boundaries are, as knowing the consequences of stepping outside those boundaries, yet deliberately choosing to do so anyway. When they disobey, they destroy their relationship with God and with the world in which they live. Through their premature aspiration to gain wisdom and be like God (Genesis 3:5), they have instead brought disorder, disharmony, and death into the world.

Were it not for the doctrines of mainstream Christianity, it would have been recognised centuries ago that the entire biblical narrative is a cohesive and themed account of the progressive growth in wisdom and understanding of Adam and Eve's descendants and that their original potential to reflect the image of God only came to fruition in Jesus of Nazareth, a man who transformed their guilt into innocence, their darkness into light, their curse into blessing, and their death into life, becoming the fullness of the *imago dei*.

The "Jesus Christ" of Christian theology renders this biblical narrative meaningless.

The Persistence of Evil

I am indebted to Jon Levenson's work, *Creation and the Persistence of Evil: The Jewish drama of Divine Omnipotence*, for some of the following observations.

The Creation account does not speak of the annihilation of malign forces, only of their being neutralised by containment. Levinson notes under the heading *The Vitality of Evil and the Fragility of Creation*:

> Creation itself offers no ground for the optimistic belief that the malign powers will not deprive the human community of its friendly and supportive environment. In the story of Noah, the ground of security is not creation, which is undone in those days, but God's mysterious oath not to destroy his world. Only that oath, only that universal covenant sworn to Noah, and nothing more, keeps human life safe from total annihilation.[2]

A dialectic between God's absolute sovereignty and the lived reality of evil unchecked underscores passages in Psalm 74 and Isaiah 51 and 54 where we find their authors urging God to once more act like the hero of old and reassert his mastery over the

---

[2] Levenson, pp 48-49.

world. For example, Isaiah 51:9-11 calls upon the "arm of the Lord" to "awaken as in the days of old". However, throughout the Hebrew Bible, the conviction that God will finally and completely triumph over malevolent forces is unquestioned and inevitable. As Levinson observes:

> …Leviathan, Amalek, Gog, and the like are symbols from different traditionary complexes for the same theological concept: the ancient and enduring opposition to the full realisation of God's mastery, the opposition destined to be eliminated at the turn of the aeon.[3] (The "Age to Come").

We see this conviction carried through into the New Testament, especially in the Book of Revelation with its radical vision of a "new heaven and a new earth" in which the "sea is no more". The "sea" of course represents the waters of chaos and darkness originally mastered at Creation.

The view to which I ascribe is that God, in a sense, released his containment of the forces of evil after Eden and will allow them to persist until the recreation of humanity and the return to a symbolic Eden in the "Age to Come". This theme of humanity reborn, a new creation in which their better impulses will no longer be undermined by their evil ones is pervasive in the New Testament whose authors drew on passages such as the following from the Book of Ezekiel:

> "I will give you a new heart and put a new spirit in you; I will remove from you your heart of stone and give you a heart of flesh. And I will put my Spirit in you and move you to follow my decrees and be careful to keep my laws" (Ezekiel 36:26-27 NIV).

Notes

See Part VIII: *Sin and Salvation* for a commentary on the teaching of Original Sin.

For an extensive commentary on the use of plural pronouns in Genesis 1:26, 3:22, 11:7, and Isaiah 6:8, see also Part VI.3: *Trinity on Trial-Proof Texts*.

---

3   Levenson, p 38..

PART XII

The Israelite God

CHAPTER ONE

The God of Israel

Ethical Monotheism

Very few ideas in the history of human thought and progress have had such a decisive impact on the course of civilisation as the Israelite concept of ethical monotheism. The true significance of this concept is that, after having reached the conclusion that there is only one God, the Israelites had gone on to universalise and spiritualise this concept in socially idealistic and ethical terms.

The Israelites perceived their God as possessing all the perfections and ideal attributes of holiness, righteousness, truth, justice, love and mercy. As a consequence, the human being created in God's image is duty bound to emulate God in the practice of all those aspects of character and virtue. Therefore, through the process of growth and refinement over centuries, there developed a comprehensive system of spiritual and intellectual ideas, and of morals, laws and ethics for the governing of life, both individually and collectively.

It is important to recognise that the emergence of monotheism amongst the ancient Israelites is a phenomenon that itself cannot be rationally explained, as the late Professor Nahum Sarna observed:

> There is absolutely no parallel in the ancient Near East for a people resisting the current universal religious thought patterns, challenging the prevailing world views and producing a national religion and literature that in its fundamentals goes against the stream of the entire existing tradition of which historically, culturally and geographically it is a constituent part. The phenomenon defies all attempts at rational explanation, for a linear, evolutionary development of monotheism from polytheism is not otherwise attested.[1]

The One and Indivisible God

The *Shema Yisrael* is a declaration of faith, a pledge of allegiance to the one God of Israel:

---

1   Sarna, Nahum M. *Paganism and Biblical Judaism: Great Confrontations in Jewish History*. The J. M. Goodstein Lecture Series on Judaica, 1975, edited by Stanley M. Wagner and Allen D. Breck. Denver: University of Denver, Department of History, 1977/5737, reprinted in *Studies in Biblical Interpretation* Philadelphia: Jewish Publication Society, 2000/5760, p. 17.

> Hear, O Israel: The LORD our God is one LORD: And thou shalt love the LORD thy God with all thine heart, and with all thy soul, and with all thy might. And these words, which I command thee this day, shall be in thine heart: And thou shalt teach them diligently unto thy children, and shalt talk of them when thou sittest in thine house, and when thou walkest by the way, and when thou liest down, and when thou risest up (Deuteronomy 6:4-7 KJV).

The *Shema* encapsulates the monotheistic essence of Israel. It has such central significance that, even today, it is recited by observant Jews in the mornings and evenings and is traditionally a Jew's last words on Earth.

This belief in God's absolute "Oneness" refutes the plurality of gods and asserts that the Israelite God is the only true existence. There is absolutely nothing in the New Testament which contradicts this biblical teaching of the Oneness of God. When Jesus was asked by a scribe what was the most important of all the commandments, he answered by reciting the *Shema*:

> ...The first of all the commandments is, Hear, O Israel; The Lord our God is one Lord: And thou shalt love the Lord thy God with all thy heart, and with all thy soul, and with all thy mind, and with all thy strength: this is the first commandment (Mark 12:29-30 KJV).

This single statement by Jesus himself reduces to dust all the doctrinal debris constructed around his person. To replace the indivisibility of the God of Israel, so explicitly reinforced by Jesus, into the doctrine of the Trinity and claim that any created being, especially the Jewish Jesus, possesses God's own qualities, that he is co-eternal, co-existent and uncreated, was and is profoundly shocking to Jews both ancient and modern. The Trinitarian doctrine has precluded any possible rapport between the Jewish people and Creedal Christianity.

The Victorious God

See Part XI.6: *In the Beginning-The End of the Beginning* for a commentary on God's victory over the forces of chaos and darkness at Creation and also in that same Chapter a commentary on the *Persistence of Evil*.

The Interventionist God

YHWH, the one God of Israel, was not perceived as a nature deity like the gods of the surrounding peoples but rather as a deity who intervened in the history of mankind in general, and of the Israelites in particular. Consider the following passage from the Book of Kings:

And he said, Go forth, and stand upon the mount before the LORD. And, behold, the LORD passed by, and a great and strong wind rent the mountains, and brake in pieces the rocks before the LORD; but the LORD was not in the wind: and after the wind an earthquake; but the LORD was not in the earthquake: And after the earthquake a fire; but the LORD was not in the fire: and after the fire a still small voice (1 Kings 19:11-12 KJV).

Authorial intent in this passage is to contrast the nature deities of peoples such as the Canaanites with the one true God of Israel. YHWH is not to be found in the wind, or the earthquake, or the fire, but is one who speaks to mankind in a *qol demama daqqa*, "a still small voice", and who intervenes on their behalf.

Regardless of what modern cultural anthropologists, historians, biblical critics and sundry other academics have to say about the pre-Christian era, it is important to realise that the persons populating the entire Bible believed in the history described in the Hebrew scriptures, as only a cursory glance at the New Testament will demonstrate.

These Israelites believed that their God had intervened on their behalf to deliver them from bondage in Egypt, had revealed the Word of God to Moses at Sinai, and that from among all the peoples of the earth, God had appointed them to be the bearers of this revealed Word.

Without that belief in intervention, the books of the Bible would never have been written. Christianity would not exist, Jesus himself would have remained unknown to us, and the entire course of human history would be radically different if not for the fact that the authors of those books believed in an interventionist God.

The Unchanging God of the Fathers

The God of the Israelites is eternal, immortal and invisible, transcending time, matter and space. The qualities of timelessness and deathlessness are not subject to change of any kind as they stand outside the forces of change.

The Israelites peopling the pages of the New Testament, including Jesus and all his disciples, worshipped and served the same unchanging God as did their ancestors:

> The God of Abraham, Isaac and Jacob, **the God of our fathers**, has glorified his servant Jesus… (Acts 3:13 NIV).

> And he (Ananias) said, "**the God of our fathers** appointed you (Paul) to know his will, to see the Righteous One and to hear a voice from his mouth" (Acts 22:14 ESV).

> ...so worship I (Paul) **the God of my fathers,** believing all things which are written in the law and in the prophets (Acts 24:14 KJV).

On the day of John the Baptist's circumcision, his father Zechariah uttered his famous song of praise, a song that is a magnificent encapsulation of faith and hope in the God of Israel, the same God of Israel worshipped and served by his ancestors. Its crucial importance is ignored: its substance never addressed by those whose responsibility it is. As such, it is reproduced in full here:

> Blessed be the Lord God of Israel, for he has visited and redeemed his people, and has raised up a horn of salvation for us in the house of his servant David, as he spoke by the mouth of his holy prophets from of old, that we should be saved from our enemies and from the hand of all who hate us; to show the mercy promised to **our fathers** and to remember his holy covenant, the oath that he swore to our father Abraham, to grant us that we, being delivered from the hand of our enemies, might serve him without fear, in holiness and righteousness before him all our days. And you, child, will be called the prophet of the Most High; for you will go before the Lord to prepare his ways, to give knowledge of salvation to his people in the forgiveness of their sins, because of the tender mercy of our God, whereby the sunrise shall visit us from on high to give light to those who sit in darkness and in the shadow of death, to guide our feet into the way of peace (Luke 1:68-79 ESV).

This one passage sounds the death knell for the masquerade that passes for Christianity today. It contradicts almost every aspect of orthodox theology as well as challenging accepted theories about gospel dating and transmission, about the messianic role, about the identity of the people of God, and so on. (These theories are discussed in full elsewhere in this work.)

Always beyond

On the one hand, the human capacity for reasoning and logical deduction would draw us in the direction of denying a supreme being and accepting that we have created a god in our own image in order to give purpose and meaning to human life. On the other hand, the design, the beauty, and the intricate interweaving of the vast cosmic forces on which all life depends draw us in the direction of denying random mutation as an explanation satisfactory to those same reasoning powers. We humans think of this being in anthropomorphic terms and refer to it with personal pronouns and suchlike since we have no other means of describing a being we call "God" who at the same time appears both intimately concerned with humanity yet remote and beyond the human capacity for comprehension.

CHAPTER TWO

Man and his Purpose

According to the Creation allegory in Genesis, the Israelite God did not create humans to be lackeys and to perform menial tasks for the gods, as did the gods in the Babylonian epic *Enuma Elish*. Rather than humans being simply an afterthought of the gods, as in other such epics, they were created to reflect God's own image, the *imago dei*, and were expected to reflect God's righteous behaviour, thereby demonstrating God's presence in the world.

Man, being created in the image of God, is therefore not subject to any force other his own sense of morality, justice and righteousness: he is free to choose good or evil. This choice is made explicit for us in Genesis Chapter 3 which portrays humans who know what God's boundaries are, who know the consequences of stepping outside those boundaries, and who deliberately choose to do so anyway.

When the humans disobey, they destroy their relationship with God and with the world in which they live. Through their premature aspiration to be like God (Genesis 3:5), they have instead brought disorder, disharmony, and death into the world.

The story of Eden demonstrates that if humans freely choose to do evil, then humans also freely choose to live in a state of separation from God. God's purpose for man is that he will redeem himself, will freely choose to reject his separation from God and symbolically re-enter Eden. (See Part X.3: *Aftermath-Heaven* and Part XI.6: *In the Beginning-The End of the Beginning*.)

To achieve this purpose for mankind, God established an unbreakable Covenant with the entire Israelite people to be the servants and champions of his revealed Word which would find its expression in a holy and righteous society, an ideal Kingdom on Earth. All Israel's intellectual, spiritual and moral resources were to be dedicated to building this Kingdom which was to serve as a model for the nations so that "the earth will be filled with the knowledge of the LORD as the waters cover the sea" (Isaiah 11:9), thereby bringing redemption to all mankind.

In order that this goal may be furthered, God delegates authority to ordinary men and women to be instruments of his will. He fills these vessels of redemption with his "spirit" which, depending on the purpose of the moment, manifests in aspects of God's character such as "word", "righteousness" and "wisdom".

CHAPTER THREE

Manifestations

The Glory Cloud

The Hebrew Scriptures contain numerous references to a "glory cloud", sometimes referred to as the *Shekinah*. The word *Shekinah* derives from the Hebrew שָׁכַן (*shakan*), which means to dwell, settle or abide. It has come to signify the majestic presence or manifestation of God which descended to dwell among men. The word occurs in passages that speak of God dwelling either in the Tabernacle or among the people of Israel. For example:

> And let them make me a sanctuary, that I may dwell (*shakan*) in their midst (Exodus 25:8 ESV).

This "glory cloud" or *Shekinah* protected the Israelites after the Exodus, received Moses on Sinai, carried Elijah to Heaven, and protected Jerusalem for a time. (See also Exodus 14:19, 40:34; 1 Kings 8:10, 2 Chronicles 7:1, and the book of Ezekiel which contains interesting passages about the movements of this glory cloud.) The cloud was envisaged as descending from the abode of God (Heaven) at certain times, and then returning. The following passage from Exodus illuminates our understanding of the concept:

> When Moses went up on the mountain, the cloud covered it, and the glory of the Lord settled on Mount Sinai. For six days the cloud covered the mountain, and on the seventh day the Lord called to Moses from within the cloud. To the Israelites the glory of the Lord looked like a consuming fire on top of the mountain. Then Moses entered the cloud as he went on up the mountain. And he stayed on the mountain forty days and forty nights (Exodus 24:15-18 NIV).

Commentators have not given the concept the attention it deserves seeing that it plays such a major role in the Hebrew Scriptures and in the New Testament. In passages where this glory cloud is referenced, it is often paired with its perceived origin, viz. "clouds of heaven". For example, consider the following:

> I saw in the night visions, and, behold, one like the Son of man came with the clouds of heaven, and came to the Ancient of days, and they brought him near before him. And there was given him dominion, and glory, and a kingdom, that all people, nations, and languages, should serve him: his dominion is an

everlasting dominion, which shall not pass away, and his kingdom that which shall not be destroyed (Daniel 7:13-14 KJV).

And then shall appear the sign of the Son of man in heaven: and then shall all the tribes of the earth mourn, and they shall see the Son of man coming in the clouds of heaven with power and great glory (Matthew 24:30 KJV).

And when he had spoken these things, while they beheld, he was taken up; and a cloud received him out of their sight (Acts 1:9 KJV).

…Hereafter shall ye see the Son of man sitting on the right hand of power, and coming in the clouds of heaven (Matthew 26:64 KJV cf. Mark 14:61-64).

The voice from the cloud

The glory of the LORD dwelt on Mount Sinai, and the cloud covered it six days. And on the seventh day he called to Moses out of the midst of the cloud (Exodus 24:16 ESV).

Compare the above passage from Exodus with the following New Testament passages referencing the voice from the cloud:

While he yet spake, behold, a bright cloud overshadowed them: and behold a voice out of the cloud, which said, This is my beloved Son, in whom I am well pleased; hear ye him (Matthew 17: 5 KJV cf. Mark 9:7, Luke 9:34).

"Father, glorify your name!" Then a voice came from heaven, "I have glorified it, and will glorify it again." The crowd that was there and heard it said it had thundered; others said an angel had spoken to him. Jesus said, "This voice was for your benefit, not mine" (John 12:28-31 NIV).

For when he received honor and glory from God the Father, and the voice was borne to him by the Majestic Glory, "This is my beloved Son, with whom I am well pleased," we ourselves heard this very voice borne from heaven, for we were with him on the holy mountain. (2 Peter 1:16-18 ESV).

An understanding of the "glory cloud" concept will facilitate an understanding of the Ascension and passages which speak of Jesus "coming with clouds" and similar. (See Part X.3: *Aftermath-Heaven* and Part XV: *Resurrection.*)

CHAPTER FOUR

The Holy Spirit

The two New Testament Greek words used to denote the Holy Spirit are *hagios* and *pneuma*, words which closely approximate the Hebrew term *ruach kodesh* (holy breath/wind/spirit) and the equivalent term *ruach el/elohim* (spirit of God).

The concept of the Holy Spirit of God is so closely related to that of the *Shekinah*, signifying the majestic presence or manifestation of God descending to dwell among men, that the author of Psalms envisages the spirit of God and the presence of God as parallel concepts:

> Do not cast me from your presence or take your Holy Spirit from me (Psalm 51:11 NIV).

According to the Hebrew Scriptures and the New Testament, the "*ruach kodesh*" (holy spirit) or the "*ruach el/elohim*" (spirit of God) comes to rest on humans who have been chosen to fulfill God's purposes for mankind. Humans thus filled with the presence and spirit of God, such as the prophets, are regarded as personifications of God's character attributes such as "word", "righteousness", "wisdom" and etcetera.

In the Hebrew Scriptures:

> And Pharaoh said unto his servants, Can we find such a one as this is, a man (Joseph) in whom the Spirit of God is? (*ruach elohim*) (Genesis 41:38 KJV).

> The Spirit (*ruach*) lifted me up and brought me to the exiles in Babylonia in the vision given by the Spirit of God (*ruach elohim*). Then the vision I had seen went up from me (Ezekiel 11:24 NIV).

In the New Testament, the Spirit of God rests on Jesus, the disciples, and on all those sent by God and who speak the words of God:

> The Spirit (*pnuema*) of the Lord is upon me, because he hath anointed me to preach the gospel to the poor…(Luke 4:18 KJV).

> When they deliver you over, do not be anxious how you are to speak or what you are to say, for what you are to say will be given to you in that hour. For it is not you who speak, but the Spirit (*pnuema*) of your Father speaking through you (Matthew 10:19-20 ESV).

> For the one whom God has sent speaks the words of God, for God gives the Spirit (*pneuma*) without limit (John 3:34 NIV).

These Israelite concepts have been re-conceptualised and manipulated into the framework of orthodox theology. Instances of their misuse have been demonstrated elsewhere in this work, especially in Part IV.3: *Virgin Birth and Incarnation-The Gospel of Matthew*.

Truth or Lies

If there is one major premise of the entire Bible it is the eternal conflict between truth and lies. Paul identified this conflict as the cause of what he perceived to be the evils of this world:

> For they exchanged the truth of God for a lie, and worshiped and served the creature rather than the Creator, who is blessed forever. Amen (Romans 1:25 NASB).

In an obvious reference to the serpent (Hebrew: *nachash*) of Eden, Jesus stated that the devil *(diabolos)* is the father of lies:

> Ye are of your father the devil, and the lusts of your father ye will do. He was a murderer from the beginning, and abode not in the truth, because there is no truth in him. When he speaketh a lie, he speaketh of his own: for he is a liar, and the father of it (John 8:44 KJV).

Jesus also stated to Pilate that bearing witness to truth was the reason for his birth:

> Pilate therefore said unto him, Art thou a king then? Jesus answered, Thou sayest that I am a king. To this end was I born, and for this cause came I into the world, that I should bear witness unto the truth. Every one that is of the truth heareth my voice (John 18:37 KJV).

To which Pilate responded with those immortal words "what is truth?" Pilate would find himself quite at home in these days of subjective relativism where truth is what you *believe*. Contrary to modern perspectives where belief and opinion masquerade as truth, Jesus understood that truth has an objective, intrinsic value independent of external circumstance or human perception. Only a sincere and honest hunger for truth allows us to probe our biases, consider and justly weigh the evidence, and use our reasoning powers to arrive at logical conclusions.

Since, according to the Bible, the conflict between truth and lies is the crux of the human problem, readers will hopefully forgive the following lengthy list of biblical exhortations to bear witness to truth, to love and value it, and to serve God in spirit and truth.

From the Hebrew Scriptures

> Now therefore fear the LORD, and serve him in sincerity and in truth… (Joshua 24:14 KJV).

> The Lord is near to all who call on him, to all who call on him in truth (Psalm 145:18 NIV).

> Thus says the LORD, "I will return to Zion and will dwell in the midst of Jerusalem. Then Jerusalem will be called the City of Truth, and the mountain of the LORD of hosts will be called the Holy Mountain" (Zechariah 8:3 NASB).

From the New Testament

> And the Word was made flesh, and dwelt among us, (and we beheld his glory, the glory as of the only begotten of the Father,) full of grace and truth (John 1:14 KJV).

> But the hour is coming, and is now here, when the true worshipers will worship the Father in spirit and truth, for the Father is seeking such people to worship him (John 4:23 ESV).

> God is spirit, and his worshipers must worship in the Spirit and in truth (John 4:24 NIV).

> And I will pray the Father, and he shall give you another Comforter, that he may abide with you for ever; Even the Spirit of truth; whom the world cannot receive, because it seeth him not, neither knoweth him: but ye know him; for he dwelleth with you, and shall be in you (John 14:16-17 KJV).

> Sanctify them through thy truth: thy word is truth (John 17:7 KJV).

> But we ought always to thank God for you, brothers and sisters loved by the Lord, because God chose you as firstfruits to be saved through the sanctifying work of the Spirit and through belief in the truth (2 Thessalonians 2:13 NIV).

> Stand firm, therefore, having fastened the belt of truth around your waist, and having put on the breastplate of righteousness (Ephesians 6:14 ISV).

> Who will have all men to be saved, and to come unto the knowledge of the truth (1 Timothy 2:4 KJV).

The Hebrew Scriptures state that God had a controversy with the people because there was no truth, no goodness, no knowledge of God in the land (Micah 6:2; Hosea 4:1). If there was no knowledge of God in the land of the ancient Israelites, it was certainly not the fault of the Israelite prophets. If there is no knowledge of God today, it is certainly not the fault of the authors of the New Testament but can be sheeted home to that vast array of theologians and teachers who have reposed trust in doctrines and traditions rather than in the words of Jesus of Nazareth and taught others to do likewise.

Humans are required to make choices based on the reasoning powers with which they have been endowed, "Come now, and let us reason together, saith the Lord..." (Isaiah 1:18). Because Jesus said that all who are "of the truth" shall hear his voice, it is incumbent upon those who would be his followers to:

- seek to establish the "truth";
- without fear or favour;
- on the basis of deductive reasoning.

When Jesus said, "Thy word is truth" (John 17:17), he was referring to the Hebrew Scriptures, the only "word" of God in existence at that time. No Christian Church can teach that which negates this statement by its founder therefore teachings which conflict with those of the Hebrew Scriptures must be rejected on that basis.

Nor should any Christian Church teach that which negates the New Testament and the teachings of Jesus, for he said:

> But you are not to be called rabbi (teacher), for you have one teacher, and you are all brothers (Matthew 23:8 ESV).

When one reflects on the manner of Jesus' teaching—in the open air, in a fishing boat—and then reflects upon the gilded palaces denoted by some as "houses of worship", consideration should be given to the manner in which God should be worshipped. On this matter, the entire Bible is in agreement.

PART XIII

The Israelite Messiah

CHAPTER ONE

Great Expectations

The hope of Israel, as expressed in the Hebrew Scriptures, was the establishment on earth of the Kingdom of God under the kingship of an "anointed" one, a "Messiah".

After the Exodus, YHWH was seen as a deliverer who had saved his people through his human agent, Moses. Out of the welter of messianic expectations and longings arising from successive waves of tribulation, disaster and disappointment, an idea arose that YHWH would one day send another deliverer—a prophet like Moses— who would save his people from their enemies.

The prophets, each building and enlarging upon the expectations of his predecessors, finally developed a complete picture of this deliverer, an ideal King-Messiah who would inaugurate the eschatalogical Messianic Age, God's Kingdom on earth, a holy and righteous Kingdom of brotherhood, peace and justice modelled on a restored, perfected, twelve-tribed Kingdom of David.

All Israel's intellectual, spiritual and moral resources were to be dedicated to building this holy and righteous society, the radical political and national components of which were not envisioned as separate from the ethical and universal but formed part of a unified whole. This Kingdom of Israel was to serve as a model for the nations.

The King-Messiah would sit on the throne of this Kingdom and, because of God's dynastic promises to David, it was envisioned that he therefore must be a biological "son of David", hence of the Israelite tribe of Judah.

In the course of fulfilling his mission, it was envisioned that the Messiah would prove himself to be the greatest of all the prophets of righteousness in the line which began with Moses in Egypt. Because both the Messiah, individually, and the people of God, collectively, are spoken of by the prophets in terms of grief, humiliation and suffering, it was therefore envisioned that the glorious reign of God would emerge only after their passage through the refining furnace of affliction which would burn off the dross of the reign of man. This advent period, also likened to the travail of a woman in childbirth, was termed by later Rabbis as the "birth pangs of the Messiah".

All these elements, together with the suggestive force of other passages in the Hebrew Scriptures, came to constitute criteria which the anointed one was expected to satisfy on his appearance. Then, as now, in the more rarified air of academia, there existed messianic speculations of greater purity, of more exquisite transcendence, of more exalted spirituality, of loftier learning and insight but, by the time of Jesus, a great majority of the "simple" people awaited the promised Messiah of the house of David who would deliver them from the tribulations of the Roman yoke and establish God's Kingdom of peace, justice and righteousness in its place. [1]

And so it was when Jesus was born "in the days of Herod the King".

---

[1] Fredriksen, Paula. *From Jesus to Christ: The Origins of the New Testament Images of Jesus*. Yale University Press, 2000, pp.141-42.; Vermes, Geza. *Jesus the Jew*. Fortress Press: Philadelphia, 1981, pp, 130-140.

CHAPTER TWO

The Unexpected Messiah

Section 1

A selection of criteria the messiah was expected to satisfy on his appearance was:

1. he would be an Israelite of the tribe of Judah;
2. he would be descended from King David of the tribe of Judah and entitled by birth to sit on David's earthly throne;
3. he would usher in the Kingdom of God on earth;
4. he would be a deliverer like the prophet Moses who would save the Israelites from their enemies;
5. he would restore and gather into one the scattered tribes of Israel;
6. he would cleanse the world by fire.

The interpretive principle of the New Testament is the way in which it reconciles all these Israelite messianic expectations with the reality of the Messiah they were preaching.

In regards to Points 1 and 2, the New Testament records that they were indeed fulfilled literally (See Part IV: *Virgin Birth and Incarnation*). The New Testament authors claim that Points 3 through 6 were also fulfilled in Jesus although through unusual but substantial and lasting ways. A brief overview follows.

Ushering in the Kingdom of God

Point 3: Followers of Jesus are united in a spiritual Kingdom of God in existence since the Resurrection. (Further analysis of the Kingdom of God appears elsewhere in this work.)

Saving the Israelites from their enemies

Point 4: Before the Israelite people could be "saved" from their enemies, like Moses had done, they first had to be saved from themselves by emulating the moral and ethical principles Jesus had lived and died for. Before an external change, there had to be internal renewal. Without internal renewal, without being "born again" into a new way of thinking and acting, external problems would simply keep repeating themselves.

Restoring and gathering Israel

Point 5: The Resurrection was a foreshadowing signal to Israelites living in the Diaspora that they would one day be "resurrected" from their dispersion, regarded as a type of death, and ingathered to Israel to form the Kingdom of God to be ruled over by God's Messiah. (See also Part VII.4: *Paul-Paul and his Theology*.)

Consuming the world by fire

Point 6: The word of God made flesh in Jesus was like a fire, the fire of the Day of the Lord of prophecy, which burned up the stubble of false values and false standards, leaving nothing behind. (See discussion of biblical fire in Part X.4.3: *Aftermath-Hell-Biblical Fire*.)

Notes

Although the authors claimed that Jesus fulfilled messianic expectations in these unexpected ways, they proposed a more literal fulfillment at some future time.

Messianic criteria points 3, 5 and 6 are addressed in a more comprehensive manner elsewhere in this work. However, the Prophet like Moses (Point 4) is most suitably placed within the present framework.

Section 2

A Dead Messiah

The average Israelite, including the disciples, believed that when the Messiah came he would rule throughout the Messianic age (John 12:34). There was certainly no thought of a crucifixion-resurrection for this anointed one. A dead Messiah was something altogether outside the messianic paradigm.

According to the New Testament, the priestly-military junta ruling Jerusalem had unwittingly condemned Jesus because the expectations which revealed his death and resurrection were hidden.

Even though Jesus had repeatedly stated that he must go to Jerusalem to suffer, die, and be resurrected (e.g. Matthew 16:21; Mark 8:31; Luke 9:22), the disciples did not, or could not, quite come to terms with what he was telling them. Only a few short hours before his death, three of his closest associates, John, Peter and

Mary Magdalene, "knew not the scripture that he must rise again from the dead" (John 20:9, Luke 18:33-34). If these scriptures referencing the Messiah's death and resurrection were hidden, where then should we look?

> He said to them, "This is what I told you while I was still with you: Everything must be fulfilled that is written about me in the Law of Moses, the Prophets and the Psalms" (Luke 24:44 NIV).

The Law of Moses and the Prophets were the source material from which messianic expectations were thought to have been drawn so for Jesus to direct his followers to also search the Psalms was unusual. We will follow the direction of Jesus and focus on the Psalms, but first a brief glance at texts stating that the death and resurrection of Jesus could be found in the Law and the Prophets.

Peter's address to fellow Israelites:

> This is how God fulfilled what he had predicted through the voice of all the prophets—that his Messiah would suffer (Acts 3:18 ISV).

Paul's address to the Jews of Thessalonica:

> And Paul went in, as was his custom, and on three Sabbath days he reasoned with them from the Scriptures, explaining and proving that it was necessary for the Christ to suffer and to rise from the dead, and saying, "This Jesus, whom I proclaim to you, is the Christ" (Acts 17:2-3 ESV).

Paul's address to King Agrippa:

> But God has helped me to this very day; so I stand here and testify to small and great alike. I am saying nothing beyond what the prophets and Moses said would happen—that the Messiah would suffer and, as the first to rise from the dead, would bring the message of light to his own people and to the Gentiles (Acts 26:22-23 NIV).

It is unclear which particular passages above that Peter and Paul were referencing. However, both before and after their lifetimes, many rabbis and sages regarded the so-called "suffering servant" of Isaiah 52:13-53:12 as the most notable of the messianic themes in the Hebrew Scriptures so it is more than likely that this passage should be uppermost in their minds.

Other sages such as Rashi have interpreted Isaiah 53 as referring to the whole nation of Israel rather than to an individual. However, in Matthew's Gospel we find Jesus presented as the "corporate" Israelite, as the one standing for the many, so both interpretations are correct. (See Part IV.3: *Virgin Birth and Incarnation-Matthew's Gospel* for a comprehensive analysis of Matthew's corporate Israelite.)

Section 3

The Messiah of the Psalmist

In searching the Psalms, the problem which confronts us is to determine what method we should use to bring to light the hidden references to the Messiah. There is no better course to adopt than to allow the New Testament authors to open our minds, just as Jesus opened their minds. We have a sure guide to what was in their minds by their acknowledgement of certain Psalms being fulfilled in Jesus. Particular references to his death are:

> All they that see me laugh me to scorn: they shoot out the lip, they shake the head…(Psalm 22:7 KJV cf. Matthew 27:39).
>
> They part my garments among them, and cast lots upon my vesture (Psalm 22:18 KJV cf. Mark 15:24; Luke 23:34; Matthew 27:35; John 19:24).
>
> My God, my God, why have you forsaken me? Why are you so far from saving me, so far from my cries of anguish? (Psalm 22:1 NIV cf. Mark 15:34; Matthew 27:45-26).
>
> Into Your hand I commit my spirit; You have ransomed me, O LORD, God of truth (Psalm 31:5 NASB cf. Luke 23:46).
>
> He keeps all his bones; not one of them is broken (Psalm 34:20 ESV cf. John 19:36. See also Exodus 12:46).
>
> They put gall in my food and gave me vinegar for my thirst (Psalm 69:21 NIV cf. Matthew 27:48; Mark 15:36; Luke 23:36).
>
> Even my close friend in whom I trusted, who ate my bread, has lifted his heel against me (Psalm 41:9 ESV cf. John 13:18; Matthew 26:23; Luke 22:21).

Many statements about the anticipated and also the post-Resurrection status of Jesus are taken from Psalms 110 and 118. For example:

> …The LORD said unto my Lord, Sit thou at my right hand, until I make thine enemies thy footstool (Psalm 110:1 KJV cf. Matthew 22:44; Mark 12:36; Luke 20:42-43; Acts 2:34-35; Hebrews 1:13).

> The stone the builders rejected has become the cornerstone. The LORD has done this, and it is marvelous in our eyes (Psalm 118:22-23 NIV cf. Matthew 21:42; Mark 12:10-11; Luke 20:17; Acts 4:11; Ephesians 2:20; 1 Peter 2:7).

Consider also the following passage from Acts in which we discover that Jesus did not become the *Only Begotten Son of God, born of the Father before all ages,* as is the Creedal assertion, but on the day of his Resurrection:

> God hath fulfilled the same unto us their children, in that he hath raised up Jesus again; as it is also written in the second psalm, Thou art my Son, this day have I begotten thee (Acts 13:33 cf. Psalm 2:7 KJV).

The Psalms are also referenced in many recorded incidents in the life of Jesus. For example:

> For he shall give his angels charge over thee, to keep thee in all thy ways. They shall bear thee up in their hands, lest thou dash thy foot against a stone (Psalm 91:11-12 KJV cf. Matthew 4:6; Luke 4:11).

> For zeal for your house consumes me, and the insults of those who insult you fall on me (Psalm 69:9 NIV cf. John 2:17; Romans 15:3).

> You love righteousness and hate wickedness; therefore God, your God, has set you above your companions by anointing you with the oil of joy (Psalm 45:7 KJV cf. Hebrews 1:9).

> Blessed is the one who comes in the name of the LORD! Let us bless you from the LORD's house (Psalm 118:26 ISV cf. Mark 11:9; Matthew 23:39; Luke 13:35; John 12:13).

Direct and indirect New Testament references to the Psalms are too numerous to list so the reader is encouraged to study the contexts from which they were drawn as they were not chosen at random—there is a systematic pattern of choice which is vital to an understanding of the role of the Messiah and of Kingdom eschatology.

There can be no question that such a diligent and contextual search will expose the fact that the doctrines of mainstream Christianity continue to be sustained only through recourse to artificial contrivance and theological sophistry.

The prophetic expectation was that the God of Israel would anoint a man with his power and Holy Spirit, clothe him with the garments of salvation, and appoint him to reign as King over an earthly Kingdom. It is preposterous for any to suggest that the God of Israel, of whose sacred name the Messiah was to stand in awe, was to become one of his own created beings, or that the anointed one was to be something other than a man born of the seed of David "according to the flesh".

Section 4

A False Assumption

The most basic difference between Christianity and Judaism through the ages is that the Jewish people are still waiting for the Messiah. Jesus could not be the Messiah, they say, because of expectations relating to the Messianic Age which he did not fulfill. Christianity and Judaism start with the same assumption that the Hebrew Scriptures predict only one appearance of the Messiah. However, when all the expectations are collected and analysed, it emerges that such an assumption is false. The reality is this:

- Jesus said that everything written about him in the Law of Moses, the Prophets, *and the Psalms* must be fulfilled (Luke 24:44);
- When studying the Messianic expectations contained in all these sources, it emerges that they cannot all be fulfilled by one man at one time;
- Thus these sources speak of *two* appearances of the Messiah in addition to his appearance in Messianic Age;
- Since the first appearance was already past, the New Testament adds further information about the second of these appearances before the Messianic Age when Jesus will appear in "power and glory".

Consider now the verses preceding verse 9 of Psalm 41 which the New Testament authors state was fulfilled in Jesus:

> The LORD will strengthen him upon the bed of languishing: thou wilt make all his bed in his sickness. I said, LORD, be merciful unto me: heal my soul; for I have sinned against thee. Mine enemies speak evil of me, When shall he die, and his name perish? And if he come to see me, he speaketh vanity: his heart gathereth iniquity to itself; when he goeth abroad, he telleth it. All that hate me whisper together against me: against me do they devise my hurt. An evil disease, say they, cleaveth fast unto him: and now that he lieth he shall rise up no more. Yea, mine own familiar friend, in whom I trusted, which did eat of my bread, hath lifted up his heel against me (Psalm 41:3-9 KJV cf. John 13:18; Matthew 26:23; Luke 22:21).

The so-called "suffering servant" theme of Isaiah 52:13-53:12 has long been recognised in Jewish interpretive tradition as having distinct parallels with Psalm 88 in terms of theme and language. Since Jesus self-identified with this "suffering servant" (Luke 22:37), it would therefore be wise to also consider what Psalm 88 reveals:

> I am counted with them that go down into the pit: I am as a man that hath no strength: Free among the dead, like the slain that lie in the grave, whom thou rememberest no more: and they are cut off from thy hand. Thou hast laid me in the lowest pit, in darkness, in the deeps. Thy wrath lieth hard upon me, and thou hast afflicted me with all thy waves. Selah. Thou hast put away mine acquaintance far from me; thou hast made me an abomination unto them: I am shut up, and I cannot come forth (Psalm 88:4-8 KJV).

From just these two passages in Psalms 41 and 88, we can readily see that they speak of a man who has an "evil disease" and whose bed has to be turned because the sickness is long-term; of a man who is still living yet counted among the dead; of a man who is "shut up and cannot come forth". It goes without saying that none of these descriptions could be applied to the life of Jesus as presented in the New Testament yet they are undoubtedly messianic through contextual and thematic associations.

All of the above will no doubt appear as a revelation to many readers. The "further information" in the New Testament, referred to above, was provided by Jesus himself, as we will see in Part XV.12: *Resurrection-Signs of the Times.*

CHAPTER THREE

The Prophet like Moses

When considering any of the acts, sayings, and descriptions of Jesus, the following passage from Deuteronomy must be a first principle of interpretation:

> The LORD thy God will raise up unto thee a Prophet from the midst of thee, of thy brethren, like unto me; unto him ye shall hearken; According to all that thou desiredst of the LORD thy God in Horeb in the day of the assembly, saying, Let me not hear again the voice of the LORD my God, neither let me see this great fire any more, that I die not. And the LORD said unto me, They have well spoken that which they have spoken. I will raise them up a Prophet from among their brethren, like unto thee, and will put my words in his mouth; and he shall speak unto them all that I shall command him (Deuteronomy 18:15-18 KJV).

That these words had no fulfillment at the close of the Torah is evidenced in the final verses of Deuteronomy:

> Since then, no prophet has risen in Israel like Moses, whom the Lord knew face to face, who did all those signs and wonders the Lord sent him to do in Egypt—to Pharaoh and to all his officials and to his whole land. For no one has ever shown the mighty power or performed the awesome deeds that Moses did in the sight of all Israel (Deuteronomy 34:10-12 NIV).

The New Testament teaches that Jesus was this promised prophet like Moses. In the Book of Acts, for example, we find that Stephen was stoned for making this precise claim. Readers are urged to consult Acts Chapter Seven for themselves and consider the various elements of Stephen's argument.

Jesus himself said of the Hebrew Scriptures that "the scripture cannot be broken". The following passages demolish the orthodox doctrinal position of the Christian churches as the parallels drawn between Moses and Jesus cannot refer to anyone but a normal, non-divine human.

One chosen from among the brethren

Philip found Nathanael and told him, "We have found the one Moses wrote about in the Law, and about whom the prophets also wrote—Jesus of Nazareth, the son of Joseph" (John 1:45 NIV cf. Acts 3:22; 28:23).

For Moses truly said unto the fathers, "A prophet shall the Lord your God raise up unto you of your brethren, like unto me; him shall ye hear in all things whatsoever he shall say unto you" (Acts 3:22 KJV).

This is that Moses, which said unto the children of Israel, "A prophet shall the Lord your God raise up unto you of your brethren, like unto me; him shall ye hear" (Acts 7:37 KJV).

The Mediator of the New Covenant

For this reason He is the mediator of a new covenant, so that, since a death has taken place for the redemption of the transgressions that were committed under the first covenant, those who have been called may receive the promise of the eternal inheritance (Hebrews 9:15 NASB).

The worker of wonders and signs

This man led them out, performing wonders and signs in Egypt and at the Red Sea and in the wilderness for forty years (Acts 7:36 ESV).

Ye men of Israel, hear these words; Jesus of Nazareth, a man approved of God among you by miracles and wonders and signs, which God did by him in the midst of you, as ye yourselves also know (Acts 2:22 KJV).

Then those men, when they had seen the miracle that Jesus did, said, This is of a truth that prophet that should come into the world (John 6:14 KJV).

Beholding the face of God

Since then, no prophet has risen in Israel like Moses, whom the LORD knew face to face (Deuteronomy 34:10 NIV).

For Christ entered not into a holy place made with hands, like in pattern to the true; but into heaven itself, now to appear before the face of God for us (Hebrews 9:24 ASV).

The reflector of glory

When Moses came down from Mount Sinai, with the two tablets of the testimony in his hand as he came down from the mountain, Moses did not know that the skin of his face shone because he had been talking with God. Aaron and all the people of Israel saw Moses, and behold, the skin of his face shone, and they were afraid to come near him (Exodus 34:29-30 ESV).

After six days Jesus took with him Peter, James and John the brother of James, and led them up a high mountain by themselves. There he was transfigured before them. His face shone like the sun, and his clothes became as white as the light (Matthew 17:1-3 NIV).

The Forty Days Transition

Then I went up to the mountain to receive the two stone Tablets of the Covenant that the LORD had established with you. I stayed on the mountain for 40 days and nights without eating food or drinking water (Deuteronomy 9:9 ISV).

To whom also he shewed himself alive after his passion by many infallible proofs, being seen of them forty days, and speaking of the things pertaining to the kingdom of God (Acts 1:3 KJV).

Summary

The New Testament teaches that Jesus was:

- the prophet from among the brethren, just like Moses;
- the mediator of the New Covenant, just as Moses was the mediator of the Old Covenant;
- the worker of signs and wonders, just like Moses;
- the one whom God knew "face to face", just like Moses;
- and the one whose shining face was a reflection of God's glory…just like Moses.

CHAPTER FOUR

Jesus Anointed

In the very first words of the New Testament, we encounter the term "Jesus Christ".

The word "Christ" is an Anglicised term for the Greek Χριστός (*Khristós*). *Khristós* is the Greek equivalent of the Hebrew מָשִׁיחַ (*Mashiach*) meaning "Anointed one". The *Mashiach* refers to a person chosen by the God of Israel to be his vice-regent on behalf of the people Israel.

Over the course of ancient Israelite history, prophets, priests and kings had taken office by having oil poured over their heads, thus becoming anointed ones. However, these *Mashiach* (Messiahs), such as those mentioned in the passages below, had served only for temporary or specific purposes:

> Then Samuel took a flask of olive oil and poured it on Saul's head and kissed him, saying, "Has not the LORD anointed you ruler over his inheritance?" (1 Samuel 10:1 NIV).
>
> And Zadok the priest took an horn of oil out of the tabernacle, and anointed Solomon. And they blew the trumpet; and all the people said, God save king Solomon (1 Kings 1:39 KJV).

Foreigners could also serve as Messiahs in order to perform a vital function:

> Thus saith the LORD to his anointed, to Cyrus, whose right hand I have holden, to subdue nations before him; and I will loose the loins of kings, to open before him the two leaved gates; and the gates shall not be shut (Isaiah 45:1 KJV).

The term מָשִׁיחַ (*Mashiach*) appears 39 times in the Hebrew Scriptures and in every case it is translated into English as "anointed". In the New Testament, however, where it refers to Jesus, its Greek equivalent *Khristós* is left untranslated and simply Anglicised. We are entitled to ask why? (In the case of proper names like Jesus, a Latin/English transliteration of the Greek *Iēsou* (*Yeshua*), we should of course adhere as closely as possible to the original but *Khristós* is not a proper name: it is a descriptive title.)

The words "Jesus Christ" invite no question, but the words "Jesus anointed" immediately pose questions for the reader—anointed by whom and for what purpose? If the term had been translated into English, we would never have been subjected to the proliferation of Christologies based on concepts such as the "total Christ" and the "cosmic Christ". Any Christology based on the concept of the "total Anointed one" or the "cosmic Anointed one" is of course inherently ridiculous and would again pose the questions that should have been asked all along—anointed by whom and for what purpose? Whether wittingly or unwittingly, by failing to translate the Greek word *Khristós* into its English equivalent "anointed", translators have achieved several outcomes:

- concealed the fact that there were other Israelite "Christs" (Messiahs) before the time of Jesus;
- masked the premise upon which every book of the New Testament is based;
- muted the questions that should have arisen about the person, nature and role of the Israelite Messiah;
- caused millions of Christians to assume that "Christ" is a name and not a title.

It is often asserted that Paul used the word "Christ" as a name. If we translate it into English, however, we see that Paul was calling Jesus the "Anointed one", which is merely a shorthand way of referring to the man he at other times described more fully as the "Lord Jesus anointed". This type of assertion deflects attention away from the fact that, just like all the other writers of the New Testament, Paul was stating his belief that Jesus was the Israelite Messiah, the Anointed one of God.

There is a reluctance to fully grasp the implications arising from New Testament claims about the Israelite Messiahship of Jesus and the reason is extremely simple—nowhere in the Hebrew Scriptures is there a single hint that the Messiah was to be anything other than a normal man anointed by God to be his instrument of intervention in human affairs.

(As far as non-canonical sources are concerned, it is asserted that in works such as 1 Enoch there were expectations of a divine, pre-existent Messiah but these assertions are merely the result of reading Jewish texts through the lens of Christian theology. See James VanderKam for full discussion of 1 Enoch.) [2]

---

[2] VanderKam, James. *From Revelation to Canon: Studies in the Hebrew Bible and Second Temple Literature.* Brill, 2002.

CHAPTER FIVE

The Ideal Israelite

Notes

Although the terms "Jew" and "Jewish" are incorrect and misleading renderings of their Greek New Testament equivalents, we will nevertheless follow the pattern of common usage lest it be too confusing for readers. Note also that the consequences arising from the use of these incorrect and misleading terms are addressed elsewhere in this work.

Terms approximating "Jewish religion" refer to the overall religious framework of the day and are not intended to imply a lack of diversity in religious thought.

The religion of Jesus

Jesus was not only a Jew by accident of birth but he was also a Jew by faith, temperament and spirit: an apocalyptic teacher who observed Torah, frequented Temple and synagogue, and kept the Jewish religious festivals. He was a Jew bent on the uniquely Jewish business of preaching the coming Kingship of God, speaking always from within the Jewish religion and not once abandoning the faith of his ancestors. His teachings, like those of his followers, reflect a distinctive ethnicity and culture.

Jesus was fully immersed in the Hebrew Scriptures. He garnered spiritual support in his battle with the wilderness temptations by quoting three times from the book of Deuteronomy. He began his public ministry by quoting from the Book of Isaiah. He and his followers referred to the Hebrew Scriptures as the "word of God" and quoted from many of its books and from every major division of the *Tanakh*—Torah, Prophets, Sacred Writings.

He taught radical obedience to God and a new way of living. He did not come to abolish the Law, he said, but to add the new commandment of love to the Law—to "fulfill" it. He did not come to call his people out of their religion but to inspire them to take its precepts to heart. He did not preach renunciation of this world for another but advocated radical change in the world of the here and now.

The preferred teaching method of Jesus was the parable, parables which have similar themes and structures to those of other great Jewish sages. Indeed, as Brad Young has argued in *Jesus and his Jewish Parables*,³ without a familiarity with rabbinic parables, it is difficult to fully understand Gospel parables. Young's study of Jesus' parables further demonstrates just how close Jesus was to his own people and to the religious thought of his day.

The Lord's Prayer (Matthew 6:9-13) is thoroughly Jewish and, as Samuel Sandmel said:

> [it]could readily have appeared without change in Rabbinic literature. ⁴

When Jesus was asked what the greatest commandment was, he began by quoting the *Shema*, the foundational statement of the Jewish religion, just as an observant Jew would:

> ...The most important is, Hear, O Israel: The Lord our God, the Lord is one. And you shall love the Lord your God with all your heart and with all your soul and with all your mind and with all your strength. The second is this: You shall love your neighbor as yourself. There is no other commandment greater than these (Mark 12:29-31 ESV cf. Deuteronomy 6:4-5; Leviticus 19:18).

The second commandment echoes the injunction of that other great Jewish sage Hillel, who was still teaching at the time of Jesus' birth.

The author of Luke takes particular pains to present the life of Jesus as thoroughly informed and characterised by the Jewish religion: from the day when his parents present him to the Temple to fulfill the Law of Moses, until the day of the crucifixion when Luke provides a meaningful insight into Jesus the observant Jew by recording Jesus' cry from the cross which, even today, is part of a standard Jewish deathbed confession, "Into your hands I commit my spirit..." (Psalm 31:5).

The life of Jesus, both in word and deed, set an example for man that by universal emulation had the potential to change the world, but that potential was very soon diverted and distorted into a form of Christianity which indoctrinated its believers with anti-Jewish thought and anti-Jewish doctrines. A wholesale ignorance and disregard of Jesus' self-identification with the Jewish religion and the Jewish people persisted from the post-apostolic age until modern times. Before the Enlightenment, Paul's statement that all Israel would be saved (Romans 11:26) was taken to refer to Christians. The possibility that he was referring to his own people was never even considered. As recently as the early 20th Century, the German Assyriologist and

---

3   Young, Brad H. *Jesus and his Jewish Parables*. Paulist Press, 1989.

4   Sandmel, Samuel. *Judaism and Christian Beginnings*. Oxford University Press: New York 1978, p. 358.

Semitist, Freidrich Delitzsch, not only denied the Jewish origins of Christianity but went so far as to claim that Jesus was a Gentile, i.e. a non-Israelite.

This failure to recognise or understand the fact that Jesus was committed to his own religion and to own people has had profound historical consequences for both Jews and Christians. (The subject of Anti-semitism is addressed elsewhere in this work.)

CHAPTER SIX

A Right Hand Man

As pointed out in Chapter Two, Psalm 110:1 is cited several times in the New Testament:

> ...The LORD says to my lord: "Sit at my right hand until I make your enemies a footstool for your feet" (Psalm 110:1 NIV cf. Matthew 22:44; Mark 12:36; Luke 20:42-43; Acts 2:34-35; Hebrews 1:13).

Proponents of mainstream doctrines often cite these verses to support their claims despite the fact there is neither consistency of application nor understanding in their arguments. Is Jesus a co-ruler with God? Does he hold his position as the Son of God? Is he actually the YHWH of the Hebrew Scriptures? Or does he rule as part of the Trinity? etcetera, etcetera...

It is a shameful indictment that by this, the 21st Century, the necessity still exists for making some elementary observations on the use of figurative language. Consider the following passages from the Hebrew Scriptures:

> I saw the LORD sitting on his throne, and all the host of heaven standing by him on his right hand and on his left (1 Kings 22:19 KJV).

> Your right hand, LORD, was majestic in power. Your right hand, LORD, shattered the enemy (Exodus 15:6 NIV).

> Oh sing to the LORD a new song, for he has done marvelous things! His right hand and his holy arm have worked salvation for him (Psalm 98:1 ESV).

And from the New Testament:

> ...who has gone to heaven and is at the right hand of God, where angels, authorities, and powers have been made subject to him (1 Peter 3:22 ISV).

> After the Lord Jesus had spoken to them, he was taken up into heaven and he sat at the right hand of God (Mark 16:19 NIV).

> God exalted him at his right hand as Leader and Savior, to give repentance to Israel and forgiveness of sins (Acts 5:31 ESV).

It is a supreme irony that the words of Stephen, who was stoned for claiming that Jesus was the "prophet like Moses", i.e. a normal, non-divine human, should have his final words taken out of context and used to promote the teaching that Jesus is literally sitting/standing on the right hand of God in heaven:

> But Stephen, full of the Holy Spirit, looked up to heaven and saw the glory of God, and Jesus standing at the right hand of God. "Look," he said, "I see heaven open and the Son of Man standing at the right hand of God" (Acts 7:55-56 NIV).

Those who have read George Orwell's *1984* will be familiar with the concept of "doublethink" and realise how hard must be the struggle to reconcile belief that there is only one God, somehow incorporating Jesus, and at the same time believe that Jesus is distinct from God and sitting at his "right hand". This necessity for "double-thinking" is imposed only by confused and inconsistent teachings.

In reality, there was no confused thinking in the minds of the Apostles and authors of the New Testament. Those men were merely presenting Jesus as, what we in the vernacular would say, God's "right hand man". This image of Jesus falls into the same category as other images which are obviously figurative, such as rending the veil of the Holy of Holies which separated man from God; as the ladder providing access to God; and as the pathway of reconciliation with God. These images speak of spiritual truths rather than physical realities.

Another critical yet overlooked factor is that this period of figuratively "sitting at the right hand of God" in Heaven has a time limit, as we can see from the "footstool" reference which draws on the Book of Psalms:

> The LORD says to my Lord: "Sit at my right hand, until I make your enemies your footstool" (Psalm 110:1 ESV).

When the "enemies" have become the "footstool" of Jesus, the New Testament affirms that he will finally take up the appointment promised to his mother, will finally reign as King on a earthly throne:

> He shall be great, and shall be called the Son of the Highest: and the Lord God shall give unto him the throne of his father David: And he shall reign over the house of Jacob for ever; and of his kingdom there shall be no end (Luke 1:32-33 KJV).

It is indeed ironic that so much of what is intended to be taken figuratively is taken literally, and yet the promise to Mary, one thing that the author certainly intended to be taken literally, is taken either figuratively or ignored completely.

CHAPTER SEVEN

Minister Plenipotentiary

The simple biblical principle of humans standing in the place of God is either unrecognised or ignored. When the scripture authors state that God "did" something, it is always understood that the "doing" was actually "done" by humans chosen by God to implement his purposes on Earth. Biblically speaking, God must always be praised and given credit for putting into the hearts and minds of humans the will and spirit to do his work.

Throughout the New Testament, Jesus is presented as God's minister plenipotentiary, an agent invested with an authority superior to all the others who had preceded him. This perception of Jesus is a reflection of the Jewish understanding of agency, viz. the agent was regarded as the person himself. According to The Encyclopedia of the Jewish Religion:

> *Agent* (Heb. *Shaliah*): The main point of the Jewish law of agency is expressed in the dictum, "a person's agent is regarded as the person himself" (Ned. 72b; Kidd. 41b). Therefore any act committed by a duly appointed agent is regarded as having been committed by the principal, who therefore bears full responsibility for it with consequent complete absence of liability on the part of the agent.[5]

The delegation of God's authority to principal agents is called "anointing". The passage below from the Gospel of Luke does not lend itself to any sort of misinterpretation or manipulation. It demonstrates very clearly that Jesus is not to be equated with God in any way, shape or form; that he is a human being embedded in a human community; but with the essential difference that he has been "anointed" to act on behalf of God:

> And he came to Nazareth, where he had been brought up. And as was his custom, he went to the synagogue on the Sabbath day, and he stood up to read. And the scroll of the prophet Isaiah was given to him. He unrolled the scroll and found the place where it was written (Isaiah 61:1), "The Spirit of the Lord is upon me, because he has anointed me to proclaim good news to the poor. He has sent me to proclaim liberty to the captives and recovering of sight to the blind, to set at liberty those who are oppressed, to proclaim the year of the Lord's favor." And he rolled up the scroll and gave it back to the attendant and

---

5 Werblowsky, R. J. Zwi. *The Encyclopedia of the Jewish Religion.* ed. Geoffrey Wigoder. Adama Books: New York, 1986, p.15.

sat down. And the eyes of all in the synagogue were fixed on him. And he began to say to them, "Today this Scripture has been fulfilled in your hearing" (Luke 4:16-21 ESV).

As can be seen clearly, the concept of anointing humans to carry out God's will was not simply a relic from the past but was a living and active concept in the New Testament. (This concept has a very long history and has been carried through to our own times. Just like many of her ancestors, Queen Elizabeth II was anointed on the occasion of her crowning, and the future heirs to the British throne will be similarly anointed.)

CHAPTER EIGHT

The Author of Life

Consider the following passages:

> In him was life, and the life was the light of men (John 1:4 ESV).
>
> You killed the author of life, but God raised him from the dead. We are witnesses of this (Acts 3:15 NIV).
>
> That which was from the beginning, which we have heard, which we have seen with our eyes, which we have looked upon, and our hands have handled, of the Word of life (1 John 1:1 KJV cf. Philippians 2:16).

These words reveal the purpose and meaning of the New Testament. When it is recognised that Jesus created "life", was the architect of the New Creation not of the old, then other texts supposedly supporting the Pre-existence and Deity teachings can finally be understood.

For instance, the following texts apply to the New Creation of Life, the new Heavens and the New Earth brought into existence by and through Jesus. They do not apply to the old Creation recorded in Genesis:

> Yet for us there is but one God, the Father, from whom all things came and for whom we live; and there is but one Lord, Jesus Christ, through whom all things came and through whom we live (1 Corinthians 8:6 NIV).
>
> Who is the image of the invisible God, the firstborn of every creature: For by him were all things created, that are in heaven, and that are in earth, visible and invisible, whether they be thrones, or dominions, or principalities, or powers: all things were created by him, and for him: And he is before all things, and by him all things consist. And he is the head of the body, the church: who is the beginning, the firstborn from the dead; that in all things he might have the preeminence (Colossians 1:15-18 KJV).
>
> And from Jesus Christ, who is the faithful witness, and the first begotten of the dead, and the prince of the kings of the earth (Revelation 1:5 KJV).

As can be seen from these last two passages, Jesus is the firstborn of all creation because he is the firstborn/first-begotten from the dead, the first-fruits of many brethren to follow who, together, constitute the Kingdom of God. (See also Psalm 89:26-27; 1 Corinthians 15:20.)

CHAPTER NINE

A Man of Authority

One prime conflict in the New Testament, particularly as presented in John's Gospel, is about authority. What is it? Who has it?

The New Testament posits that God had delegated authority to Jesus to speak and act in his name. The disciples recognised that Jesus had this authority. So did a Roman Centurion (Luke 7:1-8). The religious establishment did not recognise his authority because they had a great investment in maintaining their own authority.

So what is the nature of this authority? What did Jesus say and do to convince certain people that he possessed an authority directly from God. Many heard what he said and many saw what he did, but not all became his disciples.

Let us imagine the dilemma facing the disciples when they first encountered Jesus. John's Gospel leaves no doubt as to the essence of this dilemma. It portrays Jesus as the representative of the values of God and the Jerusalem religious establishment as representative of the values of God's opposition.

So what choices do the disciples have?

- Do they continue to place their trust in their own religious establishment? Do they turn a blind eye to the self-righteous arrogance and hypocrisy of their leaders who, as Jesus said, built tombs to the prophets killed by their own spiritual ancestors? Do they continue to recognise their authority and their teachings because it's part of their tradition? *or*

- Do they place their trust in the moral authority of the values of God which are now being preached to them by Jesus?

The reason why only some chose Jesus and what he represented over the religious establishment and what it represented was because the same values present in Jesus were already present within those who chose to follow him and they naturally resonated and responded to each other.

The values which Jesus of Nazareth embodied: truth versus manipulation, distortion and deception; the spirit of the law rather than the letter; humility versus arrogance; personal integrity versus institutional formalism; objective attitudes versus subjective attitudes; and so on, are universal and timeless and cannot be confined to either place or time.

Therefore, the superior claim of moral authority over any other form of authority is a major message of the New Testament. (Essentially, these same choices face all humans all of the time, albeit in disguised contexts.)

Jesus, who received his authority from God, delegated some of that authority to the disciples, but only for the purpose of preaching the gospel of the Kingdom and only because he knew them personally.

The crucial question is: can the authority deriving from a set of personal, internal values ever be delegated to a non-personal, external entity? The New Testament assurance is that, in the absence of Jesus, the Holy Spirit of God would guide his followers. Just as Jesus appealed to values already present in his followers at that time, so also does the Spirit appeal to values already present in his followers yesterday, today, and tomorrow. The Spirit's galvanising influence is internal and personal rather than external and corporate.

If this spirit were to be named the Spirit of Truth, for example, it could only appeal or resonate with those individuals in whom a love of truth is already present. And so it goes with all values which are interior to the life of individuals.

Choices

If Jesus of Nazareth were to appear today, he would be unrecognisable in terms of the Virgin Conception/Birth, the Incarnation and the Trinity, doctrines supposedly based on the New Testament. How then would we recognise him? Our predicament would mirror that of the disciples who had to choose between the teachings, authority and weight of tradition represented by the Judean elites, and the weight of moral authority represented by the values and principles espoused by Jesus.

The disciples chose Jesus and what he represented over the Judean elites and what they represented.

Delusions

In their self-righteous arrogance, the Judean elites asserted that Jesus could not be the representative Israelite, the "chosen of the Lord" because he did not meet with *their* approval. They laboured under the delusion that the choice was a matter for *them*. The churches of Christendom are labouring under the same delusion. They, in turn, assert that the "chosen of the Lord" must meet with *their* approval, as proclaimed through their doctrines.

Neither the Jerusalem establishment then, nor the Christian establishment now, will have any say in the matter. It is God who has chosen Jesus of Nazareth and it is God who will make him King, as it is written:

Why do the nations conspire and the peoples plot in vain?
The kings of the earth rise up and the rulers band together
against the Lord and against his anointed, saying,
"Let us break their chains and throw off their shackles."
The One enthroned in heaven laughs; the Lord scoffs at them.
He rebukes them in his anger and terrifies them in his wrath, saying,
"I have installed my king on Zion, my holy mountain" (Psalm 2:1-8 NIV).

CHAPTER TEN

A Priest Forever

The author of the Book of Hebrews asserts that Jesus is the new High Priest of Israel:

> And being made perfect, he became the source of eternal salvation to all who obey him, being designated by God a high priest after the order of Melchizedek (Hebrews 5:9-10 ESV).

The Law of Moses stipulated that priests must belong to the tribe of Levi and be descendants of a particular Levite, Aaron. Israelites were very aware of the qualifications for the priesthood and if someone claimed to be a priest but could not produce the required genealogy, he was disqualified (see Ezra 2:62).

The author of Hebrews recognised that Jesus, being a descendant of the tribe of Judah, was disqualified from the priesthood under the Law:

> He of whom these things are said (Jesus) belonged to a different tribe, and no one from that tribe has ever served at the altar. For it is clear that our Lord descended from Judah, and in regard to that tribe Moses said nothing about priests (Hebrews 7:13-14 NIV).

In order to overcome this obstacle, the author drew on two sources from the Hebrew Scriptures. Firstly from Genesis 14:

> After Abram's return from defeating Chedorlaomer and the kings who were with them, the king of Sodom went out to meet with him in the Shaveh Valley (that is, the King's Valley). King Melchizedek of Salem brought out bread and wine, since he was serving as the priest of God Most High. Melchizedek blessed Abram and said, "Abram is blessed by God Most High, Creator of heaven and earth, and blessed be God Most High, who has delivered your enemies into your control." Then Abram gave him a tenth of everything (Genesis 14:17-20 ESV).

Then from Psalm 110:

> The LORD hath sworn, and will not repent, Thou art a priest for ever after the order of Melchizedek (Psalm 110:4 KJV).

The author then presented a quite ingenious argument that Jesus can be regarded as the new High Priest by virtue of the fact that the priesthood existed in the person of Melchizedek long before either Levi or his descendant Aaron were born:

> This Melchizedek was king of Salem and priest of God Most High. He met Abraham returning from the defeat of the kings and blessed him, and Abraham gave him a tenth of everything. First, the name Melchizedek means "king of righteousness"; then also, "king of Salem" means "king of peace." Without father or mother, without genealogy, without beginning of days or end of life, resembling the Son of God, he remains a priest forever (Hebrews 7:1-3 NIV).

Authorial intent is quite clear. Firstly, Melchizedek was "without father or mother, without genealogy", meaning that he did not come from a line of priests. Secondly, Melchizedek was "without beginning of days or end of life", meaning that his priesthood was "forever", i.e was not subject to term limits like Levitical priests (see Numbers 4:3 cf. 8:24-25). Melchizedek resembled the "son of God" in all these aspects. Therefore, if Melchizedek, who had no priestly genealogy, can be a priest forever recognised by the patriarch Abraham, then Jesus can also be a priest forever despite having no priestly genealogy.

Knowing the Hebrew Scriptures, specifically the Law of Moses, contemporary readers would have understood all the points which the author intended to convey. They would never have imagined that, centuries later and far removed from its Israelite setting, so little would be known of these matters that some would take these statements literally and develop some preposterous theories, including claims that Melchizedek is a pre-incarnation of Jesus and that the plurality of the Godhead is therefore established.

However, no further time, effort or space can be wasted on these spurious claims as these passages from the Book of Hebrews are instructive in ways other than those for which they are commonly cited, not the least being that they include a clear statement that Jesus is descended from the tribe of Judah (Hebrews 7:13-14).

Of perhaps more importance is the information to be gleaned from the High-Priestly analogy for it clarifies several other New Testament statements by and about Jesus.

Coming with the Clouds of Heaven

> In my vision at night I looked, and there before me was one like a son of man, coming with the clouds of heaven. He approached the Ancient of Days and was led into his presence (Daniel 7:13 NIV).

> ...they will see the Son of Man coming on the clouds of heaven with power and great glory (Matthew 24:30 ESV).

The son of man coming to God with the clouds of Heaven evokes the Day of Atonement when the High Priest entered the Jerusalem Temple's Holy of Holies, into God's presence, surrounded by clouds of incense. He symbolically ascended from Earth to God's abode in Heaven, and as near-contemporary texts show, on his return to the people from the inner sanctuary, the High Priest is a plenipotentiary of God's own power and glory, symbolically descending from Heaven down to Earth. (Note that God was believed to rule through an opening in the sky directly above the Jerusalem Temple, the *axis mundi*, the place of connection between God in Heaven and his covenant people on Earth.)

Plenipotentiary of God's own Power and Glory

> "For whoever is ashamed of Me and My words in this adulterous and sinful generation, the Son of Man will also be ashamed of him when He comes in the glory of His Father with the holy angels" (Mark 8:38 NASB cf. Mark 3:26; Matthew 16:27).

The Son of Man of the Gospels comes clothed in the "glory of his Father", just as the High Priest, when clothed in his sacred garments, embodied the glory of God (Exodus 28:2, 40).

This perception of Jesus is of course a reflection of the Jewish understanding of agency viz. the agent was regarded as the person himself. According to *The Encyclopedia of the Jewish Religion*:

> *Agent* (Heb. *Shaliah*): The main point of the Jewish law of agency is expressed in the dictum, "a person's agent is regarded as the person himself" (Ned. 72b; Kidd. 41b). Therefore any act committed by a duly appointed agent is regarded as having been committed by the principal, who therefore bears full responsibility for it with consequent complete absence of liability on the part of the agent.[6]

In his ceremonial role, the High Priest was God's representative—his "image". This Jewish understanding of agency casts further light on other New Testament passages such as:

---

6 Werblowsky, R. J. Zwi. *The Encyclopedia of the Jewish Religion*. ed. Geoffrey Wigoder. Adama Books: New York, 1986, p.15.

> In their case the god of this world has blinded the minds of the unbelievers, to keep them from seeing the light of the gospel of the glory of Christ, who is the image of God (2 Corinthians 4:4 ESV).

Although the High-Priestly analogy is made most explicit in the Book of Hebrews, it can be seen clearly in the above passage that other New Testament authors such as Paul also portrayed Jesus using language and descriptive terminology most suited to the contemporary perception of the High Priest as the image of God who reflects the glory of God.

In addition to all the above, the author of Revelation depicts Jesus as the Son of Man dressed in the distinctive foot-length robe and golden girdle that the High Priest wore on the Day of Atonement:

> And in the midst of the seven candlesticks one like unto the Son of man, clothed with a garment down to the foot, and girt about the paps with a golden girdle (Revelation 1:13 KJV cf. Josephus, Antiquities [7])

---

[7] Flavius Josephus. *Antiquities of the Jews* in *The Works of Flavius Josephus*, Book III, Chapter vii. Transl. William Whiston. Milner and Sowerby: Halifax, 1864, p.73.

CHAPTER ELEVEN

The Saviour

The Hebrew Scriptures teach that Almighty God is the Saviour of Israel:

> For I am the LORD thy God, the Holy One of Israel, thy Saviour (Isaiah 43:3 KJV).

Apologists claim that because the New Testament also describes Jesus as a "Saviour", this means that he is to be equated with God. Yet another Deity assertion, yet another overlooked fact that, according to the Hebrew Scriptures, God delegates authority to perform all his works on Earth to humans of his choice.

The English word "saviour" derives from the Greek σῴζω *(sózó)* and the Hebrew root יָשַׁע *(yasha)*, both of which mean to "save" or "deliver". The Hebrew name *Yeshua* is a shortened form of *Yehoshua*, the name of *Joshua* the successor of Moses. It is derived from YH, a shortened form of YHWH and the Hebrew verb root *yasha*. Because of the meaning of the name "Jesus", a transliteration of *Yeshua*, Joseph was instructed to name him accordingly:

> She will bear a son, and you shall call his name Jesus (Yeshua), for he will save his people from their sins (Matthew 1:21 ESV).

However, works of "salvation" had been delegated to others long before the time of Jesus. Just two examples should suffice:

> But when the people of Israel cried out to the LORD (YHWH), the LORD (YHWH) raised up a deliverer *(yasha)* for the people of Israel, who saved *(yasha)* them, Othniel the son of Kenaz, Caleb's younger brother (Judges 3:9 ESV).

> And the people said unto Saul, Shall Jonathan die, who hath wrought this great salvation *(yasha)* in Israel?... (1 Samuel 14:45 KJV).

Just as the other humans mentioned above, Jesus was delegated authority by God to perform a "saving" role:

> The Spirit of the Lord God is upon me...I will greatly rejoice in the LORD, my soul shall be joyful in my God; for he hath clothed me with the garments of salvation, he hath covered me with the robe of righteousness (Isaiah 61:1,10 KJV quoted partly in Luke 4:18-19. See also Psalm 98:1).

In addition to Jesus and other individual Saviours, the whole people of Israel were delegated this role by Jesus:

> Ye worship ye know not what: we know what we worship: for salvation is of the Jews (John 4:22 KJV).

Forgiving Sin

An interpretive principle of the New Testament is that Jesus is depicted as God's minister plenipotentiary on Earth, a man anointed (invested) with full power and authority to speak and act in the name of the God of the Israelites. (See Isaiah 61:1; Luke 4:17).

The concept of delegated authority exercised by a plenipotentiary appears to be quite incomprehensible to those who promulgate the doctrines of mainstream Christianity. The assertion is that if Jesus had no claim to equality with God, then he had no right to forgive sins. The most quoted passage is taken from Mark 2:5-12 when Jesus is in Capernaum. It must be quoted in full to grasp a sense of the exchange between Jesus and the scribes:

> When Jesus saw their faith, he said unto the sick of the palsy, Son, thy sins be forgiven thee. But there were certain of the scribes sitting there, and reasoning in their hearts, Why doth this man thus speak blasphemies? who can forgive sins but God only? And immediately when Jesus perceived in his spirit that they so reasoned within themselves, he said unto them, Why reason ye these things in your hearts? Whether is it easier to say to the sick of the palsy, Thy sins be forgiven thee; or to say, Arise, and take up thy bed, and walk? But that ye may know that the Son of man hath power on earth to forgive sins, (he saith to the sick of the palsy,) I say unto thee, Arise, and take up thy bed, and go thy way into thine house. And immediately he arose, took up the bed, and went forth before them all; insomuch that they were all amazed, and glorified God, saying, We never saw it on this fashion (Mark 2:5-12 KJV).

Before proceeding, it is important to recognise the following conventions and practices followed by Israelites in the 1st Century AD:

- The forgiveness of sin is a prerogative of God;

- In Hebrew language usage, passive voice statements such as "thy sins be forgiven thee" are pious conventions used to avoid accidentally invoking the name of God; [8]
- These passive voice statements about God's prerogatives always imply that God is the doer of the action;
- It is Jesus presuming to act on God's behalf that the scribes object to.

In Matthew's parallel account of the incident recorded in Mark, we find that the multitude "marvelled" that God had "given such power unto men". According to the author, Jesus is one of these "men", therefore a created being—the ultimate theological spoiler:

> And, behold, they brought to him a man sick of the palsy, lying on a bed: and Jesus seeing their faith said unto the sick of the palsy; Son, be of good cheer; thy sins be forgiven thee. And, behold, certain of the scribes said within themselves, This man blasphemeth. And Jesus knowing their thoughts said, Wherefore think ye evil in your hearts? For whether is easier, to say, Thy sins be forgiven thee; or to say, Arise, and walk? But that ye may know that the Son of man hath power on earth to forgive sins, (then saith he to the sick of the palsy,) Arise, take up thy bed, and go unto thine house. And he arose, and departed to his house. But when the multitudes saw it, they marvelled, and glorified God, which had given such power unto men (Matthew 9:2-8 KJV).

Just as Jesus, the minister plenipotentiary, had been delegated his authority to forgive sins by God, so also were the disciples delegated the same authority by Jesus:

> Jesus said to them again, "Peace be with you. As the Father has sent me, even so I am sending you." And when he had said this, he breathed on them and said to them, "Receive the Holy Spirit. If you forgive the sins of any, they are forgiven them; if you withhold forgiveness from any, it is withheld" (John 20:21-23 ESV).

In all cases, however, God is perceived to be the one from whom forgiveness flows.

Note

The Apostle Peter, it is asserted, was the first Pope of the Roman Catholic Church. Through a chain of transmission starting with God, passing through Jesus and then

---

8   The term "Heaven," as in Matthew's "Kingdom of Heaven," is another pious substitute for "God."

through Peter, the priests of that church claim the delegated authority to forgive sins. (See Part IX: *The Papacy*)

Atoning for Sin

Both the Hebrew Scriptures and the New Testament draw clear distinctions between intentional and unintentional sin, and between individual and corporate atonement. A failure to recognise these distinctions is certainly the basis for all the disputations on this subject between the various denominations of Christendom and has given rise to all the flawed teachings about sin and its atonement.

In the Hebrew Scriptures

The shedding of blood

Israelites were forbidden to eat blood. Blood was sacred and it was considered that the most fitting use for something sacred was upon the altar:

> For the life of the flesh is in the blood, and I have given it for you on the altar to make atonement for your souls, for it is the blood that makes atonement by the life. Therefore I have said to the people of Israel, No person among you shall eat blood, neither shall any stranger who sojourns among you eat blood (Leviticus 17:11-12 ESV).

The Holy of Holies

The Holy of Holies was that part of the Tabernacle of the Temple which was regarded as possessing the utmost degree of holiness. So sacred was this space that the High Priest was permitted to enter only once a year on the Day of Atonement.

On that Day of Atonement, the High Priest offered up the innocent blood of unblemished animals to make a corporate, vicarious atonement for the whole people of Israel for sins they had committed *in ignorance*:

> Now if you as a community unintentionally fail to keep any of these commands the Lord gave Moses…and if this is done unintentionally without the community being aware of it, then the whole community is to offer a young bull for a burnt offering as an aroma pleasing to the Lord, along with its prescribed grain offering and drink offering, and a male goat for a sin offering. The priest is to make atonement for the whole Israelite community, and they will be forgiven, for it was not intentional and they have presented to the Lord for their wrong a food offering and a sin offering. The whole Israelite community and

the foreigners residing among them will be forgiven, because all the people were involved in the unintentional wrong (Numbers 15:22-26 NIV).

The shedding of blood under the Mosaic Law did not vicariously atone for an individual's intentional sin: it was merely a corporate and symbolic atonement for sins committed *in ignorance*. The Israelites were warned throughout the Hebrew Scriptures that there was no vicarious atonement for individual intentional sin, as we can see just a few verses later in Numbers 15:

> But the person who does anything with a high hand, whether he is native or a sojourner, reviles the LORD, and that person shall be cut off from among his people. Because he has despised the word of the LORD and has broken his commandment, that person shall be utterly cut off; his iniquity shall be on him (Numbers 15:30-31 ESV).

And again in the Book of Exodus:

> The next day Moses told the people, "You committed a great sin, and now I'll go up to the LORD, and perhaps I can make atonement for your sin." Moses returned to the LORD and said, "Please, LORD, this people committed a great sin by making a god of gold for themselves. Now, if you will, forgive their sin—but if not, blot me out of your book which you have written." The LORD told Moses, "Whoever sins against me, I'll blot him out of my book (Exodus 32:30-33 ISV).

Moses' plea was denied on the basis that he could not suffer vicariously for *corporate intentional sin*. See also Jeremiah 31:30; Psalm 49:7; Deuteronomy 24:16; and 2 Kings 14:6 where it is made clear that neither can there be vicarious atonement for *individual intentional sin*.

In the New Testament

Corporate Atonement

The Israelite concept of vicarious corporate atonement is reinforced in the New Testament, especially in the Book of Hebrews. Whereas under the Mosaic Law, the High Priest once a year atoned for the unintentional sins of corporate Israel by making a sacrificial offering of the blood of "unblemished" animals in the Holy of Holies, the author of Hebrews teaches that the New Covenant's High Priest, as the representative of corporate Israel, made a sacrificial offering of his own "unblemished" blood to atone for the "sins of the people committed in ignorance":

...but into the second (the Holy of Holies), only the high priest enters once a year, not without taking blood, which he offers for himself and for the sins of the people committed in ignorance (Hebrews 9:7 NIV).

The atoning blood of Jesus was to be offered once only:

> Nor did he go into heaven to sacrifice himself again and again, the way the high priest goes into the Holy Place every year with blood that is not his own. Then he would have had to suffer repeatedly since the creation of the world. But now, at the end of the ages, he has appeared once for all to remove sin by his sacrifice (Hebrews 9:25-26 ISV).

The Mosaic sacrificial system had begun with blood and had now ended with blood. The slate had been wiped clean.

The Pauline Perspective

The story of the Garden of Eden presents us with the failings of mankind portrayed in an allegory. "Adam" simply means "man" and is derived from the Hebrew *ha adamah* which means "the ground" or "the earth". "Eve" simply means "living one" or "source of life".

Paul identifies the sins of Adam, symbolic of mankind, as:

- exchanging the truth of God for a lie (Romans 1:25);
- worshipping and serving the creature rather than the Creator (Romans 1:25);
- disobedience to the commands of the Creator (Romans 5:19).

Paul taught that by subordinating the will of his own flesh, by choosing the truth of God instead of lies, and by choosing obedience to God instead of disobedience, Jesus restored man to his position as it existed in the beginning—the *imago dei*. Hence, Paul describes Jesus as the "last Adam":

> So it is written: "The first man Adam became a living being," the last Adam, a life-giving spirit (1 Corinthians 15:45 NIV).

(As noted in Part VIII: *Sin and Salvation*, the sins of Adam are not the types of sin that we in the English-speaking world commonly associate with the word, e.g. murder, theft, bearing false witness and etcetera. Rather, they are the types of sins for which there could be a corporate atonement.)

Life not death

Paul argued that death rather than sin had been the common inheritance of mankind ever since Adam and Eve disobeyed God (Romans 6:23). But now, new life was available for those who, in a spiritual sense, crucified the old man after the fashion of Adam and resurrected the new man after the fashion of Jesus (1 Corinthians 15:21-22).

Because blood symbolised life, and we have new life in Jesus, Paul depicts Jesus as corporately atoning once only for the sins of Adam and purging them with redeeming blood (see Leviticus 17:11). Paul's description of Jesus as the "last Adam" completely discredits the doctrine of Original Sin. Even if mankind had inherited sin from Adam, then that inheritance would have ceased automatically with the "last Adam".

The claim that only a divinity can atone for corporate sin leaves the concept of atonement utterly devoid of meaning. Only a normal man fashioned after the first Adam, subject to all the weaknesses and temptations of the first Adam, can make such corporate atonement.

Individual Atonement

While Living

Individual sins deliberately committed with a so-called "high hand" were considered to be a total rejection of God and his Covenant and placed a person outside of any relationship with God.

The Israelites had been consistently warned that there was no vicarious atonement for individual intentional sin—no atonement through the ritual blood sacrifices that had become a "cover" for such sin in the minds of some. By the time of Jesus, ritual observance of the letter of the Law while ignoring the obligations of its spirit was commonplace among those members of the Jerusalem establishment charged with upholding the Mosaic Law. Their exaggerated show of ritual observance was no more than a pretense, a convenient cover for the sin of failing to fulfill their most important duties, and was roundly condemned by Jesus:

> Woe to you, scribes and Pharisees, hypocrites! For you tithe mint and dill and cummin, and have neglected the weightier provisions of the law: justice and mercy and faithfulness; but these are the things you should have done without neglecting the others (Matthew 23:23 NASB).

Jesus warned that there would henceforth be no more excuses, no more cover for sin that the Law had been seen to provide, but that every individual was fully responsible for his or her own sin:

> If I had not come and spoken to them, they would not be guilty of sin; but now they have no excuse for their sin (John 15:22 NIV)

(Note also that this statement by Jesus is another rebuttal of the doctrine of Original Sin which, in effect, replaces the cover for sin that the Mosaic Law had been seen to provide in the minds of some.)

Biblically speaking, the only way it has ever been possible for an individual to atone for his or her own intentional sin and to receive God's forgiveness is through prayer and repentance followed by good works and righteous behaviour. (See for example Psalm 51:16-17; Psalm 32:5; Daniel 4:27; Micah 6:6-8.)

When Dead

For 1st Century Israelites, death was a process, not a moment in time. Mourning would continue for a year as the body underwent decomposition, considered a type of penal atonement for the dead person's sins which were thought to be embedded in the flesh and to dissolve along with the body.

After a year of decay and purification, the bones were often collected and placed in a stone box called an ossuary, which was just long enough to accommodate the thigh bones. It was believed that the bones retained the personality and that God would use these bones to support new flesh for the Resurrection (see Ezekiel 37 and his vision of the Valley of Dry Bones).

The day of placing the bones in the ossuary, a type of second burial, would mark the end of the family's mourning period and the beginning of hope in eventual reunion and Resurrection. These cultural practices and beliefs are the context in which the Resurrection accounts were written. (See also Part XIV.9: *Trial and Death-Burial* for Israelite Burial Customs.)

CHAPTER TWELVE

The End of the Charge

In the anti-introspective, collectivist Mediterranean society of the First Century AD, "love" always possessed the underlying meaning of attachment to God or group of persons. In this society, there was no term for an internal state that did entail a corresponding external action. "Love" always meant appropriate public actions which supported the well-being of the persons to whom one was attached.

The type of love most commonly referenced in today's popular culture is characterised mainly by self-interest, a weak sentimentality and an excess of emotion. The type of love embodied in Jesus of Nazareth, however, is of an entirely different order— strength of character, determined will, sacrifice of self-interest, and a clear head unclouded by an excess of feeling. And, yes, one that will lay down its life for others if necessary (John 15:13).

For Jesus, love of God and love of neighbour were the greatest commandments of the Law (Matthew 12:29-31).

The simplicity and purity of this teaching did not prove sufficient to the Hellenist-Latin Fathers and still does not prove sufficient today. The minds of said Fathers were set in the key of a different structure to that of the Israelite prophets and apostles, thus the doctrines built up around the person of Jesus are a reflection of their non-Israelite philosophy and theology.

Many ecclesiastics and theologians reason that because these doctrines have been taught for so many years, they are thus endowed with weight, with truth. The only truth in this view is that they have been taught long enough to become "traditional". Jesus told the Pharisees that they made "void the word of God" by their tradition (Mark 7:13). Those who rely on tradition to bolster their arguments stand in precisely the same position as their spiritual ancestors.

The prophetic expectation was that God would anoint a man with his power and Holy Spirit, clothe him with the garments of salvation, and appoint him King forever, over both Israelite and non-Israelite. The Israelites had very definite ideas about this man and these were recorded in the books of the Hebrew Scriptures. Many Christians are unaware of what exactly the Israelites did expect and this ignorance has facilitated the building up of the erroneous doctrines of mainstream Christianity.

The emphasis today is placed upon some creed or confession of faith rather than upon this message of good tidings:

> But the end of the charge is love out of a pure heart and a good conscience and faith unfeigned: from which things some having swerved have turned aside unto vain talking; desiring to be teachers of the law, though they understand neither what they say, nor whereof they confidently affirm (1 Timothy 1:5-7 ASV).

This simple message brings hope and a sense of human dignity to all. No matter their station in life, all can play a role in establishing the Kingdom of God on Earth. Mainstream doctrines can deliver no such message. If Jesus of Nazareth walked the earth today, he would not measure up to the false criteria established by these doctrines. He would perhaps be branded a heretic, a malcontent, a blasphemer, and a troublemaker, just as he was in the First Century AD.

Of one thing we can be reasonably certain: a great body of so-called "Christians" would be in the forefront of those shouting "away with him" (Acts 21:36).

CHAPTER THIRTEEN

Ignorance or Deception?

In the very first words of the New Testament, the author of Matthew affirms that Jesus is the Anointed one of God, the Israelite Messiah. The ramifications of New Testament affirmations such as this have been ignored by vast numbers of theologians and biblical scholars throughout these many centuries.

The New Testament authors state many times that Jesus is the Messiah according to the Hebrew Scriptures. If so, then it follows naturally that non-Israelite, pagan and Hellenist-inspired doctrines such as the Virgin Conception/Birth, the Incarnation and the Trinity are not to be found anywhere in either the Hebrew Scriptures or the New Testament.

Despite all the evidence one can provide, some theologians and biblical scholars committed to their doctrinal positions continue to deflect attention away from the Israelite roots of the New Testament documents by posing such inane and frankly ignorant questions as:

- Was Jesus really the Israelite Messiah?
- If he was, did he know it?
- If he knew it, why didn't he just come right out and say so?

To ask these questions is not only to display one's inability to perceive the premise on which every document of the New Testament is based, but also to demonstrate one's *naiveté* about the dangers of living under Roman occupation when dime-a-dozen Israelite messianic pretenders were promptly executed. It makes one question whether these theologians and biblical scholars actually read the entirety of the available documents or only those sections which they assume will uphold their doctrinal positions.

Jesus certainly believed he was the expected Davidic Messiah—it was confirmed by John at his baptism. His withdrawal into the wilderness informs his struggle with the ramifications of his heightened self-awareness. After this period of internal battle was resolved in the positive, one of his first public appearances was in the synagogue of his home town of Nazareth:

> And he came to Nazareth, where he had been brought up. And as was his custom, he went to the synagogue on the Sabbath day, and he stood up to read.

> And the scroll of the prophet Isaiah was given to him. He unrolled the scroll and found the place where it was written:
>
> "The Spirit of the Lord is upon me, because he has anointed me to proclaim good news to the poor. He has sent me to proclaim liberty to the captives and recovering of sight to the blind, to set at liberty those who are oppressed, to proclaim the year of the Lord's favor." And he rolled up the scroll and gave it back to the attendant and sat down. And the eyes of all in the synagogue were fixed on him. And he began to say to them, "Today this Scripture has been fulfilled in your hearing" (Luke 4:16-21 ESV).

After this initial proclamation in Nazareth, and its less than encouraging reception, Jesus confined himself to making more oblique references to his Messiahship by using particular language and particular titles, by acting in particular ways, and by applying Scriptural passages to himself. To do otherwise would have resulted in his premature death.

When Jesus judged the time to be right, he openly proclaimed his Messiahship by acting out a well-known passage from Zechariah:

> Rejoice greatly, O daughter of Zion; shout, O daughter of Jerusalem: behold, thy King cometh unto thee: he is just, and having salvation; lowly, and riding upon an ass, and upon a colt the foal of an ass (Zechariah 9:9 KJV cf. Matthew 21:4-5).

The "multitude" accompanying Jesus certainly understood that by riding into Jerusalem on an ass, he was publicly proclaiming to be the expected Davidic Messiah:

> And the multitudes that went before him, and that followed, cried, saying, "Hosanna to the son of David: Blessed is he that cometh in the name of the Lord; Hosanna in the highest" (Matthew 21:9 KJV).

The majority of theologians and biblical scholars are reluctant to grasp fully the implications arising from the Israelite messiahship of Jesus for an excellent reason—nowhere in the Hebrew scriptures is there a single hint that the Messiah was to be anything other than a normal man anointed by God to be his instrument of intervention in human affairs.

To avoid confronting this dilemma, the majority theological and academic theory encouraged is that the Gospels were orally transmitted, gradually embellished, and only committed to writing decades after the crucifixion in a language (Greek) and a culture (Hellenist) far removed from their original Israelite setting.

This theory serves three purposes:

1. Scholars can re-frame the Gospels in a Hellenist context far removed from their Israelite setting;
2. Delay in composition brings the Gospels closer to the writings of the Hellenist church fathers, thus blurring the distinction between the two;
3. Because the Gospels are allegedly the product of a long period of gradually embellished oral tradition, sayings attributed to Jesus could have been put into his mouth by later Christians. Thus passages from the Gospels can be accepted or rejected at will and theories developed according to one's own philosophical or theological preferences. This latitude has led to some very strange and extreme views of Jesus, as any cursory enquiry will demonstrate.

If Jesus is really the Israelite Messiah according to the Scriptures, as the New Testament states plainly, then all of the Hellenist-Latin doctrines of the Church are bogus. There are not enough superlatives in the English language to describe the magnitude of mainstream Christianity's betrayal of the Israelite Jesus, his Israelite disciples, and all the authors of the New Testament.

See Part II: *Documents* for a comprehensive analysis of the language, dating, and target groups of the New Testament materials.

PART XIV

Trial and Death

CHAPTER ONE

Introductory Notes

The history of the Roman Province of Judea during the decades surrounding the life and death of Jesus is vastly complicated and cannot be reproduced in detail here. The following Chapters, therefore, represent only a simplified account.

Ethnocentrism

1st Century AD Mediterranean peoples were ethnocentric. When reading the New Testament we should always be aware of the social boundaries existing between Israelites (in-groups) and everyone else (out-groups). Israelite in-group attitudes were derived from the perception of shared values existing within the sub-groups of family, village community, and country-dweller.

Religion and State

Ancient Israel did not separate various aspects of its society into modern categories. Hence, there was no distinction between religion and politics. All aspects were embedded in the social structure of the day. Take, for example, the Jerusalem Temple compound which served as an economic centre, as a military fortress, and as a place of religious observance. The view that Christians should be concerned only with religious issues is based on the assumption that the priests and scribes with whom Jesus interacted were solely focused on religious questions and were not part of the state apparatus. This view betrays a lack of knowledge of the conditions in Judea in the 1st Century AD. The government of the day was a coalition of king, aristocratic families, high government officials, Roman military representatives and the ruling elites of the priesthood. The High Priests, Annas and Caiaphas, both appointed by the Roman authorities, were two such members of the elite priestly establishment (John 18:13).

Family

Great emphasis was placed on family tradition and continuity. At least from the period of the Babylonian Exile, (see Ezra and Nehemiah), genealogies, the purity of blood, and the symbolic importance of the twelve tribes were basic. Significant social roles such as the priesthood, requirements for admission to the temple, and appropriate marriage depended on genealogical purity.

Betrothal and Marriage

To begin the process, the prospective bridegroom would negotiate an agreement with the head of the prospective bride's family. If successful, the bridegroom would go to his own father's house where he would prepare either an existing room or build a separate room for himself and his new bride. To complete the betrothal and marriage process, the bridegroom would take his bride to the room in his father's house that he had prepared beforehand where they would begin their life together. Note how this custom illuminates Jesus' statement in John 14:2, "In my Father's house are many rooms: if it were not so, I would have told you. I go to prepare a place for you".

Note that Simon Peter's mother-in-law resided in Simon's house along with Andrew (Mark 129-30), presumably also with Simon and Andrew's wives and children.

Limited Goods

Unlike the modern Western world with its abundance of goods, 1st Century Israel was a society of limited goods. To exist within a society of limited goods meant that one could not be described as a "rich" person owning many goods without the existence of its corollary—a "poor" person deprived of goods. This reality can be most instructive when reading New Testament passages about the interactions between Jesus and the "rich young ruler" for example.

Honour-Shame

Concern for one's honour permeated every aspect of life in Mediterranean antiquity. Honour served as the prime indicator of social position and prescribed how persons should interact with superiors, inferiors and equals in appropriate ways. Public insults must be challenged to defend one's honour. All of the trial exchanges between Pilate and the Jerusalem elites, and between Pilate and Jesus, are set within the framework of this honour-shame society.

CHAPTER TWO

Dating

The world of Jesus of Nazareth was a Roman world. The Roman system of reckoning the passage of time was from the foundation of the city—*ab urbe condita*—usually rendered as AUC. In the year now known as 532 AD, a monk named Dionyisus Exiguus of Scythia Minor calculated that Jesus of Nazareth was born on 25 December 753 AUC. The Roman year 754 AUC was then determined to be year 1 of the Christian era. The terms *anno Domini* (AD) and *before Christ* (BC) are used for our current system of reckoning the passage of time based on this supposed year of the birth of Jesus. Unfortunately, the monk's calculations were erroneous, as we will see.

The New Testament states that, "Jesus was born in Bethlehem of Judea in the days of Herod the king" (Matthew 2:1). As Jesus was born before the death of Herod, fixing the year of Herod's death is of particular importance. (The calculation of exact dates in the period being notoriously difficult, scholars of course disagree. However, for our purposes, a reasonable approximation of the year of Herod's death is sufficient.)

Josephus, perhaps drawing on the records of Herod's friend, Nicholaus of Damascus, fixes the date as follows:

> So Herod, having survived the slaughter of his son (Antipater) five days, died, having reigned thirty-four years, since he had caused Antigonus to be slain, and obtained his kingdom; but thirty-seven years since he had been made king by the Romans. [1]

Josephus dates Herod's death by three events:

- Five days after the execution of his son Antipater;
- Thirty-four years after he "obtained his kingdom" through the beheading of Antigonus (see below—fixed at 37 BC);
- Thirty-seven years after "he had been made king by the Romans" (see below—fixed at 40 BC).

According to the above, Herod died circa 3 BC. The New Testament records that

---

[1] Flavius Josephus. *The Wars of the Jews.* Accessed 1 May 2018. http://data.perseus.org/citations/urn:cts:greekLit:tlg0526.tlg004.perseus-eng1:1.665

after Jesus was born, Herod the Great sought to destroy him. It is difficult to estimate how long a period elapsed between the birth of Jesus and the death of Herod, some scholars proposing as early as 6 BC. Regardless of the exact year, the one fact of which we can be certain is that Jesus was born before or during 3 BC.

CHAPTER THREE

Personalities of the Period

Augustus: 62 BC-14 AD

Great-nephew of Julius Caesar, Augustus (formerly known as Octavian) became the first Emperor of Rome in 31 BC after the battle of Actium and ruled from that time until 14 AD. Augustus was the reigning Roman Emperor when Jesus was born.

Tiberius: 16/11/42 BC-16/3/37 AD

Tiberius reigned as Roman Emperor from 14-37 AD, but jointly 1 year earlier. The "word of God" came to John the Baptist in the 15th year of Tiberius (Luke 3:1) which equates to 27-28 AD. Tiberius was still Emperor at the time Jesus was crucified.

The Herodian Dynasty

The authors of the New Testament; Josephus, the Jewish historian; Nicolaus of Damascus, the chronicler attached to the court of Herod the Great; Strabo, the Greek historian, geographer and philosopher; and Philo, the Jewish philosopher; as well as numerous Roman sources all contribute to our knowledge of the complicated history of the Herodian dynasty. Source material is readily available for interested readers so rather than attempt to describe in detail the shifting political alliances, the numerous dynastic inter-marriages and internecine power struggles which comprise this complicated history, the following is a just a brief overview of those facts of which we can be reasonably certain. (If the birth and death years of any members of the Herodian dynasty are not known with any degree of certainty, they are not noted.)

The First Generation

Herod the Great: 73 BC-3 BC

The Herod associated in the New Testament with the birth of Jesus is Herod the Great, born between 74-72 BC into a leading Idumean family. The Idumeans, who lived south of Judea, were forcibly converted to Judaism by the Hasmonean ruler, John Hyrcanus I around 120 BC. (Herod was called "Great" by Josephus, not in the ordinary sense we would associate with "greatness", but rather to distinguish him from the other, younger Herods, viz. "greater in age".)

Through a series of shifting political alliances and complex stratagems, Herod was eventually entrusted with the client-kingship of Judea by Octavian (later Augustus) and the Roman Senate in 40 BC although his administration was not secured until 37 BC. Until his death in 3 BC, and with firm Roman backing, Herod would rule as client-king over the territories of Judea, Idumea, Samaria and Galilee, as well as over further regions in southern Syria and northern Transjordan.

During his reign, Herod built palaces in Jerusalem and Herodium, the fortresses of Masada and Antonia, and the Port of Caesarea Maritima. However, the jewel in his crown was the reconstruction of the Second Temple, together with a surrounding complex now known as the Temple Mount, the building of which began in 19 BC. The Temple itself was substantially larger and higher than the original Second Temple erected after the partial return from the Babylonian exile (Ezra 6:16). Work continued long after Herod's death and was not completed until the procuratorship of Albinus in 62-64 AD, a few years before its destruction in the first rebellion against Rome in 70 AD.

Even though the compound would not be completed for decades, the scale of the work was remarked upon by Jesus and a disciple:

> As Jesus was leaving the temple, one of his disciples said to him, "Look, Teacher! What massive stones! What magnificent buildings!" "Do you see all these great buildings?" replied Jesus. "Not one stone here will be left on another; every one will be thrown down" (Mark 13:1-2 NIV)

These "magnificent buildings" were destroyed by the Romans in 70 AD and the "massive stones" to which Jesus referred were indeed "thrown down". (The partially excavated foundations of the Temple Mount, the Western Wall of which is the holiest site in Judaism, are visible today, as are the great piles of stones thrown down from the heights by the Romans. Together with the remains of the Fortress Masada, the Fortress Antonia, the Port of Caesarea Maritima, and the various other Herodian building projects, they bear witness to the breathtaking scope of one man's ambitions.)

Upon his death, after much manoeuvering and disagreement between interested parties, the Emperor Augustus decided to divide his territory among Archelaus, Antipas and Philip, three of Herod's surviving sons.

The Second Generation

Herod Archelaus

Herod Archelaus, son of Herod the Great and Malthace, full brother of Antipas. Archelaus ruled as Ethnarch of Judea, Samaria, and Idumea from 3 BC-6 AD, at which time Augustus judged him incompetent to rule, banished him to Gaul, and combined the provinces of Samaria, Judea proper, and Idumea into Judea Province. This enlarged province was ruled by a succession of Roman Prefects until 41 AD, Herod Agrippa I from 41-44 AD, and thereafter by Roman Procurators and Legates until the year 135 AD.

Herod Antipas

Herod Antipas, son of Herod the Great and Malthace, full brother of Archelaus. Antipas ruled as Tetrach of Galilee and Perea from 3 BC until he was eventually banished to Gaul in 39 AD. Antipas married Herodias, his brother's ex-wife and his own half-niece. He is of course most known to readers of the New Testament as ordering the beheading of John the Baptist at the instigation of Herodias (Matthew 14:3-10; Mark 6:17-28) after John denounced them publicly on the grounds that the law forbade a man to marry his brother's divorced wife (see Leviticus 18:6). Upon receiving a report that Herod wanted to kill him, Jesus called him "that fox" (Luke 13:31-32). He also played a part in the trial of Jesus (Luke 23:7). The building projects for which he is most renowned are the cities of Tiberias on the western shore of the Sea of Galilee, and Sepphoris, a few miles north-west of Nazareth.

Philip

Philip, son of Herod the Great and Cleopatra of Jerusalem, half-brother of Archelaus and Antipas. Philip ruled as Tetrarch over Gaulanitis (the Golan heights), Batanaea (or Basan, the southern part of modern Syria), and Trachonitis and Auranitis (Hauran) until his death in 34 AD. (There is deal of disagreement surrounding the identity of the "Philip" mentioned in Matthew 14:3 in connection with the death of John the Baptist. However, there is considerable evidence that he was not Philip the Tetrarch but yet another half-brother of Archelaus and Antipas.)

The Third Generation

Herod Agrippa I

Son of Aristobulus IV and Berenice, grandson of Herod the Great and Mariamne, brother of Herodias and Herod of Chalcis. Ruled Judea Province from 41-44 AD. He was the "King Herod" who had James killed, who arrested Peter (Acts 12:1-2,6), and the one who was later struck dead (Acts 12:19-23).

Herodias

Daughter of Aristobulus IV and Berenice, granddaughter of Herod the Great and Mariamne, sister of Herod Agrippa I and Herod of Chalcis. Herodias divorced her first husband (Philip) and married his brother Herod Antipas, her own half-uncle, a marriage which led to a public denunciation by John the Baptist on the grounds that the law forbade a man to marry his brother's divorced wife (see Leviticus 18:6). Herodias followed her husband Antipas into exile in 39 AD.

The Fourth Generation

Herod Agrippa II

Last Roman client-king of the Herodian dynasty. Son of Herod Agrippa I, great-grandson of Herod the Great, brother of Berenice, Mariamne, and Drusilla (second wife of the Roman procurator Antonius Felix). Agrippa inherited the small Syrian Tetrachy of Chalcis in 48 AD upon the death of his uncle Herod of Chalcis. In 53 AD, the Emperor Claudius made him ruler over the territories previously held by his great-uncle Philip and those of Lysanius of Abila in exchange for the Tetrarchy of Chalcis. It was before Agrippa, his sister Berenice, and the Roman Procurator Porcius Festus that Paul the Apostle pleaded his case at Caesarea Maritima (Acts 25:23-27).

Other Prominent Persons

> "In the fifteenth year of the reign of Tiberius Caesar—when Pontius Pilate was governor of Judea, Herod tetrarch of Galilee, his brother Philip tetrarch of Iturea and Traconitis, and Lysanias tetrarch of Abilene—during the high-priesthood of Annas and Caiaphas, the word of God came to John son of Zechariah in the wilderness" (Luke 3:1-2 NIV).

The author of the Gospel of Luke records that the "word of God" came to John the Baptist in the "fifteenth year" of the reign of Tiberias Caesar when Pontius Pilate was governor of Judea and Annas and Caiaphas were High Priests.

Pontius Pilate

As Tiberias had begun to rule jointly as Emperor in 13 AD, and as fourteen years had already passed, the "fifteenth year" of his reign corresponds to the period extending from 27-28 AD.

This timeframe accords with the record of secular history. Pontius Pilate was *Praefectus* (Prefect) of Judaea from 26-36 AD. In 36 AD, Vitellius, the Imperial Legate and Governor of Syria, decided to remove Pilate from office for ordering a massacre of Samaritans. Without waiting for the Emperor Tiberias to name a replacement, Vitellius sent his colleague Marcellus to assume control of Judea and Samaria. Upon the Emperor's death in 37 AD, this interim arrangement became a *de facto* appointment. (Extra-biblical source material about Pilate can be found in such works as those of the Roman historian Tacitus; the Jewish historian Josephus; and the Jewish philosopher Philo of Alexandria.)

The record of both biblical and secular history was verified in 1961 when archaeologists uncovered a plaque fragment at Caesarea Maritima. The plaque, written in Latin, was imbedded in a section of steps leading to the Amphitheatre. The fragment's inscription has been reconstructed as follows:

> Pontius Pilatus, Prefect of Judea, has dedicated to the people of Caesarea a temple in honor of Tiberius.

Annas and Caiaphas

Note: Apart from the New Testament, the writings of Josephus are the primary source material for both Annas and Caiaphas.

Annas, also called Ananus, son of Seth. In 6 AD, after the Romans had deposed Archelaus, Ethnarch of Judea, Samaria, and Idumea, Annas was appointed by Quirinius, the Roman Governor of Syria, as the first High Priest of the newly formed Roman Province of Judea. Annas served as official High Priest until 15 AD when he was deposed by the governor, Valerius Gratus.

Although officially removed from office, as head of a family which had produced five High Priests since the beginning of the Herodian period, he remained influential both politically and socially through a network of familial relationships, not the least of which was his position as father-in-law of the later High Priest Joseph Caiaphas.[2] A measure of the power and shared responsibility still remaining in the hands of Annas during the ministry of Jesus can be gauged by consulting Luke 3:2, John 18:22, and Acts 4:6.

In 18 AD, the same Roman governor, Valerius Gratus, who had deposed Annas three years earlier, appointed Annas' son-in-law Joseph Caiaphas as High Priest in Jerusalem. He remained in office under Gratus' successor, Pontius Pilate, until he was deposed in 36 AD by Vitellius, the governor of Syria. Caiaphas was succeeded by his brother-in-law Jonathan, a son of Annas.

In November 1990, workers found an ornate limestone ossuary while paving a road in the Peace Forest south of the Abu Tor neighborhood of Jerusalem. This ossuary appeared authentic and contained human remains. An Aramaic inscription on the side was thought to read, "Joseph son of Caiaphas" and, on this basis, the bones of an elderly man found in the ossuary were considered to belong to the High Priest Caiaphas. Since the original discovery, this identification has of course been challenged by some scholars on various grounds. The bones were reburied

---

2 Jewish Encyclopaedia article: *Annas*. Accessed 13 May, 2018. http://jewishencyclopedia.com/articles/1554-annas

on the Mount of Olives while the ossuary itself is now in the custody of the Israel Antiquities Authority.

Quirinius

In 6 AD, Publius Sulpicius Quirinius was appointed governor of the Province of Roman Syria and ordered to carry out a census of the newly-formed Province of Judea. The following passage in Luke has occasioned much heated debate:

> In those days Caesar Augustus issued a decree that a census should be taken of the entire Roman world. (This was the first census that took place while Quirinius was governor of Syria.) And everyone went to their own town to register (Luke 2:1-3 NIV).

It is assumed that the census referred to here by Luke is identical to the census of Quirinius in 6-7 AD which was held at least ten years after the birth of Jesus. However, it appears to have gone largely unnoticed when addressing this particular issue that Luke, in addition to his Gospel, was also the author of the Book of Acts.

Consider the following:

> After him Judas the Galilean rose up in the days of the census and drew away some of the people after him. He too perished, and all who followed him were scattered (Acts 5:37 ESV).

Luke is here referring to the census of Quirinius in 6-7 AD when Judas the Galilean rebelled. That census was the one that all Israel remembered, and they remembered Quirinius mostly because of the census that he directed.

In his Gospel account, Luke sets out to distinguish between the one he speaks of in Acts 5:37, and the one which took place when Jesus was born:

> This was the first census that took place while Quirinius was governor (*hēgemoneuontos*) of Syria (Luke 2:2 NIV).

Many official population surveys were taken throughout the Roman empire during the time of Augustus. Luke is speaking of another census which took place before the census of 6-7 AD. He would certainly have spoken of *the census*, rather than *the first census* if in fact he had only known of one.

Another objection raised by critics is that, while it is certain that Quirinius was governor of Syria in 6 AD, there is no evidence that he held that official title at any previous time—specifically, during the reign of Herod (before 3 BC). However, in

Luke 2:2, the participial form of *hegemon*, i.e. *hēgemoneuontos* is used. The translation of the passage should therefore read:

> This was the first census that took place when Quirinius was governing (*hēgemoneuontos*) Syria.

It may seem a fine distinction but it should be kept in mind that, elsewhere in his writings, Luke is extremely careful to provide us with the exact titles of about a dozen officials that can be historically corroborated by external sources (see for example Acts 13:4-5, 7, 13; 14:12; 16:20; 17:6; 17:34; 18:12). Likewise is he careful to avoid stating in 2:2 that Quirinius is the *Governor* of Syria but rather that he was *governing* Syria in some capacity.

This interpretation accords with what we know from secular history. Gaius Sentius Saturninus was appointed official Governor of Syria from 9 BC-7 BC, after whom came Quinctilius Varus who was the official Governor from 6 BC until after the death of Herod the Great. Whilst it is known with certainty that these two were the official Governors of Syria from 9 BC until after Herod's death, it is also known with certainty that, after being appointed Consul by Caesar Augustus in 12 BC, Quirinius was also in the area conducting military campaigns during the periods in question.

Quinctilius Varus, noted for his harsh rule and high taxation, had become the target of mass protests and was the face of popular anti-Roman sentiment. It is not surprising therefore that a different Roman official, Quirinius, should be tasked by Augustus with conducting the *first census* referred to by Luke. (The measure of his success is that he was also tasked with conducting the subsequent census.)

Much critical energy is spent on a misguided attempt to refute something that Luke does not say, namely that Quirinius was official Governor of Syria twice. However, regardless of all the above, consider the introduction to his Gospel:

> Many have undertaken to draw up an account of the things that have been fulfilled among us, just as they were handed down to us by those who from the first were eyewitnesses and servants of the word. With this in mind, since I myself have carefully investigated everything from the beginning, I too decided to write an orderly account for you, most excellent Theophilus, so that you may know the certainty of the things you have been taught (Luke 1:1-4 NIV).

With Luke's assurances in mind, consider the following questions:

Is it reasonable to assert that Luke, otherwise renowned for his meticulous research and impeccable first-hand sources, would have made such an glaring error that could be *fact-checked at that time* and used against the fledgling Jesus movement? (On the issue of impeccable first-hand sources, see also Part IV.4,5,6: *Virgin Birth and Incarnation-The Gospel of Luke I, II, III* in which the reader will find that Luke names the biological father of Jesus.)

Is it reasonable to assume that modern academics and theologians millennia removed from these historical circumstances could possibly know more about the situation than the man on the spot—Luke himself?

CHAPTER FOUR

The Conflict

The prophets of old

Around the Roman year 783 AUC (30 AD), an itinerant preacher from the country, known to his contemporaries as Jesus of Nazareth (*Yeshua HaNotzri*), travelled to Jerusalem and began addressing the crowds when they gathered in the Temple precincts each day. (It is perhaps a little known fact there was unlimited freedom of speech in the Jerusalem of the Roman period.)

Attitudes towards Jesus polarised rapidly—his reputation had preceded him.

Jesus focused on those in Israel who, for one reason or another, had been excluded from the assembly of God's people, arguing that the place of assembly is wherever God's people strive to obey and honour God in line with the Torah, regardless of whether or not they obeyed the purity rules which the Torah prescribed. In essence, the Torah was made for people, not people for the Torah.

Love of God, compassion, and practical attachment to one's neighbour as to oneself, were priorities ranking higher than the sacrificial system administered by the priestly class. This approach, perceived as *passé* and quaint by city elites, was reminiscent of the prophets of old and resonated in the countryside. It is no surprise therefore that Jesus, coming from the countryside himself, could readily be perceived by some as a prophet in the tradition of Elijah, Isaiah or Jeremiah (Matthew 16:14; Mark 6:15; Luke 9:8).

The city elites

Struggles over the Hasmonean succession, political turmoil during and after Herod the Great's reign, and ever-encroaching Roman military might, all produced a myriad of political coalitions, alliances and disputes. The sources for this period give only a small window into the waxing and waning fortunes of numerous individuals and families who comprised the apex of the elite power structure centred in Jerusalem.

Pre-eminent amongst this elite class were the Sadducees and Herodians, the aristocracy of the day. They derived their power, prestige and status from accumulated family honour and the genealogical purity of their birth. (See Part IV: *Virgin Birth and Incarnation* for more on the crucial importance of genealogy.) Of lesser social standing, but nonetheless wielding greater influence in the religious sphere, were members of the priesthood and the retainer class, including Pharisees, Scribes, teachers of the Law, and other officials.

There was marked disagreement between the Sadducees and Pharisees about the Law code that should govern the behaviour of all Israelites. The Sadducees insisted that laws be restricted to the "word of God", i.e. the written Law of Moses, while the Pharisees allowed for a growing tradition of oral Law. The growth of these traditions amongst the Pharisees and teachers of the Law was roundly criticised by Jesus:

> You are destroying the word of God through your tradition that you have handed down. And you do many other things like that (Mark 7:13 ISV).

These Jerusalem elites had a monopoly on education and controlled channels of information through the orthodoxy of the synagogues, both in city and country.

A litany of complaints

Jesus was accused by members of these elites and other unspecified persons of being a troublemaker who stirred up the people in Galilee, Judea and Jerusalem (Luke 23:5); of blasphemy ((Matthew 26:65; Mark 14:64; Luke 5:21; John 10:33); of being demon-possessed and insane (John 10:20); of making treasonable claims (John 19:12); of being a wine-bibber and a glutton (Luke 7:34); of being a law-breaker (Mark 2:24; Luke 6:2; John 9:16); of being a con-man (John 7:48); and of being uncouth and common (Luke 11:38, Mark 7:2, Matthew 15:2).

CHAPTER FIVE

The Last Supper

Before proceeding with the Gospel accounts of the arrest, trial, and death of Jesus, a few words about the Last Supper are in order.

The Last Supper accounts found in the Synoptic Gospels would appear to suggest that Jesus' last meal with his disciples was the traditional Passover Feast. Against the testimony of the Synoptics stands the Gospel of John, which dates the crucifixion to the "day of Preparation for the Passover" (John 19:14). According to John, Jesus died just when the Passover sacrifice was being offered and before the festival began at sundown. Consider these verses from Mark and Luke:

> And on the first day of Unleavened Bread, when they sacrificed the Passover lamb, his disciples said to him, "Where will you have us go and prepare for you to eat the Passover?" (Mark 14:12 ESV).
>
> Then came the day of Unleavened Bread on which the Passover lamb had to be sacrificed. Jesus sent Peter and John, saying, "Go and make preparations for us to eat the Passover" (Luke 22:7-8 NIV).

Yet Mark and Luke *appear* to contradict themselves as they subsequently state that Jesus was crucified on the Day of Preparation. All four Gospels agree on this point (Matthew 27:62; Mark 15:42; Luke 23:54; John 19:14, 31, 42). The Day of Preparation for the Passover Feast began at sundown and ended the following sundown. During this 24-hour period, the Passover lambs were sacrificed, usually in the afternoon a few hours prior to being consumed at the Passover Feast. It is obvious that if Jesus was crucified on the Day of Preparation, he could not have already observed the Passover with his disciples.

It stretches credulity to assert that the Gospel authors would forget what they had already written and contradict themselves in subsequent chapters. An alternative explanation should therefore be sought.

That explanation may lie in the fact that the terms "Feast of Unleavened Bread" and "Passover" were used in different senses by different authors of the period. Strictly speaking, the Passover was one 24-hour period within the Feast of Unleavened Bread (which lasts for seven days), but the term "Passover" can be applied to the whole seven days. The best example of this application is taken from Luke himself, "Now the Feast of Unleavened Bread drew nigh, which is called the Passover" (Luke 22:1).

Since the primary goal of this work is to examine mainstream Christian doctrine, it is beyond our scope to delve further into this issue. However, a few observations may still be rewarding:

- The entire reason for the institution of the Passover Feast was to commemorate the eve of the Exodus when the Israelites ate a sacrificed lamb with bitter herbs and unleavened bread prior to their departure from Egypt. Exodus Chapter 12 commands the Israelites to repeat this practice every year, performing the sacrifice before sundown and then consuming it after the sun has set;

- Yet nowhere in any of the Gospel accounts is there a direct or indirect mention of a lamb actually being sacrificed, or the consumption of that lamb and bitter herbs—the obligatory food—at the last supper;

- Unlike the Synoptic authors, the author of John says nothing about the disciples making preparations for the Passover. He simply refers to the last supper as the "evening meal" (13:29);

- Mark states that the Judean elites wanted to covertly arrest and kill Jesus, "but not during the feast," they said, "or there may be a riot among the people" (Mark 14:1-2);

- John states that preparations for the Passover Feast were still in progress when Jesus was brought before Pilate (18:28);

- John provides the further detail that Jesus was crucified at the time when the Passover lambs were slain by citing Exodus 12:46 (John 19:36);

- One of John's central themes is his presentation of Jesus as the Paschal Lamb of God, dying on the cross as the Passover lambs were being sacrificed in the Temple (see also 1 Corinthians 5:7–8).

Based solely on the preponderance of evidence, notwithstanding the two verses in Mark and Luke, it is likely that Jesus, knowing he would not live long enough to celebrate the traditional Passover with his disciples, gathered them together for one last meal, a commemorative meal conducted as if it were indeed the Passover. This last meal, this "Last Supper", took place at the beginning of the Day of Preparation, i.e. beginning after sundown, some 24 hours before the traditional Passover Feast would commence. During this 24-hour period, Jesus ate his last meal with his disciples, was arrested on the Mount of Olives, was interrogated by the Judean elites, Pilate and Herod, and was crucified and died on a Roman cross.

Transubstantiation

Note

This doctrine is taught in one form or another, under one name or another, by most Christian churches. However, as the Roman Catholic form of the doctrine is perhaps its most extreme expression, we will here examine only official Catholic teaching.

The term "transubstantiation", with reference to the Eucharist, first made its appearance at the The Fourth Lateran Council in 1215 and was canonised at the Council of Trent in 1551.

In Session 13, Chapter 4 of the Council proceedings we read:

> Because Christ our Redeemer said that it was truly his body that he was offering under the species of bread, it has always been the conviction of the Church of God, and this holy Council now declares again, that by the consecration of the bread and wine there takes place a change of the whole substance of the bread into the substance of the body of Christ our Lord and of the whole substance of the wine into the substance of his blood. This change the holy Catholic Church has fittingly and properly called Transubstantiation. [3]

In the Canons attached to Session 13, we read:

> *Canon I.* If anyone denies that in the sacrament of the most Holy Eucharist are contained truly, really and substantially the body and blood together with the soul and divinity of our Lord Jesus Christ, and consequently the whole Christ, but says that He is in it only as in a sign, or figure or force, let him be anathema.
>
> *Canon II.* If anyone says that in the sacred and holy sacrament of the Eucharist the substance of the bread and wine remains conjointly with the body and blood of our Lord Jesus Christ, and denies that wonderful and singular change of the whole substance of the bread into the body and the whole substance of the wine into the blood, the appearances only of bread and wine remaining, which change the Catholic Church most aptly calls transubstantiation, let him be anathema.

This doctrine is not merely a relic of mediaeval thinking. Under the heading "Christ present in the Eucharist through Transubstantiation", the 1965 Papal Encyclical *Mysterium Fidei* by Pope Paul VI states that:

> ...we have to listen with docility to the voice of the teaching and praying

---

3 *The Council of Trent: Session XIII; Chapter IV.* Accessed 10 August 2018 at http://www.thecounciloftrent.com/ch13.htm

Church. Her voice, which constantly echoes the voice of Christ, assures us that the way in which Christ becomes present in this Sacrament is through the conversion of the whole substance of the bread into His body and of the whole substance of the wine into His blood, a unique and truly wonderful conversion that the Catholic Church fittingly and properly calls transubstantiation.[4]

This doctrine is based on a gross, literalistic interpretation of the spiritual words of the Israelite Jesus for whom such pagan practices as eating human flesh and drinking human blood would have been abhorrent in the extreme. Nevertheless, the Roman Catholic Church teaches that when one partakes of the Eucharist, one is actually eating the flesh of Jesus and drinking his blood. It is a distortion of the Last Supper meal and the Israelite "table of the Lord" fellowship concept.

That it is an absurd interpretation can be demonstrated by reference to two examples.

The first, from the Hebrew Scriptures, occurred during the days of King David:

> Now three of the thirty captains went down to the rock to David, into the cave of Adullam; and the host of the Philistines encamped in the valley of Rephaim. And David was then in the hold, and the Philistines' garrison was then at Bethlehem. And David longed, and said, Oh that one would give me drink of the water of the well of Bethlehem, that is at the gate! And the three brake through the host of the Philistines, and drew water out of the well of Bethlehem, that was by the gate, and took it, and brought it to David: but David would not drink of it, but poured it out to the LORD, And said, My God forbid it me, that I should do this thing: shall I drink the blood of these men that have put their lives in jeopardy? for with the jeopardy of their lives they brought it. Therefore he would not drink it…(1 Chronicles 11:15-19 KJV).

David did not refuse the water because it had suddenly become blood. He refused it because it had been brought at the risk of life, and "the life of the flesh is in the blood" (Leviticus 17:11). Jesus' words at the Last Supper were uttered in the same spirit as those of David, with the only difference being that Jesus spoke of himself.

The other example is taken from the Gospel of John, Chapter 6. Jesus identified himself as "bread from heaven" and told the people that, "He that eats my flesh and drinks my blood has eternal life and I will raise him up at the last day" (6:54).

Jesus was not recommending cannabalism—the words he spoke were "spirit and life" (6:63). To eat Jesus spiritually is to partake of the Word of Life, sent as a gift

---

4   *Mysterium Fidei: Encyclical on the Holy Eucharist.* Pope Paul VI, September 3 1965. Accessed 10 August 2018 at http://w2.vatican.va/content/paul-vi/en/encyclicals/documents/hf_p-vi_enc_03091965_mysterium.html

from Heaven. It is noteworthy that some of his disciples did not understand what his words really meant and so "went back and walked no more with him" (6:64). The misunderstanding of these disciples is essentially the same misunderstanding responsible for the doctrine of Transubstantiation. To accept this doctrine is to be chastised by Jesus, just as they were.

The apostle Paul deals with the question in 1 Corinthians 10:16-21. In his dissertation he speaks of those who partake of the "table of the Lord" as being "one loaf" and "one bread". Jesus and his followers are of *one spiritual flesh and blood*. It follows logically, therefore, that if the flesh and blood of Jesus is consumed with the bread and wine of the Eucharist, then those who hold to the doctrine of Transubstantiation are actually eating themselves.

All that being said, what is the true significance of this memorial meal for Christians?

> For I received from the Lord what I also delivered to you, that the Lord Jesus on the night when he was betrayed took bread, and when he had given thanks, he broke it, and said, "This is my body, which is for you. Do this in remembrance of me." In the same way also he took the cup, after supper, saying, "This cup is the new covenant in my blood. Do this, as often as you drink it, in remembrance of me." For as often as you eat this bread and drink the cup, you proclaim the Lord's death until he comes (1 Corinthians 11:23-26 ESV).

CHAPTER SIX

Betrayal

Note

The inherited family surname is a relatively recent phenomena. Until this modern emergence, other means of distinguishing one individual from another had to be devised. The most common of these identifiers were derived from occupations, or places of origin, or the name by which a family head was known.

Judas Iscariot

According to all four Gospel authors, Jesus was betrayed by one of his own, the disciple Judas Iscariot. Whilst all four tell virtually the same basic story, the emphasis, perspective and detail of each differs.

Consider for example Matthew 26:15 where the author draws on the Book of Zechariah as means of establishing relevance for his readers:

> Then I said to them, "If it seems good to you, give me my wages; but if not, keep them." And they weighed out as my wages thirty pieces of silver. Then the LORD said to me, "Throw it to the potter"—the lordly price at which I was priced by them. So I took the thirty pieces of silver and threw them into the house of the LORD, to the potter"(Zechariah 11:12-13 ESV).

The author apparently misidentifies his source as Jeremiah. However, when Matthew quotes from the Hebrew Scriptures, he most often attributes his source only to the "prophet" (see for instance Matthew 1:22; 2:5; 13:35 and etcetera). It is most likely therefore that the name of Jeremiah was inserted by a subsequent copyist and incorrectly attributed.

Consider also how Satan is introduced into the story by Luke and John (Luke 22:3; John 13:2). John adds a further element by stating that Judas was motivated by avarice (John 12:4-6).

Minor story variations, in some cases the result of individual authors employing the literary style of *Midrash* to a greater or lesser degree, is only to be expected. If four separate authors were given a story to write about today, we would most likely find their accounts to be consistent overall, but we would certainly find that the emphasis, perspective, and detail would differ. Each of them would highlight what is felt most strongly and ignore or pass over lightly what is considered peripheral or unimportant.

The same latitude, it seems, is rarely afforded the authors of the New Testament. (See notes on *Midrash* in following Chapter.)

Motivation

Many theories have been advanced about the motives of Judas, some based on the meaning of his identifier *Iscariot*. There can be little doubt that the word comprises two parts, the first deriving from the Hebrew *ish* (man). It is the second part, *Keriot*, which has been the subject of much controversy. *Keriot*, derived from *Keriah*, is the generic Hebrew word for a village or town, but is also the name of a particular town in the Negev desert near the boundary with Edom (Joshua 15:25). Still others claim that by using the word *Iscariot*, the Gospel authors meant to identify Judas with the Sicarii, a group of Jewish resistance fighters dedicated to the violent overthrow of the Romans. Of course, this putative identification allows for the dissemination of other theories about the motivations of Judas.

This author is of the view that there are no secret meanings to be gleaned from the name *Iscariot* and agrees with the Jewish Encyclopaedia that the word simply means *the man from the town of Keriot*.[5] (Note that in John 6:71, the father of Judas is named as Simon Iscariot.)

None of the theories so far advanced about the motives of Judas carry the ring of authenticity. In the absence of any real evidence, this author will take the liberty of advancing yet another theory based solely on observation of universal human behaviours—human nature is nothing if not consistent.

A personal take

When travelling around the countryside with Jesus and the other disciples, Judas could accept the occasional conflict with relative equanimity because their opponents lacked any real power or influence. However, when finally in Jerusalem, and witnessing at first hand the power, the authority, and the weight of tradition represented by the establishment, he felt weak and vulnerable. The prior declaration by Thomas—"let us also go (to Judea), that we may die with him" (John 11:16)—would have perhaps been recalled with increasing alarm. In this state of heightened awareness of impending danger, his loyalty to Jesus began to recede into the background. The money-changing incident in the Temple finally triggered his need to disassociate himself from what was now inevitable: a final showdown between Jesus and the priests, which would necessarily involve the Romans. Judas panicked, fearing now for his own personal safety, and the rest is history. Too late, he realised the

---

[5] Jewish Encyclopaedia Article *Judas Iscariot*. Accessed 27 May, 2018. http://www.jewishencyclopedia.com/articles/9033-judas-iscariot

enormity of his betrayal, and that rest is also history. One important detail that should be kept in mind is that the father of Judas was identified by the author of John's Gospel as "Simon Iscariot" (John 13:26). Just as in other honour-shame societies, which persist to our own times, any shame attaching to Judas would also fall upon his family, who would be bound to retrieve their honour in some way. It is quite possible that, in addition to the factor of remorse, taking his own life may have been perceived by Judas as a way to retrieve his family's honour. But all this is pure conjecture.

A Parallel Betrayal

The major aim of the New Testament is to demonstrate that Jesus was the expected Davidic King-Messiah. Towards this end, the Gospel authors drew many thematic parallels between Jesus and King David.

One intriguing and usually unrecognised parallel is between the betrayal of Jesus by Judas, and the betrayal of King David by Ahithopel.

Ahithopel, who had been David's chief counsellor, betrayed his King by participating in the rebellion of David's son, Absalom. A reading of 2 Samuel Chapters 15-17 will provide some intriguing similarities between Judas/Jesus and Ahithophel/David:

- It was thought by the conspirators that the death of one man would guarantee the safety of all the people (2 Samuel 17:3 cf. John 11:50);

- Judas and Ahithophel both plan to carry out their betrayal at night when Jesus and David were "weak" (2 Samuel 17:1 cf. John 13:30);

- Jesus and David both cross the Kidron Valley (2 Samuel 15:23 cf. John 18:1), before praying for deliverance on the Mount of Olives (2 Samuel 15:31 cf. Mark 14:26);

- Judas and Ahithophel both hang themselves after the betrayal (2 Samuel 17:23 cf. Matthew 27:5).

It is difficult to determine the extent to which the individual Gospel writers used the *Midrashic* style and tailored the Judas betrayal story to fit the overall theme of identifying Jesus with King David. However, all these accounts were written after the fact and after a period of reflection. It is not reasonable to suggest that Judas himself was aware of these parallels at the time, or that he was consciously working towards some unspecified goal which would ultimately lead to his own death. (See Notes on *Midrash* in following Chapter.)

CHAPTER SEVEN

Arrest and Interrogation

General Notes

- Since this work is in English, we will confine our remarks on this topic to the English version but its content applies equally to all translations of the Greek New Testament regardless of era, language or version;

- The Greek word *Ioudaios,* always translated into English in an ethnic sense as "Jew/s," should in the majority of cases be translated into English in a geographic sense as "Judean/s". This is particularly so in the case of John's Gospel. Because it is set in Jerusalem and portrays the priestly establishment as the main force of opposition to both God and Jesus, the word *Ioudaios* appears seventy-one times compared to five times in Matthew and Luke and seven times in Mark. Therefore, throughout this work, where the word "Jew/s" refers to the Jerusalem establishment, it should always be taken to mean "Judean/s".

- Concern for one's honour permeated every aspect of life in Mediterranean antiquity. Honour served as the prime indicator of social position and prescribed how persons should interact with superiors, inferiors and equals in appropriate ways. Public insults must be challenged to defend one's honour. All of the trial exchanges between Pilate and the Jerusalem elites, and between Pilate and Jesus, are set within the framework of this honour-shame society.

- It is often claimed that the Gospel authors paint a sympathetic picture of Pilate whereas, in fact, Pilate was noted for his viciousness and cruelty by contemporary sources. It is not, therefore, credible to assert that Pilate had any interest whatsoever in the fate of Jesus. Pilate's sole interest lay in maintaining his public honour and, by extension, that of Rome. Together with the interpretive principles outlined above, this is the lens through which it is advisable view all the Gospel accounts.

- The Jerusalem Sanhedrin (Council) consisted of seventy-one members, comprising scribes, elders, prominent members of the high priestly families, and the High Priest, who also served as the president of the body. The Roman rulers of Judea had given authority to this Council to hear causes which fell within its jurisdiction, with the limitation that a capital sentence pronounced by the Council was not valid until confirmed by the Roman Prefect or Procurator.

- Although the four Gospels appear to indicate that the whole Council was in agreement that Jesus should be delivered to Pilate for judgement, all four nevertheless point to one dissenting member—Joseph of Arimathea—while the author of John includes another dissenter named Nicodemus.

- To think in terms of a modern trial process when reading the Gospel accounts is anachronistic. The purpose of a trial in the ancient Mediterranean was not to discover truth and mete out justice. Rather, the purpose of a trial among social equals was to dishonour and shame the opponent. By contrast, the purpose of a trial for social inferiors such as Jesus was simply to mete out punishment. In the judgement of his accusers, if he were not guilty, he would not be standing before Pilate. The only question is: what punishment does he deserve?

Notes on Midrash

If one is familiar with the Israelite literary style of *Midrash*, and knows a little about the major themes of the Hebrew Scriptures, it is quite a simple matter to identify passages where New Testament authors, perceiving that the events of Jesus' life and death were invested with a much deeper meaning than the bare circumstances would suggest, enlivened those events by analogous association with prior events already holding great significance for a contemporary reader.

Hence we see an abundance of *Midrashic* analogy between individual events in the life of Jesus and previous events in the national life of Israel, the purpose of which was to demonstrate Jesus' central role in the redemptive plan of God.

When the author of Luke wrote the book of Acts, he put into Paul's mouth a sermon full of quotations and references to the Hebrew scriptures demonstrating that, in his day, sermons for Jesus followers were composed according to the *Midrashic* fashion.

As far as the Gospels are concerned, we see the style of *Midrash* most strikingly employed by Matthew. However, as demonstrated elsewhere in this work, the Gospel accounts found in our Greek New Testament are third or fourth generation translations of notes, documents, witness statements and so on originally composed in Hebrew at a very early date. As such, we would expect all four Gospels to contain passages written in the *Midrashic* style.

See also Part II.9: *The Documents-Understanding Literary Styles*.

Notes on Language

The majority Christian theological and academic view is that the Gospels were orally transmitted, gradually embellished, and not committed to writing (Greek) until decades after the crucifixion, first by Mark.

However, as demonstrated in Part II.7: *The Documents-The Language of the Gospels*, the Greek Gospels we have today are replete with Hebrew idioms, literalisms, thought patterns, literary devices and syntactical structures. Indeed, sections contain such slavishly transparent transliterations that they can only be based on Hebrew originals. These sections are mainly those which record the words of Jesus and those of his opponents. Luke's Gospel is the most remarkable in this regard.

These intricacies and peculiarities of the Hebrew language could not possibly have survived years of oral transmission, particularly in a foreign Hellenist environment far removed from their source, before being committed to writing.

The authors of the original Greek Gospels arranged their accounts according to their own particular purposes, including the degree to which their target readers were familiar with *Midrashic* analogies. They utilised documents, notes, witness statements and so on, reproducing in whole or in part the various sayings, incidents, parables and the like in no consistent temporal or logical relationship to one another. This compilation process naturally resulted in the loss of the original chronology of events, in textual variants, and the inclusion or otherwise of certain passages according to authorial discretion. What is truly remarkable, however, is the coherent, homogenous, and self-consistent point of view that was preserved throughout.

As for the prevailing view of Markan priority, among the many indications that Matthew was the first of the three Synoptic Gospels is the fact that, in Mark, Hebraic-style expressions that were too awkward or harsh in Greek were frequently eliminated altogether. Incidentally, this was the view of Augustine who thought that Mark followed Matthew and was a type of shorter version.

When reading the Gospel accounts of the life of Jesus, and especially those relating to his arrest, interrogation, crucifixion and death, it is helpful to keep the above in mind.

Section 1

Matthew's Account

In summary, the members of the establishment have had enough. Jesus has challenged their honour publicly and now they must have satisfaction by whatever means necessary, including those normally employed by the elites: stealth (26:3-5); bribery (26:14-16); false witnesses (26:60); trumped-up accusations before the Roman governor (27:12); inciting the mob against Jesus (27:20); and, finally, mocking him as he hung naked and shamed on a Roman cross (27:41-42). According to Pilate, Jesus' accusers during this whole process are motivated by "envy", i.e. Jesus has publicly challenged their honour and now they must have satisfaction (27:18).

Matthew 26:1-5

After the money-changing incident in the Temple and his public denunciation of the establishment's self-righteous arrogance, greed and hypocrisy, Jesus knows that the establishment will seek his death. He warns his disciples that the Passover is only two days away and that he expects to be "handed over to be crucified" at that time.

Meanwhile, the chief priests and the elders of the people assemble in the palace of Caiaphas the High Priest. They cannot arrest Jesus during the Passover festival without risking a riot among the people so they scheme to arrest and kill him in secret.

Matthew 26:14-16

The first step in the process begins. Judas goes to the chief priests and asks for a reward in exchange for giving them advance warning of the movements of Jesus. The price is agreed. They pay him thirty pieces of silver and, from that moment, Judas seeks for an opportunity to betray Jesus.

Matthew 26:17-29

On the First Day of the Festival of Unleavened Bread, the disciples ask Jesus where they should prepare the Passover meal for him (see *The Last Supper* in a previous Chapter). He directs them to go into the city (Jerusalem) to an unidentified man and to tell this man that the "teacher" (Jesus) and his disciples will celebrate Passover at this man's house. (For indications that this was a pre-arranged covert operation, see relevant commentary on Mark and Luke in following pages.)

During the evening meal, as the group are reclining at the table, Jesus tells the disciples that he knows about the secret plot to be rid of him and also that one of them will betray him. Judas displays a lack of shame in saying, "Surely, not I Lord?"

Jesus assures Judas that he knows all about the plot and warns of the consequences of such shameful and dishonourable behaviour. Judas again demonstrates his lack of shame by repeating, "Surely, not I Rabbi?" Jesus then responds to Judas by saying, in effect, "Yes it is you".

Matthew 26:30-35

After the meal, Jesus and his disciples depart for the Mount of Olives. Israelite belief was that the Messiah would come from God on Passover evening and enter through the Golden Gate into the Temple. (The Mount of Olives is situated directly across the Kidron Valley from the Golden Gate, which is now sealed.)

Jesus predicts Peter's disloyalty and again states that his is fully aware of the secret plot to be rid of him.

Matthew 26:36-56

The group enters the Garden of Gethsemane. Several hours pass. Jesus upbraids the disciples for falling asleep while he prays. A large crowd from the chief priests and the elders, with Judas in the lead, now arrive in the Garden. The fact that they are armed with swords and clubs means that they expect some type of resistance.

Judas greets Jesus with the pre-arranged signal of a kiss and the authorities move in to arrest him. One of those with Jesus strikes the High Priest's slave with a sword. Jesus rebukes him and then contrasts his own behaviour with that of the authorities: he represents the light; they the darkness. The disciples flee.

Matthew 26:57-68

Upon his arrest, Jesus is taken to the house of Caiaphas, the High Priest. Matthew reports that those who judge and condemn Jesus are representatives of the Jerusalem establishment, including the High Priest, the chief priests, and the council of elders. It is they who have most to lose if the forthcoming Kingdom of God preached by Jesus were indeed to materialise. (Peter had been following at a distance and now sits with the guards in the courtyard to see how it will all end.)

The accusers have been seeking evidence to put Jesus to death and now false witnesses come forward to testify against him. When Jesus refuses to answer the charges, the High Priest demands a response, "Are you not going to answer…?" Jesus' continued silence finally calls forth from Caiaphas the question which will serve as an excuse for a charge of blasphemy, "tell us whether you are the Messiah, the son of God". Jesus is aware of their attempts at entrapment so responds to the question indirectly with, "You have said so". However, he then follows with a direct challenge to the authority of the High Priest, "but I tell you, from now on you will see the son of man seated at the right hand of the Power and coming on the clouds of heaven".

This direct challenge prompts Caiaphas to tear his own robe and declare Jesus guilty of "blasphemy". The tearing of the robe symbolises the type of blasphemy to which Caiaphas refers—Jesus has failed to show proper reverence to the position of the god-ordained High Priest and has attempted to rip apart the social system over which the High Priest presides.

Then the gathering determines that Jesus is worthy of death and some proceed to spit in his face, to strike and to slap him. This is the outcome of the first public attempt to destroy Jesus.

Matthew 26:69-75

Jesus had told Peter that he would betray him three times. Peter had insisted that he would not (26:30-35). It is the fact that Peter did not fulfill his word of honour given to Jesus in the presence of others that is particularly shameful according to Israelite values of the time.

Matthew 27: 1-10

Early in the morning, the chief priests and elders devise plans to have Jesus executed. A decision is made to hand him over to Pilate. When Judas realises the full extent of his betrayal, he tries to hand the "thirty pieces of silver" back to the chief priests and elders. They refuse. Judas throws the money into the Temple, and subsequently hangs himself. The priests claim it is unlawful to put "blood money" into the Temple treasury so they decide to purchase "the potter's field" and use it as a place to bury foreigners.

Interrogation by Pilate

Matthew 27: 11-31

In the very first words of his Gospel, Matthew proclaimed Jesus to be the Messiah (i.e. King of the Jews). So, when Jesus stands before Pilate, Matthew has the governor ask the question, "Are you the King of the Jews (Judeans)?" to which Jesus responds, "You say so".

Therefore, it is not surprising to find that even though the chief priests and elders level "many charges" against Jesus, to which he offers no response, Matthew does not describe just what these charges are because they are peripheral and not as important as the central issue which, for him, is the messiahship of Jesus. Thus we see that four times in this passage, Jesus is referred to as either the "one who is called Messiah" or as the "King of the Jews (Judeans)".

Pilate knows that Jesus is being accused to satisfy the honour of his accusers (here called "envy"), so he decides to thwart their plans by engaging in a theatrical display involving a man called Jesus Barabbas. Pilate's wife now sends word that she has received a divine communication (a dream) that Jesus is an innocent man.

Throughout Matthew's Gospel, we have seen Jesus proclaimed as the son of God, a term of honour. In verses 15-23 we now see a role reversal: a mob incited by the elites clamouring for the release of a man with no honour, the prisoner Barabbas, in preference to Jesus. The shaming and degradation process is complete.

Consider now what is arguably the most infamous passage in the entire Bible, certainly the one with the most devastating consequences:

> So when Pilate saw that he was gaining nothing, but rather that a riot was beginning, he took water and washed his hands before the crowd, saying, "I am innocent of this man's blood; see to it yourselves" (verse 24).
>
> And all the people answered, "His blood be on us and on our children!" (verse 25). Note that *be* is not in the original Greek.
>
> Then he released for them Barabbas, and having scourged Jesus, delivered him to be crucified (Matthew 27:24–26 ESV).

If one were to accept what has been the historically dominant view of verse 25, then this bloodthirsty mob, incited by the elites, who cry out, "his blood (be) upon us and on our children", allegedly invoke God's curse upon the entire Jewish people and their descendants who are condemned to forever share in the murder of Jesus and to forever wander the world without a home, destitute and eternally punished by God and Christians. This view first surfaced in the writings of the early church fathers in the Second Century AD, became universally entrenched by the Middle Ages, and persists to this day.

Points for consideration

- All the exchanges between Pilate and Jesus, between Pilate and the Jerusalem elites, and between Pilate and the mob, are set within the framework of a Mediterranean honour-shame society, characterised by the back and forth trading of honour challenges and ripostes.

- The same author who wrote verse 25, which allegedly condemns the entire Jewish people and their descendants in perpetuity, just a few verses later draws on Ezekiel's Vision of the Valley of Dry Bones and the promised resurrection of the Jewish people and their permanent restoration to the land of Israel. (See following Chapter for an analysis of Matthew's "signs" accompanying the death of Jesus.)

- Consider Pilate's words, "I am innocent of this man's blood" and compare them with those of his wife who said, "Have nothing to do with that innocent man, for I have suffered terribly in a dream today because of Him". The theatrical show of ritual hand-washing was intended, firstly, to insult the Judean priests by mocking their purification rules concerning the washing of hands after shedding the innocent blood of sacrificial victims (see Deuteronomy 21:1-9) and, secondly, to allay his wife's superstitions.

- The Matthean phrase "his blood on us and on our children" is not a Jewish bloodthirsty cry or a Jewish self-curse. It is a formulaic recitation of Israelite law indicating responsibility and its consequences for a transgression of the Law, a crime, or a death in the eyes of God. See Leviticus 20:9,11; Deuteronomy 19:10; Joshua 2:19; 2 Samuel 1:16; Jeremiah 26:15; 51:35; Ezekiel 18:13; and especially 2 Samuel 3:28-29 and 1 Kings 2:32-33.

- The concept of multi-generational punishment had been specifically outlawed by God. See for example Ezekiel 18:20:

- Contemporary sources attest to the fact that Pilate was a vicious and brutal man. It is not, therefore, credible to insist that Pilate had any interest whatsoever in the fate of Jesus. His apparent reluctance to condemn Jesus is based on his loathing of the Jerusalem priesthood, his inclination to thwart their plans, which he knows are based on their desire to satisfy their honour (here called "envy"), and his obligation to defend Rome's honour against any Judean insults. A failure to recognise cultural context and practices has led to the belief that Matthew condemns the entire Jewish people in perpetuity while at the same time exonerating Pilate.

- There had never been any doubt about the final outcome: the fate of Jesus had already been sealed when he was reported to have claimed to be King of the Judeans. To claim kingship over the Judeans was sedition: a challenge, not only to Pilate but to the Emperor.

- Romans were extremely superstitious and believed that dreams were divine communications. Apart from the sobering effect of Roman superstition, introduced by Matthew through the agency of Pilate's wife, the entire interrogation process was a charade, an amusement for Pilate, conducted at expense of Jesus. (In Matthew, it is Pilate's wife who is portrayed as having the typical Roman superstitious nature whereas, in John, the focus shifts to Pilate who is also typically Roman in this regard.)

Jewish historian Haim Cohen observes the terrible judgment wrongly made against the Jews because of the prevalence of the anti-Jewish interpretation of Matthew 27:25. He writes:

> None of the many charges leveled at the Jews…has held so obdurately against them as unassailable proof of guilt and responsibility for the crucifixion as has this exclamation of theirs "His blood be upon us and our children". [6]

New Testament scholar David Catchpole documented Jewish views of the trial of Jesus and writes:

> For Jesus' own *via dolorosa* had tragically and shamefully become a blood-stained path for his fellow countrymen of later generations. [7]

Section 2

Mark's Account

As in Matthew's Gospel, the chief priests and the teachers of the law have had enough and are plotting to arrest Jesus by stealth and kill him by whatever means necessary, including those means normally employed by Mediterranean elites: stealth; bribery of Judas (14:10-11); false witnesses (14:56-58); trumped-up charges before the Roman governor (15:3); inciting the mob (15:11); and, finally, the mocking and public shaming as Jesus hangs on the cross (15:31-32).

Mark 14:1-2

It is two days before Passover and the chief priests and scribes are plotting to take Jesus by stealth and kill him because they fear that Jesus' supporters may riot if the arrest is carried out in public, during the Festival.

Mark 14:10-11

The stealth process begins with the bribing of Judas. The chief priests are "greatly pleased" and promise payment. Judas begins to look for an opportunity to hand Jesus over to them.

---

6   Cohen, Haim. *The Trial and Death of Jesus of Nazareth*. Konecky & Konecky, 2000, p.171

7   Catchpole, David. *The Trial of Jesus: A Study in the Gospels and Jewish Historiography from 1770 to the Present Day*. Brill, 1971, p.xi

Mark 14:12:25

On the First Day of Unleavened Bread, when the Passover lambs are sacrificed, the disciples ask Jesus where they will make preparations to eat the Passover (see Last Supper Notes). Jesus tells two of the disciples to go into the city (Jerusalem), meet a man carrying a jar of water, and follow this man to a house. They are to say to the owner of the house that the "teacher" wishes to know where the guest room is that he may eat the Passover there with his disciples. The owner will show them to a large upper room, furnished and ready. For Jesus, Jerusalem is a dangerous place to be at night so the fact that a man would be carrying a jar of water, a job reserved for women, tells us that this is a pre-arranged covert operation.

When they had gathered together in the room and the disciples had taken their places for the communal meal, Jesus tells them that he is aware of the secret plot to kill him and that it is one of those sharing that meal who will betray him. One by one, they protest saying "Surely not I". Jesus does not identify Judas but merely says that it is indeed one of them and warns of the consequences of such shameful and dishonourable behaviour. Jesus predicts Peter's disloyalty.

Mark 14:26:31

After supper, Jesus and the disciples go to the Mount of Olives. Jesus tells them he is fully aware of the plot about to unfold and of Peter's coming disloyalty. Jesus also tells them that they will move back to Galilee after he has been "raised up".

Mark 14:32:52

The group enters the Garden of Gethsemane. Jesus, Peter, James and John separate from the other disciples. Three times Jesus moves away from the core group and three times he returns to find them sleeping. It appears that the disciples had not understood the import of Jesus' prior warnings about the plot to take him by stealth as they would have certainly remained on guard if they had.

Judas arrives accompanied by a crowd armed with swords and clubs, sent from the chief priests, the teachers of the law, and the elders. By being so armed, they expect resistance. Jesus then contrasts his own behaviour with that of the authorities: he preaches openly by day in the crowded Temple; they make their moves by stealth at night in a place where there will be few witnesses. The disciples desert Jesus and flee. He is left alone to face the enemy.

The reference here to the young man wearing only a linen cloth appears to prefigure the death and resurrection of Jesus. Before the resurrection, Mark claims that Jesus is wrapped only in a linen cloth as he is laid in the tomb. After the resurrection, a young man wearing a white robe takes his place in the tomb. (There was a common belief in angelic beings so perhaps this incident is a remnant of an earlier tradition which the author does not explain.)

Mark 14:53-65

Jesus is arrested and taken that same night to a gathering comprising the High Priest, all the chief priests, the elders and the scribes. The chief priest and the whole Sanhedrin had been seeking evidence against Jesus but failed to find any so now they arrange for false witnesses to testify against him. However, their witnesses could not agree with each other.

As in Matthew's account, when Jesus refuses to answer the charges, the High Priest demands a response, "Are you not going to answer…?" Jesus' continued silence finally calls forth from Caiaphas the question which will serve as an excuse for a charge of blasphemy, "tell us whether you are the Messiah, the son of God". Jesus is aware of their attempts at entrapment so responds to the question indirectly with, "You have said so". However, he then follows with a direct challenge to the authority of the High Priest, "but I tell you, from now on you will see the son of man seated at the right hand of the Power and coming on the clouds of heaven". This direct challenge prompts Caiaphas to tear his own robe and declare Jesus guilty of "blasphemy". The tearing of the robe symbolises the type of blasphemy to which Caiaphas refers—Jesus has failed to show proper reverence to the position of the god-ordained High Priest and has attempted to rip apart the social system over which the High Priest presides.

The whole gathering declares Jesus worthy of death. After being spat on and struck with fists, the guards take him and beat him.

Mark 14:66-72

Jesus had told Peter that he would betray him three times. Peter had insisted that he would not (26:30-35). It is the fact that Peter did not fulfill his word of honour given to Jesus in the presence of others that is particularly shameful according to Mediterranean values of the time. The chief priests, the elders, the scribes and the whole Sanhedrin hold another meeting the next morning, at which time they "make plans" and then hand Jesus over to Pilate (15:1).

Interrogation by Pilate

Mark 15:2-20

It is not necessary to lay out Mark's account in detail as it is virtually the same as that of Matthew except for the following:

- there is no mention of Pilate's wife;

- there is no mention of the hand-washing incident;
- there is no mention of the mob's response, "His blood (be) on us and on our children";
- Pilate accedes to the mob's wishes in order to "please" them, rather than to avoid a riot, as in Matthew's account.

Section 3

Luke's Account

Note

The role of Satan (Hebrew שָׂטָן *Shatan*) was to test one's loyalty to God, hence this being engages in lies and deception. Abnormal behaviour, whether good or bad, was usually attributed to some external force. As Judas begins to act completely out of character with his previous identification as "one of the twelve", his abnormal behaviour is attributed to Satan. (Refer also to John's account.)

Luke 20:20-47

As in the other Synoptic accounts, the elites have had enough and are plotting to arrest Jesus by stealth and kill him.

Spies are planted in his audience by the scribes and chief priests (19:19). These spies attempt to trap Jesus with loaded questions. Luke adds a political dimension by stating that their intent is to hand him over to the "jurisdiction and authority of the governor". However, the spies are unable to outwit Jesus or to diminish him in the eyes of the people so they fall silent. Some Sadducees also ask Jesus a question designed to embarrass him but once again Jesus outwits his opponents. The scribes congratulate him on his answer to avoid diminishing their own standing in the eyes of the people. In the hearing of all, Jesus then challenges the scribes by labelling them as self-righteous and greedy hypocrites.

Luke 22:1-38

The Passover is approaching and the chief priests and the scribes are looking for ways to be rid of Jesus, for they "fear" the people. Satan "enters" Judas and he goes to the chief priests and the officers of the temple police and offers to find a way to betray Jesus. They are "delighted". Together they agree upon a price and Judas then watches for an opportunity to betray Jesus when "no crowd was present".

On the Day of Unleavened Bread, when the Passover lambs are sacrificed, Jesus instructs Peter and John to prepare the Passover (see Last Supper Notes). When Peter and John ask where it should be eaten, Jesus tells them to go into the city (Jerusalem), meet a man carrying a jar of water, and follow this man to a house. They are to say to the owner of the house that the "teacher" wishes to know where the guest room is that he may eat the Passover there with his disciples. For Jesus, Jerusalem is a dangerous place to be at night so the fact that a man would be carrying a jar of water, a job reserved for women, tells us that this is a pre-arranged covert operation. (Note that Luke identifies Matthew's "disciples" and Mark's "two disciples" as Peter and John.)

The meal begins and Jesus takes his place at the table. Jesus' statement that he had "eagerly desired" to eat the meal with his disciples underscores the importance of table fellowship. As this type of meal was primarily a family occasion, it also points to Jesus' recognition that he and his disciples are a type of surrogate family.

Given that the group are a type of surrogate family, the actions of Judas, through his betrayal, and Peter, through his disloyalty, would have been regarded as all the more shameful and dishonourable. Unlike Matthew's account, Luke does not record any direct response from Judas when Jesus says he is about to be betrayed by one who has his hand on this table of fellowship. Towards the end of the meal, Luke records a group of Jesus' sayings.

Luke 22:39-54

When Jesus was in Jerusalem, he taught every day in the Temple and spent every night on the Mount of Olives (21:37-38). So, after the Passover meal, Jesus and his disciples go at their customary place. Jesus withdraws from the group, about a "stones throw" away, and prays. Having predicted Peter's disloyalty, Jesus now displays his own loyalty to God by praying, "Father, if you are willing, take this cup from me; yet not my will, but yours be done".

Judas, one of the twelve, arrives with a crowd. As "one of the twelve," his behaviour is particularly shameful. He approaches Jesus and is greeted with those immortal words: "Judas, are you betraying the Son of Man with a kiss?"

One of those with Jesus strikes the servant of the High Priest, cutting off his ear. Jesus intervenes, heals the servant, and then contrasts his own behaviour with that of his opponents: he represents the light, they the darkness.

Luke 22:54-62

Jesus is arrested and led to the house of the High Priest. Peter follows at a distance and sits in the courtyard with others around a fire. Three of these people insist that Peter is an associate of Jesus and three times Peter denies that he is although his Galilean accent would have certainly given him away. The rooster crows. In this account, Jesus turns to look at Peter and then Peter remembers that Jesus had predicted his disloyalty and he "wept bitterly".

Luke 22:63-71

The men who are guarding Jesus begin mocking him, beating him, and insulting him in various ways. At daybreak, Jesus is led before the council comprising the chief priests and the teachers of the law.

Luke's account of their interrogation of Jesus is similar but less detail-oriented than those of Matthew and Mark. This minimal approach gives the impression of an author intent on moving forward as quickly as possible to record what are, for him, the more important incidents to follow.

Interrogation by Pilate

Note

Although Luke is the only author who records that Jesus also appeared before Herod Antipas, it should be kept in mind that Luke has demonstrated throughout his account of the life of Jesus that he has access to information unavailable to other Gospel authors. See for example Part IV.4,5,6: *Virgin Birth and Incarnation-The Gospel of Luke I, II, III* for Luke's specific and personal information about Mary.

Luke 23:1-25

The whole assembly then leads Jesus to Pilate.

Matthew and Mark both refer specifically to the charge that Jesus claimed to be the royal Messiah but, although they mention other charges, they do not specify what those other charges were. Luke fills in some gaps for us: perverting the nation; forbidding others to pay taxes to the Emperor; and, when Pilate seems uninterested in those charges, the elites insist that this perverted teaching has been spread throughout the land, stirring up the people throughout all Judea and Galilee. The implication here is that there are witnesses everywhere who could confirm this. (See John's account for the only mention of the blasphemy charge.)

When Pilate learns that Jesus is a Galilean and therefore under Herod's nominal jurisdiction, he seizes the opportunity to trifle with the plans of the elites and sends Jesus to Herod who, according to Luke, is present in Jerusalem and had been hoping to see Jesus perform a *sémeion* (miracle or sign).

As Herod is questioning Jesus at length, the Judean elites stand by "vehemently accusing him". Jesus refuses to answer Herod's questions and does not react to the accusations of the elites. (Note that an inferior's refusal to answer questions is a tacit claim to superiority in honour-shame societies.)

Herod and his guards mock Jesus, clothe him in a robe appropriate to royal status, and send him back to Pilate. This mocking of Jesus as "King of the Judeans" was a grievous insult to the elites so it is no surprise to find that, having made common cause against them, Luke reports that Herod and Pilate became friends whereas they had once been enemies. ("Friend", in that context, is a term implying a relationship of mutual benefaction.)

Pilate then calls together the chief priests, the leaders, and the people (the mob). The mob, incited by the elites, clamour for the release of a man called Barabbas in preference to Jesus. (Luke adds a parenthetical explanation that Barabbas had been thrown into prison for an insurrection in the city, and for murder.) Pilate attempts to thwart their plans three times but, in the end, he accedes to their demands. (See Matthew's account in previous pages for a cultural and contextual analysis of Pilate's interactions with Jesus, with the elites, and with the mob.)

Section 4

John's Account

John's account of these events includes more detailed information about the Judean establishment's involvement in the arrest and interrogation process. Consequently, it opens a wider window into their motivations so we will draw it into sharper focus.

John 11: 45-57

After hearing a disturbing report of the raising of Lazarus, the chief priests and the Pharisees call a meeting of the Sanhedrin. They express fears that if they allow Jesus to continue performing signs, many will believe in him and this will inevitably lead to intervention by the Romans who will "take away both our temple and our nation (Judean people)".

Caiaphas, who was "High Priest that year", is of the view that "it is better for you that one man die for the people than that the whole nation (Judean people) perish". John then explains that by making this statement, Caiaphas had unwittingly prophesied that not only would Jesus die for the Judean people but also that the scattered children of God (all Israelites) would be gathered together and united by his death. (See Part XV: *Resurrection*.)

From that day forward, the establishment plot to take the life of Jesus. Jesus is aware of this because he ceases to appear publicly among the people of Judea. As Passover approaches, "many" go up from the country to Jerusalem and wonder amongst themselves if Jesus will put in an appearance. John again tells us that the chief priests and Pharisees had given orders to be on the lookout for Jesus so they could take him into custody.

John 12:4-19

Mary, the sister of Lazarus, anoints the feet of Jesus with a quantity of the very expensive oil of spikenard. As keeper of the group's money, Judas protests that the oil should have been sold and the proceeds given to the poor. The author makes two parenthetical remarks. Firstly, he again describes Judas as the one who would betray Jesus (see 6:64, 71). Secondly, he asserts that Judas cares nothing for the poor and was known to divert money from the common fund for his own purposes. (John knows nothing about the thirty pieces of silver in the Synoptic accounts.)

We discover that the chief priests have decided to also kill Lazarus because his raising from the dead had resulted in "many" Judeans believing in Jesus.

Upon reports that Jesus is on his way to Jerusalem, those who had witnessed the raising of Lazarus and those who had heard about the raising, together with a crowd who had come to celebrate Passover in the city, take up palm branches and go out to meet him. They hail Jesus as their king. The "Pharisees" bemoan that "the whole world has gone after him".

John 13:1-17:26

Before the Passover Festival, John tells us that Jesus knows his hour has come. He adds a parenthetical remark that Jesus loved his own right to the end. Unlike the Synoptics, John does not mention any of Jesus' preparation instructions for the Last Supper. The "evening meal" is already in progress when John begins his account of proceedings.

Satan has already entered into the heart of Judas and prompted him to betray Jesus. Judas has unwittingly fulfilled Psalm 41:9 by his actions, "Even my close friend, whom I trusted, he who shared my bread, has lifted up his heel against me". Jesus tells the disciples that one of them will betray him. When they question him, rather than identify Judas by name, Jesus responds obliquely by giving them a signal—the one to whom he gives a piece of dipped bread is the one who will betray him. When Jesus gives the bread to Judas, we are again told that Satan prompted the betrayal. By here identifying Judas as the son of "Simon Iscariot", John embeds Judas within a family group. (Note that in this honour-shame society, any shame attaching to Judas would also fall upon his family, who would be obligated to restore family honour by some means.)

John emphasises that Judas leaves "at night", again signifying that this betrayal is by stealth. The very fact that he leaves at all is proof that Judas has yielded to Satan's deceptions. (Abnormal behaviour, whether good or bad, was usually attributed to some external force. As Judas begins to act completely out of character with his previous identification as "one of the twelve", his abnormal behaviour is attributed to Satan.)

As in the Synoptics, Jesus predicts Peter's disloyalty.

John then provide us with an extended account of Jesus' final discourse to his disciples and his practical examples of how they should behave towards one another. Most readers would be well aware of the sayings of Jesus found in this section so we will make no further comment except to remark that we are left with the impression that the disciples are not only mystified by the exchanges between Jesus and Judas but also that they do not fully understand the symbolic language style preferred by Jesus.

John 18:1-18

Jesus and his disciples cross the Kidron Valley and enter the Garden of Gethsemane. Judas, "the traitor", knows that the group often met there at night so he guides "a detachment of soldiers (temple military not Roman) and some officials from the chief priests and the Pharisees to the garden". Jesus identifies himself to the arresting party and asks that the disciples not be arrested with him. Simon Peter intervenes and strikes Malchus, a servant of the High Priest. Jesus commands him to put away his sword.

The arresting party takes Jesus into custody, binds him, and first brings him to Annas, the father-in-law of Caiaphas. John again reminds us that Caiaphas was High Priest that year and also that Caiaphas was the one who had "advised the Judean leaders that it would be good if one man died for the people". (Annas had been the former High Priest and, as pointed out previously, still held a measure of authority.)

John here introduces another participant in the story. Peter and "another disciple" follow Jesus. This "other disciple" is known to the High Priest so he is allowed into the courtyard while Peter remains outside at the gate until this other disciple intervenes and Peter is then allowed entry. The guard at the gate asks Peter if he belongs to the Jesus group. Peter denies that he does. (As in the Synoptic accounts, Peter denies Jesus a second and third time "before the rooster crows".)

The disciple whom Jesus loved

The identity of John's "other disciple" is a question that has troubled the minds of scholars for many generations. Although we cannot know with certainty, it is certainly possible to make reasonable inferences based on the following factors:

- The "other disciple" is one who is known to the High Priest, and whose word is sufficient to gain entry to the High Priest's courtyard. Such a person can only be a member of the Judean elites;
- The "one whom Jesus loves" is present at the last meal and reclines next to him. It is therefore likely that he accompanied Jesus and the other disciples to Gethsemane and, along with Peter, followed Jesus after his arrest;
- The "one whom Jesus loves" is present at the crucifixion (John 19:26) and is the same person as "other disciple" (John 20:2);
- The "one whom Jesus loves" has already been identified as Lazarus by John (John 11:3, 36).

All these factors point to Lazarus as the most likely candidate for the "other disciple" since, as far as we know, he is the only follower of Jesus who could be considered a member of the Judean elites.

John 18:19-24

John has already recorded in verse 13 that Caiaphas was High Priest that year, yet in verse 19 he names Annas as the High Priest. (This would lead us to assume that the title of "High Priest" could be held by more than one man at one time and again witnesses to the degree of authority still held by Annas.)

Annas questions Jesus "about his disciples and his teaching". Jesus responds by saying that he had spoken openly in the synagogues and in the temple so why doesn't Annas ask those who had heard him speak? An inferior's refusal to answer questions is a tacit claim to superiority in honour-shame societies so by refusing to answer Annas directly, Jesus has broken the rules and dishonoured the High Priest. An official strikes him in the face, a corresponding dishonour. Jesus reacts to this blow by asking a question to which Annas can have no suitable rejoinder and which, in effect, catches Annas on the horns of a dilemma:

> "…If what I said is wrong, bear witness about the wrong; but if what I said is right, why do you strike me?" (John 18:23 ESV).

With nothing determined, Annas finally sends him to Caiaphas. John does not tell us the outcome of Jesus' appearance before Caiaphas but passes straight on to Pilate.

Interrogation by Pilate

John 18:28-40; 19:1-16

The Judean leaders take Jesus from Caiaphas to the official residence of the Roman Governor (the Praetorium) early in the morning of the day before the Passover Feast which will begin at sundown, i.e. the next day according to the reckoning of 24-hour days at that time.

In order to avoid ritual defilement and render themselves unclean to eat the Passover meal, the Judean leaders will not enter. As noted previously, the relationship between Pilate and the Jerusalem priesthood was one of mutual loathing and hostility. John here gives us an insight into one of the factors underpinning such animosity—it would defile the Jerusalem priesthood to enter Pilate's unclean residence. Given that the "civilised" Romans are masters of most of the known world, and given that the Judeans and their "barbaric" customs are merely the insignificant people of a remote outpost of empire, Pilate's state of mind at this insult can only be imagined.

However, the Romans rely on the Judean elites to help maintain order, so it is Pilate's duty to meet with them. He goes "outside" and asks what charges they bring against Jesus. They reply, in effect, that if Jesus were not already guilty, they would not have brought him to Pilate. Pilate's response that the Judeans should condemn Jesus by their own laws allows the real issue to surface—the Judeans could not make the charge of "blasphemy" stick so they want Jesus executed for claiming to be a King.

Pilate summons Jesus "inside" Roman space, into the "unclean" Roman presence. Pilate's opening question confirms that the charge brought against Jesus is his claim to be King of the Judeans. Jesus responds by asking whether Pilate has followed his career himself, or whether he is simply repeating the accusations of his captors. Pilate's rejoinder, "Am I a Judean?" emphasises the fact that it was his fellow Judeans who had spied on Jesus and captured him as a criminal.

Jesus then responds to Pilate's initial question, "Are you the King of the Jews?":

> "…My kingdom is not of this world. If my kingdom were of this world, my servants would have been fighting, that I might not be delivered over to the Jews (Judeans). But my kingdom is not from the world" (John 18:36 ESV).

(See Part X.3.3: *Aftermath-Heaven-An Ethical Kingdom* for the various uses of the term "world" in John's Gospel.)

As Jesus has just stated that he has a kingdom, Pilate assumes he has his answer:

> Then Pilate said to him, "So you are a king?" Jesus answered, You say that I am a king. For this purpose I was born and for this purpose I have come into the

world—to bear witness to the truth. Everyone who is of the truth listens to my voice" (John 18:37 ESV).

Jesus has cleverly turned the question away from one of kingship towards one which, for Romans, more properly belongs in the realm of philosophy—truth versus lies. As a Roman, Pilate naturally retorts with that immortal rhetorical question, "What is truth?"

When he leaves the Praetorium, Pilate announces to the Judeans waiting outside that he finds no crime in Jesus. According to Roman trial procedures, this should have been the end of the matter. Pilate, however, has something else in mind—a public shaming of the Jerusalem elites by challenging their honour. In this honour-shame society, challenges to honour must be defended and so begins a back-and-forth trading of challenges and ripostes between Pilate, his soldiers, and the Judeans, beginning with Pilate's offer to release "the King of the Judeans" according to the custom of releasing a prisoner at Passover. Embedded in this offer is a two-fold insult to the Judeans:

- Firstly, Pilate names Jesus as the King of the very Judeans who had brought him to Pilate as a criminal;
- Secondly, by putting forward a low-born Galilean as the Judean King, Pilate has heaped on Judean heads insult upon insult.

The Judean response is equally insulting both to Pilate and to Rome: they prefer the thief Barabbas, an enemy of Roman order. Pilate's response to this insult is to have Jesus scourged. The soldiers dressing Jesus up as a King and mocking him is their response to the Judean insults to Pilate's honour.

Pilate once again comes out of the Praetorium and once again tells the Judeans that he finds no basis for a charge against Jesus. He then offers another insult by publicly presenting Jesus clothed as a mock king. The chief priests and Temple officials are outraged to see Jesus dressed like their king and they shout, "Crucify! Crucify!"

With their renewed insistence on Jesus' public humiliation, Pilate tells them to crucify Jesus themselves (the subtext here is "if you dare" since that act would be a challenge to Roman authority). Pilate pronounces a verdict of innocence a third time. Now the Judeans revert to the original charge of blasphemy:

> "The Jews answered him, "We have a law, and according to that law he ought to die because he has made himself the Son of God" (John 19:7 ESV).

This clever introduction of the term "son of God" reminds Pilate that one of the titles of the current Emperor Tiberius is *Divi filius* (son of a god).

John records that Pilate now becomes *"more* afraid". If Pilate becomes *more* afraid at this point, when did he first begin to have an apprehension about Jesus? It is obvious by his next question to Jesus—"Where are you from?"—that his apprehension originally stemmed from Jesus' previous interactions with him, which are quite remarkable given their context. Being a man of authority himself, he realises that Jesus has not responded in a manner befitting a social inferior but as a man possessing authority, as a social equal, answering questions either obliquely or with questions of his own. Jesus is thus an unknown quantity to Pilate, a man whose real origins cannot be fathomed, a source of apprehension for any superstitious Roman. Now his original apprehension has been heightened by the Judeans' insinuation that Jesus has claimed a title properly belonging to the Emperor.

Jesus' refusal to quell his apprehension and answer the question about his origins challenges Pilate's honour because silence is a tacit claim to superiority. This refusal calls forth Pilate's remonstration that he has the superior authority, the authority of life or death. Jesus responds that God is the source of all power and that Pilate would have no power over Jesus if it had not been given to him "from above".

The Judeans had hoped that Pilate's hand would be forced by their insinuation that Jesus had claimed a title belonging to the Emperor but they had not reckoned with the Roman superstitious nature which, after this last exchange with Jesus, governs Pilate's final intention to release him. The Judean leaders will not be denied and now challenge Pilate himself:

> …"If you release this man, you are not Caesar's friend. Everyone who makes himself a king opposes Caesar" (John 19:12 ESV).

Now that his allegiance to Caesar is challenged, concern for his own honour overcomes all apprehension deriving from his superstitious Roman nature. However, before yielding to the Judeans, he delivers one final insult to their honour by referring to Jesus as "your King":

> When Pilate heard this, he brought Jesus out and sat down on the judge's seat at a place known as the Stone Pavement (which in Aramaic is Gabbatha). It was the day of Preparation of the Passover; it was about noon. "Here is your king," Pilate said to the Jews. But they shouted, "Take him away! Take him away! Crucify him!" "Shall I crucify your king?" Pilate asked. "We have no king but Caesar," the chief priests answered. Finally Pilate handed him over to them to be crucified (John 19:13-16 NIV).

Blasphemy Notes

Whereas the Synoptic Gospels note that other charges were levelled against Jesus, only the author of John specifies that the charge was "blasphemy". As noted above, the precise reason for this charge was:

> "The Jews answered him, "We have a law, and according to that law he ought to die because he has made himself the Son of God" (John 19:7 ESV).

When Jesus was originally accused of blasphemy for claiming to be the son of God, he had quoted a passage from Psalm 82:6 demonstrating that their accusation was false because those to whom the word of God came were themselves regarded as "gods" or "exalted ones":

> Jesus answered them, "Is it not written in your law, I said, Ye are gods? If he called them gods, unto whom the word of God came, and the scripture cannot be broken; Say ye of him, whom the Father hath sanctified, and sent into the world, Thou blasphemest; because I said, I am the Son of God?" (John 10:34-36 KJV cf. Psalm 82:6)

As his accusers level this same charge before Pilate, they already know it to be false and merely a pretext for his arrest.

Rabbi Morris Goldstein agrees that claiming to be a "son of God" did not constitute blasphemy:

> According to the Mishnah,[8] only misuse of the Tetragram, the sacrosanct name of God, constitutes blasphemy. [9]

Consider also Paul's statement in Acts 13:27-28:

> For those who live in Jerusalem, and their rulers, recognizing neither him nor the utterances of the prophets which are read every Sabbath, fulfilled these by condemning him. And though they found no ground for putting him to death, they asked Pilate that He be executed (Acts 13:27-28 NASB).

---

8   *Mishnah.* The primary work of Jewish legal theory collected and categorised circa 200 AD.

9   Goldstein, Rabbi Morris. *Jesus in the Jewish Tradition.* Macmillan: New York, 1950, p 26.

CHAPTER EIGHT

Crucifixion

Section 1

Matthew's Account

Matthew 27:32-50

As they go out (from the City) the Romans *compel* a Simon from Cyrene to carry the cross. (Taking into account descriptions of criminals carrying cross beams by the ancient Roman authors Plautus and Plutarch, modern scholars take this to mean that only the cross beam (*patibulum*) is intended here.) As the cross beam belongs to Rome, the word *compel* here accurately reflects the Roman soldiers' entitlement to have the local population carry their gear for one Roman mile (about a thousand paces).

Matthew tells us that the crucifixion site is called "Golgotha" (cf. Hebrew: *gulgoleth*) and adds a parenthetical explanation that the word means "place of a skull" (Greek: *kranion*). He then alludes to two Psalms in succession:

> There they offered Jesus wine (Greek: *oinos*) to drink, mixed with gall (Greek: *cholē*); but after tasting it, he refused to drink it (Matthew 27:34 NIV cf. Psalm 69:21).
>
> And they crucified him, and parted his garments, casting lots: that it might be fulfilled which was spoken by the prophet, They parted my garments among them, and upon my vesture did they cast lots (Matthew 27:35 KJV cf. Psalm 22:18).

Items of clothing, all stitched by hand, were of supreme importance in this society of limited goods being, as they so often were, one's only possessions.

All four Gospels record that an inscribed sign was placed over the head of Jesus. This sign, known as a *titulus* (Latin for "legal charge"), served two purposes: firstly, by declaring Jesus as the King of the very Judeans who had brought him to Pilate as a criminal, it served as the ultimate Roman insult to the Judean elites and, secondly, it served as a warning to those who would take Rome's place in the governorship of Judea.

While all four Gospels tell us that Jesus was crucified between two men, only Matthew, Mark and Luke identify them as either "thieves" or "criminals". John simply says "two others".

Matthew once again alludes to the Psalms in the following passages:

> Then were there two thieves crucified with him, one on the right hand, and another on the left. And they that passed by reviled him, wagging their heads (cf. Psalm 22:7), And saying, Thou that destroyest the temple, and buildest it in three days, save thyself. If thou be the Son of God, come down from the cross. Likewise also the chief priests mocking him, with the scribes and elders, said, He saved others; himself he cannot save. If he be the King of Israel, let him now come down from the cross, and we will believe him. He trusted in God; let him deliver him now, if he will have him: for he said, I am the Son of God. The thieves also, which were crucified with him, cast the same in his teeth (Matthew 27:38-44 KJV).

This is the high point of satisfaction for those who plotted it all from the beginning. There can be no greater revenge than what is described here. As Jesus hangs naked and nailed to a Roman cross he is subject to the utmost in public humiliation while his enemies—the chief priests, scribes and elders—gloat and deride him. While Matthew and Mark tell us that two malefactors join in the taunting, Luke tells a different story (see Part X.3.4: *Aftermath-Heaven-Paradise* for Luke's version of events).

> From noon until three in the afternoon darkness came over all the land. About three in the afternoon Jesus cried out in a loud voice, "Eli, Eli, lemasabachthani? (which means "My God, my God, why have you forsaken me?" cf. Psalm 22:1). When some of those standing there heard this, they said, "He's calling Elijah." Immediately one of them ran and got a sponge. He filled it with wine vinegar, put it on a staff, and offered it to Jesus to drink (cf. Psalm 69:21). The rest said, "Now leave him alone. Let's see if Elijah comes to save him." And when Jesus had cried out again in a loud voice, he gave up his spirit. (Matthew 27:45-50 NIV).

The Signs

Matthew 27:51-54

Surrounding the death of Jesus are a number of signs indicative of God's presence.

The first of these, the previous reference to three hours of darkness over all the land in verse 45, is most likely a *Midrashic* analogy to the ninth plague of Egypt when three days of darkness over all the land was one of the signs of Israelite deliverance from Egyptian bondage (Exodus 10:21-22).

This author has translated the following verses from the Greek in order to draw attention to Matthew's use of five passive voice verbs in succession:

> And behold the veil of the sanctuary *was torn* in two from top to bottom and the land (of Israel) *was shaken* and the rocks *were split* and the tombs *were opened* and many bodies of the saints (Greek: *hagios*: sacred, holy) who had fallen asleep *were raised* (Matthew 27:51-52 Author translation).

The use of passive voice verbs to describe divine acts is a pious convention intended to avoid accidentally invoking the name of God.[10] This use of the "divine passive" (*passivum divinum*) is a feature that is very common in Matthew. Thus it is God who rends the veil, shakes the earth, splits the rocks, opens the tombs, and raises the dead. Whilst drawing attention to the New Testament use of the "divine passive" may appear unnecessary in this context, its significance will become apparent when considering the accounts of Resurrection appearances. (See Part XV.4: *Resurrection-The eye-witnesses.*)

One of the most prominent themes of Matthew's Gospel is his affirmation that Jesus fulfilled prophecy, evidenced by his use of at least fifty quotations and allusions to the Hebrew Scriptures sprinkled throughout the text. Based on the multiple allusions to Ezekiel 37, Daniel 12 and Isaiah 26 (and possibly other texts) found in the passage above, it is clear that he never intended any of these signs to be taken literally. Rather, he is using *Midrashic* analogies to anticipate and describe the transition to new life that the Resurrection of Jesus will foreshadow for all Israel.

The Rending of the Veil

Matthew states that the veil of the sanctuary (Greek: *naos*) was torn in two from top to bottom. The use of the word *naos* (properly a divine dwelling place) indicates that the veil to which Matthew refers must be the inner veil that separated the Holy of

---

10 The word "Heaven," as in Matthew's "Kingdom of Heaven", is another pious substitute for the word "God".

Holies from the Holy Place rather than the outer veil that covered the entrance to the Holy Place and separated it from the outer Court.

The sanctuary to which Matthew refers is the heavenly sanctuary after which the earthly sanctuary is patterned. The rending of its veil from top to bottom symbolises the removal of the barrier between God and man. Consider this passage from the Book of Hebrews:

> But when the Messiah came as a high priest of the good things that have come, he went through the greater and more perfect tent that was not made by human hands and that is not a part of this creation. Not with the blood of goats and calves, but with his own blood he went into the Most Holy Place once for all and secured our eternal redemption…
>
> Thus it was necessary for these earthly copies of the things in heaven to be cleansed by these sacrifices, but the heavenly things themselves are made clean with better sacrifices than these. For the Messiah did not go into a sanctuary made by human hands that is merely a copy of the true one, but into heaven itself, to appear now in God's presence on our behalf (Hebrews 9:11-12, 23-24 ISV).

The Raising of the Holy Ones

The coming resurrection of Jesus foreshadows the promised resurrection of all Israelites and their return to the land of Israel. The shaking of the land and the splitting of the rocks symbolically opens the graves and prepares the way for this promised resurrection. Matthew's symbolism is drawn mainly from Ezekiel 37, Daniel 12 and Isaiah 26. Consider Ezekiel's vision of the Valley of Dry Bones and the shaking (Hebrew: *raash*-used of earthquakes):

> So I prophesied as I was commanded: and as I prophesied, there was a noise, and behold a shaking (*raash*), and the bones came together, bone to his bone (Ezekiel 37:7 KJV).
>
> Therefore prophesy and say unto them, Thus saith the Lord GOD; Behold, O my people, I will open your graves, and cause you to come up out of your graves, and bring you into the land of Israel (Ezekiel 37:12 KJV).

Consider also the following passages from Daniel 12 and Isaiah 26, which are alluded to several times by New Testament authors including Matthew:

> And many of them that sleep in the dust of the earth shall awake, some to

everlasting life, and some to shame and everlasting contempt (Daniel 12:2 KJV cf. Matthew 25:46; John 5:28-29, 11:24; Acts 24:15).

But your dead will live, Lord; their bodies will rise—let those who dwell in the dust wake up and shout for joy—your dew is like the dew of the morning; the earth will give birth to her dead (Isaiah 26:9 NIV).

The resurrected ones come out of the tombs "after" Jesus' resurrection":

They came out of the tombs *after* Jesus' resurrection and went into the holy city and appeared to many people. When the centurion and those with him who were guarding Jesus saw the earthquake and all that had happened, they were terrified, and exclaimed, "Surely he was the Son of God!"(Matthew 27:53-54 NIV).

This further confirms that verses 51-54 are anticipatory symbolic descriptions of the impact of the resurrection of Jesus and the consequent resurrection of many Israelites to come whose entry into the holy city foreshadows their return to the land of Israel.

By putting words into the mouth of a Roman, who serves the purpose of validating Matthew's previous descriptions of Jesus as a son of God, he goes one step further and claims that the resurrection will also impact non-Israelites.

Matthew mentions Galilean women who see everything "from a distance". Among these women are Mary Magdalene, Mary the mother of James and Joseph, and the mother of Zebedee's sons (James and John: Matthew 10:2). Two of them, Mary Magdalene and the "other" Mary, will soon be witnesses at the tomb (verse 61).

Section 2

Mark's Account

Mark's account of the crucifixion is virtually the same as that of Matthew so it is not necessary to repeat ourselves except to note the differences.

1. In Matthew's account, Jesus is mocked because he claimed to be a "son of God". In Mark, we find them mocking his claim to be the "Messiah, the King of Israel". On its surface, this variation may appear inconsequential yet it is of vital importance when considering the major claims of mainstream theology. (See Part V.4: T*he Divine Court-Appeals to Descriptions and Titles.*)
2. Unlike Matthew, Mark uses only two signs indicative of God's Presence—the rending of the Temple Veil and the validation by a Roman. Like

Matthew, however, Mark also anticipates and symbolically describes the impact that the resurrection will have on Israelites and non-Israelites alike.

3. Among Mark's Galilean women who were looking on "from a distance" are Mary Magdalene, Mary the mother of James the younger and Joseph, and Salome who is substituted for Matthew's "mother of Zebedee's sons". (This may be the same woman but we have no way of knowing for certain.) As in Matthew, the two Marys will soon be witnesses at the tomb.

Section 3

Luke's Account

Compared to the accounts of Matthew and Mark, Luke omits little but adds much. Luke introduces his Gospel by stating that he has "investigated everything carefully from the beginning" using material originally sourced from eyewitnesses. This forensic approach may account for the inclusion of details missing from Matthew and Mark. (See Part IV.4,5,6:*Virgin Birth and Incarnation-The Gospel of Luke I, II, III* for an analysis of Luke's insider knowledge and impeccable sources.)

Luke 23:26-49

As in Matthew and Mark, Simon from Cyrene was compelled to carry the cross beam. Luke adds that Simon was "coming from the country" and that he was positioned "behind Jesus".

A "great number" of people follow Jesus, among whom are women beating their breasts and wailing on account of him. Breast-beating was normally a gesture of women, being used by men only in the most dire of circumstances, according to Josephus (*Antiquities* 7.252).

But Jesus turned to them and said:

> …Daughters of Jerusalem, weep not for me, but weep for yourselves, and for your children. For, behold, the days are coming, in the which they shall say, Blessed are the barren, and the wombs that never bare, and the paps which never gave suck. Then shall they begin to say to the mountains, Fall on us; and to the hills, Cover us. For if they do these things in a green tree, what shall be done in the dry? (Luke 23:28-31 KJV).

In this passage, Jesus quotes or alludes to the Hebrew Scriptures several times and also make a veiled reference to his role as Messiah:

- The expression "daughters of Jerusalem" is found several times in the Song of Solomon;

- Jesus foreshadows the impending destruction of Jerusalem in 70 AD by quoting this passage from Hosea 10:8, "Then they will say to the mountains, 'Cover us!' and to the hills, 'Fall on us!'" In sharp contrast to the prevailing attitudes of his day, so terrible will be this destruction that childless women will regard themselves as blessed. (Note that nowhere in the New Testament is the destruction of Jerusalem referred to as a past event. See Part II.5: *The Documents-Dating the New Testament Documents*);

- His reference to the green and dry trees is taken from Ezekiel 20:47 where the prophet envisions a destruction so encompassing that it will burn even the green trees, "...I am about to set fire to you, and it will consume all your trees, both green and dry..." The people who heard these words understood their essential meaning—"If this terrible thing can happen to me, how much more to you?";

- At the same time, some of these people would have understood that Jesus was making a veiled reference to his Messianic role because the term "green tree" was interpreted by the sages of his day as a Messianic title.

As in Matthew and Mark, Luke alludes to the Psalms in his account of the crucifixion:

> Two other men, both criminals, were also led out with him to be executed. When they came to the place called the Skull, they crucified him there, along with the criminals—one on his right, the other on his left. Jesus said, "Father, forgive them, for they do not know what they are doing." And they divided up his clothes by casting lots (cf. Psalm 22:18). The people stood watching, and the rulers even sneered at him. They said, "He saved others; let him save himself if he is God's Messiah, the Chosen One." The soldiers also came up and mocked him. They offered him wine vinegar (cf. Psalm 69:21) and said, "If you are the king of the Jews, save yourself." There was a written notice above him, which read: THIS IS THE KING OF THE JEWS (Luke 23:33-38 NIV).

All four Gospels record that an inscribed sign was placed over the head of Jesus. This sign, known as a *titulus* (Latin for "legal charge"), served two purposes: firstly, by declaring Jesus as the King of the very Judeans who had brought him to Pilate as a criminal, it served as the ultimate Roman insult to the Judean elites and, secondly, it served as a warning to those who would take Rome's place in the governorship of Judea:

While Matthew, Mark and John refer briefly to two malefactors being crucified with Jesus, only Luke tells us an expanded version. One of these men joined in the mockery of Jesus but the other was reported to have exclaimed that while he was worthy of death, Jesus was not. The following exchange between the two men has been used countless times by advocates of an other-worldly Heaven:

> Then he said, "Jesus, remember me when you come into your kingdom." Jesus answered him, "Truly I tell you, today you will be with me in paradise (*paradeisos*)" (Luke 23:42-43 NIV).

For a comprehensive analysis of this passage, and its correct punctuation, see Part X.3: *Aftermath-Heaven*.

Like Matthew and Mark, Luke refers to the three hours of darkness "over all the land". He also provides us with a meaningful insight into Jesus the observant Jew by recording his cry from the cross which, even today, is part of a standard Jewish deathbed confession, "Into your hands I commit my spirit…" (Psalm 31:5).

Like Mark, he does not refer to any of Matthew's other signs but only to the rending of the Temple veil and to the statement by the Roman. The centurion does not validate Jesus as either a son of God or the Messiah, as in Matthew and Mark, but simply refers to him as a "righteous" man. Given the polytheistic world of the Romans, it is interesting that Luke has him take a step further and validate the one God of Israel:

> Now when the centurion saw what was done, he glorified God, saying, Certainly this was a righteous man (Luke 23:47 KJV).

Luke records that "all his acquaintances", as well as the women who followed him from Galilee, watched from a distance.

Section 4

John's Account

As pointed out elsewhere in this work, John portrays Jesus as the representative of God's values, and portrays the Judean priestly establishment centred in Jerusalem as the representative of the opposite values. For example, truth versus lies; the spirit of the law rather than the letter; humility versus arrogance; personal integrity versus institutional formalism. These values of God and Jesus are those which should be reflected in the behaviour of Israel as a community. We therefore find that John's crucifixion account is not designed around a chronology of events but rather around the symbols and fulfillment statements which will appeal to the shared history and shared values of his community of Jesus followers.

John 19:16-37

Like Matthew, Mark and Luke, John states that the place of crucifixion was called "Golgotha". Unlike the Synoptic authors, however, John does not mention Simon from Cyrene but states that Jesus carried his cross (cross-beam) *himself*, thus implying that Jesus had purposes of his own.

He passes over the act of crucifixion rather quickly in order to emphasise the act of placing and lifting the cross of Jesus between two others. This emphasis is designed to draw our attention to the statement made by Jesus in John 3:14:

> And as Moses lifted up the serpent in the wilderness, even so must the Son of man be lifted up (John 3:14 KJV).

Jesus is here alluding to a passage from the Book of Numbers:

> And the LORD said to Moses, "Make a fiery serpent and set it on a pole, and everyone who is bitten, when he sees it, shall live." So Moses made a bronze serpent and set it on a pole. And if a serpent bit anyone, he would look at the bronze serpent and live (Numbers 21:8 ESV).

Jesus is "lifted up" so all Israel assembled for the Passover Festival may see him and live.

All four Gospels record that an inscribed sign was placed over the head of Jesus:

> Pilate also wrote an inscription and put it on the cross. It was written, 'JESUS THE NAZARENE, THE KING OF THE JEWS'. Therefore many of the Jews read this inscription, for the place where Jesus was crucified was near the city; and it was written in Hebrew, Latin and in Greek. So the chief priests of the Jews were saying to Pilate, "Do not write, 'The King of the Jews'; but that He said, 'I am King of the Jews'. Pilate answered, "What I have written I have written" (John 19:19-22 NASB).

Note: The New American Standard version is chosen for reproduction above as it is one of the few which translate the Greek word Ἑβραϊστί *(Hebraisti)* correctly as "Hebrew" whereas most versions render Ἑβραϊστί as "Aramaic".

Throughout his Gospel, John has drawn attention to Jesus' origins in Nazareth so he adds the words "Jesus of Nazareth" to the *titulus*, offering an even more grievous insult to the Judean establishment. Not only is Jesus presented as their King but also as one hailing from Galilee, from a class of people considered to be uneducated peasants.

Only John notes that "many" Judeans read the sign, that the crucifixion site was "near the city", and that the *titulus* was written in "Hebrew, Latin and Greek". These three languages reflect the population then present in Jerusalem: Judeans (Hebrew); Romans (Latin); and Diaspora Israelites present in Jerusalem for Passover (Greek).

We are told that the chief priests are so outraged at the *titulus* insult that they ask Pilate to amend the wording. Of course Pilate refuses: he has already gained a level of satisfaction for the previous insults offered to Rome by the Judean elites and he now presses home his advantage.

Roman soldiers had a legal right to a condemned persons belongings. The soldiers divide the four outer garments between themselves but they cast lots for the inner garment, the seamless tunic (Greek: *chitōn*). These events are singled out by John for a special emphasis not found in the Synoptics, allowing him to once again take up his theme that they were foretold and therefore a fulfillment of scripture:

> They divide my clothes among them and cast lots for my garment (Psalm 22:18 NIV).

The tearing of a garment can point to a division between groups as, for instance, when the prophet Ahijah tears his garment into twelve pieces, symbolising coming Israelite tribal divisions (see I Kings 11:30). By drawing special attention to the undivided tunic, John is signalling to his Jesus community that not even the Romans have the power to cause division between them.

Women represented no threat to Roman order and we find that fact reflected in all four Gospels which tell of women permitted to witness the crucifixion, although the Synoptics have them watching from a distance. These women are significant characters in the Gospel stories because they serve as witnesses to Jesus' crucifixion, death, burial, and the empty tomb.

John, however, tells a different story. Rather than watching from a distance, the women are near enough to interact with Jesus. John introduces these women as the "mother of Jesus", his mother's sister, Mary (the wife) of Clopas, and Mary Magdalene. John then introduces "the disciple whom Jesus loved", who seems to emerge out of nowhere and is somehow attached to "mother of Jesus".

When Jesus sees the pair standing together, he addresses them both:

> When Jesus saw his mother and the disciple whom he loved standing nearby, he said to his mother, "Woman, behold, your son!" Then he said to the disciple,

"Behold, your mother!" And from that hour the disciple took her to his own home (John 19:26-27 ESV).

Given the consistent use of symbols and scriptural allusions designed to draw on his readers' shared history and tradition, we must suspect that John is telling us something more than would be apparent from a cursory reading of this passage.

In accordance with the collectivist culture of the day, persons who represent some typical quality are often deliberately left unnamed by John to heighten that particular quality. What, then, do the qualities that the "mother of Jesus" and the "disciple whom Jesus loved" represent?

The "mother of Jesus"

The unnamed "mother of Jesus" was present at the wedding in Cana and now is present at the crucifixion. (In both cases, Jesus addressed her simply as "woman".) As John has now referred to the unnamed "mother of Jesus" for a second time, we can assume he is signalling to his readers that this woman holds a symbolic significance far deeper than that indicated by a simple biological relationship.

Many times throughout the scriptures we find a woman symbolising all Israel. For example, both John and Matthew view Jesus' ride into Jerusalem as a fulfillment of a well-known passage from the Book of Zechariah where the "daughter of Zion" and the daughter of Jerusalem are symbols of Israel:

> Rejoice greatly, O daughter of Zion! Shout aloud, O daughter of Jerusalem! Behold, your king is coming to you; righteous and having salvation is he, humble and mounted on a donkey, on a colt, the foal of a donkey. (Zechariah 9:9 ESV cf. John 12:15, Matthew 21:5).

Consider also the following passage from Jeremiah, quoted by Matthew, where Rachel represents all the mothers in Israel:

> Thus says the LORD: "A voice is heard in Ramah, lamentation and bitter weeping. Rachel is weeping for her children; she refuses to be comforted for her children, because they are no more" (Jeremiah 31:15 ESV c.f. Matthew 2:18).

Especially significant in this context is a passage from Revelation Chapter 12. To correctly identify the woman in this passage, it is necessary to refer back to Genesis 37:9-10 where we find that the sun, the moon, and the twelve stars represent Joseph's father Jacob, his mother Rachel, and his eleven brothers. In other words, the whole house of Israel:

> And there appeared a great wonder in heaven; a woman clothed with the sun,

> and the moon under her feet, and upon her head a crown of twelve star. And she being with child cried, travailing in birth, and pained to be delivered. And there appeared another wonder in heaven; and behold a great red dragon, having seven heads and ten horns, and seven crowns upon his heads. And his tail drew the third part of the stars of heaven, and did cast them to the earth: and the dragon stood before the woman which was ready to be delivered, for to devour her child as soon as it was born. And she brought forth a man child, who was to rule all nations with a rod of iron: and her child was caught up unto God, and to his throne (Revelation 12:1-5 KJV).

Regardless of biology, the "mother of Jesus" symbolises all Israel. All Israel has given birth to the Messiah and has therefore been symbolically present at his birth and now at his death. She represents the qualities of the Israelite who will continue to remain faithful to Jesus, regardless of circumstance, from birth to death, from beginning to end.

The "disciple whom Jesus loves"

As the beloved disciple is the only disciple present at the crucifixion and the one to whom Jesus entrusts "his mother", he represents the qualities of trust, loyalty, and love. Just as the care of the "mother of Jesus" can be entrusted to the disciple, so also can the care of the Jesus group community be entrusted to him; just as he has remained loyal to Jesus even to the extent of endangering his own life by being the only male present at the crucifixion, so also will he remain loyal to the Jesus group community even in the most dire of circumstances; just as he has demonstrated abiding love to Jesus, so also will he demonstrate that love to the community and obey Jesus' final instruction to "love one another as I have loved you".

Then:

> After this, Jesus, knowing that all things had already been accomplished, to fulfill the Scripture, said, "I am thirsty." A jar full of sour wine was standing there; so they put a sponge full of the sour wine upon a branch of hyssop and brought it up to His mouth. Therefore when Jesus had received the sour wine, He said, "It is finished!" And He bowed His head and gave up His spirit (John 19:28-30 NASB).

Jesus is aware that his work, everything that was expected of him, is now fully accomplished. To fulfill the scripture one last time, he says "I thirst". This statement, together with the triple mention of the "sour wine" (vinegar) are allusions to Psalm 69:21, "They put gall in my food and gave me vinegar for my thirst".

There is a much deeper significance to the final words of Jesus than a first reading would suggest. What John intends to convey can be discovered by referring back to Chapter Seven:

> On the last and greatest day of the festival (the Feast of Tabernacles), Jesus stood and said in a loud voice, "Let anyone who is thirsty come to me and drink. Whoever believes in me, as Scripture has said, rivers of living water will flow from within them." By this he meant the Spirit, whom those who believed in him were later to receive. Up to that time the Spirit had not been given, since Jesus had not yet been glorified (John 7:37-39 NIV).

Prior to his death and resurrection, the "spirit" had not yet been given to those who believe in Jesus. At the resurrection, Jesus is "glorified" and the "spirit" is passed on at Pentecost to the believers.

John records none of the signs accompanying the death of Jesus that we find in the Synoptic Gospels but moves quickly on to his most important theme—the conflict of values between Jesus and the Jerusalem elites. The elites, he tells us, have plans for Jesus even in death and have been considering the consequences of having him hanging on the cross on the day of Preparation. They wish to hasten his death and remove him from sight before sundown in order to keep holy a "great Sabbath", i.e. a Sabbath on which the Passover also falls. This atmosphere of haste certainly rings true given what we know about the laws relating to work on the Sabbath day, especially on a "great Sabbath", and the law that bodies of executed criminals must be buried before sunset:

> And if a man has committed a crime punishable by death and he is put to death, and you hang him on a tree, his body shall not remain all night on the tree, but you shall bury him the same day, for a hanged man is cursed by God (Deuteronomy 21:22-23 ESV).

The elites ask Pilate to have the legs of the crucified men broken and their bodies removed. (Breaking the legs of a crucified person hastened death by suffocation.) Having already gained satisfaction for their previous insults to Rome, and knowing that he will soon require their assistance to maintain order during the Passover festival, Pilate agrees.

> So the soldiers came, and broke the legs of the first man and of the other who was crucified with Him; but coming to Jesus, when they saw that He was already dead, they did not break His legs. But one of the soldiers pierced His side with a spear, and immediately blood and water came out. And he who has seen has testified, and his testimony is true; and he knows that he is telling the truth, so that you also may believe. For these things came to pass to fulfill the

Scripture, "Not a bone of him shall be broken." And again another Scripture says, "They shall look on him whom they have pierced" (John 19:32-37 NASB cf. Zechariah 12:10; Revelation 1:7).

These two features—not breaking the legs and piercing the side—are omitted from the other Gospels. For John, however, they are so important that he immediately makes a witness statement testifying to their truth in order to underscore one of his central themes that Jesus is the "Lamb of God who takes away the sins of the world" (John 1:29; 1:36). Note that, in this in-group context, the "sins of the world" is the sin of Israel's dishonouring of the God of Israel.

To understand why this theme assumed such central importance for John, we must first revisit the Israelite deliverance from Egyptian bondage. The Exodus occupies such a central place in both the Hebrew Scriptures and the New Testament that the account of the Passover Lamb sacrifice merits reproducing at length:

> Then Moses summoned all the elders of Israel and told them, "Choose sheep for your families, and slaughter the Passover lamb. Take a bundle of hyssop and dip it in the blood that is in the basin, and apply some of the blood in the basin to the lintel and the two doorposts. None of you is to go out of the doorway of his house until morning, because the LORD will pass through to strike down the Egyptians, and when he sees the blood on the lintel and the two doorposts, the LORD will pass over the doorway, and won't allow the destroyer to enter your houses to strike you down. You are to observe this event as a perpetual ordinance for you and your children forever. When you enter the land that the LORD will give you, just as he promised, you are to observe this ritual. And when your children say to you, 'What does this ritual mean?' you are to say, 'It is the Passover sacrifice to the LORD, who passed over the houses of the Israelis in Egypt when he struck down the Egyptians but spared our houses.'" Then the people bowed down and worshipped (Exodus 12:21-27 ISV).

> The Lord said to Moses and Aaron, "These are the regulations for the Passover meal: No foreigner may eat it. Any slave you have bought may eat it after you have circumcised him, but a temporary resident or a hired worker may not eat it. It must be eaten inside the house; take none of the meat outside the house. Do not break any of the bones. The whole community of Israel must celebrate it" (Exodus 12:43-47 NIV).

When we read this Exodus account, it is clear why John has drawn attention to these two features. By not breaking the legs of Jesus, the soldiers unwittingly drew a parallel between Jesus and the Passover sacrificial lamb, the bones of which must not be broken and by piercing the side of Jesus and causing an "immediate" flow of blood and water, the soldier unwittingly drew a parallel with the blood of the sacrificial lamb which protected the Israelites from death. John reasoned that, just as in the days of Moses when the Lamb's blood was sprinkled on the doorframes with a bunch of hyssop to protect the Israelites from physical death, so also the blood of Jesus, the Lamb of God, will symbolically protect the followers of Jesus from spiritual death. (Note also John's previous mention of "hyssop" in 19:29.)

The secondary significance of this last feature is John's attestation that the "blood and water" came out *immediately*, i.e. *spurted*. This is an allusion to the scribal Pharasaic requirements for the fitness quality of a sacrificial animal. If blood spurts forth when it is found dead, or at the point of death, the animal is declared to be a fitting sacrifice.

In addition to the theme of the Passover sacrificial lamb embedded in John's crucifixion account, consideration should also be given to at least two of the additional sacrificial allusions found in John's Gospel:

- It is the paramount function of the priest to serve God in the Temple by the offering of sacrifices. It is not surprising therefore to find that, throughout John's account, it is the High Priest and other chief priests who orchestrate the death of Jesus, thus unintentionally offering up Jesus as a fitting sacrifice upon the altar;

- Jesus is bound when arrested (18:12) just like Isaac, the son of Abraham and Sarah who was bound prior to the intended sacrifice (see John 3:16; Genesis 22: 1-12). In Israelite lore, all sacrifices offered on Jerusalem's altar received their merit from the *Akedah* or "binding of Isaac". (See Part V.4.3: *The Divine Court-Appeals to Descriptions and Titles-The only-begotten son*.)

Although John does not mention a specific time of death, the Synoptic Gospels point to around 3 p.m. The Jewish Encyclopaedia states that the Passover Lambs were sacrificed on the eve of the Passover at 3 p.m or, in case the Passover fell on a Friday, at 2 p.m. [11] So Jesus died at around the same time as the Passover Lambs were being sacrificed in the Temple, further explaining John's description of Jesus as the "Lamb of God".

There can be little doubt that, within the crucifixion account, John has embedded symbols of great significance to his Israelite Jesus group. (Whilst it can present a challenge to modern readers to grasp all this symbolism, John's contemporary readers would have understood it all perfectly well.)

---

11 Jewish Encyclopaedia Article: *Passover Sacrifice*. Accessed 19 September 2018
http://www.jewishencyclopedia.com/articles/11934-passover-sacrifice

Notes

In the anti-introspective, collectivist culture of the First Century AD, terms describing internal states always imply corresponding external behaviours. To have the internal states of "love" and "loyalty" means to outwardly express that love and loyalty in word and deed.

Whatever the medical reasons may be, the Roman soldiers certainly believed Jesus was dead when "blood and water" immediately flowed from the wound. While the Synoptic Gospels all *report* that Jesus was dead, John aims to *prove* that Jesus was truly dead by providing us with these additional details.

CHAPTER NINE

Burial

Section 1

Burial Customs in First Century Judea

For 1st Century Israelites, death was a process, not a moment in time. It was customary for the Jerusalem elites to lay out the dead on a shelf in a tomb carved out of the limestone bedrock outside the city. Mourning would then begin and continue for a year as the body underwent decomposition, which was considered a type of penal atonement for the dead person's sins, thought to be embedded in the flesh and to dissolve along with the body.

After a year of decay and purification, the bones were often collected and placed in a stone box called an ossuary or bone box, which was just long enough to accommodate the thigh bones. It was believed that the bones retained the personality and that God would use these bones to support new flesh for the resurrection. (See Ezekiel Chapter 37 and his Vision of the Valley of Dry Bones.)

The day of placing the bones in the ossuary, a type of "second" burial, would mark the end of the family's mourning period and the beginning of hope in eventual reunion and resurrection. These cultural practices and beliefs are the context in which the resurrection accounts were written.

Although the four Gospels appear to indicate that the whole Council was in agreement that Jesus should be delivered to Pilate for judgement, all four nevertheless point to one dissenting member—Joseph of Arimathea—while the author of John includes another dissenter named Nicodemus. It is Joseph of Arimathea who takes the body of Jesus and lays it in a tomb to begin the decay and atonement process. This penal process is interrupted if the body disappears.

To claim that Jesus was resurrected is to claim that the judgement of the elites was *wrong* and therefore God overturned the death sentence, taking Jesus from death to resurrection without the intermediate period of decay and atonement because there was no guilt in his flesh.

The theological assertion that the death of Jesus was *right* and required by God to take away the sins of individuals for all time stands in sharp contrast to the biblical teaching that there is no vicarious atonement for individual, intentional sin, whether past, present or future. The reader is referred to Part VIII.2: *Sin and Salvation-Sin and its Atonement* for a commentary on this subject.

For now, all that is necessary is to consult the Book of Hebrews which states unequivocally that Jesus, as the New Covenant's High Priest and representative of corporate Israel, made a sacrificial offering of his own "unblemished" blood once and forever to atone for the unintentional failures of corporate entities such as the Law of Moses, the Israelite people, and the Priesthood. The blood of Jesus was offered *once only for the past corporate sins of Israel*. This single corporate atonement was to stand forever (Hebrews 9:25-26).

Note that for the family of the deceased, the loss of a body shortly after death would have been a greater calamity than the death itself—the dead person would be unable to atone for any evil deeds committed in life, and the family would be unable to prepare the bones for eventual resurrection.

Section 2

Burial Site

Whilst it is not necessary for the purposes of this work to deal with this subject, a few relevant remarks may nevertheless pique the interest of readers who may, if they so desire, then take up in more depth what is an extremely complex subject.

All the Gospel authors state that the crucifixion site was known as the "place of a skull". Matthew, Mark and John provide its Aramaic equivalent "Golgotha" (Latin: *Calvaria*). The most promoted candidate for the site of Golgotha is the Church of the Holy Sepulchre, standing a little over half a kilometre walk from the Western (Wailing) Wall of the Temple Mount. Ever since this Church was dedicated in 335 AD, many millions of Christian pilgrims have visited the site and it is widely venerated today as the place of Jesus' death and burial.

The reasons for choosing this particular site to build the Church are given in the following extract from the Catholic Encyclopaedia:

> Helena, the mother of the Emperor Constantine, conceived the design of securing the Cross of Christ, the sign of which had led her son to victory (at Milvian Bridge). Constantine himself, having long had at heart a desire to honour "the place of the Lord's Resurrection", "to erect a church at Jerusalem near the place that is called Calvary", encouraged her design, and giving her

imperial authority, sent her with letters and money to Macarius, the Bishop of Jerusalem. Helena and Macarius, having made fruitless inquiries as to the existence of the Cross, turned their attention to the place of the Passion and Resurrection, which was known to be occupied by *a temple of Venus erected by the Romans in the time of Hadrian, or later*. The temple was torn down, the ruins were removed to a distance, the earth beneath, as having been contaminated, was dug up and borne far away. Then, "beyond the hopes of all, the most holy monument of Our Lord's Resurrection shone forth" (Eusebius, "Life of Constantine", III, xxviii). Near it were found three crosses, a few nails, and an inscription such as Pilate ordered to be placed on the Cross of Christ.[12]

To give the Encyclopaedia article its due, it does go on to list the following objection made by the anonymous "some":

> The accounts of the finding of the Holy Sepulchre thus summarized have been rejected by *some* on the ground that they have *an air of improbability*, especially in the attribution of the discovery to "an inspiration of the Saviour", to "Divine admonitions and counsels", and in the assertions that, although the Tomb had been covered by a temple of Venus for upwards of two centuries, its place was yet known.

Let us just say "improbable" indeed and raise some further objections of our own:

- Although there is no mention of this site by any source prior to the 4th Century AD, the article blandly asserts that Helena and Macarius "turned their attention to the place of the Passion and Resurrection" as if it were already well-known and well-established;

- The article encapsulates the remarkable credulity of the 4th Century AD: an age of pious frauds; pagan superstitions; proliferating relics and saints; and an increasing adaptation of pagan holidays into Christian Festivals and pagan sites into Christian places of pilgrimage;

- The Church of the Holy Sepulchre is one such site, originally the location of the pagan Temple of Venus erected by the Emperor Hadrian circa 135 AD.

Let us now see what, if anything, can be determined about the site of Jesus' crucifixion and burial.

---

12 Catholic Encyclopaedia Article: *Holy Sepulchre*. Accessed 21 August 2018 http://www.newadvent.org/cathen/07425a.htm

We know for certain that the crucifixion took place outside Jerusalem's city walls (John 19:20). What we don't know for certain is whether the site of the Church of the Holy Sepulchre was inside or outside the walls at that time. Scholars of all disciplines remain divided. If inside, it cannot be the correct site. If outside, then it is a possible candidate if we disregard the following considerations and objections.

The Book of Hebrews

Perhaps the most significant objection can be found in certain passages from the Book of Hebrews, which are of such importance on many levels that they warrant reproducing in full.

> But when Christ came as high priest of the good things that are now already here, he went through the greater and more perfect tabernacle that is not made with human hands, that is to say, is not a part of this creation. He did not enter by means of the blood of goats and calves; but he entered the Most Holy Place once for all by his own blood, thus obtaining eternal redemption. The blood of goats and bulls and the ashes of a heifer sprinkled on those who are ceremonially unclean sanctify them so that they are outwardly clean. How much more, then, will the blood of Christ, who through the eternal Spirit offered himself unblemished to God, cleanse our consciences from acts that lead to death, so that we may serve the living God! (Hebrews 9:11-14 NIV).
>
> Nor did he enter heaven to offer himself again and again, the way the high priest enters the Most Holy Place every year with blood that is not his own. Otherwise Christ would have had to suffer many times since the creation of the world. But he has appeared once for all at the culmination of the ages to do away with sin by the sacrifice of himself (Hebrews 9:25-26 NIV).

Firstly, the author alludes to the Day of Atonement when the High Priest once a year atoned for the unintentional sins of corporate Israel by making a sacrificial offering of the blood of unblemished animals in the Holy of Holies and explains that Jesus, as the New Covenant's High Priest and representative of corporate Israel, made a sacrificial offering of his own unblemished blood once and forever to atone for the unintentional failures of corporate entities such as the Law of Moses, the Israelite people, and the Priesthood.

Secondly, the author's inclusion of the phrase "the ashes of a heifer" in 9:13 demonstrates that he is alluding also to the mysterious unblemished Red Heifer sacrifice, nine of which had been performed since the time of Moses according to the *Mishnah* (Parah 3:5).

A detailed analysis of the origins and purpose of the Red Heifer sacrifice would consume too much of the reader's attention so, briefly, the purpose of the sacrifice was to cleanse Israel from Levitical defilement by contact with a dead body. The chosen heifer was taken *outside the camp*, wholly burnt, and its ashes used for ritual purification from the greatest defilement of all—death. This sacrifice, unlike other sin offerings, was a sacrifice made *once for all Israelites* (at least as long as the ashes of the previous Red Heifer lasted). Consider the common element of taking the bodies *outside the camp* in the following sacrificial rituals. Note also in Hebrews 13 that Jesus suffered *outside the gate*.

The Day of Atonement

> For the bodies of those animals whose blood is brought into the holy places by the high priest as a sacrifice for sin are burned outside the camp. So Jesus also suffered outside the gate in order to sanctify the people through his own blood. Therefore let us go to him outside the camp and bear the reproach he endured. (Hebrews 13:11-13 ESV cf. Leviticus 16:27).

The Red Heifer

> The Lord said to Moses and Aaron: "This is a requirement of the law that the Lord has commanded: Tell the Israelites to bring you a red heifer without defect or blemish and that has never been under a yoke. Give it to Eleazar the priest; it is to be taken outside the camp and slaughtered in his presence. Then Eleazar the priest is to take some of its blood on his finger and sprinkle it seven times toward the front of the tent of meeting" (Numbers 19:1-4 NIV).

The Mount of Olives

The Mishnah states that this Red Heifer sacrifice was performed *outside the camp*, on the Mount of Olives which lies directly east of the Temple Mount:

> And they would make a ramp from the temple mount to the mount of anointing [the Mount of Olives], arches on top of arches, and [hollow] domes over the foundations, because of graves of the deep, for on it the priest who would burn the heifer, and the heifer and all its helpers would leave to the mount of anointing. [13]

---

13 *Mishnah Parah 3:6*. Accessed 22 August 2018
    https://www.sefaria.org/Mishnah_Parah.3.5?lang=bi&with=all&lang2=en

Why was this location chosen?

The Red Heifer sacrifice was performed on the Mount of Olives in a direct line of sight to the entrance of the Temple on its eastern side. According to the Mishnah, this location made it possible for the priest who sacrificed and burned the Red Heifer to look directly through the opening of the vestibule into the Temple when the blood was sprinkled:

> All of the walls that were there [around the Temple] were high except for the Eastern wall, so that the Kohen who would burn the [red] heifer could stand on top of Mount of Anointing [Olives] and see the opening of the vestibule [over the eastern wall] the time that he sprinkled the blood [of the red heifer].[14]

The author of Hebrews used the phrase "outside the camp" twice in 13:11-13. Together with his previous allusion to the Red Heifer sacrifice in 9:13, it is clear that he is drawing a parallel between Jesus and this sacrificial victim, and perhaps telling us where Jesus was crucified. Is this parallel enough for us to make an informed judgement? Or are there any other indications that Jesus was crucified on the Mount of Olives? The Mount certainly holds great historical and symbolic significance for the authors of the Hebrew Scriptures and of the New Testament, as we can see by reference to the following:

- The Book of 2 Samuel records King David's flight from Jerusalem in an easterly direction towards the summit of the Mount of Olives (2 Samuel 15:30);

- The *Shekinah* (Glory Cloud), a manifestation of God's presence, came to fill the First Temple built by King Solomon (1 Kings 8:10-11; 2 Chronicles 5:13-14; 7:2; cf. Revelation 15:8). The prophet Ezekiel envisions the *Shekinah* leaving this Temple to stand on the Mount of Olives (Ezekiel 11:23), and then returning to a future Temple from the east (Ezekiel 43:2);

- The prophet Zechariah envisions the Day of the Lord when YHWH will "stand on the Mount of Olives" and the mount will be "split in two from east to west" (Zechariah 14:4);

- Jesus prophesies from the Mount of Olives about the end of the age and the *parousia* (Matthew 24:3; Mark 13:3-4);

- Jesus' final entry into Jerusalem takes place by way of Bethphage and

---

14 Mishnah Middoth 2:4. Accessed 23 August 2018
    https://www.sefaria.org/Mishnah_Middot.2.4?lang=bi&with=all&lang2=en

Bethany on the Mount of Olives (Mark 11:1; Luke 19:29, 37; cf. Matthew 21:1). He weeps over the fate of Jerusalem while descending the Mount of Olives on his way into the city (Luke 19:41);

- While in Jerusalem, Jesus teaches in the Temple by day and spends every night on the Mount of Olives (Luke 21:37; cf. Mark 11:19; John 8:1);

- Jesus spends his last night on earth on the Mount of Olives (Matthew 26:30; Mark 14:26; Luke 22:39);

- The ascension takes place in the vicinity of Bethphage on the Mount of Olives (Luke 24:50-51; cf. Acts 1:9-12). See also Part XV.6: *Resurrection-The Parallels.*

We have established that the Mount of Olives holds great historical and symbolic significance for biblical authors. Although the combination of suggestive forces points us in that direction, we have not yet established with any degree of certainty the site of the crucifixion and burial.

Extra-Biblical Sources

Are there any secular sources which may lead us further in our deliberations? In this author's opinion, there is only one source of sufficient worth to warrant our attention—the writings of Benjamin of Tudela.

Benjamin of Tudela, a major figure in medieval geography and Jewish history, was a 12th Century Spanish traveller who visited Europe, Africa and Asia. His descriptions of Western Asia preceded those of Marco Polo by a hundred years. He possessed a vast knowledge of languages, was widely educated, and is considered a reliable source about the geography and ethnography of the Middle Ages.

Benjamin of Tudela made the following observations in his *First Letter from Jerusalem* dated circa 1165 AD:

> From the valley of Jehoshaphat (the valley through which flows Kidron Brook), the traveler immediately ascends the Mount of Olives, as this valley only intervenes between the city and the mount. After the ruins of the Temple, the Mount of Olives is the most important site at Jerusalem. King Solomon built upon this mount. The prophet Zechariah is buried at its foot, in large and ancient burial grounds. *Christians consider the mount holy, believing it to be the site of the arrest and crucifixion of Jisho the Nazarene...*[15]

---

15 Jewish Encyclopaedia article: *Benjamin of Tudela*. Accessed 10 November 2017. http:www.jewishencyclopedia.com/articles/2988-benjamin-of-tudela

Further Factors

Geography

It was Roman policy to punish criminals in public places where their shame and degradation could be witnessed by the maximum numbers of persons possible. According to the Gospels of Matthew and Mark, Jesus was crucified in a place where passers-by could see him, i.e. beside a road, so another factor in our considerations should be to determine the location of the Jerusalem-Jericho road. This road is referenced several times in ancient sources:

- King David and his allies escape from Jerusalem and proceed to Jericho via the Kidron Valley and the Mount of Olives (2 Samuel 15:23-16:14);
- King Zedekiah's escape from Jerusalem and subsequent capture by the Babylonians on the plains of Jericho circa 587 BC (2 Kings 25:1-4);
- Jesus' journey from Jericho to Jerusalem (Mark 10:46-11:11);
- The Tenth Roman Legion ordered to proceed "by way of Jericho" and camp on the Mount of Olives before laying siege to Jerusalem in 69 AD (*History of the Jewish War against Rome*: Josephus 5.42.69).

Spirituality

Israelites have sought since antiquity to be buried on the Mount of Olives. According to tradition, when the Messiah comes he will descend its slopes and then enter Jerusalem through the Golden Gate (the barricaded double gate in the eastern wall of the Temple Mount). Consequently, the area today serves as one of Jerusalem's main cemeteries and contains tens of thousands of graves.

Summing up

Despite the suggestive force of all the contributing factors so far presented, the crucifixion and burial sites still cannot be determined with any degree of certainty. Perhaps the only positive outcome of the above investigation is an agreement that we should regard with skepticism all claims of certainty about this issue.

Note

The Most Holy Place (Holy of Holies) was the inner sanctuary within the Temple. It was separated from the outer sanctuary, the Holy Place, by an inner veil. Another veil, the outer veil, covered the entrance to the Holy Place and separated it from the outer Court. The High Priest could pass through the inner veil only once a year on the Day of Atonement to offer the blood of sacrifice and incense before the mercy seat, symbolically entering the presence of God. A knowledge of Temple architecture will illuminate certain passages in the New Testament, especially those found in the Book of Hebrews.

Section 3

The Gospel Accounts

Whilst there are variations in the details, the accounts consistently describe how Jesus was buried in a tomb by Joseph of Arimathea. As all four accounts tell a similar story, it is only necessary to highlight their differences.

In Matthew, Joseph is a rich disciple of Jesus while in Mark he is a prominent member of the Sanhedrin who is also looking for the Kingdom of God. In Luke, he is a good and righteous Judean member of the Sanhedrin while John states only that he is a secret disciple through fear of the Judeans.

The four Gospels all relate how Joseph of Arimathea asked Pilate for the body of Jesus. Only Mark, however, tells us that Pilate was "surprised" that Jesus was already dead and sent a centurion to confirm the report.

Matthew, Mark and Luke all describe the tomb as "cut out of rock". Matthew, Mark and John describe it as "new". Only in Matthew does the tomb belong to Joseph of Arimathea and only in John are the tomb and the place of crucifixion located near each other in a garden.

Jesus is wrapped in a "clean linen cloth" in Matthew, while in Mark and Luke he is simply "wrapped in linen". Only John tells us that Joseph of Arimathea is accompanied by Nicodemus, "the man who earlier had visited Jesus at night" (3:1-15), and that Nicodemus brought with him a mixture of myrrh and aloes weighing about 100 pounds. John adds that the two men wrap the body of Jesus in "strips of linen" together with the spices and that this preparation of the body is done in accordance with Judean burial customs.

All four Gospels confirm that a stone was rolled over the entrance. In Matthew and Mark, it is Joseph of Arimathea who seals the tomb himself.

Matthew and Mark tell us that Mary Magdalene and another Mary were witnesses to where the body of Jesus was laid. For Luke, these witnesses are women who had "come with Jesus from Galilee" and who then depart and prepare spices and perfumes to anoint the body. However, Luke adds, "they rested on the Sabbath in obedience to the commandment". John fails to mention these women witnesses.

Embalming

Among the Israelites, the bodies of great men were buried with a large quantity of spices (see 2 Chronicles 16:14 for an account of the burial of King Asa).

By specifying such a vast quantity of embalming material, the author of John means to imply that the burial of Jesus is one befitting a King and that his burial linen is reminiscent of Psalm 45:8 where the King's robes "are fragrant with myrrh and aloes and cassia".(Psalm 45 is undoubtedly a messianic text as it is quoted in Hebrews Chapter One as finding fulfillment in Jesus.)

According to the author of Luke, the women who had come with Jesus from Galilee also prepare embalming material.

PART XV

Resurrection

CHAPTER ONE

Introduction

If the Israelites peopling the pages of the New Testament had not believed in the resurrection of Jesus, we would have no New Testament and the Hebrew Scriptures themselves would have had relevance only for Jewish communities which, even today, represent only a tiny fraction of humanity. We would never have known that Jesus existed at all and we would never have heard about the golden rule and similar maxims that have elevated and energised millions throughout these long centuries.

Therefore, we have an obligation to at least attempt to understand what the authors of the New Testament intended to convey when they so confidently asserted the resurrection of Jesus.

Many Christians today are finding it increasingly difficult to accept the commonly-held belief that the New Testament teaches the physical resuscitation of a corpse. For critical thinkers with minds nurtured on the principles of science and natural laws, acceptance of this commonly-held belief is impossible. For we know that any person who has witnessed the transition from life to death understands on an intellectual level that there is no return from brain death.

However, were Paul and the other authors of the New Testament actually teaching the physical resuscitation of a corpse? Or did their use of this term convey an entirely different set of concepts to contemporary Israelites?

Although a daunting task, we will nevertheless attempt to understand what the teaching of the resurrection meant for Israelites of the 1st Century AD and, by engaging in that process, we may draw out meaning of great significance for present and future generations. While engaged in this attempt to open our modern minds to such understanding, it would be wise to keep in the forefront the following quote from William Shakespeare's Hamlet:

> There are more things in heaven and earth, Horatio, Than are dreamt of in your philosophy. (Hamlet, Act 1, Scene V)

Notes on Corporate Personality

Although Christians living in every age have questioned the meaning of the resurrection, the question has often taken a personal form— what does it mean for me, for the individual? To frame the question in such personal terms betrays not only an anachronistic view of the nature of Israelite society in the 1st Century AD, but also a lack of understanding of modern Jewish society today.

For the Israelites of old, and for the Jews of today, life is a communal event. In the words of the Jewish scholar Nicholas de Lange:

> To be a Jew means first and foremost to belong to a group, the Jewish people, and the religious beliefs are secondary, in a sense, to this corporate allegiance.[1]

Most prayers were, and still are, communal, as we see in the "Lord's Prayer". An old Hasidic saying goes like this, "A prayer which is not spoken in the name of all Israel is no prayer at all". [2]

Central to the idea of Israelite community is the concept of *corporate personality*. From ancient times, the entire community, past, present and future, was seen as one personality, as "a living whole, a single animated mass of blood, flesh and bones".[3] Even today, at Passover, modern Jews are required to think of themselves as personally taking part in the Exodus and receiving the Torah at Sinai.

As set out above, from the Israelites at Sinai to their descendants of today, the concept of the *corporate personality* has remained unchanged.

Notes on Mythology

Many academics and sundry other critics have claimed that the resurrection stories in the New Testament are just a recycling of similar mystery myths about vegetation deities whose repeated deaths and resurrections depicted the annual cycle of nature.

What these critics fail to recognise is that the New Testament authors take pains to demonstrate that the death and resurrection of Jesus has nothing at all to do with the cyclical nature myths of other peoples. They do so by specifically denying the two major attributes of these other myths:

- Jesus was not a deity like the vegetation gods—he was just a man like other men;

- Jesus does not die and resurrect continually like the vegetation gods—he died just once to atone for the past corporate sins of Israel.

---

1 De Lange, Nicholas. *Judaism*. Oxford University Press: New York, 1986, p. 4.

2 Buber, Martin, ed. *Ten rungs: Hasidic Sayings*. Schocken Books: New York, 1947, p. 31.

3 Robinson, H. Wheeler. *Corporate Personality in Ancient Israel*, rev. ed. Fortress Press: Philadelphia, 1980, p. 28. Quotation from W. Robertson Smith. *Lectures on the Religion of the Semites*, 2nd ed. A.& C. Black: London, 1894, pp. 273-74.

The assertion that Jesus was a deity like the vegetation gods destroys this vital distinction. Yet despite having relegated the New Testament accounts of the death and resurrection of Jesus to the realm of myth, we still witness a variety of critics continuing to pick over the remains of the cadaver in the hopes of gleaning a little justification for their remaining Creedal commitments.

How many have lost faith in Jesus and even in God because of all this? The damage wrought by the mythology assertion is incalculable.

CHAPTER TWO

Roadblocks

One of the most significant of Israelite Messianic expectations was that the Messiah, when he came, would fulfill the ancient promises found in the Hebrew Scriptures that the Israelite Diaspora community would one day be symbolically "resurrected" from their exile, which was regarded as a type of "death", and be in-gathered to the land of Israel to form the Kingdom of God under the rule of God's Messiah. (See for example Ezekiel 37:1-14.)

The New Testament theme that the resurrection of Jesus represented the foreshadowing of these ancient promises, one day to be fulfilled literally, has been relegated to the shadows, emerging briefly in the works of theologians and academics, and then dismissed into the darkness once again.

The major cause of this centuries-long state of darkness is of course the imposition of a thick layer of mainstream doctrine rendering the New Testament virtually meaningless. As an examination of these doctrines forms the major part of this work, we will here address only the effects of additional contributing factors which, taken together with the malignant force of mainstream belief, can never be reversed—they have already done their diabolical work.

Section 1

Supersessionism

The most egregious of these contributing factors is the teaching of *Supersessionism*, more recently known as *Replacement Theology*. This theological concept was first developed by such men as Justin Martyr (circa 100 - 165 AD), Irenaeus of Lyon (circa 130 - 202 AD) and Origen of Alexandria (185 - 254 AD).

It asserts that because the majority of Israelites in the 1st Century AD did not accept Jesus as their Messiah, God poured out his wrath upon them and destroyed both nation and Temple in 70 AD. God also terminated his Covenants with the Israelite people and transferred them to the followers of Christianity who are the new people of God. Christianity is the true Israel and the sole heir to God's Covenant blessings.

Church Fathers indulged themselves in tirades of demonisation and condemnation, which only increased in fervour and ferocity when Christianity was declared the official religion of the Roman Empire in 380 AD. Charged with "deicide", denounced as "Christ-killers", and accused of bizarre blood rituals, Jews were to suffer many centuries of mob violence and state-sanctioned vitriol which straightened and paved the path towards its inevitable end in the gas chambers.

Of course, in the wake of the Holocaust, many mainstream Christian churches began the work of hand-washing, back-tracking, modifying, excusing, and even attempting to undo the teaching of Supersessionism. But there will be no redemption for the major institutions of Christianity.

Section 2

Anachronism

Anachronisms have plagued biblical scholarship since the immediate post-apostolic period: from the time that the New Testament writings passed from their Israelite milieu into the hands of Hellenists and Latinists unto this very day.

We should take account of the fact that although some may question the "historicity" of the events recorded in the New Testament, the documents did not suddenly spring fully-formed to life like Athena from the head of Zeus: they emerged in real time, from within the historical, political, religious and cultural context of the surrounding Israelite society.

If intellectual honesty is the goal, then we cannot retroject onto this ancient Israelite society those Hellenist-based teachings which have dominated the religious landscape ever since the creedal formulations of Nicea. Neither can we impose upon the New Testament ideas drawn from our present forms of modern, liberal democracies, new age teachings, eastern spiritualities, and so on. For far too long, this scriptural sifting of the New Testament and its characters—accept the best and reject the rest—has been made to serve popular whims, religions, ideologies and philosophies.

To sweep away all this clutter requires no less than a revolution in thinking, even though it may be considered offensive to modern sensibilities. De-cluttering the mind requires a conscious effort to first empty the mind of its previous, and perhaps cherished, beliefs and be prepared to begin at the beginning with Israelite Messianic expectations as they existed in the 1st Century AD. (See Part XIII.2: *The Israelite Messiah-The Unexpected Messiah* for a detailed analysis of these expectations.)

Section 3

A Messianic Expectation

As noted at the beginning of this Chapter, one of the most significant of Israelite Messianic expectations was that the Messiah, when he came, would fulfill the ancient promises found in the Hebrew Scriptures that the Israelite Diaspora community would one day be symbolically "resurrected" from their exile, which was regarded as a type of "death", and be in-gathered to the land of Israel to form the Kingdom of God under the rule of God's Messiah. (A detailed description of the places to which the twelve tribes of the House of Israel were dispersed is provided in Part I.2: *The Context-Centres of Israelite Life in the 1st Century AD*). For now, is it only necessary to recognise that the in-gathering of these exiles and the establishment of the Kingdom of God was a key messianic function.

Since all the authors of the New Testament claimed that Jesus was the Israelite Messiah, it is only to expected that we would find this key function ascribed to Jesus before, during, and after his lifetime:

> He shall be great, and shall be called the Son of the Highest: and the Lord God shall give to him the throne of his father David: And he shall reign over the house of Jacob forever; and of his kingdom there shall be no end (Luke 1:32-33 KJV).

> These twelve Jesus sent forth, and commanded them, saying, Go not into the way of the Gentiles, and into any city of the Samaritans enter ye not: But go rather to the lost sheep of the house of Israel. And as ye go, preach, saying, The kingdom of heaven (God) is at hand (Matthew 10:5-7 KJV).

> But one of them, Caiaphas, who was high priest that year, said to them, "You know nothing at all; you do not understand that it is expedient for you that one man should die for the people, and that the whole nation should not perish." He did not say this of his own accord, but being high priest that year he prophesied that Jesus should die for the nation, and not for the nation only, but to gather into one the children of God who are scattered abroad (John 11:49-52 ESV).

As we see below in Peter's address to his fellow Israelites, the "good news" of the New Testament is for "all the house of Israel":

> Therefore let all the house of Israel know assuredly, that God hath made that same Jesus, whom ye have crucified, both Lord and Christ (Acts 2:36 KJV).

This fact is either completely overlooked, or its importance is diminished. Consider also that Jesus appointed "twelve" disciples because of their symbolic connection with the "twelve" tribes of Israel.

(Note that the "house of Jacob" (Luke 1:33), later renamed Israel, comprised the original twelves tribes.)

Section 4

Hellenism

By the time of Jesus, Hellenism had been the dominant culture of the peoples of the Greco-Roman world for centuries. Israelite intellectuals and others of similar social classes had not been immune to its influence. For example, in the writings of Philo of Alexandria we can see Hellenist philosophy tailored to suit Israelite sensibilities.

The Pharisees also had been highly influenced by Hellenist thought, especially by Plato's philosophy of the immortal soul, which also permeates most of Christian thought and doctrine. This philosophy of the soul holds that man is a duality composed of a pre-existent immortal soul imprisoned within a physical body. Only upon death can the immortal soul of man be released from this body and return to its metaphysical home.

Unlike the Pharisees, the Sadducees denied the philosophy of duality and held to the Scriptural view that man is an indivisible entity. For the Sadducees, there was no post-mortem existence of any kind—no consciousness, no rewards or punishments, only oblivion in the grave. However, Jesus argued that the Sadducees were only partially correct in their assessment of Scriptural teachings and that they had overlooked certain key components which indicated that there was a type of post-mortem existence, a type of "life" in the mind of God. (In forthcoming pages, we will examine these components in greater depth.)

Section 5

Eternity

The Greek nouns *aionas* and *aionon* are plural forms of the Greek *aion*, which simply means an "eon" or "age". The word *aion* always means a period of time. Otherwise it would be impossible to account for its plural forms, or for such qualifying expressions as "this age", or the "age to come" (see for example Matthew 12:32; 1 Corinthians 2:6; Ephesians 1:21). It is only necessary to reference one verse to recognise the inherent contradictions in English translations of all forms of the Greek word *aion:*

> In the hope of eternal life (*zóé aiónios*), which God, who does not lie, promised before the beginning of time (*pro chronōn aiōniōn*) (Titus 1:2 NIV).

If *aiónios* is translated as "eternal" in the first part of the verse then, to be consistent, the final *pro chronōn aiōniōn* must be translated as "before eternal times", which makes no sense whatever as it should be self-evident that "eternity" has no beginning and no ending. Common sense, however, seems to be on permanent, doctrinal by-pass for some translators.

The concept of "eternity" or "endlessness" was not conveyed by the Greek word *aion* or any of its various forms until theologians assigned such meanings to them centuries after the New Testament was written. Once it is recognised that *aion* denotes an "age" or "ages", and that *aionios* means "age-lasting", it can also be recognised that the doctrines of eternal punishment, eternal heaven, eternal life, and so on, are completely without foundation. The Biblical promise of "Eternal Life" (*zóé aiónios*) actually means "age-long life in the age to come":

> And this is what he promised us—eternal life (*zóé aiónios*) (1 John 2:25 NIV).

This "age to come" of which John speaks is the longed-for Messianic age, the age of the kingship of God on Earth, described in the New Testament as the Kingdom of God.

Note

Greek words take many different forms all deriving from the same basic root. To avoid unnecessary complexity, only the basic root forms and their meanings are reproduced in this work.

Section 6

Faith is not blind

During his lifetime, Jesus spoke of a resurrection for those who have "faith" or "belief" in him. Before proceeding, it is necessary to determine the correct meaning of the Greek word translated into English as "faith", and its derived forms, or as "belief", and its derived forms.

In traditional Israelite terms, to have "faith" (Hebrew: *emunah*) meant to have steadfast faithfulness towards the God of Israel and to trust that God would act on behalf of Israelites. This trust and faithfulness was expressed by appropriate behaviour towards God and other Israelites.

In the New Testament, the authors supplied the Greek word *pístis* to reflect the meaning of its Hebrew counterpart *emunah*.

In the majority of cases, the Greek *pístis* has been translated into English as "faith", derived from the Latin *fides*, or as "belief", derived from the Latin *cred*. Unfortunately, the English words "faith" and "belief" have come to imply little more than an unquestioning acceptance of the doctrines and creeds of religion. If we define these terms in their original Hebrew and Greek contexts, we will see that "blind belief" played no part in the thinking of Israelites.

emunah (Hebrew: אֱמוּנָה)

The first definition of *emunah* in Brown, Driver and Briggs Hebrew-English Lexicon is "firmness, steadfastness, fidelity". Also implied in the word are the concepts of trustworthiness, faithfulness, reliability, and the like. For example, in Romans 1:17 and Galatians 3:11, Paul quotes the final words of Habbakuk 2:4. The majority of English translations render these words as, "…the righteous shall live by faith", wheras the correct translation should be, "…the righteous shall live by his faithfulness (*emunah*)".

The Israelite concept of *emunah* is therefore not an intellectual assent to a creed or list of doctrinal propositions but implies trust in someone or something and steadfast faithfulness to someone or something.

pistis (Greek Πίστις)

The word *pístis* is found in the writings of the ancient Greeks including those of Aristotle, Plato, Herodotus, and etcetera. The Liddell and Scott Greek-English Lexicon is used by every student of ancient Greek in the English-speaking world and is an essential library item in universities. The first definition of *pístis* in Liddell and Scott is "trust in others".

New Testament "faith" and "belief" in Jesus is not blind belief in a set of religious doctrines but unwavering trust that God has once again acted on behalf of Israelites by sending them Messiah Jesus, a man declared righteous by God, a man who is to establish the Kingdom of God on Earth, and whom God has raised from the dead. In John's Gospel in particular, we find that "belief" in Jesus means trust that he represents the values and principles of God and not those of God's opposition. One became a follower of Jesus by demonstrating commitment to those same values and principles which brought him to his death.

Unquestioning acceptance of doctrine—blind belief—produced a credulity throughout Christendom which became indifferent to the laws of nature and which deprecated reason, research and learning. A craving for the miraculous and supernatural created ever new superstitions or sanctioned, under the form of relic-worship, old pagan forms of belief. One has only to consider the centuries of religious warfare and the multitude of victims slain on the altar of dogmatism to appreciate just how devastating, how diabolical, and how "un-Christian" blind belief can be. Surely a warning for our times with the rise of yet another deadly band of blind believers.

The reader is encouraged to keep these roadblocks in mind as we attempt to navigate our way to a clearer understanding of the resurrection teachings in the New Testament.

CHAPTER THREE

Altered States

Before proceeding with an analysis of the New Testament accounts of the resurrection, it must be pointed out that all other events recorded in the New Testament are subject to reasonable interpretation using comparative textual analysis, cultural context, and the various literary styles outlined in Part II.9: *The Documents-Understanding Literary Styles.*

As demonstrated elsewhere in this work, the doctrines of mainstream Christianity such as the Virgin Conception/Birth, the Incarnation, and the Trinity, are not based on the teachings of the New Testament. The resurrection, however, is central to New Testament teachings so it is incumbent upon us to discover a reasonable interpretation leading to an understanding of what it meant to the authors and to Israelites of the 1st Century AD.

Cultural anthropologists, historians and neuroscientists recognise that, especially in ancient societies, there existed a prevalent phenomenon known as an "altered state of consciousness". The normal conscious state is awake and alert, allowing us to know where we are, when our experience is taking place, and the difference between self and someone else. An altered state of consciousness is an experience which modifies one or more of the properties of consciousness, such as the relationship of the individual to the self, to the body, to the sense of identity, to other people, and to the surrounding time and space. As we know from experience, our dreams transport us into such an altered state of consciousness. (Falling into a similar category are the states of trance, reverie, and meditation.)

Modern Western society generally denies the human capacity for trances, visions and experiences of altered reality and tends to label all such phenomena as irrational. Any report of an experience of altered reality is usually attributed to dreams or to the use of mind-altering drugs. However, in many other societies throughout the world, all in varying stages of technological and scientific advance, altered states of reality are commonly reported and accepted as normal. To take modern Western society as the norm by which all others should be judged is anachronistic in the extreme.

Reality Consensus

Every culture develops a consensus of what constitutes "reality". Apart from religious considerations, the consensus of what constitutes reality in the modern West is firmly circumscribed by the dictates of modern science. However, before this age of science, the consensual reality of many cultures, including that of ancient Israel, was vastly different to our own.

Many centuries before the Gospels were written, Israelites believed that the God of Israel had intervened in their history in various ways including through prophetic visions and angelic visitations. These visions and visitations were acceptable and believable phenomena because they occurred within an Israelite consensus of what constituted reality.

As with the Israelites of old, so also did the later Israelites peopling the pages of the New Testament believe in divine intervention, prophetic visions, and angelic visitations. As with the personalities, so with the authors who quoted countless times from the writings of the Israelite prophets. If we are to arrive at a reasonable understanding of the resurrection, then the experiences of all these people must be considered seriously and interpreted from within the framework of *their* consensual reality, not of ours.

New Testament Experiences

Jesus and his core group members appear to have had the ability to enter into an altered state of consciousness. Apart from dreams and angelic visitations, the New Testament records the following major instances of alternate reality experiences.

The Baptism by John

After being baptised by John, Jesus experiences an alternate reality vision as he is coming up out of the water. He sees Heaven torn open and the Spirit descending upon him in the form of a dove, followed by the sound of God's voice coming from Heaven saying, "You are my beloved Son; with you I am well pleased" (Mark 1:9-11; cf. Matthew 3:13-17; Luke 3:21-22).

The Wilderness Temptation

After his baptism, and after he has been proclaimed as God's son, Jesus is led by the Spirit into the wilderness for forty days during which time he experiences an alternate reality vision in which he undergoes a loyalty test set by "Satan", who represents the forces of opposition to God. Jesus is reported as outwitting the tempter's game of deception before being attended by ministering angels, who serve and strengthen those who remain loyal to God (Luke 4:1-13; cf. Matthew 4:1-11; Mark 1:12-13).

The Water Walking

This event is reported as a visionary experience of the disciples. Although it strains our credulity, the story records a real experience of a real event in alternate reality. In Matthew's account we find a description of the transition from one reality to another when Peter's doubt causes him to exit alternate reality and return to the world where walking on water is impossible (Matthew 14:22-33; cf. Mark 1:12-13; Luke 3:21-11).

The Transfiguration

Even to this day in Mediterranean culture, solutions to problems and concerns often reveal themselves in altered states of consciousness experiences such as dreams, visions, trances, and the like. The Transfiguration achieves the purpose of reassuring Peter, James and John that they should listen to Jesus more so than even Moses and Elijah, representing the Law and the Prophets.

The Road to Damascus

Whilst Paul had been a persecutor of the disciples and other followers of Jesus, and was neither an eye-witness nor one who had interacted with Jesus personally, the effects of his experience on the Damascus road were no less profound and life-changing for him as encounters with the resurrected Jesus had been for the disciples and other eye-witnesses.

As an aid to comprehension, consider Paul's experience on the road to Damascus and then his next experience in the Jerusalem Temple:

> "But it happened that as I was on my way, approaching Damascus about noontime, a very bright light suddenly flashed from heaven all around me, and I fell to the ground and heard a voice saying to me, 'Saul, Saul, why are you persecuting Me?' "And I answered, 'Who are You, Lord?' And He said to me, 'I am Jesus the Nazarene, whom you are persecuting.' "And those who were with me saw the light, to be sure, but did not understand the voice of the One who was speaking to me. "And I said, 'What shall I do, Lord?' And the Lord said to me, 'Get up and go on into Damascus, and there you will be told of all that has been appointed for you to do.' "But since I could not see because of the brightness of that light, I was led by the hand by those who were with me and came into Damascus. "A certain Ananias, a man who was devout by the standard of the Law, and well spoken of by all the Jews who lived there, came to me, and standing near said to me, 'Brother Saul, receive your sight!' And at that very time I looked up at him. "And he said, 'The God of our fathers has appointed you to know His will and to see the Righteous One and to hear an utterance from His mouth. 'For you will be a witness for Him to all men of

what you have seen and heard. 'Now why do you delay? Get up and be baptized, and wash away your sins, calling on His name.'

"It happened when I returned to Jerusalem and was praying in the temple, that I fell into a trance, and I saw Him saying to me, 'Make haste, and get out of Jerusalem quickly, because they will not accept your testimony about Me.' (Acts 22:6-18 NASB).

Referring to the road to Damascus experience, Ananias tells Paul that the "God of our Fathers" has appointed him to *see* the righteous one and to *hear* words from his mouth. Referring to the Temple experience, Paul *sees* and *hears* the Lord speaking to him. Consider the common elements of these two experiences. The voice of the Lord on the Damascus road telling Paul to, "Get up and go on into Damascus" and the voice of the Lord in the Jerusalem Temple telling him, "Make haste, and get out of Jerusalem immediately". Since these instructions are so similar in nature, one of which Paul attributed to a "trance", it is most likely that both instances can be safely categorised as altered state of consciousness experiences, especially when we also consider the following passage from 2 Corinthians.

Paul begins this passage in the first person. However, in order to show his humility and not ascribe to himself the honour of what he is about to relate, he switches to the third person to speak of a "man in Christ" who experiences visions and revelations from the Lord. The "man in Christ" is undoubtedly Paul himself:

> I must go on boasting. Although there is nothing to be gained, I will go on to visions and revelations from the Lord. I know a man in Christ who fourteen years ago was caught up to the third heaven. Whether it was in the body or out of the body I do not know—God knows. And I know that this man—whether in the body or apart from the body I do not know, but God knows—was caught up to paradise and heard inexpressible things, things that no one is permitted to tell (2 Corinthians 12:1-4 NIV).

The ancients knew only the visible sky which was divided into two "heavens". The first, or lower heaven, is what we would term the localised atmosphere of the Earth. The second, or higher heaven, was the layer containing all other visible bodies—the sun, the moon, the planets, and the stars. It was believed that the invisible abode of God lay above these two layers of visibility and was variously known as the "highest heaven", or the "heaven of heavens", and is here given the term the "third heaven" by Paul. By equating this "third heaven" with "paradise", where he encounters the ineffable, Paul is stating that his experiences come from the God of Israel. The type of language he uses— "Visions and revelations from the Lord" and "whether in the body or out of the body I do not know"— is exactly the type of language a 1st Century Israelite would use to describe altered states of consciousness experiences.

Note

The term "paradise" has two meanings: God's own abode in the "heaven of heavens" and the original human paradise of Eden patterned on God's heavenly abode. The Kingdom of God on Earth is envisioned as a symbolic return to this paradise of Eden from which we were cast out (Isaiah 51:3; Ezekiel 36:35).

CHAPTER FOUR

The eye-witnesses

Before the crucifixion, the followers of Jesus believed that he was their long-awaited Davidic Messiah who was about to establish the Kingdom of God on Earth. After the crucifixion, the beliefs of his followers died with him. Perhaps they wondered if Jesus had been just another Messianic pretender after all.

After the resurrection, however, appearances of Jesus to the eye-witnesses cannot be dismissed as examples of those alternate reality experiences noted in the previous Chapter. They alone would not be sufficient to account for the miraculous and life-long transformation in the lives of his followers whose willingness to preach the "good news" even at the cost of their own lives is simply inexplicable if we attribute these appearances to simple altered states of consciousness experiences.

Given the interactions between Jesus and the resurrection eye-witnesses recorded in the New Testament, we have no option but to conclude that we are dealing with a phenomenon infinitely more profound. Therefore, whilst it is the aim of this work to explore reasonable scenarios satisfactory to the modern mind, there can be no such explanation for the experiences of the eye-witnesses.

Two important factors most often overlooked is that all the witnesses, including Paul and others, were chosen beforehand by God and *enabled to see* the resurrected Jesus:

> We are witnesses of all the things He did both in the land of the Jews (Judeans) and in Jerusalem. They also put Him to death by hanging Him on a cross. "God raised Him up on the third day and granted that He become visible, not to all the people, but to witnesses who were chosen beforehand by God, that is, to us who ate and drank with Him after He arose from the dead (Acts 10:39-41 NASB).
>
> Before long, the world will not see me anymore, but you will see me. Because I live, you also will live (John 14:19 NIV).

Paul also speaks of this witness enabling:

> For I delivered to you as of first importance what I also received: that Christ died for our sins in accordance with the Scriptures, that he was buried, that he was raised on the third day in accordance with the Scriptures, and that he appeared to Cephas, then to the twelve. Then he appeared to more than five hundred brothers at one time, most of whom are still alive, though some have

fallen asleep. Then he appeared to James, then to all the apostles. Last of all, as to one untimely born, he appeared also to me (1 Corinthians 15:3-8 ESV).

In the above passage are six statements which use passive voice verbs in the original Greek. Paul's use of these passive voice verbs is a pious substitution known as the "divine passive" (*passivum divinum*), originally intended to avoid accidentally invoking the sacred name, and commonly used when describing acts of God. Thus, Paul is saying that God *caused* Jesus to be buried, *caused* him to be raised, and *caused* him to appear to all the disciples, to five hundred brothers, to James and the apostles, and finally to Paul.

It is not possible to overstate the importance of these factors. If the New Testament authors were writing about the resuscitation of a corpse, then that earthly body would possess the same essential properties as it had previously. However, if only the chosen witnesses were enabled to see and interact with Jesus, then his resurrected body was so profoundly different in substance that it was invisible to everyone else.

The Transformation Body

Whilst the eye-witnesses give us a wraith-like impression of Jesus when they tell of sudden appearances and disappearances, they also record their ordinary interactions such as touching him, speaking with him, eating and drinking with him, and walking with him "on the road to Emmaus" (Luke 24:15).

Consider especially the experience of Thomas recorded in John's Gospel:

> On the evening of that first day of the week, when the disciples were together, with the doors locked for fear of the Jewish (Judean) leaders, Jesus came and stood among them and said, "Peace be with you!" After he said this, he showed them his hands and side. The disciples were overjoyed when they saw the Lord…Now Thomas (also known as Didymus), one of the Twelve, was not with the disciples when Jesus came. So the other disciples told him, "We have seen the Lord!" But he said to them, "Unless I see the nail marks in his hands and put my finger where the nails were, and put my hand into his side, I will not believe." A week later his disciples were in the house again, and Thomas was with them. Though the doors were locked, Jesus came and stood among them and said, "Peace be with you!" Then he said to Thomas, "Put your finger here; see my hands. Reach out your hand and put it into my side. Stop doubting and believe" (John 20:19-27 NIV).

While incidents such as the one recorded above imply that Jesus was recognisable simply by physical characteristics, others imply that he was not. Consider his appearance to Mary Magdalene, who initally thought that he was the "gardener" until he began to speak to her (John 20:14-16), and to the two disciples on the road to Emmaus who were "kept from recognising him" until he ate with them and "their eyes were opened" (Luke 24:16-31).

We must conclude therefore that the pre-resurrection body of Jesus was not identical to his post-resurrection body which, although possessing concrete substance, had undergone some profound transformation.

Before his death, Jesus is portrayed as a free agent acting under his own volition. After the resurrection, he makes no appearances under his own volition and is therefore no longer a free agent. Whatever the composition of his body, God is in complete control of his appearances and disappearances, and the choice of eye-witnesses. This *before* and *after* distinction again speaks of a profound transformation of the resurrected body.

Plumbing the depths of a phenomenon which will always defy modern scientific explanation is of lesser importance, however, than an understanding of the resurrection's meaning and significance to 1st Century Israelites, to which we will turn our attention in forthcoming Chapters.

Note

The Transfiguration, the Resurrection, and the Ascension, are all thematically entwined. The New Testament accounts of these events will be explored more fully in forthcoming Chapters.

CHAPTER FIVE

The empty tomb

Notes

Anyone who has witnessed the process of dying and its aftermath knows that brain death is irreversible. Therefore, we will not approach this topic on the premise that the New Testament authors were teaching the resuscitation of a corpse. Rather, we will focus on the search for alternative possibilities.

In this Chapter, we will just make a few remarks on what the Gospel authors have to tell us before moving on to identify themes associated with the resurrection from within the context of 1st Century Israelite life.

Section 1

Matthew

> After the Sabbath, at dawn on the first day of the week, Mary Magdalene and the other Mary went to look at the tomb. There was a violent earthquake, for an angel of the Lord came down from heaven and, going to the tomb, rolled back the stone and sat on it. His appearance was like lightning, and his clothes were white as snow. The guards were so afraid of him that they shook and became like dead men. The angel said to the women, "Do not be afraid, for I know that you are looking for Jesus, who was crucified. He is not here; he has risen, just as he said. Come and see the place where he lay. Then go quickly and tell his disciples: 'He has risen from the dead and is going ahead of you into Galilee. There you will see him. Now I have told you'."
>
> So the women hurried away from the tomb, afraid yet filled with joy, and ran to tell his disciples. Suddenly Jesus met them. "Greetings," he said. They came to him, clasped his feet and worshiped him. Then Jesus said to them, "Do not be afraid. Go and tell my brothers to go to Galilee; there they will see me."
>
> While the women were on their way, some of the guards went into the city and reported to the chief priests everything that had happened. When the chief priests had met with the elders and devised a plan, they gave the soldiers a large sum of money, telling them, "You are to say, 'His disciples came during the night

and stole him away while we were asleep'. If this report gets to the governor, we will satisfy him and keep you out of trouble." So the soldiers took the money and did as they were instructed. And this story has been widely circulated among the Jews (Judeans) to this very day (Matthew 28:1-15 NIV).

As pointed out in Matthew's account of the crucifixion (Part XIV.10), the death of Jesus is accompanied by a number of signs indicative of God's presence. Based on the multiple allusions to Ezekiel 37, Daniel 12 and Isaiah 26 (and possibly other texts) found in Matthew 27:51-52, it is clear that he never intended any of these signs to be taken literally. Rather, he is using *Midrashic* analogies to anticipate and describe the transition to new life that the resurrection of Jesus will foreshadow for all Israel. The shaking of the land (the earthquake) and the splitting of the rocks symbolically opens the graves and prepares the way for this promised resurrection.

In the above passage, Matthew calls on the same signs (the earthquake) and the splitting of the rocks (rolling back the stone), to tell us that the transition to new life is no longer the foreshadowing of 27:51-52, but has now become a reality.

Matthew specifies that the earthquake is caused by an "angel of the Lord" descending from heaven, i.e. breaking through from the realm of God which lay beyond the vault of the firmament of the sky directly above the Jerusalem Temple. We are told that this angel has the appearance of "lightning", i.e. like a sudden flash of brilliance, and that his clothes were "white as snow". This description calls to mind the appearance of the Ancient of Days (Daniel 7:9; 10:6), and of the Transfigured Jesus (Mark 9:3; Luke 9:29).

Matthew's "angel of Lord" functions as a herald of joyful news: first appearing to Joseph in a dream to announce the birth of the Messiah and now appearing to announce the Messiah's resurrection.

The angel's purpose in rolling back the stone is to allow the women to see inside the empty tomb and to remind the disciples about what Jesus had told them in Chapter 26:32, "But after I have risen, I will go ahead of you into Galilee".

The women now encounter Jesus himself. The appearances of both the "angel of the Lord" and the crucified Jesus are best described as events experienced in altered states of consciousness, evidenced by the inclusion of descriptions of the angel's clothing— like "lightning" and "white as snow"— which are indicative of divinely-appointed messengers.

Jesus delivers to them the same message as did the angel of the Lord—remind the disciples to go to Galilee.

When the body of Jesus disappears, the chief priests and elders are yet again faced with dishonour before Pilate. Matthew tells us that, true to form in their treatment of Jesus, the elites deal with the situation by resorting to their usual tactics of bribery and the spreading of false rumours, all in the hope of preserving their honour.

Section 2

Mark

> When the Sabbath was past, Mary Magdalene, Mary the mother of James, and Salome bought spices, so that they might go and anoint him. And very early on the first day of the week, when the sun had risen, they went to the tomb. And they were saying to one another, "Who will roll away the stone for us from the entrance of the tomb?" And looking up, they saw that the stone had been rolled back—it was very large. And entering the tomb, they saw a young man sitting on the right side, dressed in a white robe, and they were alarmed. And he said to them, "Do not be alarmed. You seek Jesus of Nazareth, who was crucified. He has risen; he is not here. See the place where they laid him. But go, tell his disciples and Peter that he is going before you to Galilee. There you will see him, just as he told you." And they went out and fled from the tomb, for trembling and astonishment had seized them, and they said nothing to anyone, for they were afraid (Mark 16:1-8 ESV).

After the Sabbath, very early on the first day of the week, i.e. Sunday, the same three Galilean women of Chapter 15:40 are bringing anointing spices to the tomb and discussing their concerns about the removal of the sealing stone. When they arrive at the tomb, however, they find that the "very large" stone has been rolled away.

Unlike Matthew, there is no mention of the symbolic earthquake and Matthew's "angel of the Lord" is now a young man dressed in a white robe sitting inside the tomb. However, they are both visions experienced in an altered state of consciousness, evidenced by the inclusion of a description of the clothing—a "white robe"—which is indicative of a divinely-appointed messenger. Regardless of the variations in the two accounts, Matthew's "angel of the Lord" and Mark's young man dressed in a white robe deliver the same message to the women.

Unlike Matthew and Luke who report that the women obeyed their instructions and relayed the message to the disciples, the women in Mark are so afraid that they say nothing to anyone, which leads us to the much-disputed ending of Mark.

Verses 9-20 are absent from two of the oldest and best Greek manuscripts, the Codex *Sinaiticus* and Codex *Vaticanus*. In addition, the fourth-century church fathers Eusebius and Jerome noted that almost all Greek manuscripts available to them lacked verses 9–20. Even so, the verse 8 ending is abrupt and appears unfinished so we are left with the problem of omitting these verses. However, scholars are agreed that, on the basis of vocabulary, style, and lack of subject continuity, verses 9-20 do not belong to the original Markan account. Unless some verifiable original ending of Mark is miraculously uncovered, we must unfortunately finish our commentary at verse 8.

Note

In Chapter 14:51, Mark made a somewhat curious reference to a young man wearing nothing but a linen garment who followed Jesus from Gethsemane after his arrest. This young man, after being seized, presumably by his clothing, fled away naked leaving his garment behind. Mark's intent is not clear. Are we supposed to identify the young man at Gethsemane with the young man in the tomb? We cannot be certain. Like this young man, however, the women also flee from the scene.

Section 3

Luke

On the first day of the week, very early in the morning, the women took the spices they had prepared and went to the tomb. They found the stone rolled away from the tomb, but when they entered, they did not find the body of the Lord Jesus. While they were wondering about this, suddenly two men in clothes that gleamed like lightning stood beside them. In their fright the women bowed down with their faces to the ground, but the men said to them, "Why do you look for the living among the dead? He is not here; he has risen! Remember how he told you, while he was still with you in Galilee: 'The Son of Man must be delivered over to the hands of sinners, be crucified and on the third day be raised again'." Then they remembered his words. When they came back from the tomb, they told all these things to the Eleven and to all the others. It was Mary Magdalene, Joanna, Mary the mother of James, and the others with them who told this to the apostles. But they did not believe the women, because their words seemed to them like nonsense. Peter, however, got up and ran to the tomb. Bending over, he saw the strips of linen lying by themselves, and he went away, wondering to himself what had happened (Luke 24:1-12 NIV).

All the Gospels record that the empty tomb was discovered early in the morning on the day after the Sabbath, i.e. Sunday. According to Luke, "the women who had come with him from Galilee" (23:55) made the discovery.

These women are reported as being puzzled by the empty tomb until they suddenly see "two men in clothes that gleamed like lightning" standing beside them. This is once again best described as an experience taking place in an altered state of consciousness, evidenced by the description of clothes that "gleamed like lightning", which description most fittingly applies to divinely-appointed messengers.

As in Matthew and Mark, the women are told that Jesus is risen. Unlike Matthew and Mark, however, these men don't deliver a message to pass on to the disciples but ask the women to recall what Jesus had said to them when they were still in Galilee, "The Son of Man must be delivered over to the hands of sinners, be crucified and on the third day be raised again".

The women recall Jesus' words and leave the tomb. Mary Magdalene, Joanna, and the mother of James are named by Luke as being included in the women who report back to the eleven remaining disciples and "all the others". Unsurprisingly, Luke tells us that their report is met with disbelief by all but Peter who runs to the tomb and finds no body but just the strips of linen in which it was wrapped. Peter goes away, Luke tells us with remarkable understatement, "wondering to himself what had happened".

Section 4

John

> Now on the first day of the week Mary Magdalene came to the tomb early, while it was still dark, and saw that the stone had been taken away from the tomb. So she ran and went to Simon Peter and the other disciple, the one whom Jesus loved, and said to them, "They have taken the Lord out of the tomb, and we do not know where they have laid him." So Peter went out with the other disciple, and they were going toward the tomb. Both of them were running together, but the other disciple outran Peter and reached the tomb first. And stooping to look in, he saw the linen cloths lying there, but he did not go in. Then Simon Peter came, following him, and went into the tomb. He saw the linen cloths lying there, and the face cloth, which had been on Jesus' head, not lying with the linen cloths but folded up in a place by itself. Then the other disciple, who had reached the tomb first, also went in, and he saw and believed;

for as yet they did not understand the Scripture, that he must rise from the dead. Then the disciples went back to their homes.

But Mary stood weeping outside the tomb, and as she wept she stooped to look into the tomb. And she saw two angels in white, sitting where the body of Jesus had lain, one at the head and one at the feet. They said to her, "Woman, why are you weeping?" She said to them, "They have taken away my Lord, and I do not know where they have laid him." Having said this, she turned around and saw Jesus standing, but she did not know that it was Jesus. Jesus said to her, "Woman, why are you weeping? Whom are you seeking?" Supposing him to be the gardener, she said to him, "Sir, if you have carried him away, tell me where you have laid him, and I will take him away." Jesus said to her, "Mary." She turned and said to him in Aramaic, "Rabboni!" (which means Teacher). Jesus said to her, "Do not cling to me, for I have not yet ascended to the Father; but go to my brothers and say to them, 'I am ascending to my Father and your Father, to my God and your God'." Mary Magdalene went and announced to the disciples, "I have seen the Lord"— and that he had said these things to her (John 20:1-18 NASB).

Whereas in John's account, only Mary Magdalene discovers the empty tomb, all four Gospels nevertheless tell a consistent story about the day and time of the discovery.

The order of events is reversed here. Mary first runs to tell Peter and the "other disciple, the one whom Jesus loves". (See Part XIV.7: *Trial and Death-Arrest and Interrogation-John's Account* for the possible identity of the "other disciple".)

After hearing Mary's report, both disciples run to the tomb. Although the beloved disciple outstrips Peter, he defers and allows Peter to enter the tomb first. While Peter *sees* the linen cloths and "the face cloth, which had been on Jesus' head, not lying with the linen cloths but folded up in a place by itself", the beloved disciple both *sees* and *believes*. Although neither of them understand how to interpret the meaning of the empty tomb with the help of Scripture, by telling us that the beloved disciple *believes*, John intends us to know that while interrupting the burial process with a resurrection was not a thought that had occurred to Peter, the beloved disciple understands that God has intervened in some unknown way.

It is unclear where Mary had been during this time but after the disciples return to their lodgings, Mary is pictured as once more present at the tomb. While weeping in the garden, she stoops down to look inside. Mary knows that the tomb is empty because she had previously told the disciples that, *"They* have taken the Lord out of the tomb, and *we* do not know where they have laid him". (Although we may wonder to whom "they" and "we" refer, it is language typical of collectivist societies.)

Mary sees "two angels in white" sitting where the body of Jesus had lain, one at the head and one at the feet. In Matthew, an angel of the Lord is dressed in white clothing; in Mark, a young man is dressed in white clothing; in Luke, two men are dressed in bright clothing; and here in John, two angels are dressed in white clothing. Regardless of these variations, clothing descriptors such as white, bright, or shining are indicators that they are messengers carrying out the will of God and that they are visions experienced in alternate reality.

Mary had already told Peter and the beloved disciple that her greatest concern about the empty tomb was the loss of the body. Now she responds in essentially the same manner to the angels when they ask her why she is weeping? *They* have stolen the body of Jesus and she doesn't know where it is. Like Peter, she does not consider that God's interruption of the burial process results in resurrection.

After giving her answer to the angels, Mary turns around and sees another vision, this time of Jesus. However, she doesn't recognise him and assumes he is the "gardener." Jesus asks the same question as the angels did: why is she weeping? Mary responds by voicing her greatest concern for the third time—the loss of the body.

Jesus calls Mary by her name and only then does she recognise him. She in turn calls him by the Aramaic name "Rabboni" (Teacher). Jesus tells her:

> "Do not cling to me, for I have not yet ascended to the Father; but go to my brothers and say to them, 'I am ascending to my Father and your Father, to my God and your God'." (John 20:17 NASB).

There cannot be any prohibition on Mary touching his body because he allowed others to later interact with him in physical ways. Perhaps she had "bowed down with her face to the ground" as had the women in Luke or "clasped his feet and worshipped him" as had the women in Matthew. Whatever the case, there is certainly an atmosphere of haste in this verse because Jesus has *not yet* ascended to the abode of God. It cannot be overstated that John's consensual reality, and that of his contemporaries, was vastly different to our own. Therefore, although difficult for us to comprehend, he intends his readers to understand by the words *not yet* that Mary's vision of Jesus exists in some intermediate form of alternate reality. He is not of the same substance as other beings existing in alternate reality, such as Moses and Elijah at the Transfiguration, but of an entirely different order.

The purpose of this suspended or intermediate state is to enable temporary communications between Jesus and his disciples in order that they may be convinced of his living presence in alternate reality and that they will therefore receive and obey his final instructions before he is permanently gone from the physical world.

Mary returns from the tomb and announces to the disciples that she had seen the Lord and that he had said these things to her.

Notes

Mary's greatest concern is the loss of Jesus' body. Because it has disappeared, it is now unable to undergo the penal process of decay and atonement for sins of the flesh and neither can the bones be prepared for eventual resurrection. Mary's vision of Jesus convinces her that God has intervened in this process of decay and atonement and, since he has already been raised to life, his bones need not be prepared for an eventual resurrection. Mary is comforted: her greatest concern has been allayed. Jesus now lives in an alternate reality where he will continue to live for her and for all his followers. (See Part XIV.9.1: *Trial and Death-Burial-Burial Customs in 1st Century Judea.*)

Section 5

The Body

Despite any attempt at a reasonable interpretation of the events described above, we are still left with one unanswered, or perhaps unanswerable question—what happened to the body of Jesus?

Angels

It is neither necessary nor useful to punctuate this section with a broad-based discussion of the Biblical concept of "angels". Rather, we will address the concept only as it relates to an understanding of the resurrection.

Israelites of the 1st Century AD believed that each person was assigned a protective spirit or "guardian angel". Jesus articulated this same belief:

> "See that you do not despise one of these little ones. For I tell you that their angels in heaven always see the face of my Father in heaven" (Matthew 18:10 NIV).

Consider also this passage from Acts Chapter Twelve which is reproduced below in two sections for the purposes of illustration:

> Now when Herod was about to bring him out, on that very night, Peter was sleeping between two soldiers, bound with two chains, and sentries before the door were guarding the prison. And behold, an angel of the Lord stood next to him, and a light shone in the cell. He struck Peter on the side and woke him, saying, "Get up quickly." And the chains fell off his hands. And the angel said

to him, "Dress yourself and put on your sandals." And he did so. And he said to him, "Wrap your cloak around you and follow me." And he went out and followed him. He did not know that what was being done by the angel was real, but thought he was seeing a vision. When they had passed the first and the second guard, they came to the iron gate leading into the city. It opened for them of its own accord, and they went out and went along one street, and immediately the angel left him. When Peter came to himself, he said, "Now I am sure that the Lord has sent his angel and rescued me from the hand of Herod and from all that the Jewish (Judean) people were expecting" (Acts 12:5-11 ESV).

When this had dawned on him, he went to the house of Mary the mother of John, also called Mark, where many people had gathered and were praying. Peter knocked at the outer entrance, and a servant named Rhoda came to answer the door. When she recognized Peter's voice, she was so overjoyed she ran back without opening it and exclaimed, "Peter is at the door!" "You're out of your mind," they told her. When she kept insisting that it was so, they said, "It must be his angel" (Acts 12:12-15 NIV).

Peter believes he's having a vision when the "angel of the Lord" appears in his cell. From all the carefully recorded details of the escape, however, we can deduce that this was no ethereal vision but most likely an actual human, perhaps a sympathetic insider. Whatever the case, the person is portrayed as having been sent by God to break Peter out of prison.

When the "many people" gathered at the house of Mary, the mother of John Mark, are told that Peter is knocking at the door, they refuse to believe it and exclaim that, "It must be his angel".

Articulated in these passages from Matthew 18:10 and Acts 12:5-15 are two interconnected concepts:

1. An actual human can be viewed as an "angel of the Lord" if he is carrying out the will of God, as in Acts 12:5-11 above;

2. Every person has a representative "guardian angel", an "angel of the Lord" originating from the abode of God (Matthew 18:10). This "angel of the Lord" can appear as a visionary representative of this person, as in Acts 12:12-15.

Into which category do the messengers at the tomb fall? Are they "guardian angels" representing the actual humans who removed the body? Or are they actual humans viewed as "angels of the Lord" because they are seen to be carrying out the will of God? Regardless of whether they were described as "men" or "angels," all four

Gospels tell us that the messengers wore clothing which indicated that they had been divinely-appointed.

The only conclusion we can draw from all the above is that the Gospel authors were telling that all was done according to the purposes of God. Whilst it may not be enough to satisfy the modern mind, it was certainly enough to satisfy the minds of their contemporaries who believed absolutely in an interventionist God.

Note

The English word "angel" is derived from the Greek *aggelos* which is, in turn, derived from the Hebrew *malak* meaning "messenger". For example, the name of the prophet Malachi means "my messenger". See also Hebrews 13:2 where the "angels" are obviously human, "Do not neglect to show hospitality to strangers, for thereby some have entertained angels unawares".

A personal conjecture

There is one "empty tomb" scenario that this author has considered, but it is just conjecture, nothing more.

The Gospels all record that the body of Jesus was removed from the cross and buried in haste because of the approaching Sabbath, beginning at sunset on Friday. The prohibition against work on the Sabbath ended around sunset on Saturday and the empty tomb was discovered around sunrise the next morning. Thus we are left with a period of approximately twelve hours during which the body could have been removed.

All the parties involved in the discovery of the empty tomb, and those who were subsequently told about it, were certainly surprised and shocked so we will discount the women and Jesus' core disciples. Who, then, is the person most likely to have removed the body?

We are told by all the Gospel authors that Joseph of Arimathea, acting in haste, took the body of Jesus and laid it in a tomb. In Matthew's Gospel, Joseph took the body of Jesus and "placed it in his *own new tomb* that he had cut out of the rock". Matthew didn't just add these details about the tomb to fill up space: his contemporary readers would have understood what their inclusion meant.

It was customary for the Jerusalem elites to lay out the dead on a shelf in a tomb carved out of the limestone bedrock outside the city. Such rock-cut tombs were expensive and reserved for family members. The fact that the tomb is described as Joseph's *own new tomb* meant that no members of Joseph's family had as yet been buried there. If Jesus' body were permitted to remain there for the year-long decay and atonement process, then no members of Joseph's family who died in the interim could be buried there together with a body belonging to a total stranger.

While Israelite traditions in this regard were certainly observed more rigorously than our own, it nevertheless remains to this day a custom for families of a certain status or ethnic origin to own expensive tombs reserved for themselves alone. It would strike us as highly unusual if we were reading a list of names inscribed on such a family tomb only to discover among them the name of a total stranger.

We know that Jesus was buried in haste because of the approaching Sabbath. Perhaps Joseph of Arimathea had always planned to move the body from his family tomb once the Sabbath was over. If that is the case, then removal would have occurred during the twelve hours between sunset Saturday and sunrise Sunday.

Only Matthew tells us that there were guards at the tomb when the women arrived on the Sunday morning. However, when the guards report the empty tomb to the elites, the elites bribe the guards to spread abroad a rumour that the body was stolen while the guards slept (see Matthew 28:1-15). If the guards are so easily bribed, then they could have been bribed to leave their posts for a time by anyone with sufficient resources, such as Joseph of Arimathea who is described by Matthew as "rich".

In John's Gospel we find that Joseph of Arimathea was "a disciple of Jesus, but secretly because he feared the Jewish (Judean) leaders" (John 19:38). If Joseph did indeed remove the body, then it was in his own best interests that no word of such removal would find its way to the elites. Thus, none but Joseph himself, and perhaps a trusted retainer, would ever know the truth.

It cannot be overstated that the above is purely personal conjecture. There is not enough evidence on which to base a conclusion. It is presented to readers simply as an exercise of the mind.

CHAPTER SIX

The Parallels

The parallels between the accounts of the Transfiguration, Resurrection and Ascension, and the accounts of Moses at Sinai and Elijah at the Jordan, are so significant that they cannot be understood independently of each other, much less ignored as they largely have been.

Before proceeding, however, it is once again important to draw attention to the fact that the original New Testament stories were steeped in *Midrash*, a traditional storytelling style which was readily understood by Israelites both at home and in the Diaspora (see Part II:8: *The Documents-Understanding Literary Styles*). The authors also made use of other literary styles such as parallelism, allegory, typology and pesher, but it is not necessary for us to involve ourselves any further in all this scholarly minutiae.

What *is* necessary for us to keep in mind is that the Transfiguration, Resurrection and Ascension stories were only written because the wisdom conferred by hindsight enabled the authors to discern the central role which Jesus had played in the redemptive history of Israel—a role which would have been far from evident at the time the actual events were being played out.

This post-resurrection awareness compelled the authors to interpret the meaning of Jesus' life by reference to previous redemptive acts of God and to present him as the final act in the great redemption drama planned from Creation. Even though theologians and academics have appropriated the writings of the New Testament as their own special and private preserve, it must be emphasised that one does not have to be an expert in Israelite literary styles to comprehend the way in which the authors sought to identify Jesus as the promised "prophet like Moses" (see Part XIII.3: *The Israelite Messiah-The Prophet like Moses*). Note that in Acts Chapter Seven, Stephen was stoned for making this very same claim. Note also that, among all those present, Jesus was "visible" only to Stephen.

Section 1

Transfiguration

Consider the following account of the Transfiguration and its four unmistakable parallels with the account of Moses at Sinai.

> And after six days Jesus took with him Peter and James, and John his brother, and led them up a high mountain by themselves. And he was transfigured before them, and his face shone like the sun, and his clothes became white as light. And behold, there appeared to them Moses and Elijah, talking with him. And Peter said to Jesus, "Lord, it is good that we are here. If you wish, I will make three tents here, one for you and one for Moses and one for Elijah." He was still speaking when, behold, a bright cloud overshadowed them, and a voice from the cloud said, "This is my beloved Son,a with whom I am well pleased; listen to him" (Matthew 17:1-5 ESV cf. Mark 9:2-7; Luke 9:28-35).

The three named witnesses

> Then He said to Moses, "Come up to the LORD, you and Aaron, Nadab and Abihu and seventy of the elders of Israel, and you shall worship at a distance. "Moses alone, however, shall come near to the LORD, but they shall not come near, nor shall the people come up with him" (Exodus 24:1-2 NASB).

The Shining Countenance

> And it came to pass, when Moses came down from mount Sinai with the two tables of the testimony in Moses hand, when he came down from the mount, that Moses knew not that the skin of his face shone by reason of his speaking with him (Exodus 34:29 ASV).

The Glory Cloud

> When Moses went up on the mountain, the cloud covered it, and the glory of the Lord settled on Mount Sinai…(Exodus 24:15-16 NIV).

An analysis of the "glory cloud" appears in Part XII.3: *The Israelite God-Manifestations* and will be explored further in the forthcoming Ascension section.

The voice from the cloud

> ...For six days the cloud covered the mountain, and on the seventh day the Lord called to Moses from within the cloud (Exodus 24:16 NIV).

In addition to the "voice from the cloud" references in the Synoptic Gospel accounts of the Transfiguration, consider also additional New Testament references to a voice from Heaven:

> Father, glorify your name." Then a voice came from heaven, "I have glorified it, and I will glorify it again!" The crowd standing there heard this and said that it was thunder. Others were saying, "An angel has spoken to him." Jesus replied, "This voice is for your benefit, not for mine" (John 12:28-31 ISV).

> For we did not follow cleverly devised stories when we told you about the coming (*parousía*) of our Lord Jesus Christ in power, but we were eyewitnesses of his majesty. He received honor and glory from God the Father when the voice came to him from the Majestic Glory, saying, "This is my Son, whom I love; with him I am well pleased. "We ourselves heard this voice that came from heaven when we were with him on the sacred mountain (2 Pet. 1:16-18 NIV).

Section 2

Resurrection

The third day in the morning

> And the LORD said unto Moses, Go unto the people, and sanctify them to day and to morrow, and let them wash their clothes, And be ready against the third day: for the third day the LORD will come down in the sight of all the people upon mount Sinai (Exodus 19:10-11 KJV).

> On the morning of the third day there was thunder and lightning, with a thick cloud over the mountain, and a very loud trumpet blast. Everyone in the camp trembled (Exodus 19:16 NIV).

At the Sinai event described above, the power of God was demonstrated before all the people on the *third day in the morning*. Just as at Sinai, all the Gospels record that the power of God was also demonstrated on the *third day in the morning* by the resurrection:

> Early on the first day of the week, while it was still dark, Mary Magdalene went to the tomb and saw that the stone had been removed from the entrance (John 20:1 ESV cf. Matthew 28:1; Luke 24:1; Mark 16:2).
>
> Him God raised up the third day, and shewed him openly; Not to all the people, but unto witnesses chosen before of God, even to us, who did eat and drink with him after he rose from the dead (Acts 10:40-41 KJV).

The only difference between the two accounts is that the resurrection power of God was not demonstrated to all the people, as at Sinai, but only to pre-selected witnesses.

> Before long, the world will not see me anymore, but you will see me. Because I live, you also will live (John 14:19 NIV).

The fact that this difference is specifically noted in the above passage, and in Acts 10:41, is evidence that the events at Sinai were being referenced in the resurrection accounts.

The forty days

> When I went up on the mountain to receive the tablets of stone, the tablets of the covenant that the Lord had made with you, I stayed on the mountain forty days and forty nights; I ate no bread and drank no water (Deuteronomy 9:9 NIV).
>
> To whom also he shewed himself alive after his passion by many infallible proofs, being seen of them forty days, and speaking of the things pertaining to the kingdom of God (Acts 1:3 KJV).

Section 3

Ascension

Accounts of the Ascension appear only in the Book of Acts, the Gospel of Luke, and in the disputed ending of Mark (verses 9-20). We will focus our attention on the account in Acts:

> When they therefore were come together, they asked of him, saying, Lord, wilt thou at this time restore again the kingdom to Israel? And he said unto them, It is not for you to know the times or the seasons, which the Father hath put in his own power. But ye shall receive power, after that the Holy Ghost is come upon you: and ye shall be witnesses unto me both in Jerusalem, and in all Judaea, and

in Samaria, and unto the uttermost part of the earth. And when he had spoken these things, while they beheld, he was taken up; and a cloud received him out of their sight. And while they looked stedfastly toward heaven as he went up, behold, two men stood by them in white apparel; Which also said, Ye men of Galilee, why stand ye gazing up into heaven? this same Jesus, which is taken up from you into heaven, shall so come in like manner as ye have seen him go into heaven (Acts 1:6-11 KJV).

The "cloud" referenced in the above passage has not received the attention it deserves from theologians and academics of various stripes so we will now attempt to make up for their shortcomings.

The Glory Cloud

The Hebrew Scriptures contain numerous references to a "glory cloud", sometimes referred to as the *Shekinah*. The word *Shekinah* derives from the Hebrew שָׁכַן (*shakan*), which means to "dwell", "settle" or "abide". It has come to signify the majestic presence or manifestation of God which descended to "dwell" among men. The word occurs in passages that speak of God dwelling either in the Tabernacle or among the people of Israel. For example:

> And let them make me a sanctuary, that I may dwell (*shakan*) in their midst (Exodus 25:8 ESV).

This "glory cloud" or *Shekinah* protected the Israelites after the Exodus, received Moses on Sinai, carried up Elijah to Heaven, and protected Jerusalem for a time. (See also Exodus 14:19, 40:34; 1 Kings 8:10, 2 Chronicles 7:1, and the book of Ezekiel which contains interesting passages about the movements of this glory cloud.)

The Transfiguration and Ascension accounts both refer to this glory cloud which has always been envisioned by Israelites as *descending* from the abode of God (Heaven) at certain times, and then *ascending* from whence it came.

The following passage from Exodus, briefly referred to in the Transfiguration section, illuminates our understanding of the concept:

> When Moses went up on the mountain, the cloud covered it, and the glory of the Lord settled on Mount Sinai. For six days the cloud covered the mountain, and on the seventh day the Lord called to Moses from within the cloud. To the Israelites the glory of the Lord looked like a consuming fire on top of the mountain. Then Moses entered the cloud as he went on up the mountain. And he stayed on the mountain forty days and forty nights (Exodus 24:15-18 NIV).

In passages where this glory cloud is referenced, it is often paired with its perceived origin, viz. "clouds of heaven". For example, consider the following:

> I saw in the night visions, and, behold, one like the Son of man came with the clouds of heaven, and came to the Ancient of days, and they brought him near before him. And there was given him dominion, and glory, and a kingdom, that all people, nations, and languages, should serve him: his dominion is an everlasting dominion, which shall not pass away, and his kingdom that which shall not be destroyed (Daniel 7:13-14 KJV).

And now observe how New Testament authors other than Luke/Acts applied this glory cloud concept:

> And then shall appear the sign of the Son of man in heaven: and then shall all the tribes of the earth mourn, and they shall see the Son of man coming (*erchomai*) in the clouds of heaven with power and great glory (Matthew 24:30 KJV).
>
> ...Again the high priest asked him, and said unto him, Art thou the Christ, the Son of the Blessed? And Jesus said, I am: and ye shall see the Son of man sitting on the right hand of power, and coming (*erchomai*) in the clouds of heaven (Mark 14:61-62 KJV).
>
> Then they (the two witnesses) heard a loud voice from heaven saying to them, "Come up here." And they went up to heaven in a cloud, while their enemies looked on (Revelation 11:12 NIV).

As is evident, the concept of the glory cloud was in the forefront of the minds of New Testament authors when they wrote their accounts of the Transfiguration and the Ascension. (See also Part XII.3: *The Israelite God-Manifestations*)

Taken to Heaven

The Son of Man coming to God with the clouds of heaven evoked the Day of Atonement when the High Priest entered the Jerusalem Temple's Holy of Holies and symbolically ascended into God's presence (Heaven) surrounded by clouds of incense. And as near-contemporary texts show, on his return to the people from the inner sanctuary, the High Priest symbolically descended from Heaven down to Earth. (Note that God was believed to rule through an opening in the sky directly above the Jerusalem Temple, the *axis mundi*, the place of connection between God in Heaven and his covenant people on Earth.)

Just as Jesus disappeared into Heaven, so also did Elijah the prophet:

And it came to pass, when the LORD would take up Elijah into heaven by a whirlwind, that Elijah went with Elisha from Gilgal…And it came to pass, as they still went on, and talked, that, behold, there appeared a chariot of fire, and horses of fire, and parted them both asunder; and Elijah went up by a whirlwind into heaven (2 Kings 2:1,11 NIV).

Summing up

The accounts of the Transfiguration, Resurrection and Ascension associate Jesus with Moses and Elijah, the two greatest figures in Israel's redemptive history, thus reinforcing the New Testament claim that Jesus is the ultimate redeemer, the King-Messiah of the House of David, the fulfillment of God's ancient promises to the Israelite ancestors.

Note

The original New Testament accounts were steeped in *Midrash*, a traditional storytelling style which was readily understood by Israelites both at home and in the Diaspora (see Part II.8: *The Documents-Understanding Literary Styles*). Doing *Midrash* means enlivening a current event and investing it with a deeper meaning by analogous association with a prior event already holding great significance for a contemporary reader. Hence we see an abundance of *Midrashic* analogy between individual events in the life of Jesus and previous events in the national life of Israel, the purpose of which was to demonstrate Jesus' central role in the redemptive plan of God. We therefore see variations according to the presence of absence of *Midrash*, and even the level of *Midrash*, in the individual accounts.

CHAPTER SEVEN

Three Days

Note

In a previous Chapter we examined the phrase "the third day in the morning" and drew attention to the parallels between Moses at Sinai and the accounts of the resurrection. Now we will attempt to discover the meaning of other references attached to the "third day" theme and how they relate to our understanding of the resurrection.

Section 1

Determining Death

Throughout history, the ability to determine whether death was actual or apparent was limited to observation of the body over a period of time. Only in the modern age has technology provided the means of establishing actual death with certainty.

Ancient Israelites were aware of the possibility that death may only be apparent and made provisions allowing for the body to be visited for a period of up to three days to check if death's processes had begun in earnest:

> One may go out to the cemetery for three days to inspect the dead for a sign of life, without fear that this smacks of heathen practice. For it happened that a man was inspected after three days, and he went on to live twenty-five years; still another went on to have five children and died later.[4]

Those readers of the Gospel accounts who were acquainted with well-established mourning rituals including checking on the condition of the body and anointing it with spices would have no reason to wonder why the women visited the tomb on the Sunday morning after the Sabbath restrictions. The particulars of these accounts would also have offered readers further confirmation as to their truth and accuracy. (It is an interesting observation that the author of Matthew found it important to

---

[4] Tractate Semahot 8.1: Babylonian Talmud. This Tractate reflects customs begun at least as early as the 1st Century AD because it pre-supposes the wide-spread practice of burial in cave-tombs which had begun at a much earlier date.

emphasise that the followers of Jesus were more faithful to these rituals than were the elites who attempted to thwart the process by the posting of guards and the sealing of the stone, details found only in his Gospel.)

The Raising of Lazarus

Corresponding to the above rituals was the common belief that the spirit of the deceased lingered around the body for three days before finally returning to God on the fourth day. Besides describing events surrounding the raising of Lazarus, the account from John's Gospel also includes elements of great import which are the subject of commentaries appearing elsewhere in this work. Selected extracts from John's account are reproduced below followed by observations on the most striking elements:

> Now a man named Lazarus was sick. He was from Bethany, the village of Mary and her sister Martha. (This Mary, whose brother Lazarus now lay sick, was the same one who poured perfume on the Lord and wiped his feet with her hair.) So the sisters sent word to Jesus, "Lord, the one you love is sick." When he heard this, Jesus said, "This sickness will not end in death. No, it is for God's glory so that God's Son may be glorified through it." Now Jesus loved Martha and her sister and Lazarus. So when he heard that Lazarus was sick, he stayed where he was two more days, and then he said to his disciples, "Let us go back to Judea" (John 11:1-6 NIV).

> "…Our friend Lazarus has fallen asleep; but I am going there to wake him up." His disciples replied, "Lord, if he sleeps, he will get better." Jesus had been speaking of his death, but his disciples thought he meant natural sleep So then he told them plainly, "Lazarus is dead, and for your sake I am glad I was not there, so that you may believe. But let us go to him" (John 11:11-15 NIV).

> On his arrival, Jesus found that Lazarus had already been in the tomb for four days (John 11:17 NIV).

> Jesus said to her (Martha), "Your brother will rise again." Martha answered, "I know he will rise again in the resurrection at the last day." Jesus said to her, "I am the resurrection and the life. The one who believes in me will live, even though they die; and whoever lives by believing in me will never die. Do you believe this?" "Yes, Lord," she replied, "I believe that you are the Messiah, the Son of God, who is to come into the world" (John 11:23-27 NIV).

> Jesus, once more deeply moved, came to the tomb. It was a cave with a stone laid across the entrance. "Take away the stone," he said. "But, Lord," said Martha, the sister of the dead man, "by this time there is a bad odor, for he has been there four days." Then Jesus said, "Did I not tell you that if you believe, you

will see the glory of God?" So they took away the stone. Then Jesus looked up and said, "Father, I thank you that you have heard me. I knew that you always hear me, but I said this for the benefit of the people standing here, that they may believe that you sent me." When he had said this, Jesus called in a loud voice, "Lazarus, come out!" The dead man came out, his hands and feet wrapped with strips of linen, and a cloth around his face. Jesus said to them, "Take off the grave clothes and let him go" (John 11:38-44 NIV).

Observations

- The belief noted above that the spirit lingered around the body for three days before finally departing on the fourth explains why Jesus delayed his return to Judea for *two more days* after hearing the news that Lazarus was sick and did not arrive until Lazarus had been dead for *four days*. If he had returned sooner, it could be asserted that Lazarus was not really dead and therefore not really raised. Just as in his crucifixion account, where the author set out to demonstrate that Jesus was truly dead by introducing details not found in the Synoptic Gospels, so also is he asserting that Lazarus was truly dead.

- The disciples appeared not to understand when Jesus told them that Lazarus had *fallen asleep* and that he was going to *wake him up*. However, when Jesus told Martha that, "Your brother will rise again," she responded with, "I know he will rise again in the resurrection at the last day". These statements by both Jesus and Martha reflect the Biblical proposition that the dead are just sleeping in the earth until the resurrection at the last day. (In forthcoming Chapters, this subject will be explored in greater depth. (See also Part X.2: *Aftermath-Immortal Souls*)

- When asked if she believes Jesus' statement, "I am the resurrection and the life. The one who believes in me will live, even though they die; and whoever lives by believing in me will never die", Martha responds by saying, "I believe that you are the Messiah, the Son of God, who is to come into the world". She thus connects the resurrection with the Messiah, which reflects the twin expectations that the Messiah would gather into one all the children of Israel who were dispersed abroad and establish the Kingdom of God on Earth in the land of Israel. (This dispersion, known as the Diaspora, was regarded as a symbolic death and return to Israel as a symbolic resurrection.)

- The parallels with Jesus' own resurrection are obvious: a stone across the entrance to a cave tomb and linen wrappings with a separate face cloth. Only John provides us with the face cloth detail in his account of the raising of Jesus. He is therefore implying to his readers that the raising of Lazarus prefigures the raising of Jesus, just as the raising of Jesus prefigures the eventual raising of all God-fearing Israelites. (This interconnected network of themes defies a brief and concise analysis. However, in forthcoming Chapters we will attempt to provide an account which will be as minimally tedious as is possible.)

- Although John is obviously drawing these parallels, there was a profound difference between the *before* and *after* bodies of Lazarus and Jesus. Lazarus continued to act under his own volition, just as he did before, and he was visible to all, just as he was before. Jesus, however, did not continue to act under his own volition, as he had done before, his appearances were controlled by God, unlike they had been before, and he was visible only to a pre-chosen few, unlike he was before.

John's Gospel centres on the collision of spiritual values between Jesus and the Jerusalem elites. Jesus represents spiritual life, they represent spiritual death. When the elites judge and kill Jesus and God responds by overturning their judgement and restoring Jesus to life, John's message to his readers is that life will always conquer death. Perhaps, then, we should regard the raising of Lazarus as John's readers would have done—as a case of life being the spiritual victor in its battle with death rather than as a case of either actual resurrection or the revival of one apparently dead.

Note that reports of the raising of Lazarus lead to the plot to kill Jesus (John 11:45-53).

Section 2

Counting the days

The Gospels are in agreement that the crucifixion took place around three hours after midday on a Friday afternoon. Critics have used the following prediction by Jesus to cast doubt on the veracity of the crucifixion accounts:

> For just as Jonah was three days and three nights in the belly of the great fish, so will the Son of Man be three days and three nights in the heart of the earth (Matthew 12:40 ESV).

Jesus used this phrase "three days and three nights" once only, and then when quoting from the Book of Jonah:

> Now the LORD provided a huge fish to swallow Jonah, and Jonah was in the belly of the fish three days and three nights (Jonah 1:17 NIV).

It is asserted by some that the only way Jesus could have been in the tomb for "three days and three nights" is if the crucifixion happened the day before, i.e. Thursday afternoon.

However, the Israelite method of reckoning the passage of time cannot be compared to our own. Their day began at sunset and ended the following sunset, a period of twenty-four hours known as a "day and a night". Whilst a "day and a night" could refer to the entire period of twenty-four hours, it could also refer to any period falling within. For example, the period of time between 3 p.m. and sunset on Friday was reckoned as a whole "day and a night" because it belonged to the twenty-four day which began on the previous evening, Thursday, at sunset. From Friday at sunset until Saturday at sunset was an actual twenty-four hour "day and a night". The period of time from sunset on Saturday until sunrise on Sunday was also reckoned as a whole "day and a night" because it belonged to the twenty-four day which had begun some twelve hours previously on the Saturday at sunset. (See also article from Jewish Encyclopaedia [5].)

Although complicated to our way of thinking, the "three days and three nights" did not necessarily mean a period of seventy-two hours but a period which included portions of "three days and three nights". In the case of Jesus, his body was placed in the tomb about thirty-nine hours before the tomb was discovered to be empty.

Since Jesus quoted from the Book of Jonah found in the Hebrew Scriptures, perhaps the best demonstration of the elastic use of the terminology is found in another passage from the Hebrew Scriptures:

> Then Esther replied to Mordecai, "Go and gather all the Jewish people who are in Susa and fast for me. Don't eat or drink for three days, night or day. Both I and my young women will also fast in the same way, and then I'll go in to the king, even though it's against the law. And if I perish, I perish." Then Mordecai left and did everything that Esther had ordered him. On the third day, Esther put on her royal attire and stood in the inner courtyard of the palace in front of the king's quarters… (Esther 4:15-5:1 ISV).

---

5 Jewish Encylopaedia Article: *Day*. Accessed 16 October 2018
   http://www.jewishencyclopedia.com/articles/5007-day

Consider and compare also the elastic use of the terminology by Jesus himself when speaking of his death and resurrection, "three days and three nights" (Matthew 12:40), "after three days" (Mark 8:31), "in three days" (John 2:19), "on the third day" (Matthew 16:21; 17:23; 20:19; Luke 24:46).

In this age of atomic clocks, our lives are regulated by the precise measurement of the passage of time. It is unwise to hold the ancients to the same measure of precision when they had only the observed movements of celestial bodies to guide and regulate their lives.

Section 3

From death to life

Perhaps the most definitive and concise New Testament statement about the "third day" theme is found in Paul's First Letter to the Corinthians. According to Paul, Jesus had to rise on "the third day" in accordance with the Scriptures:

> For I delivered unto you first of all that which I also received, how that Christ died for our sins according to the scriptures; And that he was buried, and that he rose again the third day according to the scriptures… (2 Corinthians 15:3-4 KJV).

According to Paul, the events surrounding the crucifixion and resurrection were foretold in the Scriptures and he is now passing that information on to his readers. Paul, an Israelite with a Pharisaic background, schooled in the Scriptures from childhood, would not have made this claim with such assurance if he had not been convinced of its veracity. Although many of his contemporary readers would have known on what Scriptures he based his claim, Paul makes no specific references so we are left to discover them for ourselves.

One of the Scriptures on which Paul perhaps relied in part was a passage from the Book of Hosea:

> Come, and let us return unto the LORD: for he hath torn, and he will heal us; he hath smitten, and he will bind us up. After two days will he revive us: in the third day he will raise us up, and we shall live in his sight (Hosea 6:1-2 KJV).

However, given that Paul sets all of his teachings within the framework of the Abrahamic Covenant, perhaps the story of the *Akedah* or "binding of Isaac" found in Genesis Chapter 22 held the most significance for him. As well as the "three days" theme, verses 2-18 include motifs which form the basis of many New Testament teachings other than those of Paul so the reader is encouraged to study the passage in its entirety.

The story of the attempted sacrifice of Isaac has no doubt puzzled many. We read that Abraham hears a voice telling him to sacrifice Isaac, despite prior promises from God that his posterity, land and blessings would be established only through Isaac. The answer to this puzzle is found in the Book of Joshua where we find that Abraham's ancestors had served "other" Gods:

> And Joshua said unto all the people, "Thus saith the LORD God of Israel, Your fathers dwelt on the other side of the flood in old time, even Terah, the father of Abraham, and the father of Nachor: and they served other gods" (Joshua 24:2 KJV).

The journey towards the place of sacrifice, which Abraham reaches on the "third day", symbolises progressive revelation of the one, true God and the passage from death to life foreshadowing the crucifixion and resurrection. The God who had called Abraham to Canaan to serve him is not one of the "gods" of his ancestors. This God would not renege on his promises; both he and Isaac would return; God would provide the lamb; and even if Isaac's death were required, God could raise him to life. When Isaac was spared, Abraham received him back in a figure from the dead. The author of the Book of Hebrews provides us with Abraham's reasoning:

> By faith Abraham, when he was tried, offered up Isaac: and he that had received the promises offered up his only begotten son, Of whom it was said, That in Isaac shall thy seed be called: Accounting that God was able to raise him up, even from the dead; from whence also he received him in a figure (Hebrews 11:17-19 KJV).

Abraham's faith in the power of God was established and his absolute obedience extolled and rewarded. The practice of human sacrifice is explicitly repudiated, both then by the "angel of the Lord", and later by prophets such as Micah (6:7) and Jeremiah (7:31).

CHAPTER EIGHT

Community Promises

As noted previously, the Messiah when he came was expected to fulfill the ancient promises to the Israelite Diaspora that they would one day be resurrected from exile and in-gathered to the land of Israel to form the Kingdom of God under the rule of God's Messiah. Perhaps the most definitive and striking example of the resurrection promise is found in the Book of Ezekiel.

Strange as it may seem, Ezekiel's vision of the Valley of Dry Bones, written circa 570 BC during the Babylonian exile, is not only dismissed by the adherents of teachings such as Supersessionism, but also for reasons strategic and political. Although it is an ancient vision of promise, and although legions may wish it away, it would be intellectually dishonest to ignore its modern fulfillment and visible impact on the world stage. It is therefore worth considering the passage in its entirety:

> The hand of the LORD was upon me, and carried me out in the spirit of the LORD, and set me down in the midst of the valley which was full of bones, And caused me to pass by them round about: and, behold, there were very many in the open valley; and, lo, they were very dry. And he said unto me, Son of man, can these bones live? And I answered, O Lord GOD, thou knowest. Again he said unto me, Prophesy upon these bones, and say unto them, O ye dry bones, hear the word of the LORD. Thus saith the Lord GOD unto these bones; Behold, I will cause breath to enter into you, and ye shall live: And I will lay sinews upon you, and will bring up flesh upon you, and cover you with skin, and put breath in you, and ye shall live; and ye shall know that I am the LORD.

> So I prophesied as I was commanded: and as I prophesied, there was a noise, and behold a shaking, and the bones came together, bone to his bone. And when I beheld, lo, the sinews and the flesh came up upon them, and the skin covered them above: but there was no breath in them. Then said he unto me, Prophesy unto the wind, prophesy, son of man, and say to the wind, Thus saith the Lord GOD; Come from the four winds, O breath, and breathe upon these slain, that they may live. So I prophesied as he commanded me, and the breath came into them, and they lived, and stood up upon their feet, an exceeding great army.

> Then he said unto me, Son of man, these bones are the whole house of Israel: behold, they say, Our bones are dried, and our hope is lost: we are cut off for our parts. Therefore prophesy and say unto them, Thus saith the Lord GOD;

> Behold, O my people, I will open your graves, and cause you to come up out of your graves, and bring you into the land of Israel. And ye shall know that I am the LORD, when I have opened your graves, O my people, and brought you up out of your graves, And shall put my spirit in you, and ye shall live, and I shall place you in your own land: then shall ye know that I the LORD have spoken it, and performed it, saith the LORD (Ezekiel 37:1-14 KJV).

Consider also the following selection of other resurrection promises:

> Thy dead men shall live, together with my dead body shall they arise. Awake and sing, ye that dwell in dust: for thy dew is as the dew of herbs, and the earth shall cast out the dead (Isaiah 26:19 KJV).

> Behold, I will gather them out of all countries, whither I have driven them in mine anger, and in my fury, and in great wrath; and I will bring them again unto this place, and I will cause them to dwell safely (Jeremiah 32:37 KJV).

> "The days are coming," declares the Lord, "when the reaper will be overtaken by the plowman and the planter by the one treading grapes. New wine will drip from the mountains and flow from all the hills, and I will bring my people Israel back from exile. They will rebuild the ruined cities and live in them. They will plant vineyards and drink their wine; they will make gardens and eat their fruit. I will plant Israel in their own land, never again to be uprooted from the land I have given them"(Amos 9:13-15 NIV).

By the time the New Testament came to be written, these expectations of resurrection, in-gathering, and Kingdom had not yet been fulfilled. The authors were therefore faced with the challenge of convincing readers that the expectations had found their fulfillment, but in totally unexpected ways. Their arguments developed along the following lines. (See also Part XIII.2: *The Israelite Messiah-The Unexpected Messiah*.)

The communal resurrection of the exiles

Although the tribes of Israel still remained scattered in the dispersion, they argued that the resurrection of Jesus was a *foreshadowing* of this communal promise of resurrection and in-gathering envisioned by prophets such as Ezekiel in his vision of the Valley of Dry Bones. For example, in Matthew 27:51-52, the author draws multiple allusions to this passage in his account of the crucifixion.

The Kingdom of God

Although the Kingdom of God in the land of Israel under the rule of God's Messiah had not yet been established, they argued that a *foreshadowing* "spiritual" kingdom had been in existence since the resurrection. Although the authors claimed that Jesus fulfilled messianic expectations in these unexpected ways, their arguments propose a more literal fulfillment at some future time. As noted previously, it should be kept in mind that the Kingdom of God, the Kingdom of Heaven, the Messianic Age, and the Age to Come, are interchangeable terms implying the same conditions and the same promises.

CHAPTER NINE

Individual Promises

Individual resurrection was largely a theological concept emerging from an Israelite culture which believed in a God of life whose power and promises could not be broken by death. God had the power to overcome all obstacles and every hostile power standing in the way of his great promises of life to them. Not even death, man's greatest adversary, could hold man in the grave if God willed otherwise.

Whilst this concept remained within the sphere of theological and philosophical debate, disagreement between parties could be tolerated. However, it was a totally different matter to claim that the concept could be found in the Hebrew Scriptures. (The three recorded cases described in forthcoming pages were unprecedented and usually categorised as incidents of temporal resuscitation.)

The concept of individual resurrection from actual death was therefore rejected outright by groups such as the Sadducees, whom we would perhaps describe as *sola scriptura* people.

However, regardless of its contentious nature, the New Testament authors and major characters argued that both a communal and an individual resurrection had been promised in the Hebrew Scriptures.

When Paul said "for now we see through a glass, darkly", he could never have imagined how immeasurably darker would those reflections and shadows appear to us in the modern world so a note of caution before moving forward to New Testament teachings. Because the authors viewed the resurrection of Jesus as the foreshadowing of both a communal and individual resurrection, some of the source texts on which they rely may apply to one, or the other, or to both. They defy consensus categorisation today, as they have done in the past, and will do so in the future. Therefore, the wise course is to assume that the texts apply to both, thus everything is gained and nothing lost.

Authorial Sources

Although the consensus of higher-critical opinion is that belief in an individual resurrection of the dead was unattested before the Book of Daniel, the New Testament authors certainly reject this consensus.

Before turning our attention to the New Testament, however, let us first deal with the consensus text from the Book of Daniel, generally regarded as one that cannot be taken as anything other than literal. The following extracts are reproduced from The Soncino Books of the Bible: *Daniel, Ezra, Nehemiah*:

> And at that time Michael shall stand up, the great prince who standeth for the children of they people; and there shall be a time of trouble, such as never was since there was a nation even to that same time; and at that time thy people shall be delivered, everyone that shall be found written in the book. And many of them that sleep in the dust of the earth shall awake, some to everlasting life, and some to reproaches and everlasting abhorrence…But go thou thy way till the end be; and thou shalt rest (in the grave cf. Isaiah 57:2), and shalt stand up to thy lot, at the end of the days (Soncino, Daniel 12:1-2, 13).

In his commentary on this Chapter, Dr. Judah Slotki notes that:

> This chapter is generally taken by Jewish authorities to refer to the remote future which will herald the advent of the Messianic era.[6]

Dr. Slotki's term, "the Messianic era", is simply another way of referring to the Kingdom of God, the Kingdom of Heaven, the Messianic Age, and the Age to Come. As noted previously, it should be kept in mind that these are interchangeable terms implying the same conditions and the same promises.

The New Testament authors and major characters certainly did not accept that the Book of Daniel was the first in which the concept of individual resurrection was to be found. Consider the following selection of statements by Paul, Jesus, and Peter.

When Paul was on trial before the Sanhedrin, he skillfully diverted attention away from himself and made use of the animosity between the Sadducees and the Pharisees by saying that the real charge against him was because he had been preaching the resurrection of the dead:

> But when Paul perceived that the one part were Sadducees, and the other Pharisees, he cried out in the council, Men and brethren, I am a Pharisee, the son of a Pharisee: of the hope and resurrection of the dead I am called in question. And when he had so said, there arose a dissension between the Pharisees and the Sadducees: and the multitude was divided. For the Sadducees say that there is no resurrection, neither angel, nor spirit: but the Pharisees confess both (Acts 23:6-8 KJV).

---

6   Slotki, Dr. Judah J. Soncino Books of the Bible: *Daniel, Ezra, Nehemiah*. ed. Rev. Dr. A Cohen. The Soncino Press: London, 1970, pp 100-101.

Paul says he is on trial because of his "hope of the resurrection from the dead". From what sources do his hope spring? In the very next chapter of Acts, when on trial before Governor Felix, he enlightens us while at the same time dividing his opposition once again:

> However, I admit that I worship the God of our ancestors as a follower of the Way, which they call a sect. I believe everything that is in accordance with the Law and that is written in the Prophets, and I have the same hope in God as these men themselves have, that there will be a resurrection of both the righteous and the wicked (Acts 24:14-15 NIV).

The Law of Moses and the Prophets are Paul's sources, which he confirms yet again in Acts 26 when testifying before King Agrippa:

> To this day I have had the help that comes from God, and so I stand here testifying both to small and great, saying nothing but what the prophets and Moses said would come to pass: that the Christ must suffer and that, by being the first to rise from the dead, he would proclaim light both to our people and to the Gentiles (Acts 26:22-23 ESV).

Coming events casting their shadows before

Whilst it is clear that the New Testament authors and major characters drew their concept of an individual resurrection from the Hebrew Scriptures, the source texts on which they relied remain uncertain. Let us therefore raise some possibilities.

Three episodes of "raisings" are found in the *Ketuvim* (Writings) of the Hebrews Scriptures. Elijah raised a widow's son (2 Kings 17:20-23), Elisha raised a Shunammite's son (2 Kings 4:34-35), and Elisha's bones raised a dead man when the latter's body touched the prophet's bones (2 Kings 13:20-21). It is notable that these incidents involved "prophets", i.e. those to whom the word of God came, and that all were attributed to God's power to triumph over death. Although they are not directly referred to in the New Testament, there can be little doubt that they were regarded as types and shadows which influenced perceptions that physical death was reversible.

Consider the following passage:

> Now when John heard in prison about the deeds of the Christ, he sent word by his disciples and said to him, "Are you the one who is to come, or shall we look for another?" (Matthew 11:2-3 ESV).
>
> And Jesus answered them, "Go and tell John what you hear and see: the blind receive their sight and the lame walk, lepers are cleansed and the deaf hear,

and the dead are raised up, and the poor have good news preached to them" (Matthew 11:4-5 ESV).

Verse 5 is an amalgamation of various texts from the Hebrew Scriptures, notably from Isaiah 35:5-6 (where there is reference to the blind, deaf, and lame) and Isaiah 61:1 (where good news is preached to the poor). Whilst we cannot be certain, Jesus' reference to the dead who "are raised up" could be allusions to various passages which appear to speak of resurrection such as Isaiah 26:19; 1 Samuel 2:6; Job 19:25-27; Psalm16:9-10; and of course Daniel 12:13.

The problem which faces us is that passages from the Hebrew Scriptures most often speak of a symbolic communal resurrection so, once again, we must assume that texts which speak of this communal resurrection were understood by the authors of the New Testament to be types and shadows of a future physical resurrection for individuals.

Jesus stated clearly that the Psalms were a major key to understanding his resurrection:

> Then he told them, "These are the words that I spoke to you while I was still with you—that everything written about me in the Law of Moses, the Prophets, and the Psalms had to be fulfilled" (Luke 24:44 ISV).

By extension, therefore, we can expect that passages which speak of hope for the consequent resurrection life beyond death for all those who "believe" in Jesus can be found in the Psalms. In forthcoming pages, a selection of relevant passages from the Psalms will be examined.

Before we can move on to the New Testament's resurrection teachings, we must first grasp the nature of the promises attached to the establishment of the earthly Kingdom.

CHAPTER TEN

The Kingdom of God

Note on Matthew's Gospel

During the Second Temple period, the commandment against taking the name of YHWH in vain was so strictly interpreted that pious substitutions were used to avoid unintentionally pronouncing the sacred name. Given that Matthew's Gospel is totally focused on Israelite norms, it is not surprising therefore to find the author substituting the term Kingdom of Heaven for the term Kingdom of God found in the remainder of the New Testament.

The Kingdom of God (Heaven) is also referred to as the Messianic Age or the Age to Come. All terms imply the same conditions and the same promises. On that premise, and for the sake of simplicity, we will use the term Kingdom of God in this Chapter.

Before the Resurrection

The hope of Israel was the restoration of the throne of David under the kingship of an "anointed one" (Messiah) at his one and only appearance. For example:

> Of the greatness of his government and peace there will be no end. He will reign on David's throne and over his kingdom, establishing and upholding it with justice and righteousness from that time on and forever. The zeal of the LORD Almighty will accomplish this (Isaiah 9:7 NIV cf. Psalm 89:19-29).
>
> And there was given him dominion, and glory, and a kingdom, that all people, nations, and languages, should serve him: his dominion is an everlasting dominion, which shall not pass away, and his kingdom that which shall not be destroyed (Daniel 7:14 KJV).

The hope for this ideal Kingdom of God was expressed in the synagogue liturgy at the time, "may it come soon—in your lifetime". Jesus came preaching this very same hope. He taught that his activity and presence among them was a sign that God's redemptive reign was now coming upon them, was now breaking through among people who were making God's will their will (e.g. Luke 16:16).

When Jesus told the disciples, "I tell you the truth, some who are standing here will not taste death before they see the Kingdom of God" (Luke 9:27), they naturally assumed that they would live to see its inauguration. However, the disciples were not the only ones who were expecting the immediate establishment of the Kingdom:

> Those who went ahead and those who followed shouted, "Hosanna! Blessed is he who comes in the name of the Lord! Blessed is the coming kingdom of our father David! Hosanna in the highest heaven!" (Mark 11:9-10 NIV).

Jesus had to correct this assumption with statements such as, "I go to prepare a place for you" (John 14:2), and the parable concerning a certain nobleman who went into a "far country" to receive a Kingdom and then returned (see Luke 19:11-27). In the following passage, Jesus makes it quite clear that he would reign on this earthly throne in a future period he named "the regeneration":

> And Jesus said unto them, Verily I say unto you, that ye who have followed me, in the regeneration when the Son of man shall sit on the throne of his glory, ye also shall sit upon twelve thrones, judging the twelve tribes of Israel (Matthew 19:28 KJV cf. Matthew 25:31; Luke 22:29-30; Daniel 7:27).

Jesus promises his disciples that they also will also sit on thrones, "in the regeneration". Scant, if any, attention has been paid to this statement so we will explore its meaning in a forthcoming Chapter.

After the Resurrection

Before his death, Jesus had told the disciples and others that the earthly Kingdom would not be inaugurated until his return from a "far country". After the resurrection, the disciples still hoped he was about to establish the Kingdom so Jesus was forced to correct them once again:

> When they therefore were come together, they asked of him, saying, Lord, wilt thou at this time restore again the kingdom to Israel? And he said unto them, It is not for you to know the times or the seasons, which the Father hath put in his own power (Acts 1:6-7 KJV).

While the authors of the New Testament recorded the hopes of the contemporaries of Jesus, they themselves were under no such misapprehensions and preached that the kingdom and resurrection promises would be fulfilled in two phases.

For those who hold to the view that the fullness of the Kingdom of God is already in existence and being ruled by Jesus from "heaven", it must be stressed that Gabriel's promise to Mary that her son would sit on the throne of David has not yet been fulfilled. Just as David's throne was always an earthly throne, so also is this Kingdom an earthly Kingdom:

> He shall be great, and shall be called the Son of the Highest: and the Lord God shall give unto him the throne of his father David: And he shall reign over the

house of Jacob for ever; and of his kingdom there shall be no end (Luke 1:32-33 KJV).

The author of the Book of Revelation drew on Daniel 7:14 to assure his readers that the concept of an earthly Kingdom had not been abandoned and that, in the fullness of time, the following would come to pass:

> And the seventh angel sounded; and there were great voices in heaven, saying, The kingdoms of this world are become the kingdoms of our Lord, and of his Christ; and he shall reign for ever and ever (Revelation 11:15 KJV).

The establishment of this Kingdom, a holy and righteous Kingdom of brotherhood, peace and justice modelled on a restored and perfected Kingdom of David, is the culmination of the hope of Israel.

CHAPTER ELEVEN

Now, but not yet

Introductory Notes

It must be made perfectly clear that it is not necessary to believe in God, or in Jesus, or in the resurrection, or in anything at all. What is necessary, however, is the living of a life which mirrors the principles and values espoused by Jesus, whether one knows it or not. For God, blind belief is nothing: character in action is everything. (See also a previous Chapter: *Roadblocks: Faith is not Blind* for a definition of the terms "faith" and "belief".)

In all cases, the English words "eternal" and other forms signifying "endlessness" have been incorrectly translated from the original Greek. (See a previous Chapter: *Roadblocks: Eternity* for the correct translation of these Greek words.)

The Age to Come is also referred to as the Kingdom of God (Heaven) or the "Messianic Age". All terms are synonymous and imply the same conditions and the same promises.

Section 1

Authorial Teachings

When the ancient promises of resurrection, in-gathering, and kingdom were not fulfilled in the lifetime of Jesus, the New Testament proposed a spiritual kingdom and a spiritual resurrection which were foreshadows of a future fulfillment. Of most concern to the authorities was the fact that the apostles were teaching this foreshadowing resurrection:

> And as they spake unto the people, the priests, and the captain of the temple, and the Sadducees, came upon them, Being grieved that they taught the people, and preached through Jesus the resurrection from the dead (Acts 4:2 KJV).

Paul preached that entry into the future kingdom and the future resurrection could be ensured in the here and now for those who, in a spiritual sense, crucified the old man after the fashion of Adam and resurrected the new man after the fashion of Jesus. In the here and now, his followers may know the power of his resurrection and walk in newness of life, that endless life which Jesus shares with his followers because he continues to live in them.

Because Paul and other New Testament authors focused in large measure on these spiritual aspects of kingdom and resurrection, we must turn to statements made by the living Jesus for an expanded understanding of the resurrection teachings.

It emerges from the Gospel accounts that while his contemporaries seemed oblivious to such an outcome, Jesus also understood that these promises would not be fulfilled in a literal sense in his own lifetime and therefore taught the same two-phased fulfillment. That this was a totally radical concept and not at all reflective of Messianic expectations as they understood them to be is evidenced by, for example, Nicodemus' confusion when Jesus spoke of an enabling spiritual rebirth, "you must be born again". (John 3:5-7)

Section 2

The Teachings of Jesus

Crucial to an understanding of the resurrection is an assessment of relevant teachings issuing from the mouth of Jesus himself while yet living, as recorded in the Gospels. None of these teachings have been fully explored due to attitudes which favour doctrinal imperatives over rigorous inquiry. This grave dereliction of duty by those entrusted with the teaching of erstwhile followers of Jesus can only be rectified by an honest appraisal of texts emerging from a culture vastly different to our own and separated in time by thousands of years. Key elements of these teachings are revealed in exchanges with contemporaries such as the Pharisees, the Sadducees, Martha the sister of Lazarus, and various others.

His sources

We have noted the sources from which New Testament authors such as Paul drew their resurrection teachings. Before proceeding to an analysis of Jesus' teachings, it is also necessary to confirm his source material. By comparing his teachings with those of his major adversarial groups, the Pharisees and Sadducees, we can not only confirm his sources but also eliminate certain teachings which owe their existence to alien influences far removed from an Israelite milieu.

The Pharisees and Sadducees

The Pharisees had been highly influenced by Hellenist thought, especially by Plato's philosophy of the soul. This philosophy of the soul holds that man is a duality composed of a pre-existent immortal soul imprisoned within a physical body. Only upon death can the immortal soul of man be released from the body and return to its metaphysical home. We are indebted to the contemporary historian Flavius Josephus for the following description of Pharisaic belief:

> …they (the Pharisees) also believe that souls have an immortal vigour in them, and that under the earth there will be rewards or punishments, according as they have lived virtuously or viciously in this life; and the latter are to be detained in an everlasting prison, but that the former shall have the power to revive and live again; on accounts of which doctrines they are able to greatly persuade the body of the people… [7]

It is clear from passages such as the one below that Jesus rejected the Hellenist-inspired teachings of the Pharisees, as described above by Josephus:

> "You (the Pharisees) are destroying the word of God through your tradition that you have handed down. And you do many other things like that" (Mark 7:13 ISV).

However, he shared their view that there was an individual resurrection although their conceptualising of it was incorrect. (Luke's parenthetical remark in Acts 23:8 that the "Sadducees say that there is no resurrection, and that there are neither angels nor spirits, but the Pharisees believe all these things", is further confirmation that the Pharisees believed in resurrection.)

It should be more than apparent that mainstream Christian teachings in respect of immortal souls, rewards and punishments immediately upon death, and so forth, are virtually identical to those of the Pharisees. These teachings therefore stand under the same condemnation by Jesus for the same reason—they destroy the word of God with Hellenist-inspired teachings and traditions.

As noted previously, the Sadducees held to what they believed was the strict scriptural view that man is one indivisible entity and could not be separated into soul and body components. They also held to the following scriptural statements that there was no post-mortem independent existence of any kind, no consciousness, no rewards or punishments, only oblivion in the grave:

> His spirit departs, he returns to the earth; In that very day his thoughts perish (Psalm 146:4 NASB).

---

[7] Flavius Josephus. "Antiquities of the Jews" in *The Works of Flavius Josephus*, xviii, Chapter 1. Transl. William Whiston. Milner and Sowerby: Halifax, 1864, p. 390.

> For the living know that they shall die: but the dead know not any thing, neither have they any more a reward; for the memory of them is forgotten... Whatsoever thy hand findeth to do, do it with thy might; for there is no work, nor device, nor knowledge, nor wisdom, in the grave, whither thou goest (Ecclesiastes 9:5,10 KJV).

Jesus agreed with the Sadducees that the Hebrew Scriptures were the "word of God" and the paramount source for teaching, although he disagreed with their view that the concept of individual resurrection was not to be found therein. Thus we find him arguing with the Sadducees and pointing out the error of their ways. One of these exchanges in particular deserves our full attention. When the Sadducees attempted to mock Jesus by telling him a story which they thought displayed the absurdity of resurrection, they received much more than they had expected for he responded with a statement that not only displayed their ignorance of scripture but contained layers of meaning crucial to our understanding of more than just the resurrection theme, as we will see:

> ...The people of this age marry and are given in marriage. But those who are considered worthy of taking part in the age to come and in the resurrection from the dead will neither marry nor be given in marriage, and they can no longer die; for they are like the angels. They are God's children, since they are children of the resurrection (Luke 20:34-36 NIV).

This statement by Jesus is not about marriage: it is about worthiness to enter the "age to come". Consider all the elements contained in these verses:

- By posing such an absurd dilemma, the Sadducees belong to the people "of this age";
- This dilemma will never present itself to people worthy of taking part in the "age to come";
- Therefore, since the "age to come" is actually the Messianic age, the Sadducees have demonstrated their unworthiness to take part in the Messianic age;
- By making such authoritative statements about the Messianic age, Jesus is making an implicit claim to the role of Israel's Messiah;
- Besides the resurrection, the Sadducees also did not believe in angels or spirits (Acts 23:8). By adding mention of angels who never die, Jesus is not only challenging their philosophy in this regard but also their view of what it means to be "alive".

Consider the next verses:

> Now that the dead are raised, even Moses shewed at the bush, when he calleth the Lord the God of Abraham, and the God of Isaac, and the God of Jacob. For he is not a God of the dead, but of the living: for all live unto him (Luke 20:37-38 KJV).

Jesus is here reminding the Sadducees of Moses and the burning bush where God referred to the patriarchs as if they were still alive although their bodies had long been in the grave (Exodus 3:6). In accordance with the scriptural statements reproduced previously (Psalm 146:4; Ecclesiastes 9:5,10), Jesus is not teaching any type of post-mortem consciousness or independent soul-existence here but rather that the patriarchs continue to "live" in what may be termed the "mind" of God.

As we will discover in forthcoming pages, the proposition is that if God has the power to create Adam by breathing the spirit of life into a lump of clay, then God can re-create and re-breathe the patriarchs, and everyone else, if he so wills because "for all live unto him".

As is clear from all the above, the sole foundation for Jesus' resurrection teachings was the "word of God" as found in the Hebrew Scriptures. After the resurrection, we find Jesus confirming that foundation:

> And he said unto them, These are the words which I spake unto you, while I was yet with you, that all things must be fulfilled, which were written in the law of Moses, and in the prophets, and in the psalms, concerning me (Luke 24:44 KJV).

Now that we have established the sole source for Jesus' resurrection teachings, we may proceed on the basis that our enquiries must likewise be restricted to the "word of God" as found in the Hebrew Scriptures.

Section 3

Teaching Keys

One of the first things the author of John's Gospel tells us about Jesus is that "in him was life" (John 1:4). The Gospel is all about life overcoming death so it is no surprise therefore to find that it contains the most revealing texts about the resurrection and also the associated life-giving concepts such as John's description of Jesus as the "bread of life":

I am that bread of life. Your fathers did eat manna in the wilderness, and are dead. This is the bread which cometh down from heaven, that a man may eat thereof, and not die. I am the living bread which came down from heaven: if any man eat of this bread, he shall live for ever: and the bread that I will give is my flesh, which I will give for the life of the world (John 6:48-51 KJV).

Consider the following key passage in which Martha, the sister of Lazarus, provides us with a clear and unambiguous statement of what the contemporary followers of Jesus believed about death and its immediate aftermath:

Then said Martha unto Jesus, Lord, if thou hadst been here, my brother had not died. But I know, that even now, whatsoever thou wilt ask of God, God will give it thee. Jesus saith unto her, Thy brother shall rise again. Martha saith unto him, I know that he shall rise again in the resurrection at the last day. Jesus said unto her, I am the resurrection, and the life: he that believeth in me, though he were dead, yet shall he live: And whosoever liveth and believeth in me shall never die…(John 11:21-26 KJV).

Martha believes there is only the grave until that last day resurrection comes. Jesus assures her that all who believe in him, even though they will eventually sleep in the grave, have already undergone a spiritual resurrection and passed from death to life with God, thus enabling their resurrection "at the last day". This concept is re-inforced by Jesus in the following passage, divided into two sections so as to highlight the two-phased resurrection:

Very truly I tell you, whoever hears my word and believes him who sent me has eternal life and will not be judged but has crossed over from death to life.

Very truly I tell you, a time is coming and has now come when the dead will hear the voice of the Son of God and those who hear will live. For as the Father has life in himself, so he has granted the Son also to have life in himself. And he has given him authority to judge because he is the Son of Man. Do not be amazed at this, for a time is coming when all who are in their graves will hear his voice and come out—those who have done what is good will rise to live, and those who have done what is evil will rise to be condemned (John 5:24-29 ESV).

This first section refers to the spiritual resurrection of the present: those who hear his voice and "believe" in him have already crossed over from spiritual death to life with God. The second section contains a direct allusion to the literal resurrection found in the book of Daniel:

> And at that time shall Michael stand up, the great prince which standeth for the children of thy people: and there shall be a time of trouble, such as never was since there was a nation even to that same time: and at that time thy people shall be delivered, every one that shall be found written in the book. And many of them that sleep in the dust of the earth shall awake, some to everlasting life, and some to shame and everlasting contempt (Daniel 12:1-2 KJV).

Consider the following selection of statements from the Synoptic Gospels where Jesus also speaks of the two-phased resurrection:

> Therefore I tell you, every sin and blasphemy will be forgiven people, but the blasphemy against the Spirit will not be forgiven. And whoever speaks a word against the Son of Man will be forgiven, but whoever speaks against the Holy Spirit will not be forgiven, either in this age or in the age to come (Matthew 12: 31-32 ESV).

> "Truly I tell you," Jesus said to them, "no one who has left home or wife or brothers or sisters or parents or children for the sake of the kingdom of God will fail to receive many times as much in this age, and in the age to come eternal life" (Luke 18:29-30 NIV).

On other occasions, Jesus spoke solely of resurrection in the Age to Come:

> And this is the Father's will which hath sent me, that of all which he hath given me I should lose nothing, but should raise it up again at the last day. And this is the will of him that sent me, that every one which seeth the Son, and believeth on him, may have everlasting life: and I will raise him up at the last day (John 6:39-40 KJV).

> But when you give a banquet, invite the poor, the crippled, the lame, the blind, and you will be blessed. Although they cannot repay you, you will be repaid at the resurrection of the righteous (Luke 14:13-14 NIV).

Having concluded our enquiries regarding the two-phase teachings of kingdom and resurrection, the reader would perhaps expect us to move naturally on to an assessment of teachings regarding the *parousía* (presence), and the Messianic Age. However, we must first draw attention to the man whose role was that of pre-cursor to the Messiah, a subject that has been often overlooked, or else restricted in scope.

CHAPTER TWELVE

Elijah

The herald of the Messiah

After the altered state of consciousness experience of the Transfiguration when Peter, James and John saw Moses and Elijah speaking with Jesus, the following incident took place:

> And his disciples asked him, saying, Why then say the scribes that Elias must first come? And Jesus answered and said unto them, Elias truly shall first come, and restore all things. But I say unto you, That Elias is come already, and they knew him not, but have done unto him whatsoever they listed. Likewise shall also the Son of man suffer of them. Then the disciples understood that he spake unto them of John the Baptist (Matthew 17:10-13 KJV).

Here we find Jesus agreeing with the scribes that Elijah must precede the appearing of the Messiah and also stating to his disciples that John the Baptist was that man. This precursor expectation was based on verses from the Book of Malachi:

> Behold, I am going to send you Elijah the prophet before the coming of the great and terrible day of the LORD. He will restore the hearts of the fathers to their children and the hearts of the children to their fathers, so that I will not come and smite the land with a curse (Malachi 4:5-6 NIV).

Jesus had previously stated publicly that John the Baptist was the man to whom the following verse from Malachi referred:

> This is he of whom it is written, "Behold, I send my messenger before your face, who will prepare your way before you" (Matthew 11:10 ESV cf. Malachi 3:1).

Additional direct allusions to the Book of Malachi are found in the angel's announcement of the forthcoming birth of John the Baptist:

> And many of the children of Israel shall he turn to the Lord their God. And he shall go before him in the spirit and power of Elias, to turn the hearts of the fathers to the children, and the disobedient to the wisdom of the just; to make ready a people prepared for the Lord (Luke 1:16-17 KJV cf. Malachi 4:5-6).

And after his birth, in the Song of Zechariah:

> And thou, child, shalt be called the prophet of the Highest: for thou shalt go before the face of the Lord to prepare his ways (Luke 1:76 KJV cf. Malachi 3:1).

Compare also the following descriptions of John the Baptist and Elijah where we find that both men were identifiable by the same items of clothing that they wore:

> John wore clothing made of camel's hair, with a leather belt around his waist (Mark 1:6 NIV cf. Matthew 3:4).

> The king asked them, "What kind of man was it who came to meet you and told you this?" They replied, "He had a garment of hair a and had a leather belt around his waist." The king said, "That was Elijah the Tishbite" (2 Kings 1:7-8 NIV).

The authors of Mark and Matthew could hardly make more direct statements of intent to their readers. Yet despite their intent, and despite all the categorical statements by Jesus, by the angelic herald, and by Zechariah, it has been asserted that the following passage in John's Gospel demonstrates that John the Baptist was *not* Elijah:

> And this is the testimony of John, when the Jews (Judeans) sent priests and Levites from Jerusalem to ask him, "Who are you?" He confessed, and did not deny, but confessed, "I am not the Christ." And they asked him, "What then? Are you Elijah?" He said, "I am not." "Are you the Prophet?" And he answered, "No." So they said to him, "Who are you? We need to give an answer to those who sent us. What do you say about yourself?" He said, "I am the voice of one crying out in the wilderness, 'Make straight the way of the Lord,' as the prophet Isaiah said" (John 1:19-23 ESV).

However, just like the Judean leaders who asked John if he was Elijah, those who make this assertion have failed to recognise that John was actually confirming his identity in an oblique fashion—making "straight the way of the Lord"—but, for reasons known only to himself, did not want to say so openly. While the authors of Matthew and Mark reported John's use of this passage from Isaiah to identify himself, we must consider that Jesus referred us instead to those passages from the Book of Malachi reproduced above.

To agree with Jesus that John the Baptist was Elijah is to take a course that is fraught with danger for some sectors of the Christian establishment so it is quite understandable that they should wish to downplay its significance. The danger as they see it the foreshadowing principle espoused by the New Testament: if Elijah was the herald of the Messiah's public appearance in the 1st Century AD, then it follows naturally that he must also fulfill the same role and announce the imminent public appearance of the Messiah. Elijah will, of course, appear as a man of flesh and blood just as he did then. The unknown implications of all this are challenging for those who have considered the matter fully.

Note that the role of Elijah as pre-cursor of the Messiah is so pervasive in Jewish thought that it has become associated with some of the most beloved Jewish holidays, blessings, and rituals. For example, at the conclusion of every Sabbath, it is customary for Jews to sing songs imploring the Almighty to send Elijah with the good news that their redemption and comfort is at hand. For the same purposes, a fifth cup of wine called the "Cup of Elijah" is symbolically set aside for the prophet at the Passover *Seder*.

The Trumpet

One important point not to be overlooked is the use made of the Trumpet (*Shofar*) in the Hebrew Scriptures where it is mentioned seventy two times in various contexts. As well as an obvious literal function, a blast from the Trumpet has metaphorical implications and applications: it can be likened to the voice of a man warning of the coming of an event of great significance for Israel, e.g. the prophet Ezekiel (33:1-7); or it can be likened to the voice of God at Sinai. For our purposes, it is significant to note that the prophet Joel associates a warning blast of the *Shofar* with the coming of the "day of the Lord":

> Blow ye the trumpet in Zion, and sound an alarm in my holy mountain: let all the inhabitants of the land tremble: for the day of the LORD cometh, for it is nigh at hand (Joel 2:1 KJV).

Jesus used this same imagery of the Trumpet when speaking of his coming in "power and glory":

> Then will appear the sign of the Son of Man in heaven. And then all the peoples of the earth will mourn when they see the Son of Man coming (*erchomai*) on the clouds of heaven, with power and great glory. And he will send his angels with a loud trumpet call, and they will gather his elect from the four winds, from one end of the heavens to the other (Matthew 24:30-31 NIV).

Articles in *The New Testament Teaching on the Second Coming* found in *The Catholic Commentary on the Holy Scripture* contain some remarkable observations about Elijah in his role as precursor to the Messiah. The article, *The Trumpet of the Archangel*, lists various occasions on which the trumpet was sounded in ancient Israel before proceeding with:

It is befitting, then, that a trumpet-call should announce the final coming of the King (Revelation 11:15), should summon mankind—initiating an eternal festival of victory for the just, declaring grief and destruction and endless expiation for the wicked. Fitting too it is that the voice of an archangel should make that proclamation with the trumpet of God. Whoever this high herald may be, he will perform a function similar to that of the precursor of the glorified Messias of whom Mal 4:5 says: 'Behold I will send you Elias the prophet, before the coming of the great and dreadful day of the Lord'—Elias whose second coming John the Baptist prefigured when the Kingdom of God was proclaimed for the first time, Lk 1:17; Mt 11:14.[8]

An immediately subsequent article, *The Sign of the Son of Man*, states that, "Ancient writers favour the idea that this sign is a luminous cross. *We venture to suggest that the return of Elias, forerunner as he is to be, may be the sign indicating that the Son of man is about to appear*".

Note Paul's use of this imagery when speaking of a "secret" associated with the resurrection which begins with the "last trumpet" blast (2 Corinthians 15:51-52; 1 Thessalonians 4:16).

---

[8] Hodous, E. J. *The New Testament Teaching on the Second Coming*. In B. Orchard & E. F. Sutcliffe (Eds.), *A Catholic Commentary on Holy Scripture*. Thomas Nelson: Toronto; New York; Edinburgh. 1953, p. 835.

CHAPTER THIRTEEN

Signs of the Times

Section 1

A False Assumption

The most basic difference between Christianity and Judaism through the ages is that the Jewish people are still waiting for the Messiah. Jesus could not be the Messiah, they say, because of expectations relating to the Messianic Age which he did not fulfill. While both Christians and Jews base their arguments on the same material from the Hebrew Scriptures, and start with the same assumption that these Scriptures predict only one appearance of the Messiah, they reach conclusions which are contradictory.

When all the expectations are collected and analysed, it emerges that both parties are labouring under a false assumption. The reality is this:

- Jesus tells us that *everything* that is written about him in the Law of Moses, the Prophets, *and the Psalms must be fulfilled* (Luke 24:44);
- When we do study the Messianic expectations contained in all these sources, we find that they cannot all be fulfilled by one man at one time, thus they speak of two appearances of the Messiah in addition to his appearance in the Messianic Age;
- Since the first appearance was already past, the New Testament adds further information about the second of these appearances before the Messianic Age when Jesus will appear in "power and glory".

Consider for example the verses immediately preceding verse 9 of Psalm 41 which Jesus himself states was fulfilled by the betrayal of Judas:

> The LORD will strengthen him upon the bed of languishing: thou wilt make all his bed in his sickness. I said, LORD, be merciful unto me: heal my soul; for I have sinned against thee. Mine enemies speak evil of me, When shall he die, and his name perish? And if he come to see me, he speaketh vanity: his heart gathereth iniquity to itself; when he goeth abroad, he telleth it. All that hate me

whisper together against me: against me do they devise my hurt. An evil disease, say they, cleaveth fast unto him: and now that he lieth he shall rise up no more (Psalm 41:3-8 KJV).

Yea, mine own familiar friend, in whom I trusted, which did eat of my bread, hath lifted up his heel against me (Psalm 41:9 KJV cf. John 13:18).

The so-called "suffering servant" of Isaiah 52:13-53:12 has long been recognised in Jewish interpretive tradition as having distinct parallels with Psalm 88 in terms of theme and language. Considering the legitimate analogies that can be drawn between the "suffering servant" and the life of Jesus, it would therefore be wise to reflect on what Psalm 88 has to tell us:

I am counted with them that go down into the pit: I am as a man that hath no strength: Free among the dead, like the slain that lie in the grave, whom thou rememberest no more: and they are cut off from thy hand. Thou hast laid me in the lowest pit, in darkness, in the deeps. Thy wrath lieth hard upon me, and thou hast afflicted me with all thy waves. Selah. Thou hast put away mine acquaintance far from me; thou hast made me an abomination unto them: I am shut up, and I cannot come forth (Psalm 88:4-8 KJV).

Even from this small sampling, we can readily see that Psalms 41 and 88 speak of a man who has an "evil disease" and whose bed has to be turned because his sickness is long-term; of a man who is still living yet counted among the dead; of a man who is "shut up" and "cannot come forth". It goes without saying that none of these descriptions could be applied to the life of Jesus as presented in the New Testament yet they are undoubtedly messianic through contextual and thematic associations.

As noted in Part XIII.2: *The Israelite Messiah-The Unexpected Messiah*, all of the above will no doubt appear as a revelation to many readers. The "further information" in the New Testament, referred to above, was provided by Jesus himself, as we will see.

Section 2

Notes

For a comprehensive analysis of the "cloud" imagery, see Part XII.3: *The Israelite God-Manifestations*.

The abode of God was believed to be beyond the great visible vault of the sky thus one looked *up* towards the abode of God if a divine act was perceived to be in progress. In the following passage from Acts, the same Greek word has been translated as either "heaven" or "sky". These confusing inconsistencies of translation are driven by theological assertions about the existence of an other-worldly heaven for humans. In all cases, the correct translation is "sky".

Goings and Comings

A New Testament passage which deals with Jesus' departure and reappearance is found in the Book of Acts:

> Then they gathered around him and asked him, "Lord, are you at this time going to restore the kingdom to Israel?" He said to them: "It is not for you to know the times or dates the Father has set by his own authority. But you will receive power when the Holy Spirit comes on you; and you will be my witnesses in Jerusalem, and in all Judea and Samaria, and to the ends of the earth." After he said this, he was taken up before their very eyes, and a cloud hid him from their sight. They were looking intently up into the sky as he was going, when suddenly two men dressed in white stood beside them. "Men of Galilee," they said, "why do you stand here looking into the sky? This same Jesus, who has been taken from you into heaven, will come back in the same way you have seen him go into heaven" (Acts 1:6-11 NIV).

The interpretation of this passage is supposed to lie in the somewhat similar references to Jesus as, for example, "coming in the clouds with great glory and every eye shall see him" (Revelation 1:7). That this is not the meaning of the text is obvious from the following:

- The disciples were told distinctly *not* to look into the sky;
- The departure was witnessed by a mere handful and was unheralded;
- As his reappearance was to be in like manner, it would be unheralded except by those who perceive the signs of the times;
- Jesus was born, grew up, died, and departed as an ordinary man, albeit in a transformed body. His unheralded appearance will follow the same natural processes.

Section 3

Defining Presence

We will begin by defining the Greek word *parousía*, most often translated into English as *coming*. Liddell and Scott's *A Greek-English Lexicon*, 1968, p. 1343, gives as the first definition of *parousía* the English word *presence*.

Parousía literally means "being alongside". It is drawn from the preposition *pará* (alongside) and *ousia* (being). The word occurs 24 times in the New Testament: Matthew 24:3, 27, 37, 39; 1 Corinthians 15:23, 16:17; 2 Corinthians 7:6, 7; 10:10; Philippians 1:26, 2:12; 1 Thessalonians 2:19, 3:13, 4:15, 5:23; 2 Thessalonians 2:1, 8, 9; James 5:7, 8; 2 Peter 1:16, 3:4, 12; 1 John 2:28.

To translate *parousía* into English as *coming* is not appropriate for any of these 24 instances. If the authors wished to express the idea of *coming*, they could have used a Greek word such as *eleusis* (Acts 7:52) or *erchomai* (Matthew 24:30) where it is correctly translated into English as *coming*. Moreover, the English word *coming* conveys the idea of motion towards something whereas *presence* conveys the idea of resting beside something. The incorrect translation of *parousía* also has significant ramifications when considering statements such as the following by Paul:

> For what is our hope or joy or crown of boasting before our Lord Jesus at (in) his coming (*parousía*)? Is it not you? (1 Thessalonians 2:19 ESV).

If this passage had been translated correctly, we would see that Paul is assuring his brethren that they will one day stand in the *presence* of Jesus. Paul could not have meant that they would stand at his *coming* for, if this were so, they would have been resurrected already, thus causing conflict with the passage in 1 Corinthians 15 where he speaks of the resurrection order:

> But Christ has indeed been raised from the dead, the firstfruits of those who have fallen asleep. For since death came through a man, the resurrection of the dead comes also through a man. For as in Adam all die, so in Christ all will be made alive. But each in turn: Christ, the firstfruits; then, when he comes (*parousía*), those who belong to him (1 Corinthians 15:20-23 NIV).

Innumerable theories and belief systems have sprung into life because of incorrectly translating *parousia* as *coming* rather than as *presence*, as we see in the passage above. In reality, Paul's statement is quite simple and clear: Jesus will be raised first, then when he is present, "those who belong to him".

Section 4

The Presence

As pointed out previously, the Bible speaks of two appearances of the Messiah in addition to his appearance in the Messianic Age. Accounts which throw a great deal of light on this subject are found in Chapter 24 of Matthew, Chapters 17 and 21 of Luke, and Chapter 13 of Mark. All these accounts record that when the great buildings of the Temple had been pointed out to him by the disciples, Jesus had warned that, "there will not be left here one stone upon another that will not be thrown down". In Luke and Mark, the disciples respond by asking Jesus for a sign indicating *when* this catastrophe was about to happen. In Matthew, however the disciples' question is framed differently:

> Tell us, when will these things be, and what will be the sign of your coming (*parousía*) and of the end of the age? (Matthew 24:3 ESV).

In this verse, the Greek word *parousía* has been incorrectly translated into English as "coming". A sign of Jesus' presence is totally different to a sign of his coming. If the end of the age were to co-incide with his coming, then there would be no need for any further sign.

By virtue of its insertion at a critical point, Jesus' response to their question must be of great significance yet the conventional interpretation of the so-called "Second Advent" glosses over it altogether. In the accounts of both Matthew and Luke, Jesus uses the exact same phrase as a sign of his presence and describes this appearance as sudden, similar to the behaviour of lightning, which appears and disappears in a flash. We are also informed in Luke 17:25 that this appearance is subsequent to his rejection by "this generation".

Compare these accounts:

> For as the lightning comes from the east and shines as far as the west, so will be the coming (*parousía*) of the Son of Man. Wherever the corpse is, there the vultures will gather" (Matthew 24:28 ESV).
>
> And they said to him, "Where, Lord?" He said to them, "Where the corpse is, there the vultures will gather" (Luke 17:37 ESV).

In Matthew, the disciples ask for a sign of Jesus' presence whereas in Luke the disciples ask "Where?" Whilst it can be assumed that much of this private conversation has gone unrecorded, such a question seems out of keeping with the trend of the discussion. Their question is, in effect, "where shall we look?"

In both accounts, Jesus draws their attention to the way in which circling birds of prey are an indication of dead flesh laying on the ground. For the disciples to ask Jesus where they should look to find him, and for him to answer that they should look for his dead body, means that they must have believed that all of them would be present on this Earth at some future time. The "corpse" of Jesus was to be a sign of mutual recognition. There is no other possible meaning one can draw from this exchange, although many have offered a variety of scenarios which do not stand up to any contextual test. For example, some have argued that the "vultures" refer to the eagle standards of the Roman legions swooping down on Jerusalem during the first Jewish revolt (66-73 AD), but this ignores Luke's context and cannot explain the purpose of any sudden appearance and disappearance of Jesus at that time, marked only by his existence as a "corpse".

Section 5

The Tribulation

In all these accounts, Jesus speaks of signs warning that a great destruction was about to come:

> For nation will rise against nation, and kingdom against kingdom, and there will be famines and earthquakes in various places. All these are but the beginning of the birth pains... So when you see the abomination of desolation spoken of by the prophet Daniel, standing in the holy place (let the reader understand)...then there will be great tribulation, such as has not been from the beginning of the world until now, no, and never will be. And if those days had not been cut short, no human being would be saved. But for the sake of the elect those days will be cut short (Matthew 24:7-8,15, 21-22 ESV).

When speaking of the "great tribulation" to take place at the end of the age, Jesus likened it to an event which would soon take place—the destruction of Jerusalem by the Romans in 70 AD. He spoke of this more immediate destruction in guarded terms and, not wishing to name Rome openly, instead used Daniel's prophecy of "the abomination of desolation" to identify the destroying power. (See Daniel 9:27; 11:31; 12:11).

Jesus' statement that, "All these are but the beginning of the birth pains" has gone largely unremarked. As noted in Part XIII: *The Israelite Messiah*, because both the Messiah, individually, and the people of God, collectively, are spoken of by the prophets in terms of grief, humiliation, and suffering, it was therefore envisioned that the glorious reign of God would emerge only after their passage through the refining furnace of affliction which would burn off the dross of the reign of man. This advent period, also likened to the travail of a woman in childbirth, was termed by later Rabbis as the "birth pains of the Messiah".

Section 6

The Sign of the Son of Man

Jesus gave his disciples two signs of recognition during their private conversation and it is crucial to keep their respective timelines in mind. The sign of the "corpse" was to be an indicator of his presence on earth before the tribulation, else the disciples would have no need of a further sign other than the tribulation itself. Whilst all the Synoptic Gospels describe events associated with the tribulation in the same terms, only the author of Matthew inserts the appearing of the "sign of the Son of man in heaven" into the sequence of events which occur after the tribulation:

> Immediately after the tribulation of those days shall the sun be darkened, and the moon shall not give her light, and the stars shall fall from heaven, and the powers of the heavens shall be shaken: And then shall appear the sign of the Son of man in heaven: and then shall all the tribes of the earth mourn, and they shall see the Son of man coming (*erchomai*) in the clouds of heaven with power and great glory. And he shall send his angels with a great sound of a trumpet, and they shall gather together his elect from the four winds, from one end of heaven to the other (Matthew 24:29-31 KJV).

Luke adds one further piece of information, telling us that just as it was in the days of Noah and Lot, so also will people be eating and drinking, buying and selling, planting and building "on the day when the Son of Man is revealed" and thus be taken completely unawares (Luke 17:26,30).

Section 7

Observations

It is extremely unwise to make claims of certainty regarding the contents of the above-quoted passages. Jesus himself said he did not know "the day or the hour". If he was not privy to knowledge kept within the bounds of God's own authority, the only thing we can be certain of is uncertainty. Nevertheless, we can establish possibilities by comparing Matthew's "sign of the Son of man in heaven" and its attendant phenomena with other signs and their attendant phenomena which, taken together, may paint a scenario for us to ponder.

Before we begin, let us dwell on the remarkable fact that many believe in the literal application of the words, "Immediately after the tribulation of those days shall the sun be darkened, and the moon shall not give her light, and the stars shall fall from heaven, and the powers of the heavens shall be shaken". This uncritical belief is simply a reflection of the general lack of knowledge about biblical symbols. So, what do the symbols of the sun, the moon and the stars represent? Consider the following passage, taking note that Revelation's "sign" of the woman and Matthew's "sign of the Son of Man" both appear in "heaven":

> A great sign appeared in heaven: a woman clothed with the sun, with the moon under her feet and a crown of twelve stars on her head (Revelation 12:1 NIV).

The identification of this woman can be found in Genesis 37:9-10 where the people of Israel are described with exactly the same symbols—the sun (Jacob), the moon (Rachel), and the twelve stars (the twelve patriarchs).

Consider Jesus' prophecy of events which will take place *before* the tribulation, "For nation (*ethnos*) will rise against nation, and kingdom against kingdom…" The reference to "nations" and "kingdoms" indicates that Jesus is here speaking of ethnic outsiders, i.e. non-Israelites.

Now that we have identified the woman Israel, we can see that the tribulation itself and its attendant phenomena—the darkness of the sun and the moon and the toppling of the stars — refers to a catastrophe to befall ethnic insiders, thus Israelites. It is also clear that if the heavenly bodies are symbols, then so also are the "heavens" in which they exist.

Taken together with Luke's reference to "the day when the Son of Man is revealed" (Luke 17:30), it is obvious that the "sign of the Son of Man in heaven" is some identifying factor through which the Messiah will become known to the symbolic heavenly bodies, i.e. to Israelites. As noted in a previous Chapter, the CCHS article, *The Sign of the Son of Man*, suggests that the return of Elijah may be the sign that the Son of Man is about to appear. If this is the case, it is Elijah himself who will reveal the identity of the Messiah.

Notes

When considering the "great tribulation such as has not been from the beginning of the world until now, no, and never will be", we should keep in mind that, for the Jewish descendants of the ancient Israelite people, the insanity of this world was at its zenith during those years leading up to and including the Holocaust.

An important point to note here is that Jesus describes the Israelite-specific "great tribulation" event in the same terms as the "day of the Lord" prophecies found in Joel 2:2,10; 3:14-15. Although this hoped-for day was to mark God's glorious restoration and final salvation of Israel (e.g. Ezekiel 36), the expectation was that it would only be realised after the Israelites had passed through such a "great tribulation" (e.g. Amos 5, Zephaniah 1, Joel 1, Zechariah 14).

Section 8

Summing Up

Conclusions drawn from the material presented in this Chapter can be summarised by the following points:

- The Ascension of Jesus was unheralded. Those present were told that Jesus would reappear just as he went and not to look into "heaven" for him;
- After the Ascension, there was to be another unheralded appearance of Jesus who would be present on earth for a time and who then, like lightning, would disappear from view;
- This appearance would be prior to the tribulation and marked by the sign of the "corpse";
- The common belief that Jesus has been in "heaven" sitting at the right hand of God since the Ascension cannot be reconciled with Jesus' statement identifying himself as a "corpse". Obviously, to be finally reduced to a "corpse", one must first be born as a living human;

- The tribulation and its attendant phenomena—the darkness of the sun and the moon and the toppling of the stars—refers to a catastrophe to befall the Israelite people;

- The "sign of the Son of Man in heaven" occurs after the tribulation. As noted in a previous Chapter, the CCHS article, *The Sign of the Son of Man*, suggests that the return of Elijah may be the sign that the Son of Man is about to appear (see note on Elijah);

- If one rejects an unheralded appearance by Jesus, subsequent to that of the 1st Century AD, but before his public appearance in "power and glory", then one must either reject the "corpse" statements by Jesus or offer some alternative and plausible explanation.

CHAPTER FOURTEEN

Resurrection Revelations

It has been asserted that analysis of the Book of Revelation is notoriously difficult for scholars given that it is a genre combining three literary styles described as apocalyptic, epistolary, and prophetic. However, such excuses cover the reality that most difficulties stem from an unwillingness to correctly define context and terminology for fear that it will subject core teachings to unwanted scrutiny.

The Book of Revelation does what it says on the cover—it reveals things unknown about the future by means of apocalyptic visions contained within a circulating epistle. It is not possible in this work to devote space sufficient for even a brief analysis so we must confine ourselves to referring to relevant passages when necessary and to keep in mind that, throughout the work, the author depends in part on the prophetic Books of Daniel and Ezekiel. Those to whom this epistle was addressed would have been well aware of this reliance and able to draw meaning from imagery, concepts, symbols and themes already familiar to them. For us, however, it may appear to be an uphill battle to recover what appears to have been lost in the mists of time. Nevertheless, we must make the attempt.

That being said, we will now analyse the following resurrection passage from the Book of Revelation:

> I saw thrones on which were seated those who had been given authority to judge. And I saw the souls of those who had been beheaded because of their testimony about Jesus and because of the word of God. They had not worshiped the beast or its image and had not received its mark on their foreheads or their hands. They came to life and reigned with Christ a thousand years. (The rest of the dead did not come to life until the thousand years were ended.) This is the first resurrection. Blessed and holy are those who share in the first resurrection. The second death has no power over them, but they will be priests of God and of Christ and will reign with him for a thousand years (Revelation 20:4-6 NIV).

Compare this "resurrection" (regeneration) with events described below by Paul in his First Letter to the Corinthians:

> But Christ has indeed been raised from the dead, the firstfruits of those who have fallen asleep. For since death came through a man, the resurrection of the dead comes also through a man. For as in Adam all die, so in Christ all will

be made alive. But each in turn: Christ, the firstfruits; then, when he comes (*parousía*), those who belong to him (1 Corinthians 15:20-23 NIV).

Points for consideration

- In Revelation 20:4-6, those seated on thrones with the authority to judge is an obvious reference to the "regenerated" disciples (Matthew 19:28);

- In addition to the disciples and others specified in Revelation, this resurrection (regeneration) includes all those named by Jesus (Matthew 8:11; Luke 13:28-29) in connection with the same event, viz. Abraham, Isaac, Jacob, and all the prophets. (See *The Banquet* in forthcoming Chapter: *Hiding in Plain Sight*);

- When Paul speaks of Jesus as the "firstfruits" of those who are raised from the dead in 1 Corinthians 15:20-23, he is initially referring to the resurrection of Jesus in 30 AD and then foreshadowing the future resurrection (regeneration) spoken of in Revelation;

- Jesus will also be the "firstfruits" of this future resurrection;

- The implications arising from the mistranslation of *parousía* in verses such as 1 Corinthians 15:23 cannot be overstated. Since Jesus is not *coming* from somewhere else, he will be *present* (*parousía*) on this Earth at the future resurrection of "those who belong to him".

We will explore the method of resurrection (regeneration) in more depth in a forthcoming Chapter: *Hiding in Plain Sight*.

Notes

As pointed out previously, Jesus' statement identifying himself as a "corpse" (Matthew 24:28; Luke 17:37) cannot be reconciled with the common belief that Jesus has been in heaven sitting at the right hand of God since the Ascension. Obviously, to be finally reduced to a "corpse", one must first be born as a living human.

The reader is no doubt aware of the ever-expanding numbers of bizarre and outlandish theories based on the so-called "mark of the beast". These theories conveniently overlook passages in Revelation 7:3; 9:4; 14:1; and 22:4 where the servants of God also bear a seal or "mark". The concept here is drawn from Ezekiel 9:4-6 where the servants of God are symbolically "marked" or identified as such by their outward opposition to evil. In Revelation, the opponents of God are also "marked" or identified as such by their outward acceptance of evil. Acceptance or rejection of evil is demonstrated by character in action, "every good tree bears good fruit, but a bad tree bears bad fruit". Servants of God had been persecuted in various ways because their character in action had demonstrated publicly that they reject the evils inherent in every society.

The "thousand year" reign is also known in certain quarters as the "Millenium". There are of course those who insist on a literal period of one thousand years. However, if we look at the Greek word *chilioi* (thousand) we find that it was chosen because its meaning (10 x 10 x 10) symbolised completeness. The "thousand years" refers to an unknown period of time, also known as the Messianic Age, during which Jesus is expected to destroy all earthly power structures before overcoming death, the greatest of all human enemies (1 Corinthians 15:24-26).

CHAPTER FIFTEEN

Double Jeopardy

In Revelation 20:11, what is commonly called the "great white throne judgement" period is introduced. (This period corresponds with "the end" spoken of by Paul in 1 Corinthians 15:23-26 when the works of the Kingdom age are completed.)

> Then I saw a great white throne and the One seated on it. Earth and heaven fled from His presence, and no place was found for them. And I saw the dead, great and small, standing before the throne. And there were open books, and one of them was the Book of Life. And the dead were judged according to their deeds, as recorded in the books. The sea gave up its dead, and Death and Hades gave up their dead, and each one was judged according to his deeds. Then Death and Hades were thrown into the lake of fire. This is the second death—the lake of fire. And if anyone was found whose name was not written in the Book of Life, he was thrown into the lake of fire (Revelation 20:11-15 KJV).

Commentaries on various aspects of this "great white throne judgement", such as the reference to a "Lake of Fire", appear in Part X:4.2: *Aftermath-Hell-Lake of Fire* so, in this Chapter, we will just make some relevant remarks beginning with the observation that there would be no need for the dead to be raised after the so-called Millennium to face this final judgement if judgement had already been passed upon them immediately after their deaths.

Whilst the majority of Protestant Christian denominations have diverse and apparently ever-changing views and, in some cases, appear to have adopted a *laissez faire* approach, the Roman Catholic Church, being meticulous in terms of doctrine and practice, has correctly perceived the serious nature of the problem and devised the theory of two judgements— "particular" and "general".

According to this theory, the immortal soul is separated from the body upon death and immediately faces a "particular" judgement which will decide the soul's eternal destiny. Depending on the outcome, the soul is either granted entrance to Heaven or sentenced to damnation in Hell. Then, at the end of times, the soul is summoned from either Heaven or Hell and re-united with its body in a "general resurrection". The same irreversible decree is pronounced at the general judgement, after which time the soul is sent back either to Heaven or to Hell for all eternity, this time in company with its body.

Aside from the fact that this theory is grossly offensive to the God of justice, mercy and love, it is remarkable that so many should accept a concoction so glaringly based on the necessity to bolster and preserve related teachings.

Finally, let us lay to rest all teachings that insist on judgement immediately upon death by considering once again the case of Lazarus, the brother of Mary and Martha. According to these teachings, the following sequence of events had to have transpired:

- Lazarus has died and his immortal soul has separated from his body;
- his dead body now lays in the grave;
- his soul has been judged and has either entered an eternal Heaven or been consigned to an eternal Hell;
- Jesus summons him from the grave after four days;
- the corollary of which is that his soul must be summoned from either Heaven or Hell to be re-united with his four-days dead body;
- after which Lazarus lives again through the trials of this life;
- before being once more consigned to his eternal abode;
- keeping in mind that his eternal destiny was already decreed at the time of his first death.

Note: For a commentary on the raising of Lazarus, see Chapter Seven: *Three Days*.

CHAPTER SIXTEEN

Hiding in Plain Sight

Notes

Within the Christian churches and their many denominations, further divided into conservative and liberal wings, there is a significant amount of confusion regarding what happens after death. Whilst it is not possible here to detail the bewildering array of teachings currently in vogue, the following examples will serve the purpose of illustration.

Some hold that after death, everyone sleeps until the final judgment, after which everyone will be sent either to Heaven or Hell. Others believe that at the moment of death, people are instantly judged and sent to their eternal destinations. Still others claim that when people die, their souls/spirits are sent to a temporary Heaven or Hell to await a final resurrection, a final judgment, and then consigned to their eternal destination.

Regardless of their differences, however, the common element binding them all together is the concept of immortal souls. All teachings based on this concept are ultimately derived from Hellenist philosophy, particularly Plato's philosophy of the soul. Briefly stated, this philosophy holds that man is a duality composed of a pre-existing immortal soul imprisoned within a mortal body. Only upon death can the immortal soul of man be released from this body and return to its metaphysical home. This philosophy pervades almost all Christian doctrine and practice and gave rise to the traditional teachings of other-worldly soul destinations called Heaven and Hell and a soul fate called Eternal Life.

These traditional teachings about soul destinations have caused many millions to spend their last moments on Earth in abject terror of what may befall them, and those they leave behind to spend countless hours in prayer for the souls of the dearly-loved departed.

In stark contrast to these teachings based on Hellenist dualism, ancient Israelite thought held that man is one indivisible entity created by God to serve the Creator's purposes on Earth. There is no escape to some other world: the earth is man's home and ever will be. Man is expected to glorify God daily with all his actions, including with his bodily functions. He is expected to pursue justice, righteousness, mercy, and the knowledge of God with every fibre of his being in the physical world.

The Death State

The Bible does not speak of the independent existence of disembodied souls, as does Christian doctrine. Rather, the Bible teaches that there is no post-mortem existence of any kind and that the dead sleep in the dust of the earth until awakening in the resurrection. Jesus himself described the dead Lazarus as "sleeping", then "waking" (John 11:11). Although the dead are conscious of nothing, and after a time are dead to the world also, Jesus taught that they continue to live in what may be termed the "mind" of God for to him "all are alive" (Luke 20:38 cf. Romans 4:17).

The Pattern

Whatever their variations, the doctrines of Heaven and Hell and their total subjugation of any independent thought have successfully masked what should have been obvious from the very beginning. So dominant are these teachings that the unmistakable meaning of words and phrases used by Jesus and his contemporaries have been ignored, or simply overlooked. The mechanism by which the Bible envisions man awakening from the sleep of death is possible only through careful analysis, and only by those willing to cast aside preconceived notions about the meaning of death and resurrection.

If we begin by using the following statement by Jesus as a lens through which to view other statements by Jesus and his contemporaries, a consistent pattern of thought will be revealed, brightening the darkness of centuries.

The Sadducees did not believe in the resurrection so, in the passage below, Jesus reminds them of Moses and the burning bush where God referred to the patriarchs as if they were still alive although their bodies had long been in the grave (Exodus 3:6):

> But in the account of the burning bush, even Moses showed that the dead rise, for he calls the Lord "the God of Abraham, and the God of Isaac, and the God of Jacob." He is not the God of the dead, but of the living, for to him all are alive (Luke 20:37-38 NIV).

The Banquet

The Bible speaks of no other existence for mankind but the one we have always shared together—this Earth. To complete the cycle of human life on Earth, it was envisioned that we must symbolically return to the Eden from which we were expelled and to our previous state of being ruled by God and not by man. This ideal reign, known as the Kingdom of God, would emerge only after passage through the refining furnace of affliction which would burn off the dross of the reign of man. Also envisioned was an ideal earthly King who would be appointed by God to sit upon the throne of this Kingdom and rule as viceroy of the God of Israel.

The final establishment of this Kingdom would be such a joyous occasion that it was likened to a celebratory banquet. According to Jesus, guests at this banquet would include "Abraham, Isaac, and Jacob" (Matthew 8:11) and, in the parallel statement found in Luke 13:28-29, "all the prophets". Moses and Elijah, being the greatest of the prophets, are included in this group. In a previous Chapter, it was noted that Jesus made several categorical statements to the effect that John the Baptist was Elijah, one of these prophets to whom he here refers. The reason behind the naming of these persons was that all of them, beginning with Abraham, were perceived as having contributed towards the Kingdom's establishment. After the passage of millennia, their collective efforts culminate in a symbolic banquet.

Perhaps the most fitting analogy for us is to imagine being present at a stage play in which a series of events begins immediately after the introduction of the story and builds up to the climax. Throughout the play, the individuals players are given only their own parts in the various Acts or Scenes, but they work collectively towards an ideal objective. In the final Scene, all the loose ends of the plot are tied up, and a satisfactory resolution accomplished. At the end of the performance comes the curtain call when the individuals return to the stage to be recognised by the audience for their performance and to take a final bow. Consider now the method through which all these leading players named by Jesus are enabled to return to the stage after sleeping in the dust of the earth for millennia.

The regeneration

In addition to the persons named above as being present at the celebratory banquet, Jesus also named his disciples:

> And Jesus said to them, "Truly I say to you, that you who have followed Me, in the regeneration when the Son of Man will sit on His glorious throne, you also shall sit upon twelve thrones, judging the twelve tribes of Israel" (Matthew 19:28 NASB cf. Revelation 20:4).

The crucial word used by Jesus in this passage is "regeneration", translated from the Greek *paliggenesia*. The literal meaning of *paliggenesia* is "born again". It is formed from *pálin* (again) and *génesis* (birth). (This word is also used to refer to the concept of a foreshadowing spiritual rebirth/resurrection but the context of this passage rules out that interpretation.)

Confirmation that the concept of regeneration was widespread among the contemporaries of Jesus is found in passages where the thoughts of some automatically turned in that direction:

Now when Jesus came into the district of Caesarea Philippi, he asked his disciples, "Who do people say that the Son of Man is?" And they said, "Some say John the Baptist, others say Elijah, and others Jeremiah or one of the prophets"(Matthew 16:13-14 ESV cf. Mark 6:15; Luke 9:8; John 1:21).

These "people," these contemporaries of Jesus, knew that he had been born and raised among them, thus the only possible meaning to be drawn from this passage is that these people believed in the concept of regeneration. The only logical means consistent with the teachings of Jesus by which he, the disciples, all the prophets, the patriarchs, and many others could be present in the Kingdom of God on Earth is by being born again into a new body—literally. Without embodiment, there is no possibility of meaningful existence.

The proposition underlying all these statements by Jesus and his contemporaries is that if God has the power to create Adam by breathing the spirit of life into a lump of clay, then God can re-create and re-breathe the patriarchs, and everyone else, if he so wills because "to him all are alive". Since these concepts first were articulated amongst the Israelite people, it is not surprising to find that certain sectors within Judaism have likewise concluded that without embodiment on this Earth, meaningful existence is impossible.

CHAPTER SEVENTEEN

Timelines

As noted previously, Jesus told his disciples he did not know "the day or the hour" when he spoke of the tribulation and other events indicating his unheralded presence on Earth and his subsequent public appearance in "power and glory". If he was not privy to knowledge kept within the bounds of God's own authority, the only thing we can be certain of is uncertainty. That being said, however, a comparative analysis of the resurrection and kingdom teachings noted in previous Chapters reveals for us a possible timeline of events for us to consider. A sampling of references is included with each point.

1. The "firstfruits" resurrection of Jesus (1 Corinthians 15:20-23). The sign of the "corpse" marks his *presence* on earth before the tribulation (Matthew 24:28; Luke 17:37);

2. The resurrection of those who "belong to him". Included in this group are the disciples, those who had not worshipped the beast or his image, and those persons and groups named by Jesus as being present at the banquet celebrating the inauguration of the Kingdom, i.e. Abraham, Isaac, Jacob, and all the prophets. Moses and Elijah, being the greatest of the prophets, are included in this group. Whether the resurrection of all these persons is conducted in stages, or simultaneously, is left vague, perhaps deliberately. All we know for certain is (a) that the disciples are present at the unheralded appearance of Jesus, marked by the sign of the "corpse", and (b) that certain persons and groups named by Jesus are alive at the time of the symbolic celebratory banquet (1 Corinthians 15:20-23; Revelation 20:4-6; Matthew 8:1, 17:10-13, 19:28; Luke 13:28-29);

3. The "great tribulation" (Matthew 24:21);

4. After the "great tribulation", the "sign of the Son of Man" appears in "heaven", i.e. to the heavenly bodies which represent Israel. As noted in a previous Chapter, the CCHS article, *The Sign of the Son of Man*, suggests that the return of Elijah may be the sign that the Son of Man is about to appear;

5. Just as in the 1st Century AD, Elijah the prophet must be present at this time to herald the public appearance of the Messiah (Matthew 11:10; Luke 1:16-17, 76; Malachi 3:1; 4:5-6). Note that John the Baptist/Elijah was the one who revealed the identity of the Messiah at his first public appearance so

it is likely that after Elijah's return (the "sign"), he will reveal the identity of the Messiah either before or simultaneously with his appearance in "power and glory";

6. Jesus appears in "power and glory" (Matthew 24:29-30; Mark 13:24-26);

7. Inauguration of the Kingdom (Matthew 8:11; Luke 13:28-29) promised in Isaiah 9:7; Daniel 2:44, 7:13-14; Luke 1:3-33);

8. The Kingdom Age during which earthly power structures are overturned and enemies made a "footstool" for Jesus (Psalm 110:1; Matthew 22:44; Hebrews 2:8; I Corinthians 15:24-28);

9. Authority returned to God (2 Corinthians 15:24-28);

10. General resurrection (Daniel 12:1-2; Revelation 20:11-15).

Notes

When considering the "great tribulation" spoken of by Jesus, we should keep in mind that, for the Jewish descendants of the ancient Israelite people, the insanity of this world was at its zenith during those years leading up to and including the Holocaust.

The author of the Book of Hebrews asserts that Jesus is the new High Priest of Israel (Hebrews 5:9-10). The Son of Man of the Gospels comes clothed in the "glory of his Father" (Matthew 16:27; Mark 8:38), just as the High Priest, when clothed in his sacred garments, embodied the glory of God (Exodus 28:2, 40).

Therefore, phrases such as "the Son of Man coming on the clouds of heaven, with power and great glory" (Matthew 24:30) should be considered from within the context of the Day of Atonement when the High Priest entered the Jerusalem Temple's Holy of Holies and symbolically ascended into God's presence (Heaven) surrounded by clouds of incense. And as near-contemporary texts show, on his return to the people from the inner sanctuary, the High Priest symbolically descended from Heaven down to Earth reflecting God's own power and glory. It is in that sense that Jesus "comes on the clouds of heaven with power and great glory". See also Part XIII.10: *The Israelite Messiah-A Priest Forever.*

CHAPTER EIGHTEEN

Choices

As demonstrated previously, the Bible speaks of two appearances of the Messiah in addition to his appearance in the Kingdom Age. As also demonstrated previously, Jesus gave his disciples the sign of the "corpse" which would mark his presence on earth before the "great tribulation". This appearance would be unheralded and only the disciples would understand its significance. The reason for this unheralded appearance of the Messiah is nothing if not a divinely inspired plan befitting the God of justice.

It must be stated once again that Jesus was a totally unexpected Messiah. His message did not conform with the prevailing messianic expectations, nor did the circumstances surrounding him appear to conform with these projections. The reality was that, before his death, the expectations that revealed his crucifixion and resurrection were in a sense hidden from view for a very good reason: had they been visible to all from the outset, no one would have been presented with a choice. Besides challenging their authority on many levels, those who crucified Jesus chose to do so because he represented the very antithesis of their grandiose teachings about the Messiah.

It is made abundantly clear in the New Testament that the disciples and other followers of Jesus knew nothing about these hidden expectations: theirs were the same as the majority of the "simple" folk—they awaited the promised Messiah of the house of David who would deliver them from the tribulations of the Roman yoke and establish God's Kingdom of peace, justice and righteousness in its place. Plumbing the depths of Scripture in order to find the Messiah was the concern of scholars, not of fishermen and the like, so we find that the disciples and other followers of Jesus made their choice on an entirely different basis. Rather than place their trust in the authority of the religious establishment to interpret Messianic teachings, they chose rather to trust in the moral authority of the values which Jesus embodied, such as truth versus lies, manipulation, distortion and deception; the spirit of the law rather than the letter; humility versus arrogance; and personal integrity versus institutional formalism.

If Jesus were to make an unheralded appearance today, as he assured his disciples he would, and challenge the teachings of the religious establishment, just as he did then, he would certainly be unidentifiable in terms of church doctrines such as the Virgin Conception/Birth, the Incarnation and the Trinity. Just as before, he would be the antithesis of these erroneous and grandiose teachings.

Should the current religious establishment expect to find itself in a more favoured position than that of the Judean establishment? Should they expect to have the comfortable certainty that the Judeans did not? Just as before, they will have no outward signs or clouds of glory to guide them. They will be faced with essentially the same choice. When provided with the evidence that their grandiose teachings about him are nothing but a tissue of lies, will they choose to uphold those teachings and brand him a heretic, a blasphemer, a companion of undesirables, or a malcontent, just as did their spiritual forefathers? Will they prove to be no less fraudulent and spiritually bankrupt and be in the forefront of those shouting "away with him"?

Or will they make the same choice as did the disciples and other followers of Jesus? This process of separating the "wheat from the chaff", is designed to fully and finally expose those who have been only masquerading as the representatives of Jesus.

Notes

In the previous Chapters of Part XV, we addressed only those teachings which bear directly on an understanding of the resurrection. Related concepts only mentioned in passing are addressed in more detail elsewhere in this work.

As noted in various places throughout this work, the Messiah was expected to fulfill the ancient promises to the Israelite Diaspora that they would one day be symbolically resurrected from exile and in-gathered to the land of Israel to form the Kingdom of God under the rule of God's Messiah. In the New Testament, this restoration of Israel is inextricably entwined with the resurrection of Jesus.

PART XV

The Israelite People

CHAPTER ONE

Introduction

Notes

It is beyond the capacity or scope of this work to record a history of the Israelite people beginning with the call of Abraham. Rather, we will begin our journey in the 1st Century AD. In Part I: *The Context*, readers will find essays on particular aspects of Israelite life in the 1st Century so we will not repeat them here.

The task of separating the entwined maze of mainstream Christian doctrine and associated teachings into discrete and coherent strands has proved immensely difficult. This work has been arranged according to topical divisions which, it is hoped, has made it easier for the reader to navigate. However, readers are aware by now that essays applicable to one or more of these divisions have, of necessity, been repeated in whole or in part if deemed essential to a thorough explication of the subject under examination. This pattern must continue through to the end of this work so the readers' further indulgence is sought.

Evolution

From the Law, the Prophets and the Writings of the Hebrew Scriptures, through to the books of the New Testament, what is laid out for us is the evolution of the human mind. A gradual development from darkness into light. It is our greatest anthropological storehouse and would be valuable for that reason alone. It marks the progress of human ethical and intellectual development and an evolution in human thinking about the nature of God.

From a tribal God of the Israelites only, a god among many gods, who first lived on a mountain, then was carried about in a box, who was vengeful and terrible, and who could be approached only with fear and appropriate ceremony, all the way through to the perception that there is only one God, a God who was not vengeful but full of endless mercy, a God who did not have to be appeased, a God of love and truth who did not have to be approached through ceremony, but could be approached privately through prayer. From the birth of the first Adam, made in the potential image of God, through to the death of Jesus, the last Adam, and thereafter the resurrection of a new creature, a man realising the full potential of humanity, a man finally made in the *imago dei*, the image of God.

If not for the writings of the Israelite people, the core principles of the Ten Commandments, specifically the prohibitions against murder, theft and perjury, would never have become the basis for so many of the world's legal codes. We would never have known that concepts such as justice, peace, equality and, above all, the sanctity of human life, were first articulated in the Hebrew Scriptures. We would never have known that Jesus existed at all and we would never have heard about the golden rule and other New Testament maxims that have elevated and energised millions.

The debt we all owe to these ancient peoples is vast. And yet some of their descendants, the tribe of Judah, have been demonised and delegitimised throughout these long centuries by those whose motives primarily stem from the concept of "replacement theology", otherwise known as the teaching of "Supersessionism", and the consequent need to demonstrate Jewish unworthiness to remain the "people of God".

The religious leaders in Jerusalem are rightly held accountable for the crucifixion of one Jew. The teaching of Supersessionism must rightly be held accountable for the lives of six million. Those who continue to preach this doctrine unwittingly stand in the ashes of the dead. Essays on Supersessionism are repeated in relevant sections of this work as this teaching is the source of centuries of festering hostility towards the Jews, boiling over into the occasional pogrom, but finding its inevitable and ultimate realisation in the Holocaust.

Social context of the First Century AD

Ethnocentrism

1st Century AD Mediterranean peoples were ethnocentric. When reading the New Testament we should always be aware of the social boundaries existing between Israelites (in-groups) and everyone else (out-groups). Israelite in-group attitudes were derived from the perception of shared values existing within the sub-groups of family, village community, and country-dweller.

Religion and State

Ancient Israel did not separate various aspects of its society into modern categories. Hence, there was no distinction between religion and politics. All aspects were embedded in the social structure of the day. Take, for example, the Jerusalem Temple compound which served as an economic centre, as a military fortress, and as a place of religious observance. The view that Christians should be concerned only with religious issues is based on the assumption that the priests and scribes with whom Jesus interacted were solely focused on religious questions and were not part of the state apparatus. This view betrays a lack of knowledge of the conditions in Judea in the 1st Century AD. The government of the day was a coalition of king, aristocratic families, high government officials, Roman military representatives and the ruling elites of the priesthood. The High Priests, Annas and Caiaphas, both appointed by the Roman authorities, were two such members of the elite priestly establishment.

Family

Great emphasis was placed on family tradition and continuity. At least from the period of the Babylonian Exile, (see Ezra and Nehemiah), genealogies, the purity of blood, and the symbolic importance of the twelve tribes were basic. Significant social roles such as the priesthood, requirements for admission to the temple, and appropriate marriage depended on genealogical purity.

Betrothal and Marriage

To begin the process, the prospective bridegroom would negotiate an agreement with the head of the prospective bride's family. If successful, the bridegroom would go to his own father's house where he would prepare either an existing room or build a separate room for himself and his new bride. To complete the betrothal and marriage process, the bridegroom would take his bride to the room in his father's house that he had prepared beforehand where they would begin their life together. Note how this custom illuminates Jesus' statement in John 14:2, "In my Father's house are many rooms: if it were not so, I would have told you. I go to prepare a place for you".

Note that Simon Peter's mother-in-law resided in Simon's house along with Andrew (Mark 129-30), presumably also with Simon and Andrew's wives and children.

Limited Goods

Unlike the modern Western world with its abundance of goods, 1st Century Israel was a society of limited goods. To exist within a society of limited goods meant that one could not be described as a "rich" person owning many goods without the existence of its corollary—a "poor" person deprived of goods. This reality can be most instructive when reading New Testament passages about the interactions between Jesus and the "rich young ruler" for example.

Honour-Shame

Concern for one's honour permeated every aspect of life in Mediterranean antiquity. Honour served as the prime indicator of social position and prescribed how persons should interact with superiors, inferiors and equals in appropriate ways. Public insults must be challenged to defend one's honour. All of the trial exchanges between Pilate and the Jerusalem elites, and between Pilate and Jesus, are set within the framework of this honour-shame society.

A "chosen" people

The Israelites, the "chosen" people of the Hebrew Scriptures, were not chosen for greater favour, as is all too evident by their history, but for greater responsibility—the responsibility of being the instruments through which would come to pass the Abrahamic promise to spiritually bless all nations with the true knowledge of God and to be a light to the non-Israelites nations.

Many of those who freely accept that the Israelite Jesus was chosen by God to be a blessing to many individuals appear to have difficulty in accepting or even recognising that the nation Israel was chosen by God for the same but more-comprehensive reason—to be a blessing to the non-Israelite nations. (See also Part IV.3: *Virgin Birth and Incarnation-The Gospel of Matthew* for Matthew's presentation of Jesus as the "corporate" Israelite.)

There is a general failure to understand that the responsibilities of these chosen people were not intended to be shouldered only by the two tribes of Judah and Benjamin (plus a sprinkling of Levites), now known as the "Jews", but by the whole twelve tribes. It must be said, however, that because the Jews were the only tribes remaining in the land in New Testament times, the responsibility has been visibly carried by them since then. The possible identity of the so-called "ten lost tribes" was once a hotly-debated topic in certain quarters but has now faded from any discourse or reference. Suffice to say that if the identity, location and numbers of these peoples who had been exiled from the land of Israel circa 720 BC was still known in the time of Josephus in the First Century AD, then they did not just disappear from the world:

> Wherefore there are but two tribes (the Jews) in Europe and Asia subject to the Romans, while the ten tribes (Israelites) are beyond the Euphrates till now, and are an immense multitude, and not to be estimated by numbers. [1]

---

1 Josephus, *Antiquities*, XI.5.2

CHAPTER TWO

Note

The Greek New Testament has been translated into many different languages over time. If translators of all these versions had correctly identified the various categories of persons all designated as *Ioudaios* in the New Testament, that word would not have become the most consequential single word in human history. Since this work is in English, we will confine our remarks on this topic to the English version but its content applies equally to all translations of the Greek New Testament regardless of date, language or version.

The Judeans

There is no distinction drawn between the various categories of persons all designated as "Jew/s" (*Ioudaios*) in English versions of the New Testament. Whilst an understanding of the particularities of Israelite life is both complex and challenging, such understanding should not have been beyond the capacity of professionally qualified translators. No attempt has been made to determine both context and authorial intent and differentiate accordingly: all *Ioudaios* are carelessly lumped together and translated into English as "Jew/s".

Persons designated in the English New Testament as "Jew/s" could fall into one or more of the following categories:

1. Descendants of the Israelite tribe of Judah who lived in the Roman Province of Judea, worshipped at the Temple in Jerusalem, and followed the Law of Moses;

2. Descendants of the Israelite tribe of Judah regardless of where they lived. For instance, Jesus was a Jew because he belonged to the tribe of Judah even though he came from Galilee;

3. Persons who followed the customs and practices of the Judeans regardless of where they lived. For instance, Paul self-identified as a "Jew" because he followed the customs and practices of the Judeans who worshipped at the Temple in Jerusalem even though he came from Tarsus and belonged to the Israelite tribe of Benjamin.

Note that Jesus falls into categories 2 and 3 above: not only did he belong to the Israelite tribe of Judah but he also followed the customs and practices of the Judeans who worshipped at the Temple in Jerusalem.

Correctly identifying the category of person the author has in view at any one time is daunting but not impossible if context is studied and fully appreciated. Given the fact that the word rendered into English as "Jew" was to become perhaps the most important single word in all of human history, the consequences of not differentiating between the various categories of *Ioudaios* mentioned in the New Testament can hardly be overestimated.

Note

Some scholars assert that the word *Ioudaios* always means "Judean" but they fail to take into account the other categories of *Ioudaios* mentioned in the New Testament.

The Gospel of John

The Gospel of John has been used to foment anti-Semitic sentiment for nigh on two thousand years. Because it is set in Jerusalem and portrays the ruling priestly elites as the main force of opposition to both God and Jesus, the Greek word *Ioudaios* appears seventy-one times compared to five times in Matthew and Luke and seven times in Mark. There has been a universal failure, or perhaps unwillingness, to recognise that in John's Gospel, this word *Ioudaios*, always translated into English in an ethnic sense as "Jew", should most often be translated into English in a geographic sense as "Judean".

When John uses the word *Ioudaios* in a condemnatory sense, he is always referring to the elites ruling from Jerusalem. He is certainly not referring to those descendants of the tribe of Judah then living in Galilee, such as the Jewish Jesus and the Jewish disciples, or the many Jews then living in the Diaspora. (See Part 1.1,2: *Context-Setting the Scene* and *Centres of Israelite Life in the 1st Century AD* for a description of Israelite tribal distributions.)

CHAPTER THREE

Jesus the Jew

Notes

The people known to the English speaking world as "Jews" originally comprised the Israelite tribes of Judah and Benjamin with a sprinkling of Levites. Over time, however, these people became known collectively as "Jews" so we will use this term for the sake of simplicity.

The term "Jewish religion" refers to the overall religious framework of the day and is not intended to imply a lack of diversity in religious thought.

The religion of Jesus

Jesus was not only a Jew by accident of time and place but he was also one by faith, by temperament and by spirit, an apocalyptic teacher who observed Torah, frequented Temple and synagogue, and kept the Jewish religious festivals, a Jew bent on the uniquely Jewish business of preaching the coming Kingship of God.

Jesus immersed himself in the Hebrew Scriptures and taught always from within the Jewish religion, not once abandoning the faith of his ancestors. He garnered spiritual support in his wilderness battle with temptation by quoting three times from the book of Deuteronomy. He began his public ministry by quoting from the Book of Isaiah. He and his followers referred to the Hebrew Scriptures as the "word of God" and quoted from many of its books and from every major division of the *Tanakh* (Torah, Prophets, Sacred Writings).

Jesus taught radical obedience to God and a new way of living. He did not come to abolish the Law of Moses but to add the new commandment of love to the Law, to "fulfill" it. Jesus did not come to call his people out of their religion but to inspire them to take its precepts to heart because the time of reckoning was near. He did not preach future change in some otherworldly place but advocated change in the real world of the here and now.

The preferred teaching method of Jesus was by the use of parables which have similar themes and similar structures to those of other great Jewish sages. Indeed, as Brad Young has argued in Jesus and his Jewish Parables,[2] without a familiarity with rabbinic parables, it is difficult to fully understand Gospel parables. Young's study of

---

2 Young, Brad H. *Jesus and his Jewish Parables*, Paulist Press: 1989.

Jesus' parables further demonstrates just how close Jesus was to his own people and to the religious thought of his day. The Lord's Prayer (Matthew 6:9-13) is thoroughly Jewish and, as Samuel Sandmel stated:

> ...(it) could readily have appeared without change in Rabbinic literature.[3]

When Jesus was asked what the greatest commandment was, he began by quoting the *Shema*, the foundational statement of the Jewish religion, just as an observant Jew would:

> "...The most important is, 'Hear, O Israel: The Lord our God, the Lord is one (Deuteronomy 6:4). And you shall love the Lord your God with all your heart and with all your soul and with all your mind and with all your strength' (Deuteronomy 6:5). The second is this: 'You shall love your neighbor as yourself' (Leviticus 19:18). There is no other commandment greater than these" (Mark 12:29-31 ESV).

This second commandment echoes the injunction of that other great Jewish sage Hillel, who was still teaching at the time of Jesus' birth.

The author of Luke takes particular pains to present the life of Jesus as thoroughly informed and characterised by the Jewish religion: from the day when his parents present him to the Temple to fulfill the Law of Moses until the day of the crucifixion when Luke provides a penetrating insight into Jesus the observant Jew by recording Jesus' cry from the cross which, even today, is part of a standard Jewish deathbed confession, "Into your hand I commit my spirit" (Psalm 31:5).

The life of Jesus, both in word and deed, set an example for man that by universal emulation had the potential to change the world, but that potential was very soon diverted and distorted into a form of Christianity which indoctrinated its believers with anti-Jewish thought and anti-Jewish doctrines.

A wholesale ignorance and disregard of Jesus' self-identification with the Jewish religion and the Jewish people persisted from the post-apostolic age until modern times and has had profound consequences both for Jews and for Christians. Before the Enlightenment, few even considered the possibility that when Paul said that all Israel will be saved (Romans 11:26), he referred not to the Christian Church but to the Israelite people.

---

3   Sandmel, Samuel. *Judaism and Christian Beginnings*. Oxford University Press: New York, 1978, p. 358

CHAPTER FOUR

Supersessionism

Supersessionism, more recently known as Replacement Theology, is the theological concept that because the majority of Jews in the First Century AD did not accept Jesus as their Messiah, God poured out his wrath upon them and destroyed both nation and Temple in 70 AD. God also terminated his covenants with the Israelite people and transferred them to the followers of Christianity who are the new people of God. Christianity is the true spiritual Israel and the sole heir to God's Covenant blessings.

This concept was first developed by such men as Justin Martyr (circa 100-165 AD), Irenaeus of Lyon (circa 130-202 AD), and Origen of Alexandria (185-254 AD). Fathers of the church indulged themselves in tirades of demonisation and condemnation, which only increased in fervour and ferocity when Christianity was declared the official religion of the Roman Empire in 380 AD. Charged with "deicide", denounced as "Christ-killers", and accused of bizarre blood rituals, Jews were to suffer many centuries of mob violence and state-sanctioned vitriol which straightened and paved the path towards its inevitable end in the gas chambers.

For an example of the anti-Jewish, supersessionist triumphalism endemic to Christianity, consider this statement made by Cardinal Michael Faulhaber, who ordained the current Pope Emeritus Benedict XVI in Freising Cathedral on June 29, 1951. In his 1934 book, *Judaism, Christianity and Germany*, he tried to distance Christianity from the Jewish people and at the same time justify the inclusion of the Hebrew Scriptures into the Christian Canon:

> By accepting these books (the Hebrew scriptures) Christianity does not become a Jewish religion. *These books were not composed by Jews*; they are inspired by the Holy Ghost, and therefore they are the word of God, they are God's books. The writers of them were God's pencils, the psalmsingers were harps in the hand of God, the prophets were announcers of God's revelation...We must acknowledge that the sacred Scriptures of the Old Testament have contributed material a great permanent value for the construction of the social order for all time. Social activity has assumed a different form in matters of detail, for example in legislation for the poor or in the administration of justice, but its fundamental ideas are these universal values for civilisation which come to us as a priceless heritage from the sacred books of pre-Christian Judaism. *This wealth of thought*

> *is so unique among the civilised nations of antiquity that we are bound to say: People of Israel, this did not grow in your garden of your own planting. This condemnation of usurious land-grabbing, this war against the oppression of the farmer by debt, this prohibition of usury, is not the product of your spirit.*[4]

Whilst vicious tirades such as these were nothing new or surprising, for a Cardinal Prince of the Church, to commit such anti-Jewish vitriol to writing at that crucial time is nothing less than criminal. Statements such as these would go on to bear terrible fruit. Unless this age-old attitude of mind is kept firmly in the forefront of memory there is little hope of guarding against history repeating itself.

Anti-Semitism is once more on the rise, especially in Europe, and the Catholic Church, for one, appears to be lapsing into frighteningly familiar ways if recent developments are any indication. For example, the campaign to canonise Pope Pius XII and the recent re-communication of a Holocaust-denying Bishop of the Society of St. Pius X cause distress to the Jewish people generally and make it abundantly clear that the Church's attitude to them remains essentially the same as it always has been—one of contempt.

---

4   Faulhaber, His Eminence, Cardinal Michael, Archbishop of Munich. *Judaism, Christianity and Germany,* Translated by Rev. George D Smith, Macmillan: New York, 1934.

CHAPTER FIVE

Notes

The series of Jewish-Roman wars which took place between 66-135 AD resulted in the extensive depopulation of Judean communities. By this time, however, due to the Assyrian and Babylonian exiles of previous centuries, great numbers of Jews and Israelites had already been dispersed throughout the Roman Empire, and also eastwards beyond the sway of Rome into the territories held by the client kings of the Parthian Empire. (See Part I.2: *The Context-Centres of Israelite Life in the First Century AD*)

Poison Pens

Systematic villification and demonisation of the people English speakers have come to know as "Jews" began about a century after the death of Jesus with the Christian apologist Justin Martyr and only increased in fervour and ferocity when Christianity was declared the official religion of the Roman Empire in 380 AD. This now state-sanctioned vitriol was to rain down relentlessly upon the heads of the Jews throughout these long centuries, all the while smoothing a path to the gas chambers. It is not possible in this work to devote sufficient space to catalogue all the accusations levelled against the Jewish people, nor to list all the sufferings inflicted upon them throughout these long centuries. This record is exceptionally well-documented elsewhere so we will just provide a few outstanding examples of writings which contributed in large measure to the poisonous atmosphere of Europe before turning our attention to their consequences.

In *After the evil: Christianity and Judaism in the shadow of the Holocaust*, Richard Harries, former Church of England Bishop of Oxford, provides a succinct overview of the main theological arguments of the early Church fathers, as well as the legislative structure of the Church's anti-Judaism down the ages, from the second century through to the twentieth:

> *The Jews are Christ killers.* "It is because you shed the precious blood that there is now no restoration, no mercy anymore and no defence…through your madness against Christ you have committed ultimate transgression." (St. John Chrysostom, *The Sixth Oration Against the Jews*)
>
> "*Why was the temple made desolate?*…It was because they killed the son of their benefactor, for he is coeternal with the Father. (St. Hippolytus, *Contra Judaas 1*)

Israel has been replaced by Christianity. "On the rejection of Israel and the election of the gentiles, the Lord said to Moses, 'Let me alone that I may destroy these people and make of you a great nation'...it thus follows clearly that everything concerning these people is an adumbration, image, prefiguration and symbol of that which had been written for us—Upon whom the end of the ages have come." (St, Jerome, *On the Promised Land*)

The wandering Jew. "You can hear the wailing and lamentations of each of the prophets...over the calamities which will overtake the Jewish people because of their impiety to him who had been foretold...how their kingdom would be utterly destroyed after their sin against Christ...and they would be dispersed among the gentiles throughout the whole world, with never a hope of any cessation of evil or breathing space from troubles." (Eusebius of Ceasarea, *Demonstrations of the Gospel 1.7*)

The Jews are eternally reprobate. "Groaning and trembling shall you be upon the earth, here no one can fail to see that in every land where the Jews are scattered, they are in terrified subjection to the immensely superior number of Christians...to the end of the seven days of time the continued preservation of the Jews will be a proof to believing Christians of the subjection merited by those who, in the pride of their kingdom, put the Lord to death." (St. Augustine, *Reply to Faustus the Manichean*)

The Jews are depraved. "The demons inhabit the very souls of the Jews as well as the places where they gather. If you call the synagogue a brothel, a den of vice, the devil's refuge, Satan's fortress, a place to deprave the soul, an abyss of every conceivable disaster, or whatever you will, you are still saying less than it deserves." (St. John Chrysostom, *The Sixth Oration Against the Jews*)

This theological outlook was reflected in legislation. Although some church laws were occasionally enacted to protect Jews and allow them to practise their own religion, the majority were hostile; forbidding marriage or adultery with Jews, eating with them, using fields blessed by them, receiving gifts from them, entering synagogues or converting to Judaism, the penalty for which was death. Not surprisingly, all this hateful teaching and legislation resulted in very direct suffering for Jewish communities. There were massacres of Jews along the Rhine in 1096 by the Crusader army. There was a massacre of Jews at York in 1190. In 1290 all Jews were expelled from England and in the fifteenth century Jews were first massacred and then expelled from Spain. Along with the Reformation came Martin Luther's extreme hostility to Jews followed up by centuries of pogroms and massacres taking place against a backdrop of Jewish depiction in art and literature as the personification of evil. Allegedly Jewish features were caricatured in order to depict the negation of everything that was Christian and good. Judas Iscariot became a symbol for Jews.[5]

Anti-Judaism and Anti-Semitism

It is a tribute to the integrity of some Christian clergymen that they are prepared to acknowledge Christianity's role in what is undoubtedly the greatest shadow and stain on the collective conscience of the human race. In his previously quoted work, *After the evil: Christianity and Judaism in the shadow of the Holocaust*, Richard Harries first describes the difference between Anti-Judaism and Anti-Semitism and then goes on to say that it is important to distinguish between Anti-Judaism and what emerged under Hitler:

> Anti-Semitism is primarily a hatred that is directed against the Jews as a race and its modern form arose is the nineteenth-century as part of various racial theories. Anti-Judaism is hostility to a religion…And the question is how far the Church's traditional anti-Judaism, its centuries-long teaching of contempt, prepared the ground and dulled people's hearts and minds, so that antisemitism could take hold with so little resistance in the people as a whole. [6]

Harries then goes on to quote extensively from James Parkes, an Anglican clergyman, whose importance as a contemporary witness to the rise of modern Anti-Semitism cannot be overestimated:

> In 1928, James Parkes went to work with the International Students Service in Geneva, where he quickly became aware of the rising tide of antisemitism and began a serious study of this pehenomenon. He was, he wrote later, 'Completely unprepared for the discovery that it was the Christian church and the Christian church alone, which turned a normal xenophobia and a normal good and bad community relations between two human societies into the unique evil of antisemitism, the most evil, and as I gradually came to realise, the most crippling sin of historic Christianity.' He published the results of his conclusions in his pioneering study The Conflict of Church and Synagogue in 1934. The major responsibility for antisemitism rested, in Parkes's view 'upon the theological picture created in Christian literature of the Jews perpetually betraying God and ultimately abandoned by him'. Parkes summarized his study in the words:

---

5 Harries, Richard. *After the evil: Christianity and Judaism in the shadow of the Holocaust*. Oxford University Press, 2003, pp. 18-20.

6 Ibid. 16.

> The Christian public as a whole, the great and overwhelming majority of the hundreds of millions of nominal Christians in the world, still believe that 'The Jews' killed Jesus. That they are a people rejected by their God, that all the beauty of the bible belongs to the Christian church and not to those by whom it was written; and if on this ground, so carefully prepared, modern anti-Semites have reared a structure of racial and economic propaganda, the final responsibility still rests with those who prepared the soil, created the deformation of the people, and so made these ineptitudes credible. [7]

James Parkes also stated clearly in an article on Anti-Semitism, written for *A Concise World History*, that there was a direct line from the teachings of the Church to the death camps of Hitler:

> That which changed the normal pattern of Jewish-Gentile relations was the action of the Christian Church. The statement is tragic, but the evidence is inescapable. **What is still more tragic is that there is no break in the line which leads from the beginning of the denigration of Judaism in the formative period of Christian history, from the exclusion of Jews from civic equality in the period of the Church's first triumph in the fourth century, through the horrors of the Middle Ages, to the death camps of Hitler in our own day.** [8]

After the Holocaust, other Christian scholars began the job of whitewashing the most rabid writings of the early Church fathers, especially those of John Chrysostom, claiming that not enough consideration had been given to the context of the times in which they lived when the general discourse was brutal and aggressive. Regardless of these protestations, nothing can change the fact that the unmistakable meaning of words such as "deicide" (killing God), or terms such as "sons of the devil" have not altered over time, carrying with them exactly the same odium and detestation then, as they would now.

At the First Council of Nicea in 325 AD, the Jews were declared as perfidious Christ-killers, as people to be avoided, converted, or persecuted. They were only absolved of the "murder" of Jesus by Pope John XXIII in 1965, a mere one thousand, six hundred and forty years later.

Note

Although Richard Harries (quoted above) reflects the generally-accepted view that

---

7   Ibid. 17

8   Parkes, James. *Anti-Semitism*: A Concise World History. Quadrangle Books, First American Edition, 1964.

historic Anti-Judaism was based on an opposition to the practices and practitioners of the Jewish religion, it is difficult to maintain that position when considering that so many attacks were based on an ideological perception of the Jewish character as being permanently and unreformably degenerate, and as being satanic in nature. According to that ideology, the Jews, no matter how few or assimilated, are perpetually engaged in conspiracies that seek to dominate, exploit, and destroy society or the world. Such attacks are about the Jews as a people, as a race, therefore they are Anti-Semitic. The more correct position would be that a current of hatred towards the Jews as a people, exacerbated by a hatred of the Jewish religion, has always been present in the fulminations of the Christian churches and their acolytes but certainly found its ultimate expression in later race-based theories. (Making a fine distinction at this late stage may appear unimportant but it will become relevant in a forthcoming Chapter when we turn our attention to the religious institution which has demonstrated throughout history the most relentless opposition to the Jewish people.)

CHAPTER SIX

"Superior" Hellenist-Western thought

The Germanic school of Western philosophy is rooted in Hellenist thought. Hellenist thought was "spiritual, cosmic, and universal", unlike Jewish thought which was "narrow-minded, exclusive, and legalistic". Through Kant, Schopenhauer, Hegel, Fichte, Bauer, et al, German philosophy displayed a horror and detestation of Judaism. This horror and detestation simply mirrored the thought of the religious authorities from the Church Fathers onwards.

As if all this anti-Jewish thought had not spawned enough hatred and violence over the centuries, it took an even more deadly turn when German philosophers and religious scholars began to think about religion in terms of Darwinian biology. Once Anti-Judaism became suffused with a pseudoscientific racism based on ethnicity, i.e. Anti-Semitism, that age-long Christian legitimisation, nurturing and popularisation of Jew-hatred reached its final and devilish expression when actualised through the authority of the German State.

The purpose of going over all the above is to focus attention on the greatest paradox in history—through fear, loathing, demonisation and isolation of everything Jewish, Christianity itself attended humanity's descent into the abyss, yet all of Christianity's foundational documents are based on Jewish thought.

Post-Holocaust, many theologians reacted with an equal and opposite horror and detestation of anti-Judaism. This new opposition, plus the discovery of the Qumran texts, found many biblical scholars reassessing and reorienting their theologies. Learned tomes stressing the "Jewishness" of Jesus now proliferate on bookshelves.

Even though the majority of biblical scholars today strongly support the Jewish background to the life and teachings of Jesus, most are unwittingly adopting anti-Jewish positions which go largely unrecognised as such because they take subtle and indirect forms. For example, to continue to teach the doctrine of the Incarnation is to keep alive in the minds of Christians that original charge of "deicide" (killing God) levelled against the Jews.

So, even though they have cast off the more recent philosophies of overt anti-Judaism/Semitism, they still remain hopelessly ensnared in the doctrines devised by the Church fathers whose minds, just like their German philosophical descendants, were conditioned by the more "spiritual", the more "cosmic", the more "universal", and the more "superior" Hellenist thought.

The "assembly of God" was intended to be built upon the foundation of the Jewish apostles and the Jewish prophets with the Jewish Jesus as the chief cornerstone (Ephesians 2:20) so this challenging question posed by Abraham Heschel should give Christians reason to pause and think:

> The vital question for the Church is to decide whether to look for roots in Judaism and consider itself an extension of Judaism, or to look for roots in pagan Hellenism and consider itself the antithesis of Judaism.[9]

Heschel's question pinpoints the essential choice facing Christians. It is important to keep in mind at all times that the election of Israel was never abolished and that non-Israelite followers of Jesus can be considered part of the people of God only by spiritual adoption. Jesus preached radical transformation to his contemporaries at a pivotal point in their history. At this pivotal point in Christian history, if the Churches wish to redeem themselves and be included in the people of God, they must rebuild themselves on the foundation of the Jewish apostles and the Jewish prophets, with the Jewish Jesus as the chief cornerstone.

Jesus castigated the religious leaders of his time for not understanding their own scriptures. It could be argued that the Christian churches have a more serious case to answer. They ostensibly preach Jesus of Nazareth while, at the same time, through their doctrine, they misrepresent him and actually further the viewpoint of those who crucified him. The personality cult built up around the person of "Jesus Christ" effectively destroys the central figure with far greater definition than the crucifixion itself accomplished.

---

9 Heschel, Abraham J. *The Insecurity of Freedom.* Schocken Books: New York, 1972, pp. 169-70.

CHAPTER SEVEN

Millennial Rivals

Notes on terminology

- *Roman Catholic Church*: The Roman Catholic Church refers to the Latin Church of the Catholic communion headquartered in Rome, in contradistinction to the 21 other particular Churches of the Catholic communion, including the Byzantine, Alexandrian, Armenian, Antiochian and Chaldean Catholic Churches;

- *Bishop of Rome*: The Bishop of Rome is also known as the Pope or the Supreme Pontiff and exercises world-wide dominion over the congregations of the Roman Catholic Church;

- *Holy See, Apostolic See, Vatican, Papacy*: These terms all refer to the central government comprising the Bishop of Rome (the Pope) and the Curia which is headquartered in the independent Vatican City State enclave in Rome.

This work is primarily concerned with the false teachings and false claims of the Christian churches and how those distortions of the New Testament led to the centuries-long persecution of the Jewish people with its inevitable result. This work is unapologetically about placing the responsibility where it belongs. Not on individuals but on the Christian institutions which still teach the same anti-Jewish doctrines and distortions, thus providing a continuing reason for history to repeat itself.

Whilst the crimes against the Jewish people were perpetrated by all branches of Christendom, both Eastern and Western, the most relentless historical foe of the Jewish people, and now of the State of Israel, is the Roman Catholic Church.

Divine Rights

The Roman Catholic Church has never wavered from the following position articulated in *Pastor Aeternus*, the Dogmatic Constitution on the Church of Christ, issued by the First Vatican Council on July 18 1870:

> And so, supported by the clear witness of Holy Scripture, and adhering to the manifest and explicit decrees both of our predecessors the Roman Pontiffs and of general councils, we promulgate anew the definition of the ecumenical

Council of Florence, which MUST be believed by all faithful Christians, namely that **the Apostolic See and the Roman Pontiff hold a world-wide primacy, and that the Roman Pontiff is the successor of blessed Peter, the prince of the apostles, true vicar of Christ, head of the whole Church and father and teacher of all Christian people.** (*Pastor Aerternus* 3:1-4)

Pope Pius X reiterated the Church's divine rights in his 1903 Encyclical *E Supremi*: *On the restoration of all things in Christ*, in which he claims that the following text from Jeremiah 1:10 was really addressed to the Catholic Church, "Lo, I have set thee this day over the nations and over kingdoms, to root up, and to pull down, and to waste, and to destroy, and to build, and to plant". Pope Pius XI echoed these sentiments in his 1922 Encyclical *Ubi Arcano Dei Consilio*, in which he claimed that the Church is "by divine institution the sole depository and interpreter of the ideals and teachings of Christ," and that she has been "divinely commissioned to lead mankind".

The Church's opposition to the Jews as a people derives from this claim to be the sole representative of God on Earth by divine appointment through the Apostle Peter. (For the Primacy claims of the Bishop of Rome see Part IX: *The Papacy*.) Unfortunately for the Jewish people, the Church has long recognised that the Hebrew Scriptures assign the role of representative of God on Earth to the Israelites. For as long as the Jewish descendants of those ancient Israelites are a visible presence, they are a constant reminder of this uncomfortable truth. For a Church which is meticulous in terms of doctrine and practice, rival claimants cannot be tolerated.

Note on Ecumenism

Unitatis redintegratio (Restoration of Unity) is the Second Vatican Council's decree on ecumenism promulgated by Pope Paul VI on 21 November 1964. Ostensibly, it calls for the promotion of worldwide co-operation and understanding between the various Christian denominations with a view to the eventual reunification of Christendom. Unlike Eastern Christendom, the Western denominations seemed oblivious to the fact that the Holy See, in all its long history, had never willingly ceded one scrap of authority or power. It seemed to have faded from collective memory that the Bishop of Rome can never yield his primacy because to do so would be to admit that he has no authority passed on by the Apostle Peter, therefore no "Apostolic Succession" and no claim to be "Vicar of Christ" on Earth.

Only now, more than 50 years after *Unitatis Redintegratio*, can we see the results of this brilliantly designed and orchestrated ecumenical campaign—the Pope is publicly hailed as the single voice of Christianity while all around his throne lie the bloodied remnants of the Reformation.

CHAPTER EIGHT

The Holy See and the Holy Places

Unfortunately, we can do no more here than merely touch on the well-documented and extensive evidence confirming the Church's hostility towards the State of Israel, except to make a few relevant remarks and to reflect that her methods of manipulation and deception have been honed to razor-sharp effectiveness through the collective and successive efforts of the most peerless practitioners of power the world will ever know.

The first crusade to capture the sacred city of Jerusalem and the Holy Land from the Muslims, launched in 1095 by Pope Urban II, may seem like ancient history to most, but to the Holy See, with it relentless purpose and millennial views, the ownership of Jerusalem has never been off the agenda. Ever since the eventual failure of the Knights militant, the Church has waged relentless political and spiritual warfare for possession of the "Holy Places". The profoundly complex history of this war defies simple description here but its energising principle is profoundly simple, as we will see by referencing a few examples.

In May 1897, on the eve of the first World Zionist Congress in Basle, Switzerland, the Roman Catholic Church issued its first official statement on Zionism. The authoritative Jesuit journal, *Civiltà Cattolica*, let it be known that a Jewish state in the Holy Land with Jerusalem as its capital was unthinkable for the Catholic Church:

> 1827 years have passed since the prediction of Jesus of Nazareth was fulfilled, namely that is that Jerusalem would be destroyed ... that the Jews would be led away to be slaves among all the nations, and that they would remain in the dispersion till the end of the world ... According to the Sacred Scriptures, the Jewish people must always live dispersed and wandering among the other nations, so that they may render witness to Christ not only by the Scriptures ... but by their very existence. As for a rebuilt Jerusalem, which could become the center of a reconstituted state of Israel, we must add that this is contrary to the prediction of Christ Himself. [10]

---

10   *Civiltà Cattolica*, 1 May 1897. Quoted in Livia Rokach, *The Catholic Church and the Question of Palestine*. Saqi Books: London, 1987, p.11.

In no uncertain terms, the statement clarified Rome's opposition to political Zionism on both theological and political grounds and announced that the Church would never support a homeland for the Jewish people with its centre in Jerusalem.

On 26 January 1904, Theodor Herzl, the founder of the Zionist movement, met with Pope Pius X in the Vatican and sought his support for the Zionist effort to establish a Jewish state in Palestine. Herzl recorded his account of the meeting in his diary. The Pope's responses are so reflective of the Church's millennial attitude towards the Jewish people that the relevant passages are worth reproducing in full:

> We cannot give approval to this movement. We cannot prevent the Jews from going to Jerusalem—but we could never sanction it. The soil of Jerusalem, if it was not always sacred, has been sanctified by the life of Jesus Christ. As the head of the Church I cannot tell you anything different. The Jews have not recognized our Lord, therefore we cannot recognize the Jewish people.

At one point in the conversation, Herzl informed the Pope that his sole concern was with current Jewish distress and that he had hoped to avoid religious issues. The Pope was not moved and responded with:

> Yes, but we, and I as the head of the Church, cannot do this. There are two possibilities. Either the Jews will cling to their faith and continue to await the Messiah who, for us, has already appeared. In that case they will be denying the divinity of Jesus and we cannot help them. Or else they will go there without any religion, and then we can be even less favorable to them. [11]

Over the next four decades, and despite the ever-worsening position of European Jewry during the 1930's, the Holy See's position remained unchanged. By 1943, and although the Holy See undoubtedly knew about the mass extermination of the Jewish people, they would not relent, as demonstrated by the following request and response.

In March of that year, Archbishop Angelo Roncalli (the apostolic delegate to Turkey and later Pope John XXIII) transmitted a request from the Jewish Agency for Palestine that the Holy See intervene with the Slovak government to permit a thousand Jewish children to emigrate to Palestine. The request was handled by Msgr. Dominico Tardini, the Vatican's Under Secretary of State, who responded that:

---

11 Patai, Raphael. *The Complete Diaries of Theodor Herzl*, translated by Harry Zohn (New York/London: Herzl Press, Thomas Yoseloff, 1960), pp 1601-1605.

> The Holy See has never approved the project of making Palestine a Jewish home…Palestine is by this time more sacred for Catholics than…for Jews.[12]

As Rubenstein and Roth conclude in Approaches to Auschwitz:

> This response and others of a similar kind indicate that, at the time, the Vatican took a political stand on Palestine on the basis of a religious position at least as old as the First Crusade, namely, the idea that Palestine was Christ's patrimony.[13]

Also in March 1943, Secretary of State Maglioni wrote to William Godfrey, apostolic delegate to London, expressing disappointment that Britain, which had recently facilitated the immigration of Jews from all corners of Europe to Palestine, had "altered its course" and appeared to be contravening the limits on immigration outlined in the 1939 White Paper.[14] It was clear that Maglione equated Jewish immigration to Palestine with the creation of a Jewish state.

The following month, in April 1943, Maglione reflected on the "particular historical rights" held by Catholics on the Holy Places, which extended "with deep piety and devotion to Palestine itself, made sacred by the presence and memory of the divine redeemer". He concluded that their "religious feelings would be injured and they would justly feel for their rights if Palestine belonged to the Jews".[15]

The Holy See's policy remained unchanged after the War, effectively leaving half a million Holocaust survivors, now displaced persons, huddled in occupied Europe. However, as news about the horrors of the Holocaust gradually became known, so also was there a corresponding rise in sympathy for the Zionist cause, including not only from a majority of American Jewry, but also from President Harry S. Truman and a large group of US senators and congressmen. This rising tide of support for the idea of a Jewish homeland from the pre-eminent political, economic and military power in the West resulted in the Zionist lobby increasingly focusing their efforts on Washington, an investment which would pay enormous long-term dividends.

---

12 *Actes et Documents du Saint Siège relatifs à la Seconde Guerre Mondiale*, Vol 9, No. 272. (Acts and Documents of the Holy See related to the Second World War is an eleven-volume collection of documents from the Vatican historical archives compiled by Jesuit historians Pierre Blet, Angelo Martini, Burkhart Schneider, and Robert Graham.)

13 Roth, J.K. and Rubenstein, R.L. *Approaches to Auschwitz*. 2nd Ed. published by Westminster John Knox Press: Louisville, Kentucky, 2003, pp. 275.

14 Luigi Maglione to William Godfrey, 3 March 1943, *Actes et Documents du Saint Siège relatifs à la Seconde Guerre Mondiale*. Volume 9, No. 184.

15 Phayer, Michael. T*he Catholic Church and the Holocaust, 1930-1965*. Indiana University Press: Bloomingdale, 2000, p. 50.

The war over Jerusalem

The Mandate for Palestine (valid 29 September 1923–15 May 1948) was a League of Nations Mandate for British administration of the territory of Palestine and the territory of TransJordan, a separate Arab Emirate, both of which were conceded by the Ottoman Empire following World War I. The Balfour Declaration's "national home for the Jewish people" was to be established in the territory of Palestine.

The Holy See's firm opposition to a "national home for the Jewish people" was expressed several times during the debates surrounding the decision to grant Britain the Mandate.

On 29 November 1947, the UN General Assembly adopted Resolution 181 calling for the partition of Mandatory Palestine into Jewish and Arab states. The resolution envisaged a *corpus separatum* (separate entity) status for the city of Jerusalem and its environs under a special international regime to be administered by the United Nations. This resolution was viewed favorably by the Holy See. However, it was promptly rejected by the Arab states and, following the hostilities of 1948, the *corpus separatum* for Jerusalem did not eventuate.

In October of that year, Pope Pius XII issued an encyclical, *In Multiplicibus Curis*, in which he called on the peace-makers to give Jerusalem and its outskirts an "international character" and also to assure internationally guaranteed freedom of access and worship at the Holy Places scattered throughout Palestine. In April 1949, in the encyclical *Redemptoris Nostra*, Pius appealed for justice for the Palestinian refugees and repeated his call for an "international status" as the best form of protection for the Holy Places.

When the Holy See approved Resolution 181 in 1947, it did so because of the envisaged separate status of Jerusalem and not because it approved the establishment of a Jewish State. When the State of Israel was declared on 15 May 1948, *L'Osservatore Romano*, the official newspaper of the Holy See, announced to the world, including to the remnants of the slaughtered Jewish communities of Europe seeking a safe home, that its position on a homeland for the Jewish people had never changed:

> Modern Zionism is not the true heir to the Israel of the Bible, but a secular state.... Therefore the Holy Land and its sacred places belong to Christianity, which is the true Israel.[16]

---

16 Feldman, Egal. *Catholics and Jews in 20th Century America*. University of Illinois Press, 2001, p. 98.

The Holy See's ill-will lasted decades after the Jewish state was born, throughout the genocidal attacks by Arab armies only three years post-Holocaust, throughout the fledgling State's successful absorption of millions of refugees, and throughout its creation of a functioning democracy along with all the institutions of civil society. Despite all these achievements, the Holy See remained grudgingly and glacially aloof. Her position statements on the issue exuded a piety and virtue belied by her recognition of one tyrannical regime after another.

The Six Day War of 1967 permanently changed the geo-political situation in the Middle East. Israel was in firm possession of the whole of the land west of the Jordan River, including all the Holy Places.

By the early 1990's, as country after country established diplomatic relations with Israel, the Holy See's position became untenable and threatened to leave her the lone Christian voice in a Muslim chorus of intransigence. So she could continue to be relevant and influence possible peace negotiations between Israel and the Palestinians, which would include the status of Jerusalem, Rome entered into the 1993 *Fundamental Agreement between Israel and the Holy See* that paved the way for the subsequent establishment of full diplomatic relations. However, her calculated violations of this agreement demonstrate once again that there is no deception she will not entertain, there is no hypocrisy she will not tolerate, there is no calculated lie she will not tell, there is no pledge she will not break, and there is no friend she will not betray in her relentless campaign to establish "spiritual" hegemony over Jerusalem and the Holy Land because Palestine is still "Christ's patrimony" and still belongs by right to the Church. [17]

The Dreyfus Affair

Reproduced below are extracts from an article entitled *Alfred Dryefus and the "Dreyfus Affair"* accessible on the United States Holocaust Memorial Museum site.[18]

> Alfred Dreyfus, born in Alsace in 1859, graduated from the *Ecole Polytechnique* military school in Paris in 1880. After receiving specialised artillery training, he was promoted to Lieutenant in the French military in 1885. He was promoted to Captain in 1889, later becoming the only Jew serving in the French Army's General Staff headquarters in 1893.

---

17 See article series *The Holy See and the Holy Places* on this author's blog *The Race is Run*. https://raceisrun.typepad.com/weblog/2007/01/the_holy_see_an.html

18 *Alfred Dreyfus and the "Dreyfus Affair"* accessed 29 December 2018. https://encyclopedia.ushmm.org/content/en/article/alfred-dreyfus-and-the-dreyfus-affair

In the autumn of 1894, French intelligence services discovered that a secret military document (known as the bordereau) had been sent by a French officer to the military attaché of the German embassy in Paris. This was an act of treason. At the time, there was some evidence that made it unlikely Dreyfus was the author of the traitorous memorandum. Nonetheless, on the basis of handwriting analysis and out of anti-Jewish prejudice against Dreyfus, he was arrested on October 15, 1894, and court-martialed.

Dreyfus had no hope of a fair trial. The ministry of war placed a file of secret and in some cases forged documents before the tribunal that Dreyfus' attorney was not allowed to see. Further, unverified and false testimonies against Dreyfus were presented at the secret trial. The court quickly found Dreyfus guilty of treason. He was sentenced to life imprisonment.

At a public ceremony on January 5, 1895, Dreyfus was dishonorably discharged and demoted. As (according with tradition) his stripes were torn and his sword was broken, Dreyfus maintained his innocence, crying out: "Soldiers, they are degrading an innocent man! Long live France! Long live the army!" A mob that had gathered at the ceremony, incited by the antisemitic press and the writings of Edouard Drumont in *La Libre Parole*, accompanied the public degradation with calls against Dreyfus and Jews. Dreyfus was exiled to a penal colony on Devil's Island, part of an archipelago off the coast of French Guiana in South America.

With Dreyfus languishing in captivity, his family continued to challenge the verdict and claim that he was innocent. Lieutenant Colonel Georges Picquart, who had become the new head of French Intelligence Services, was never convinced of Dreyfus' guilt. In March 1896, new evidence surfaced implicating a French major, Ferdinand Walsin Esterhazy, as the German agent who had written the bordereau. Despite Picquart's efforts to investigate Esterhazy, his superiors resisted efforts to have the case reopened and eventually had Piquart reassigned to Tunisia.

Nonetheless, the proof that Dreyfus was in fact innocent reached the French senate, where Senator Auguste-Scheurer-Kestner declared Dreyfus' innocence and accused Esterhazy of being the traitor. Meanwhile, on January 13, 1898, the Socialist newspaper *L'Aurore* published an open letter from the novelist Emile Zola to the president of the republic, Felix Faure. Titled "J'accuse!" ("I Accuse"), the letter accused the government of antisemitism, lack of evidence against Dreyfus, judicial errors, and illegal jailing of Dreyfus. Novelist Zola was found guilty of criminal libel in slandering the army and had to flee to England to avoid imprisonment. He remained there until he was granted amnesty in 1899.

The front-page article made a powerful impression in France, dividing the country into two camps. The anti-Dreyfusards, comprised of the Catholic Church, the military, and the right wing, clung to the original verdict and exploited antisemitism. They feared that a reversal would lead to a weakening of the military establishment. They were opposed by the Dreyfusards, an alliance of moderate Republicans, Radicals, and Socialists. The Dreyfusards protested the innocence of Alfred Dreyfus. They also felt the case had become a test of France's ability to protect truth, justice, and the basic elements of the Rights of Man against the forces of extreme nationalism, antisemitism, and the excessive involvement of the Church in state affairs.

In the summer of 1898, the case was reopened and the original forgeries used to convict Dreyfus were discovered. Public opinion began to shift in favor of Dreyfus. The Supreme Court ordered a retrial. At the retrial in August and September 1899, the court-martial still found Dreyfus guilty of treason but reduced his sentence due to "extenuating circumstances." The President of the Republic, Emile Loubet, granted Dreyfus a pardon. On September 20, 1899, Dreyfus was set free, remarking, "The government of the Republic has given me back my freedom. It is nothing for me without my honor."

Dreyfus was not officially exonerated until July 12, 1906, by a military commission. He was readmitted into the army with a promotion to the rank of Major. A week later, he was made a knight of the Legion of Honour. Despite the toll which the years of imprisonment on Devil's Island had taken on his health, he returned to serve in the French army in World War I and was promoted to Lieutenant Colonel at the end of the war. Dreyfus died in Paris on July 12, 1935, at the age of 75.

The Dreyfus Affair had a profound impact on French politics. It revealed the tensions that existed in France following defeat in the Franco-Prussian War of 1871, divided the country between Left and Right, reflected the continuing power of antisemitism in the homeland of liberty and the Revolution, and challenged the very notion of France's identity as a Catholic nation. The Dreyfus Affair would eventually contribute to the formal separation of Church and State in France in 1905.

Jews in France and around the world were shocked that a thoroughly acculturated French Jew like Alfred Dreyfus, who had demonstrated his loyalty to the state and served in the military, could not receive a fair trial and instead became the victim of such vehement anti-Jewish hatred.

A Divine Irony

For Theodor Herzl, the founder of the Zionist movement, the Dreyfus affair demonstrated that despite the emancipation of the Jews initiated by the French Revolution and the Enlightenment, and despite thorough assimilation, nothing would solve the problem of Anti-Semitism but the creation of a Jewish State. Thus, if not for the complicity of the Catholic Church in the anti-Jewish railroading of Dreyfus, the State of Israel may never have materialised.

CHAPTER NINE

European Fascism

Fascism was a political ideology and a mass movement that dominated many parts of Europe between 1922 and 1945. Europe's first fascist leader, Benito Mussolini, took the name of his party from the Latin word *fasces*, which referred to a bundle of elm or birch rods (usually containing an axe) used as a symbol of penal authority in ancient Rome.

While there is no universally accepted definition of fascism, it is nevertheless possible to identify a number of general characteristics that fascist movements of those times tended to have in common, including aggressive and expansionist ultra-nationalism; contempt for electoral democracy and political and cultural liberalism; a belief in natural social hierarchy and the rule of elites; the suppression of individual liberties, especially freedom of speech; and centralised autocratic government headed by a dictatorial leader.

Fascist parties and movements in European countries between 1922 and 1945 included the National Fascist Party (*Partito Nazionale Fascista*) in Italy, led by Mussolini; the National Socialist German Workers' Party (*Nationalsozialistische Deutsche Arbeiterpartei*), or Nazi Party, led by Adolf Hitler; the Fatherland Front (*Vaterländische Front*) in Austria, led by Engelbert Dollfuss; the National Union (*União Nacional*) in Portugal, led by António de Oliveira Salazar (which became fascist after 1936); the Party of Free Believers (*Elefterofronoi*) in Greece, led by Ioannis Metaxas; and the *Ustaša* (Insurgence) in Croatia, led by Ante Pavelić.

Spain's fascist movement, the *Falange* (Phalanx), founded in 1933 by José Antonio Primo de Rivera, never came to power but many of its members were absorbed into the military dictatorship of Francisco Franco, which itself displayed many fascist characteristics.

In Germany

Adolf Hitler was appointed Chancellor of Germany on 30 January 1933. On 23 March 1933, eighty-three percent of the German Parliament, or *Reichstag*, passed an act which gave him the power to enact laws without permission from Parliament. This *Enabling Act* gave Hitler plenary powers and followed on the heels of the *Reichstag Fire Decree*, which had abolished most civil liberties and transferred state powers to the *Reich* government. The combined effect of the two laws was to transform

Hitler's government into a legal dictatorship. The mass media then manipulated public opinion and reinforced the power of the central Government through a vast propaganda machine using subtle techniques to dupe the German people into thinking they were receiving news and information. It may perhaps surprise some to discover that Hitler never won an election on the vote of the German people—politicians deprived them of their right to decide.

Despite the regime's stranglehold on all conventional methods of communication, news of atrocities on the Eastern Front committed by the *Einsatzgruppen* paramilitary death squads filtered through the censorship barriers. Many ordinary German civilians were horrified by these reports and began to organise resistance. For example, the non-violent White Rose movement conducted an anonymous leaflet and graffiti campaign calling for active opposition to the regime. After the core group's arrest by the Gestapo on 18 February 1943, they and many other members and supporters were sentenced to death or imprisonment. As for the ordinary German soldier, sailor or airman, he operated under the same command structure as his Allied counterpart with similar punishments for disobedience or desertion so there was little or nothing the individual could have done about the situation even if he had wanted to.

That leaves us with the German professional military class. The post-war view held that the *Wehrmacht*, the combined Army, Navy and Air Forces, had merely fought their enemies in a conventional war and was not involved in the Holocaust or other atrocities. The contrasting view today is that the *Wehrmacht* was complicit in the Holocaust and examples are cited of collaboration with the SS in committing atrocities, especially on the Eastern Front. However, just as was the case with German civilians, many examples could be cited where officers of the *Wehrmacht*, including Field Marshals and Generals, expressed disapproval of the dishonorable and brutal methods of the regime, lodged official complaints about the numerous atrocities of the *Waffen-SS*, especially the actions of the notorious Dirlewanger and Kaminski Brigades in putting down the Warsaw Uprising and, in some cases, collaborated with other resistance groups in numerous attempts to assassinate Hitler, all such attempts resulting in extremely dire consequences for the parties involved. According to an article entitled "Operation Valkyrie 1944", in Cambridge University Library's Germanic Collection:

> The most famous assassination attempt on the life of Adolf Hitler took place on July 20th 1944 at the *Wolfsschanze* or Wolf's Lair headquarters near Rastenburg, East Prussia. The plot was codenamed Operation Valkyrie and was led by the German aristocrat and army officer Claus Schenk Graf von Stauffenberg in conjunction with General Friedrich Olbricht and General Ludwig Beck of the German general staff. The plot was the culmination of a more widespread

anti-Nazi German resistance movement to overthrow Hitler and the Third Reich." In the aftermath of Operation Valkyrie, around 7,000 Germans were either executed or sent to concentration camps. There had been several abortive assassination attempts on Hitler's life before Stauffenberg finally went ahead with Operation Valkyrie.[19]

Whilst it is always dangerous to stereotype an entire group or class of people, as the foregoing demonstrates, this work is primarily about apportioning responsibility for the Holocaust so we must now identify those forces which bear the major degree of culpability.

By the time the Nazi's came to power, the teaching of Supersessionism and the resulting centuries-long demonisation of the Jewish people by the Christian Churches had contributed to a mindset of hatred which, when added to Hitler's race-based theory that the Jewish people were a type of sub-human species, enabled some to accept his "final solution to the Jewish question". History records that the "final solution", which was to be mass murder, was carried out by organisations declared "inherently criminal" by the Nuremberg Military Tribunal: the Leadership Corps of the Nazi Party; the *Schutzstaffel* (Protective Echelon or SS); the *Sicherheitsdienst* (Security Service or SD); and the Gestapo (Secret State Police).

By the outbreak of World War II, these organisations were all effectively under the control of *Reichsführer-SS* Heinrich Himmler, the head of the SS. By this time also, the SS had consolidated into its final form, which comprised three main groups: the *Allgemeine SS* (responsible for enforcing the racial policy of Nazi Germany and general policing); the *SS-Totenkopfverbände* (responsible for running the concentration and extermination camps); and the *Waffen-SS* (paramilitary combat units). Reputable sources dealing with every aspect of these groups and their crimes, including the administration of the extermination camps, are readily available for readers so we will not dignify them further but rather limit ourselves to making a few observations about enduring consequences.

As a result of successive trials held by the post-war Nuremberg Military Tribunal, a number of SS volunteers were executed, while others were tried and imprisoned by their countries. Still others either lived in exile or returned to their homeland. At this point, it is important to note that, as the war progressed, foreign volunteers and conscripts came to make up one half of the *Waffen-SS*. Volunteer foreign nationals came from such places as Belgium, the Netherlands, Croatia, Hungary, France,

---

19 Germanic Collections, *Operation Valkyrie 1944*. Cambridge University Library. Accessed 28 January 2019. http://www.lib.cam.ac.uk/collections/departments/germanic-collections/about-collections/spotlight-archive/operation-valkyrie

Romania, Spain, Switzerland, and even the UK. Therefore, the *Waffen-SS* developed into an international coalition of the willing and was not, as is commonly thought today, a purely German affair. (Note that while *Waffen-SS* units served alongside regular German units in World War II, they were never integrated into the regular army, nor were their members able to join the ranks of the German High Command.)

There are two important takeaways for the future. Firstly, it is wise to keep in mind that Hitler was not voted into office by the German people but granted his power by politicians. Secondly, those who believe that an event like the Holocaust could never happen again because the political Nazi Party no longer exists are labouring under a delusion. History teaches us that the common characteristics of fascism are timeless and boundless and any of its manifestations, such as attempts to wrest power from the voting public to an unelected bureaucracy, or attempts to transfer the power of the many into the hands of a few, or attempts to suppress freedom of conscience and freedom of speech, must be vigorously resisted. The maxim "Eternal Vigilance is the Price of Liberty" remains forever true.

CHAPTER TEN

The Holy See and European Fascism

At the outset, it must be made clear that this Chapter is directed solely at the Holy See. The inescapable fact is that the policies and attitudes of the authorities in Rome produced mixed reactions among Catholics on the ground. For example, some German Catholic religious institutions fought openly against Nazism. Catholic Bishops initially banned membership of the Nazi Party because they disapproved of Hitler's violent methods and his doctrine of "positive Christianity" although they agreed with his Anti-Communism and Nationalism. During the Holocaust period, Catholic Bishops throughout Europe sent reports of Nazi atrocities to the Holy See urging the Pope to intervene. In contradistinction, however, the Catholic Centre Party, whilst initially being the political voice of moderation and democracy in Germany, finally abandoned those principles through political expediency and enabled Hitler's rise to power.

We will now focus on the reasons why the Holy See encouraged, enabled and supported the formation, rise and establishment of 20th Century fascist movements such as those in Germany, Italy, Spain, and Portugal. Whilst we cannot provide sufficient space in this work for a detailed analysis of all the circumstances leading to the Church's involvement with these regimes, we can, however, draw the reader's attention to factors which had a significant impact on their development.

Mobilisation

Beginning in the mid 19th Century, the Church began to mobilise her religious and political resources for a battle against emerging ideologies which dared to assert that the Church should be subject to civil authorities and which challenged the divine right of the Church to exercise her influence "even to the end of the world—not only over private individuals but over nations, peoples, and their sovereign princes..." (See Papal Encyclical *Quanta Cura: Condemning Current Errors,* issued by Pope Pius XI on 8 December 1864.)

After the publication of Karl Marx's first volume of *Das Kapital* in 1869, Pope Leo XIII and Pope Pius X issued several Papal Encyclicals in which they condemned concepts such as Rationalism, Materialism, Atheism, Liberalism, Socialism, Communism, Nihilism, Separation of Church and State, and so forth. (See for example *Quod Apostolici Muneris* (28 December 1878); *Diuturnum* (29 June 1881); *Libertas Praestantissimum* (20 June 1888); *Exeunte iam Anno* (25 December 1888); *E*

Supremi (4 October 1903); *Vehementer Nos* (11 February 1906); and *Pascendi Dominici Gregis* (8 September 1907). [20]

In reaction to the abdication of Tsar Nicholas II, the collapse of Imperial Russia, and the Russian Revolution of February 1917, an increasingly fearful Church embarked upon a world-wide political and religious crusade to mobilise and unite her legions of individual Catholic men and women in opposition to what was now perceived to be the gravest challenge to Christian society— "Atheistic Communism".

This crusade only increased in vehemence and intensity when the Russian Bolshevik Government, led by Vladimir Ilyich Lenin, came to power through the October 1917 Revolution. Within a few months, the Russian Government had declared the separation of Church and State and seized all church lands. Although the initial target of the Bolsheviks was the Russian Orthodox Church, and although that Church was not in communion with the Holy See, the authorities in Rome could clearly see that the writing was on the wall for them also if Communism were allowed to spread into Western Europe. From the Holy See's point of view, the fact that an ex-seminarian of the Russian Orthodox Church, Josef Stalin, had been appointed General Secretary of the Communist Party of the Soviet Union's Central Committee on 3 April 1922 was all the proof one needed that the menace of Communism had infected even those who had once given their allegiance to Christianity.

In 1922, Count John de Salis, the British minister to the Holy See, confirmed the fear and hysteria gripping the Vatican and Pope Pius XI when he reported to the Foreign Office in London that, "Everything in the Vatican is dominated by the Pope's fear of Russian Communism, that the Soviets may reach Western Europe". [21]

While the forces of European Fascism were busy garnering support and then consolidating power in Germany, Italy, Spain and Portugal, Pope Pius XI was preparing his master stroke, which was delivered via the 23 December 1922 Encyclical *Ubi Arcano Dei Consilio*, in which he outlined a strategy to counter the current modernist evils. This strategy, to be known as "Catholic Action", would encourage, promote, and hand-pick Catholic men and women who would devote themselves to pursuing the best interests of the Church in their respective societies without the necessity of becoming priests or nuns. The effect of the policies, plans and edicts of this Pope were to transform the immense Catholic apparatus throughout the world into one giant political party, one which could easily defeat any candidate, president, or prime minister, one which could also elect its own leaders with absolute

---

20 All Papal documents referenced may be accessed on the Holy See's Website.
    http://w2.vatican.va/content/vatican/en.html

21 Rhodes, Anthony. *The Vatican in the Age of Dictators 1922-1945*. Hodder & Stoughton: London, 1973, p. 18.

allegiance to Rome. Coincidentally, or not, this Encyclical was published only seven days before the formation of the Union of Soviet Socialist Republics (USSR) on 30 December 1922.

See also the following Encyclicals of Pius XI: *Quadragessimo Anno* (15 May 1931), in which he forbids Catholics to take up either Communism or Socialism, advocates strict and watchful moral restraint enforced vigorously by governmental authority, and endorses fascist corporatism; *Caritate Christi Compulsi: On the Sacred Heart* (3 May 1932), in which he exhorts all Catholic individuals and Catholic States to strive against the "enemies of religion", and links a "satanic hatred of religion" with the Pauline "mystery of iniquity"; *Mit Brennender Sorge* (14 March 1937), addressed to all the faithful of the world about the plight of the Church in Germany; *Divini Redemptoris: On Atheistic Communism* (19 March 1937), in which he uses language such as "a satanic scourge", the "monstrous emanations of the communistic system flow with satanic logic" and "occult forces" to describe Atheistic Communism as manifested chiefly in Bolshevism. He mentions the "horrors" being perpetrated in Russia, Mexico and Spain and places "the vast campaign of the Church against world Communism under the standard of St. Joseph". In *Divini Redemptoris*, Pius XI also draws attention to his previous condemnations of Communism in the special Allocution of 1924, and in his Encyclicals *Miserentissimus Redemptor; Quadragesimo Anno; Caritate Christi; Acerba Animi; Dilectissima Nobis;* and in *Ingravescentibus Malis : On the Rosary* (29 September 1937), in which he states that just as the "Virgin Mother of God" defeated the terrible sect of the Albigenses and the Mohammedan armies at Lepanto, so too will she defeat Communism. (*Mit Brennender Sorge* and *Divini Redemptoris*, the two Encyclicals of March 1937, will be explored in more depth under a separate heading).

Although couched in religious language, these Encyclicals represented a political call to arms which was answered by Catholic Action groups, Catholic press outlets, and Catholic political organisations, all of which swung into action to further its implementation. These factors should be kept in mind when considering the following timeline which covers only crucial events leading up to 1941, at which time the results of the Holy See's enabling of European Fascism were becoming clear to all:

- **30 October 1922**: Benito Mussolini becomes Minister-President of Italy;

- **15 December 1922**: Creation of Fascist Grand Council of Italy;

- **11 February 1929**: The Lateran Treaty, also called the Lateran Pact of 1929, between the Fascist Government of Italy and the Holy See is signed by Benito Mussolini for the Italian government and by Cardinal Secretary of State Pietro Gasparri for the Papacy. The Pact reaffirms the principle established in the 4 March 1848 Statute of the Kingdom of Italy, "that the Catholic, Apostolic and Roman Religion is the only religion of the State". Through this agreement, the Holy See gains its own sovereign monarchical-sarcedotal State of Vatican City and is awarded financial reparation by the Italian State for the loss of its Papal States in 1870;

- **April 14 1931:** The Second Spanish Republic instituted;

- **9 December 1931:** Adoption of new Spanish Republican constitution. It establishes freedom of speech and freedom of association, extends suffrage to women, allows divorce, largely disestablishes the Catholic Church, and strips the Spanish nobility of any special legal status;

- **5 July 1932:** Ex-Seminarian, António de Oliveira Salazar, appointed Prime Minster of Portugal. Salazar was opposed to Democracy, Socialism, Communism and Liberalism. His political project, the New State, (*Estado Novo*) had a corporatist authoritarian structure clearly inspired by the social doctrines of the Catholic Church as defined in the Papal Encyclicals *Rerum Novarum* (1891) and *Quadragesimo Anno* (1931);

- **31 January 1933:** Adolf Hitler appointed Chancellor of Germany;

- **23 March 1933:** The *Enabling Act* gives Adolf Hitler the power to rule by decree. The Act was passed by the *Reichstag* only with the support of the Catholic Centre Party, led by Monsigneur Ludwig Kass, in coordination with the German Bishops;

- **28 March 1933:** Only five days after the passage of the *Enabling Act*, the Catholic Bishops of Germany rescind the previous ban on Catholic membership of Nazi Party;

- **3 June 1933:** Pius XI issues Papal Encyclical *Dilectissima Nobis : On persecution of the Church in Spain by the Spanish Republic*;

- **6 July 1933:** Germany's Catholic Centre Party undertakes to dissolve itself as a pre-condition of forthcoming *Reichskonkordat* between Germany and the Holy See;

- **20 July 1933:** *Reichskonkordat* between Germany and the Holy See signed in Rome by Cardinal Secretary of State Eugenio Pacelli for the Holy See and Vice-Chancellor Franz von Papen for Germany. The Concordat, ratified on 10 September 1933, guarantees the rights of Catholic Church and requires Bishops to swear an oath of loyalty to the Governor or

President of the German *Reich* upon taking office. The German Catholic Centre Party dissolves itself as a condition of the Concordat (see note on New York Times article);

- **23 October 1933**: Hitler withdraws Germany from the League of Nations with the support of the Catholic Press and several Catholic Bishops;

- **15 September 1935**: Nuremberg Laws enacted. Beginning in 1933, the German government had enacted a series of anti-Jewish laws restricting the rights of German Jews to earn a living, to enjoy full citizenship, to gain education, or to work in the civil service. The subsequent Nuremberg Laws stripped German Jews of their citizenship and forbade Jews to marry non-Jewish Germans. Note that both Catholic and Protestant clergy provided the baptismal information that made the general implementation of the race laws possible by identifying who was a Christian and, by omission, who was not;[22]

- **16 February 1936**: The Popular Front, an alliance of Socialists, Communists, and left-wing Republicans, wins National Elections in Spain;

- **July 1936**: Spanish Civil War breaks out;

- **1 October 1936**: Generalissimo Francisco Franco becomes Head of State in those parts of Spain controlled by Nationalist forces;

- **25 October 1936**: Benito Mussolini and Adolf Hitler announce a Rome-Berlin alliance—the Axis powers;

- **14 March 1937**: Pope Pius XI issues Papal Encyclical *Mit Brennender Sorge*, followed five days later by another Encyclical *Divini Redemptoris: On Atheistic Communism*. (These two Encyclicals will be addressed under a separate heading);

- **5 August 1937**: The Holy See recognises the Spanish Fascist regime of Francisco Franco;

- **9-10 November 1938**: *Kristallnacht* (Night of Broken Glass). Jewish synagogues, businesses, schools, hospitals and homes ransacked or destroyed. Thousands of Jewish men incarcerated. *Kristallnacht* is viewed by historians as the beginning of the "Final Solution to the Jewish Question";

---

22 Wilenski, Gabriel. *Six Million Crucifixions*. QWERTY Publishers, 2010, p. 254.

- **2 March 1939**: At this crucial juncture, ten days before the Austrian *Anschluss*, Cardinal Secretary of State, Eugenio Pacelli, becomes Pope Pius XII (see separate article);

- **12 March 1939**: The *Anschluss*. Nazi Germany annexes Austria;

- **15 March 1939**: German troops enter Prague, completing invasion of Czechoslovakia;

- **1 April 1939**: Francisco Franco takes control of the whole of Spain. As leader, he is known as *Caudillo de España, por la gracia de Dios* (Leader of Spain, by the grace of God);

- **1 September 1939**: Outbreak of World War II. Nazi Germany invades Poland. Ultimate target is the "Judeo-Bolshevik" regime of the Soviet Union;

- **7 May 1940**: The Holy See and Salazar's Portugal sign Concordat. Catholicism recognised as State religion;

- **2 June 1941**: *Operation Barbarossa*: Nazi Germany invades Soviet Union. General Franco sends official offer of military support to Hitler on the condition that Spanish troops are deployed only in the struggle against Communism. Hitler accepts. The Spanish Blue Division is incorporated into the German Army and deployed along the Russian front.

Note

The New York Times edition of 21 July 1933 published on page five a report of the signing of the *Reichskonkordat* by Pacelli and von Papen. Astoundingly, on the same page, just three columns to the right, was a story advocating that the League of Nations should send a committee to "Hitlerland" to investigate the pretexts on which "hundreds of thousands of unoffending German Jews have been imprisoned, tortured and lodged in hells on earth called detention camps".

Mit Brennender Sorge - on the Church and the German Reich

When criticism began to be levelled at the Holy See for its failure to condemn Jewish persecution in Germany, the 14 March 1937 Encyclical *Mit Brennender Sorge* (With Burning Concern) was cited as an example of attempts at intervention. It must be said that only the Holy See would dare to cite this document as proof of its righteous attitude towards the Jewish people as it has nothing whatever to do with condemning Jewish persecution. On the contrary, it incited hatred towards them as a people, essentially describing them as "crucifiers" and as "torturers". Lurking beneath its convoluted and pious language is the old charge of "deicide":

> Whoever wishes to see banished from church and school the Biblical history and the wise doctrines of the Old Testament, blasphemes the name of God, blasphemes the Almighty's plan of salvation, and makes limited and narrow human thought the judge of God's designs over the history of the world: he denies his faith in the true Christ, such as He appeared in the flesh, **the Christ who took His human nature from a people that was to crucify Him**; and he understands nothing of that universal tragedy of the Son of God who to **His torturer's sacrilege** opposed the divine and priestly sacrifice of His redeeming death, and made the new alliance the goal of the old alliance, its realization and its crown. (para 16)

Mit Brennender Sorge did not condemn Nazism as such, only its "idolatrous" aspects. What is did condemn wholeheartedly was the concept of a *Reich* Church, a German National Church based on race, i.e. the German race, set up in opposition to the indivisible, Universal Church (Rome). It condemned the concept of German racial superiority seeing that the Universal Church consists of all races, it condemned interference in church affairs, and it expressed a great desire for the restoration of true peace between Church and State:

> Faith in the Church cannot stand pure and true without the support of **faith in the primacy of the Bishop of Rome**...Should men, who are not even united by faith in Christ, come and offer you **the seduction of a national German Church**, be convinced that it is nothing but a denial of the one Church of Christ and the evident betrayal of that universal evangelical mission, for which a world Church alone is qualified and competent. (para 22)

> He who searches the hearts and reins (Psalm vii. 10) is Our witness that **We have no greater desire than to see in Germany the restoration of a true peace between Church and State**. (para 43)

The Church reserved its condemnation of political systems for Atheistic Communism.

Divini Redemptoris - On Atheistic Communism

The Encyclical *Divini Redemptoris: On Atheistic Communism* was published on 19 March 1937. The timing of its publication is very revealing. Any effect *Mit Brennender Sorge* may have had on German political attitudes was nullified by the publication of *Divini Redemptoris* just five days later. The Church's desire in *Mit*

Brennender Sorge to see a restoration of peace between the Church and the Nazi State contrasts sharply with the warlike tone of *Divini Redemptoris*.

The fate of "Our Beloved Spain" lay heavy on the heart of whoever did in fact write this Encyclical, be it Pius XI or Eugenio Pacelli, at that time Cardinal Secretary of State. It incites hatred against all those opponents of the "Leader of Spain by the Grace of God", Fascist Dictator Franco, by using such words and phrases as "satanic scourge", "diabolical", "atrocious barbarity", "sons of darkness", and so forth. The message to all Catholics everywhere was crystal clear: no matter how bad Fascism in Germany and Spain may be, Communism was infinitely worse. [23]

Note

The Holy See never once condemned Fascism, Nazism, or similar movements as it had once condemned, for instance, Liberalism in the Nineteenth Century, or Socialism and Communism in the Twentieth Century.

---

[23] All Papal documents referenced may be accessed on the Holy See's Website. http://w2.vatican.va/content/vatican/en.html

CHAPTER ELEVEN

Pope Pius XII

Section 1

Background

Eugenio Maria Giuseppe Giovanni Pacelli was born in Rome on 2 March 1876. He studied philosophy at the Gregorian University, learned theology at Sant Apollinare, studied Canon Law, and was ordained a priest in 1899. He entered the Secretariat of State for the Vatican in 1901. On 23 April 1917, in what was to prove a decisive event, Pacelli was appointed Papal Nuncio to Bavaria. Three years later, on 23 June 1920, he was appointed Nuncio to Germany and, ten years after that, on 7 February 1930, he was appointed Cardinal Secretary of State by Pope Pius XI. At a crucial juncture, on 2 March 1939, just ten days before the Austrian *Anschluss*, Pacelli was elevated to the Papacy to become Pope Pius XII.

As Pope, Pacelli held three official positions: Supreme Head of the Roman Catholic Church and in direct communication with bishops throughout the world; Head of State of the Vatican City State with his own diplomatic corps; and the Bishop of Rome who is "infallible" when teaching officially (*ex-cathedra*) on matters of faith and morals. (Papal infallibility is the dogma in Catholic theology that, by action of the Holy Spirit, the Pope is preserved from even the possibility of error when he solemnly declares or promulgates to the Universal Church a dogmatic teaching on faith as being contained in divine revelation, or at least being intimately connected to divine revelation. It is also taught that the Holy Spirit works in the body of the Church, as *sensus fidelium*, to ensure that dogmatic teachings proclaimed to be infallible will be received by all Catholics. This doctrine was defined dogmatically in the First Vatican Council of 1870.)

Pacelli's views therefore, whether defined as "infallible" or not, had the capacity to influence in a decisive and concrete way the hundreds of millions of Catholics living in Europe during the period of his Pontificate, which lasted from 2 March 1939 until his death at Castel Gandolfo on 9 October 1958.

Section 2

Shaping Influences

The Jesuits

From his seminary days until his death, Pacelli regarded Rome's Jesuit priests as his special mentors. Many of the staff from his days as Papal Nuncio in Germany would remain with him for the rest of his life, including his advisor, Jesuit Father Robert Leiber, and Sister Pascalina Lehnert—housekeeper, friend and adviser for 41 years. Considering the close association between the Roman-born Pacelli and the Roman-based Jesuits, the views and attitudes expressed in their journal *La Civiltà Cattolica* must be taken into account when considering his shaping influences.

La Civiltà Cattolica

Rome's Vatican-reviewed Jesuit journal, *La Civiltà Cattolica* (Catholic Civilization), has been in continuous publication since 1850 and is among the oldest of Italian Catholic periodicals. The journal is directly revised by the Secretariat of State of the Holy See and must receive approval before publication. A sampling of the journal's attitude towards Jews is altogether frightening.

Jesuit Father Guiseppe Oreglia de San Stefano, in a series of articles published in *La Civiltà Cattolica* between February 1881 and December 1882, claimed that Jewish killing of Christian children for the Paschal Feast was "all too common" in the East and that using that blood of a Christian child was "binding on the conscience of all Hebrews". Every year, it went on, the Jews "crucify a child", who "must die in torment". The journal again turned the spotlight on the Jews in a series of 1890 articles republished in pamphlet form as *Della questione ebraica in Europa* (Rome 1891) aimed at exposing the Jewish contributions to the formation of the modern liberal nation-state. The author/s claimed that the Jews had instigated the French Revolution in order to gain civic equality, which they then used to insert themselves into key positions with the ultimate aim of controlling state economies and establishing their "virulent campaigns against Christianity". The Jews were "the race that nauseates"; "an idle people who neither work nor produce anything"; and "who live on the sweat of others". The pamphlet concluded with a call for the abolition of "civic equality" and for Jewish segregation.[24]

In 1898, as Pacelli was completing his studies for the priesthood, *La Civiltà Cattolica* was proclaiming the guilt of Alfred Dreyfus (see article in Chapter 8: *The Dreyfus*

---

24 Wilenski, p. 28.

Affair). The journal's editor, Father Raffaele Ballerini, continued to proclaim Dreyfus' guilt even after his pardon, claiming that the Jews had "bought all the newspapers and consciences in Europe" in order to acquit him. Ballerini concluded that "wherever Jews had been granted citizenship" the outcome had been the "ruination" of Christians or the massacre of the "alien race". [25]

The journal continued to publish anti-Jewish slurs in the following decades although they did drop the "blood" libels. According to an article in the *Encyclopaedia Judaica*:

> Three years after the advent of the Third Reich, the review actively competed with Nazi propaganda, setting out in detail all the arguments for Christian antisemitism as distinguished from the racial antisemitism of the Nazis. The Jews, stated the writer, "have become the masters of the world" (vol. 87, 1936, no. 37–8); "Their prototype is the banker, and their supreme ideal to turn the world into an incorporated joint-stock company" (ibid, 39–40). In search of a solution to the "Jewish Question" Civiltà analyzed Zionism. Would the Jews, asked the writer, once they had realized the Zionist state, "give up their messianic aspiration to world domination and preponderance, both capitalistic and revolutionary? Besides, what would be the attitude of the Christians when they saw the Holy Places in Jewish hands?" (vol. 88, 1937, no. 2, 418–31). As Civiltà Cattolica saw it, the only way to salvation was through conversion.
>
> Throughout World War II (1939–45), Civiltà's silence over the fate of the Jews echoed that of Pius XII. Later, the "unprecedented cruelty of the massacres of Jews and Poles," and "the horror of concentration camps, gas and torture chambers," were mentioned in an article which raised doubts about the very principle and objectivity of the Nuremberg trials and stated, among other things, that "conceding even that, on the diplomatic ground, Germany had been the one to set the gunpowder on fire, historically, they had been compelled to do so" (vol. 97, 1946, issue 2297).[26]

The Jews and Communism

While serving as Papal Nuncio to Bavaria in 1919, Pacelli found himself at the centre of a local Communist Party revolution struggling to take advantage of the chaos in postwar Munich. Pacelli wrote about the incident in a letter to Secretary of State Gasparri, describing the revolutionaries and their chief, Eugen Leviné at their headquarters in the former royal palace:

---

25   Cornwell, John. *Hitler's Pope: The Secret History of Pius XII*. Viking Penguin: New York, 1999, p. 24

26   Jewish Virtual Library Article: *Encyclopaedia Judaica: La Civiltà Cattolica*. Accessed 7 May 2019. https://www.jewishvirtuallibrary.org/la-civilt-cattolica

The scene that presented itself at the palace was indescribable. The confusion totally chaotic, the filth completely nauseating; soldiers and armed workers coming and going; the building, once the home of a king, resounding with screams, vile language, profanities. Absolute hell. An army of employees were dashing to and fro, giving out orders, waving bits of paper, and in the midst of all this, a gang of young women, of dubious appearance, Jews like all the rest of them, hanging around in all the offices with provocative demeanor and suggestive smiles. The boss of this female gang was Levine's mistress, a young Russian woman, a Jew and a divorcee, who was in charge. And it was to her that the nunciature was obliged to pay homage in order to proceed. **This Levine is a young man, about 30 or 35, also Russian and a Jew. Pale, dirty, with vacant eyes, hoarse voice, vulgar, repulsive, with a face that is both intelligent and sly."** [27]

Whilst Eugen Leviné himself was certainly a Jew, Pacelli had no way of knowing the ethnic background of all the persons to whom he refers. While this letter demonstrates his fear and loathing of Jews and Communists based on political grounds, his stereotypical descriptions of these individuals emphasising their physical and moral repulsiveness also demonstrates an anti-Semitic scorn and contempt for them as a people.

Note

The term Communism embraces a wide variety of ideologies and political movements sharing the core theoretical values of common ownership of wealth, economic enterprise and property, and the incorporation of state atheism into political regimes. Bolshevism is one such movement. A common but incorrect assumption is that the founders of such movements were all Jews and atheists and that Jews alone were the originators of the 1917 Bolshevik Revolution in Russia.

Nazism

In 1921, Adolf Hitler became the supreme leader or *Fuehrer* of the National Socialist German Workers Party, also known as the Nazi Party, which had been founded in Germany in 1920. After the failed *coup d'état* known as the Beer Hall Putsch which took place in Munich on 8-9 November 1923, Adolf Hitler was arrested and charged with treason. The Putsch generated front page headlines in newspapers around the world and his subsequent 24-day trial gave Hitler enormous publicity and a ready-made platform from which to spread Nazi propaganda throughout Germany and the wider world. He was found guilty of treason and sentenced to five years jail in

---

[27] Vatican Secretariat of State Archive. Baviera, Fasc. 42, Folio 37. Letter from Pacelli to Gasparri, 18 April 1919.

Landsberg Prison. Whilst in Landsberg, Hitler dictated *Mein Kampf* (My Struggle) to his fellow prisoners Emil Maurice and Rudolf Hess. On 20 December 1924, having served only nine months, he was released. Volume I of *Mein Kampf* was published in 1925 and Volume II in 1926.

Besides being notorious for its aggressive stance against political enemies, and its expansionist foreign policy aimed at gaining more *Lebensraum* (living space) for the German people in Eastern Europe, *Mein Kampf* is also an expression of Hitler's *Weltanschauung* (a term much used by him and signifying a world-encompassing philosophy of life). His *Weltanschauung* was a mixture of racism, anti-Semitism and social Darwinism, most effectively delivered to a very Christian Germany within a wrapper of religious zeal. For example, the type of sentiments expressed in the following extract from *Mein Kampf* were repeated elsewhere in the work and also in many of his speeches:

> And so I believe to-day that my conduct is in accordance with the will of the Almighty Creator. **In standing guard against the Jew I am defending the handiwork of the Lord.**[28]

These ideas were repeated over and over again in his conversations, writings and speeches and he never deviated from them to any significant degree. Although Hitler's *Weltanschauung* tapped into ideas already popular in Christian Germany, he nevertheless failed to win an election on the vote of the German people.

Having access to what is generally recognised as the most well-informed intelligence network in the world, and being present to witness and report on the formation of the Nazi Party, the Beer Hall Putsch in Munich, Hitler's trial, the publication of *Mein Kampf*, and Hitler's steady rise to prominence and power, there can be no serious denial that Papal Nuncio Pacelli was well-acquainted with Nazism and its virulent hatred of Jews and Communists. As noted previously, it is a view which he shared.

During his years in Germany, Pacelli had become a *Germanophile*—a lover of all things German. Besides being fluent in the German language, he had expressed a great love of the German people and their culture, particularly their great musical composers such as Bach and Beethoven. He would later be known in the Vatican as *il papa tedesco* (the German pope).

---

28 Hitler, Adolf. *Mein Kampf*. Volume I, Chapter II. Translated from the German by James Murphy. Available at Project Gutenberg Australia. Accessed 13 January 2019 http://gutenberg.net.au/ebooks02/0200601.txt

On 20 July 1933, the *Reichskonkordat* between Germany and the Holy See was signed in Rome. In the authoritative work on the history of Nazi Germany, *The Rise and Fall of the Third Reich*, William L. Shirer observes that:

> The agreement, signed on behalf of Germany by Papen and of the Holy See by the then Papal Secretary of State, Monsignor Pacelli, later Pope Pius XII, was hardly put to paper before it was being broken by the Nazi Government. But coming as it did at a moment when the first excesses of the new regime in Germany had provoked worldwide revulsion, the Concordat undoubtedly lent the Hitler government much badly needed prestige. [29]

By the time he was elected Pope, Pacelli had said very little in public about Adolf Hitler beyond a speech given before 250,000 Lourdes pilgrims on April 28 1935 in which he said, "The (Nazis) are in reality only miserable plagiarists who dress up old errors with new tinsel. It does not make any difference whether they flock to the banners of social revolution, whether they are guided by a false concept of the world and of life, or whether they are possessed by *the superstition of a race and blood cult*". (As noted in the previous Chapter article *Mit Brennender Sorge*, the condemnation of what Pacelli here terms a "race and blood cult" had nothing whatever to do with Jews.)

Section 3

The Holocaust

We have already laid out how Pacelli's attitudes to Jews were perhaps shaped by his Jesuit mentors, and how his attitudes to Communism and Nazism must have been shaped by his residency in Germany between 1917 and 1928. How that combination of attitudes affected the role played by him as Pope during the period up to and including World War II has been the subject of much heated debate between his apologists and his critics, resulting in the publication of numerous works devoted to the topic. It is not possible here to analyse all of this material in any depth so we must confine ourselves to a few brief examples, beginning in 1938, of his attitude towards Jews and his situational responses to the catastrophe facing European Jewry.

In his role as Cardinal Secretary of State, Pacelli had been the personal representative of the Pope at the International Eucharistic Congress which took place in Budapest

---

29 Shirer, William L. *The Rise and Fall of the Third Reich: A History of Nazi Germany*. Simon and Schuster: New York, 1960, p. 324.

between 25–30 May 1938. It is undeniable that a diplomat of Pacelli's stature must have known of the anti-Semitic legislation in the process of being formulated in the Hungarian Parliament at the very moment of his presence in Hungary's Capital. In his Congress address, Pacelli spoke of the "wonderful atmosphere of love, the contribution of Christianity", which prevailed during the Congress period. Despite this "atmosphere of love", and despite the fact that the Jews were not mentioned by name, Pacelli still managed to speak indirectly of the Jews "whose lips curse him (Christ) and whose hearts reject him even today". [30]

Upon his elevation to the Papacy on 2 March 1939, Pacelli's actions belied his more restrained public statements. For example, just a few weeks later, in April 1939, he lifted the ban on the rabidly anti-Communist and anti-Semitic *Action Francaise* movement in France.

Throughout the Holocaust years, Pius XII was constantly besieged with pleas for help on behalf of the Jews. For example, in the spring of 1940, the Chief Rabbi of Palestine, Isaac Herzog, asked the Secretary of State, Cardinal Luigi Maglione, to intercede to keep Jews in Spain from being deported to Germany. He later made a similar request for Jews in Lithuania. The Pope did nothing.[31]

In October 1941, the Assistant Chief of the US delegation to the Vatican, Harold Tittman, asked the Pope to condemn the atrocities being perpetrated against the Jewish people. The response came that the Holy See wanted to remain "neutral", and that condemning the atrocities would have a negative influence on Catholics in German-held lands.[32]

On 22 June 1940, the Second Armistice at Compiègne was signed by France and Germany. Germany occupied the north and west coasts of France and their hinterlands, Italy took control of a small occupation zone in the south-east, while the Vichy regime, led by Marshal Philippe Pétain, retained the unoccupied territory in the south, known as the *zone libre*. Between July 1940 and August 1941, statutes were enacted by the Vichy regime depriving Jews of citizenship and preventing them from holding public office. When Pope Pius XII was asked by Pétain if the Holy See objected to such anti-Jewish legislation, he replied that the church condemned racism, but did not repudiate *every* rule against the Jews.[33] On another occasion, the Vichy

---

30 Herczl, Moshe Y. *Christianity and the Holocaust of Hungarian Jewry*. New York University Press: New York, 1993, pp. 93-94

31 *Encyclopedia of the Holocaust: Vol 3*. Israel Gutman, editor-in-chief. Macmillan: New York, 1995, p. 1136.

32 Perl, William R. *The Holocaust Conspiracy: An International Policy of Genocide*. Shapolsky Publishers: New York, 1989, p. 206

33 Ibid. Gutman, *Encyclopedia of the Holocaust*, p. 1137

ambassador to the Holy See informed Pétain that the Holy See did not consider the legislation in conflict with Catholic teachings, as long as they were carried out with "charity" and "justice". [34] Even as he was speaking about "charity" and "justice", Jews were being rounded up and detained in internment camps before being deported by train to the East. A total of some 76,000 French Jews, among them 11,000 children, were murdered in Auschwitz. Most of the deportations left France from the concentration camp of Drancy in Paris. The last transport left France in August 1944 while the battle for Paris was being fought. Of all the Jews deported from France to the extermination camps in the East, a total of some 2,500 survived.

Throughout 1942, reports flooded into the Holy See from its own diplomatic corps, its own Catholic Bishops in both Eastern and Western Europe, from foreign diplomats accredited to the Holy See, from various Jewish agencies and individuals, and from ordinary Catholic priests and laypersons. The Holy See received accounts of the massacre of Jews from at least nine different countries where the Holocaust was taking place, including occupied Poland.[35] Messages to the effect that the Pope was losing his "moral authority" due to his failure to condemn Nazi atrocities also began to pour in from countries where the Holocaust was not taking place, including the United States, Great Britain, Brazil, Uruguay, Peru, and Cuba.

In late August 1942, after more than 200,000 Ukrainian Jews had been murdered, the Metropolitan Archbishop of the Ukrainian Greek Catholic Church, Andrey Sheptytsky, wrote a letter to the Pope in which he described the German government as a regime of terror and corruption more diabolical than that of the Bolsheviks. The Pope replied by quoting verses from the Psalms and advising Sheptytsky to "bear adversity with serene patience".[36]

Despite this constant flow of information from so many reputable sources, Cardinal Secretary of State Luigi Maglione repeatedly and publicly stated that the Holy See was unable to confirm atrocity reports. For example, on 18 September 1942, Monsignor Giovanni Battista Montini, the future Pope Paul VI, wrote, "The massacres of the Jews reach frightening proportions and forms". [37] Yet that same month, when Myron C. Taylor, President Roosevedlt's personal envoy to the Holy See, warned the Pope that his silence was endangering his moral prestige, Secretary

---

34   Ibid. Perl, T*he Holocaust Conspiracy*, p. 200.

35   Phayer, Michael. *The Catholic Church and the Holocaust 1930-1965*. Indiana University Press: Bloomington. 2000 p. 48.

36   Hilberg, Raul. *Perpetrators, Victims, Bystanders: The Jewish Catastrophe 1933-1945*. Harper Perennial: New York, 1993, p. 267

37   Ibid. Perl, *The Holocaust Conspiracy*, p. 206.

of State Maglione responded on the Pope's behalf that it was impossible to verify rumors about crimes committed against the Jews.[38]

In the closing months of 1942, Myron Taylor and Britain's Envoy Extraordinary and Minister Plenipotentiary to the Holy See, Francis d'Arcy Osborne, put considerable pressure on the Pope to speak out about the Holocaust.

On 10 December 1942, the Minister of Foreign Affairs of the Polish government-in-exile, Count Edward Raczynski, issued a 16-page note to the Allied Governments entitled *The Mass Extermination of Jews in German Occupied Poland*. In response, on behalf of the Allies, the United States and British Governments issued the following *Joint Declaration by Members of the United Nations*:

> The attention of the Belgian, Czechoslovak, Greek, Jugoslav, Luxembourg, Netherlands, Norwegian, Polish, Soviet, United Kingdom and United States Governments and also of the French National Committee has been drawn to numerous reports from Europe that the German authorities, not content with denying to persons of Jewish race in all the territories over which their barbarous rule has been extended, the most elementary human rights, are now carrying into effect Hitler's oft-repeated intention to exterminate the Jewish people in Europe.
>
> From all the occupied countries Jews are being transported in conditions of appalling horror and brutality to Eastern Europe. In Poland, which has been made the principal Nazi slaughterhouse, the ghettos established by the German invader are being systematically emptied of all Jews except a few highly skilled workers required for war industries. None of those taken away are ever heard of again. The able-bodied are slowly worked to death in labor camps. The infirm are left to die of exposure and starvation or are deliberately massacred in mass executions. The number of victims of these bloody cruelties is reckoned in many hundreds of thousands of entirely innocent men, women and children.
>
> The above-mentioned governments and the French National Committee condemn in the strongest possible terms this bestial policy of cold-blooded extermination. They declare that such events can only strengthen the resolve of all freedom-loving peoples to overthrow the barbarous Hitlerite tyranny. **They reaffirm their solemn resolution to insure that those responsible for these crimes shall not escape retribution, and to press on with the necessary practical measures to this end.**

---

38 Ibid. Gutman, *Encyclopedia of the Holocaust*, p. 1137.

When Assistant Chief of the United States delegation to the Holy See, Harold Tittman, asked Secretary of State Maglione if the Pope could issue a similar proclamation, Maglione said the Papacy was "unable to denounce publicly particular atrocities". [39]

However, all this combined pressure eventually drew a promise from Secretary of State Maglione that the Pope would speak about the issue, which he did in his 1942 Christmas address broadcast on Vatican Radio. The transcript of this broadcast contained 27 words about the Holocaust buried within 26 pages of text. The 27 words about the Holocaust did not mention the Jews by name.

In January 1943, Wladislaw Raczkiewicz, president of the Polish government-in-exile, again appealed to the Pope to publicly denounce Nazi violence. Bishop Konrad von Preysing of Berlin did the same, at least twice. Pius XII refused. [40]

Neither the Pope nor Secretary of State Maglione shared with the outside world any of the reports which the Holy See continued to receive until the end of 1944. Neither did they share their terrible knowledge with any of the Catholic resistance groups such as those in Germany, Poland and France. Not once in all his many letters to German Bishops did Pius XII share with them the reports he began to receive in 1942 about mass extermination centres in occupied Poland. Rather, he recalled with fondness his years in Germany and commiserated with them about their bombed-out cities and churches.

During the last few decades, a veritable sea of apologists have mounted a campaign to rescue this Pope's reputation, even going so far as to agitate for his canonisation, a move which generally causes great distress to the Jewish people. These apologists point to a limited number of cases before and during his Papacy when he intervened on behalf of Jews. However, when examined, some of these cases relate to *quid-pro-quo* agreements where the Holy See would receive something in return for its co-operation, some relate to Jews who had converted to Catholicism, and others relate to later stages of the war when it became evident to the Pope that Germany would be defeated. Perhaps the UN Joint Declaration that "...those responsible for these crimes shall not escape retribution..." began to exercise his mind.

Apologists offer a variety of reasons as to why Pius XII was not a stronger public advocate for the Jews: a fear of Nazi reprisals; the idea that private intervention could accomplish more; the anxiety that acting against the German government could provoke a schism among German Catholics; the church's traditional role of

---

39 Hilberg, Raul. *The Destruction of the European Jews*. Holmes & Meier: New York, 1985, p. 315.

40 *Holocaust*. Israel Pocket Library. Keter Publishing House: Jerusalem, 1974, p. 134.

being politically neutral; the fear of the growth of Communism were the Nazis to be defeated; and, the most risible of all, fear that his public speech would have no effect and might harm the Jews. The only truthful reason given by his apologists is his fear of Communism.

All of these arguments, however, overlook or ignore the single fact that, with the enormous authority and prestige attaching to the Papacy, Pius XII could have issued at any time during 1942 a public statement declaring that it was sinful and morally reprehensible for any professing Christian, of whatever denomination, to collaborate, to aid, or to abet in any way the genocide then taking place.

Note

In *We Remember*, the 1998 statement on the role of the Catholic Church in the Holocaust, it is claimed that Pope Pius XII saved "hundreds of thousands of Jewish lives". It is an absurd claim. It is perhaps fitting that the man who had refused to intervene on behalf of the Jews of Europe should be forced to witness a few years later the establishment of a Jewish homeland in "Christ's Patrimony" from the isolated heights of his Papal Throne.

Section 4

Escape

When the Third Reich was defeated, many of its senior Nazi criminals, such as Josef Mengele and Adolf Eichmann, escaped justice through a notorious smuggling system known as the "ratlines" which operated via a network of Vatican contacts spread throughout Europe. There is also ample evidence that members of the Catholic clergy in Rome itself were involved in fabricating documents and new postwar identities for Nazis.

Names of personnel and Vatican embassies in Rome are documented in a declassified "top secret" report to the US State Department, compiled in 1947 by agent Vincent La Vista, titled "Illegal Emigration Movements in and through Italy".[41]

The report lists twenty-two Vatican relief and welfare organisations in Rome, representing various nations such as Austria, Hungary and Germany, which were engaging in, or suspected of engaging, in illegal emigration. The directors of all these

---

[41] This de-classified record dated 15 May 1947 is addressed to Herbert J. Cummings. It is date-stamped 14 July 1947 by the Department of State, Office of American Republic Affairs. One copy was originally sent to the American Legation in Vienna. The report's declassification No. is NND760050.

agencies were Catholic clerics. It is a disturbing fact that the report provides evidence that Catholic clergy representing the Vatican used the International Committee of the Red Cross as part of the chain of documentation enabling legal and illegal emigration from Europe. Vatican representatives would provide and verify identities of persons of a certain national group. These persons would then be issued with passports by the ICRC. Agent La Vista noted that many persons in the International Red Cross were pro-German and that persons of nations formerly allied with Germany were successful in obtaining documents.

In one notorious case, the Italian Delegation of the International Committee of the Red Cross issued Adolf Eichmann with a 1948 false passport (No. 100940) under the name of "Ricardo Klement", facilitating his escape to Argentina. The passport also bears the stamp and signature of the then Argentine vice-consul in Genoa, Pedro Solari Capurro. Readers may view a facsimile of this passport on the NBC News Website.[42]

Since the Papacy of Pius XII continued until 1958, his apologists have also been forced to deny his complicity in the smuggling of Nazi war criminals out of Europe. However, these denials fly in the face of the documentary evidence presented by Uki Goni in his book *The Real Odessa: How Perón Brought the Nazi War Criminals to Argentina*. Goni cites previously unavailable material from the Public Record Office in London and from the United States National Archives and Record Administration which clearly demonstrates that Pius XII knew that ecclesiastical institutions in Rome were hiding war criminals.[43]

Section 5

The Final Analysis

The answer to the oft-asked question of why Pope Pius XII did not speak out against the Holocaust is quite simple. His decision to remain silent was based upon a tried and true maxim, "the enemy of my enemy is my friend".

From the day Eugenio Pacelli was appointed as Papal Nuncio to Bavaria in 1917, through his elevation to the Papacy as Pope Pius XII in 1939, until the day he realised that Germany would be defeated, his overarching concern was to bolster and

---

42 Eichmann's False Passport. *NBC News*. Accessed 9 May 2019. http://www.nbcnews.com/id/18946600/ns/us_news-giving/t/nazi-eichmanns-phony-passport-found/#.XNOIYy9L124

43 Goni, Uki. *The Real Odessa: How Perón Brought the Nazi War Criminals to Argentina*. Second Edition. Granta Books, 2002.

advocate a strong Christian Germany as the only possible bulwark against atheistic Communism. Hitler and Nazism were merely incidental elements which could be embraced or rejected by him at will. Pius XII was faced with a simple choice—speak out about what was happening to the Jews, mainly in very Catholic Poland, or keep silent and allow Hitler to continue the great work of destroying atheistic Communism forever. The lives of millions of Jews were not enough to outbalance the weight of the Holy See's sacred hatred of atheistic Communism which ensured she would remain silent in the face of the greatest barbarism in all of human history.

Notes

The Holy See never made an official protest to the Nazi regime about its political-social system; about its concentration camps; or about its persecution of Liberals, Democrats, Socialists, Communists and Jews. It never protested the loss of independence of Austria and Czechoslovakia; the takeovers of Denmark, Belgium, Holland and France; or the Nazi Lebensraum policies resulting in the invasion of Poland and the campaign against Soviet Russia.

The Holy See protested only when her spiritual or material interests were at stake, such as, for example, the attempt to set up a German Reich Church (see *Mit Brennender Sorge*). When she did issue a protest, almost all were worded mildly and accompanied by promises and offers of co-operation with the Nazi State.

CHAPTER TWELVE

The State of Israel

Section 1

Misnomers

Although its origins are still debated, the word "Palestine" is believed to be derived from the Egyptian and Hebrew word *peleshet*. Roughly translated to mean "rolling" or "migratory", the term was originally used to describe an area of free city-states along the Mediterranean Coastal Plain, including Gaza and Ashdod, that were settled by the Philistines circa 1100 BC. These Philistine people had no ethnic, linguistic or historic connection with the peoples of Arabia. After crushing the 2nd Century AD revolt of Shimon Bar Kokhba (132 AD), the Romans regained Judea and named it *Syria-Palaestina* in an attempt to minimize Jewish identification with the land. Thereafter Latin texts kept the last Roman name for the area alive. Under the Ottoman Empire (1517-1917), it was used as a general term to describe the land south of Syria: it was never an official designation. In fact, many Ottoman Turks and Arabs who lived in this area during this time period referred to the area as Southern Syria and not as Palestine. After World War I, the name "Palestine" was applied to the territory that was placed under the British Mandate. This area included not only present-day Israel but also present-day Jordan.

On 29 November 1947, the UN General Assembly adopted Resolution 181 calling for the partition of Mandatory Palestine into Jewish and Arab states. Since the Arab population living in the area had never been designated as "Palestinians", the Resolution does not refer to the creation of a "Palestinian" state for the "Palestinian" people.

Although it is misleading to describe the Arab peoples of the region as "Palestinian/s", we will however use this designation in forthcoming pages to avoid unnecessary confusion.

Section 2

Zionism

Zionism is a political movement based on the assertion that the Jewish people, like any other people, has the right to self-determination and a right to a national home in their historic homeland. Although the dream of return to the land of Israel had always been present in Jewish cultural and religious life during the two millennia of exile, it remained just a dream until its modern ideological expression began to take shape in the nineteenth century when various thinkers such as Moses Hess and Leon Pinsker wrote the first Zionist ideological manifestos and pro-Zionist groups began to organise Jewish immigration to the land of Israel on a small scale.

The first Zionist congress in August 1897, organised by Theodor Herzl, turned what had previously been an intellectual movement into a real political force with the clear goal of establishing a national home for the Jewish people which would be guaranteed by international law. The first stage on the way to achieving this Jewish national home was the Balfour Declaration of 2 November 1917 which was secured for the Zionist organisation through the efforts of Dr. Chaim Weizmann and others. In this declaration, the British government "viewed with favor the establishment in Palestine of a national home for the Jewish people".

Section 3

The British Mandate

In July 1922, the League of Nations entrusted Great Britain with a Mandate for the territory of Palestine which had been conceded by the Ottoman Empire following World War I. Great Britain was called upon to facilitate the establishment of the Balfour Declaration's "national home for the Jewish people" within the Mandate territory.

The preamble of the mandate document declared:

> Whereas the Principal Allied Powers have also agreed that the Mandatory should be responsible for putting into effect the declaration originally made on November 2nd, 1917, by the Government of His Britannic Majesty, and adopted by the said Powers, in favour of the establishment in Palestine of a national home for the Jewish people, it being clearly understood that nothing should be done which might prejudice the civil and religious rights of existing

non-Jewish communities in Palestine, or the rights and political status enjoyed by Jews in any other country.

In September 1922, the League of Nations and Great Britain decided that this national home would be established only in the area between the west bank of the Jordan River and the Mediterranean Sea, an area which constituted one-quarter of the territory included in the Mandate. (Maps depicting the difference between the intended homeland area of 1922 [44] and the greatly reduced reality of 1947 [45] are available on the Jewish Virtual Library Website.)

Article 6 of the Mandate states that:

> The Administration of Palestine, while ensuring that the rights and position of other sections of the population are not prejudiced, shall facilitate Jewish immigration under suitable conditions and shall encourage, in co-operation with the Jewish agency referred to in Article 4, **close settlement by Jews on the land, including State lands and waste lands not required for public purposes.**

All of western Palestine, from the Jordan River to the Mediterranean Sea, including the West Bank and Gaza, remains open to Jewish settlement under international law until a legally binding document—a peace treaty between Arabs and Jews that was called for in UN Security Resolutions 242 and 338—changes its status. The territories that are today referred to as "occupied" should in reality be referred to as "disputed".

This legal situation should be kept in mind when considering the issue of Jewish settlements in what is now called the "West Bank", some of which settlements have existed throughout the centuries of Ottoman rule while others were settled under British Mandatory administration prior to the establishment of the State of Israel. Whilst this issue has become the major weapon in the arsenal of Israel's opponents, and leaves her open to criticism, for Israel it is a matter of security. When Israel withdrew from Gaza, all her settlements were dismantled. The results were disastrous, to say the least. She does not wish to make the same mistake again. Maintaining a Jewish presence in what would otherwise be an entirely hostile Palestinian sea goes some way to prevent territorial amalgamation of those hostile forces.

---

44 Map of pre-1948 Palestine: The British Mandate (1921-1923) Accessed 12 February 2019. https://www.jewishvirtuallibrary.org/map-of-the-british-mandate-1921-1923

45 Map of the UN Partition Plan 1947. Accessed 12 February 2019. https://www.jewishvirtuallibrary.org/map-of-the-un-partition-plan

Section 4

Independence

On 29 November 1947, after the UN General Assembly adopted Resolution 181 to partition Palestine into Jewish and Arab States, Britain announced the termination of its Mandate over Palestine, to take effect on 15 May 1948. On 14 May 1948, one day before the Mandate's termination, the Declaration of the Establishment of the State of Israel was proclaimed by David Ben-Gurion, the Executive Head of the World Zionist Organization, Chairman of the Jewish Agency for Palestine, and soon to be first Prime Minister of Israel.

A few hours after the Declaration of Independence, the armies of Egypt, Iraq, Lebanon, Syria, and Transjordan (now Jordan) invaded the territory of the new Jewish state, locking Israel into a life-and-death struggle. The Jewish people faced these armies alone, with their backs to the last shores of hope remaining to them. The fledgeling Israeli Defence Force, which included Holocaust survivors, won this desperate battle which, had it been lost, would certainly have represented the "final solution" to the Jewish question and history's last curtain call.

An Armistice Agreement between Israel and Egypt was finally signed on 24 February 1949, followed by similar agreements with Jordan, Lebanon and Syria over the next few months. The Armistice Agreement between Jordan and Israel is of particular importance because it was at Jordan's insistence that the armistice demarcation line, the famous "Green Line", not be recognised as an international border but only as a line separating armies. The drawing of the "Green Line" superseded entirely the partition lines proposed and voted on by the United Nations in the Partition Plan of 1947, and which Israel had accepted in the Israeli Declaration of Independence. (The Arab leaders had repeatedly rejected any permanent partition of Mandatory Palestine.)

At the end of hostilities in 1949, Jordan controlled areas spanning both sides of the Jordan River. Its Hashemite rulers began referring to the kidney-shaped area as the "West Bank", and so it remains in popular use today.

To analyse or to comment even briefly on the vast web of complicated interactions between Israel and her Arab neighbours would consume far too much space in this work so we will address only those interactions with the most far-reaching of consequences, beginning with the Six-Day war of 1967.

Section 5

The Six-Day War

In the weeks leading up to the war, Egyptian and Syrian leaders repeatedly declared that war was coming and that their objective was to wipe Israel off the map. Just days before the conflict erupted, Israel passed word to Jordan via the UN and the United States urging Jordan's King Hussein not to tie his country's fate to that of Egypt and Syria. Egypt's President, Gamal Abdel Nasser, demanded the removal of UN peacekeeping forces that had been in the area for the previous decade to prevent conflict. The UN complied with Nasser's demands, with the result that there remained no buffer zone between the Arab armies then being mobilised and deployed and the Israeli forces of a country one-fiftieth the size of Egypt and just nine miles wide at its narrowest point.

Egypt then blocked Israeli shipping lanes in the Red Sea, effectively preventing Israel's only maritime access to trading routes with Asia and Africa. This step was regarded as an act of war by Israel. The United States spoke about joining with other countries to break the blockade but did not act. France, which had been Israel's principal arms supplier, announced a ban on the sale of weapons on the eve of the war, leaving Israel in potentially grave danger if a war were to drag on and require the re-supply of arms. (It was not until the next year that the United States stepped into the breach and sold vital weapons systems to Israel.)

On the eve of the Six Day War, the situation on the ground was as follows: the West Bank and East Jerusalem were in Jordanian hands; the Gaza Strip and the Sinai Peninsula were under Egyptian control; and the Golan Heights, which were regularly used to shell Israeli communities far below, belonged to Syria.

On 5 June 1967, five Arab armies attacked Israel. In the course of this war, Israel seized all these territories of the former Mandatory Palestine from Egypt, Jordan and Syria. After winning this war of self-defense, Israel had hoped that its newly-acquired territories would be the basis of a "land-for-peace" accord so approaches were made to the relevant parties. The formal response came on 1 September 1967 when the Arab League Summit Conference in Khartoum issued what has become known as the *Three No's* Declaration—no peace, no recognition, no negotiation with Israel.

Regardless of the Arab League's declaration, on 22 November 1967, the United Nations sought to create an enduring solution to the conflict and passed Security Council Resolution 242. Operative Paragraph One affirms that:

> The fulfillment of Charter principles requires the establishment of a just and lasting peace in the Middle East which should include the application of both the following principles: withdrawal of Israeli armed forces from territories occupied in the recent conflict; termination of all claims or states of belligerency and respect for and acknowledgment of the sovereignty, territorial integrity and political independence of every State in the area and their right to live in peace within secure and recognized boundaries free from threats or acts of force.

The resolution called for the implementation of the "land-for-peace" formula, and for Israel's withdrawal from territories it had occupied in 1967 in exchange for peace with its neighbors. This land-for-peace formula eventually served as the basis of the Egypt–Israel Peace Treaty of 1979, in which Israel withdrew from the Sinai peninsula and Egypt withdrew its claims to the Gaza Strip in favor of the Palestine Liberation Organisation, and the Israel–Jordan Peace Treaty of 1994, in which Jordan withdrew its claims regarding the West Bank in favor of the Palestine Liberation Organisation and recognised the Jordan River as the boundary of Jordan.

Although there were Israel-Syria negotiations throughout the 1990's aimed at normalising relations with a view to an Israeli withdrawal from the Golan Heights, no agreement could be reached. Thus, skirmishes around the Green Line in the Golan Heights continue to this day.

Section 6

Terrorism

Beginnings

Palestinian/Arab spokesmen commonly claim that Palestinian terrorism is the result of the Israeli occupation of the West Bank and Gaza, adding that the violence will cease only when the "occupation" is ended. Despite this claim, it should be recalled that Palestinian/Arab rejectionist factions, such as Hamas and Hezbollah, repeatedly declare that even if Israel were to fully withdraw from the territories, they will continue their attacks since they deny Israel's basic right to exist.

More importantly, however, the basic premise of the claim that the occupation causes terrorism is historically flawed because such terrorism against Israel existed prior to the establishment of the State in May 1948. For example, Arab terrorism was rampant during waves of anti-Jewish riots in 1920-21; during the disturbances of 1929 (which included the massacre of the Jewish community in Hebron); during the Arab Revolt of 1936-39; and in many other recorded incidents throughout the pre-state period. The terrorism campaign intensified in the period prior to the UN Partition Resolution of November 1947 and led to the joint Arab invasion of 1948-49. Far from being caused by the occupation, this deplorable violence can be traced back to the beginning of the renewed Jewish settlement of the Land of Israel in the 1880's.

The PLO

In the late 1950's, Yasser Arafat co-founded Fatah, the "Movement for the National Liberation of Palestine". His *modus operandi*, and thus Fatah's, was the sneak attack on soft Israeli targets, the better to maximise carnage and fear. After the first few failed attempts, the organisation soon perfected its methods, successfully attacking villages and civilian infrastructure.

The Arab League established the Palestine Liberation Organisation on 2 June 1964 as an umbrella organisation representing several political and armed groups with varying ideological orientations including Arafat's Fatah. Its stated purpose was, and still is, the "liberation of Palestine" through armed struggle. On 4 February 1969, Arafat was elected Chairman of the PLO, a position he held until his death in 2004. The most notorious of the terror groups affiliated with the PLO were Arafat's own Fatah, the Fatah-affiliated Black September, and the Popular Front for the Liberation of Palestine (PFLP).

Before the 1967 War, Palestinian terrorists struck at targets in Israel, often in cooperation with neighboring states. After the war, the Palestinians used terrorism to internationalise the conflict. Arafat and his affiliates soon became innovators in a tactic later refined by Al-Qaeda—the civilian airliner as a weapon of terror.

Terrorism analysts date modern international terrorism to 22 July 1968 when the Popular Front for the Liberation of Palestine (PFLP) hijacked an Israeli El Al flight travelling from Rome to Tel Aviv. However, the most notorious wave of hijackings began on 6 September 1970 when PFLP terrorists hijacked TWA flight 741 from Frankfurt to New York and SwissAir flight 100 from Zurich to New York, diverting them both to a disused airstrip in the Jordanian desert known as Dawson Field. Terrorists also hijacked Pan Am flight 93 from Amsterdam and diverted it to Beirut and then on to Cairo where they destroyed it with explosives. El Al officials thwarted another hijacking attempt on their flight from Amsterdam. On 9 September, another PFLP sympathizer seized a British Overseas Airways Corporation flight in Bahrain and brought it to the same Jordanian airstrip as the first two. Whilst the majority of the 310 hostages were transferred to Amman and freed on 11 September, the terrorists segregated the flight crews and Jewish passengers, keeping 56 hostages in custody. On 12 September, prior to the announced deadline, the PFLP used explosives to destroy the three airliners. (PFLP leader, George Habash, had planned the hijackings after Jordan and Egypt agreed to an "in-place" cease-fire with Israel, ending the so-called "War of Attrition" which followed the Six-Day War.)

These multiple, coordinated hijackings precipitated a crisis culminating in the conflict known as "Black September", which was fought in Jordan between the Jordanian Armed Forces under the leadership of King Hussein, and the Palestine Liberation Organisation under the leadership of Yasser Arafat.

In 1972, a group of Palestinian terrorists affiliated with Arafat's Fatah and calling themselves "Black September" shocked the world by killing 11 Israeli athletes and a German policeman during the Summer Olympic Games in Munich. Targeting the Olympic Games, one of the only true symbols of peace and co-operation between nations, was a step too far even for the PLO so the Black September organisation was disbanded in 1973 and, in an attempt to regain some global acceptance and legitimacy, Arafat eventually called a halt to PLO attacks on targets outside of Israel.

In October 1974, the Arab League recognized the PLO as the "sole legitimate representative of the Palestinian people", and granted it full membership. A month later, on 13 November 1974, Arafat addressed the UN General Assembly, becoming the first representative of a non-member organisation to speak to the world body. He appealed to the UN to enable the Palestinians "to establish national independent sovereignty" over their own land. In his most memorable lines, Arafat said, "Today I have come bearing an olive branch and a freedom fighter's gun. Do not let the olive branch fall from my hand. I repeat: Do not let the olive branch fall from my hand". After the speech, the PLO was granted observer status at the UN and its right to self-determination was recognised. The status of the PLO as the organisation leading the Palestinian national struggle is based on this official recognition it received from the Arab League and the UN.

Authorities date the period of bloody conflict known as the "First Intifada" (Palestinian Uprising) as beginning in 1987 and ending either at the end of 1991 with the convening of the Madrid Peace Conference, or in 1993 with the beginning of the Oslo Peace Process. The difficulty with pinpointing dates is that violence and terrorism were daily facts of life both before and after the uprising, so the only means of determining its beginning and ending points is by counting the numbers of victims. Whatever the case, the Oslo Peace Process marked a strategic change in Israeli policy. Negotiations, concessions, and co-operation with terrorists now replaced Israel's semi-legendary anti-terrorist strategy, which had once spelled out the opposite principles—no negotiation, no concessions, and no co-operation with terrorists.

The Peace Process

The Oslo Accords I and II are a complex set of agreements between the Government of Israel and the Palestine Liberation Organization (PLO) which marked the beginning of the Peace Process. In 1993, Israel's foreign minister, Shimon Peres, held a series of secret negotiations with representatives of the PLO in Oslo, Norway. In early September, Yasser Arafat sent a letter to Israeli Prime Minister Yitzhak Rabin stating that the PLO recognised Israel's right to exist, accepted UN Resolutions 242 and 338 (which called for lasting peace with Israel in exchange for Israel's withdrawal to its pre-1967 borders), and renounced terrorism and violence. In response, Israel officially recognised the PLO as the representative of the Palestinian people. On 13 September, on the lawn of the White House in Washington, Rabin and Arafat signed the *Declaration of Principles on Interim Self-Government Arrangements*, known as the Oslo I Accord, agreeing to set up Palestinian self-government over a period of five years in exchange for Palestinian partnership in matters of Israeli security. The most contentious issues, including Jerusalem, final borders, Jewish settlements in the West Bank and the Gaza Strip, and the return of Palestinian refugees, were set to be discussed after that five-year period.

On 4 May 1994, a follow-up treaty to Oslo I, officially called the *Agreement on the Gaza Strip and the Jericho Area*, was signed by Arafat and Prime Minister Rabin. Israeli military withdrawal from much of the Gaza Strip and the West Bank town of Jericho was stipulated. The Palestinian National Authority (PNA) and Palestinian security forces were also established under the terms of this agreement.

On 24 September 1995, the *Interim Agreement on the West Bank and the Gaza Strip* known as the Oslo II Accord, was first signed in Taba (Sinai Peninsula, Egypt) by Israel and the PLO and then, four days later, on 28 September 1995 by Rabin and Arafat in Washington. This agreement sought to implement Oslo I and defined the security, electoral, public administration and economic arrangements which would govern the West Bank and Gaza during the interim period of five years from the date of the *Agreement on the Gaza Strip and the Jericho Area* of 4 May 1994 until permanent settlement was reached in accordance with Security Council Resolutions 242 and 338. (On 4 November, just a few days after signing Oslo II, Rabin was assassinated by an Israeli ultranationalist radically opposed to Rabin's peace initiative and particularly to the signing of the Oslo Accords, viewed by some as a capitulation to terror.)

In subsequent years, the interim process put in place under the Oslo Accords failed to achieve any meaningful results so on 5 July 2000, US President Bill Clinton announced an invitation to Israeli Prime Minister Ehud Barak and Yasser Arafat to come to Camp David, Maryland, in order to continue their negotiations. The precedent for such an invitation was the Camp David Accords of 1978 when

President Jimmy Carter was able to broker a peace agreement between Egypt, represented by President Anwar Sadat, and Israel represented by Prime Minister Menachem Begin.

The Summit convened on 11 July and ended on the 25 July with no agreement having been reached. Both the US and Israel blamed the summit's failure on Arafat because of his rejection of what both Rabin and Clinton believed to be reasonable proposals. The vision of recognition, and of peace and security in exchange for land, turned out to be a mirage which evaporated right before Israeli eyes when the Second Intifada erupted at the end of September. Arafat was accused of trying to secure by insurrection what he did not win at the negotiating table. This series of riots was characterised by Palestinian suicide bombers attacking Israeli buses, cafes, restaurants and other public places, and by Israel's crackdowns and closures in response. By the time it petered out in 2005, 1,100 Israelis and around 3,000 Palestinians had died. The Second Intifada had a dramatic and negative effect on Israeli-Palestinian relations and was widely regarded as marking the end of the Peace Process begun in 1993 with Oslo I.

In a strange twist of fate, or something else, just 1 year and 17 days after Arafat was welcomed into the very heart of the United States by the President, a terrorist attack in New York City would signal a new reign of terror by forces who had drawn their inspiration to use hijacked civilian airliners as weapons of terror from Arafat himself.

Despite his 1993 renunciation of violence and terrorism, and the recognition of Israel's right to exist in peace, his promises and assurances were proven to be hollow and deceitful, and his intentions just as murderous as ever, as we can see by his statement just a few short months after signing Oslo II:

> We will not bend or fail until the blood of every last Jew from the youngest child to the oldest elder is spilt to redeem our land! [46]

Until the day he died in 2004, and regardless of any public statement to the contrary, Arafat never wavered in his determination to destroy the State of Israel. While he is often described as the "Father of Palestine", he would be more accurately described as the "Father of Terrorism", his true legacy.

The Oslo Accords led to the creation of the Palestinian National Authority (PNA), an interim self-governing body meant to facilitate transfer of power from Israel to a future Palestinian independent State. Mahmoud Abbas, a co-founder with Arafat

---

[46] In his speech '*The Impending Total Collapse of Israel*', Stockholm, Sweden, 30 January 1996, as quoted in *The Legacy of Islamic AntiSemitism: From Sacred Texts to Solemn History*. Bostom, Andrew. Prometheus Books, 2008, p. 682

of the Fatah Party, has been Chairman of the PLO since Arafat's death in 2004, President of the Palestinian National Authority since 2005, and Chairman of the Fatah since 2009.

On 29 October 2018, the PLO Central Council suspended its former recognition of Israel and halted all forms of joint security and economic coordination until Israel recognised a Palestinian State within the pre-1967 borders with East Jerusalem as its capital. It also announced its immediate withdrawal from agreements with Israel, including the Oslo Accords.

Israel has been subjected to ceaseless rocket and mortar attacks from the Gaza Strip since the unilateral disengagement in 2005. To also withdraw from the West Bank to the pre-1967 border (the armistice Green Line) without any legally-binding peace agreement in place would leave her open to the same remorseless attacks from enemies sworn to her destruction. This move demonstrates that the PLO has never been serious about recognising Israel, has never been interested in peace, and has never departed from its original goal of "liberating Palestine' through armed struggle".

Hamas

The Islamic Resistance Movement, also known as Hamas, was founded in 1987 as a national, ideological and organisational alternative to the PLO. The movement, an offshoot of the Muslim Brotherhood in Egypt, created a military wing, the Izz al-Din al-Qassam Brigades, to pursue armed struggle against Israel with the aim of liberating Palestine "from the river to the sea" and replacing Israel with a Palestinian State.

The Covenant

The Hamas Covenant, originally issued on 18 August 1988, is a comprehensive manifesto comprised of 36 separate articles, all of which promote the basic Hamas goal of destroying the State of Israel through Jihad (Islamic Holy War). It views the "problem of Palestine" as a religious-political Muslim issue, and the Israeli-Palestinian confrontation as a conflict between Islam and the "infidel Jews". It strictly forbids giving up one inch of Palestine, which is presented as sacred Islamic land. With regard to international relations, the Covenant manifests an extremist world-view which is as anti-Western as Al-Qaeda, ISIS, and similar terrorist organisations. Detailed excerpts from the Covenant can be accessed on the Israeli Embassies Site.[47]

On 1 May 2017, in Qatar's capital Doha, a new political document was issued by Hamas leader-in-exile, Khaled Meshaal. While the 1988 founding Covenant called for the takeover of all of Mandatory Palestine, including present-day Israel, the new

---

47 *The Hamas Covenant*. Accessed 17 February 2019
    https://embassies.gov.il/holysee/AboutIsrael/the-middle-east/Pages/The%20Hamas-Covenant.aspx

document states its acceptance of the pre-1967 borders as the basis for a Palestinian State with Jerusalem as its capital. But it does not go so far as to fully recognise Israel and does not relinquish its goal of "liberating all of Palestine". The document also falls short of accepting the two-state solution that is assumed to be the end product of the Oslo Accords between Israel and the PLO. It asserts that Hamas is opposed to the "Zionist project", not the religion of Judaism, making a distinction between those who are adherents of the Jewish religion and the "Zionist Israeli citizens who occupy Palestinian lands". While the 1988 Covenant affirmed its ties to the Muslim Brotherhood by mentioning it six times, the new document asserts the movement's strict Palestinian credentials as a "liberation movement" that uses Islam as its main ideological component.

Analysts see this document as an attempt to walk a fine line between Western supporters and its fighters on the ground. On the one hand, it employs moderate language which seeks to avoid international isolation given that the Western world has now experienced Islamic terrorism on a large scale and will no longer tolerate the type of language employed by terrorist groups such as Al-Qaeda and ISIS. On the other hand, hardliners can still claim that the group is not recognising Israel's right to exist. It is unclear if the 1988 Covenant will be superseded by a new Covenant based on this political document.

Regardless of the contents of this document, which was designed to relieve pressure from the West, the reality is that Hamas leaders call for the genocide of all Jews and the destruction of Israel on a daily basis.

Lessons from Gaza

On 15 August 2005, Israel's plan of unilateral disengagement from the Gaza Strip was implemented. The purpose of the plan, proposed by Prime Minister Ariel Sharon, was to improve Israel's security and international status in the absence of peace negotiations with the Palestinians. With the implementation of the plan, Israel Defense Forces (IDF) installations and forces were removed and thousands of Israeli citizens living in settlements were evicted. By 22 September 2005, Israel's withdrawal from the entire Gaza Strip was completed and the PNA took control.

The Israelis left a fully-functioning economic infrastructure which, they had hoped, would form the basis for a working civil society existing in peace alongside Israel and that this would be the prelude to further withdrawals from the West Bank and, eventually, to two States, Israel and Palestine, peacefully coexisting side by side. The reality was somewhat different. Palestinians destroyed much of the economic infrastructure and their terror groups immediately began firing rockets and mortars at Israeli civilians across the Gaza border.

The Middle East Quartet, consisting of the United Nations, the European Union, the United States and Russia, had been set up in 2002 to mediate Middle East peace negotiations and to support Palestinian economic development and institution-building in preparation for eventual statehood. After Hamas staged an armed *coup d'état* in June 2007 and wrested control of the Gaza Strip from the Palestinian National Authority, the Quartet announced that it would negotiate with Hamas if it met three preconditions—renounce violence; accept Israel's right to exist; and agree to be bound by agreements previously signed by the PNA. These terms were refused and Hamas was consequently excluded from talks.

Following a lengthy period during which Hamas bombarded southern Israel unopposed, Israel finally responded in an attempt to cripple Hamas weapons facilities in Gaza. The ensuing conflict in December 2008 and January 2009 (Operation Cast Lead) resulted in a high casualty count on the Palestinian side. Even before the war ended, the UN Human Rights Council met at the behest of the Organization of the Islamic Conference in a special session to condemn the Israeli assault and to call for a mandate to carry out a fact-finding mission designed to investigate the conflict. The Goldstone report,[48] written by this mission, said little about Hamas but much about Israeli "war crimes". Some voices stood out against the report and its methodology. One of the most emphatic was that of a senior British soldier, Colonel Richard Kemp MBE, a former commander of British forces in Afghanistan and a veteran of action in the 1990-91 Kuwait war and elsewhere. On 16 October 2009, he testified before an emergency session of the Human Rights Council. Colonel Kemp's address reveals the methods of Israel's opponents so comprehensively and compellingly that it should be compulsory reading for all those who are wont to criticise Israel from the comfort of their fireside armchairs. A complete transcript of his address is reproduced below and is also available to view online at UN Watch:

> I am the former commander of the British forces in Afghanistan. I served with NATO (North Atlantic Treaty Organization) and the United Nations; commanded troops in Northern Ireland, Bosnia, and Macedonia; and participated in the Gulf war. I spent considerable time in Iraq since the 2003 invasion and worked on international terrorism for the UK Government's Joint Intelligence Committee.
>
> Mr. President, based on my knowledge and experience, I can say this: During Operation Cast Lead, the Israeli Defence Forces did more to safeguard the

---

48 *Human Rights in Palestine and Other Occupied Arab Territories: Report of the United Nations Fact-Finding Mission on the Gaza Conflict.* UN Human Rights Council, New York, 15 Sept, 2009. Accessed 18 February 2019. https://www2.ohchr.org/english/bodies/hrcouncil/docs/12session/A-HRC-12-48. https://www2.ohchr.org/english/bodies/hrcouncil/docs/12session/A-HRC-12-48.pdf

rights of civilians in a combat zone than any other army in the history of warfare. Israel did so while facing an enemy that deliberately positioned its military capability behind the human shield of the civilian population. Hamas, like Hizballah, are expert at driving the media agenda. Both will always have people ready to give interviews condemning Israeli forces for war crimes. They are adept at staging and distorting incidents.

The IDF faces a challenge that we British do not have to face to the same extent. It is the automatic, Pavlovian presumption by many in the international media and international human rights groups that the IDF are in the wrong, that they are abusing human rights. The truth is that the IDF took extraordinary measures to give Gaza civilians notice of targeted areas, dropping over 2 million leaflets and making over 100,000 phone calls. Many missions that could have taken out Hamas military capability were aborted to prevent civilian casualties. During the conflict, the IDF allowed huge amounts of humanitarian aid into Gaza. To deliver aid virtually into your enemy's hands is, to the military tactician, normally quite unthinkable. But the IDF took on those risks.

Despite all of this, of course, innocent civilian lives were lost. War is chaos and full of mistakes. There have been mistakes by the British, American, and other forces in Afghanistan and in Iraq, many of which can be put down to human error. But mistakes are not war crimes. More than anything, the civilian casualties were a consequence of Hamas's way of fighting. Hamas deliberately tried to sacrifice its own civilians.

Mr. President, Israel had no choice apart from defending its people to stop Hamas from attacking them with rockets. And I say this again: The IDF did more to safeguard the rights of civilians in a combat zone than any other army in the history of warfare. [49]

Predictably, Kemp's testimony was greeted with relief by Israel, but dismissed as bizarre by those States and groups preferring to base their opinions on Goldstone's "evidence". Opponents of Israel do not wish to draw international attention to the fact that, in contrast to Hamas, which targets Israeli civilians while using its own civilians as human shields, Israel only attacked terrorist infrastructure such as Hamas security installations, rocket-launching sites, weapons stockpiles and factories, and the tunnels used to smuggle in weapons and explosives. Unfortunately, while the majority of casualties belonged to Hamas and other terrorist groups, the practice of recklessly

---

49 *UK Commander challenges Goldstone Report.* UN Watch. 16 October 2009. Accessed 18 February 2019. https://www.unwatch.org/dramatic-u-n-testimony-uk-commander-challenges-goldstone-report/

and callously siting these facilities in civilian areas meant that there were inevitable civilian casualties despite Israel's best efforts to avoid this outcome.

Two more major conflicts erupted in subsequent years: Operation Pillar of Defense (2012) in response to the continuing barrage of rockets fired at Israeli civilians; and Operation Protective Edge (2014) in response to the kidnapping and murdering of three Israeli teenagers by two Hamas militants. Despite the fact that no other country in the world would be expected to tolerate such attacks on its civilian population, these Israeli operations have on the whole resulted in the same condemnation of Israel by those who are united with Hamas in their desire to portray Israel as the wicked aggressor, and the Palestinians as helpless, innocent victims of a bullying, far more powerful neighbor.

Between 30 March 2018 and 15 May 2018, tensions surrounding the US Embassy relocation to Jerusalem escalated into violence on the Gaza-Israel border. On 18 May, the UN Human Rights Council convened a *"Special Session on the deteriorating human rights situation in the occupied Palestinian territory"*. In a breathtaking display of hypocrisy, representatives presented statements critical of Israel on behalf of such stellar examples of commitment to human rights as the PLO, Iraq, Qatar, the United Arab Emirates for Arab Group, and Syria.

The Human Rights Council provided yet another forum for Government and non-Government organisations deeply opposed to Israel to attack with impunity. Statements by Israel, the United States and UN Watch were critical of the Council for its prejudgement, its wilful blindness, its blatant partiality, its hypocrisy, and for its eager acceptance of lies and distortions.

The Session finally adopted a resolution to dispatch an independent, international commission of inquiry to investigate all violations of international humanitarian law and international human rights law in the context of large-scale civilian protests in the "occupied" Palestinian territory. The resolution was adopted by a vote of 29 in favour, two against, with 14 abstentions.

All statements presented to the *"Special Session on the deteriorating human rights situation in the occupied Palestinian territory"* can be accessed on the Office of the High Commissioner for Human Rights website. [50]

---

50 Office of the High Commissioner for Human Rights. *Special session on the deteriorating human rights situation in the occupied Palestinian territory.* Accessed 19 February 2019. Morning Session: www.ohchr.org/EN/HRBodies/HRC/Pages/NewsDetail.aspx?NewsID=23104&LangID=E
Afternoon Session: https://www.ohchr.org/en/NewsEvents/Pages/DisplayNews.aspx?NewsID=23107&LangID=E

Notes

As pointed out previously, the Oslo Accords led to the creation of the Palestinian National Authority (PNA), an interim self-governing body meant to facilitate transfer of power from Israel to a future Palestinian independent State. Mahmoud Abbas, a co-founder with Arafat of the Fatah Party, has been Chairman of the PLO since Arafat's death in 2004, President of the Palestinian National Authority since 2005, and Chairman of the Fatah since 2009.

Section 7

Nations United

When the United Nations debated the future of the Mandate of Palestine in 1947, world opinion was powerfully affected by news of the Holocaust and the plight of Jewish refugees. This momentary humanitarian advantage succeeded in mobilising public opinion on their behalf. Almost as soon as it became clear that the Jews had won their war for independence, however, forces hostile to the Jewish people and to the State of Israel began to reassert themselves.

If an unbiased observer were to listen to United Nations debates and read its resolutions, the observer would conclude that its principal purpose is to censure a tiny country called Israel. Since around 1967, the full weight of the UN gradually but deliberately turned against the country it helped to bring to birth by General Assembly resolution only twenty years earlier. The result today is that many of the UN's political organs, specialised agencies, and bureaucratic divisions have been subverted by a relentless propaganda war against the Jewish state, causing them to stray from their founding purposes and constitutional frameworks.

In the *Palais des Nations* corridor of the European headquarters of the UN in Geneva, this prejudice is displayed in a series of giant panels devoted to the Palestinian cause. Every day, the visual message that the Palestinians are the world's greatest human rights victims—and, by implication, that Israel is the world's worst human rights abuser—is absorbed by hundreds of UN country delegates, employees, and non-governmental activists as they pass by.

The UN's obsession with censuring Israel at every turn directly affects all citizens of the world for it constitutes a severe violation of the sovereign equality principle guaranteed by the 1945 UN Charter and underlying the 1948 Universal Declaration of Human Rights. It challenges the principle of UN universal standards for when a standard is applied selectively, it loses its very meaning.

This does not mean that Israel should be above the law. It is perfectly legitimate to criticise Israel if there is a well-documented reason for so doing. But to launch such a decades-long obsessive campaign speaks loudly of an unstated agenda masquerading as high-minded activism.

The grossly disproportionate and one-sided anti-Israel resolutions caused the then UN Secretary General, Kofi Annan, to criticise the UN Human Rights Council in 2006 for its "disproportionate focus on violations by Israel" while neglecting other parts of the world such as Darfur.[51]

On 21 June, 2007, Reuters reported that his successor, Ban Ki-Moon, "joined Western nations on Wednesday in criticizing the world body's own Human Rights Council for picking on Israel as part of an agreement on its working rules". [52]

In the same article, Alejandro Wolff, once deputy US permanent representative at the UN, accused the Council of having "a pathological obsession with Israel". It was for good reason that Israel's legendary statesman and one of its founding fathers, Abba Eban, once remarked about the UN, "If Algeria introduced a resolution declaring that the earth was flat and that Israel had flattened it, it would pass by a vote of 164 to 13 with 26 abstentions". [53]

These anti-Israel resolutions and related debates consume an astonishing proportion of the UN's time and resources. In 2013, the UN General Assembly in New York adopted 21 Israel-related condemnations and a total of only four related to the rest of the world combined. The time spent by UN ambassadors on drafting, debating, and enacting these anti-Israel resolutions was time not spent on passing a single resolution for the victims of mass killings, terrorist bombings, bloody police crackdowns, and other massive human rights abuses which took place elsewhere that year. The UN Human Rights Council, populated primarily with despots and rogues, finds it difficult to condemn these abuses but seems to delight in attacking a tiny nation surrounded by 30 million Arabs who are taught that the residents of that tiny nation are no better than animals. The almost complete segregation of Israel from the community of nations points to the end game—the nullification of Israel's legitimacy

---

51 *UN Secretary General's Address to mark International Human Rights Day.* 8 December 2006. Accessed 11 May 2019. https://www.un.org/sg/en/content/sg/statement/2006-12-08/secretary-generals-address-mark-international-human-rights-day

52 *U.N.'s Ban faults rights council over Israel.* Reuters Report, 21 June 2007. Accessed 11 May 2019. https://www.reuters.com/article/us-rights-council-un/u-n-s-ban-faults-rights-council-over-israel-idUSN2030978520070621

53 *UNESCO Denies Jewish History.* The New York Jewish Week in the Times of Israel, 20 October 2016. Accessed 11 May 2019. https://jewishweek.timesofisrael.com/unesco-denies-jewish-history/

as a nation. There is a chilling familiarity in all of this. One of the world's oldest stories is playing out before our eyes yet again.

Section 8

World Opinion

Politicians, academics, media outlets, celebrities, and moralising armchair critics propagate and perpetuate a revisionist and contextless portrayal of Israel with a type of religious zeal virtually indistinguishable from any other belief system of times past. They continue to describe the Arab ethnic groups living in the West Bank and the Gaza Strip as "Palestinians" despite the fact that the term is a modern political creation which has no basis in fact and never had any international or academic recognition prior to the advent of the Palestine Liberation Organisation in 1964.

They continue to focus on the sufferings of the Palestinians but not on the price paid by the ordinary Israeli citizen who lives in a permanent state of preparedness for war and/or terror attacks and that the cost of this preparedness is ruinous taxation. They never draw attention to the fact that the Arab States with all their petro-trillions have done little or nothing to help their own people in the West Bank and the Gaza Strip during the last fifty years or so because to alleviate their situation would be to diminish their usefulness as a club to wield against the State of Israel.

They will listen carefully to the plight of the "poor Palestinians", who are simply pawns for the Arab League, and wring their hands over the issue of "refugees". No mention is made of the 800,000 Jews who were ejected from Arab lands during the 1948 conflict, losing lives or livelihoods and property estimated at 80 billion in today's dollars. Those Jewish refugees were taken in by new State of Israel. Arabs who abandoned their properties at the urging of the Arab aggressors were never taken in by their own people so they remain today a political pawn used by the Arab League, Hamas, and the PLO's Fatah Party.

When regional Arab States discriminate against, brutalise, and slaughter their own citizens, it is almost accepted as the norm. Yet when Israel shoots tear gas or rubber bullets at Palestinians, it is front page news and presented as proof that Israel is anti-democratic, apartheid, and/or the biggest offender of human rights and perpetrator of "war crimes" in the world. Yet one has only to consider, for example, the ongoing Syrian civil war to recognise that even the Palestinians have a better and safer life than most of their Middle Eastern brethren.

Israel's opponents, mainly in the West, always claim that they are not anti-Semitic. They are just opposed to the policies and actions of the State, they say. However, if we consider the virulent strain of hatred on full display between December 2008 and January 2009, when Israel responded to unremitting Hamas attacks on her civilian population and attempted to cripple Hamas weapons facilities in Gaza, we may conclude that the surface hysteria masked a vicious underlying strain of ancient prejudice.

If it were not so, there would be no explanation for the failure to condemn on an equal or greater scale the genuine human rights abuses occurring around the world every day. If it were not so, there would be no explanation for the language of protest using terms such as "massacre" and "slaughter" which determined the issue before it could even be verified. If it were not so, there would be no explanation for the unreasoning, deranged, and over-and above hatred expressed daily in the streets, on campuses, in newspapers, and on radios and televisions. If it were not so, there would be no explanation for the expression of values which are diametrically opposed to all that the West is supposed to believe in—tolerance and truth, the free exchange of opinions, the clear-headedness of thinkers and teachers, the modernity of outlook. To dare to publicly deviate a fraction of a moral millimetre from the prevailing orthodoxy about Israel is to invite abuse, jeers, and even the questioning of one's own humanity.

Despite Israel's best efforts to avoid civilian casualties and only attack terrorist infrastructure, the reckless and callous Hamas practice of siting such infrastructure in the midst of civilian populations, in effect using these civilians as human shields, resulted in innocent casualties. Why was there no mass protest against Hamas who make a virtue of endangering their own civilian population and who, as everyone knows but many choose to discount, have been firing rockets and mortars into Israeli towns and endangering Israeli civilians for years? The original withdrawal from Gaza and the dismantling of the settlements was a sufficient signal of magnanimous and peaceful intent, yet it was not reciprocated with the smallest gesture. And the question has to be asked whether a Jewish state, however magnanimous and conciliatory, will ever be accepted in the Middle East.

Certainly, the continuing and most horrifying accusation of all is when Israelis are labelled "Nazis" and the situation of the people in Gaza likened to that of the Jews in the Warsaw Ghetto. Is is possible that these accusers are really ignorant of the conditions in the Warsaw Ghetto in the early 1940's where around 100,000 Jews and Romany Gypsies died of engineered starvation and disease and another quarter of a million were transported to the death camps? Could they really be ignorant of the horrors attending the Warsaw Uprising in 1943 when around 13,000 were killed and the remaining 50,000 or so sent to be murdered in Madjanek or Treblinka? Or are they simply playing upon ignorance and uncritical emotional reaction to draw support for their campaigns? While the death of every innocent Palestinian in Gaza is one death too many, there is not the slightest similarity either in intent or in deed between Gaza and the Warsaw Ghetto.

Given the state of our world, characterised as it is by regular occurrences of pitiless warfare and the resulting deaths of thousands of innocent men, women and children, there can be only one explanation for singling out Israel above any of these perpetrators and invoking the spectre of Warsaw and that is to turn the knife in their most recent deadly wound and portray the Jews rather than the Nazis as shameless, pitiless murderers. In a reversal of the laws of cause and effect, this portrayal cancels out any lingering collective guilt about what happened to them in the Holocaust because their actions of today prove retrospectively that they had retribution coming to them yesterday.

It is not anti-Semitism, they say, it is just criticism of the State, pure and simple. What is really pure and simple and obvious to all but the perpetrators is the Jew-hatred that is so acculturated and ingrained that the haters don't even recognise it in themselves. That same millennial Jew-hatred which is the only explanation for the otherwise inexplicable reaction to even the slightest infraction of a moral and ethical code reserved only for Israel, and imposed only on Israel.

No matter how much Israel is despised, or by how many, of one thing we all can be absolutely certain: Israelis will never give up the homeland that their ancestors yearned for throughout their millennial persecutions and wanderings. The sooner their adversaries realise and accept this certainty, the sooner the first steps in the long road to peace can be taken. Meanwhile, "world opinion" with its double standards and unbridled hypocrisy continues to eat away at the trust and confidence Israel once placed in the international community. (With the recent softening of attitudes in certain Arab quarters, hopes have been raised that the tide may be turning. However, it is yet to be determined whether this represents a genuine change or heart or is simply a necessary re-balancing of alliances in the face of larger external threats to the region.)

Israel's first responsibility is to ensure its own survival. It has attempted to do so with as much restraint and responsibility as is possible in the circumstances. It is a testament to the tenacity of its citizens that they have not already been overrun by Arab zealots intent on finishing the job that, despite their best efforts, the European anti-Semites failed to do during World War II.

Section 9

Church or State

The justification for Jewish suffering has primarily been the charge of "deicide". For this "crime", the Jews as a people had been condemned to wander the earth in perpetuity while Christians had replaced the Jews as the "people of God". The very fact of millennial Jewish sufferings served to confirm this view in the minds of some. The establishment of the State of Israel, however, presented a challenge and an affront to this view of the "wandering Jew" and there can be little doubt that, in some quarters, adopting a position hostile to the State of Israel is merely a substitute for a deeper animosity.

For example, the Roman Catholic and mainstream Protestant Churches champion the cause of Palestinian Nationalism and, employing the rhetoric of the Middle East Council of Churches, portray Israel as the "oppressor". They are, in essence, caught in a trap of their own devising because if they were to champion the cause of Israel, or even take a neutral position, it would be an admission that the teaching of Supersessionism and their view of the perpetually "wandering Jew" was wrong. If wrong, then Christians as a group are not, and never were, the "people of God", except through a process of individual spiritual adoption. At the opposite end of the scale are those such as evangelical Christian groups who generally hold the view that Israel's restoration is according to the will of God.

It is perhaps the greatest continuing irony in history that the Jewish Jesus, preached as the Israelite Messiah by the Jewish apostles who cited their proofs from the Hebrew Scriptures, has been used as a weapon against his own Jewish people throughout two millennia. A classic case of the Scriptural prohibition on "boiling the kid in its mother's milk".

The catalogue of crimes against the Jewish people, much of it committed in the name of so-called "Christianity", is the most shameful, the most truly wicked expression of man's inhumanity to man that it is possible to conceive. If there is a devil, a *shatan*, then this monstrous exhibition must surely be its crowning achievement against the people who provided us with the likes of Moses and Jesus.

Section 10

The Promises

For the Israelite people, dispersion from their own land was regarded as a type of symbolic "death" while ingathering to the land a type of symbolic "resurrection". Perhaps the most definitive and striking example of the promise of resurrection and ingathering to the land of Israel is found in the prophet Ezekiel's Vision of the Valley of Dry Bones, written circa 570 BC during the Babylonian exile:

> The hand of the LORD was upon me, and carried me out in the spirit of the LORD, and set me down in the midst of the valley which was full of bones, And caused me to pass by them round about: and, behold, there were very many in the open valley; and, lo, they were very dry. And he said unto me, Son of man, can these bones live? And I answered, O Lord GOD, thou knowest.
>
> Again he said unto me, Prophesy upon these bones, and say unto them, O ye dry bones, hear the word of the LORD. Thus saith the Lord GOD unto these bones; Behold, I will cause breath to enter into you, and ye shall live: And I will lay sinews upon you, and will bring up flesh upon you, and cover you with skin, and put breath in you, and ye shall live; and ye shall know that I am the LORD.
>
> So I prophesied as I was commanded: and as I prophesied, there was a noise, and behold a shaking, and the bones came together, bone to his bone. And when I beheld, lo, the sinews and the flesh came up upon them, and the skin covered them above: but there was no breath in them. Then said he unto me, Prophesy unto the wind, prophesy, son of man, and say to the wind, Thus saith the Lord GOD; Come from the four winds, O breath, and breathe upon these slain, that they may live. So I prophesied as he commanded me, and the breath came into them, and they lived, and stood up upon their feet, an exceeding great army.
>
> Then he said unto me, Son of man, these bones are the whole house of Israel: behold, they say, Our bones are dried, and our hope is lost: we are cut off for our parts. Therefore prophesy and say unto them, Thus saith the Lord GOD; Behold, O my people, I will open your graves, and cause you to come up out of your graves, and bring you into the land of Israel. And ye shall know that I am the LORD, when I have opened your graves, O my people, and brought you up out of your graves, And shall put my spirit in you, and ye shall live, and I shall place you in your own land: then shall ye know that I the LORD have spoken it, and performed it, saith the LORD (Ezekiel 37:1-14 KJV).

Consider also the following selection of similar promises:

> I will surely gather My people from all the lands to which I have banished them in My furious anger and great wrath, and I will return them to this place and make them dwell in safety (Jeremiah 32:37 NIV).
>
> And I will bring again the captivity of my people of Israel, and they shall build the waste cities, and inhabit them; and they shall plant vineyards, and drink the wine thereof; they shall also make gardens, and eat the fruit of them. And I will plant them upon their land, and they shall no more be pulled up out of their land which I have given them, saith the LORD thy God (Amos 9:14-15 KJV).

To these promises was added the rule of the righteous King:

> Behold, the days come, saith the LORD, that I will raise unto David a righteous Branch, and a King shall reign and prosper, and shall execute judgment and justice in the earth. In his days Judah shall be saved, and Israel shall dwell safely: and this is his name whereby he shall be called, The Lord our Righteousness. Therefore, behold, the days come, saith the LORD, that they shall no more say, The LORD liveth, which brought up the children of Israel out of the land of Egypt; But, The LORD liveth, which brought up and which led the seed of the house of Israel out of the north country, and from all countries whither I had driven them; and they shall dwell in their own land (Jeremiah 23:5-8 KJV).

The King-Messiah, when he came, was expected to be the agent through which these ancient promises would be fulfilled. The disciples certainly expected that the death and Resurrection of Jesus would signal the restoration of the Kingdom:

> Then they gathered around him and asked him, "Lord, are you at this time going to restore the kingdom to Israel?" (Acts 1:6 ISV).

By the time the New Testament came to be written, however, these promises had not yet come to pass so the authors argued that the death and resurrection of Jesus foreshadowed the communal Israelite resurrection from the spiritual death of dispersion and their ingathering to the land, as we can see quite clearly in this passage from John's Gospel:

> But one of them, Caiaphas, who was high priest that year, said to them, "You know nothing at all. Nor do you understand that it is better for you that one man should die for the people, not that the whole nation should perish." He did not say this of his own accord, but being high priest that year he prophesied that Jesus would die for the nation, and not for the nation only, but also to gather into one the children of God who are scattered abroad (John 11:49-52 ESV).

All these texts confound the teaching of Supersessionism.

Notes

See Matthew 27:51-52 where the author draws multiple allusions to Ezekiel's Vision of the Valley of Dry Bones in his account of the Crucifixion. See Part XIII.2: *The Israelite Messiah-The Unexpected Messiah* for an analysis of Israelite messianic expectations. See also Part VII.4.2: *Paul-Paul and his theology-The Covenants* for Paul's presentation of Jesus as restorer and gatherer of Israel.

A final word

On the one hand, the human capacity for reasoning and logical deduction would draw us in the direction of denying a supreme being and accepting that we have created a god in our own image in order to give purpose and meaning to human life. On the other hand, the design, the beauty, and the intricate interweaving of vast cosmic forces on which all life depends draw us in the direction of denying random mutation as an explanation satisfactory to those same reasoning powers. If one were to seek an answer to this dichotomy, one need look no further than a map to see recorded there the greatest true miracle in all of human history—the existence of the State of Israel. That an obscure people, sifted among all the nations of the earth, should keep a recognisable identity throughout centuries of persecution and now find themselves once more living in the land of Israel and calling Jerusalem their Capital is the ultimate proof of a plan of redemption rolled out over millennia. The architect of this plan is a being or force we think of in anthropomorphic terms and refer to with personal pronouns and suchlike since we humans have no other means of describing a power we call "God" who at the same time appears both intimately concerned with humanity yet remote and beyond the human capacity for comprehension.

If not for the momentary mobilisation of favourable public opinion when news of the Holocaust pricked at many a conscience, the State of Israel would not exist. Considering the terrible price that had to be paid for that small scrap of land, it is advisable to keep in mind that the consequences of this indictment of humanity may not yet have run their full and final course:

> Though the mills of God grind slowly; Yet they grind exceeding small;
> Though with patience He stands waiting, With exactness grinds He all.[54]

---

54 Proverb translated into English by Henry Wadsworth Longfellow in *Retribution, Poetic Aphorisms, 1846*. Hugh Rawson; Margaret Miner, eds. (2006). *God*. The Oxford Dictionary of American Quotations. Oxford University Press: Oxford. p. 289.

Select Bibliography

Ausubel, Nathan. *The Book of Jewish Knowledge*. Crown Publishers: New York, 1979.

Brown, F., Driver, S.R., Briggs, C.A. *A Hebrew and English Lexicon of the Old Testament*. Clarendon Press: Oxford, 1968.

Carmignac, Jean. *The Birth of the Synoptics*. Franciscan Herald Press: Chicago, 1987.

Gesenius, Wilhelm. *Gesenius' Hebrew Grammar*. Eds. Kautzsch, E and Cowley, A. E. Clarendon Press: Oxford, 1910.

Josephus, Flavius. *Antiquities of the Jews* in *The Works of Flavius Josephus*. Transl. William Whiston. Milner and Sowerby: Halifax, 1864.

Leningrad Codex B19A (L) in *Biblica Hebraica Stuttgartensia*. Deutsche Bibelgesellschaft: Stuttgart, 1983.

Levenson, Jon.D. *Creation and the Persistence of Evil: The Jewish Drama of Divine Omnipotence*. Princeton University Press: Princeton, New Jersey, 1988.

Malina, B.J, Pilch, J.J. *Social Science Commentary on the Letters of Paul*. Augsburg Fortress: Minneapolis, 2006.

Malina, Bruce J. Rohrbaugh, Richard L. *Social-Science Commentary on the Synoptic Gospels*. Second Ed. Fortress Press: Minneapolis, 2003.

Mowinckel, Sigmund. *He That Cometh: The Messiah Concept in the Old Testament and Later Judaism*. Transl. G.W. Anderson. Abingdon: Nashville, 1954.

Robinson, Bishop John A.T. *Redating the New Testament*. Wipf & Stock: Oregon, 2000.

Rubenstein, Richard L., Roth. John K. *Approaches to Auschwitz: The Holocaust and its Legacy*. Revised Ed. Westminster John Knox: Louisville, London, 2003.

Salderini, Anthony J. *Pharisees, Scribes and Sadducees in Palestinian Society*. Wm.B.Eerdmans & Dove Booksellers: Michigan, 1988.

Slotki, Rev. Dr. Israel W. *Soncino Books of the Bible*. Ed. Rev. Dr. A.Cohen. The Soncino Press: London, 1970.

Tresmontant, Claude. *The Hebrew Christ: Language in the Age of the Gospels*. Franciscan Herald Press: Chicago, 1989.

Weingreen, J. *A Practical Grammar for Classical Hebrew*. Second Ed. Clarendon Press: Oxford, 1975.

Wixted, E.P. *The Race is Run*. Regent Press: Brisbane, 1952.

www.ingramcontent.com/pod-product-compliance
Lightning Source LLC
Chambersburg PA
CBHW020312010526
44107CB00054B/1810